Labour Questions in the Global South

Praveen Jha • Walter Chambati
Lyn Ossome
Editors

Labour Questions in the Global South

palgrave
macmillan

Editors
Praveen Jha
Centre for Economic Studies and Planning School of Social Sciences
Jawaharlal Nehru University
New Delhi, India

Walter Chambati
Sam Moyo African Institute for Agrarian Studies (SMAIAS)
Harare, Zimbabwe

Lyn Ossome
Makerere University
Kampala, Uganda

ISBN 978-981-33-4634-5 ISBN 978-981-33-4635-2 (eBook)
https://doi.org/10.1007/978-981-33-4635-2

This Palgrave Macmillan imprint is published by the registered company Springer Nature Singapore Pte Ltd.
The registered company address is: 152 Beach Road, #21-01/04 Gateway East, Singapore 189721, Singapore

Preface

Labour Questions in the Global South is the eighth book in the publication series of the Agrarian South Network (ASN), a tri-continental network comprising of the researchers from Africa, Asia and Latin America. The network is coordinated by the team at the Sam Moyo African Institute of Agrarian Studies (SMAIAS) in Harare, in collaboration with academics and activists in Africa, Asia and Latin America; both the Institute and the network were founded by Professor Sam Moyo, one of the leading Marxist scholars of the developing world.

The core concerns of the ASN focus on the political economy of world development and aim to contribute to global debates on the multi-faceted challenges of our times, namely the agrarian, environmental, and development crises. Its theoretical interventions have enabled it to expand the debate on the forms of primitive accumulation and semi-proletarianization under contemporary capitalism. These contributions have been chronicled in many publications of the network and its members, and more specifically in different issues of *Agrarian South: Journal of Political Economy*, which is sustained by the network. Many of the authors in this book belong to the editorial and editorial advisory board of the journal.

The genesis of this volume lies in the South-South Conference, 'Labour Questions in the Global South' which the ASN hosted at the Jawaharlal Nehru University in collaboration with Centre for Informal Sector and Labour Studies (JNU), the then African Institute of Agrarian Studies (now renamed as SMAIAS), International Centre for Development and

Decent Work (University of Kassel) and Action Aid India, between 18–20 November, 2015. Tragically, this was also the last conference attended by Sam Moyo, who we lost in a car accident at the end of this Conference in New Delhi. After a gestation period of about two years, the theme of the Conference also became the major theme of the 2017 Annual Agrarian Studies Summer School at Harare. Scholars, young and old, presented their papers on the structural changes within contemporary capitalism and also documented the diverse trajectories of changes within labour relations. The understanding of the patterns of semi-proletarianisation resulting from the corporatisation of agriculture and other natural resources was advanced during these workshops and has formed the basis of this book. Some of the articles were first published in a special issue of the *Agrarian South: Journal of Political Economy* in April 2017.

This book is a compilation of some of the essays which were published in different issues of the Journal in different periods of time. The value of the book is also enhanced by many unpublished pieces that are included in its contents. As such, the essays in the book may be classified into three broad themes: Some conceptual issues at the current juncture; trends and forms of vulnerable and informal labour in different regions of the world; and studies on agrarian systems and forms of semi-proletarianisation. The attempt is to give readers a good sense of the multiple ways in which the labouring poor have been integrated into the contemporary capitalist system.

The editors would like to thank all the institutions and individuals who have contributed to the making of the book. As mentioned earlier, the book is a collective effort borne out of several meetings, conferences and the editorial board of the journal, Agrarian South. All these initiatives have been undertaken by ASN. We would like to thank the faculty, students and staff of Centre for Informal Sector and Labour Studies and the Centre for Economic Studies and Planning, JNU which hosted the first conference that led to this book. We would also like to thank Action Aid India, the secretariat of the Global Labour University and the staff and faculty of the International Centre for Development and Decent Work which partly sponsored the 2015 seminar and has been collaborating with the ASN on many issues of core concern in this volume. The editorial board of the Journal and the trustees and staff of the Sam Moyo African Institute for Agrarian Studies have been behind this project for the last couple of years now. We would like to thank them for their support and cooperation in this endeavour. We are grateful to all the contributors for their patience, and commitment to this volume. Last but not the least, we would like to acknowledge the valuable contribution from the editors and staff of Springer and thank them for their support in publication of this book.

New Delhi, India — Praveen Jha
Harare, Zimbabwe — Walter Chambati
Kampala, Uganda — Lyn Ossome

Contents

Notes on Contributors

Joseph Awetori Yaro is Professor of Human Geography at the University of Ghana. He has authored several publications in these broad developmental themes and has contributed to a range of policy strategies for agriculture, land tenure and climate change. He is the co-editor of the book entitled *Adaptation to Climate Change and Variability in Rural West Africa* (Springer 2016).

Muryatan S. Barbosa is Professor of International Relations and of the Post-Graduate Program in World Political Economy, Federal University of ABC (UFABC), São Paulo, Brazil. He works with themes related to Pan-Africanism, African Union, Global South and Black Brazilian Thought.

Sheila Bhalla is a renowned economist and Professor Emeritus at the Jawaharlal Nehru University, New Delhi, India and a visiting professor at the Institute for Human Development. She has written widely on political economy of agriculture, rural labour and employment. She was a member of the National Task Force on unorganised sector statistics which was set up by the National Commission on Enterprises in the Unorganised Sector.

Walter Chambati is Executive Director of The Sam Moyo African Institute for Agrarian Studies (SMAIAS), Harare, Zimbabwe, Associate Editor of *Agrarian South: Journal of Political Economy* and Research Fellow at the College of Graduate Studies, School of Transdisciplinary Research and Graduate Studies at the University of South Africa (UNISA). He has written extensively on land, labour and agrarian relations in Zimbabwe and Southern Africa. Some of his published works include

Land and Agrarian Reform in Zimbabwe (CODESRIA 2013) (along with Sam Moyo), and *Rethinking the Social Sciences with Sam Moyo* (along with Praveen Jha and Paris Yeros).

Bernardo Mançano Fernandes is Professor of Geography at São Paulo State University (UNESP), Presidente Prudente, São Paulo, Brazil, and UNESCO Chair in Territorial Development and Education for the Countryside.

Eryka Galindo is a research scholar at the Institute for Latin American Studies at Freie Universität Berlin, Germany; She earned her Master in Sociology from the University of Brasília, Brazil. She has done research on rural trade unionism, feminisms, organization, and social participation of women workers in rural areas.

Yu Huang is Assistant Professor of Anthropology at the Minzu University of China. She has written widely on the themes of Science and Technology Studies (STS), robotization and industrial automation, labour studies, environmental anthropology, and agrarian change. She is also one of the associate editors of *Agrarian South: Journal of Political Economy.*

Ricardo Jacobs is Assistant Professor in the Department of Global Studies at the University of California, Santa Barbara. His research focuses on the global political economy of urbanization, ecology and agrarian change, with a focus on Africa. His work examines how global capitalism and class struggle shapes race, ethnicity, indigeneity, gender and class at the local and global level.

Praveen Jha is Professor at the Centre for Economic Studies and Planning, and Adjunct Professor, Centre for Informal Sector and Labour Studies, School of Social Sciences, Jawaharlal Nehru University, New Delhi, India. He is one of the editors of the *Agrarian South: Journal of Political Economy.* His most recent books include *Reclaiming Africa: Scramble and Resistance in the twenty-first Century* (edited with Sam Moyo and Paris Yeros) (Springer, 2019), *Rethinking Social Sciences with Sam Moyo* (along with Paris Yeros and Walter Chambati), and *Labouring Women: Issues and Challenges in Contemporary India* (along with Avinash Kumar)..

Trywell Kalusopa is Professor at the University of Namibia in the Faculty of Humanities & Social Sciences. He has also previously worked at the University of Zambia, University of Botswana and University of Zululand,

South Africa. He is the founding executive director of the Zambia Institute for Labour Research & Development (ZILARD).

Joseph Kofi Teye is an Associate Professor and Director of the Centre for Migration Studies (CMS) of the University of Ghana. He is also an Associate Professor of Migration and Development in the Department of Geography and Resource Development of the University of Ghana. He has been associated with several interdisciplinary research projects with DFID, EU, and other international agencies.

Kin Chi Lau is Associate Professor and program coordinator for the Centre for Cultural Research and Development and an adjunct Associate Professor of cultural studies at Lingnan University in Hong Kong, China. She is also associated with Global University of Sustainability and has co-authored *The Struggle for Food Sovereignty*.

Arup Mitra is Professor and Dean in the Faculty of Economics (FE) at the South Asian University (SAU), New Delhi, India. His book, *Insights into Inclusive Growth, Employment and Wellbeing* (Springer 2013) received Professor S. R. Sen best book award, 2019. He has also been a contributing author of *Encyclopedia of Life Support Systems* and *Encyclopedia of Sustainability*.

Grasian Mkodzongi (PhD) is Executive Director at Tropical Africa-Land and Natural Resources Research Institute (Tropical Africa LNRRI) based in Harare Zimbabwe. His current research focuses on the interface of agrarian change, natural resource extraction and rural livelihoods in Zimbabwe and the Southern African region.

Sirisha Naidu is an Associate Professor of Economics at the University of Missouri-Kansas City. Her areas of research include radical feminist political economy, land, environment, labour and women's work and processes of social reproduction. She has written widely in peer-reviewed journals such as *Agrarian South*, and *Economic and Political Weekly*, among others.

Lyn Ossome (PhD) is Senior Research Fellow at the Makerere Institute of Social Research, Makerere University and Associate Editor of *Agrarian South: Journal of Political Economy*. Her research and teaching focus on politics and feminist political economy, with specializations in gendered labour, land and agrarian studies, and the political economy of gendered violence. She is the author most recently of *Gender, Ethnicity and Violence in Kenya's Transitions to Democracy: States of Violence.*

Archana Prasad is Professor at the Centre for Informal Sector and Labour Studies, JNU and one of the Associate editor of *Agrarian South: Journal of Political Economy.* She has written widely on political economy of development with focus on resistance, women, ecology and adivasis. Her most recent published works include *The Red Flag of the Warlis: A History of an Ongoing Struggle* (2017, with Marathi translation in 2020) and *Struggling for Nation Building: History of All India Bank Officers Association* (2018).

Satyaki Roy is Associate Professor at the Institute for Studies in Industrial Development, New Delhi, India. He works on the political economy of industrialization and his current focus is on global hegemony and value capture from developing economies through production networks and financialisation. His most recent book is *Contours of Value Capture: India's Neoliberal Path of Industrial Development.*

Marcelo C. Rosa is a visiting researcher at the Centre for African Studies and an Associate Professor of Sociology at the University of Brasilia, Brazil. His work in the field of sociology is dedicated to the development, teaching and exchanging of the theories of the south in the Social Sciences. He is one of the editors and founders of the *Agrarian South: Journal of Political Economy.*

Anamitra Roychowdhury is Assistant Professor and teaches economics at Jawaharlal Nehru University, New Delhi, India. His areas of interest include development economics, labour economics, Indian economy and macroeconomics. He has published widely in peer-reviewed journals and he is the author of *Labour Law Reforms in India: All in the Name of Jobs.*

Vitor Eduardo Schincariol is Associate Professor of Political Economy and Economic History and Coordinator of the Postgraduate Program in World Political Economy at the Federal University of ABC (UFABC), São Paulo, Brazil. He is also a Research Associate at the School of Oriental and African Studies (SOAS), University of London (UK) and one of the associate editors of *Agrarian South: Journal of Political Economy.* His most recent book is *Society and Economy in Venezuela, An Overview of the Bolivarian Period*, 1998–2018 (Springer, 2020).

Naubahar Sharif is Associate Professor in the Division of Social Science and Division of Public Policy at The Hong Kong University of Science and Technology with research interests in automation and innovation policy in Hong Kong and Southern China. He has authored numerous articles in leading peer-reviewed journals.

Hanjabam Isworchandra Sharma is Assistant Professor, Department of Economics, Manipur University, India. The focus of his research is on agriculture, labour economics and resource economics. He has also been associated with several interdisciplinary research projects.

Issa G. Shivji is Emeritus Professor of Public Law at the University of Dar es Salaam. He chaired the Tanzania Presidential Commission of Inquiry into Land Matters in 1990–1992. He works on the Agrarian Question in Africa and is a founding member of the Agrarian South Network. He has written widely, and his most recent work is the three volume series *Development as Rebellion: A Biography of Julius Nyerere*, which he co-authored with two of his colleagues.

Ch. Priyoranjan Singh is Professor, Department of Economics, Manipur University, India. His areas of interest are agriculture, demography and international trade. He is also serving as an expert committee member for policy formulation in Department of Agriculture, Department of Horticulture, and Department of Veterinary & Animal Husbandry, Government of Manipur.

Tsui Sit is Associate Professor of the Rural Reconstruction Institute at Southwest University, Chongqing. Her areas of research include globalization, rural reconstruction and cultural studies. She is one of the Associate Editors of *Agrarian South: Journal of Political Economy.* She is also one of the founding members of Global University of Sustainability.

Gertrude Dzifa Torvikey is Programme Officer of the journal *Feminist Africa* based at the Institute of African Studies, University of Ghana. Her research focuses on gender and agrarian livelihoods. Her most recently published papers are 'Labour Casualisation and Youth Employment in Ghana's Private Formal Sector' (2018) in IDS Bulletin Volume 49 No 5, Institute of Development Studies, Sussex U.K. and, 'The Political Economy of Agricultural Commercialisation in Ghana' (along with J. Teye) (2018) in *Journal of Peasant Studies*, Volume 44 No 3.

Tiejun Wen is a renowned Chinese economist and is also Professor and Dean of the School of Agricultural Economics and Rural Development at the Renmin University of China in Beijing. He is well known for his work with the New Rural Reconstruction Movement in China. He has published several books and, along with his team of researchers, is a contributor to journals like *Monthly Review.*

Erebus Wong is a senior researcher for the Centre for Cultural Research and Development at Lingnan University in Hong Kong, China. His work focuses on the political economy of China, and contemporary finance capitalism.

Paris Yeros is Professor in the faculties of Economic Sciences, Sciences and Humanities, and World Political Economy at the Federal University of ABC, São Paulo, Brazil. He has been a visiting fellow in universities and institutes in Brazil, South Africa and Zimbabwe, and has written on labour and agrarian relations in Africa and the world economy. He is editor of *Agrarian South: Journal of Political Economy.*

List of Figures

List of Tables

CHAPTER 1

Introduction

Praveen Jha, Lyn Ossome, and Walter Chambati

Structural transformations within the current phase of neoliberal capitalism have put considerable pressure on the well being of workers, by bringing about fundamental changes which have exacerbated inequalities through the reconfiguration of labour relations in multiple ways. The diverse trajectories of these developments have resulted in the deepening of informality today which forms the foundation of flexible labour relations which are central to contemporary accumulation regimes. This book provides a rich mosaic of essays which illustrate different aspects of these changes and their diverse manifestations, in several multiple regional, national and socio-political contexts. The perspectives presented here are a result of several years of tri-continental collaboration within the Agrarian South Network. Some of the papers were published earlier in *Agrarian South: Journal of Political Economy*, which brought out a special issue on

P. Jha (✉)
Centre for Economic Studies and Planning, School of Social Sciences, Jawaharlal Nehru University, New Delhi, India

L. Ossome
Makerere University, Kampala, Uganda

W. Chambati
Sam Moyo African Institute for Agrarian Studies (SMAIAS), Harare, Zimbabwe

P. Jha et al. (eds.), *Labour Questions in the Global South*,
https://doi.org/10.1007/978-981-33-4635-2_1

the 'Labour Questions in the Global South' in 2017. In this introduction we provide a broad overview of the themes addressed in this volume.

A *longue durée* perspective on the history of capitalism provides important insights into the complex dynamic of structural transformations at the current juncture. It is clear that despite enormous increases in global wealth and unprecedented levels of productivity, workers across the world have faced the brunt of deepening uneven development and sharpening of inequities. Over the last few decades, increasing rates of accumulation have put under considerable pressure, almost all markers of the well being of workers, namely, the generation of employment and livelihoods, wage share, conditions of work, and so on; these have been impacted by the thrust of State do away with regulations and take measures that deepen informality, rather than those that provide better conditions of employment. In the large parts of the Global South, accounting for more than three-fourths of the global labour force, informality has been the norm and only small segments of workers account for the organised/formal and have the 'privilege' of reasonable labour rights. But, the 'decent' working conditions of even this small segment have come under threat due to structural transformations brought about by the ascendency of neoliberalism with its multiple trajectories and manifestations in different spatial and social contexts.

However, despite this diversity, contemporary neoliberal capitalism is characterised by a couple of common structural features two of which are worth highlighting here. The first is the ascendency and domination of neoliberal finance capital which, for almost half a century, has resulted in the reconstitution of power within the *global capitalist class structure and the balance between different components of capital.* This asymmetrical reconfiguration is loaded in the favour of 'capital as finance', which is distinctly international in character and thrives on the cooperation between the bourgeoisie and the political elite across countries. Consequently sovereign States and their espoused objectives of development take a back seat and supra-national Bretton Woods institutions (World Bank and IMF) and several other powerful actors become the dominant force in directing capital investments and structuring labour relations. This results in the emergence of a new global order in facilitating institutional arrangements to further the interests of the transnational capitalist class, segments of which may also be located in some countries of the South. The asymmetrical power equation between the North and the South is illustrated by relatively stable Northern origins and headquarters of the top 100 multi-national enterprises (MNEs); in 2012 only 16 of the top 100 MNEs belonged to 'developing countries' and China and this number went up to 17 in 2017, thus showing that more than 80 per cent of the lead MNEs continued to be headquartered in the Global North (UNCTAD 2018, p. 29). Such an uneven concentration of capital in the so-called developed countries underlines the current changes within the world of work and has largely been reflected in flexible arrangements of labour and the semi-proletarianisation of the peasantry, occurring because of new forms and the continuous process of primitive accumulation. These forms are marked by the reducing share of manufacturing industries in the top 100 MNEs, whereas there has been a significant increase in the share of financial and digital MNEs, especially those driven by platform economies and technology, with China making the most gains amongst the countries of the South (UNCTAD 2018, p. 29). Therefore, the composition and content of capital flowing from North to South changed with technological and financial giants dominating the flows; though Foreign Direct Investment (FDI) inflows decreased between 2012 and 2018 in the developed world, they remained stagnant in the economies of the South; the inflows from so-called developed countries in fact did not decrease much and remained at 71 per cent of the total FDI inflows; the rest being dominated by China, and South Korea (UNCTAD 2018, p. 6). Therefore the integration of the South into a globalised neoliberal world economy is embedded in 'uneven and combined' development of contemporary capitalism, where new forms of primitive accumulation have led to a more generalised process of semi-proletarianisation and deepened and reconfigured informality.

The second major marker of contemporary global capitalism that we flag here is the 'de-centring' of production, characterised by a shift of production from advanced capitalist countries to a select countries of the Global South; it is a result of the process of the changing dynamics of the capital-labour-state 'compacts' which have resulted in the reorganisation of production. This internationalisation of production has enabled metropolitan capital to strengthen its presence to take advantage of, inter alia, relatively inexpensive labour and raw materials as well as to tap the markets through the development of, what have popularly been described as Global Commodity Chains (GVCs), Global Value Chains (GVCs), Global Supply Chains (GSCs) or Global Production Networks (GPNs). However, as discussed elsewhere (Jha 2016), these concepts do not adequately capture the resultant relative 'de-segmentation' of the world economy which changed the dynamics of labour utilisation, labour reserves, conditions of work and so on. In other words, the historical process of the creation and extraction of surplus value from the South not only takes place outside the 'Chains', as they have been described in popular literature, but is endemic and systemic in all its manifestations. Hence we use the all encompassing conceptual term 'Global Value Systems' (GVSs), to describe the transnationalisation of contemporary capitalism whose geographical and temporal spread is connected with interlocked processes across the globe (Jha and Yeros 2019).

Further, the emergence, maintenance and expansion of these value systems are propelled by interconnected processes: The continuous primitive accumulation (in all its older and newer forms); and the concomitant creation and expansion of labour reserves or what Marx called Relative Surplus Population (RSP) (Jha et al. 2017). It is pertinent to look at both these aspects in their new manifestations, especially under more segmented (though not necessarily decentralised) production systems. One good example of the foundational processes of contemporary primitive accumulation is the second wave of land grabs, free expropriation of nature and adverse integration of smallholder farmers into supply chains, which have been highlighted through recent research in several parts of the world (for details see Moyo et al. (2019)). These show that labour contracts and arrangements in agrarian settings have been structured through the penetration of the large corporations, which are characterised by a shift towards finance capital and developments in biotechnology and other frontier areas. These have resulted in mergers and acquisitions facilitating and increasing the penetration to corporations in all segments of the agricultural production system. For example, as the Atlas reports, two US corporations (DuPont and Dow Chemical) have already merged, Chem China has bought the Swiss company Syngenta, and the German chemical giant Bayer is going to take over the US-based company, Monsanto; net outcomes of these mergers would result in a control of over 60 per cent of the markets for commercial seeds, agricultural chemicals and genetically modified plants (Heinrich Boll Stiftung 2017, pp. 12–14). Similarly, the domination of post-harvest processed food markets by big corporations such as Nestle, Kraft, Associated British Foods (ABF), are also well known. Moreover, the new contractual arrangements in mining, forestry and fisheries also exhibit the same tendencies, which alter the terms of engagement between big capital and petty producers, many of who are semi-proletarianised workers. Emerging forms of primitive accumulation and control over land and nature, therefore, have diverse and complex manifestations which fuel labour reserves through regulatory changes which have manifested themselves in what are popularly termed as 'precariat', 'flexi-contracts', 'agency work', 'platform work' and so on. This mass of workers labour under extremely fragile and vulnerable conditions and overwhelming majority of them make a living through a collection of diverse economic activities, spanning agricultural and extractive activities, across rural and urban areas and at times even across international boundaries. One may, justifiably, quibble over fine-tuning of the relevant concepts, but it would be hardly off the mark to consider this large and heterogeneous segment as being co-terminus with Marx's Relative Surplus Population (RSP) (Jha and Yeros 2019).

The character of the RSP under contemporary capitalism may be gauged from the data on unemployment and underutilisation of labour as provided by the International Labour Organisation (ILO) database. As per the analysis of the ILO, unemployment is not an adequate indicator of labour absorption in the economy. Hence two other categories may be used to gauge a greater extent of labour reserves: 'time related underemployment' (people are working less than stipulated number of hours) and 'potential labour force' which consists of people who are looking for jobs, but are unavailable to work at a particular point in time (or 'unavailable jobseekers'). It is possible to recast this vast pool of the 'unemployed' as the stock/latent reserve; whereas the 'time rated underemployment' may be termed as the floating labour force which is in and out of work which can be described as a flow reserve. The newly peddled category of 'potential labour force' is in fact a stagnant labour reserve, which is waiting to seek work if the circumstances change (ILO 2020).

Table 1.1 indicates a clear divide between the North and the South as far as the presence of labour surplus and reserves is concerned. It is evident that part-time work or time rated underemployment is very high in both Africa and Latin America. They also have higher unemployment rates than any other region, thereby showing the existence of stock reserves. It is not coincidental that these 'reserves' exist in regions which have experienced continuous processes of large land grabs; this in turn has led to the expropriation of populations resulting in burgeoning 'labour reserves', that form almost one fifth of the total labour force. An important feature to note is that there is a concentration of labour surpluses even within the regions: For example, Sub-Saharan Africa and Southern Asia had time rated underemployment rates which were much higher than the rates of the African and Asian continents respectively, especially for females and

Table 1.1 Region-wise dimensions of labour reserve, 2018

Region		*World*	*Africa*	*Latin America and Caribbean*	*Northern America*	*Asia and the Pacific*	*North, South and West Europe*	*Eastern Europe*
Total	Ur*	5.39	6.87	7.95	4.11	4.34	7.56	5.11
	TRU**	4.76	10.64	7.41	0.80	3.67	4.72	1.07
	PLF***	3.41	5.93	5.59	0.89	2.51	4.47	1.91
	TLR****	13.55	23.44	20.94	5.79	10.52	16.74	8.09
Female	Ur*	5.57	7.59	9.43	4.02	3.91	7.82	4.84
	TRU**	5.33	11.91	8.40	0.77	3.76	6.13	1.11
	PLF***	4.83	8.17	8.33	0.92	3.46	5.45	2.18
	TLR****	15.73	27.66	26.15	5.71	11.13	19.40	8.13
Youth	Ur*	13.51	10.91	17.94	8.80	13.54	15.74	15.31
	TRU**	6.43	12.13	8.29	1.03	4.42	7.12	1.96
	PLF***	8.27	10.54	12.04	2.35	6.66	10.32	5.94
	TLR****	28.20	33.58	38.27	12.18	24.61	33.17	23.20

* Unemployment rate; ** Time rated underemployment; *** Potential Labour Force; **** Total labour reserve

Source: https://www.ilo.org/shinyapps/bulkexplorer46/?lang=en&segment=indicator&id=LUU_2LU2_SEX_AGE_GEO_RT_A, accessed on 13 April 2020

youth. Similarly, there is also concentration of 'potential labour force' among women and youth, along with intra-regional concentrations in specific nations and amongst different social groups (ILO 2019).

The RSP furthermore gives rise to the question regarding what is happening to those whom capital daily expends, and to the conditions of survival of the growing labour reserves which capital can neither absorb nor sustain. Even for those marginally employed, below-minimum wages compel resorting to a cornucopia of livelihood strategies in order to survive. As such, besides wage labour, petty commodity production and peasant agriculture in combination now constitute income/livelihood activities for the vast majority of semi-proletarianised households. Furthermore, these activities increasingly depend on access to land, including forests, private land and common lands. Labour questions in the global south therefore articulate existing and new agrarian questions, (among them that of gendered labour, caste, ethnicity etc.), which structure the contours of capitalist exploitation and dispossession. As such while agriculture is increasingly peripheral to GDP in most countries of the South, its relevance ought to be understood in light of peasant production, its gendered, ethnic and other components, that retain fundamental connection to the labour relations described above.

The deepening and reconfiguration of informality with the transnationalisation of capital is further evident in rising trend of informal labour and part-time work within the 'wage and salaried' segment is increasing throughout the world. As a recent publication by ILO (2018) states 'the share of employees in informal employment in the formal sector represents 27.4 per cent of total informal employment among employees worldwide and up to 42 per cent in Latin America and the Caribbean and more than half in developed countries from Europe and Central Asia' (ILO 2018, p. 16). In addition to this large labour surplus concentrations in different parts of the global South house a bulk of the informal labour; informality comprises more than 80 per cent of the family and small enterprises and two-thirds of the formal employment in peripheral capitalist economies classed as 'developing and emerging' nations. Here we may note that the rate of growth of informality is higher among women and rural workers. Regions with high dependence on agriculture like Sub-Saharan Africa and Southern Asia record an unprecedented level of informality, which may be above 90–95 per cent. In contrast the degree of informality in Latin America is just above 50 per cent, but almost two-thirds of young and women workers are in informal labour (ILO 2018).

The above-mentioned multiple trajectories are embedded within the wider structural transformations in contemporary capitalism. The essays in this volume not only map the different facets in different regional and national settings, but also provide important empirical and theoretical insights into the contemporary history of capitalism from a Southern perspective. In this sense the chapters presented here make significant contributions to our understanding of neoliberalism today.

The Chapters

Given the diverse nature and scope of the contributions, the sequence of the chapters presented follows a broad thematic logic. The first five contributions provide a broad conceptual overview of the themes which foreground the other essays in this volume. In the context of the conceptual background, the next 14 essays in the volume may be broadly classified into two broad themes: Informal labour and its vulnerability and conditions of labour and semi-proletarianisation in rural settings. Within this broad classification, the contributions provide important illustrations about the complex relationship between persistent informality in labour relations and semi-proletarianisation.

The first essay by Praveen Jha and Paris Yeros, 'Labour Questions: Back to the Drawing Board, Yet Again', is primarily concerned with labour's landscape in the Global South. It outlines one of the central kernels of Marxist Political Economy, beginning with the brilliant analysis in the Communist Manifesto of 1848, by Karl Marx and Friedrich Engels, which is about the inexorable, ruthless and brutal march of Capital, that seeks to hammer and subordinate whatever opposition comes in its way; no 'Chinese Wall' is safe, and through its relentless complex journey, with primitive accumulation at its core, in particular via colonial conquests, a 'combined and uneven' global capitalist system is shaped. In other words, it argues that the dynamics of 'Global South' can hardly be understood without comprehending its inexplicable connections with 'Global North', at different stages in approximately five centuries of capitalism and, equally importantly, at the current juncture.

In the context of this discussion, the next essay, 'The Concept of 'Working People' by Issa Shivji interrogates Walter Rodney's concept of the 'working people' in order to explore the possibilities of a broad unity against the emerging contradiction with capital. The author traces the intellectual journey of the term and contends that the concept of the 'working people' has more political potency and validity than 'worker-peasant alliance'. It is of higher relevance on a conceptual scale because it can enable us to theorise real-life struggles against neoliberalism.

Another dimension of the character of the working class is elaborated by Sirisha Naidu and Lyn Ossome in their contribution, 'The Agrarian Question of Gendered Labour'. The authors provide a conceptual lens to analyse the agrarian transitions in relation to social reproduction. This interface, they argue, has been largely ignored and a focus on 'reproduction of life' can provide a useful way of adding to the contemporary debate. Further the current academic engagement with the concepts of 'self-exploitation' and 'subsidy' are inadequate to understand the multifaceted character of women's labour, which has both reproductive and productive dimensions. A consideration of both these through the prism of the 'reproduction of life' has important implications for the understanding of the strategies needed for egalitarian agrarian transformations.

As indicated earlier, one of the central structural feature of contemporary capitalism is the emergence of global value systems that helps to maintain and increase the rate of accumulation by extracting surplus value from workers of the South. Satyaki Roy outlines the dynamics of value capture in his contribution 'Rent and Surplus in Global Production Network: Identifying Value Capture from the South'. Roy reviews the existing literature and points out the limitations in the in existing frameworks which study Global Production Networks (GPN) which focus on rent seeking behaviour by different actors at different nodes and production points. Instead, he delineates the processes of surplus creation and realisation, thus explaining how value is captured by lead firms and big players within the network. The contribution contends that value and surplus may be generated outside process of formal relations instituted by GPNs. This can only be analysed with a study of the dynamics of the inclusion and exclusion of firms and the relative position of individual capital.

The creation and maintenance of labour reserves through continuous processes of primitive accumulation is a necessary precondition for capitalist accumulation. However the study of this process has been neglected since the 1970s; rather the concept of 'informal sector' and 'informal economy' has replaced the analytical focus on labour surpluses in scholarly and policy debates. This lacunae is the focus of the essay by Sheila Bhalla titled, 'From "Relative Surplus Population" and "Dual Labour Markets" to "Informal" and "Formal" Employment and Enterprises'. The contribution traces the intellectual history of the concepts 'informal' sector and 'informal economy' from Karl Marx to Arthur Lewis, Barry Bluestone, Keith Hart and S. V. Sethuraman. Through this history, it shows how Marxian dynamics of 'relative surplus population' has been replaced by the concept of 'informal economy'. In doing so, the essay also provides some insights into the dynamic role of population pressure on agriculture in many countries of the Global South. Bhalla concludes by pointing out that current frameworks employed by agencies like the International Labour Organisation have a very narrow focus, and this also influences their policy prescriptions.

The themes laid out in the first five essays contextualise the other essays which draw attention to the diverse trends in different regional and national contexts. The contribution, 'Labour Trends in Latin America and the Caribbean in the Current Crisis', by Vitor Eduardo Schincariol, Muryatan Barbosa and Paris Yeros provides a broad overview of the process that has led to a deepening of informality in the region between 2008 and 2016. This assessment is done of the basis of the analysis of demographic trends, employment structure, trends in unemployment and wages and the trajectory of social, racial and gender inequalities. The authors contend that the informal or low productivity sector has expanded even while rural exodus has persisted in the post-2008 crisis period. Further, though the economic boom of the 2000s had some positive distributional effects, it made limited inroads into the established racial and gender hierarchies, which found expression in persisting super-exploitation and extreme levels of violence and mass incarceration.

Another explanation of the rural-urban dynamic with respect to informal arrangements is provided by Arup Mitra, in his chapter 'Informal Economy: Persistence and Meagreness'. Using the data of the National Sample Survey (2009–2010), the study constructs an index to delineate the well being of informal labour for India. It examines the phenomenon of contractualisation and ancillarisation and their impacts on work. It argues that with the similar level of skill endowment and other demographic characteristics, an individual may have the possibility of being better off in terms of real earnings and other indicators in a city that has the growth momentum. Therefore it is not correct to surmise that an informal sector is uniformly stagnant; its spatial variations lay emphasis on its potential to provide better sources of livelihood in the broad context of economic growth. Such a conclusion has policy implications which are also elaborated in this contribution.

The nuanced conclusions of Mitra's chapter may be contextualised in the chapter by Anamitra Roychowdhury in his essay 'Whatever Happened to Employment: India's Recent Record from a Nationally Representative Sample'. The study contends that the neoliberal economic order has been the principal guiding force of managing the Indian economy for close to three decades. This has given rise to two challenges, namely, rise in inequality and dismal performance on the employment front. The essay discusses the challenges on the employment front in a period that coincides with the first term of the right-wing populist government. The author contextualises the discussion of the results of the Periodic Labour Force Survey (2017--2018) within the broad employment trends in South Asia.

The transformations in the quality of employment are explored further by Grasian Mkodzongi in 'Primitive Accumulation and Exploitative Labour Relations in Zimbabwe's Artisanal and Small Scale Gold Mining Sector'. Through the case study of Mhondro Ngezi district, the author highlights the links between Zimbabwe's fast track land reforms and expansion of artisanal gold mining. This contribution sees artisanal gold mining as a part of a new wave of primitive accumulation which is studied through a focus on labour dynamics and environmental degradation and maps the exploitative and violent labour management practices of the employers and makes a case for a more proactive involvement of the State and political establishment in regulating the sector.

The changing labour dynamics under contemporary capitalism is also the focus of Yu Huang and Naubahar Sharif's contribution 'From "Labour Dividend" to "Robot Dividend": Technological Change and Workers Power in South China'. Drawing on Beverly Silver's concept of the 'structural power of workers', the authors focus on the dialectical relationship between technological change and workers bargaining power in the light of the growing demand for robots in China since 2013. A detailed analysis of the labour arrangements and practices in the factories of South China shows a dual tendency in labour dynamics: While a 'labour shortage' and high turnover rate might epitomise workers' increasing marketplace power, the rising labour costs that result might jeopardise workers' interests, as employers are incentivised to use robots to replace human labour. The essay refutes the technological determinism of mainstream economists, which views labour as a static and passive force awaiting capital's manipulation. It also cautions against an opposite tendency that champions workers' power as inherently insurmountable with respect to machines. While stressing the need for more research on this theme, the authors conclude that the large-scale adoption of automation equipment will, in all likelihood, create a homogenised workforce and revolutionise shop floor control. Therefore, it is time for workers in the Global South to unite and fight strategically.

The challenges for trade unions in the context of the changing dynamics in the world of work are explored by Trywell Kalusopa in the African context. In his contribution, 'Wither African Trade Union Movements?' Kalusopa indicates that the intricate nexus of colonialism, post-colonialism and unfettered capitalism has been the stimulus for trade unions to broaden the scope of their struggles beyond the shop floor and to embrace liberation. The author suggests strategies, which can enable trade unions to build alliances with global trade unions and become more effective in their changing national contexts.

As mentioned earlier, the engagement with deepening informality in the world of work is also influenced by the structural changes within the agrarian structure in the South. Essays from diverse regional, national and local settings point towards the multiple trajectories of semi-proletarianisation, which have characterised the contemporary agrarian question and its influence on the extent and character of labour reserves.

In his study of 'Changing Forms of Wage Labour in Zimbabwe's New Agrarian Structure', Walter Chambati examines the changing nature of farm wage labour in the context of the extensive redistributive land reform since 2000. Using field research from two districts with contrasting agro-ecology and socio-economic patterns, the essay shows that hiring of wage labour is not only done by the large-scale capitalist farms after the reforms; under the new agrarian structure, the peasantry not only employs an expanded base of unpaid family labourers, but also 'informal' wage labour. Though the character and conditions of employment of such labour are qualitatively different from the full and part-time labour of the past, the super-exploitation of agrarian wage labour continues. It is reflected by the payment of poor wages and differing degrees of the institution of the residential labour tenancy in both the old and new farm compounds. Landlessness and/or land shortage continues to be a key characteristic of farm wage labourers as in the past suggesting the persistence of the labour reserve dynamic.

While the Zimbabwean case shows the impact of state-led land reforms on the agrarian structure, the Brazilian case highlights the process of 're-peasantisation which has occurred as a result of the land occupation struggles. In the essay entitled 'Re-peasantisation, Resistance and Subordination: The Struggle for Land and Agrarian Reform in Brazil', Bernardo Mancano Fernandes analyses the history of peasant formation, particularly focusing on the formation of the Landless Rural Workers' Movement (MST) and its contribution in recreating the peasantry through land occupations. The author discusses the manner in which the transformative idea of the 'family farm', as promoted by MST, has been co-opted into a model of State supported capitalist agriculture. As a result the newly formed peasantry started seeing itself as an appendage to the capitalist model of development and therefore there is an urgent need to construct and reimagine an alternate model of peasant agriculture. The contribution highlights the ideological challenges confronting any contemporary project for peasant emancipator in the global South.

To a certain extent, the notion of re-peasantisation is also supported by Priyoranjan Singh and Hanjabam Isworchandra Sharma in their essay 'Peasants in Manipur: Agrarian Change, Land Tenure and Emerging Patterns of Peasantisation in India'. The contribution studies methods by which peasants seek to further their survival by enhancing their own 'autonomy' through farming intensification and diversification. They map the agrarian changes taking place in the North Eastern State of Manipur and highlight the important changes in the traditional land tenure system. The authors make an in depth study of two villages and contend that in times of food and employment stress, culture and social norms are capable of innovating and fine-tuning themselves to re-order the very structure of production, distribution and appropriation. These social innovations have give little room for private appropriation and consequently the slogan of 'Back to the farm' seems to be re-emerging among the peasantry in the region.

The capacity of the peasantry to resist and survive in the age of finance capitalism is highlighted in the case of China by Tsui Sit, Erebus Wong, Kin Chi Lau and Tiejun Wen in their contribution, 'Re-organising Peasant Labour for Local Resilience in China'. The essay makes a case study of the local initiatives in Puhan and contextualises it in an in-depth analysis of the macroeconomic framework. It focuses on the double-cost imposed on the South through the financialisation of grain markets and the measures taken by the Chinese State to counter this tendency through the programme, 'new socialism in the countryside', which was focused on building local self-reliance among the peasantry. The authors show that local initiatives in Puhan provide some important lessons for the study of alternative forms of peasant agriculture. Echoing other essays in this volume, they emphasise the importance of fostering social relations that form the basis of interdependence, mutual support and recognition. These reaffirm the genuine wealth of the people and do not give priority to the monetary value determined by capitalistic relations. Hence the social organisation of peasants and agricultural workers form an important part of the strategy to build an alternative to a finance driven approach.

The relationship between land and labour is one of the central issues in studying the capacity of small peasants to withstand the onslaught of capital in neoliberal ties. The contribution titled 'Changing Labour Relations in Commercial Agrarian Landscapes in Ghana' by Joseph Awetori Yaro, Gertrude Dzifa Torvikey and Joseph Kofi Teye, focuses on this aspect. Through its primary survey the study shows that employment and labour relations in different agricultural landscapes are shaped, not only by the distinctive features of the different agricultural models, but also by intergenerational class and gender norms. This focus on the social relations of production has important implications for the policy makers who are implementing the models of agrarian commercialisation in neoliberal times.

Furthering the debate, Archana Prasad, in her contribution entitled 'Adivasi Women, Agrarian Change and Forms of Labour in Neoliberal

India', focuses on the complex relationship between class, gender and community in processes of semi-proletarianisation of adivasi (or tribal) groups. The different dimensions of the gendered nature of semi-proletarianisation and proletarianisation of the adivasi social groups after neoliberal reforms are also examined. The author argues that the integration of the adivasis into the world of work in general, and adivasi women in particular, has been a result of agrarian distress and macroeconomic trends that have structured the patterns of dispossession, displacement and urbanisation in the last two decades leading to rising labour mobility amongst adivasi women. Patterns of work and employment over two decades of economic reforms also show that 'class' and not 'community' has played an important part in the gendered division of labour within adivasi communities.

The implications of changing agrarian structures in different regional and national contexts have important implications for the possibilities for organising peasants and rural workers against the contemporary capitalist order. This theme is the focus of the contribution of Eryka Galindo and Marcelo Rosa, titled 'The Historical Transformations in the "Rural Worker" Category in Brazil and Effects on Labour Unionism Politics'. Focusing on transformations in the work of National Confederation of Farm Workers Confederação Nacional dos Trabalhadores Rurais Agricultores e Agricultoras Familiares (CONTAG), the authors argue that any study of unionism needs to be grounded in a larger understanding of the 'labour question'. The emergence of new political actors in the countryside has contributed to changes in the discourse and the modus operandi of unions, which have had to be increasingly more connected to a range of social subjects demanding recognition and advocacy for their agenda. At the same time, these new political actors also drew attention to the diversity of occupations and types of work in the countryside, calling into question the vision of the rural worker as a homogeneous category unified by common interests.

Unionism only represents one important dimension in organising rural workers; the self-organisation of workers is also another dimension that needs some attention in the emerging literature. Ricardo Jacobs deals with this aspect in the last essay of this volume which is titled 'Insurgent Working Class Self-Organisation Beyond the Workplace: Land, Labour and Livestock in the City'. Focusing on the self-organisation of workers who do livestock rearing, the author argues that the insurgent semi-proletarians and their self-organisation are a critical component of the anti-capitalist struggles of the twenty-first century. Further, the presence self-organisation in urban spaces of reproduction is also indicative of the co-presence of different temporalities that give rise to a counter politics in cities in South Africa, and more broadly in the entire Global South. This is evident in the fact that struggles of rural workers in urban settings have resulted in a contemporary 'urban agrarian politics'; a phenomenon which has been neglected, both, by present day activists and researchers.

The diverse perspectives presented in this book show that a comprehensive mapping of labour in neoliberal times needs to take into account the ascendency of finance capitalism and other major attributes of global value systems at the current juncture. Investigations of the contemporary labour questions involve a better understanding of new patterns of informality in labour relations, multiple aspects of the re-structuring of the land and labour dynamic, and the changing rural-urban dynamic. The volume also highlights the need for further research on the intimate links between 'the labour questions' and the 'agrarian question' in both rural and urban regions.

Bibliography

ILO. (2018). *Men and Women in the Informal Economy: A Statistical Picture.* Geneva: International Labour Organisation.

ILO. (2019). *World Employment and Social Outlook.* Geneva: International Labour Organisation.

ILO. (2020). *World Employment and Social Outlook.* Geneva: International Labour Organisation.

Jha, P. (2016). Global Production Network: Whats Labour Got to Do With it. In A. Truger, E. Hein, M. Heine, & F. Hoffer (Eds.), *Monetary Markets, Labour and Development: Feschschrift for Hansjorg Herr.* Marburg: Metropolis Verlag.

Jha, P., & Yeros, P. (2019, August). Global Agricultural Value Systems and the South: Some Critical Issues at the Current Juncture. *Agrarian South: Journal of Political Economy, 8*(1-2), 14–29.

Jha, P., Moyo, S., & Yeros, P. (2017). Capitalism and 'Labour Reserves'. In C. Chandrasekhar & J. Ghosh (Eds.), *Interpreting the World to Change It: Essays for Prabhat Patnaik.* New Delhi: Tulika.

Jha, P., Moyo, S., & Yeros, P. (2019). Reclaiming Africa: Scramble and Resistance in 21st Century, Springer, Singapore.

Stiftung, H. B. (2017). *Agrifood Atlas: Facts and Figures About Corporations that Control What We Eat.* Berlin: Heinrich Boll Stiftung.

UNCTAD. (2018). *World Invesment Report 2018.* Geneva: United Nations Council for Trade and Development.

PART I

Conceptualising Labour Questions in the Global South

CHAPTER 2

Labour Questions in the South: Back to the Drawing Board, Yet Again

Praveen Jha and Paris Yeros

Introduction

The fact that the world of work across the globe, under contemporary capitalism, confronts multiple challenges is hardly news. For over decades now, since the ascendency of neoliberalism from 1970s onward, the overall thrust has been characterised by a range of adverse processes for indicators typically associated with well-being of workers, be it employment and livelihood generation, wages and labour incomes, forms of contract, etc., to name only a few. In general, the trajectories of transition have generated huge concerns, if not despair, for large swathes of working people. Although the broad trends since the 1970s have been characterised by a degree of unevenness, inter-temporally and spatially, important adverse outcomes such as growing inequalities and declining share of labour incomes, increasing job and remuneration polarisation, accelerated

---

P. Jha (✉)
Centre for Economic Studies and Planning, School of Social Sciences, Jawaharlal Nehru University, New Delhi, India

P. Yeros
Federal University of ABC, São Paulo, Brazil

P. Jha et al. (eds.), *Labour Questions in the Global South*,
https://doi.org/10.1007/978-981-33-4635-2_2

dilution of standard employment relations etc. have been near-universal across countries, including in the advanced ones. There is indeed a large body of incontrovertible evidence and burgeoning literature, documenting and analysing these and other pitfalls pertaining to transformation trajectories in the world of work.

As the title suggests, this essay is primarily concerned with labour's landscape in the Global South. However, one of the central kernels of Marxist Political Economy, beginning with the brilliant analysis in the Communist Manifesto of 1848, by Karl Marx and Friedrich Engels, is about the inexorable, ruthless and brutal march of Capital, that seeks to hammer and subordinate whatever opposition comes in its way; no 'Chinese Wall' is safe, and through its relentless complex journey, with primitive accumulation at its core, in particular via colonial conquests, a 'combined and uneven' global capitalist system is shaped. In other words, dynamics of 'Global South' can hardly be understood without comprehending its inextricable connections with 'Global North', at different stages in approximately five centuries of capitalism and, equally importantly, at the current juncture. We hardly need to labour this argument, which has almost universal acceptance in framing analytical paradigms within (Marxist) political economy tradition, to engage with historical capitalism.

Sure enough, recognition of this critical connect (across space and time), and its implications for theory, has certainly not led to homogenised, simplistic narratives among Marxists; on the contrary, significant differences and major contestations, some of these irreconcilable, abound! However, it is not our purpose here to engage with the relevant debates. While acknowledging multiplicity of trajectories, across time and space, it seems reasonable to go along with the widely held view that the three continents of Africa, Asia and Latin America, as colonies or semi-colonies, lost massively through a whole range of mechanisms associated with primitive accumulation, and were ***structurally deformed***, to serve the North.[1] There is a very large and impressive literature that endorses such a perspective.[2]

Economic historians have amassed compelling evidence that even as late as middle of the eighteenth century; the contemporary Third World was at least at par, if not ahead of the First World, not only in agriculture, but also with respect to the index of non-agricultural and per capita incomes (Bairoch 1995; Kuznets 1971; Maddison 2007). Subsequently, the 'West' started moving ahead of the 'Rest' and the widening gap between the two became a surge in due course. Of course, as is well acknowledged, there is more to the material progress of the West over the Rest, than mechanisms of colonialism, or later, imperialism and neo-colonialism. However, the economic stranglehold of the former over the latter has to be a critical component, in any reasonable account of the combined and uneven development of capitalism since its inception, and to comprehend persistent structural and other economic challenges in the South.

As said earlier, this essay is not an attempt to engage with capitalist transitions and their diversities in the South, even at a high level of generality; but a recall of the above noted conclusion, we suggest, is absolutely necessary not only from the perspective of a minimalist historical backdrop, but also for appropriate framing of the present. Without such an acknowledgment, contemporary socio-economic challenges in the South, including persistent mass poverty and utter vulnerability of the world of work can hardly be investigated. We will do well to remember that primitive accumulation and Imperialism are integral to every stage of capitalism, whatever be the differences in their forms, scale and intensity.

Thus an engagement with labour questions in the South at the current juncture needs to be situated in contemporary global capitalism, which has been broadly neoliberalism, with all its variations across regions and countries, for the last half a century or so. Further, during this period, there are important *differentia specifica* of capitalism, compared to its earlier stages, which are central to the relationships between metropolitan capital and the rest of the world, along with major changes in productive forces. In an overall context of intensification of neoliberal globalisation, through so called structural reforms, there has been, inter alia, a spectacular acceleration of financialisation of accumulation and trans-nationalisation of capital, including in production, along with the rise of Big Tech and automation. These have resulted in profound restructuring of economic landscapes – nationally and internationally – and accumulation regimes, with major implications for the present and future of work. As already noted at the outset, world of work has been under huge stress through multiple channels, including dwindling of employment opportunities, compression of social protection, dismantling of labour regulation, assault on trade unions, rising inequalities and overall precarisation.

Apart from these brief introductory remarks, and just about a couple of words as conclusion, this chapter has two substantive sections. First of these flags a couple of major markers central to contemporary neoliberal capitalism and sketches out, conceptually their implications in reconfiguring the material and socio-political prospects for labouring women and men, particularly in the Global South. The subsequent section outlines the core of an analytical framework rooted in Marxian Political Economy, and is better than any other theoretical alternative in our judgment, to comprehend the world of work in general and seeks to bring in sharp relief its implications and linkages for labour questions at the current juncture; in other words, thus section underscores the significance and urgency of getting back to the drawing board yet again.

Neoliberalism and Contours of World of Work

The fact the global capitalist system entered into a new episode of globalisation since the early 1970s, after approximately four decades of nationally regulated regimes in large measure, post the WWII and along with decolonisation of much of the third world, is well acknowledged, across the ideological spectrum from the 'Left' to the 'Right'. There is a huge literature examining and analysing this historical transition inter –temporally and for different regimes and countries, which we cannot engage with here even in broad brush strokes, but a couple of words may be in order.

This shift, spread over the 1970s to 1990s, had its philosophical moorings and policy justification in the presumed supremacy of the market in delivering efficient economic outcomes. To put it bluntly, this presumption was akin to religious fervour among the market devouts who hardly bothered to have any substantive engagement with either theory or history of actual experiences. Given the balance of forces, the ideological warfare against post-WWII state-led strategies of economic transformation, and equally importantly, against the idea and models of existing socialism, succeeded in 'discrediting' them. Of course the pitfalls, contradictions, and challenges of *dirigiste* regimes, collapse of the Soviet bloc, setbacks to socialist system in general and their embracing of markets in varying degrees were very useful in relentless ideological onslaughts. However, the point worth stressing here is that there was not even a pretence among the market-fundamentalists to have an assessment of the contrasting and competing perspectives, or even an elementary consideration of bare facts and figures.[3] Thus, the so-called 'Washington Consensus', as economist John Williamson put it, became the ruling orthodoxy; this 'manufactured consensus' by Capital and its ideologues, with active support of 'States' almost everywhere, managed to steamroll all dissenting voices. This is the backdrop of the 'Ten Commandments' or 'righteous' principles of economic policies, including privatisation of public enterprises and services, financial and trade liberalisation, deregulation, among others, as discussed in detail by Williamson. The crux of these, as one would expect, was utterly simple, "leave the economy to the market; it knows and does the best for it".

Sure enough, we have had varieties of neoliberalism, depending on the domestic contestations within each context, and, of course, the designs and power of imperialism, of which Pinochet dictatorship seizing control of Chile (1973), with direct US backing was an early major illustration. As is well known, US imperialism has often treated Latin America as its own backyard in imposing its writ, but the continent has also been a powerful site of anti-imperialist struggles. The simple point is: varieties of neoliberalism (or capitalism in general) have to be investigated as the dialectics of the national and the global tendencies of capitalist accumulation processes, and resistances to these in search of progressive alternatives. Thus, on the one extreme, we have almost 'textbook versions' of neoliberalism, which are illustrations of brutal assaults on the system by capital and driven by unadulterated market orthodoxy. We have already mentioned the case of Chile in early 1970s, which was one such regime, after Allende was dislodged and the 'Chicago Boys' had field day; subsequently in several other countries in Africa, Asia and Latin America, we get cases of extreme neoliberal models. On the other extreme, we have illustrations of far more 'reticent neoliberalism', e.g. in erstwhile citadels of 'welfare state capitalism' or socialist countries that have embraced the market rather cautiously without surrendering to several commandments of the Washington consensus. In fact for the latter category such as China, Vietnam or Cuba, there are strong contestations as to whether it is appropriate to label these as neoliberal systems or state capitalism (if not still a variety of socialism).

These matters, relating to 'varieties of neoliberalism', have been discussed extensively in the literature with a focus on country specific dialectics and specific trajectories of resistances and other relevant themes. Substantive debates around visions and prospects of progressive transformations, located within careful political economy frameworks abound. It is neither feasible, nor our intention here to interrogate this complex terrain. Given the core objective of this paper, our argument is rather straight forward: it is undeniable that the last half a century has been a phase of ascendency for *Laissez Faire* economic regimes across the world, resulting in profound socio-economic transformations everywhere. There has been much triumphalist celebration on the Right of getting free markets in the driver's seat yet again and the Left has discussed and analysed the current phase of 'capitalist globalisation' or 'neoliberal globalisation', with considerable concern for prospects of progressive socio-economic alternatives. As stressed earlier, each context and place requires careful, in depth analysis; however it is crystal clear that capitalist accumulation strategies and tendencies have acquired tremendous momentum everywhere in recent years and are reconfiguring the world of work, with serious adverse implications. We now turn to provide a brief overview of these relevant linkages.

Current phase of globalisation is characterised by at least a couple of novel features, in comparison with earlier episodes of globalisation, along with a continuation and accentuation of several others. One major difference is the dominance of 'capital-as-finance' in global economy, as never before. This is a kind of 'Finance Capital' whose primary thrust is remarkably different from the one that Hilferding and Lenin had analysed around late 19th and early 20th centuries, which was one of relatively greater synergy between 'capital-in-production' and 'capital-as-finance'. To be sure, rifts and tensions between these two have been a part of multiple competitions characterising components of capital, as emphasised by Marx and several of his eminent successors, including Lenin. Nonetheless the kind of disjunction between the two witnessed during the recent decades, has been unprecedented. The subject has received considerable attention by a number of Marxist scholars and heterodox economists, (for example Samir Amin (2013), Gerald Epstein (2005), Harry Magdoff and Paul Sweezy (1987), Mariana Mazzucato (2017), Prabhat Patnaik (2016a, b), Robert Pollin (2012) and Paul Sweezy (1994), among others), underlining and emphasising the fact that the 'New Finance' has almost been a hindrance to expansion of productive systems, and that there has been growing financialisation of accumulation.[4] As Sweezy put it way back in 1994, "Traditionally financial expansion has gone hand in hand with prosperity in the real economy. Is it really possible that this is no longer true, that now in the late twentieth century the opposite is more nearly the case; in other words, that financial expansion feeds not on a healthy real economy but a stagnant one? The answer to this question, I think is yes it is possible, and it has been happening" (Sweezy 1994).

There is indeed a large literature on the ascendency and dominance of finance capital in the current phase of globalisation and on multiple implications of unprecedented growth in financialisation[5] in global economy. It is quite clear that growing financialisation of accumulation has impacted adversely a whole range of macro-economic outcomes, including investments in real economy, as the new finance chases immediate speculative gains.[6] Further, as Patnaik has often emphasised in his several illuminating contributions, apart from incessantly running after speculation, and thus contributing to an effective squeeze on capital-in-production at large, new finance seriously undermines economic policy space very significantly for the States, particularly in the South, and compresses public investments and expenditures in general. In short, there is a double whammy, via both the market and the State, on real economy, with huge deleterious consequences for the world of work primarily through contraction of employment.

The relationship between Finance and real economy has played out in complex ways, at different junctures of capitalism, including the present; however, depredations of the latter by the former in the contemporary neoliberal era appear to be unprecedented. It would seem that the worst fears of John Maynard Keynes, one of the greatest economists of all time, and a great well-wisher of capitalism, regarding unregulated and footloose finance, have come true. Writing in the 1930s, about untrammelled finance, he was seriously apprehensive about the 'best brains of the Wall Street' essentially indulging in betting and speculation, and warned that if "the capitalist development of a country becomes a by-product of the activities of a casino, the job is likely to be ill-done" (Keynes 1936 p. 159). Several well-known economists in the heterodox traditions who were close associates of Keynes, or were much influenced by him, such Joan Robinson and Hyman Minsky, made significant contributions to our understanding of the debilitating consequences of unregulated finance; in particular, an overall reorientation of the banking sector to speculative finance and its disastrous consequences for productive activities in general.

The second notable feature of the current episode of globalisation, with profound implications for the world of work, is relatively much larger direct engagement of the metropolitan capital in the third world through investments in production, resulting in considerable and unprecedented dilution of the traditional division of labour.[7] This has facilitated substantial diffusion of economic activities from North to select destinations in South, across several sectors. Thus, transnational deepening of economic connectedness in the last half a century or so has been accompanied by considerable reconfiguration in spatial organisation, generally through the so-called offshore outsourcing platforms, much of it in Asia and Latin America as the major action hubs. By the first decade of twenty first century, in case of manufacturing for instance, China became the major node, the so-called 'factory of the world', whereas for the IT-enabled offshore services outsourcing, India emerged as the critical platform, earning the sobriquet of the 'office of the world'. Apart from these two countries as major exemplifiers of the noted offshoring trends, there are a number of other significant destinations in the Global South, along with a few countries in Central and Eastern Europe, which are connected in these transnational webs through investments, production, trade, etc.

Although, inflows in direct investment from the Global North has been critical to the above noted trans-nationalisation, it is worth noting that there has been increased incorporation of countries in the South not only in trade of final goods and services, but increasingly for components and tasks, without these countries being recipients of FDIs, in a whole range of economic activities. For instance, the remarkable success of India's IT-enabled exports in services since the early 1990s, across a broad range in terms of skills and subsectors, has been fuelled by domestic firms through opportunities of inserting themselves in global demands and requirements. Thus, increased incorporation of producers in the South, to cater to the global, in particular Northern demand, from agricultural commodities to the top end of the service segments, as part of the global production and consumption systems, is yet another important dimension of contemporary capitalism. Frequently it happens on terms and conditions significantly different from old fashioned trade patterns, through relatively complex contracts pertaining to several aspects of transactions.

The fact that the production of many commodities is dispersed/fragmented/segmented through splitting up of particular task is indeed an important dimension of contemporary economic arrangements. Models of assembly line, mass production, where raw materials were brought to the factory door and final product exited it, is much less significant now. Initially, the transition to dispersed production was largely confined to outsourcing of tasks within national boundaries; with the ascendancy of neoliberal globalisation, many of these tasks are performed through offshore outsourcing, much of it to the select destinations in the South.[8]

Typically, model of dispersion is one where high value, non-production tasks such as R&D, design, branding, up-market retail etc. are retained in the North and 'low-end activities' (in terms of their share in total value) tend to get relocated to the South. In case of quite a few commodities, there have been dramatic exits of production from well-known centres in the North, such as that of automobile sector from Detroit in the USA, reducing them to rust-belts. In general, there has been substantial shift of material production, either entirely, or of its major components, especially in case of 'polluting' activities. Thus it is hardly surprising that the share of manufacturing output as well as workforce employed in it, for the North in total global manufacturing has come down significantly since the 1980s.[9]

In short, a globalised regime of production dispersed across countries, whose core features have been sketched in the foregoing, is a major marker of contemporary neoliberalism; some of the attributes of this regime, as suggested, are indeed specific to the current phase of capitalism. As it happens, much of the scholarly literature has described it as Global Supply Chains (GSCs)/Global Value Chains (GVCs)/Global Commodity Chains (GCCs)/Global Production Networks (GPNs), among others. Sure enough, all these labels offer important and considerable insights, both analytical and empirical. However, as discussed elsewhere (Jha and Yeros 2019), in our assessment they suffer from inadequate consideration of political economy and historical trajectories of capitalism. In particular, the 'immanent tendencies', or the 'laws of motion' of the system (as Marxist political economists put it) are hardly engaged with in any substantive manner by the above characterisations. Our preferred analytical expression for encapsulating the developments under consideration is *Global Value Systems* (GVSs) which of course have a much longer history, beginning with colonialism, but with powerful ***differentia specifica*** for the current juncture. For reasons of space, we avoid getting into the relevant details[10] here; however, it is worth flagging a couple of issues of obvious significance in contextualising the ascendency of the above-sketched regime.

As already noted, expansion and deepening of the current phase of internationalised accumulation has been co-terminus with ascendancy of neoliberalism since the 1970s; in other words, the backdrop of the transition to neoliberalism, and its subsequent unfolding, are important structural and political correlates, critical to any analysis of the global accumulation trajectories during the last half century. It is widely acknowledged that the late 1960s onward, there was a palpable crisis of profitability in metropolitan countries, for a variety of reasons, both domestic and external, including increased power of organised labour, decolonisation of a large number of countries in the third world and varying degrees of assertion by the newly independent countries in their respective economic policies with help from the socialist bloc, successive oil crisis of 1970s, defeat of the US in Vietnam, among others. It was this backdrop which set the context for successful assault by capital and its allies on existing models of 'regulated capitalism' of the post-WWII period, which indeed had delivered, and was delivering a better material deal to the working classes and masses at large. It is not for nothing that the regulated post-WWII regulated capitalism has often been described as the 'golden age of capitalism'.

The second issue to note here is that the actors who subsequently were central in the unfolding of the current episode of globalisation, namely the giant firms, many of them already trans-national/multinational companies, were waiting in the wings to take forward the neoliberal accumulation regimes. It is worth recalling that the first generation of eminent Marxist scholars such as Lenin, Bukharin, Luxemburg, among others had already noted around a century ago, the emergence and power-in-making of such actors. To recall a succinct and sharp word on it from Lenin, from his preface to Bukharin's important contribution, *Imperialism and the World Economy* (Bukharin 1929 [Reprint 1950] p. Preface): "At a certain in the development of exchange, at certain stage in the growth of large-scale production, namely at the stage that was reached approximately at the end of the nineteenth and the beginning of the twentieth centuries, commodity exchange had created such an internationalisation of economic relations, and such an internationalisation of capital, accompanied by such a vast increase in large-scale production, that free competition began to be replaced by monopoly". As we know well, by the middle of the twentieth century, further growth in economic heft and power of international corporations was recognised across the board, especially within Marxist political economy. Paul Baran (1957), Paul Sweezy and Paul Baran (1966), Paul Sweezy (1994), Andre Gundar Frank (1967), Amiya Bagchi (1982), Stephen Hymer (1979), Samir Amin (1974), and several other scholars, during the 1960s and 1970s, within the Marxist tradition, came up with profound contributions in their investigations of the role of multinational corporations in strengthening imperialism. It was evident that working of the 'laws of concentration and centralisation of capital' had reached a stage that had made large capital in the North much more capable and ambitious in controlling global economic systems.

These two features of the material-political context contributed significantly to the prospects of neoliberal transition since the 1970s. Further, major technological breakthroughs such as container revolution in transportation and remarkable leaps in information processing in the IT sector, effectively resulted in shrinking of space and time, which also led to considerable cost reductions in economic transactions and played a huge role in facilitation of global dispersion of production. These developments, in turn, with ascendancy of neoliberalism, accelerated concentration and centralisation of capital, and consequently economic power through multinational corporations in the North. In short, it became a virtuous tango that fed on, and supported, each other, and the net outcome is, as Amin elaborates and analyses in his *Capitalism in the Age of Globalisation* (Amin 1997), effectively a 'capitalism of generalised monopolies', with giant transnational corporations headquartered in the North controlling the key economic areas, such as technology and finance, among others. Thus, it is a bunch of monopolistic corporations who are lords and masters of the current globally dispersed production and accumulation regimes. As noted by Screpanti, this system of centralised control but decentralised production is one where "expansion of foreign direct investments involves a constant flow of profits from the South to the North, that is, from Periphery to the Centre of the imperial power of multinational capital" (Screpanti 2014 p. 19), reiterating a point made by Baran and Sweezy more than five decades ago.

We do not wish to pursue and examine any further the vibrant and growing literature on alternative analytical approaches engaged with the nitty-gritty of the transition to the current accumulation regime of globally dispersed production systems, outlined in the foregoing. However, two points are in order, given the core concerns of this paper. First, in identifying major proximate correlates for mobility of capital from North to South, both through direct investments as well as through increased incorporation into production without requirements of substantial investments, 'global labour arbitrage' (an expression often attributed to Stephen Roach when he was chief economist of Morgan Stanley) has often been given pride of place; given the huge gaps in real wages between the North and the South (especially in terms of hard currency, such as USD and Euro, exchange rates), there is general agreement that wage hierarchy has been a major contributor to the relocation of economic activities from the former to the latter. This explanation is certainly valid, and has a longer history in the Marxist tradition, rooted in the analysis of the globalisation of TNCs. For instance, well-known and important contributions by Barnett and Muller (1974), Hymer (1979), among others, had emphasised the significance for the search for low unit labour costs as a powerful tool in business strategies underlying oligopolistic rivalry, in extraction of super-profits and rents from the third world countries, by the TNCs headquartered in the North. Huge amount of evidence has been marshalled by Marxist scholars (and others) for a few decades now, corroborating the importance of wage hierarchies that have benefitted TNCs immensely.[11] It is clear from all the major data sources that wage costs in developing countries are a small factor, in percentage terms often in single digits, of the wages in developed countries (for details see Immanuel Ness (2015) and Intan Suwandi (2019).

While the importance of global labour arbitrage is indeed a major driver in the current episode of globalisation, it obviously needs to be contextualised in the evolution of imperialism, in particular, structural and systemic changes underlying it which have unleashed new strategies of accumulation, as we have indicated in the foregoing. Furthermore, in the current neoliberal regime, economic relationship between North and South is of a kind where, beyond labour, there are huge cost differences and thus possibilities of 'arbitrage' along various other axes, such as land and a host of natural resources, industrial safety norms, environmental regulations etc. In short, overall regulatory regimes vis-à-vis capital in the South is not only much weaker than in the North, for several historical reasons we need not get into here, but the gap between the two may have widened further during the recent decades since 1970s, as several countries in the South have been scrambling to attract and retain capital, leading to a virtual 'race to the bottom'. Thus, it is important to situate the ascendancy of the current phase of GVSs in the larger complex of *'labour-nature-regulation arbitrage'*, which has had major implications for capital-labour dynamics both in the North and South.

One powerful outcome, as noted by a large number of scholars (Amin, Stiglitz, Patnaik and others), is worsening of the prospects for work, wages, and overall working conditions in the North itself.[12] Effectively, what we have is a process of 'globalisation of labour reserves', itself, more than ever before. Whereas the wages in third world economies remain largely connected to subsistence levels, in part due to the high and persistent levels of relative surplus population, real and potential mobility of capital threatens and compels workers to a relatively more vulnerable regime in advanced countries. Thus, the 'de-segmentation' of the 'traditionally-enforced pattern of international division of labour', to use Patnaik's expression, has contributed to a context where wages continue to be under pressure all around, whereas labour productivity keeps rising everywhere due to incessant technological changes (central to capitalist competition) and increased encroachment of more capital intensive methods of production. An obvious outcome of the inter-play of these, and other relevant on-going structural changes is, as documented extensively, a marked compression of wage share in national outputs almost in every country of the world, (for a couple of recent contribution on this theme see (Ness 2015; ILO 2017; Suwandi 2019; Basu 2016)).

This brings us to the second point pertaining to the world of work that we need to flag about in the current context of globally fragmented but connected value systems. The fact of an increase in the share of surplus across most countries, and in the total global output, aggravates the problem of aggregate demand for well-known Marxian and Keynsian reasons.[13] As effective demand gets squeezed overall level of economic activity gets curtailed; thus, ceteris paribus, higher the share of surplus and more prolonged the tendency of wage-squeeze, greater is the problem of effective demand. Such a denouement, in its extreme, may result in stagnation or even recession, with huge employment challenges and other adverse impacts on every aspect of the world over. Experience of recent decades, since the 1980s, provide ample testimony to a protracted crisis and deep distress to the lives of working people almost everywhere. Although there are notable differences across countries and particular sub-phases during the current neoliberal era, the fact of growing employment and livelihood challenges are widely acknowledged with expressions such as 'jobless growth' gaining currency across ideological divides in academic and policy discourses.

Combination of the above noted depressing effect on inducement to invest in material production due to worsening income distribution, and the ascendancy of capital-as-finance, discussed earlier, has been critical in shackling capital-in-production worldwide, contributing to not only 'jobless' but 'job-loss' growth trajectories in many countries, and thus to an increase in size of relative surplus population globally and in unleashing a range of lethal outcomes for the world of work in general.

This brings us to the third major, and much talked about, feature during the current episode of globalisation, namely the dramatic technological transformations and their implications for what often gets labelled euphemistically as 'future of work' in popular discourses. Clearly, the technological advances, or the development of 'Productive Forces', to use the standard Marxist expression, during the last half a century or so have been absolutely breath-taking, both in terms of content and pace. Between the so-called Third Industrial Revolution, that had gained considerable ground by 1970s, the crux of which was fantastic leaps in the structure, processes and speed of information, computing and processing, to the Fourth one, with its core features as artificial intelligence, robotics, automation, deep machine learning and big data, modes of production and production relations (again to use well-known Marxist concepts), have undergone phenomenal reconfigurations globally, and these are very much 'works in progress'. For reasons of space, it is impossible for us to engage in this paper with already considerable, and burgeoning, literature on various dimensions of the so-called 'Industry III' and 'Industry IV', and their implications for world of work.[14] Nonetheless, couple of remarks, very briefly, are in order.

First, the argument that the fears of labour displacement due to on-going technological advances is a 'misplaced' one, as we have 'frequently been there and seen it all' in different waves of technological disruptions and changes in the history of capitalism, may itself well be a misplaced one, as the current phase could very well be a sharp rupture from the past in unprecedented ways.[15] The future is uncertain but it seems quite clear that, over a relatively short period of about four to five decades, the global economy has undergone very significant acceleration in labour-saving changes in technology leading to exacerbation of unemployment, even if experiences across countries are uneven. Furthermore, in addition to contributing to this squeeze on the jobs, equally, if not more important concerns relating to on-going trends have been that of the quality of jobs, working conditions, dismantling of even rudimentary social protections and regulations, flattening of trade unions, and on each one of these we have growing evidence from different corners of the world. Given that the ascendancy of the third and fourth industrial revolutions have been largely co-terminus with the rise and consolidation of the other important features pertaining to the current phase of neoliberalism noted above, it is indeed difficult to separate significance of any one of the multiple correlates in a stark and precise manner, as they are inextricably connected with each other. However, what seems certain is that the technological changes are jettisoning a great deal of spatially well-defined dimensions of production, through online digital labour platforms, reconfiguring the interactions between workers and machines through robotisation, artificial intelligence etc., and thus leading to new regimes of labour processes and business models.[16] How the future will unfold is obviously uncertain, as it depends, not only on technological changes, but equally importantly, on social and political contestations. Nonetheless, circumstantial evidence at the current juncture seems to suggest significant contribution of these changes to growing labour reserves and increased vulnerability of workers in the global economy.

Yet another important attribute of neoliberalism that we must note here, even if only in passing, that has huge implications for world of work, is the aggravation of the multiple forces of primitive accumulation. As noted right at the outset, primitive accumulation is a permanent feature of capitalism. Rise of neoliberalism fundamentally means a return to 'spontaneous capitalism' (to use an expression from Marxist authors such as Oscar Lange and Prabhat Patnaik), which means that the system gets increasingly driven by its own immanent tendencies and laws of motion, and a major outcome of such an order is strengthening of the forces of primitive accumulation in a comprehensive sense. Consequently, we have an accentuation in the processes of 'accumulation through dispossession' (as Harvey put it), and 'accumulation through encroachment' (to use Patnaik's expression) in general, as well as the "deepening of super-exploitation by the offloading of the costs of social reproduction unto the expanding of labour reserves themselves, and unto women and the most oppressed social layers in particular" (Yeros and Jha 2020 p. 83). For the world of work, particularly in the South, a major implication of such a transition is the strengthening of the tendency to destroy petty production, in all its forms, which had enjoyed a degree of protection in the *dirigiste* era. Such a process obviously aggravates the problem of growing labour reserves through displaced producers joining its ranks in substantial numbers.

Before we close this section, a couple of extremely important caveats are in order. In the foregoing, we have highlighted major systemic changes and features central to the current episode of globalisation, that are important in an analysis of labour questions, with particular focus on the South. However, we need to go beyond these and engage with other critical aspects of capitalist transformation trajectories, globally and locally, both in *longue duree* and conjunctural perspectives, to engage with the relevant issues in a fuller fashion. Given the level of abstraction adopted in this paper, and its focal concerns, such a task is clearly not feasible here. However, even at the highest level of generality it is important to flag that issues relating to nature and ecology are absolutely critical in shaping the world of work everywhere, as is widely recognised in contemporary political economy literature. Growing ecological crisis, or the 'metabolic rifts', created by relentless greed of capital, has reached a point that seriously threatens the planet Earth, posing profound challenges to not only livelihoods and work, but well-being of humanity in general. Given our focus in this paper, we have not managed to explore the multi-dimensional ecological assaults of capitalism; however, as noted above, ascendancy of the neoliberal order necessarily implies that the tendencies and pace of the processes of primitive accumulation get evermore strengthened and reckless, taking the system's contradictions around natural resources and environmental sustainability to dangerously new levels.

Finally, another caveat we need to note is that, given the level of abstraction our discussion here has been unable to get into profound issues and features pertaining to race, caste, ethnicity, patriarchy and gender, which are inextricably enmeshed with capitalist accumulation processes. 'Divide and rule' has always been central to capitalist control strategies and a variety of segmentative and discriminatory tactics, along the above noted axes, are critical markers of the world of work everywhere, and need to be investigated thoroughly.

Framing the Current Conjuncture

As suggested in our introductory remarks, primary purpose of this section is to underpin a couple of core building blocks central to the Marxist analytical framework of the world of work under capitalism, which help us understand several processes highlighted in the foregoing, and other important outcomes at the current juncture. Given the Marxist assumption that the fundamental motivation of capitalism, namely ceaseless accumulation, driven by maximum possible surplus extraction from workers, basic constitutive blocks of such a framework hinge on the structure of the labour process and overall control strategies to facilitate optimal outcomes for capital. This obviously has a wide canvas and our brief remarks in the following focus only on a couple arguments of immediate significance for this paper.

As is well-known, the abstract, stylised core of Marxist analysis in *Das Kapital* and other important contributions is a model of spontaneous system driven by its own 'laws of motion', in an incessantly competitive framework. With reference to labour, among the most profound laws that shape trajectory of spontaneous capitalism is what Marx framed as 'the absolute general law of capitalist accumulation', the essence of which is:

> The greater the social wealth, the functioning capital, the extent and energy of its growth, and, therefore, also the absolute mass of the proletariat and

> the productiveness of its labour, the greater is the industrial reserve army. The same causes which develop the expansive power of capital, develop also the labour power at its disposal. The relative mass of the industrial reserve army increases therefore with the potential energy of wealth. But the greater this reserve army in proportion to the active labour army, the greater is the mass of a consolidated surplus population, whose misery is in inverse ratio to its torment of labour. The more extensive, finally, the lazarus layers of the working class, and the industrial reserve army, the greater is official pauperism. *This is the absolute general law of capitalist accumulation*. Like all other laws it is modified in its working by many circumstances, the analysis of which does not concern us here ((Marx 1887 [Reprint 1995–1996] p. 450), emphasis added).

This law is central to an understanding of dynamics of world of work under capitalism and critical to comprehending labour reserves or relative surplus population. The conclusions that Marx reached using this law – namely inevitability of labour reserves as intrinsic, permanent and absolutely important to cyclical as well as secular functioning of capitalism – are not only among his remarkable insights, but unparalleled till date in the history of economic analysis to explain persistence unemployment and other important features of capitalist labour regimes. For Marx, perennial existence of labour reserves is not only an outcome of 'valorisation of capital', but in fact a general condition of capitalist accumulation process.[17] Such a framework of a *competitive* capitalist system distinguishes the Marxist tradition sharply, in fact irreconcilably so, from all other major analytical paradigms in economics, including the much respected Keynesian paradigm in heterodox economic analysis.[18]

Relentless 'valorisation of capital' versus 'de-valorisation of labour power' in Marx's narrative has several major consequences for the world of work including a perennial unstable relationship between the 'active labour reserve army' and the 'relative surplus population', continuous reconfiguration of these broad categories and their constituents etc. His discussion of the different components of the RSP, which he categorised *floating, latent and stagnant*, and how they connect with circuit of capital, at particular junctures as well as in *longue duree* perspective, are extremely insightful and persuasive. Essentially outcomes for the world of work are shaped by overall accumulation regimes, which have complex and multiple correlates, inter alia, economic-structural and political, both internal and external to a country. Further it is suggested that more spontaneous a system, higher would be the probability of a range of stark and adverse outcomes for labour, including a relatively powerful tendency of labour repulsion, compared to labour absorption. In such a system, prospects of gains for workers are extremely limited at best, as suggested by Marx and Engels in most of their writings. In fact, they advance the claim of inevitable polarisation, with growing poverty for workers at one pole along with growing wealth at another, for capital. The proposition has been much debated but remains an extremely powerful insight pertaining the working of capitalism. Sure enough, the polarisation thesis and conception of poverty are quite complex and have multiple dimensions, including a range of social and political questions.[19] However, the fact of worsening or stagnant material lot for workers has a strong association with spontaneous capitalism in Marx's analysis, as indeed analytical tradition following in his footsteps, through the so-called 'immeserisation thesis'.

Again, there are different ways of interpreting and investigating the immeserisation thesis, starting form a worsening of wage income for working people, on an average, which cannot guarantee access to a well-defined consumption basket, which had been the case at an earlier comparable point in time. Although both Marx and Engels occasionally hint at such an interpretation,[20] and there is substantial evidence to corroborate such immeserisation across time and space,[21] it seems to us that Marx's claim of "growing misery of workers" is better interpreted with reference to overall conditions of work, including multiple vulnerabilities, drudgery etc. along with monetary returns to labour power. Another common interpretation of the immeserisation thesis focuses not on absolute but relative impoverishment around money-metric and other indicators; in other words, such an approach highlights growing inequalities, or polarisation, across different critical spaces to establish the claim of relative impoverishment of the working classes.

Consistent with Marx's Absolute General Law of Capitalist Accumulation, the fact of the growing proportion of the reserve army, to the active labour army, can be considered a powerful indicator, in a *systemic sense*, of growing impoverishment. This claim gains further credence in a context where ensuring the basic sustenance of those constituting the labour reserves falls on the shoulders of the active labour army, as well as on the intensification of unpaid labour expended on social reproduction mainly by women, a feature common to large parts of the Global South even today. Yet another simple, but a powerful and telling measure of growing misery is the following: as capitalism evolves, incessant technological progress tends to reduce the socially necessary labour hours required to produce the 'wage basket', whereas the length of the working day does not go down proportionately, thus increasing the gap between what a worker gives and what she gets, measured in terms of total labour hours. This utterly simple point, borne out of the history of capitalism in large measure, is a compelling substantiation of the immeserisation thesis.

In short, Marx's remarkable conclusions regarding immeserisation of workers and inevitable polarisation constitutes a rich terrain, analytically and empirically, and are of critical importance in framing the relevant discourses on the world of work under capitalism. Essential claim here is: spontaneous capitalism, given its laws of motion, is driven by relentless commodification of labour (aided and abated by forces of primitive accumulation), perennial and growing labour reserves, inexorable immeserisation of workers, and polarisation of wealth and poverty, within and across countries. In our reading of Marx, it is important to assess the claim of 'worsening' of worker's condition with respect to totality of her situation, including what Marx, somewhat polemically, highlighted as "accumulation of misery, the torment of labour, slavery, ignorance, brutalisation, and moral degradation", in his critique of the prevailing regime. Processes that generate such outcomes are indeed complex and require careful investigations locally and globally, and any Marxist narrative must engage with these issues adequately. However, as Marx put it while referring to the General Law of Capitalist Accumulation, "like all other laws, it is modified in its working by many circumstances", which deserve serious investigations. There are two arguments that we wish to flag in this context.

First, even in a context of spontaneous capitalism, struggles of organised workers can achieve substantial collective gains against capital, as we know well from different junctures in history. In fact, Marx himself notes significance of such actions, which is not surprising given the centrality of political struggles in his theory, in several of his writings all through, and makes forceful case for building organisations of workers, nationally and internationally, and planned cooperation among them. For instance, he highlights the victory of workers in gaining a ten hour working day, legally approved in England in 1847, in his Inaugural Address to the First International, as major success of organised struggle of workers, and lauds this achievement, when the capitalist class "succumbed to the political economy of the working class". We may recall quite a few instances form history of capitalism when workers, through organisation and cooperation, have successfully achieved collective gains even in contexts structurally seemed heavily stacked against them. Taking an example from the present for instance, the way the neo-liberal tide has been confronted since the early 2000s in several countries in Latin America, with notable gains, offer crucial insights on agency of labour. As one would expect, there is a huge literature on these issues within the Marxist tradition and we are not in a position to engage with these any further here.[22] Simple point worth stressing here is: Marxian political economy must not be interpreted in crude and narrow deterministic frameworks.

This brings us to the second argument we wish to flag here: without undermining the agency of labour in any way, it is obvious that the larger structural context, consisting not only of the economic but other core features of accumulation regime, are crucial in shaping the overall political economy of labour at any juncture. As we know, historical capitalism has had a range of accumulation regimes with distinctly different prospects for trajectories of economic transformation, each having specific linkages and possibilities for incorporation of labour power and other dimensions pertaining to the world of work. Analytically and empirically, this has been a rich terrain within Marxian scholarship, investigating varieties within capitalism, 'articulation' versus disarticulation', making of the 'core' and 'periphery', issues of uneven development, unequal exchange and so on. We briefly touched on the making of the North and South, right at the outset of this paper in an overarching frame of global accumulation that ushered in capitalism, driven by colonialism and imperialism.

Of course, we have, at a high level of generality, worthwhile attempts at typologies of regimes, inter-temporally and across countries, that provide huge insights and powerful messages. Any adequate consideration of these issues is impossible within the scope of this paper. However, for illustrative purposes, and especially its relevance to the South, we may recall Amin's stylised distinction between two regimes, namely, a 'self-centred system' and a 'peripheral system' respectively (Amin 1974), during the post WWII period, with their roots in Marx's well-known 'departmental schemes' in *Capital*, (Marx 1893 [1956 Reprint] p. Chapter 19). Primary analytical concern of Amin is to contrast a relatively virtuous circuit of accumulation, which also entails better outcomes for the world of work, with a comprador, parasitic mode, i.e. the peripheral system which has little to offer to its own working people (For further details (Amin 1974; Jha et al. 2017)), a regime characteristic of many countries in the South during the post WWII era. However, as we also know, during this period of regulated capitalism, a handful of countries in the South were able to embark on relatively autonomous transformation trajectories, often with public sector-led industrialisation, occasionally substantial land reforms, etc., which resulted in respectable economic outcomes, including for labour; the so-called 'East Asian Miracle' cases were, economically speaking, considered as most impressive among these.

Not that these countries were beyond orbit of imperialism or early neo-colonialism; yet as we suggested in one of our recent paper, "a number of peripheral states-- beyond the revolutionary states of China, Vietnam and Cuba – were sufficiently radicalised to retain substantial autonomy and sustained an anti-imperialist posture in the spirit of Bandung, without succumbing immediately to the dictates of neoliberal rule. And, in fact, nationalism in the liberated peripheries generally still showed a commitment to social and economic development, even if it remained deficient in democratic content, and even if when it gravitated to the Western camp" (Yeros and Jha 2020). Ascendency of neoliberalism, or late neo-colonialism, has made it exceedingly difficult, structurally, for the South, the pursuit of relatively autonomous economic transformation and social development, and indeed the outcomes for the world of work. As discussed in the preceding sections, neoliberalism as a system unleashes a number of major processes which militate against labour at large, through multiple mechanisms that we highlighted, in the dominated periphery. Countries in the South through their willing or forced submission, get trapped in what Samir Amin (following Andre Gunder Frank) christened as *lumpen-development*, which is fundamentally anti-labourist. We have already flagged a number of relevant features and outcomes in this regard, to close this section it may useful to point out, very briefly, a couple of indicators pertaining to a worsening state of flux for labour, drawing on the ILO data.

As mentioned in an earlier paper (Jha et al. 2017), both for conceptual and empirical reasons, it is not feasible to have very good operational markers, with the help of global databases, for estimating the relevant and crucial Marxist categories such as the RSP and its components etc. Nonetheless, in spite of serious limitations, a broad-brush sketch pertaining to some of the major indicators may certainly be noted from the data bases of the ILO, such as the Key Indicators of Labour Markets. Using this source, a well-known distinction may be made between two broad categories; 'non-vulnerable workers' (consisting mainly of Wage and Salaried Employees), and 'vulnerable' (constituting Own Account or Self Employed and Contributing Family Workers); we take the former as a proxy for 'active labour force'. If we do so, the estimate for 2019, of the share of Wage and Salaried Employees in total global labour force is about 53 percent. As one would expect, there are stark differences between the North and the South; for Europe and North America the relevant ratios are around 85 percent, whereas for Sub Saharan African and South Asia, these are in the range of 24 to 30 percent. Although during the last couple of decades, globally there is a small improvement in the share of regular and salaried workers, it is also a fact that informality of different kinds has deepened considerably among them, for which we do not have comparable information globally.[23] It is also the case that these figures refer to the economically active population excluding not only the aged but also the young under 15, who are heavily concentrated in the South and remain unaccounted for in both paid and unpaid labour, especially girls.

Between 2000 and 2019, global count of workers increased from about 2.6 to 3.29 billion, which as a proportion of total world population for these two respective years shows a decline from about 61 to 57 percent; further, for the latter year, the share of the North in total global labour force has come down marginally, from about 18 to 15 percent, and the South currently accounts for about 85 percent of the global labour force. Based on the labour force participation numbers, it would appear that due to several challenges highlighted earlier, even the most basic indicator for the world of work, e.g. participation, conveys a worrisome message. What we seem to have, at least for the last couple of decades, is the phenomenon of so-called 'discouraged worker effect' in operation. For the U.S., East Asia and South Asia, estimates for those who have opted out of labour force are 25 million, 145 million and 275 million respectively; globally the projected count is about 740 million. It is worth stressing here that for very large segments of workers in the South, opting out basically underlines ultimate hopelessness and despair.

We have already pointed out earlier that the information relating to wage rates, wage share etc., from all major global data sources, generally paint a grim picture for the recent decades, although, with notable variations across regions and countries, which require much closer investigation; unfortunately we are not in a position to undertake this task here. However, the moot point is: labour questions in the South (or in the North) can hardly be addressed by relying on currently dominant frameworks of spontaneous capitalism or tinkering on its margins, a conclusion which is as old as Marxian political economy itself; hence our insistence in this paper to return to such a 'drawing board', yet again.

Concluding Remarks

As we see it, global capitalism has been in a state of profound protracted crisis, with huge and persistent challenges for working people across the world, and more so for those in the South. Central project for the political economy of labour currently has to be framed in a comprehensive strategy of rolling back the globally dominant model of corporate controlled lumpen capitalism, fashioned and driven in large measure by the imperial centres. This model, which is hegemonic on a global scale, is akin to a pyramid, characterised by a handful of giant monopolies mostly headquartered in the North, and a massive RSP located largely in the South; the former reaping the imperialist rents, and the huge mass of working people in the latter trapped in pauperisation. As long as such a model remains hegemonic, there is no escape from persistent polarisation, and precariarisation of the working masses, inherent in such a model.

However, as Amin says, 'Yet, this autumn of capitalism does not coincide with a "springtime of peoples" which implies that workers and peoples in struggle have made an accurate assessment of the requirements, not to "end crisis of capitalism" but to "end capitalism". This has not happened or not yet' (Amin 2019). In other words, for political economy of labour, the road is possibly a long and hard one, but one can hardly visualise any other promising road. The essence of the challenge is to work for a system, which functions 'without the existence of a class of masters employing a class of hands', to borrow a gem of an expression from Marx again.

Notes

1. It is worth recalling Karl Marx's well-known statement on some of the powerful and rapacious mechanisms associated with early capitalism: "The discovery of gold and silver in America, the extirpation, enslavement and entombment in mines of the aboriginal population, the beginning of the conquest and looting of the East Indies, the turning of Africa into a warren for the commercial hunting of black-skins, signalised the rosy dawn of the era of capitalist production. These idyllic proceedings are the chief momenta of primitive accumulation. On their heels treads the commercial war of the European nations, with the globe for a theatre. It begins with the revolt of the Netherlands from Spain, assumes giant dimensions in England's Anti-Jacobin War, and is still going on in the opium wars against China, &c" (Marx 1887 [Reprint 1995–1996] p. 533).

2. For some of the major contributions, supporting such a conclusion, see Samir Amin (1973, 1976), Amiya Bagchi (1982, 2005), Paul Baran (1957), Eduardo Galeano (1973), Peter Magubane (1979), Irfan Habib (1995), Eric Williams (1966), Walter Rodney (1972), Joseph Inikori and Engerman, ed. (1992), Prabhat Patnaik (1995, 2009), and Utsa Patnaik and Prabhat Patnaik (2016).
3. As mentioned, there is a huge literature on these issues and some of the useful references include: David Harvey (2005), Erik Reinert, Jayati Ghosh and Rainer Kattel (2016), Robert Pollin et al. (1998), Ha Joon Chang (2002), Lucia Pradella and Thomas Marois ed. (2014).
4. Epstein offers a simple and useful definition: "Financialisation means the increasing role of financial motives, financial markets, financial actors and financial institutions in the operation of domestic and international economies" (Epstein 2005 p. 3).
5. Empirical measures of financialisation are tricky, complex and controversial. However, there are relatively simple estimates which are robust indicators of the phenomena. One such measure is the ratio of the value of global financial transactions to the value of transactions in global trade. As per a recent estimate by Thomson and Dutta, this ratio was 2:1 in 1973 and increased to a whopping 90:1 by 2004. As per the same estimate, for the year 2017, value of the global trade for the entire year happened to be USD 17.88 trillion, whereas valuation of *daily financial transactions* in the same year stood at USD 5.1 trillion (Thomson, et al., 2018).
6. As Patnaik puts it, "The new finance is not separate from industry, since even capital employed in industry is not immune to the quest for speculative gains, but industry does not occupy any special place in the plan for this finance capital.... This is basically what the process of financialisation involves, namely an enormous growth of capital as finance, pure and simple and its quest for quick speculative gains" (Patnaik 2010).
7. As Patnaik notes, a fundamental difference contemporary globalisation compared to the earlier phases is "the fact that the current episode is characterised by a mobility not just of capital-as –finance across the globe but also of capital-in-production" (Patnaik 2016a, b p. 3). He goes on to suggest that had such a feature (e.g. direct investment from the North to the South) characterised earlier episodes of globalisation, "the division of the world into an advanced and backward segment would not have occurred" (Patnaik 2016a, b).
8. Adam Smith had emphasised the 'division of labour' as among the most important contributor to the wealth of nations; whatever be the merits of his claims, for an enthusiastic Smithian on this matter the current state of the division of labour, going beyond the firm, far and wide across the world, would be a dream come true!

9. As John Smith notes, “In 1980s half of the world’s industrial workers lived in Europe, Japan, and North America, i.e. the imperialist nations. Since then, in just three decades, their numbers have declined in absolute terms by around a quarter, while the export-led expansion of the industrial workforce in low-wage countries has grown rapidly and now comprises 80 percent of the world’s industrial workers” (Smith 2013).
10. Interested readers may refer to Praveen Jha and Amit Chakraborty (2014) and Praveen Jha and Paris Yeros (2019) for brief overviews of the relevant arguments.
11. For a sample of recent important contributions, interested readers may refer to several articles by Foster and his colleagues in Monthly Review. Further, there are quite a few impressive books engaging with this theme during the last two decades; Samir Amin (2010 and 2011), (2010; 2011) Ernesto Screpanti (2014) Immanuel Ness (2015), Intan Suwandi (2019), John. B. Foster and Robert McChesney (2012), Stephanie Barrientos (2019) and Dev Nathan et al. (2016), are among persuasive and easily accessible treatments of the subject, most of these within Marxist Political Economy.
12. As noted by Stiglitz, for a male worker in the United States, real wage over a period of more than five decades (between 1968 and 2011), did not increase, which is indeed one of the starkest indicators of the increased pressure on workers at large in economically the most powerful country in the world (Stiglitz 2013).
13. Highlighting the tendency of the growing hiatus between the ‘vectors of world real wages and productivity’, Patnaik notes, “A rise in the share of surplus in total output has the effect ceteris paribus of reducing aggregated demand....for a simple reason highlighted by authors like Michal Kalecki (1954), Josef Steindl (1976), and Paul Sweezy and Paul Baran (Sweezy and Baran 1966), namely that the consumption-income ratio is higher for wage-earners than for surplus-earners. Such a shift therefore has the effect of reducing aggregate consumption, and hence aggregate demand for any given level of investment” (Patnaik 2016a, b p. 9).
14. For a good overview of the relevant trends, implications etc. interested readers may refer to *Inception Report for the Global Commission on the Future of Work* (ILO 2017).
15. As the 2017 ILO report observes, “while the prevailing evidence of past technological developments suggests that waves of technological change result in short-term job destruction followed by the creation of jobs, today’s technological advances are emerging at an unprecedented rate and changing work in ways not seen before” (ILO 2017 p. 10).
16. As already stated, there is a large and growing literature on these issues, and to mention a couple of helpful references, readers may look at Christian

Fuchs (2014), Ursula Huws (2010, 2014), Janine Berg et al. (2018) and International Labour Organisation (2017).

17. To quote Marx: "But if a surplus labouring population is a necessary product of accumulation or of the development of wealth on a capitalistic basis, this surplus population becomes conversely the lever of capitalist accumulation, nay a *condition of existence of the capitalist mode of production.* It forms a disposable industrial reserve army that belongs to capital as absolutely as if the latter had bred it at its own cost. Independently of the limits of the actual increase of population, it creates for the changing needs of the self-expansion of capital, a mass of humans always ready for exploitation" ((Marx 1887 [Reprint 1995–1996] p. 444) emphasis added).
18. We have discussed these issues briefly in an earlier work (Jha et al. 2017).
19. Marx's well-known and much discussed proposition in Chapter 25 of *Capital Volume 1* that, "in proportion as capital accumulates, the situation of the worker, be his payment high or low, must grow worse" (Marx 1887 [Reprint 1995–1996] p. 451), is an obvious and clear statement beyond a simply construed material conception, and hints at his deep and abiding engagements with issues of alienation, conditions of freedom etc. as critical constituents of human poverty. In fact, contrary to popular perception, that capitalism is conducive to realisation of individual freedom, whereas socialism is antithetical to it, Marx's claim is exactly the opposite; rule of capital, for him, was "the most complete suspension of individual freedoms" (Marx, 11857–61 [Reprint 1993] p. 652).
20. In his 1867 address of the General Council of the International Working Men's Association, Marx refers to the unchecked functioning of "the iron rule of supply and demand" (read as spontaneous capitalism) *reducing* the "producers of all wealth to a starvation diet". Likewise in his Inaugural Address to the First International in 1864, reflecting on the situation of the English industrial working class, Marx says, "it is a great fact that the misery of the working masses has not diminished from 1848 to 1864, and yet this period is unrivalled for the development of its industry and the growth of commerce" (Marx 1864).
21. Drawing on an impressive array of scholarship on the English experiences, Ranadive notes that, "not only was there a qualitative deterioration over 1795–1840 in the living standard of workers, but relative to other classes in English society, the deterioration stood out in sharp contrast.…While the deterioration set in after 1770, the critical year was 1795 when the 'battle of the loaf' started with the labourer being driven from a wheaten, to a potato diet" (Ranadive 1987 p. 45). In a recent and very impressive contribution to theorising imperialism, Patnaik and Patnaik (2016), highlights absolute worsening in the plight of working people with reference to

accessing even minimum nutrition norms in the countries of the South at different junctures.

22. We may mention a couple of important references for readers interested in pursuing it further: Hal Draper (1978), Eric Olin Wright (2000), Beverly Silver (2003).
23. In case of India, for instance, within the so-called formal sector, there has been a huge increase in the share of officially defined informal workers.

Bibliography

Amin, S. (1973). *Neocolonialism in West Africa*. s.l.: Penguin.

Amin, S. (1974). *Accumulation on a World Scale*. New York: Monthly Review Press.

Amin, S. (1976). *Unequal Development: An Essay in Social Formation of Peripheral Capitalism*. Sussex: Monthly Review Press.

Amin, S. (1997). *Capitalism in the Age of Globalisation*. London: Zed.

Amin, S. (2010). *The Law of World Wide Value*. New York: Monthly Review Press.

Amin, S. (2011). *Global History: A View from the South*. Cape Town: Pamazuka Press.

Amin, S. (2013). *The Implosion of Contemporary Capitalism*. New York: Monthly Review Press.

Amin, S. (2019). The New Structure of Imperialism. *Monthly Review, 71*, 3.

Bagchi, A. K. (1982). *Political Economy of Underdevelopment*. Cambridge: Cambridge University Press.

Bagchi, A. K. (2005). *Perilous Passage: Mankind and the Global Ascendancy of Capital*. London: Rowman and Littlefield.

Bairoch, P. (1995). *Economics and World History: Myths and Paradox*. Chicago: University of Chicago Press.

Baran, P. (1957). *The Political Economy of Growth*. New York: Monthly Review Press.

Barrientos, S. (2019). *Gender and Work in Global Value Chains*. Cambridge, UK: Cambridge University Press.

Basu, K. (2016). Globalization of Labor Markets and the Growth Prospects of Nations. *Journal of Policy Modeling, 38*, 4.

Berg, J., et al. (2018). *Digital Labour Platforms and the Future of Work: Towards Decent Work in Online World*. Geneva: International Labour Organisation.

Bukharin, N. 1929 [Reprint 1950]. *Imperialism and the World Economy*. [Reprint 1950].

Chang, H. J. (2002). *Kicking Away the Ladder: Development Strategy in Historical Perspective*. s.l.: Anthem Press.

Draper, H. (1978). *Karl Marx's Theory of Revolution: The Theory of Social Classes*. New York: Monthly Review Press.

Epstein, G. (2005). *Financialization and the World Economy*. Cheltenham: Edward Elgar.

Foster, J. B., & McChesney, R. (2012). *The Endless Crisis: How Finance Capital Produces Stagnation and Upheavel from USA to China* (p. 2012). New York: Monthly Review Press.

Frank, A. G. (1967). *Capitalism and Underdevelopment in Latin America.* New York: Monthly Review Press.

Fuchs, C. (2014). *Digital Labour and Karl Marx.* New York: Monthly Review Press.

Galeano, E. (1973). *The Open Veins of Latin America: Five Centuries of Pillage of a Continent.* New York: Monthly Review Press.

Habib, I. (1995). *Essays in Indian History: Towards a Marxist Perception.* Delhi: Tulika Books.

Harvey, D. (2005). *A Brief History of Neoliberalism.* Oxford: Oxford University Press.

Hess, M. (2018). Global Production Networks. In D. Richardson (Ed.), *The International Encyclopedia of Geography: People, the Earth, Environment, and Technology* (Vol. 13). Hoboken: Wiley Blackwell.

Huws, U. (2010). *The Making of the Cybertariat.* Beijing: University of Beijing Press.

Huws, U. (2014). *Labour in a Global Digital Economy: The Cybertariat Comes of Age.* New York: Monthly Review Press.

Hymer, S. (1979). *The Multinational Corporation.* Cambridge: Cambridge University Press.

ILO. (2017). *Inception Report for the Global Commission on the Future of Work.* Geneva: International Labour Organisation.

Inikori, J., & Engerman, S. (Eds.). (1992). *The Atlantic Slave Trade: Effects on Economies, Societies and Peoples in Africa, the Americas, and Europe.* Duke University Press: Durham.

Jha, P., & Chakraborty, A. (2014). *Post Fordism, Global Production Networks and Implications for Labour: Case Studies from National Capital Region, India.* Delhi: Institute for Studies in Industrial Development.

Jha, P., & Yeros, P. (2019). Global Agricultural Value Systems and the South: Some Critical Issues at the Current Juncture. *Agrarian South: Journal of Political Economy, 8*, 1–2.

Jha, P., Moyo, S., & Yeros, P. (2017). Capitalism and Labour Reserves. In C. P. Chandrasekhar & J. Ghosh (Eds.), *Interpreting the World to Change It: Essays for Prabhat Patnaik.* Delhi: Tulika Books.

Kalecki, M. (1954). *Theory of Economic Dynamics: An Essay on Cyclical and Long-Run Changes in Capitalist Economy.* London: Allen and Unwin.

Keynes, J. M. (1936). *The General Theory of Employment, Interest and Money.* London: Palgrave Macmillan.

Kuznets, S. (1971). *Economic Growth of Nations: Total Output and Production Structure.* Cambridge: Harvard University Press.

Maddison, A. (2007). *The World Economy (Two Volumes)*. s.l.: OECD.
Magdoff, H., & Sweezy, P. (1987). *Stagnation and Financial Explosion* (p. 1987). New York: Monthly Review Press.
Magubane, P. (1979). *Political Economy of Race and Class in South Africa*. New York: Monthly Review Press.
Marx, K. (1864). Inaugural Address and Provisional Rules of the International Working Men's Association, Along with the "General Rules". *Marx and Engels Internet Archive*. [Online] October 21–27, 1864. [Cited: August 20, 2020.] https://www.marxists.org/archive/marx/works/1864/10/27.htm
Marx, K. (1887 [Reprint 1995–1996]). *Das Capital, Volume 1: The Process of Capitalist Production*. USSR: Progress Publishers.
Marx, K. (1893 [1956 Reprint]). *Das Capital Volume 2: The Process of Circulation of Capital*. Moscow: Progress Publishers.
Marx, K. (11857–61 [Reprint 1993]). *Grundrisse: Foundations of the Critique of Political Economy*. London, 11857–61 [Reprint 1993].
Mazzucato, M. (2017). *The Value of Everything: Making and Taking in the Global Economy*. s.l.: Pubic Affairs.
Nathan, D., Tiwari, M., & Sarkar, S. (Eds.). (2016). *Labour in Global Value Chains in Asia*. Cambridge: Cambridge University Press.
Ness, I. (2015). *Southern Insurgencies: The Coming of the Global Working Class*. London: Pluto Press.
Patnaik, P. (1995). *Whatever Happened to Imperialism and Other Essays*. Delhi: Tulika Books.
Patnaik, P. (2009). *The Value of Money*. Delhi: Tulika Books.
Patnaik, P. (2010). *Notes on Contemporary Imperialism*. https://mronline.org/2010/12/20/notes-on-contemporary-imperialism/. [Online] Monthly Review Press, December 2010. [Cited: August 17, 2020]. https://mronline.org/2010/12/20/notes-on-contemporary-imperialism/
Patnaik, P. (2016a). Capitalism and Its Current Crisis. *Monthly Review, 67*, 8.
Patnaik, P. (2016b). Globalisation and the Current Impasse of Capitalism. *networkideas.org*. [Online] International Development Economics Associates, October 28, 2016. [Cited: August 17, 2020.] http://www.networkideas.org/themes/political-economy/2016/10/globalization-and-the-impasse-of-capitalism/
Patnaik, U., & Patnaik, P. (2016). *A Theory of Imperialism* (p. 2016). New York: Columbia University Press.
Pollin, R. (2012). *Back to Full Employment*. Cambridge, MA: MIT Press.
Pollin, R., Baker, D., & Epstein, G. (1998). *Globalisation and Progressive Economic Policy*. Cambridge: Cambridge University Press.
Pradella, L., & Marois, T. (2014). *Polarising Development: Alternatives to Neoliberalism and the Crisis* (p. 2014). London: Pluto Press.
Ranadive, K. (1987). *The Political Economy of Poverty*. Hyderabad: Orient Longman.

Reinert, E., Ghosh, J., & Kattel, R. (2016). *Handbook of Alternative Theories of Economic Development*. Cheltenham: Edward Elgar.
Richard, J. B., & Robert, E. M. (Eds.). (1974). *Global Reach: The Power of Multinational Corporations*. New York: Touchstone.
Rodney, W. (1972). *How Europe Underdeveloped Africa*. London: Bogle L'ouventre Press.
Screpanti, E. (2014). *Global Imperialism and the Great Crisis: The Uncertain Future of Capitalism*. New York: Monthly Review Press.
Silver, B. (2003). *Forces of Labour: Workers' Movement and Globalization Since 1870*. Cambridge: Cambridge University Press.
Smith, J. (2013). Southern Labour: 'Peripheral' No Longer. *International Socialism, 30*, 9.
Steindl, J. (1976). *Maturity and Stagnation in American Capitalism*. New York: Monthly Review Press.
Stiglitz, J. (2013). *The Price of Inequality: How Today's Divided Society Endangers Our Future*. UK: Penguin.
Suwandi, I. (2019). *Value Chains: The New Economic Imperialism*. New York: Monthly Review Press.
Sweezy, P. (1994). The Triumph of Finance Capital. *Monthly Review, 46*, 2.
Sweezy, P., & Baran, P. (1966). *Monopoly Capitalism: An Essay on American Economic and Social Order*. New York: Monthly Review Press.
Thomson, F., & Dutta, S. (2018). *Financialisation: A Primer*. Amsterdam: Transnational Institute.
Williams, E. (1966). *Capitalism and Slavery*. New York: Capricorn Books.
Wright, E. O. (2000). Working-class power, capitalist-class interests, and class compromise. *American Journal of Sociology, 105*, 4.
Yeros, P., & Jha, P. (2020). Late Neo-Colonialism: Monopoly Capitalism in Permanent Crisis. *Agrarian South: Journal of Political Economy, 9*, 1.

CHAPTER 3

The Concept of 'Working People'

Issa G. Shivji

This chapter interrogates the concept of 'working people'. Lenin and other classical Marxists commonly used terms like labouring people, working people, or rural poor. Typically, they were used as descriptive, or, at best, as terms of political art rather than theoretical science. The inspiration in this article for the use of the term 'working people' comes from Walter Rodney. Building on previous work, the article relates the concept of working people to a modified definition of primitive accumulation under neo-liberalism, that is, as a process of surplus extraction by capital based on expropriation of a part of necessary consumption of the producer. It is argued that this is the material basis common to all sectors of what is here understood as working people.

Originally published in *Agrarian South: Journal of Political Economy, Vol. 6 No. 1*

I. G. Shivji (✉)
University of Dar es Salaam, Dar es Salaam, Tanzania

P. Jha et al. (eds.), *Labour Questions in the Global South*,
https://doi.org/10.1007/978-981-33-4635-2_3

Marxist Tradition

In this short piece, I interrogate the concept of working people by tracing my own conceptual journey to arrive at the proposition put forth here. Needless to add that the journey was a collective enterprise of radical intellectuals who believed they were engaged in emancipatory politics and not the musings of an intellectual wanderer or a 'revolutionary traveller'. (I borrow the term from John Saul (2010).) These snippets give me an opportunity to mention in passing some of the radical debates of the post-Arusha Declaration period at the leading University in Tanzania and for that matter in Africa.

Lenin and other classical Marxists commonly used terms such as labouring people, working people, rural poor and so on. Typically, they were used as descriptive or at best as terms of political art rather than theoretical science. We too used the term 'working people' in our debates as a short hand for worker–peasant alliance but never felt the need to theorize it. With the wisdom of hindsight, I can now see that even then practice demanded a theorization but we were too steeped in traditional Marxist frameworks to contemplate a departure from the 'formula' of the proletariat as the agency of the revolution. We were very familiar with the traditional categories of Marxist political economy—working class, bourgeoisie, petty bourgeoisie, lumpen proletariat, etc. In a country where the most oppressed, and perhaps exploited, was the mass of the peasantry, we readily, if somewhat lazily, fell back on the Chinese formula of worker–peasant alliance led by the working class and where the working class itself was wanting in leadership, working class leadership was substituted by the leadership of the proletarian ideology (Shivji 1976). Where would the proletarian ideology come from? Lenin gave the answer. The working class on its own is capable only of trade union consciousness; socialist consciousness is brought from outside their ranks by bourgeois intellectuals who have been exposed to a wider worldview (Lenin 1970, p. 70).

Our own Marxist theoretician Amilcar Cabral, who led the anticolonial liberation struggle in Guinea-Bissau, argued that the struggle would of necessity be led by the petty bourgeoisie provided they committed class suicide. In a classical piece, The Weapon of Theory that remains relevant to this day, Cabral argued:

> To retain the power which national liberation puts in its hands, the petty bourgeoisie has only one path: to give free rein to its natural tendencies to

> become more bourgeois, to permit the development of a bureaucratic and intermediary bourgeoisie in the commercial cycle, in order to transform itself into a national pseudo-bourgeoisie, that is to say in order to negate the revolution and necessarily ally itself with imperialist capital. In order not to betray these objectives the petty bourgeoisie has only one choice: to strengthen its revolutionary consciousness, to reject the temptations of becoming more bourgeois and the natural concerns of its class mentality, to identify itself with the working classes and not to oppose the normal development of the process of revolution. This means that in order to truly fulfil the role in the national liberation struggle, the revolutionary petty bourgeoisie must be capable of committing suicide as a class in order to be reborn as revolutionary workers, completely identified with the deepest aspirations of the people to which they belong. (https://www.marxists.org/subject/africa/cabral/1966/weapon-theory.htm)

Cabral did not live long enough to witness the miserable failure of the 'revolutionary petty bourgeoisie' of national liberation to commit suicide; instead, it went along the first path of turning itself into a voracious pseudo-bourgeoisie whether in or outside the state. The rude interruption of neoliberalism blew the lid off of whatever was left of its nationalist pretentions as it embraced imperialist dictates lock, stock and barrel resuming the plunder of natural and human resources of the colonial era. But let me return to the journey.

Rodney's Inspiration

The inspiration for the use of the term 'working people' came from Walter Rodney. Rodney taught at the University of Dar es Salaam for eight years in the Department of History (Shivji 2012). He was one of the leading participants in student struggles and an active, *albeit* noncard carrying member of the University Students African Revolutionary Front (USARF) which published the well-known student radical journal Cheche (Hirji 2010). When he returned to his native Guyana, he formed his party and called it 'Working People's Alliance' (WPA). The party was the first that brought together working people from the Indian and African communities and had a collective leadership, though, of course, Rodney remained its iconic leader.

I used the term in the book I edited called *The State and the Working People in Tanzania* (Shivji 1986b), which contained articles by young radical researchers exploring the transformation of the Tanzanian state and its relationship with the working people under the ideology of Nyerere's Ujamaa. The central thesis of the book was to show that the Tanzanian state had established its ideological and organizational hegemony over the working people (working class, peasantry and students) and in the process had become a centralized, authoritarian party-state. The term working people was used loosely as a composite noun to designate working class, peasants, lower petty bourgeoisie, etc., but not theorized as a concept. The need was not felt then, though rereading my introduction to the book today, I believe the germs of some paradigmatic shift in explaining the exploitation (not just oppression) of the peasant under capitalism were there. This was probably the first step leading to the conceptualization of working people. The argument was summarized thus:

> The peasant constitutes the major source of surplus and as such is made to yield maximum surplus product. To maximise the rate of exploitation of the peasant producer, capital lets him retain ownership of the means of production and control over the labour process so that capital may be free from bearing the costs of peasant reproduction. But this in turn means that unlike a worker who yields surplus value by sheer operation of economic forces, the peasant has to be constantly subjected to extra-economic coercion so that he continues yielding surplus to capital. The major extra-economic force is state coercion. (Shivji 1986b, p. 8)

The argument that the peasant's exploitation by capital is predicated on the fact that exploitation cuts into the peasant's necessary consumption was first developed in our article that we did for a study group of Tanzanian and Ugandan comrades on the agrarian question.[1] The article was never published but I rehashed the position in my '*The exploitation of small peasant*' (Shivji 1983) and '*The Roots of Agrarian Crisis in Tanzania—A Theoretical Perspective*' (Shivji 1987). These writings try to explain the relation between the peasant and the state in the context of overall domination by imperialism, taking as its point of departure Lenin's definition of imperialism as the monopoly stage of capitalism (Lenin 1999). Monopoly capital reaps super-profits—meaning over and above average profits—by establishing and reproducing control both at the level of production and the market. The control is rarely direct. 'It is often mediated through intermediaries, those classes and social groups in the dominated social formation who play the role of compradores' (Shivji 1987, p. 119). To be sure, the control is never absolute or complete. The process is contradictory. '[T]o the extent that commodity economy is a soil of capitalist relations and the fact that the peasant is involved in commodity production means that peasant differentiation does take place …'.(Ibid., p. 126). This tendency, which I was later to dub as 'accumulation from below' gets stuck, as it were, at the stage of rich peasant. Thus 'capitalist development in agriculture appears as if it was in a transition which has been arrested' (Ibid.) The conclusion was:

> Since the surplus is siphoned off, there is very little accumulation in agriculture. The upper echelons of the peasantry move into commercial and merchant activities—transport, hotels, guesthouses etc. rather than in the direction of capitalist farming. The latter would require investment in technology and industrial inputs both of which have a high premium and are, therefore, 'unprofitable'.
>
> What is preserved and reproduced, therefore, is an impoverished, starving middle and poor peasantry which forms the backbone of agriculture production and the source of surplus for capital. (Ibid., p. 127)

The article foreclosed the possibility of the development of fully fledged agrarian capitalism in an African periphery. The capitalism of the periphery was variously labelled as truncated, arrested, perverse, etc. (Hadjivayanis 1987; Rweyemamu 1973). Since this was the time in Tanzania of the transition from the nationalist to the neoliberal period, the debate on IMF conditionalities packaged in structural adjustment programmes (SAPs) was rife. The 1987 article argued that with open markets, withdrawal of state subsidies, privatization of land-ownership, dismantling of single-channel marketing and a free ride for foreign investment, the country would return to the classical colonial-type agrarian economy. This time around it would be worse because we would witness a rapid Latin Americanization of Africa, as Nyerere would have caricatured it. We may as well quote the results of the IMF programme predicted by my 1987 article:

> 1. gradual concentration of prime agriculture land in the hands of large, foreign corporations specializing in traditional export crops (tea, coffee, cotton etc) and luxury food (fruits, vegetables and so on) for foreign markets (the Sahelian model). This scenario can be extended as the corporations specialize in meat and dairy products for the Middle-Eastern market. In short, tropical Africa would provide cheap land and labour, while finance capital would reap super-profit. …

2. a quick development of a landless peasantry;
3. massive migration from rural to urban areas;
4. sprawling cities full of luxury, consumer goods with millions of marginalized unemployed lumpen masses living on the verge of starvation;
5. all the evils of child labour, prostitution, urban ghetto violence, etc.;
6. a political superstructure rabid with coups, assassination and pathetic subservience to foreign interests;
7. a tiny, local wealthy compradorial class shamelessly squeezing into the interstices of foreign multinationals as representatives, commission agents, real estate speculators, hoteliers and caterers, political brokers, etc.... (Ibid., p. 128)

This was written 30 years ago. Not all has come to pass, at least not in Tanzania, although it has come close. As a composite picture of the continent as a whole, however, the prophecy comes uncannily close to reality. One wishes though one would have been proved wrong! To be fair, the article did posit an alternative set of measures that would launch the country on a path towards what it called new democracy. It added a caveat that this was not a full new democratic programme. Such a programme 'would assume a fundamental change in state power—a people's power with worker–peasant alliance as the base under the leadership of the proletariat.' (Ibid., p. 130). The last formulation is traditional. The concept of the working people has not yet entered the discourse. That was to come later with the second shift in paradigmatic focus, the focus now being on accumulation, what Marx called, the 'Moses and the Prophets' of the capitalist system.

Character and Trajectory of Accumulation

In 1990, the President of Tanzania appointed a Commission of Enquiry into Land Matters (Land Commission) which I had the honour to chair. This was the first land commission to be appointed after independence. The last Commission was in 1953–1955, the East African Royal Commission, appointed by the colonial government. In a comprehensive report, the gravamen of its recommendations on land was to create conditions for individualization of land and its negotiability to allow mobility of resources from uneconomic to economic hands, as it puts it (Ingham 1955, ch. 23). In short, the underlying rationale was to create enabling environment for the development of a class of yeoman farmers. Nyerere, then the leader of the freedom movement Tanganyika African National Union, opposed it. So it never came to pass. For 40 years after independence, the land tenure system in essence remained as it was established by the colonial government in 1923 under the Land Ordinance (No. 3 of 1923).

Typical of the British legal tradition, the Land Ordinance was a masterpiece of legal craftsmanship. In less than 20 sections, it laid down the salient features of the land tenure system that endured for almost three-fourths of a century. Tanganyika was ruled as a trust territory under the mandate of the League of Nations, later the United Nations, which stipulated the supremacy of 'native' interests. Unlike neighbouring Kenya which was a colony, where all lands were crown lands, in Tanganyika all lands were declared to be public lands and

> all public lands and all rights over the same are hereby declared to be under the control and subject to the disposition of the Governor and shall be held and administered for the use and common benefit, direct or indirect, of the natives of the Territory, and no title to the occupation and use of any such lands shall be valid without the consent of the Governor. (Section 3)

In one fell swoop, the radical title or ultimate authority over land was vested in the state which had the discretionary powers over its allocation and use. Land was nationalized. The governor was empowered to grant rights of occupancy, a kind of lease, of up to 99 years to non-natives. A small settler population and other immigrant communities were given rights of occupancy while 'natives' continued to occupy land under their customary laws. Over a period of time, a doctrine of deemed right of occupancy was evolved by judicial interpretation. Courts held that natives occupied and used land by virtue of an implied consent of the governor that could be withdrawn at the governor's discretion. The land tenure system thus came to rest on a triangular relationship between the grantee of a right of occupancy who held titles, customary owners who had no titles and the state that was the custodian of radical title. The relationship between the state and the grantee was a legal relation governed by civil law; that between the state and the customary owner was an administrative relation governed by the state's policy and the relation between the grantee and a customary owner was hierarchical where the registered title was superior to a customary owner's claim. Customary laws governed the relation among customary owners. The arrangement was thus neat in law, although it did not always worked as neatly on the ground. Nonetheless, the most important implication of the land tenure system was that the rights and claims of customary owners were not secured by law against the state. The security of the big majority of peasant and pastoral communities was precarious. As and when it suited the state, they continued to occupy the land producing food for themselves and cash crops for export under the pain of minimum acreage laws—an acre of food crops and acre of cash crop, for example —enforced by criminal sanctions, whereas the relation between a grantee of a right of occupancy and the state was legal governed by civil law subject to civil remedy; that between the state and customary owner was administrative governed by fiat and subject to criminal sanctions.

From the standpoint of political economy, the state stood in the shoes of a landlord in relation to occupiers with an entitlement to ground rent. In practice, grantees of rights of occupancy—foreign plantation companies and settlers—were charged minimal rent while the element of rent from customary owners was built into various taxes and tributes, including the so-called communal labour, a euphemism for forced labour, which was often extracted from rural communities under the guise of constructing public works. Labour for plantations, mines and public works was migratory recruited from labour reserves, a system akin to indentured labour. Labour was paid what was called a bachelor wage just enough to keep body and soul together and pay cash taxes like poll tax chargeable on every adult male above an apparent age of 18 years (see generally Shivji 1986a). As the man worked on a plantation for a period of, say, nine months, the woman and children were working on family farms growing food and cash crops. The result was that the man was semi-proletarianized while the woman was peasantized, both subsidizing capital which reaped super-profits. Surplus for capital cut into necessary consumption of the producer, man and woman, who lived sub-human lives while exerting super-human labour. This was a form of primitive accumulation of capital in all its essentials.

Evidence received by the Tanzania Land Commission showed that the main grievance of the rural community was insecurity of land tenure resulting in their customary lands being arbitrarily acquired by the state and its organs—parastatals, national parks, army, prisons, bureaucracy, etc.,—without their involvement or consultation. The commission interpreted this to imply that the demand of rural producers was democratization of the land tenure system in which they would fully participate in the allocation and use of land and broadly in decision-making over their natural resources. On the issue of security of tenure, the commission took the position that this could not be decided without first identifying the path and agency of development.

The commission argued that in the debates and discourses of the 1960s and 1970s, it was believed that the small peasant was destined to disappear and that the future lay in large scale, industrialized agriculture for reasons of efficiency and productivity. Tanzania experimented with such large-scale investment and they had proved to be miserable failures. Studies had shown that the legendary inefficiency and low productivity of the small peasant was not inherent; rather it was based on deliberate policy measures of the state—for example, ensuring supply of cheap labour, charging minimal rent for land, subsidizing imports of inputs and so on—favouring large-scale producers at the expense of small one. In effect, the small-producer gave a hidden subsidy to the large ones. Such policies 'simultaneously impoverished the peasant thus perpetuating the myth of his inefficiency and low productivity while raising the profits of the large-scale holder thus upholding the latter's claim to superior economic performance' (United Republic of Tanzania 1994, p. 137).

Beginning from the premise that Tanzania was a country of small holders (it still is) and was likely to remain so in the foreseeable future, the Commission went on to recommend a land tenure structure based on providing security to the small producer while at the same time ensuring participation of peasant communities in the decision-making organs of the village. This is not the place to go into the details of the commission's recommendations. Suffice it so that its central recommendation was to divest the state of its monopoly of radical title and diversify it. The radical title in village lands would be vested in their respective village assemblies (a body of all adult residents of a village) that would be constitutionally recognized as corporate bodies and the lowest rung of local government. The radical title in national lands would be held by a National Land Commission which would be accountable to the Parliament at national level. What is of immediate interest to this chapter is the Commission's accumulation model which was summed up as follows. It needs to be quoted at length.

> [T]he Commission recognises that there are forces within the peasant and pastoral communities capable of generating, accumulating and reinvesting capital in the rural sector. These forces develop spontaneously as a result of

> differentiation in the smallholder economy. In the literature, they are often described as 'rich peasants' or kulaks. We distinguish them from capitalist farmers. Unlike the latter, the former are not simply managers and supervisors but continue to work on their land. In the past, they were identified as 'real exploiters' and thus stifled and suppressed. We believe that at this stage of our development they are one possible agency of accumulation from below or a national agrarian and pastoral development, albeit capitalist.
>
> … [I]t is quite conceivable that the rich peasantry can develop a voracious appetite for land at the expense of the large majority of the peasantry. That possibility informs our recommendations on fixing a statutory ceiling on land ownership on village lands, …. (Ibid., p. 138)

Accumulation from below was another way of denoting the classical Marxist process of accumulation by expanded reproduction. This position is pregnant with the development of, and distinguishing between, two tendencies of accumulation, that is to say, accumulation by expanded reproduction and primitive accumulation, existing not sequentially as in Marx but contemporaneously, or side by side, albeit in tension and contestation. However, a fully fledged argument on this score had to wait another 20 years.

The 1990s and 2000s was marked by an intellectually insipid neoliberal interregnum in the radical debates and discourse at the University and elsewhere. As the University was starved of resources, the faculty left in droves for greener pastures, others took up consultancies on policy research driven by donor funds and still others took off the gown and went to town to start or join donor-funded NGOs and think tanks. Basic research was undermined as theoretical debates were devalued (Chachage 2016). Revolutionary standpoints and class perspectives gave way to eclectic activism as radicals jumped on agendas set by donor agencies.

In 2009, having retired from the University of Dar es Salaam, I published a small book *Accumulation in an African Periphery: A Theoretical Framework* (Shivji 2009) under the sponsorship of REPOA (Research in Poverty Alleviation). Under the leadership of our dear friend, the late Sam Moyo, the African Institute for Agrarian Studies supported the publication. The book combined together the two theoretical shifts mentioned earlier. The two poles of the exploitation and accumulation were brought together which were: (a) at the level of production, the argument that the surplus extracted by capital cuts into the necessary consumption of the producer and (b) at the level of accumulation, the argument that the dominant form of accumulation in the neoliberal phase of capitalism in the periphery is primitive accumulation.

Besides the classical methods of primitive accumulation, like appropriation of peasant land and resources, it was argued that under neoliberalism primitive accumulation assumes new forms and becomes generalized in almost all sectors of the economy, including the so-called informal sector. The producer self-exploits him or herself just to survive while subsidizing capital.

> [P]easant labour super-exploits itself by intensifying labour in multiple occupations and cutting down on necessary consumption (Moyo and Yeros 2007, p. 84). Directly, or ultimately, the beneficiary is the dominant capital. The so called informal sector, for example, providing meagre and fragile livelihoods to thousands of people in any African city, is a kind of subsidy to capital. By over-exploiting itself, the so-called self-employed labour in the informal sector produces cheap wage goods thereby enabling proletarian labour in factories and farms, in turn, to provide cheap labour. Cheap labour and cheap food are the twin pillars on which stands the system of super-exploitation yielding super profits. Hundreds of rural youth migrating to the streets of African cities, the wamachinga, as they are called in Tanzania, are in effect subsidizing the costs of circulation of commodities, thereby enhancing the profits of merchant capital. The phenomenon of labour subsidizing capital, as opposed to the capitalist logic of labour-power exchanging at value underlying expanded reproduction, lies at the heart of the disarticulated process of accumulation, or accumulation by dispossession. Devaluation of peripheral labour and resources is the lynchpin in the exploitation and transfer of surplus from the periphery to the centre. (Shivji 2009, p. 67)

Commodification and privatization of health care, education, water, sanitation and removal of subsidies from essential foods which all formed part of the social wage goods previously means that now the poor have either to pay for it or go without. All in all, the materiality which underlies producers—peasants and pastoralists, proletarians and semi-proletarians, street hawkers selling consumer goods and peddlers selling cooked food, operators and repairers in backyard workshops—in virtually all sectors is the minimizing of their necessary consumption and maximizing their labour. I therefore proposed a modified definition of primitive accumulation under neoliberalism—the process of surplus extraction by capital based on expropriation of a part of necessary consumption of the producer. This is then the material basis common to all sectors of what I called the working people.

To be sure, the concept of the working people needs to be further theorized. What I have sketched above are only the first steps towards theorizing it. In the long durée, I have also attempted in discussions at the annual Summer Schools organized by the African Institute of Agrarian Studies to historicize the two tendencies of accumulation in the African periphery. From the Vasco da Gama era to colonialism, the dominant tendency was primitive accumulation that took the classical form of plunder of resources and human labour including turning human beings into chattels during the slave trade. Given the introduction of commodity economy, no doubt the tendency of accumulation through expanded reproduction was also introduced but this was not a dominant tendency. Following independence, various economic policies pursued by African governments, under whatever ideological rubric from nationalism, to liberalism to socialism, were meant to reinforce conditions for accumulation by expanded reproduction. The neoliberal assault with SAPs imposed by international financial institutions reinvigorated the old and new forms of primitive accumulation mentioned above. Primitive accumulation became the dominant tendency. This is schematic, but I believe, provable.

While inchoate theorization does not allow me to take a position that working people is a class—whether in itself or for itself—I can perhaps assert more definitively that it is a 'class' against capital and has great potency in political discourse and mobilization. The potency of the concept of the working people was driven home to me in a trade union rally some years ago. I translated the term 'working people' into Swahili as wavujajasho (toilers). Together with its opposite wavunajasho (exploiters), it caught popular imagination and has more or less entered common usage. I believe politically, and even conceptually, the term working people has greater potency and validity than worker–peasant alliance. I would venture to say that even as a description of the agency for transformation the concept of working people sounds more sensible and convincing than worker–peasant alliance led by the proletariat or proletarian ideology. On a conceptual scale, therefore, the concept of working people is higher than worker–peasant alliance albeit lower than the concept of working class. Only real life struggles against the neoliberal phase of capitalist imperialism will help us further to theorize the concept of working people.

Note

1. We were acquainted with the 'mode of production' debate among Indian Marxists raging then in the pages of Economic and Political Weekly, which grappled with the issue of the relation between capital and the peasant, and the class alliances that it generated. The most prominent participant in that debate whose name I fondly remember was Utsa Patnaik. I had the pleasure of meeting and interacting with her several decades later the product of which was the publication of a small book The Agrarian Question in the Neoliberal Era: Primitive Accumulation and the Peasantry (Patnaik and Moyo 2011).

References

Chachage, S. L. (2016). *Ghettoisation of Basic Research in Higher Education* (Occasional Paper No. 4). Dar es Salaam: Kavazi la Mwalimu Nyerere.

Hadjivayanis, G. G. (1987). Perverse Capitalism in Agriculture: A study of Nyandira Village. *Eastern African Social Science Review, 3*(1), 75–110.

Hirji, K. F. (2010). *Cheche: Reminiscences of a Radical Magazine*. Dar es Salaam: Mkuki na Nyota.

Ingham, J. H. (Ed.). (1955). *East Africa Royal Commission 1953–1955 Report* (Report No. Cmd 9475). Her Majesty's Stationery Office: London.

Lenin, V. I. (1970). What Is To Be Done? In V. I. Lenin (Ed.), *On Trade Unions* (pp. 68–140). Moscow: Progress Publishers.

Lenin, V. I. (1999[1917]). *Imperialism, the Highest Stage of Capitalism*. Sydney: Resistance Books. Retrieved from http://www.readingfromtheleft.com/Books/Classics/LeninImperialism.pdf

Moyo, S., & Yeros, P. (Eds.). (2007). *Reclaiming the Land: The Resurgence of Rural Movements in Africa, Asia and Latin America*. London/Cape Town: Zed Books & David Philip.

Patnaik, U., & Moyo, S. (2011). *The Agrarian Question in the Neo-liberal Era: Primitive Accumulation and the Peasantry*. Oxford: Pambazuka Press.

Rweyemamu, J. (1973). *Underdevelopment and Industrialization in Tanzania: A Study of Perverse Capitalist Industrial Development*. Oxford: Oxford University Press.

Saul, J. S. (2010). *Revolutionary Traveller: Freeze-frames from a Life*. Winnipeg: Arbeiter Ring Publishing.

Shivji, I. G. (1976). *Class Struggles in Tanzania*. New York/London: Monthly Review Press.

Shivji, I. G. (1983). The Exploitation of Small Peasant. In A. Das et al. (Eds.), *The Worker and the Working Class*. Delhi: PECCE.

Shivji, I. G. (1986a). *Law, State and the Working Class in Tanzania, c.1920–1964.* London/Portsmouth/Dar es Salaam: James Curry, Heinemann & Tanzania Publishing House.

Shivji, I. G. (Ed.). (1986b). *The State and the Working People.* Dakar: CODESRIA.

Shivji, I. G. (Ed.). (1987).The Roots of Agrarian Crisis in Tanzania: A Theoretical Perspective. *Eastern Africa Social Science Research Review, 3*(1), 111–131. Reprinted in P. G. Forster & S. Maghimbi (Eds). (1992). *The Tanzanian peasantry: Economy in crisis* (pp. 124–150). Aldershot: Avebury.

Shivji, I. G. (2009). *Accumulation in an African Periphery: A Theoretical Framework.* Dar es Salaam: Mkuki na Nyota.

Shivji, I. G. (2012). Remembering Walter Rodney. *Monthly Review, 64*(7).

United Republic of Tanzania. (1994). *Report of the Presidential Commission of Inquiry into Land Matters, Volume I, Land Policy and Land Tenure Structure.* Uppsala: Scandinavian Institute of African Studies.

CHAPTER 4

The Agrarian Question of Gendered Labour

Lyn Ossome and Sirisha Naidu

Analysis of the behaviour of the peasantry has historically focused on three main issues: perceived peasant backwardness and modernisation of peasant agriculture, the role of the agrarian economy in national economic development, and the relationship between agrarian transformations and emancipatory politics. While feminist agrarian studies have highlighted a fourth element—the gendered nature of exploitation attached to social reproduction in the process of agrarian transitions—the conceptual dimensions of this gendered labour remain vague in the literature. We seek in this chapter to address this lacuna by focusing on the labour processes associated with rural and agrarian economies through a theoretical exploration of reproductive labour as an agrarian question. We argue that under the global neoliberal economic regime and the resulting labour fragmentation, capitalist markets increasingly rely on such reproductive labours whose dimensions are now different. Beyond denoting women's historical burden of reproduction, we argue that every productive activity is a mere

L. Ossome (✉)
Makerere University, Kampala, Uganda

S. Naidu
University of Missouri, Kansas City, MO, USA
e-mail: snaidu@umkc.edu

P. Jha et al. (eds.), *Labour Questions in the Global South*,
https://doi.org/10.1007/978-981-33-4635-2_4

act of survival, disarticulated from accumulation and therefore assumes less importance to both national and global concerns. Our analysis thus argues for a shift of an exclusive focus on exploitation under capitalist value creation to survival not just of labour but of human life under phases of capitalist accumulation. We suggest that reproduction constitutes the core of the agrarian question of labour, and that it has implications for the politics of societal transformation.

Introduction

The agrarian question is situated in a literature and praxis that emerged out of attempts to understand capitalist development in conjunction with rural and agrarian economies. After freeing themselves of colonial rule in many countries in Africa and Asia, the agrarian question was meant to address both the issues of self-determination, the adoption of a development path that would benefit the people, and remedy the havoc wreaked through colonialism and imperialism.

In its classical form, the agrarian question concerned itself with the development of capitalism in agriculture and the role of agriculture in capital accumulation, class formation, and class struggle (Ramachandran 2011). Global conditions have seemingly made irrelevant the role of agriculture in capitalist development, leading some to suggest that the agrarian question and land reform are irrelevant (Bernstein 2016; Lerche 2013). Yet, others have argued that focusing the agrarian question solely on capital has meant that there has been inadequate attention to the land and peasant aspects of the agrarian question (Moyo et al. 2013).

These aspects are particularly important in those countries of Latin America, Asia and Africa where the agrarian transition has been incomplete, and vast sections of society still depend on non-capitalist production despite the dominance of capitalist modes of production and in the context of severe land and resource dispossession, ecological degradation and disasters and the declining value of labour (Araghi 2009). This also means that the agrarian question has had to assume a contemporary form in which issues of land, labour, gender, access to nature, and national sovereignty are not subsumed under the classical agrarian question of capital (Akram-Lodhi and Kay 2010; Moyo et al. 2013).

We offer in this regard, an attempt to understand the lives of the labouring classes. This is particularly relevant in the current phase of capitalism which has produced differing and fragmented forms of class formation and has impeded the development that was expected for the former colonies. In discussing the labouring classes, we consider the broad class of people whose reproduction—their life and survival—are not guaranteed within the capitalist accumulation process. Unlike capitalists and others in the professional classes who are deemed essential to the operation of the capitalist system, the labouring classes have to engage in their own reproduction. This reproduction may occur as a result of their participation in wage labour, but is not guaranteed. Rather, varying degrees of energy expenditure outside the labour market is required by wage workers, their families and their communities in order to survive, live and flourish. These have been acknowledged in the agrarian studies literature (e.g., O'Laughlin 1996; Moyo et al. 2013), but not adequately theorised.

In this chapter, we highlight the immanence of the problem of gender inequity inherent in labour processes under capitalism and manifest both in households that are reproduced on account of wage labour, but also households that rely on other forms of production that co-exist and articulate with capitalist modes of production. We classify this as the Agrarian Question (AQ) of gendered labour. It pertains to the labour that is expended in producing and reproducing life whether it is relevant for capital accumulation or not. Our objective is to offer better conceptual clarity on gender inequities inherent in agrarian societies as they relate to reproduction of the labouring classes, and decentre the labour-capital relationship to shift attention to the survival and flourishing of the working people. In turn with this clarification we also hope to advance our collective understanding of the immiseration or impoverishment of the labouring classes under capitalism.

The growing global reserve army of labour (Foster, McChesney and Jonna 2011) appears to be inadequately supported by the processes of proletarianisation. The rise of PCPs (Harris-White 2012) and the processes of semi-proletarianisation (e.g., Moyo et al. 2013) indicate the inability or unwillingness of the capitalist system to provide adequately for the reproduction of the labouring classes. The full extent of the degradation of the classes may be mitigated by women's invisible labour that participates in various productive and reproductive activities. In advanced capitalist countries, women's responsibilities for reproductive work have tended to be in the context of care work as the welfare state socialised others aspect of reproductive labour. But even in these countries, state intervention in reproduction has varied by race and ethnicity (e.g., Davis 1981). But, in many regions in the Global South responsibility for reproduction was never adequately assumed by capital or the state. Women's reproductive labour in these economies then is not merely restricted to care work and also includes participation in non-capitalist forms of production. In order to understand the AQ of gendered labour, our discussion necessarily draws on questions of land and ecological security (see Bernstein 2004; Moyo et al. 2013) which sustain the reproduction.

Feminist scholarship highlights a link between capitalist development and the exploitation both of 'free' wage labourers and fundamentally, that of non-wage labourers involved in processes of social reproduction comprising both affective and material labour (Fraser 2016). Inherent to every capitalist society as such is a social-reproductive 'crisis tendency' which arises on the one hand because social reproduction is a condition of possibility for sustained capital accumulation, and on the other because capitalism's orientation to unlimited accumulation tends to destabilise the very processes of social reproduction on which it relies (ibid). This crisis of social reproduction has taken historically specific forms through different stages of capitalist transitions: "the liberal, competitive capitalism of the 19th century; the state-managed capitalism of the postwar era; and the financialised neoliberal capitalism of our time" (ibid 2016: 100). It is in the latter period where we locate our analysis in this chapter, in which we deal with the specificity of this care deficit as it manifests in agrarian societies. Aspects of this crisis have been broadly addressed in some of the literature on the Global South (e.g. Mies 2014), but this work retains a linear historical trajectory in which underdeveloped nations are expected to follow the industrialisation trajectory of developed nations, and does not account for the specificity of agrarian societies in which capitalist accumulation is not reducible to industrialisation.

Further, past literature discusses non-capitalist production in the context of self-exploitation in specific terms related to internal household demand and the subsumption or subordination of agrarian and peasant economies to capital. Neoliberal economic policies implemented in much of the global south throughout the1990s have afforded capital the benefit of mobility, informal and flexible labour markets, and formal capital markets. However, evidence of growing unrest among peasants, and agrarian and industrial workers in many countries suggests that gains from these economic growth paths may be inequitably distributed, and demands greater attention to the conditions under which the working poor and marginalised satisfy minimum consumption and reproduce themselves (Naidu and Ossome 2016). We seek in this regard to reorient our analysis away from discussions of value creation and hence exploitation to reproduction of life, or the political economy of survival of the labouring classes under conditions of a global surplus population.

Surplus Population and Social Reproduction

The process of reproduction is historically specific and the historical development of capitalism in different contexts subject to specific economic, social, and political conditions pertaining to each context. Late capitalism's tendency towards massive depeasantisation of the countryside, accompanied by casualisation of semi-proletarianised labour has had an acute impact on agrarian households that are both articulated and disarticulated to capitalist production. In light of these tendencies we discuss below the significance of social reproduction, surplus population, and the relationship between the two.

The Basis for Capitalist Production: Reproduction of Labour

The capitalist mode of production may treat labour as a commodity, but its production and reproduction fall outside the realm of capitalist production. Under a high degree of proletarianisation, wages provide the means of subsistence for the working classes and pay for consumption of goods and services. Yet, while workers exchange the capacity to labour for a wage, the actual processes of reproducing both workers as well as those not incorporated into the value-producing economy remains within the family-household sphere. These processes include the expenditure of wages on consumption goods, production of simple-use goods and services using household labour, and acquiring and maintaining a private domestic sphere (Dickinson and Russell 1986). Necessary labour therefore is not just expended in the value-producing economy but also within the family-household, even though the latter is unwaged.

As Dickinson and Russell argue, the family household not only appears as the primary institution of individual consumption, but deceivingly "as an island of self-determination in an otherwise very large ocean of externally-manifested hierarchical power and discipline relations" (Dickinson and Russell 1986: 9). This role played by the family-household may therefore, at least in part, explain the varying degree of importance of the family in different capitalist societies even if the specific form of the heteronormative family has undergone significant changes. Primacy of wages to facilitate 'self-managed reproduction' depends on workers' access to employment and decent wages (Dickinson and Russell 1986: 10). The gap between actual consumption and consumption afforded by wage income has to be fulfilled either through state intervention or additional household production. The persistence of economic insecurity in the absence of adequate wages and state intervention forces households from working classes to engage in subsistence production and care work, and the labour expended in these activities constitute reproductive work that is often, but not exclusively, the bastion of women's invisible work. Thus, while capitalism heralds a separation of workers from the means of production and hence reproduction, this separation may not be complete as household production of goods and services is non-trivial in both advanced and less-advanced capitalist economies, even though the actual magnitude may vary regionally.

The existence and persistence of such household production particularly allows capitalists to expect the reproduction of labour in the absence of a living wage and inadequate social welfare programmes. Here we want to highlight the fact that workers simply do not earn a living wage: the expectation that becoming part of the proletariat would result in better living conditions has, in reality, not materialised particularly for workers of the Global South. This material reality expands the scope of production of simple use-values within the domestic sphere. Consequently, non-capitalist social formations of household and family labour shoulder a large proportion of the burden of meeting minimum consumption levels essential for daily and generational reproduction, and as Luxemburg (1951) suggests, continues to subsidise capital accumulation. The means of subsistence in this case are not merely acquired through the expenditure of wages, but also through means outside the capitalist mode of production. While we are not claiming a priori causality between wage labour and domestic labour, what is clear from feminist analyses is that labour performed within the household in social reproduction has a direct relation to the degree of subsidy obtained by capital though its manifestation of changes over time, space, class and race.

Social Reproduction and Relative Surplus Population

Workers not only undertake the reproduction of the current and future labour pool, but also relative surplus population. As Marx (1986: 603) noted, even though the reproduction of the labouring and relative surplus population, including pauperism, enters the '*faux frais*' of capitalism, it systematically shifts the burden on to the working classes and the lower middle-class. Surplus population, i.e., surplus relative to capital, can be divided into the floating part that constituted those who are cyclically unemployed, the latent population constituting those with insecure unemployment and those not fully integrated into capitalist production, and the stagnant population of people who are rarely employed, or are engaged in outwork and are likely to sink into pauperism (Marx 1986: 603, Li 2009; Foster et al. 2011).

Marx drew a link between the relative surplus population and capital accumulation, arguing thus:

> the greater the social wealth, the functioning capital, the extent and energy of its growth, and therefore also the greater the absolute mass of the proletariat and the productivity of its labour, the greater is the industrial reserve army. The same causes which develop the expansive power of capital, also develop the labour-power at its disposal. The relative mass of the industrial reserve army thus increases with the potential energy of wealth. But the greater this reserve army in proportion to the active labour-army, the greater is the mass of a consolidated surplus population, whose misery is in inverse ratio to the amount of torture it has to undergo in the form of labour. The more extensive, finally, the pauperized sections of the working class and the industrial reserve army, the greater is official pauperism. *This is the absolute general law of capitalist accumulation* (Marx 1977:798, emphasis in original).

The link between surplus population and capital accumulation, however, is not limited by national boundaries or by economic crisis. As the global economy has grown and integrated countries of the global north and south, albeit unevenly, it has affected the working classes and there appears to be convergence in the conditions of survival for relative surplus populations (Foster et al. 2011) impacted by economic expansion and contraction, and primitive accumulation.

When capital accumulation increases, there is a tendency to increase employment, hence reducing the relative surplus population, all else constant. This is the direct relationship that is noted between economic growth and employment, and contributes to the growth fetish. This result may manifest in a closed economy with a stagnant labour pool, but is less likely to occur in an economy under globalisation. The availability of a large global labour pool of wage workers either through the mobility of capital, vertical and horizontal integration of capital, or migration owing to a rise in the dispossessed rural population due to grabs of private and common lands, debt, or the non-viability of agrarian livelihoods that is not absorbed into the wage economy increases the possibility of relative surplus labour. Further, as the global economy has changed, decreasing labour intensity of output and de-skilling is not an uncommon phenomenon in many industries. Not only does the rate of employment generation appear to be insufficient, but also the employment structure is increasingly fragmented and characterised by informal employment in countries of the Global North and South (Mingione 1985).

Foster, McChesney and Jonna (2011) estimate that the size of the relative surplus population in the age group 25–54 years to be around 2.4 billion. This makes the surplus population 70 percent larger than the estimated 1.4 billion in the active labour army (Foster et al. 2011). The surplus population, relative to its utility to capital, is a potential reserve army of labour that is an important condition for capital accumulation. The surplus population depresses wages and keeps existing workers in check, it offers a release for workers in recessionary times, and is a pool of potential workers to draw from in times of economic booms. But acknowledging the need for a surplus population does not address how this population will be kept alive in order to be useful to capital when needed (Li 2009), and especially when this population is irrelevant and not useful to capital.

As we have already mentioned, household labour plays an important role in reproducing both the labour pool as well as the relative surplus population. In the case that the state intervenes in social welfare, it eases pressure on household labour and socialises reproduction. In societies with a high degree of social provisioning, we can expect the majority of the surplus labouring population to be either latent or floating that is affected by economic cycles, technological change and spatial changes in productive activities (McIntyre and Nast 2011). But with an increasing surplus population, the burden of these responsibilities is higher with ever decreasing means of reproduction.

As long as the cost of labour was favourable for capital accumulation and the living standards of the workers was increasing productivity, the state was able to engage in welfare primarily in countries in the North (Mingione 1985) in the postwar period. However, with higher international competition, capital mobility and global surplus population, the possibility of socialised reproduction has fallen significantly. While even in the neoliberal milieu the state does not disappear, its role has, however, shifted from the provision of collective services such as public transport to contributing money or basic consumption to ensure survival of the population that is surplus to the demands of labour, to maintain it in its 'frozen state' and maintain political consensus (Mingione 1985).

In societies in which social provisioning has been less than adequate, there exists a likelihood of a larger proportion of the stagnant population relative to floating and latent populations. Yet, in many countries of the global South the stagnant population has been displaced from agrarian and rural livelihoods and have not been integrated into the capitalist production process (Yates 2011). The existence of a large relative surplus population represents the failure of the capitalist growth model, yet is often represented as the misery that the population brings upon itself for failing to subject itself to the 'torture' represented by wage work as Marx called it (McIntyre 2011). This attitude is particularly reserved for the stagnant portion of the working classes. As society evolves its definition of who is deserving of public assistance, the stagnant working population reflects the erosion of stable and homogenous wage work and the decomposition of the solidarities of class and culture (Wacquant 2009: 4; Tyner 2013).

In most contemporary societies the state-capital nexus, even when it has taken on a significant role in provisioning, has fallen short of assuming the full costs of reproduction. Nevertheless, in states where social provisioning has been minimal, the practical problem of reproduction has been mostly disregarded (McIntyre and Nast 2011). This follows from the capitalist demand for abstract and not concrete labour such that as long as the class of labourers perpetuates itself, it does not matter which individual labourer is unable to show up for work, a fact which allows capitalists to hyper-exploit their workers without regard for their health, of well-being (Tyner 2016).

While Marx acknowledged that the burden of the relative surplus labouring population is displaced onto the working classes, historically, the burden has been particularly borne by women of these households. Beyond a particular threshold, many of these lives are expendable and the labours of the women who keep the labouring populations alive are outside the interest domain of general society and policy makers. In addition to wage work, the labouring classes may rely on other forms of production in order to satisfy reproductive needs. Some of these may be purely to satisfy consumption needs of the labouring classes while others, including petty commodity production, may be linked to capitalist relations of production through exchange, the insufficiency of only one form of reproduction in this regard suggesting extreme strain. Furthermore, the articulation of petty commodity production to wage labour and peasant production is rendered most visible through gendered labour relations, necessitating a discussion of reproduction under different labour processes operating in agrarian economies in the global south.

Development of the Global Rural Populace

Given the marginality of reproduction of the labouring classes to capital under neoliberalisation, reproduction ought to be viewed not from the perspective of capital but rather in its relation to the development of the global rural populace. We focus here on three stylised forms of production and reproduction associated with different labour processes—subsistence production, petty commodity production, and wage labour. In each of these forms, we locate the role of gendered labour.

Under the subsistence form, production may be indistinguishable from reproduction. Value takes the form of use value (though not exclusively as it also produces for consumption), and yet differentiation can occur within the narrow confines of consumption. Due to the inability to distinguish production from reproduction, gender roles, despite being delineated, do not sufficiently interact with capitalist market forces to deepen the divide, and hence the usefulness or 'productiveness' of activities is not gender delineated. Male as well as female labour may be subject to extreme exertion and drudgery in order to ensure minimum consumption when conditions of production/reproduction are unsatisfactory, and when the household is exposed to economic, socio-political or ecological shocks.

Capitalist forces, however, may impact the conditions under which subsistence production is possible. Decreasing availability and degradation of land and other natural resources may further increase the intensity of work that is required to make production and reproduction possible. Beyond a threshold, it may make subsistence production unviable as the primary source of livelihood. As Quick (2004) argues, "[t]he need for wage labour arose not from the *total* inability of labouring people to engage in production but rather from their inability to provide *in full* for the reproduction needs of the labouring family through their own labour, which takes the form of household production and the form of petty-commodity production" (emphasis in original). The specific manifestation of subsistence production under the dominant capitalist mode of production may differ significantly based on historical contexts as well as the intensity of competition between the two production processes for land and other aspects of nature (Levien 2015; Moyo et al. 2012).

Under petty commodity production (PCP), which falls within the realm of simple commodity production, wages are indistinguishable from profits. This result may be true for PCPs both in the agricultural and non-agricultural sectors. Either due to the inherent character of the production and labour process, or due to the contracts that PCPs enter into, the accumulation process is limited even if it harbours the potential to turn entrepreneurial. While the realisation of this potential is contingent on the different exchange processes and contracts entered into, at the very least PCPs aims to fulfil the subsistence requirements of rural households. There is, here too, a high potential for extreme exertion in order to compete with other capitalist and non-capitalist producers.

Harris-White's (2012) argues that since capital and labour are embodied in the same enterprise, and since the capital of PCP (land, artisanal tools, etc.) is not to be presumed fungible, the petty commodity producer does not seek to alter the material content of his/her capital in a way that would correspond to a search for profit maximisation. It follows, she argues, that there is no particular internal dynamic leading to differentiation, and that if differentiation occurs, it must be due to external dynamics.

This differentiation is observed when PCP is examined under the current conditions of neoliberal capitalism where the primary 'external force' has been markets and commodification not only of labour, but of the means of reproduction (land, nature, etc.). On a global level, the massive proliferation of secondary goods and the destruction of primary and artisanal industries appears to once again shift the question from one of capital to the pauperisation of labour. Once mainly constituting the floating component of the surplus population, PCPs now constitute an increasing bulk of the dormant and latent proportions of the relative surplus population. The defining characteristic of PCPs in the contemporary phase of neoliberal capitalism relates to its maintenance in favour of capital, by transferring the burden of ground rent to PCP and the devaluation of labour power (Saka 2014). The concentration and centralisation of capital in this period has considerably eviscerated the earnings and income pace of PCPs, including peasants and led them into a 'PCP trap by capital' such that the peasantry can sustain itself only by deepening its subjection to capital, and in which peasant labour is open to cycles of proletarianisation and re-peasantisation (Saka 2014: 100). This precarity is also imposed on those engaged in PCPs in non-agricultural sectors as well.

The cycles of proletarianisation and re-peasantisation are uneven within regions and lead to complex processes of social and class differentiation based on race, ethnicity, caste, and gender.

Gender roles in these processes may be delineated but may manifest in a host of different ways. For instance, when it creates a distinction between 'productive' work that generates income for the household, and reproductive work that may be invisible and considered unproductive, it deepens not only the sexual division of labour, but also excludes women from participating in market exchanges thus making them dependent on male members of the household in order to sustain themselves. In other cases, we observe an increased incidence of women's interaction with market forces through home-based production that is also a manifestation of gender roles within the PCP framework. Home-based work or outwork features lower in the hierarchy of informal work and is predominantly performed by women. It may be disguised wage work, or may subsidise commodity production that is controlled by male members of the household.

Women's increased and continued dependence (based on historical contexts) has two aspects because the self-exploitation that is the hallmark of PCPs is dependent not on the self-exploitation of the labour engaged in production to satisfy capital's thirst for 'value' creation, but is supported and subsidised by the productive and reproductive work by women. Their productive and reproductive roles themselves may be intertwined and interdependent. Women then take on a double burden of production and reproduction with little, if any, acknowledgment of, or compensation for their role in the capitalist production process.

A third labour process frequently observed in agrarian economies is wage labour, which is subject to specific capital-labour dynamics. Even though reproduction of workers constitutes a pre-condition for the capital-labour relationship, the production process is not geared toward the fulfilment of the reproductive needs of the workers. From the perspective of the labouring classes, who are divorced from the means of production, wage labour provides the means to reproduce themselves and hence the prime motivation for subjecting themselves to capitalist exploitation. The impacts of wage labour itself are varied depending on the informality of the employment contract, labour laws, the degree of sex, race or ethnic-based occupational segregation, and bargaining power of the wage workers.

However, even when wage employment fully satisfies the consumptive needs of the workers, household labour is still required to process consumptive goods. Care work has historically not been commodified or recognised, and has been provided by women within the household, thus subsidising the cost of reproducing the labour pool for capitalist production. In the case that women also join the ranks for wage labour, they then engage in a double-shift burden of commodified wage work and uncommodified care and other reproductive work. In either case, labour expended in reproductive activities is subject to the vagaries of the labour market and state support.

Under less than ideal conditions, particularly if conditions of reproduction are unmet by the capitalist workplace or the state, household labour is not exempt from extremely long working hours and immiseration. Numerous studies focused on Asia, Africa and Latin America suggest that neither the wage economy nor the state have been able or willing to maintain socially acceptable levels of consumption for the working classes and the growing proportion of surplus population (e.g., Kay 2000; Mooij 2000; Naidu and Ossome 2016). The resulting burden of reproduction has specific manifestations and implications in agrarian societies in which meeting the reproductive deficit is, in combination with wage labour and PCPs, also highly dependent on land, nature and the commons which retain primacy as a source of capitalist primitive accumulation.

The literature has accorded little attention to the conditions under which the rural populations reproduce themselves and enhance their standard of living. Agrarian transition since the 1970s has significantly changed the role of agriculture and peasants in economies, yet this has not resulted in the promised prosperity for the labouring classes. Labour absorption is low and at the same time there has been a marked rise in PCPs and surplus population. Hansen's (2015) observation that the challenging aspect about the re-actualisation of the theory of surplus populations today is that it is not predicated on a thesis of gradual embourgeoisement of the world, or on the homogenisation of the proletariat. The reality of surplus-populations, he argues, "poses instead the issue of a generalized crisis of reproduction, and the multitude of survival strategies that arise from it, including modes of wealth appropriation that are far short of revolution proper, women's struggles, and various forms of state and para-state violence".

Our intention in providing these stylised accounts is not to engage in a stagist thesis that advocates a linear progression from subsistence production to wage labour. Nor are we suggesting that these labour processes operate homogeneously spatially and temporally. Rather, the forms of labour processes described above represent different states of commodification in society as well as different moments of integration in capitalist societies. In reality different societies and different points in time possess a different combination of characteristics from the different labour processes discussed above. The economies of the global South have, for the most part, not witnessed a transition in which wage labour constitutes the only form of reproduction for the rural populace despite much lower contribution of agriculture to GDP and employment. Instead, subsistence production continues to thrive in rural economies, and in many economies we are also witnessing a resurgence of PCPs (Harris-White 2012), which may be carried out in conjunction with both subsistence production and wage labour.

Contemporary peasant economies often embody all three labour processes though the specificities differ based on historical and sociopolitical factors. The impact of these labour processes is also not uniform and are differentiated by class, gender, race and ethnicity depending on access to productive resources, "external extractive claims of their labour product," legal and other conditions of production, including socially provisioned "social and productive service infrastructure," and the degree of risk undertaken in the production process (Bryceson 2000). Global economic conditions have forced a high degree of livelihood diversification away from subsistence production (e.g., Harris-White 2012; Shah and Harris-White 2011). This in turn has created or intensified differentiation among peasant producers based on their reliance on PCPs and wage labour. The global economic conditions, however, do not facilitate nor have demonstrated the capacity to complete the process of full proletarianisation, hence the significant role that subsistence production continues to play in offering a way to cope with market conditions (Naidu and Ossome 2016). The semi-proletarianisation thesis that links peasant production to PCPs and wage labour has nonetheless, not sufficiently accounted for the gendered labour that sustains all three realms in more or less permanent articulation and contradiction. To the extent that neither subsistence production nor wage labour nor PCP—the primary realms of production in agrarian economies—can proceed without reliance on the reproductive realm, gendered labour poses a key contemporary agrarian question.

While there is considerable debate about whether the wage and commodity market feeds into the peasant mode of production or vice versa, the continued relevance of subsistence production indicates an on-going process of semi-proletarianisation (e.g. Kay 2000), with subsistence production offering a way to accommodate rather than escape the market (Bryceson 2000). The same appears true for PCPs as well. Though some scholarship has argued otherwise (e.g., Ellis 1998), livelihood diversity does not necessarily offer a pathway out of poverty. Further, neither subsistence production nor PCPs necessarily guarantee minimum levels of consumption for the rural populace independently. Each of these spheres of production and reproduction, however, subject different sections of rural society to varying degrees of vulnerability and security, which we elaborate below through a critique of the notion of self-exploitation.

A Critique of Self-Exploitation Viz-a-Viz Reproductive Labour

The predominant framework through which the vulnerability of peasant households has been explained in the literature has been in relation to their tendency towards self-exploitation to meet their minimum consumption needs. We have so far offered stylised accounts of three different labour processes that we are likely to encounter in contemporary agrarian economies. Despite significant differences, the literature has mainly explained their convergence through the role of self-exploitative labour in the different labour processes. However, as we argue above, the fact that gendered labour is not primarily about value production but rather about survival indicates the insufficiency of the self-exploitation framework in theorising gendered labour as an agrarian question.

Self-exploitation has been viewed as the peasantry's tendency to self-exploit in order to achieve a relationship of equilibrium between family demand satisfaction and the drudgery of labour (Chayanov 1986). Self-exploitation has also been viewed as proof of the peasantry's subordination to capital (Kautsky 1988). According to Kautsky (1988), peasants would increase their yield per unit of land under conditions of overwork and under-consumption due to the self-regulating market. Contrary to Lenin's view, capitalism would thus not be fully able to depeasantise the rural agricultural economy despite large-scale technological advancement in agriculture. Further, Kautsky believed that continuous primitive accumulation was impossible[1] without the peasantry (Kautsky 1988).

Luxemburg (1951) provides more insight into the relationship between the non-capitalist realm of production and the conditions necessary for capital accumulation. To her, it is precisely the 'primitive' conditions in the non-capitalist realm of production that allow for accumulation to a far more ruthless extent than could be tolerated under purely capitalist conditions. This non-capitalist stratum is dominated by forms of labour that are unwaged. The recognition of its articulation to capitalist accumulation compels an acknowledgement of the forms of labour that enables its reproduction outside of the wage labour relation as critical to capitalism. Stated differently, this formulation compels the recognition of women's unpaid reproductive labour as a key source of capitalist accumulation.

Following Luxemburg, the discussion of the subsidy provided by women's work to capital accumulation is a familiar theme among feminist thinkers. Deere, for instance, discusses this particularly with respect to peasant agriculture. She argues,

> [i]f the peasant unit must participate in the labour market to assure its full subsistence, then this unity[2] is broken as the non-capitalist unit is integrated into the capitalist mode of production. Semi-proletarianisation requires that the family be still in possession of the means of production from which to obtain some portion of subsistence; thus production of the means of subsistence is still tied to the reproduction of labour power. But the sale of labour power at a wage insufficient to cover at least the worker's subsistence, means that the reproduction and maintenance of labour power only results from the super-exploitation of familial labour on the unit of subsistence production. Here then, the division of labour is key in the extraction of surplus labour: women and children are mobilized to produce the means of subsistence for the production and reproduction of labour power for the labour market. The articulation between modes of production in this case assures that the surplus labour which is appropriated from the non-capitalist mode is realized as surplus value within capitalist units of production. For women's labour within the non-capitalist mode reduces the value of labour power to capital, thus the rate of surplus value is increased and capital accumulation enhanced. (1976: 13)

Deere's assertion that women's subsidy to capital constitutes actual extraction of surplus value is instructive but insufficient,[3] as is her notion of articulation (between modes of production) in this regard. We instead propose three significant ways in which to rethink women's productive and reproductive labour in the context of agrarian economies.

First, we locate the problem not just in the relation of exploitation, which lends itself in a derivative fashion to value creation for capitalist accumulation and the industrialisation myth, but rather in the requirements of sustenance and survival of households. Such a reformulation moves beyond the reproduction of various agrarian classes that sustain monopoly capitalism (that presumes gendered labour) to encompass the conditions of possibility of social reproduction (which poses gendered labour as an agrarian problem in relation to various agrarian classes).

Second, gendered labour is immanent to capital to the extent that it is crucial for the capitalist form of production, but has to reproduce itself by means other than capitalistic ones, or means not readily supplied or guaranteed in the capitalist milieu. Even when considered within non-capitalist forms of production, i.e., the conditions in which non-wage agricultural income subsidises part of the cost of labour production and semi-proletarianisation absorbs the costs of social reproduction (Moyo and Yeros), the notion of exploitation is theorised as being in constant articulation with capitalist production through the production of exchange value, and hence value for the market.

Analyses of the reproduction of the labouring classes has typically been subordinate to capitalist production. Yet, reproductive labour is rarely about competition and exchange value despite its constant articulation with capitalist production and articulation. For the labouring classes the primary concern is that of ensuring the survival of the family, household or community rather than a concern with the creation of value. In other words, the primary preoccupation is with the sustenance of life. This distinction suggests the need for an analytical shift in the analysis of value in relation to *gendered* labour. From the perspective of the working classes the distinction between production and reproduction may be irrelevant, i.e., human energy is allocated to various forms of labour processes whether categorised as 'productive' or 'reproductive' to sustain or reproduce humans (Naidu 2018). Nevertheless, the allocation of human energy continues to be gendered, racialised or ethnicised because it necessarily articulates to social institutions that support capitalist accumulation.

Third and relatedly, the peasant unit actually *produces* goods and services for its reproduction (rather than merely converting them to use value or purchasing them with wages). Such production requires some degree of uncommodified resources, mostly lands or nature that are part of the commons. When land and nature become highly commodified or degraded, then the other options are: (a) what is considered as theft or expropriation; or (b) extreme immiseration. Under the current globalised conditions of monopoly finance capitalism that has been accompanied by massive displacement and dispossession of the peasantry, the thesis of self-exploitation is not sustainable on its own. This means that for gendered labour, land and nature are also sites of contestation and competition. If we recognise that this gendered labour is essential for survival, then in addition to the workplace and markets which are primary sites for those involved in petty trade and wage labour respectively, we also are forced to contend with the fact that land, nature and gendered labour are not irrelevant despite the diminished significance of agrarian economies. They continue to allow rural households to survive despite immiserating conditions.

It is these analytical and conceptual points that concretely rearticulate the AQ of gendered labour. It is essential to fully grasp the scale of the task undertaken by reproductive labour to ensure that the labouring people, including the ever increasing surplus population, survives in the context of global capitalist accumulation which renders as insufficient independent sites of survival. Capitalist accumulation draws to a great extent from household workers whose labour does not enter into the labour market relation and is in effect concealed by wage work (e.g. Federici 2006). Moreover, under neoliberal capitalism an increasing amount of production has also been shifted to the household. This not only includes informal home work in which elements of capitalist production are carried out by household waged and unwaged labour and may be disguised wage labour or PCPs, but also significant elements of production required for consumption or what is often referred to as wage goods. Due to their historical roles as caregivers, women are particularly burdened with the drudgery of domestic labour. Yet, the work of daily reproduction of labour power and potential labour, i.e., surplus population, is being performed by men and women as they scramble to eke out a living in a global economy that appears disinvested in their survival and has increased the precariousness of their lives. Their labour appears both in the context of what has been commonly distinguished as reproductive and productive work, yet labour expended in both categories is primarily focused on ensuring survival. The AQ of gendered labour as such highlights the shifting trajectories of productive and reproductive labour under the changing phases of capitalism.

Under the current stage of capitalism, labour processes are not divorced from each other as most households engage in various kinds of labour processes including PCP, wage labour and peasant agriculture. Non-waged productive and reproductive labour, particularly that which is gendered, gains greater significance in light of the fact that capitalism's surplus populations are trying to survive under increasing unavailability of means of survival, whether they are filtered through the capitalist or non-capitalist modes of production, or through the state. The ensuing social differentiation that this causes warrants further theoretical and empirical investigations of its scholarly and political implications.

Conclusion

The agrarian question in its simplest political expression a century ago was concerned with how the mass of the peasantry could be drawn into a revolutionary movement whose main force was the proletariat. This question gains additional significance in the present milieu of neoliberal capitalism, among whose greatest casualty as we show in this chapter, has been the mass of surplus labour that does not in itself represent a class, but which places significant demands on both the peasantry and proletariat classes burdened with ensuring its survival. This surplus population is being cast into the three realms of production and reproduction: subsistence production, wage labour, and petty commodity production—none of which separately or in combination with each other appear able to secure sufficient resources and wages to support the surplus population. Given that the need for reproduction of human life exists whether or not people are employed by capital, the exponential growth of the surplus population under neoliberalism has deepened the general level of reliance on unremunerated gendered labour necessary to ensure survival of this population in the absence of state or market support. The current global conditions of capital accumulation are deepening the contradictions of increasing reliance on what is typically referred to as reproductive labour, precisely when the means of reproduction are under severe threat of capitalist appropriation and degradation.

Past literature has attempted to address the problems associated with peasant economies by offering us theoretical concepts of 'self-exploitation' and 'subsidy'. We contribute to these earlier discussions by reorienting our analysis toward reproduction of life, which is of utmost importance to the labouring classes, and shifting the focus away from value creation and exploitation. Semi-proletarianisation means that the peasant path itself constitutes significant livelihood diversity. We have attempted to capture this diversity in three stylised categories of subsistence production, PCPs, and wage employment, by showing that the survival of the labouring classes (those that labour for a wage or are categorised as the surplus population) requires a high degree of reliance on gendered labour to meet minimum consumption needs. All three realms, we argue, are integral to the agrarian economy, and yet represent no more than a desperate scramble for survival. And while it is now more apparent that they cannot be counted as accumulative strategies, it is also increasingly unclear whether they even satisfy basic consumption needs of the labouring classes. The point we emphasise in this regard is that gendered labour exists whether or not people are employed. The focus on the reproduction of *labour* as such does not sufficiently capture this rapture, and warrants greater attention to reproduction of life, whether it is useful to capital or not. Expressed as an agrarian question, this shift in the theorisation of social reproduction also contains within it the possibility of resolution of the political and social dimensions of the classical agrarian question.

The surplus population has become so massive that we do not in fact know if the labouring classes that supports it is a revolutionary subject. The mere existence of precarity is likely leading to tremendous social upheaval—an expression of extremes that could either go down a revolutionary or a reactionary path. The internal coherence of this surplus labour—that is, the present dynamics of its stabilisation—cannot be gleaned in any concrete way outside of the social relations that reproduce and socialise them as humans and potential workers on a daily basis. Furthermore, despite significant differences in the social, economic, and political context across societies, there is evidence of a degree of convergence in the conditions of reproduction faced by the working classes, particularly working-class women resulting from a patriarchy that appears to operate in tandem to the capitalist economic system (Naidu and Ossome 2018). The labour of the working classes is thus shaped as a response to a potential crisis of reproduction and the immiserating tendencies inherent in the specific context of individual countries' growth paths.

This cost of social reproduction is imposed on non-capitalist realms of the family/household, which while not exempt from the commodification of labour, time and resources, does not concretely enter into value production. As with Lenin's concern with charting a political strategy of political class alliances in a society characterised by several forms of economy, our concern here views the articulation between the peasant, petty-commodity and wage economies as fundamentally expressing an imperative for survival that approximates men and women's unpaid, unremunerated and invisible reproductive labour. We have argued elsewhere that while capitalist production enhances cooperation in the organisation of production, it also accumulates differences and divisions within the proletariat through its organisation of social reproduction (Naidu and Ossome 2016). This point is crucial, given that economic policies have ostensibly paved the way for women to participate in the wage economy without mitigating the historical burden of reproduction while at the same time also intensifying this burden on account of global economic conditions.

The implication is that the peasant economy, apart from posing the question regarding its usefulness as potentially revolutionary classes, poses the question of gender inequity due to contradictions internal to itself that require greater attention from agrarian scholars. These contradictions—what in this chapter we refer to as the agrarian question of gendered labour—compel further reflection on what kinds of solidarities the current conditions of the labour under neoliberal capitalism entail, and the particular difficulties that a peasant path upon which reproductive labour greatly relies, is likely to encounter.

Notes

1. Kautsky argued that what [this] means for the 'national' political economy is a flow of extra surplus-value extracted from impoverished peasants unable to resist the forces that dominate them. The peasant sector of the capitalist political economy is therefore a source of continuous 'primitive accumulation' (1988: xvi).
2. The unity between production of the products which constitute the family's means of subsistence and the reproduction and maintenance of labour power makes the division of labour by sex secondary as mechanisms of surplus extraction.
3. Once the capitalist mode of production is dominant within a social formation, if the articulation between modes of production is to affect capital accumulation, it must do so by increasing the mass of surplus value. For capital accumulation is predicated on the extraction of surplus labour hours from workers which, within capitalist relations of production, takes the form of the mass of surplus value (equivalent to the rate of surplus value times the employment base (Deere 1976: 11).

References

Akram-Lodhi, A. H., & Kay, C. (2010). Surveying the Agrarian Question (Part 2): Current Debates and beyond. *Journal of Peasant Studies, 37*(2), 255–284.

Araghi, F. (2009). Accumulation by Displacement, Global Enclosures, Food Crisis, and the Ecological Contradictions of Capitalism. *Review, 32*(1), 113–146.

Bernstein, H. (2004). Changing before our very eyes: Agrarian questions and the politics of land in capitalism today. *Journal of Agrarian Change, 4*(1–2), 190–225.

Bernstein, H. (2016). Agrarian Political Economy and Modern World Capitalism: the Contributions of Food Regime Analysis. *The Journal of Peasant Studies, 43*(3), 611–647.

Bryceson, D. F. (2000). Peasant Theories and Smallholder Policies: Past and Present. In D. F. Bryceson, C. Kay, & J. Mooij (Eds.), *Disappearing Peasantries: Rural Labour in Africa, Asia and Latin America*. London: IT Publications.

Chayanov, A. V. (1986). *The Theory of Peasant Economy*. Wisconsin: The University of Wisconsin Press.

Davis, A. (1981). *Women, Race and Class*. New York: Random House.

Deere, C. D. (1976). Rural Women's Subsistence Production in Capitalist Periphery. *Review of Radical Political Economy, 8*(9), 9–17.

Dickinson, J., & Russell, B. (1986). The Structure of Reproduction in Capitalist Societies. In J. Dickinson & B. Russell (Eds.), *Family, Economy and the State: Social Reproduction under Capitalism*. New York: St. Martin's Press.

Ellis, F. (1998). Household Strategies and Rural Livelihood Diversification. *Journal of Development Studies, 35*(1), 1–38.

Federici, S. (2006). *Precarious Labour and Reproductive Work*. Http:// https://caringlabor.wordpress.com/2010/07/29/silvia-federici-precarious-labor-and-reproductive-work/. Accessed 15 June 2017.

Foster, J. B., McChesney, R. W., & Jonna, R. J. (2011). The Global Reserve Army of Labor and the New Imperialism. *Monthly Review, 63*(6), 1–31.

Fraser, N. (2016). Contradictions of Capital and Care. *New Left Review, 100*, 99–117.

Hansen B. R. (2015, October 31). Surplus Population, Social Reproduction, and the Problem of Class Formation. *Viewpoints*. https://www.viewpointmag.com/2015/10/31/surplus-population-social-reproduction-and-the-problem-of-class-formation

Harris-White, B. (2012). Capitalism and the Common Man: Peasants and Petty Production in Africa and South Asia. *Agrarian South: Journal of Political Economy, 1*(2), 109–160.

Kautsky, K. (1988). *The Agrarian Question* (2 Vols). London: Zwan Publications.

Kay, C. (2000). Latin America's Agrarian Transformation: Peasantization and Proletarianization. In D. F. Bryceson, C. Kay, & J. Mooij (Eds.), *Disappearing Peasantries: Rural Labour in Africa, Asia and Latin America*. London: IT Publications.

Lerche, J. (2013). The Agrarian Question in Neoliberal India: Agrarian Transition Bypassed?. *Journal of Agrarian Change, 13*(3), 382–404.

Levien, M. (2015). From Primitive Accumulation to Regimes of Dispossession: Six Theses on India's Land Question. *Economic and Political Weekly, 50*(22), 146–157.

Li, T. M. (2009). To Make Live or Let Die? Rural Dispossession and the Protection of Surplus Populations. *Antipode, 41*(S1), 66–93.

Luxemburg, R. (1951). *The Accumulation of Capital*. London: Routledge.

Marx, K. (1977). *Capital* (Vol. I). New York: Vintage Books.

Marx, K. (1986). *Capital: A Critique of Political Economy* (Vol. 1). Moscow: Progress Publishers.

McIntyre, M. (2011). Race, Surplus Population and the Marxist Theory of Imperialism. *Antipode, 43*(5), 1489–1515.

McIntyre, M., & Nast, H. J. (2011). Bio (Necro) Polis: Marx, Surplus Populations, and the Spatial Dialectics of Reproduction and "Race". *Antipode, 43*(5), 1465–1488.

Mies, M. (2014). *Patriarchy and Accumulation on a World Scale: Women in the International Division of Labour*. London: Zed Books.

Mingione, E. (1985). Ch. 1: Social Reproduction of the Surplus Labour Force: The Case of Southern Italy. In N. Redclift & E. Mingione (Eds.), *Beyond Employment: Household, Gender and Subsistence* (pp. 14–54). Oxford: Basil Blackwell.

Mooij, J. (2000). Changing Peasantries in Asia. In D. F. Bryceson, C. Kay, & J. Mooij (Eds.), *Disappearing Peasantries: Rural Labour in Africa, Asia and Latin America*. London: IT Publications.

Moyo, S., & Yeros, P. (2005). *Reclaiming the Land: The Resurgence of Rural Movements in Africa, Asia and Latin America*. London: Zed Books.

Moyo, S., Yeros, P., & Jha, P. (2012). Imperialism and Primitive Accumulation: Notes on the New Scramble for Africa. *Agrarian South: Journal of Political Economy, 1*(2), 181–203.

Moyo, S., Jha, P., & Yeros, P. (2013). The Classical Agrarian Question: Myth, Reality and Relevance Today. *Agrarian South: Journal of Political Economy, 2*(1), 93–119.

Naidu, S.C. (2018, June 19–21). *Understanding Social Reproduction: Nature, Labour and Capitalist Accumulation*. Paper presented at the 27th Annual Conference of the International Association of Feminist Economics, New Paltz, NY.

Naidu, S. C., & Ossome, L. (2016). Social Reproduction and the Agrarian Question of women's Labour in India. *Agrarian South: Journal of Political Economy, 5*(1), 50–76.

Naidu, S. C., & Ossome, L. (2018). Work, Gender and Immiseration in South Africa and India. *Review of Radical Political Economics, 50*, 332–348.

O'Laughlin, B. (1996). Through a Divided Glass: Dualism and the Agrarian Question in Mozambique. *Journal of Peasant Studies, 23*(4), 1–39.

Quick, P. (2004). Subsistence Wages and Household Production: Clearing the Way for an Analysis of Class and Gender. *Review of Radical Political Economics, 36*(1), 20–36.

Ramachandran, V. K. (2011). The State of Agrarian Relations in India Today. *The Marxist, 27*(1–2), 51–89.

Saka, B. (2014). Petty Commodity Production in the Neoliberal Phase of Global Capitalism: The Case of Grape Production. In Çanakkale, A. Bonanno & J. S. B Cavalcanti (Eds.), *Labor Relations in Globalized Food* (Research in Rural Sociology and Development, Vol. 20), Emerald Group Publishing Limited, pp. 93–113. https://doi.org/10.1108/S1057-192220140000020004

Shah, A., & Harris-White, B. (2011). Resurrecting Scholarship on Agrarian Transformations. *Economic and Political Weekly, 46*(39), 13–18.

Tyner, J. A. (2013). Population Geography I: Surplus Populations. *Progress in Human Geography, 37*(5), 701–711.

Tyner, J. A. (2016). Population Geography III? Precarity, Dead Peasants and Truncated Life. *Progress in Human Geography, 40*(2), 275–289.

Wacquant, L. (2009). *Punishing the Poor: The Neoliberal Government of Social Insecurity.* Durham: Duke University Press.

Yates, M. (2011). The Human-as-Waste, the Labor Theory of Value and Disposability in Contemporary Capitalism. *Antipode, 43*(5), 1679–1695.

CHAPTER 5

Rent and Surplus in the Global Production Network: Identifying 'Value Capture' from the South

Satyaki Roy

Globalization in the current phase entails greater degree of interdependence between nations. The engagement of nations and capital manifests itself in cross border financial flows as well as in the emergence of a world assembly line production system. The nature of interdependence despite being asymmetric appears to be increasingly participatory for the developing countries of the South. This involves a post-colonial division of labour where the entire value creation is broken down into tangible tasks that are performed in different parts of the world. It is only after 1940s we come across this reorganization of industrial geography where regions are no

Originally published in *Agrarian South: Journal of Political Economy, Vol. 6 No. 1*

S. Roy (✉)
Institute for Studies in Industrial Development, Delhi, India

P. Jha et al. (eds.), *Labour Questions in the Global South*,
https://doi.org/10.1007/978-981-33-4635-2_5

longer differentiated from one another by the industries in which they specialize but by the particular tasks which they undertake as part of the entire production process (Lipietz 1980; Hudson 1988). The new division of labour and the process of global distribution of value added are coordinated by multinational and transnational corporations who govern the production network of transforming inputs into outputs. This not only involves physical transformation of objects confined in the providence of manufacturing but also requires capabilities to organize and source inputs from across the world, optimize costs, create brands through design and development for global marketing and hence involves a large part of service activities. Growth of manufacturing exports from the South, with intermediate goods accounting for roughly 60 per cent of global trade and the share of FDI inflows to the developing world, are the immediate indicators of increased participation of developing South in the global production structure (UNCTAD 2013). In this context, global production network (GPN) provides a heuristic device to understand the nature of global integration. The GPN framework, however, acknowledges the fact that for the developing countries mere participation in the GPN might not necessarily lead to desired gains. On the contrary, there seems to be higher concentration of rents in developed countries despite production being 'de-centred' and distributed in favour of the global South. In other words, the physical redistribution of production which has off late tilted towards the South does not in any case change the historical trend of greater share of value added being appropriated by the developed North.

The GPN framework in its various incarnations has been able to delineate the complex flows of capital, labour, knowledge and power focusing on particular sectors tracing back the concrete processes of value addition and enhancement; nevertheless, it confuses two conceptual categories, namely, rent and surplus. Adhering a rent-centric approach, as the case may be in the GPN framework, hardly allows an appreciation of the underlying fact of value capture from the developing countries by large multinational brands. This chapter using a Marxian framework explains that the asymmetry within the process of production remains hidden within the system of prices. Therefore, one needs to see the underlying turbulent process of capturing and siphoning off surplus from global South that takes place beneath the harmonious system of prices. Trade data that record gross inflows and outflows of goods and services are simply incapable of explaining the value capture. The relative position of producers in the global value chain and the production and appropriation of rent which that particular producer wants to realize is not independent of the systemic process of production, appropriation and distribution of surplus value. Therefore, it would be misleading to argue that a particular country or a region can move up the value ladder simply by upgrading its technology and by improvising governance structures at various points within the global value chain. Because of its rent-centric approach the GPN analyses seeks to resolve the problem of asymmetric distribution by 'organizational fix' articulated through two of its key notions—'upgradation' and 'governance'.

The following section revisits the genesis of the GPN framework. The third section discusses why the notion 'value-added' presumed to be measuring contributions at particular stages in the value chain would not be revealing the actual value being captured. This is further taken up in the fourth section by an exposition of the relationship between rent and surplus in the context of value chain and finally some concluding remarks.

Revisiting the GPN Framework

Commodity chain was defined by Hopkins and Wallerstein (1986) as 'a network of labour and production process whose end result is a finished commodity'. In this perspective, value chain as it is understood today was conceived as an entry point to analyse the geopolitical organization of expanding capitalism. French economists in the 1970s developed an empirical research agenda to trace the flows of commodities and identify the agents and activities within the filiere (Raikes et al. 2000). The dependency theory which was at the core of world system analyses viewed the capitalist system as a structure that reproduces hierarchy and inequality through unequal exchange. This was of course the entry point of Gereffi (1994) who pioneered in redefining value chain analyses. Subsequent scholars from the dependency school and others who emphasized the emergence of new international division of labour contributed in shaping the value chain framework (Fröbel et al. 1980; Castells and Henderson 1987; Henderson 1989; Gereffi 1995, 1999; Whitley 1996; Czaban and Henderson 1998; Dicken et al. 2001). The dependency tradition led by Gary Gereffi and others, however, conceived global value chain not just as a heuristic device to analyse global capitalism but as a distinct phase of capitalist industrialization. It went beyond the static categories of core-periphery deployed in the dependency argument and tried to comprehend the dynamics of the emerging industrial organization. In course of time, the trajectory of value chain literature took a serious turn, relying more on the empirical details of meso level or sectoral dynamics and firm level upgrading strategies rather than analysing capitalism as a system using political economic categories (Blair 2005). Henceforth, value chain analyses largely remain restricted as a heuristic framework to understand the details of various stages of production and sometimes even narrowed down to a managerial perspective of supply chain analyses (Porter 1985, 1990).

Gereffi (1994) identified three major dimensions of value chain analyses: physical input–output flows; territoriality; and governance structure. Governance and upgradation are the two most fundamental concepts of value chain analyses. Governance is about the relative positioning of power across the chain and upgradation is about how participants can increase their respective shares in the process of value addition by moving up the value ladder. Furthermore, it is argued that performance of value chains depends more on systemic efficiency than point efficiency as the governance of the system makes a significant difference even if the contributions of individual actors remain the same. The principal theoretical mould of value chain as conceived by Gereffi (1999, 2001) and Kaplinsky (1998, 2000) is that chains are repositories of economic rents[1] that emerge out of returns from scarce assets. The rents arise from differential productivity of factors because of varying degrees of entrepreneurship and barriers to entry that creates relative scarcity. This scheme of analyses is close to the Schumpeterian notion of rents. Schumpeter (1961) argued that scarcity can be created through purposive action by the entrepreneurs through the act of innovation and they derive surplus over and above the average rate of profit by constructing new scarcities. Once the innovation is diffused through competition, the producer's rent gets converted into consumer's surplus. Hence, the dynamics of the value chain and the relative position of actors that define the equation of power and profit within the chain are results of the creation and destruction of economic rents in various nodes. Sources of rents could be technological, organizational, trade rents, relational and so on. Technological rents arise from differential access to key product and process technologies which are propertied. Strategic relationships with other firms can give rise to relational rents. Scarce assets can be tangible as machines or intangible as brands and some of intermediate type like the marketing skills. Economic rents emerge at different degrees in different nodes of the value chain and that determines the power relations within the chain.

Because of increased competition the barriers to entry once created get eroded beyond a point and new scarcities need to be generated either by technological innovation or through changing the rules of governance. Hence, rents are dynamic and change according to deliberate actions of related economic actors. The governance structure in which economic actors are embedded may evolve in a way that allows certain rents to continue to accumulate while others may get depleted over time. Gereffi (1994) defined governance as 'authority and power relationships that determine how financial, material, and human resources are allocated and flow within a chain'. Gereffi et al. (2005) identified five governance structures categorizing network relations based on possible combinations of three independent variables, namely, complexity of transactions, extent of codification of information and competence of suppliers. The typology of governance structures refers to the coordination of flows of inputs and outputs regulated by various organizational forms that lie in a continuum between market and hierarchy. However, since the GPN framework largely focuses on the verticality of the relationships and the value addition that occurs in particular nodes, it can only capture a sliced view of the complex totality.

In view of broadening this framework, Sturgeon (2001) and Henderson et al. (2002) developed the notion of GPN that aims to incorporate at certain levels the social process of reproduction of knowledge, interaction between capital and labour power mediated through hierarchical layers of networks and participants. Value chain analyses of earlier versions were primarily confined to the verticality of relationships ignoring the horizontal and diagonal societal processes that constitute complex dynamics of spaces and flows. The GPN framework was therefore conceived to transcend the limitations of its predecessors. This undoubtedly enhanced the richness of description of production networks but the conceptual building blocks of understanding contribution at particular stages and distribution of gains remain more or less the same.

Macro perspectives and large number of case studies within this tradition itself started questioning the win–win proposition that global integration allows all participants to benefit by means of specializing on the basis of given endowments. Indeed, absolute income levels and the general living standards of people in developing countries have increased; population-weighted income differentials across countries have also narrowed down with the increasing global integration (Kaplinsky 2000). Yet despite this, the surprising fact is the existence of rising inequality within countries.

Furthermore, the countries that have suffered declining income shares are precisely those that have also experienced a high trade/GDP ratio. This is the backdrop of Kaplinsky's (2005, 2007) reinventing the Prebisch–Singer thesis (Singer 1950; Prebisch 1962) of unequal exchange in the context of the twenty-first century. The crux of the argument is that the decline of the barter terms of trade of commodities vis-à-vis manufacturing in Prebisch–Singer thesis was related to country endowments rather than attributes of commodities. In the present context, the barter terms of trade in manufacturing suffered a decline between developing countries and the European Union (Maizels et al. 1998). This has been attributed to rapid industrialization and exports from East Asia especially from China in the last three decades. 'Immiserizing growth', that is, falling returns with increasing economic activity, is being reflected in a decline in the unit price of exports specially in cases where countries rely heavily on simple assembly of imported inputs (Schmitz 2004; Kaplinsky 2007). Therefore, value-chain literature concludes that returns for developing countries could only increase by means of creating quasi-rents[2] that can be protected from global competition.

The value chain framework gives a snap shot view of the relationships between stages of production but provides very little scope to endogenize the existing power relations between various layers of actors. Rather it assumes the structural hierarchy as something given and therefore ignores the political economy of the perpetuation and reinforcing of such hierarchy. The other important critique of the value chain analyses is its relative neglect of the financialization of the global economy. The realm of production is increasingly being intimidated by financial interests that largely influence the flow of international capital. Consequently, the choice of location within a country and the terms of inclusion within the value chain are to a great extent determined by the requirements of finance capital. Palpacuer (2008) shows how increasing financialization and high-market capitalization by firms gives rise to performance indexes that factor in not only interests on borrowed capital but also expected returns to shareholders. Increased concern on shareholders' return shifts the focus of internal investment to high-valued activities related to product definition, marketing and consumer lending rather than manufacturing. It once again increased the importance of scale as buyers tend to deal with few suppliers who could go through stringent monitoring of supplier performance (Gibbon 2002). High pressure is put on suppliers to share price deflation and uncertainties which suppliers tend to absorb for the sake of retaining orders. This often leads to growing flexibilization, informalization and feminization of the work force.

Value Added and Value Captured

The GPN framework measures the value added in each stage of production within the network. The value added in this case is simply the difference between output and input prices in each stage. Aggregate value addition is the sum of all these values added in different stages of production. As one moves up the value ladder by way of producing more value-added output at a particular stage, *ceteris paribus*, can improve its share in the aggregate value added. Therefore, an argument is made that the relative share of a particular stage of production in the total value added will increase if efforts are made to enhance the value addition capacity of units involved in the process of production. Therefore, countries or regions participating in GPN could easily increase their share in value added by increasing their contribution by means of process and product innovation and upgradation. Measuring value added in each stage is simply accounting the difference between output and input prices but the system of prices that gives monetary expression to created values may not always match with the actual value created and measured in labour units. Transformation of values into prices[3] relates to a complex process that is embedded in the systemic architecture of interactions between production and exchange articulated within the hierarchy of capitals.

The global production structure is being recasted in two ways: one is the FDI route and the other which is emerging to be the dominant is by way of arms-length subcontracting or outsourcing. Globalization offers transnational corporations access to a global reserve army of labour. Since labour markets continue to be embedded in national settings, there is increased mobility of capital coupled with relative immobility of labour, allowing for the maintenance of differential rates of exploitation.

Production facilities are shifted to the global South because it enhances profit by replacing high waged workers by similarly skilled low waged counterparts. This is evident particularly, but not exclusively, in cases of buyer driven value chains where pressure on retailer's profit is ultimately passed on to manufacturers and contractors down the chain. Reducing costs through squeezing labour has been the usual response in such cases, and this is done either by reducing wages or by introducing piece rated work, further subcontracting to lower cost factories or drawing on illegal factories which exist only temporarily and close down without paying rents for space and wages of the workforce (Appelbaum and Gereffi 1994).

In the light of this, it should be noted that the shift in manufacturing activities in the global South which are often captured in the growth of exports have not been similarly matched by an increasing share of the South in manufacturing value added. Manufactured exports from the 55 low-wage nations increased by 329 per cent between 1990 and 2004 (434 per cent if China is included), while their combined manufacturing value added grew by just 46.3 per cent during the same period (Smith 2016). This is not only intermediate inputs that had a higher share, but more importantly because the value produced in the developing South are captured not at the point of production rather at destinations for consumption by transnational corporations. Value capture occurs not because parent firms contribute in a large measure to production activities but because they maintain control over design, development, distribution channel including the ultimate retail loop. For instance, the mark-up captured by a US company Fast Fashion dealing with T-shirts entirely produced in Bangladesh is 152 per cent over the manufacturing cost. This is even higher for K P McLane polo shirt retailed at US$175 with a profit mark up of 718 per cent and that for Hermes polo shirt the average markup amounts to 1800 per cent of the total manufacturing cost (Smith 2016). These hefty mark-ups, recorded as value added by the US company, cannot be attributable to any production activity undertaken at the USA rather the value created by Bangladeshi workers are being captured by the US company and accounted as value addition by the parent company.

A more telling example is the story of Taiwanese-owned Foxconn Technology Group located at China. It is the world's largest contract manufacturer of electronics supplying parts to Samsung Electronics, Hewlett-Packard, Sony, Apple, Microsoft, Dell and Nokia (Ngai and Chan 2012). The production of Apple's iPod, particularly, involve 41,000 jobs worldwide including 13,290 in the USA, and the rest are distributed across the outsourced centres. Only 30 out of the US workers are production workers, and the rest are retail, non-professional workers as well as professional workers. The advantage that companies like Apple derive by shifting sites of production from the developed to the developing parts of the world primarily emerges from huge difference in wages between the North and the South. The ratio of wages at Foxconn China compared to similar production work in the USA is only 3.2 per cent. Similarly, in cases of retail and professional work, these ratios are 6 per cent and 1.8 per cent, respectively. The number of workers employed in iPod-related activities is similar in the USA and China, yet the total US wage bill was $719 million and the total Chinese wage bill was $19 million in 2006 (Smith 2012). The cost of production is low because of low wages in China and the mark up accrued to domestic producers based on this cost of production if added gives the gross value of output exported by China. The value of the exported product being low the profit margin accrued by Apple has been as high as 64 per cent (Xing and Detert 2011). The gross profit is, however, shared between Apple, its North American distributors and the US government. Studies show that on an average Chinese manufacturing wages remained fairly low at 2–3 per cent of the US wages during the period 1980–2005. Despite recent increase in the legal minimum wages in China, Hokou system of household registration, student internship in factories and high labour intensity forced upon workers by the employers in large factory campuses helps in maintaining low reproduction cost (Ngai and Chan 2012). A detailed study on Nokia value chain reveals a similar story of value capture by the North. Nokia N-95 smartphone is assembled in China for final sales in the USA. The final assembly which is the main step in the physical incarnation of the product accounts only 2 per cent of the total value added while EU-27 countries including Finland capture 51 per cent of the value added because they control the branding, development, design and management (Ali-Yrkkö et al. 2011). These facts simply suggest that figures in value added do not necessarily reflect the limited contribution of lead firms in particular stages of production and the process of value creation.

The world of commodities involves production of goods and services that are of no immediate use to the producer; rather they are produced for sale, and the final objective of the capitalist is to earn profits. Since all such productive activities involve labour, skilled or unskilled, physical or mental, labour time emerges as the fundamental regulator of this social process of production whose reproduction involves the social allocation of labour time. This implies that although individual capitalists may perceive the production process as independent of the social process, they also assume that elements supporting a particular process of production would automatically fall in place without any central coordination. In other words, individual capitalist presupposes a social division of labour that is only realized by the act of exchange with other commodity producers. And in this act of exchange, is what Marx argues that in the midst of fluctuations of exchange value the 'socially necessary labour time', that is, the amount of labour time socially allocated for the production of a particular commodity asserts itself as some fundamental law that governs the social process of exchange. This labour theory of value allows us to perceive prices as determined by an underlying process that relates to labour time and also conceives value as intrinsic to the determination of prices. Therefore, distribution is not the only site which involves social relations but the process of production itself involves labour processes and hence a social determination. This social determination of production and the class processes and related asymmetries hence become relevant in determining the price structure. The value of the 'labour power' is determined in the way the values of other commodities are determined. In other words, it is determined by the amount of labour time considered to be socially necessary to produce the goods and services required to reproduce the labour power. In a globalized world, one would therefore expect that there would be a single value of labour power but that labour power is recompensed at different rates (Amin 2010). This fundamental asymmetry and heterogeneity are maintained by keeping labour immobile leading to differential rates of exploitation or unequal rates of surplus-value to exist in different parts of the world. Heintz (2006) argues that developing countries face unequal exchange because they export commodities that embody greater amount of labour in comparison with the commodities they import which require relatively lesser amount of labour. This happens because profit rates are equalized across national boundaries owing to the mobility of capital while labour is a relatively immobile factor of production, thus allowing, both differential wages and as also differential rates of exploitation at equalized rates of profit. In other words, developing countries that with a labour surplus import goods at prices that include higher wages prevailing in industrialized countries and also have to accept the equalized rates of profit arrived by competition between free-flowing capitals. But this asymmetry is hidden under the price structure. In fact, lower wages in developing countries generate higher rates of surplus-value. The higher surplus produced in the low-wage segment of the world is siphoned off and accumulated as imperialist rent by the international corporations located in the developed world. This is evident only when the underlying value relations are uncovered to explain how surplus value is being captured through lowering of wages in developing countries. Thus, the veil of value-added measured only in terms of price differentials has to be demystified in order to identify the multifold transfer of value from the periphery to the centre. Moreover, this process of determination of the rate of surplus value on the world scale and the respective rates in different nations are not independent of the conflicts and contestations that take place between different layers of capital and labour within the global and the local space.

Rent and Surplus in Global Production Network

As shown earlier, the GPN framework in its different versions relies on the notion of rent or quasi-rent of the Schumpeterian tradition. The deliberate creation of 'scarcity' through innovation in resources, technology and organization gives rise to an income stream for an extended period of time by virtue of exclusive control over some directly or indirectly tradable item which is in some crucial respects unique and non-replicable. This rent-centric view hardly recognizes the fact that the distribution of surplus across the value chain does not depend only upon specific interventions at stages of production but also gets mutually determined by the relative position of individual capital in that industry in the process of creating surplus. In other words, the return to improvements created in particular stages of production is not independent of the entire process of surplus creation and realization for the whole value chain. Rent is after all a distributed surplus. The neglect of this fact by the value chain literature perhaps explains why this literature cannot adequately integrate the process of production with an analysis of the labour processes that gives rise to surplus.

In the context of global value chains, Kaplinsky (2005) defines a special class of economic rent as quasi-rent which is a return on a resource over and above the opportunity cost of the use of that resource. Rent arises when the supply of resource is fixed and the resource itself does not get depleted by its use. As a result, a higher demand of such resources would not result in higher supply rather to higher market clearing prices in the form of rent. Quasi-rents are conceived to be temporary implying that the supply of resources is fixed only in the short run but not over a longer period of time. Technology is one of the major sources of quasi-rent and therefore firms need to innovate continuously to generate such rents. Kaplinsky (2005) also proposes a notion of composite quasi-rent which arises when returns over and above the opportunity cost of a specific resource can only be realized when it is being utilized in combination with another resource. For instance, the higher return from the use of an improved machine can only be realized when workers with specialized skills are available to operate such machines. And in such cases, returns are distributed between owners of machines and skilled workers through a process of bargain. Stretching this argument, furthermore, one can state that since capabilities of workers of different groups vary, there are differential returns to workers depending on their contribution in creating composite rents and the autonomy they derive from particular capabilities in the process of bargain. This is the neo-Ricardian tradition of analysing distribution. It essentially views production as a technical process rather than a social process and assumes capital and labour just as contending claimants in a bargaining relationship.[4]

The creation and distribution of rent is overdetermined by the production, appropriation and distribution of surplus. Marx (1959) argues that rent emerges because of differences in organic composition of capital defined by the ratio of constant to variable capital in various production processes that gives rise to surplus over and above average profit. This implies that one producing in a developing country with greater use of labour compared to the average composition of capital in that specific industry would produce more surplus value than that of a similar size of capital with average organic composition of capital. But whether such capital in the developing world would get a higher share of returns, that is, an additional profit over and above the average rate of profit depends upon how the access to or ownership of labour resources is protected and kept out of competition. In the context of agricultural rents, Marx argued that such rents exist so long the ownership of land is being protected and competition does not allow the inflow of capital from industry to agriculture. This implies that differential access to resources might give rise to returns over and above average rate of return, but the sustainability of such return as rents depends on the determination of the average rate of profit as well as the institutional structure of ownership of resources.

The amount of rent that could be generated and accrued by individual capital is not determined by the capacity of an individual to differentiate their products from other competitors, but it also depends upon how such innovations fare vis-à-vis the normal capital with average level of technology for the entire industry. Technological improvements influence the productivity of labour and hence the division between necessary and surplus labour time. This is the physical datum which bridges the relationship between market prices and value relations (Laibman 1973/1974). The notion of socially necessary labour time in Marx not only determines the value of a commodity (including that of labour power) but actually suggests the boundaries of socially accepted distribution of labour at a given point of time and space. Therefore, the production process and hence the labour process introduced by an individual capitalist have to confront the socially accepted distribution of labour and the labour processes of 'normal capital' in that specific industry. The surplus value created by the individual capital in the process of production is only potential profit and usually do not get realized as actual profit. Rather the transformation of value into prices gets mediated by the market, and prices vary because of differences in organic composition of capital vis-à-vis the normal capital. Capitals that employ higher levels of technology realize more profits than the surplus value individually generated by them and conversely those operate with a lower level of technology realize profits that are less than the surplus value generated. This precisely indicates that the realization of rent which actually emerges because of the difference between actual price and market price depends not only on the cost of production of a particular commodity but also on the determination of the market price of that product as well.

The determination of market price in Marx's Capital III rests upon a prior determination of the general rate of profit which is given by the social surplus generated out of the total social capital advanced. Thus, the cost price of the product is given by the sum of constant and variable capital advanced by individual capitalist in a particular industry. And the price of production adds up the cost of production with the individual profit realized. The individual profit realized once again is given by the share of aggregate profit in proportion to the individual capital advanced to total capital in that particular industry. The profit component of the individual capitalist is therefore the product of the average rate of profit in that industry and the individual capital advanced. The average rate of profit in a particular industry, however, is determined by the normal capital in that industry that employs average technical composition of capital. The inflow and outflow of capital from various industries determined by the underlying value relations finally leads to a converging trend towards the general rate of profit applicable for the whole economy. Therefore, the determination of the price of production as well as the difference from that to the average price are co-determined by the individual and the capitalist system of value relations as a whole. This implies that if the average technical composition of an industry moves faster than the pace of innovation of a firm within that industry, the individual firm is likely to lose out even if improvisation takes place. This perhaps provides a better clue in understanding the 'technology gap' perpetually reproduced between developed and developing countries.

Rent as an additional income over and above the average market price can exist so long it does not enter into the process of tendential equalization of the rate of profit.[5] It has to exist as a monopoly right on certain unique resources or a process of production. This monopoly right might not always follow from the concentration and centralization of capital but also from a special access to a local resource. One has to deliberately create scarcity but at the same time it should not be so unique that it goes beyond the realm of exchange (Harvey 2009). And that scarcity has to be protected by the system of property rights. Once capital from other industries is allowed to access the protected resources, then competition would eventually bring down prices to the average level. Therefore, manoeuvring the system of property relations and competition may help destroying certain monopoly rights existing in the developing world and at the same time protecting exclusive rights created in the North. This perhaps explains why the larger concentration of quasi-rents in a network of decentred production still rests with the North. The value chain framework acknowledges this asymmetry but claims to overcome that by upgrading and governance. Instead of looking into the systemic determination of prices of production informed by value relations and the underlying dynamism of differential rents this framework anchors on differential prices. And precisely because of its exclusive focus on price differentials the value chain framework ignores the labour process as a necessary datum determining the relative position of individual production process vis-à-vis the social average.

The GPN analysis limits its scope within the relationship between firms that are participating in the network. It, however, explains neither why a firm happens to be included in the network nor why one is dropped out. The dynamics within the value chain is primarily governed by the relative position of individual capital and its technical composition with reference to the normal capital that assumes average levels of technology in that particular industry. The inclusion and exclusion of firms within the global value chain and also upgrading relative positions depends upon how they could create and protect rents given the general determination of the rate of profit. Now if an individual capital within the global circuit of capital operates at a scale of production that does not allow production at a price that is at least not more than the price of production of normal capital in that industry, then that individual capital could hardly survive in the face of competition. Otherwise the smaller capital has to compromise on the rate of profit itself or take recourse to extending working hours or intensification of labour that reduces production costs. The rationale, however, is little different for small firms. Carrera (1998) using Marx's theory of ground rent argued that valorization in the case of small firms are not regulated strictly by average rate of profit of normal capitals but it actually depends upon the means of subsistence required to reproduce the family business. It is the sum of cost of production and the notional interest rate that can be derived on the liquidation value of productive assets which gives the minimum margin required for survival. The space of survival, however, depends upon the dynamics of normal capital in a specific industry. As the general level of productivity improves in a specific branch of industry, the threshold of survival for small firms also moves upwards. As a result, within a given level of technology and scale of operation, it becomes difficult for such firms to remain integrated with the value chain. Sometimes it is quite possible that smaller capitals sell at a price which is greater than the minimum level required for survival but less than the price of the average capitals. However, in such cases also, it is the buyers from smaller capitals who benefit in terms of sourcing inputs at below normal price because competition among the small enterprises eventually brings down the price at the minimum level. Hence locating industries and integrating smaller firms of developing countries in the global value chain serves the purpose of deriving surplus profit out of cheap labour available there.

Given this fact, the firms of developing countries can hardly derive any rent out of exclusive access to such labour and end up competing with each other in order to create conditions for enhancing the super normal profits of the monopolistic buyers. In other words, the 'exclusivity' and 'scarcity' that the developing South can easily garner, because of its specifics in endowments, are increasingly drawn into the realm of global capital and worldwide competition. On the contrary, the resources and inputs which historically developed in the North, especially technology- and 'knowledge'-related inputs because of their specific endowment patterns and cultural hegemony, are protected by monopoly and exclusive property rights in the form of patenting, copyrights and other measures. The political economy of institutions in fact determines which of the 'scarcities' should remain protected and which others would be increasingly drawn into the realm of competition. Therefore, creation of rent and its protection at the end of the day does not depend only on the innovative interventions by individual firms but largely on the relative position of the firm vis-à-vis average capital in a particular industry. And of course, how such innovations cater to the tastes and preferences of the buyers located in the developed North.

Conclusion

The global value chain framework provides an entry point to comprehend the process of accumulation and distribution of profits that cuts across both national boundaries and sectoral divisions. It underlines the fact that interventions, for increasing either the value added or the distribution of gains, invoke a global perspective. Studies explicitly raise serious doubts about the possibilities of developing countries reaping equal benefits because of participating in value networks. But such analysis traces the cause of this to differential power in bargain at the nodes of exchange within the value chain and underplays the crucial point that such power relations are largely determined by the impersonal forces of capitalism that drives the tendential equalization of the general rate of profit. The process of value capture can only be identified when we use the conceptual scope of surplus creation and distribution across the entire value chain. It shows that the creation of rents, which could be derived over and above average rate of profit, does not depend only on the level of innovation at that particular stage of production, but also upon how these changes fare with reference to the normal capital that employs average level of technology in that industry. The social determination of profit realized by individual capitalist shows that calculus of price differentials are the visible outcomes of an underlying turbulent process of capitalist competition, changing relative weights of individual capital and dynamics of power relations.

The GPN framework which confines its analyses to value added would expectedly be suffering from the optical illusion of not being able to see the value capture involved in this process of price determination. Moreover, the creation and protection of rents primarily rests upon how certain resources and capabilities can be kept outside the realm of competition that tend to equalize the rate of profit across firms as well as across industries. The institutional arrangements that prevent capital to invade certain exclusive resources are dependent on the political economy of emerging monopolies. In the course of globalization with the 'annihilation of space through time', local monopolies are destroyed because of declining transaction costs and due to weakening of economic barriers such as tariffs and political protections. Hence in order to reorganize monopoly structures, global capital needs to redefine institutional architecture, particularly the boundaries of institutions to design what is to be protected from global competition and the exclusive rights need be maintained. Increased penetration of economic, social and cultural relations of one nation into another has been the defining character of the current phase of globalization. As a result, exclusive rights or access to natural resources or cheap labour are increasingly being invaded by international capital. On the other hand, knowledge and technology is increasingly being codified and propertied than earlier times. Therefore, there is a structural asymmetry in the distribution of potential sources of rents and individual improvements are certainly constrained by such asymmetries. Producers in developing countries largely derive their margin by recourse to cheap labour and also competition among similar suppliers result in higher shares of value added for global buyers. In fact, instead of diffusion of knowledge asymmetric relations within the production network sometimes result in fragmentation of enterprises and erosion of skills at lower end of the value chain. The survival strategies in the face of global competition often give rise to 'footloose industries' that rely heavily on 'fluid labour' and move from one place to another. This prevents any long-term relation between capital, labour and technology. Improving governance and technological upgradation simply seizes to be options in such volatile situations. The success of individual interventions within the value chain therefore does depend not only on its intention to improve its position in the network but also on how individual producers confront the ever-changing social division of labour and capital that concretely determines the share of individual gains.

Acknowledgements The author would like to thank the anonymous referees for their valuable comments and suggestions. The usual disclaimer applies.

Notes

1. Rent as originally defined by Ricardo (1973, p. 33) in the *Principles of Political Economy and Taxation* (Chapter II: 'On Rent') as 'that portion of the produce of the earth which is paid to the landlord for the use of the original and indestructible powers of the soil'. Ricardo indicates that rent does not arise because of differential fertility of land but because of differential access to scarce resources. Later on ecnomic rent is referred to any return

that a resource attracts over and above the opportunity cost of the use of that resource.

2. Quasi-rents are special type of economic rents that are temporary in nature and arise where the supply of a resource is fixed over the short term but not for a longer term. Discussed in detail in fourth section.
3. In Capital vol. III part II, Marx discusses the distribution of surplus value between competing industrial capitals as well as between other forms of capital including commercial and financial capital and the landowning class. Marx shows how prices are linked to values and can be higher and lower than values. This transformation of values into prices is actually a process of distribution of surplus value between different capitals.
4. For a detailed discussion, see Sheikh (1982).
5. Profit rates within industry and between industry tend to equalize through competition converging towards a general rate of profit for the whole economy in the longer period. This is some average rate of profit accrued by capital that has mean or average composition at a particular point of time. Rent can exist by keeping resources or 'scarce' factors away from competition or by restricting access to such resources to other capitals. In fact, the average rate of profit is computed on that portion of social capital which enters the equalization process.

References

Ali-Yrkkö, J., Rouvinen, P., Seppälä, T., & Ylä-Anttila, P. (2011). Who Captures Value in Global Supply Chains? Case Nokia N 95 Smartphone. *Journal of Industry, Competition and Trade, 11*, 263–278.

Amin, S. (2010). *The Law of Worldwide Value*. New York: Monthly Review Press.

Appelbaum, R. P., & Gereffi, G. (1994). Power and Profits in the Apparel Commodity Chain. In E. Bonacich, L. Cheng, N. Chinchilla, & N. H. P. Ong (Eds.), *Global Production: The Apparel Industry in the Pacific Rim* (pp. 42–62). Philadelphia, PA: Temple University Press.

Blair, J. (2005). Global Capitalism and Commodity Chains: Looking Back, Going Forward. *Competition & Change, 9*(2), 153–180.

Carrera, I. J. (1998). *A Model to Measure the Profitability of Specific Industrial Capitals by Computing their Turnover Circuits* (CICP Working Paper). Buenos. Aires: Centro para la Investigación como Crítica Práctica la Investigaci'on como Cr'ıtica Pr'actica.

Castells, M., & Henderson, J. (1987). Techno-Economic Restructuring, Sociopolitical Process and Spatial Transformation: A Global Perspective. In J. Henderson & M. Castells (Eds.), *Global Restructuring and Territorial Development* (pp. 1–17). Newbury Park: SAGE Publications.

Czaban, L., & Henderson, J. (1998). Globalisation, Institutional Legacies and Industrial Transformation in Eastern Europe. *Economy and Society, 27*(4), 585–613.

Dicken, P., Kelly, P., Olds, K., & Wai-Chung Yeung, H. (2001). Chains and Networks, Territories and Scales: Towards a Relational Framework for Analyzing the Global Economy. *Global Networks, 1*(2), 89–112.

Fröbel, F., Heinrichs, J., & Kreye, O. (1980). *The New International Division of Labour*. Cambridge: Cambridge University Press.

Gereffi, G. (1994). The Organisation of Buyer-Driven Global Commodity Chains: How US Retailers Shape Overseas Production Networks. In G. Gereffi & M. Korzeniewicz (Eds.), *Commodity Chains and Global Capitalism* (pp. 95–122). Westport/London: Greenwood Press.

Gereffi, G. (1995). Global Production Systems and Third World Development. In B. Stallings (Ed.), *Global Change, Regional Response: The New International Context of Development* (pp. 100–142). New York: Cambridge University Press.

Gereffi, G. (1999). International Trade and Industrial Upgrading in the Apparel Commodity Chain. *Journal of International Economics, 48*(1), 37–70.

Gereffi, G. (2001). Beyond the Producer-Driven/Buyer-Driven Dichotomy: The Evolution of Global Value Chains in the Internet Era. *IDS Bulletin, 32*(3), 30–40.

Gereffi, G., Humphrey, J., & Sturgeon, T. (2005). The Governance of Global Value Chains. *Review of International Political Economy, 12*(1), 78–104.

Gibbon, P. (2002). At the Cutting Edge? Financialisation and UK Clothing Retailers' Global Sourcing Patterns and Practices. *Competition & Change, 6*(3), 289–308.

Harvey, D. (2009). *The Art of Rent: Globalization Monopoly and the Commodification of Culture*. Retrieved from http://www.generation-online.org/c/fc_rent1.htm.

Heintz, J. (2006). Low-Wage Manufacturing and Global Commodity Chains: A Model in the Unequal Exchange Tradition. *Cambridge Journal of Economics, 30*(4), 507–520.

Henderson, J. (1989). *The Globalisation of High Technology Production*. London: Routledge.

Henderson, J., Dicken, P., Hess, M., Coe, N., & Wai-Chung Yeung, H. (2002). Global Production Networks and the Analysis of Economic Development. *Review of International Political Economy, 9*(3), 436–464.

Hopkins, T., & Wallerstein, I. (1986). Commodity Chains in the World Economy Prior to 1800. *Review, 10*(1), 157–170.

Hudson, R. (1988). Uneven Development in Capitalist Societies: Changing Spatial Divisions of Labour, Forms of Spatial Organization of Production and Service Provision, and their Impacts on Localities. *Transactions of the Institute of British Geographers, New Series, 13*(4), 484–496.

Kaplinsky, R. (1998). *Globalisation, Industrialisation and Sustainable Growth: The Pursuit of the Nth Rent* (Discussion Paper No. 365). Brighton: Institute of Development Studies, University of Sussex.

Kaplinsky, R. (2000). *Spreading the Gains from Globalisation: What Can Be Learned from Value Chain Analysis?* (Working Paper No. 110). Brighton: Institute of Development Studies, University of Sussex.

Kaplinsky, R. (2005). *Globalization, Poverty and Inequality: Between a Rock and a Hard Place*. Cambridge: Polity Press.

Kaplinsky, R. (2007). *Capability Building in SSA: What Difference Do the Asian Drivers Make?* (SLPTMD Working Paper Series 10). Oxford: Department of International Development, University of Oxford.

Laibman, D. (1973/1974). Values and Prices of Production: The Political Economy of the Transformation Problem. *Science and Society, 37*(4), 404–436.

Lipietz, A. (1980). The Structuration of Space, the Problem of Land and Spatial Policy. In J. Carney, R. Hudson, & J. R. Lewis (Eds.), *Regions in Crisis* (pp. 60–75). London: Croom Helm.

Maizels, A., Berge, K., Crowe, T., & Palaskas, T. B. (1998). *Trends in the Manufacturing Terms of Trade of Developing Countries*. Oxford: Mimeo, Finance and Trade Policy Centre, Queen Elizabeth House.

Marx, K. (1959). *Capital* (Vol. III). Moscow: Foreign Languages Publishing House.

Ngai, P., & Chan, J. (2012). Global Capital, the State, and Chinese Workers: The Foxconn Experience. *Modern China, 38*(4), 383–410.

Palpacuer, F. (2008). Bringing the Social Context Back in: Governance and Wealth Distribution in Global Commodity Chains. *Economy and Society, 37*(3), 393–419.

Porter, M. (1985). *Competitive Advantage: Creating and Sustaining Superior Performance*. London: Macmillan.

Porter, M. (1990). *The Competitive Advantage of Nations*. London: Macmillan.

Prebisch, R. (1962). The Economic Development of Latin America and its Principal Problems. *Economic Bulletin for Latin America, 7*(1), 1–22.

Raikes, P., Jensen, M. F., & Ponte, S. (2000). Global Commodity Chain Analysis and the French Filiere Approach: Comparison and Critique. *Economy and Society, 29*(3), 390–417.

Ricardo, D. (1973; first published 1911). *The Principles of Political Economy and Taxation*. London: J.M. Dent and Sons.

Schmitz, H. (2004). Chain Governance and Upgrading: Taking Stock. In H. Schmitz (Ed.), *Local Enterprises in the Global Economy* (pp. 349–353). Cheltenham: Edward Elgar.

Schumpeter, J. (1961). *The Theory of Economic Development*. Oxford: Oxford University Press.

Sheikh, A. (1982). Neo-Ricardian Economics: A Wealth of Algebra, a Poverty of Theory. *Review of Radical Political Economics, 14*(2), 67–83.

Singer, H. W. (1950). The Distribution of Gains between Investing and Borrowing Countries. *American Economic Review, 40*(2), 473–485.
Smith, J. (2012). The GDP Illusion: Value Added Versus Value Capture. *Monthly Review, 64*(3), 86–102.
Smith, J. (2016). *Imperialism in the Twenty-First Century: Globalization, Super Exploitation and capitalism's Final Crisis.* New York: Monthly Review Press.
Sturgeon, T. J. (2001). How Do we Define Value Chains and Production Networks? *IDS Bulletin, 32*(3), 9–18.
UNCTAD. (2013). *Handbook of Statistics.* New York/Geneva: United Nations.
Whitley, R. (1996). Business Systems and Global Commodity Chains: Competing or Complementary Forms of Economic Organisation? *Competition & Change, 1*(4), 411–425.
Xing, Y., & Detert, N. (2011). *How the iPhone Widens the United States Trade Deficit with the People's Republic of China* (Working Paper Series 257). Tokyo: Asian Development Bank Institute.

CHAPTER 6

From 'Relative Surplus Population' and 'Dual Labour Markets' to 'Informal' and 'Formal' Employment and Enterprises: Insights About Causation and Consequences

Sheila Bhalla

This essay traces the intellectual history of the concepts 'informal' sector and 'informal economy' from Karl Marx to Arthur Lewis, Barry Bluestone, Keith Hart and S. V. Sethuraman.* It shows how the Marxian dynamics of 'relative surplus population' has been replaced by the concept of 'informal economy'. It also discusses the dynamic role of population pressure on agriculture in many countries of the Global South. Finally, it is suggested

Originally published in *Agrarian South: Journal of Political Economy, Vol. 6 No. 3*

S. Bhalla (✉)
Centre for Economic Studies and Planning, Jawaharlal Nehru University, New Delhi, India

P. Jha et al. (eds.), *Labour Questions in the Global South*,
https://doi.org/10.1007/978-981-33-4635-2_6

that the strategies advocated by the International Labour Organization (ILO) since the 1970s have tended to narrow the areas of investigation promoted by them.

Introduction

This article is about the 'forerunners', those who thought and wrote about the phenomenon we call today 'the informal economy', informal workers and 'unorganized' or (informal) enterprises. It provides an overview of the work of five contributors to this literature, namely, Karl Marx, W. Arthur Lewis, Barry Bluestone, Keith Hart and S. V. Sethuraman.[1]

Karl Marx

In Marx, the concept of declining employment elasticities is embedded in an account of the dynamics of the rise of raw capitalism in a developing country—the United Kingdom in the eighteenth and early nineteenth centuries—where the shift of the workforce out of agriculture was still underway, and where large numbers of non-agricultural workers were being absorbed in low quality jobs, in what today we would describe as the 'unorganized sector' or the 'informal economy'. Together with the unemployed, these people constituted what Marx called the 'relative surplus population'—relative, that is, to the demand for labour in the capitalist segment of the economy of his own time.

In this context, Marx describes the links between five phenomena: (a) declining employment elasticities, (b) the accumulation of capital, (c) the falling share of wages in national income, (d) the falling share of unorganized sector enterprises in national income and (e) increasing income inequality.[2]

Marx's exposition begins as follows:

> The growing extent of the means of production, as compared with the labour power incorporated with them, is an expression of the growing productiveness of labour. The increase of the latter [i.e., labour productivity], appears therefore, in the diminution of the mass of labour in proportion to the means of production moved by it.

He goes on: '…this growth of the means of production, as compared with the mass of the labour power that vivifies them, is reflected again in its value composition, by the increase of the constant constituent of capital at the expense of its variable constituent'.[3]

What then happens to demand for labour? While the process of capital accumulation reduces the share of labour in the production process in non-agricultural enterprises, the absolute numbers of workers may or may not rise.[4]

However, this does not apply to agriculture. The workforce shift out of agriculture is visualized as a process in which the capitalist process of accumulation pushes workers out of agriculture, just as mechanization of some agricultural operations is doing in India today. To the extent that it does so, the demand for agricultural labour falls absolutely, that is, in terms of absolute numbers, not just relatively, that is, in terms of shares.

The result is that a section of the 'agricultural population' is constantly in the process of shifting out and into an urban and non-agricultural proletariat. As long as there is a 'surplus population' in rural areas, this flow continues.

In this process, 'the agricultural labourer is therefore reduced to the minimum of wages and always stands with one foot already in the swamp of pauperism'. Workers in what Marx describes as 'domestic industry'—roughly the equivalent of the self-employed in unorganized manufacturing, trade and services of today—suffer the same fate. Their 'conditions of life' tend to sink 'below the average normal level of the working class'.[5]

As the accumulation of capital proceeds, it 'increases the concentration of that wealth in the hands of individual capitalists'. In their competition with one another, the larger capitalists, whose enterprises enjoy economies of scale, tend to beat the smaller ones by charging less for the commodities they produce. The formation of joint stock companies then 'intensifies and accelerates the effects of accumulation and speeds up the changes in the technical composition of capital which raises the constant portion at the expense of the variable portion, thus diminishing further the relative demand for labour'.[6] Thus, the process of capital accumulation produces an 'accumulation of wealth at one pole' and, at the same time, 'an accumulation of misery … at the opposite pole', in short, rising inequality.[7]

Two features of this analysis may be noted here. First, Marx visualizes the capitalist accumulation process as what has been described as a 'self-acting, self-driven order, functioning independently of the will and consciousness of the participants', and second, that he does not say how he thinks this will all end. He leaves it open-ended.[8] This is in contrast to the early dual economies and dual labour market theorists. They tended to see a happy outcome.

Lewis and Dual Market Theorists

W. Arthur Lewis, the first in a series of 'dual labour market' theorists, is best known for his 1954 paper, 'Economic Development with Unlimited Supplies of Labour'. His distinction between a 'modern' and a 'traditional' (or a 'capitalist' and a 'pre-capitalist or subsistence' sector) set the stage for subsequent writers on the 'dual economy'.

Lewis and other early writers on the dual economy focused on how low productivity and surplus labour, available at subsistence wages, especially in agriculture, could provide a window of opportunity for capital accumulation in a dynamic development context. That is, behind the original Lewis notion of a dual economy with an overcrowded informal sector, lay a theory about how sustainable development processes could take place. They would be 'sustainable' in the sense that the workers in the pre-capitalist sector would eventually get absorbed in the modern, capitalist sector.

A number of scholars built upon the Lewis model and extended it.[9] In these models, the bridge between the traditional and modern sectors is capital accumulation—that is, investment in public and private productive assets of a kind that not only raise labour productivity but also, more importantly, create increasing demand for labour in the 'modern' or 'capitalist' sector.

In all of these models, development is seen as a process by which the 'modern' sector becomes progressively more important in terms of its contribution to employment generation as well as in terms of its contribution to gross domestic product (GDP). Agriculture, as well as the rural non-farm sector, also are transformed or 'modernized' through the application of improved techniques until the modern, capitalist sector absorbs most of the surplus labour, and the informal or traditional sector shrinks to the point where the modern capitalist or 'formal' sector dominates the economic structure.[10]

The formalization of employment in these models constitutes an integral part of the development process. In this literature, however, the terms 'formal' and 'informal' were not used.

This literature raises a question: Why did these dual labour market theorists tend to be so optimistic about the outcome of this development process—the absorption of workers into the modern capitalist sector, the formalization of employment and the ultimate absorption of low productivity informal workers from agriculture and low-productivity non-agricultural enterprises? Why?

It seems that their optimism was a product of what they could see happening in their own time in countries like the United States and the United Kingdom. This was, in turn, the product of very special political, economic and technological conditions which prevailed for a couple of decades following the Second World War. These combined to produce an era of 'high growth, low unemployment, high productivity growth and the provision of social security, each of which was unprecedented in magnitude...' (Patnaik 2011, p. 8). The result was a period described later, after its inevitable demise, as the Golden Age of Capitalism.

It appears that Simon Kuznets (1965) made the same kind of mistake about inequality. He thought that at higher income levels, inequality would decline, because that was what was happening in the United States and some European countries in his time.[11]

Barry Bluestone: The Tripartite Economy

Bluestone (1970) wrote at a time when, as he himself says, '[c]ontemporary labour market analysis' was 'steeped in the human capital school of orthodox economics'. This, he said, had 'unfortunately led to the widespread belief that the poor are poor primarily because they lack marketable skills. Based on this analysis, the American Government had stressed manpower training programmes as the main route to improving the status of low paid workers and the unemployed' (ibid. 1970, p. 16).

In other words, the problem of the working poor had nothing to do with an industrial structure that was characterized by inadequate demand for labour. It was a supply problem.

In modern India, the twelfth five-year planners still had not gotten out of this old mental trap. The supply side approach critiqued in Barry Bluestone (1970) is embodied in India's Twelfth Five-Year Plan, Volume III, on Social Sectors. It starts on page 138. To expand employment opportunities, it suggests that two things need to be done. First, the focus should be on promoting labour market flexibility. This should be done 'at least in labour intensive manufacturing industries like textiles and garments, leather and footwear, gems and jewellery, food processing and so on...' The point is made in less than one page (GoI 2013, p. 139). Second, it is necessary to promote skill development. The skill development measures suggested take up 20 pages: pages 139 to 159!

Bluestone's analysis produces a very different policy prescription. His analysis begins with a description of a 'tripartite economy' consisting of a 'core economy', on the one hand, and a 'peripheral sector' plus an 'irregular economy', on the other. His core economy corresponds almost exactly to the definition given by the National Commission for Enterprises in the Unorganized Sector (NCEUS) for private, formal sector enterprises. His description of the peripheral and irregular economies matches the NCEUS definition of the set of informal sector enterprises.

His core economy is concentrated in durable goods manufacturing, the organized construction and extraction industries, and includes specifically automobile, steel, rubber, aluminium, aerospace and petroleum industries. He describes it as being characterized by high productivity, high profits, intensive use of capital, high incidence of monopoly elements and a high degree of unionization. It is 'by far the largest sector of the three in terms of financial resources' and constitutes the 'muscle' of national economic and political power (Bluestone 1970, p. 24). Workers in these industries generally get relatively high wages, superior working conditions and fringe benefits.

The peripheral economy consists mainly of agriculture, non-durable manufacturing, retail trade and sub-professional services. It is characterized by small firm size, labour intensity, low profits, low productivity, intensive product market competition, lack of unionization and low wages. It lacks the assets, 'the sheer size and the political power to take advantage of economies of scale or spend large sums on research and development' (ibid.). Workers 'trapped' in the periphery become the working poor. Even full-time workers commonly earn below poverty line incomes.

Irregular economy units are described as 'informal' and only loosely tied to the core, or formal economy, networks. The irregular workforce is characterized by informal work patterns and skill acquisition processes. It includes 'daily contract' work from gardening to plumbing, and self-employed workers engaged in what Bluestone (1970) describes as 'pseudo entrepreneurial' activity not available to them in the formal economy. Workers include non-union and non-licensed craftsmen and repairmen, street vendors and door-to-door sales workers. Although persons engaged in perfectly legal activities constitute the majority, this segment of the informal workforce also includes people engaged in illegal activities, such as drug peddling and prostitution. For many of them, mobility to the formal, or core sector, is severely limited by institutional barriers, such as membership in particular groups, gender and ethnic origin (particularly blacks), quite aside from lack of skills and other human capital characteristics.

In the American experience, efforts to reduce poverty among workers in the peripheral and irregular segments of the informal economy through massive government spending on skill upgradation, training and retraining programmes did not work. The reason was that the structure of the workforce itself was the constraint on pulling people up out of poverty. The kinds of jobs that were available to millions of fully employed workers provided below poverty line incomes. Classified by industrial sector, the bulk of the below poverty line workforce was engaged in agriculture, the manufacture of non-durable goods, retail trade and personal services. Classified by occupational category, the worst off were operatives, labourers, sales clerks and clerical workers. Bluestone's data showed that the workers' occupation and industry was a more important factor in their poverty than the skills and education they possessed.

He concluded that to raise the incomes of the working poor, deliberate public intervention aimed at altering the industrial structure and occupational structure of the workforce, may be the best way, even the only way (ibid., p. 30).

The Introduction of the Terms 'Formal' and 'Informal'[12]

Keith Hart (1973) seems to have been one of the first to use the terms 'formal' and 'informal' with respect to employment in developing countries with a large farm sector. He also used the terms 'organized' and 'unorganized' sectors to refer to the kinds of enterprises in which formal and informal job holders were employed. His anthropological fieldwork-based study in Accra, Ghana, in the late 1960s provides a solid urban grass-roots context to what 'informal' employment in the late 1960s was all about in a developing country.

Hart (1973) characterized wage employment in the organized or registered sector as 'formal' employment. Workers who are enumerated 'by surveys of establishments' are included in the formal sector. The remainder who are not covered by such surveys belong to the informal sector.[13] Thus, informal employment is viewed as a numerically large and heterogeneous residual category. Self-employment in small enterprises, especially trade, repairs and services, is treated as the typical form of informal, and commonly precarious, unorganized sector employment, and as a means of livelihood for a part of the 'reserve army of underemployed and unemployed' (ibid., p. 66). Multiple economic activities of individual workers and multiple income sources of their households characterize the typical worker in the informal sector. Illegal services and 'transfers', from drug pushing to protection rackets and petty theft are counted among 'informal income opportunities' (ibid., p. 67).

In short, from the individual workers' point of view, informal jobs act as a buffer against unemployment, while, in the aggregate, the urban informal sector serves to take up some of the slack created by inadequate rates of growth in the modern sector (ibid., p. 70).

The similarities and contrasts between Keith Hart's 1973 account of his fieldwork in Ghana during the late 1960s and Bluestone's early work published in 1970 are worth noting. What is identified as 'peripheral' and 'irregular' employment in Bluestone (1970) corresponds almost exactly to Hart's characterizations and terminology, suggesting that Keith Hart may have seen Barry Bluestone's 1970 paper before the publication of his own work. The significant difference between the two is that Barry Bluestone (1970) places his findings explicitly in a theoretical context and derives a set of important policy implications, which Hart (1973) does not.

S. V. Sethuraman: Informal Sector Enterprises and Informal Employment

Sethuraman's (1976, pp. 69–81) work marked a new stage in the run up to the international search for a set of complete and coherent definitions of informal sector enterprises and informal employment. He was in charge of the World Employment Programme of the International Labour Organization (ILO), at the time when the ILO's urbanization and employment research project initiated a series of studies on the informal sector in selected large towns in developing countries in Asia and South America.

The first effort in this direction came shortly before the publication of Hart's (1973) study. In 1972, the ILO and United Nations Development Programme (UNDP) employment mission on Kenya adopted the term 'informal sector'. Although their concern was with the generation of productive employment opportunities, their description of the informal sector focused on the characteristics of enterprises, not workers (ILO 1972).

From then on, the term 'informal sector' 'was enlisted in the cause of promoting employment, development and equity' (Sethuraman 1976, p. 73). A series of ILO-sponsored case studies of development and employment followed, all with an urban orientation. In these ILO studies, ***agriculture was excluded***, 'not only because it was less important in urban areas but ***also because the problems of informal enterprises in agriculture are significantly different and therefore best investigated separately***' (emphasis added).[14]

Thus, the process of transition from traditional rural, mainly agricultural activities to modern, largely urban and industrial activities got more or less lost to sight. Unfortunately, the ILO never sponsored parallel studies of rural areas with the same spirit and thrust. However, certain basic principles were laid down. One of them was that the definitions and coverage of the informal sector and informal employment studies needed to be aligned with country-specific grassroots realities. Or, as Sethuraman (1976, p. 72) put it, the 'characteristics of the informal sector must be deduced from analysis of the actual situation'.

A second guiding principle in the ILO urban studies questionnaires was that emphasis should be 'placed on the identification of factors that restrict the employment potential and earnings of participants in the informal sector' (ibid., p. 79). Aside from the problems of access to credit and high interest rates, and interlinked markets for output, credit and inputs, Sethuraman (1976, p. 80) mentions specifically 'access to infrastructure facilities and better technology'.

In an Appendix (ibid., p. 81) embodying the criteria suggested as guidelines for identifying informal sector enterprises for the purposes of the ILO's World Employment Programme on urbanization and employment, technology criteria were given for specified economic sectors. For manufacturing, the technology criterion was that the enterprise 'does not use any electricity in the production processes'. For construction, it was that the unit 'does not use power-operated machinery and equipment', and for transport, 'it does use any mechanical power'. (In the cases of trade and services, the use of electricity and motorization criteria was dropped.) Although the use of electricity criterion appears in the Indian definition of unorganized manufacturing, for other economic activities, the potential importance of such a technology variable has been overlooked.

In Lieu of Conclusions

By the late 1970s, agriculture, the wellspring of 'relative surplus population' in Marx, had been eliminated from the analysis in the ILO/UNDP documents on the informal sector. The focus had narrowed to the conditions of urban non-agricultural informal workers in unorganized enterprises. This puts an end to coherent studies of the ongoing working population shift from agriculture to informal employment in the cities of developing countries in Asia, Africa and South America.

Concurrently, Bluestone's insights, despite their significance for contemporary policy making in countries like India, vanished from subsequent policy-related documents, such as India's Twelfth Five-Year Plan (2012–2017) and the series of reports brought out by India's NCEUS. These include the Report on Conditions of Work and Promotion of Livelihoods in the Unorganized Sector (NCEUS 2007).

Last but not least, in the NCEUS volume entitled A Special Programme for Marginal Farmers (NCEUS 2008), there is no explicit recognition of the fact that the problems of farmers, particularly small farmers, are not going to be solved within agriculture. So, where do we go from here?

Notes

1. Reference will be made here to the following five publications: Marx (1959), Lewis (1954), Bluestone (1970), Hart (1973) and Sethuraman (1976).
2. These five phenomena are similarly linked in India today, but the literature is scattered. Two papers which cover much of the ground are Papola (2013) and Gill (2012). The Institute for Human Development (2014) provides relevant data together with an overview of recent developments in the Indian labour market.
3. For those not familiar with this terminology, constant capital is defined as depreciation on fixed assets plus the value of materials used up. Variable capital is the value of labour power. For these definitions, given with numerical examples, see Marx (1959), Chapter 9, Section 2, p. 221.
4. On this, see Marx (1959), Chapter 24, Section 2, p. 623.
5. The accounts of what happens to agricultural and unorganized sector workers are in Marx (1959), Chapter 25, Section 4, pp. 642 and 643, respectively.
6. The quoted passages are from Marx (1959), Chapter 25, Section 2.
7. This end result is described in Marx (1959), Chapter 25, Section 2.

8. On this, see Patnaik (2011), Chapter 1, especially pp. 1–7, inclusive.
9. A list, and the gist of some of their contributions, is given in Bhalla (2009), p. 4, para. 2.3 and the footnotes.
10. See Dasgupta (1974), especially Chapter 2, entitled 'Dualism and Surplus Labour'.
11. The analysis that led Kuznets to this conclusion is found in Kuznets (1965), Chapter 9, entitled 'Economic Growth and Income Inequality'.
12. This part is based on the account of Hart's classic 1973 work given in Bhalla (2009, p. 4). The original Hart paper is was published in 1973.
13. This is, or was, the approach of those who derived sector-wise unorganized sector employment estimates for India, by subtracting the organized sector estimates published by the Ministry of Labour's Directorate General of Employment and Training (DGE&T), from the NSS Usual Principle and Subsidiary Status (UPSS) employment estimates. In recent years, unit level data from the NSS has made more accurate and more elaborate cross classifications possible. See, for example, the five tables on p. 56 of the Institute for Human Development (2014).
14. The studies were published mainly in the mid-1970s. For a list, see Sethuraman (1976), footnote 1, p. 75.

References

Bhalla, S. (2009). *Definitional and Statistical Issues Relating to Workers in Informal Employment, Working Paper No. 3.* New Delhi: National Commission for Enterprises in the Unorganised Sector.

Bluestone, B. (1970). The Tripartite Economy: Labour Markets and the Working Poor. *Poverty and Human Resource Abstracts, 5*(4), 15–35.

Dasgupta, A. K. (1974). *Economic Theory and Developing Countries.* London: Macmillan.

Gill, S. S. (2012, January–March). Distribution of Income and Share of Wages in India: Labour in a Globalising Economy. *Indian Journal of Labour Economics, 55*(1), 1–21.

GoI (Government of India). (2013). *Twelfth Five Year Plan (2012–2017)* (Vol. 3, Social Sectors). New Delhi: Planning Commission.

Hart, K. H. (1973). Informal Income Opportunities and Urban Employment in Ghana. *Journal of Modern African Studies, 11*(1), 61–89. (Excerpt reprinted in Richard Jolly et al., Third world employment, problems and strategy, Penguin Education.).

ILO. (1972). *Employment Incomes and Inequality: A Strategy for Increasing Productive Employment in Kenya.* Geneva: Author.

Institute for Human Development. (2014). *India Labour and Employment Report, 2014: Workers in the Era of Globalisation.* New Delhi: Author.

Kuznets, S. (1965). *Economic Growth and Structure: Selected Essays.* New Delhi: W. W. Norton and Company.
Lewis, A. W. (1954, May 22). Economic Development with Unlimited Supplies of Labour. *The Manchester School, 22*(2), 139–192.
Marx, K. (1959). *Capital* (Vol. 1). Moscow: Foreign Languages Publishing House.
NCEUS (National Commission for Enterprises in the Unorganized Sector). (2007, August). *Report on Conditions of Work and Promotion of Livelihoods in the Unorganised Sector.* New Delhi: Author.
NCEUS (National Commission for Enterprises in the Unorganized Sector). (2008, December). *A Special Programme for Marginal Farmers.* New Delhi: Author.
Papola, T. S. (2013). Employment Growth During the Post-Reform Period. *The Indian Journal of Labour Economics, 56*(1), 1–13.
Patnaik, P. (2011). *Re-envisioning Socialism.* New Delhi: Tulika Books.
Sethuraman, S. V. (1976). The Urban Informal Sector: Concept, Measurement and Policy. *International Labour Review, 114*(1), 69–81.

PART II

Informal and Precarious Labour in Global Value Systems

CHAPTER 7

Whither African Trade Union Movement? Lessons for Restitution and Reform

Trywell Kalusopa

In Africa, the intricate nexus of colonialism, post-colonialism and unfettered capitalism has been the stimulus for trade unions to broaden the scope of their struggles beyond the shop floor to embrace liberation, democracy, promotion of economic development, social reconstruction and justice in the current neo-liberal world order. Evidence now points to the fact that trade union organisation in Africa is fragile at the national, regional and continental levels and primarily limited to the minority formal working sector with the vast majority informal workers unrepresented. Historically, among the social justice organisations, trade unions are frequently the ones with the greatest potential for mobilisation and perhaps the most enduring ones with visible legitimate national structures, ideological clarity and defined membership. However, this potential to shape the political and socio-economic reforms that can spur job-enriching growth has not been fully realised in Africa owing to several factors driven by the neo-liberal onslaught. In view of the continuously changing

T. Kalusopa (✉)
University of Namibia, Windhoek, Namibia
e-mail: tkalusopa@unam.na

P. Jha et al. (eds.), *Labour Questions in the Global South*,
https://doi.org/10.1007/978-981-33-4635-2_7

underlying conditions in the African labour markets; frail union structures and their representativeness; limited organisational abilities; questioned solidarity; imperfect social dialogue structures, the political intervention by trade unions to inspire structural transformation still remains a daunting challenge. This paper provides a critical overview of these challenging times based on desk research largely drawn from literature review and documentation on trade union development in Africa. The paper examines the state of trade unions, their organisational state, internal capacity, membership growth, campaigns and programmes essential for their strategic survival. The key national centres and their relationship with continental trade union bodies such as International Trade Union (ITUC)-Africa and Organisation of African Trade Union Unity (OATUU) are critically discussed. The influence of Global Union Federations (GUFs) and their links with ITUC and OATUU as well as national centres is also discussed and lessons drawn. Several recommendations for the strategic renewal of trade unions are presented.

Introduction

Literature affirms that in Africa, trade unions emerged as a response to the repressive capitalist colonial order (ANSA 2006; Jauch 2003; Jauch 2004; Kalusopa 2011). The post-independence embrace of the enclave economies coupled with the implementation of Structural Adjustment Programmes (SAPs) in most African countries since the 1980s created a labour market that is characterised by exclusion in terms of low wages, poverty and inequality (ANSA 2006; Kanyenze et al. 2006). The intricate interconnections of colonialism, post-colonialism and capitalism motivated African trade unions to broaden the scope of their struggles beyond the shop floor to embrace political liberation, democracy, socio-economic development, social reconstruction and justice (Kanyenze et al. 2006).

Currently, all evidence points to fact that trade union organisation in Africa is weak at the national, regional and continental levels and primarily limited to the formal sector with only the interests of a minority of the working population represented (FES 2008; Kalusopa 2011; Kalusopa and Otoo 2013). However, what is also evident is that, among the various social justice organisations, trade unions are have the greatest potential for political mobilisation (Moodley 2015), and perhaps the most capable ones with visible and legally acknowledged national structures that have clarity in defined membership (Kalusopa 2011). But this potential has not been fully realised effectively by most trade unions in Africa so as to shape the political and economic reforms and foster job-producing growth (Kalusopa 2011). In view of continuously changing underlying conditions in African labour markets; the strengthening of structures of trade unions and their representativeness; their capabilities to organise and take action inspired by solidarity; an improvement in their capabilities for social dialogue; the strengthening of capabilities for political intervention remain the biggest challenge.

This paper thus provides an overview of these challenging times backed by some desk study information largely drawn from literature review and documentation. The paper examines the trade unions, their organisational characteristics and relationship with in the current neo-liberal world order in Africa. The main objective of this paper is to ascertain the current status of trade unions in terms of union governance and administration, internal democracy, accountability and transparency in the context of how trade unions can contribute to the development process at national level and the regional in Africa. The thrust of the argument focuses on exploring the lessons for restitution and substantial reform for trade union survival in the current daunting neo-liberal times. The paper attempts to answer some of the following questions:

- What are the current structural characteristics of the trade union movement in Africa?
- How effective are trade union in their current form effective in influencing labour, socio-economic and political issues at national and regional level in Africa?
- How do internal issues in the trade unions affect the relationship between trade unions and the state in each of the countries in Africa?
- What strategies can be proffered to ensure that trade unions are ready for change in Africa?

The assumption in this article is that there is need to understand the current status of trade unions and their defined role in national and regional development in Africa. In this context, it is envisaged that such an exposition should unravel the current strength of the labour movement in terms of organisational ability; representations and representativeness; legitimacy and influence at all levels involving labour rights and working conditions; employment and life. This should also help ascertain the state of internal democracy, accountability, transparency and relationship between members, shop stewards and their leadership. Further, this article would make sound contributions towards determining new strategies to help renew trade union capacity and ensure their effective campaigning around issues affecting workers at the national, sub-region and global levels.

Methodology and Conceptual Framework

This paper relies on literature review and qualitative content analysis focusing on the internal credible reports on trade unions and some reports from selected the national federation or centres. This paper seeks to develop a better understanding of the current state of affairs of trade unions in the African region. Specifically, it focuses on both the macros and micro-level analysis of the internal challenges that largely pose threats to the very existence of these organisations, thereby rendering them ineffective in terms of meeting their objectives. In the process of determining these internal challenges, the paper envisages to assist in terms of ascertaining the sustainability of these organisations in the short, medium and long-term periods. In achieving the above, this paper was guided by a conceptual view that at regional level, internal and external factors which come into play in union renewal strategies and self-reform programmes revolve around three different dimensions:

(a) The first dimension is *external structure* or *external shape* which comprises the boundaries of the trade unions. As such, *external shape* embraces the principles that underpin the pattern of the union organisation, decisions on inclusion and exclusion, and border or demarcation lines between unions.
(b) The second dimension is *union governance*, the analysis of which centres on union democracy, representation and participation. It is thus concerned with internal union politics and relations between different groups within a union, region and beyond.
(c) The third dimension is *union administration*, which focuses on union management and the allocation of resources.

As is apparent from this conceptualisation, the scope of structural change is much broader than just finding a clear-cut technical solution for structural adjustment. It also affects the heart of the trade unions in that it defines the rules of interest representation, the rights of membership towards the leaders and much more. There are several analytical tools that can be used to operationalise this framework within the context of understanding trade union self-reform and change management. However, for this study, the adaptation of a combination of the *SWOT* and *Lewin's force-field analysis* were adopted, preferred and found useful. The SWOT analysis is a simple but useful framework for analysing any organisation's strengths and weaknesses, and the opportunities and threats it may face. It helps an organisation to focus the strengths, minimise threats, and take the greatest possible advantage of opportunities available. On the other hand, the Kurt Lewin force field analysis is a general tool for systematically analysing the factors found in complex problems. It frames problems in terms of factors or pressures that support the status quo (restraining forces) and those pressures that support change in the desired direction (driving forces). The discussions that follow were guided by this conceptual outlook.

Trade Unions in the Current Neo-Liberal Environment

Globalisation has taken a deep centre stage and now rules the world political and economic order defining the current state of the power play. The global capitalist architecture's socio-economic production system has produced and reproduced inherent structural and systemic economic enclaves with evident manifestations of steep inequalities and bruised labour relations in Africa (ANSA 2006; Kalusopa 2011). The integration of technology, trade foreign direct investment (capital) and labour are some of the most key indicators that are driving globalisation. The world is now also highly multi-lateral: IMF, World Bank, WTO are key institutions in setting the tone and agenda for the world (ANSA 2006). Globalisation has continued to pose socio-economic and political challenges to the worker in the world. The world seems to be invariably hooked to this competitive economic chain where trade and investment are transcending national boundaries and thus creating both opportunities for a few linked to the metropoles and massive failures for many (ANSA. 2006; Kalusopa and Otoo 2013).

The entire process of exploitation appears mystified under capitalism (Cooper and Hardy 2012). This is a form of ideology arising out of the capitalist system, the belief that it is simply hard work and luck which makes you successful, the implication being that those at the bottom of the pile (the workforce) are either unlucky, not hard working enough or not bright enough to rise up the social classes (Cooper and Hardy 2012).

This paper agrees with Cooper and Hardy, that nature is not constituted to create people with property and capital on one side, and people with nothing but their ability to labour on the other side of the ledger (Cooper and Hardy 2012). Evidently, it is the capitalist structural production system which produces the workless person. This therefore is admittedly created through human agency in a socio-historical process (Cooper and Hardy 2012). It is not accident or indeed hard luck that workers find themselves dispossessed of their valued labour as this is structural and systemic! Thus, the working class is largely left to itself (as a class which merely exists in itself, that is it is unconscious of its full role in the system of production) and is simply raw material for exploitation; and in the capitalist's eyes has as much value as coal, electricity and steel in production (Cooper and Hardy 2012). In that regard, the establishment of trade unions is a crucial step in the working class becoming class conscious, aware of capitalist exploitation and resisting it, no matter how piecemeal! (Cooper and Hardy 2012). Therefore, it is instructive to argue that the deliverance of the working class from exploitative capital must be the effort of the working class itself (Cooper and Hardy 2012). The point is that classes become socially significant groups only when their members become *conscious of their interests as a class* and the opposition of these interests to the interests of the other class (Cooper and Hardy 2012). As put by Marx in his discourse, in as far as "*the identity of their interests begets no community no national bond and no political organisation among them, they do not form a class*".

Accordingly, most trade unions exist for historical and ideological reasons of advancing the cause of workers and the society at large (Kalusopa 2011). They engage the working social and economic order and may either accept the existing economic order or work within that order to achieve a "*favourable set of economic terms and employment conditions, or they may seek to overthrow the existing [political and] economic system and replace it with another*" (Rainsberger 1998:1). The former strategy has been called "business unionism" or "simple unionism" while the latter strategy tends to go beyond workplace issues to deal with broader socio-economic matters that affect the workers and the people, a strategy called "social trade unionism" (ICFTU 2001[1]; Rainsberger 1998; Wood 2001). This philosophical foundation is grounded in the belief in fair social transformation and justice and aims to influence society based on its organised power, capacity to mobilise and building affective political and social alliances (ICFTU 2001:1). It is committed to workers control and democracy, and to maintaining its character as a movement. Such a trade union movement is supposed to be effective and "proactive and able to negotiate and monitor complex agreements with government and employers" as well as making meaningful contributions to national development. (ICFTU 2001:1). To any common worker, the unemployed and the larger populace, globalisation through the integration of trade, investment, capital, technology and labour has only brought about social and economic injustice. Today most African states are actively led by the neo-liberal economic paradigm that cherishes liberalisation, privatisation and restructuring, albeit in various forms. Most of them are drowsed into believing trade and foreign direct investment at all costs without a human face is that answer to development. Yet, the evidence of underdevelopment continues to persist!

The Complexion of Trade Union Organisation in Africa

The legislative and policy frameworks in most African countries recognise the existence of trade unions though with a constrained implementation environment. The most influential trade union organisations in Africa are the Nigeria Labour Congress (NLC), and the Ghana Trades Union Congress (TUC) in West Africa, the Congress of South African Trade Unions (COSATU) in the Southern Africa, and the Central Organisation of Trade Unions – Kenya (COTU-K) in East Africa. There is a long standing relationship among COSATU, TUC and NLC. In fact, as a demonstration of this influence, NLC, Ghana TUC and COSATU have had what they refer to as an annual Trilateral Conference since 2012. COTU-K has of recent times also participated in the meetings of the three without being a formal member of trilateral conference. This predates their membership of the ITUC-Africa and its predecessor, the ICFTU-Afro as well as membership to Organisation of African Trade Union Unity (OATUU). These three trade union centres have had shared education and research programmes; actively pursued various forms of exchanges, and shared perspectives on various matters of international working class interest and the struggle to advance a new and just world economic order. Thus, for example, based on its broader social vision, NLC has forged united fronts with other social movements over the years. These include the Alliance for Democratic Rights in the early/mid-80s, Women in Nigeria in the 80s, and since 2005, both the NLC and the TUC, have collaborated with the Joint Action Forum (of left/pro-labour civil society organisations) under the auspices of the Labour Civil Society Coalition (LASCO). At several times in its history, the trade union movement[2] in Nigeria has similarly formed or joined political parties.[3] It has also formulated people-oriented alternative development pathways through documents such as the *Workers Charter of Demands* and *Nigeria Not for Sale,* in the 1980s. It recently also finished drafting an *Alternative National Development Agenda.* Building a strong, virile and visionary continental trade union movement has always been a major aim of the NLC. It has thus been very active in ITUC-Africa from its inception and presently one member of staff on secondment from the NLC handles the continental body's desk on trade union and human rights.

In South Africa, COSATU remains by far the South Africa's largest and most effective trade union federation. The political policy of COSATU is based on its historical circumstances associated with the struggle against apartheid (Southall 1994). Thus COSATU posits that "*when political organisations were unbanned, the ANC, SACP and COSATU agreed to work together as a Revolutionary Alliance (Tripartite Alliance, the Alliance)*" Buhlungu (2010:1). Accordingly the alliance is based on "*short, medium to long terms goals of the National Democratic Revolution - the establishment of a democratic and non-racial South Africa, economic transformation and continued process of political and economic democratisation*". Buhlungu (2010:1). In recent years, the effectiveness of the Alliance and its usefulness for bringing about transformation has been intensely contested with its mainly large affiliate, National Union of Metalworkers of South Africa (NUMSA), and probably most militant and left-leaning affiliate leading to a break away to form South African Federation of Trade Unions (SAFTU) on 21 April, 2017. It claims to have close to 800,000 members. COSATU is currently affiliated to the ITUC, OATUU and WFTU (in June, 2018). COSATU played a leading role in the newly established BRICS trade union forum. At the second forum which was held during the Durban Summit in 2013, COSATU together with the Brazilian CUT (and against the resistance of the Chinese ACFTU) successfully negotiated that the BRICS trade unions condemn neo-colonial trade patterns in their joint declaration.[4] COSATU's future role in BRICS, on the continent and internationally will largely depend on the outcomes of the internal and reginal unity outlined above.

COTU- K is the national trade union federation of Kenya and has 36 affiliates which are drawn from the various economic industries of Kenya with over 1.5 million membership. However, trade union membership has declined over the years. When the clamour for a new Constitution started, COTU-K was one of the first organisations to champion for a new constitution. Following the political skirmishes that followed the 2007 general elections, COTU-K was the first organisation to warn the government that Kenyans wanted a new constitution. Large public meetings were held nationwide, with massive media attention. These efforts were aimed at creating a departure from the old-fashioned governance arrangements. COTU-K played a pivotal role to the adoption of the new constitution especially on championing for the inclusion of labour rights, the right of association and the right to form trade unions. Together with their Ugandan and Tanzanian trade union counterparts, Kenyan labour leaders formed the East African Trade Union Consultative Council (EATUCC) in 1988. The protocol on the free movement of labour by the East African Community (the Customs Union is already in place) will have other far-reaching effects on workers in the sub-region. Like, the other trade unions in Africa, COTU-K belongs to ITUC, seen as a gateway to European influence and international bodies; as well as to OATUU, probably seen as a historical linkage to the African Union (AU). The influence of OATUU at the AU remains a contested issue.

ITUC Africa: OATUU Relationship

At the continental level, two main trade union organisations have evolved over the years and influenced the trade union landscape. These are ITUC-Africa and OATUU. The two continental trade union centres, ITUC-Africa and OATUU, by large, share nearly the same membership, and thus duplicate their activities and roles, create fertile ground for competition, fragmentation and lack of focus. Though, in a weak position, there is also the re-emergence of the WFTU in Africa with affiliates in a few countries and an office in South Africa and makes the relationship between ITUC-Africa and OATUU even more complicated by adding a further ideological conflict component to the already difficult situation. Thus, the voice of African workers remains disjointed and weakened in their engagement over a range of issues with multilateral institutions, including the International Labour Organisation (ILO) and also with the AU. Besides, the trade union movement is disabled from developing a strategic plan for advancing the overall interests of workers in Africa. ITUC-Africa at its 2nd Congress in 2011 underlined the urgent need to place the interests of African workers above other considerations and called for action towards building a viable, united, independent and strong Pan African trade union movement that is committed to African integration, unity and emancipation and that enjoys the full confidence of workers as a result of its organisational strength, bargaining effectiveness and political assertiveness in representing their aspirations. The Congress then resolved on the development of an African trade union unity road map targeted at continental, national and industrial sector levels and which was targeted to be fully realised by 2015. There was also an explicit demand for a process towards merger between ITUC-Africa and OATUU by 2013. In furtherance of the resolution, a first meeting was held in April 2012 between the Executive Bureaus of the two organisations to kick start the process towards unification. ITUC Africa regards the issue of trade union fragmentation and the relationship with OATUU as its priority issues and underscores that fact that they have made some effort. For example, they conducted research in Benin, Senegal, Burkina Faso, and DRC and found that the causes for proliferation included inadequate internal democracy and individual ambitions. In response, it adopted the "Appeal of Lome" in 2009 and held a workshop in March 2012 with federations in Ivory Coast, Niger, and Togo to develop a plan of action towards unity. Despite signs of some kind of emerging agreement on their co-operation, the continental bodies seem destined to continue operating as separate entities in the foreseeable future. Various types of agreements were reached over the years have not led to any fundamental changes in terms of more efficient and mutually beneficial cooperation (ITUC 2012).

There are several notes of discussions with African trade union leaders at national and continental level which reveal how the two continental bodies are viewed. OATUU is seen as the primary organisation representing African interests and offering access to tripartite structures at AU level (OATUU 2014). OATUU is also seen as the organisation best placed to formulate African positions for example for the ILO. International issues on the other hand seen as being best addressed via ITUC-Africa: "*The ITUC is our channel to international solidarity*", remarked a senior African union leader. The idea to merge ITUC-Africa with OATUU seems to be based on the argument that a united African voice can be stronger. However, there are disagreements which could not be solved, for example who would lead a united African organisation.

Sub-Regional Organisations Relationship with ITUC-Africa

At the sub-regional level, there are three main functional sub-regional labour organisations that have evolved over the years that influence trade union landscape namely Southern African Trade Union Coordinating Council (SATUCC), the East African Trade Union Council (EATUC) and Organisation of Trade Unions of West Africa (OTUWA). The Organisation of Trade Unions of Central Africa (OTUCA) and Union of Arab Maghreb Trade Unions (UAMTU) are hardly functional.

These three regional bodies ae formally recognised by ITUC Africa and OATUU. There is a danger that sub-regional organisations such as SATUCC and EATUCC focus mainly on delivering TU positions on regional issues to regional bodies like SADC, EAC and ECOWAS. The so called consultative status of a Trade Union Organisation in a supranational organisation like SADC is certainly not enough to become a regional trade union organisation or movement with regional political clout. There are also signs that national union federations do not pay much attention to sub-regional work and hardly pay membership dues. Another striking fact is that sub-regional organisation like OTUWA and SATUCC want to become more inclusive by accommodating more than one national federation from each country. Often this merely means that rival national federations might come together in meetings of the sub-regional bodies but continue to act as bitter rivals at the national level. Sub-regional organisations thus will have discuss how they can facilitate greater trade union unity or at least better collaboration on common issues amongst different federations from the same country. The fragmentation amongst unions is worsened in West Africa where the union movement is split into the francophone and English speaking countries with French speaking countries usually having 5 to 8 national union centres.

Global Union Federations (GUFs) and Their Influence in Africa

There seems to still be a significant disconnect between ITUC-Africa and GUF. While ITUC-Africa focuses predominantly on influencing policies but also has programmes on organising and human and trade union rights, these programmes seem to be mostly an add-on for industrial unions on the continent. The GUFs on the other hand, focus more on direct worker participation in their campaigns and organising projects on multinationals. Most GUFs are still focusing predominantly on their own specific programmes but the annual Africa GUF Forum has created the opportunity for meaningful exchanges geared towards improved common practices. They are also a platform for GUFs to engage with continental and sub-regional bodies to achieve greater coherence of approach (GUF 2014).

The GUFS currently cooperate with ITUC-Africa in a cordial manner but without a coherent joint programme of action. Both tend to implement their respective programmes and while informing one another, these programmes are not co-ordinated with each other in any systematic manner. Co-ordination is thus limited to some of the broader common goals like achieving respect for workers' and trade union rights or campaigning against precarious forms of employment. GUF Head offices usually determine some of the overall themes for their organisations (for example quality public services) but continental and regional structures still seem to have the space to determine their own priorities within this framework. Little meaningful linkages though seem to exist with sub regional bodies like SATUCC and EATUC.

The work of GUFs around MNCs seems to be amongst the most significant trade union activities on the continent. They respond to the global organisation of capital and bring workers together across borders in a much focused and thus meaningful manner. The shop stewards' alliances are of special importance in this regard with Shoprite Checkers, Pick n' Pay, AngloGold etc. providing interesting (and encouraging) case studies (GUF 2014).

GUFs in Africa are clearly most relevant to their affiliated industrial unions while the relationship with national federations is limited. The GUF strategies of combining recruitment with research, education and campaign holds perhaps the greatest promise for improving trade union work on the continent in the years to come in dealing to the neo-liberal narrative.

Challenges of Trade Unions in Africa and Strategies for Change and Renewal

Most internal audit reports reviewed on African trade unions capacities (NALEDI 2009; FES 2008; ILO 2010; SATUCC 2017; Kalusopa 2011) present a complex and evolving challenges that call for complete renewal if these organisations are to survive. In this section, we describe these in the context of organisational characteristics (representativeness, internal democracy, resources campaign capabilities, solidarity attitudes, social dialogue involvement, and relation with political parties).

It clear and evident from literature reviewed that the transformation processes in terms of evolution, growth and decline of trade unionism in Africa could well be closely linked to the changes in the global capitalist production system, state policies, composition of the workforces and the internal trade union organisational structural dynamics and democracy (NALEDI 2009; FES 2008; ILO 2010; SATUCC 2017). The literature also underscores the diversity that can be found across various countries in the African region with regard to the functioning of trade unions and the degree of operation and challenges thereof (ILO 2010). In analysing this, it is instructive to assert that there is need for strategies that African trade unions should embrace in terms of internal characteristics and dynamics of union membership growth; union governance, trade union pluralism and proliferation; trade union representativeness and democracy; trade union-political relationships; financial independence and investments, workers' solidarity, international cooperation. These are discussed in the proceeding sections.

Trade Union Membership Growth

Relevant studies affirm that currently the neo-liberal economic agenda and globalisation has had a negative impact on trade union organisations in most African countries in terms of decline in density and union influence (FES 2008; Jauch 2003; ILO 2010; SATUCC 2017). Most of the countries have union density of between 10–20% (SATUCC 2017). This trade union density decline could be attributed to several factors such as: slow growth of the economy, failing to create jobs, retrenchments, and generally poor organisation as well as recruitment strategies employed to unionise members in Africa (Kalusopa and Otoo 2013). The strongest and most stable sector over the years in terms of union's growth has been public sector affiliates. They have had much more stable leadership, much more secured incomes and hence financially strong (Kalusopa and Otoo 2013). The second can be said to be the mining and energy sector unions which despite having lost membership over time due to retrenchments in the mining sector continues to be one of the most financially stable trade unions (Kalusopa and Otoo 2013). The trade unions with larger membership potential are those in the services sector such as wholesale, food, retail and construction. However, these are also the sectors where employment is insecure and wages too low (Kalusopa and Otoo 2013). Membership contributions are irregular, low and insignificant to keep these unions afloat. The weakest trade unions seem to those in the agricultural sector, private security and domestic work (Kalusopa and Otoo 2013). These trade unions are not only weak organisationally, but their members are the most exploited in terms of working conditions and incomes. There is rivalry and competition for membership by the unions splinters in the formal public and private sectors with no clear strategy to deal with the growing insecure unorganised service industry and informal economy (Kalusopa and Otoo 2013). In fact most of the trade union affiliates do not have functional databases for membership tracking and growth projections over years (Kalusopa 2011).

Going forward, it is therefore recommended that trade unions need to:

- Develop a clear ideological framework and firm alternative positions to counter neo-liberal economic globalisation and embark on workers education to sensitise the workers on the effects of globalisation and specifically the privatisation and outsourcing.
- Develop well targeted organisational and recruitment agenda that focuses on strengthening recruitment in the formal public sectors and extending this to the unorganised service industries and agriculture which have a weak membership base.
- Improve the amalgamation mechanisms to strengthen the national labour structures so as to counter exploitation in service industry and agriculture which have a weak membership base.
- Establish information labour management systems such as databases/databanks for easy access to membership statistics, collective bargaining trends, etc.
- Step up efforts in social dialogue to advocate for an economically living minimum wage for the vulnerable workers across the sectors.
- Work with global union federations and advance the protection of workers from globalisation onslaught in such sector such as construction and service sectors.

Trade Union Structural Characteristic, Governance and Administration

This paper affirms that greater challenge exists for most trade unions is on various dimensions of trade union governance, namely: union democracy, representation, and participation. In most cases, trade unions have reported challenges of internal union democracy, ineffective representation and poor member participation (Kalusopa and Otoo 2013; SATUCC 2017). The situations vary considerably in scale and complexity, depending on the historic development of the country concerned, the legal, political and democratic context and the trade union movement's own internal regulations and attitudes. Nonetheless, it is possible to draw overall and common conclusions. Thus, for example, several audits or studies carried out on the continent by the Africa Labour Research Network (ALRN)[5] over the past decade clearly show that on various dimensions of governance (union democracy, representation, and participation), most of the trade unions and their affiliates showed poor union democracy, ineffective representation and poor membership participation.

Going forward, it would be useful for trade union to:

- Engage in continuous capacity building to enhance the knowledge and skills in negotiations, conflict management, budgeting of the union leadership.
- Advocates for the democratisation of trade unions to entrench members' control. In that context, an ideological framework plays a decisive role in the strengthening the substance of trade union members' role, right and responsibility of making informed decisions. The ideological framework can also strengthens and enhance the relationship between union leaders and members. In addition, it could assist in promoting worker empowerment, a sense of participation and an increased understanding between employers and employees.

Trade Union Pluralism, Proliferation and Workers Solidarity

For the past decades, the systemic promotion of neo-liberal narrative has been accompanied by the growing individualism among trade unions that has undermined the future, strength and relevance of the trade union movement (ANSA 2006). This is because trade union gains depend on largely the willingness and capacity to join forces in solidarity and focus on common objectives and challenges of a particular time. In most cases, trade unions in Africa have reported trivial policy differences and personal ambitions or interests which heavily compromised trade union structures, unity in strategies, action and response to the collective needs and aspirations of workers in an efficient and responsible manner (ILO 2010). Though the freedom to associate and bargain has flourished in most countries allowing workers to freely choose the type of trade union organisation that is most suited to defending their interests, in many cases this has undermined workers' solidarity (ILO 2010). In most of the African countries where the excessive proliferation of trade unions has taken place, it is not realistic to expect the leaders of all splinter unions to agree in the short term to move towards structural realignment and reunification. Many studies (FES 2008; ILO 2010,; SATUCC 2017) show that trade union fragmentation is not only manifested through multiplicity existence of a number of duplications of trade union structures but also equally the result of a lack of structural links and coherence between unions at the lower levels in the trade union pyramid (for example, where branch and enterprise unions are not affiliated to federations and federations are not affiliated to any confederation). Yet, trade unions are supposed to provide a collective voice in solidarity for the productivity of the work place. Trade unionism requires unwavering focus, commitment and dedication. It entails personal self-sacrifice and putting others before self (Kalusopa 2011). There is need to have an inner belief to face confrontations, challenges and not to betray the trust that workers bestow on the leadership. This is can only happen if there is a clear ideological framework (Kalusopa 2011).

In that regard, if trade unions have to remain relevant, they have to:

- Channel efforts at pursuing unity in diversity and promoting solidarity which remains the cornerstones of a successful the trade union movement through various innovative forms of inter-union cooperation which strengthen the cohesion and effectiveness of trade union unity.
- Bring pressure to bear on splinter in-house small unions so that they join initiatives for more effective and structured unity in action regarding all issues on which common trade union action can be achieved or envisaged.

- Restructure and consolidate union structures through some deliberate efforts towards the merging of different types of unions into bigger and stronger sectoral unions.
- Ensure the proper exchange of information and consultation among themselves and with the lower echelons in their own organisations.
- Ensure that the rank and file members and activists are informed of such mergers and their value at designated structures such as congresses.
- Adopt of clear and equitable internal rules that include provisions for a regularly rotating leadership positions, setting and preparation of agendas and sharing of the human, financial and material costs. It is cardinal that there are constitutional limits placed on union leadership.
- Initiate processes that are targeted at convincing splinter groups to join the more genuine and representative organisations. Such efforts must propose unification of trade union structures rather than alliances based on leadership quests.
- Develop comprehensive and successful strategy with clear and well-thought-out plans of action.

Trade Union Internal Democracy and Transparency

Internal trade union democracy and transparency are among the most vital cornerstones of a viable and effective trade union organisation. They are indispensable elements not only for the preservation of the organisation's integrity, effective functioning, internal cohesion and discipline, but also for the respect and credibility of the organisation among the workers and its general public image. Literature and reports reviewed established that most countries in Africa have fairly sound legal framework to guide the functioning of trade unions. However, most of the trade unions, reported challenges with the implementation of their trade unions constitutions, clarity in election of their leaders on regular basis, entrenched "chieftainship" of leaders, and showed an incapacity to keep records and manage their constitutional obligations. The studies also affirmed evidence of poor balance in gender representation, poor national spread in the frequency of meetings within the structures, undermined local shop steward structures and inadequate technical staffing in the unions (NALEDI 2009; FES 2008; ILO 2010; SATUCC 2017).

In order for trade union to strategically renew and survive, it is important that:

- Internal democracy must be conceived and applied in a spirit of participative manner democracy, in which workers' control is at the centre and workers be the must be a principal actor and advocate.
- The principles, the rules and the outcomes of democratic decision-making have to be accepted and respected by all actors with regard to the results of trade union leadership elections.
- There must be clear and consistent constitutional guidelines and a set of rules which go with the mandate, management of trade union activities. The internal rules should determine the terms of the political and administrative responsibilities and accountability of the leadership.
- The management and monitoring of financial assets should be particularly strictly monitored in a transparent manner with clear up-to-date rules and regulations.

Dealing with Trade Unions and Politics

Trade union and political action go hand in hand in the defence of workers' and trade union rights. However, disproportionate political ambitions and involvement in party politics on the part of trade union leaders, serving personal interests rather than the cause of workers and the union, have caused a lot of damage and division within ranks of the trade union movement (ILO 2010). Many unions have now merely become conduits of political capture and mobilisation for ruling political parties. The results of such relationships – where they exist – between unions and their leaders on the one hand and political parties on the other should be openly debated and assessed at trade union congresses and other governing bodies. As a result, several national trade union centres have not been successful in their efforts to redefine the objective boundaries between trade unionism and party politics. Most study findings (FES 2008; Kalusopa and Otoo 2013; SATUCC 2017), suggest that the trade union-political party relationship is not membership driven, not well thought out, ad hoc, unstable and in flaccid state. This means that political activism on the part of trade unions remains a challenge in Africa. This then calls for trade unions to adopt the following recommendations:

- Trade unions should develop a strategic working document on their role in politics which should be endorsed by the general membership in various Congresses.

- Based on the strategic working document, work on the modalities of political activism (i.e. whether to support a particular political party, candidate, or decampaign others)
- Trade unions should embark on workers political education on their role in the political process.

Financial Independence and Organisation

There are mixed perceptions regarding the benefits of trade union investments to general membership (Kalusopa and Otoo 2013). On one hand, the union leadership who are in control of these investments argue that they are beneficial to members. On the other hand, the general membership, although not against such investments, are critical of how these investments are managed for the benefit of worker. Questions of loss of focus to plough resources for the cause of workers have been raised.

Therefore, trade union should:

- Put in place investment strategies guided by social considerations through creating an investment framework that would be approved by general membership.
- Have financial information so that there is clarity on company ownership (directorship), business strategies including business deals.
- Have clear structures clarifying the link between the companies and the accountable organs of the unions such as the finance and investment committees.
- Appointments to run investment companies should be on merit.

Coping with Newer and Global Workers Challenges

The growing importance and impact of globalisation, of macroeconomic and macro labour policies and of precarious types of work and employment and the overwhelming dominance of the informal economy are only some of the major issues to which trade unions are called upon to respond in a contemporary neo-liberal environment. The adaptation and strengthening of trade union capacities in terms of expertise, training, research and networking as well as for developing adequate policies and strategies, require an enormous investment of resources, which are scarcely available.

Therefore, if trade unions are to play any meaningful role against this background, there need for:

- Clarity and joint action by trade unions on common global thorny issues such migration, portability of social protection, regional trade, women rights, child labour, educational qualification frameworks. Such trade union positions and unity in action are also essential in connection with a variety of regional, sub-regional and international opportunities.
- Treating as a priority issue strengthening the membership and preservation of their representativeness and credibility as a workers' movement through organising the informal workers. For example, there are already numerous efforts by progressive organisations which regional trade union body like SATUCC put in place in the place to align to such informal organisation such as STREETNET that requires to be deepened. In that regard, national trade unions should adapt the constitutions and rules of engagement in order to accommodate the informal economy organisations. The question of affiliation fees will need attention in this context as well.
- Entrenching the creation of stronger alliances through cooperation with like-minded women NGOs and other civil society organisations (such as rural workers' associations) must be positively considered. Though limited in finance and scope many positive examples already exist throughout Africa and simply require guidelines and concrete action plans.
- Entrenching women trade unionist and young workers that offer the greatest potential for the broadening of the base and membership of trade unions. Women and young trade unionists must therefore be encouraged with all possible means to join trade union structures and activities at all levels. Incompatibilities between women's family responsibilities and their participation in trade union activities (for example, with regard to the time and location of activities and meetings) must be addressed more effectively.
- Adopting and enhancing gender sensitive policies in general. Many excellent strategies and action plans have been developed for this purpose and need not be mentioned here.

Regional and International Cooperation and Solidarity

A major requirement in this connection is that international, regional and national donor partners must channel their cooperation – multilateral as well as bilateral – to a maximum extent through joint trade union structures and initiatives. Ideally, this would mean working with and through joint trade union platforms.

Therefore going forward, trade unions should:

- Allocate resources with a view to giving priority support to unification-oriented activities has to be given serious consideration. This may not be easy, as it may require reviewing longstanding preferences and privileged relationships, outdated and ideologically based choices and routine programmes, among other things. However, the overriding interest should be that of building strong and effective trade unions in the many African countries.
- Seek structured unity in action at the sectoral level with the GUFS should be sought for the further expansion and improvement of these activities.

Conclusion

Like elsewhere in the world, the role of trade union organisations has developed for historical and ideological reasons in advancing the cause of workers and the society at large. Suffice to say, trade unions still remain a vehicle that can be used to effectively advance the workers cause in the Africa region. However, currently, they remain declining and inert organisations that have numerous challenges which have made them fail to deliver on their mandate of being the "vanguard" of the workers' struggle in the Africa region. This is clearly demonstrated by the admission of many trade unions of their in capacity to engage meaningfully in tripartite arrangements with structures of national government as well as on the regional and international fronts. This is because, it is only a modern, strong and progressive trade union that can be able to mobilise workers in solidarity on socio-economic issues that affect them and play a pivotal role in the face of globalisation. To achieve this it is key that there is clarity about where trade unions stand, the forces ranging against the strategic interests of the working class; who their allies are; and last but not least clarity about the international ideological warfare and what their role is in it.

This paper has presented an overview of the current state of affairs in which trade unions find themselves in the African region. Both external and internal factors that have directly or indirectly impacted negatively and positively on effectiveness of trade unions in the achievement of workers interests have been discussed. External challenges include: forces of globalisation that undermine trade union growth and development; adversarial union relationship; weak union-political party relationship; and nascent trade union international linkages. Internal challenges identified in the study relates to poor governance characterised by lack of union democracy, limited representation and participation. In addition, there were concerns about non-functioning union structures such as working committees and shop stewards. Another notable internal challenge was that, although financial investments were institutionalised, they were fraught with weak accountability and transparency mechanisms.

The paper recommends, among other suggestions, strengthening of state-trade union relationship; establishment of clearer union-political party linkage; building stronger collaboration between trade unions and other like-minded stakeholder; development of a clearer workers ideology to counter the influence of globalisation; strengthening the three federations in terms of international networking; enhancing governance and building a strong union administrative capacity. This underscores the need for ideological clarity so that trade unions adopt a proactive approach and a play a pivotal role in their countries and the region. They should also direct efforts towards globalised trade unionism in the face of increasing assaults by global capital.

Notes

1. The ICFTU is now called the International Trade Union Confederation (ITUC), formed on 1 November 2006 out of the merger with the World Confederation of Labour (WCL).
2. Before 1975; factions of it i.e. the left-leaning unions
3. These include: the National Council of Nigeria and the Cameroons, 1964; SWAFP & Labour Party, 1963/64; Nigeria Labour Party, 1989; Social-Democratic Party, 1990 & Labour Party, 2002
4. See https://www.tralac.org/news/article/5914-cosatu-attends-brics-trade-union-forum.html
5. ALRN is a network of distinguished African labour researchers. It has since 2001 provided radical labour analysis of trends, issues and social processes in Africa. It sustains a critical analysis of the nature of labour, power and the state in Africa in the context of capitalist globalisation.

References

Alternatives to Neo-Liberalism in Southern Africa (ANSA). (2006). *The Search for Sustainable Human Development in Southern Africa*. Harare: ANSA Secretariat.

Buhlungu, S. (2010). *A Paradox of Victory; COSATU and the Democratic Transition in South Africa*. Scottsville: University of KwaZulu-Natal.

Cooper, L., & Hardy, S. (2012). *Beyond Capitalism?* Winchester: Zero Books.

FES. (2008). *Trade unions in Botswana Country Report*. Gaborone: FES.

GUF. (2014). *Africa GUF Forum 2014, Report*. Johannesburg: FES.

ILO. (2010). *Trade Union Pluralism and Proliferation in French-Speaking Africa*. Geneva: ILO – Office, Bureau for Workers' Activities of the ILO (ACTRAV-ILO).

International Confederation of Free Trade Unions (ICFTU). (2001). *Strategic Perspective on the International Trade Union Movement for the 21st Century*. http://www.cosatu.org.za/doc. Accessed 10 Feb 2015.

ITUC – Africa. (2012). *Strategic Plan 2012–15*. Lome: ITUC Secretariat.

Jauch, H. (2003). Trade Unions in Southern Africa. Paper presented to *'Futures for Southern Africa' a Symposium Organised Jointly by Catholic Institute for International Relations (CIIR/ICD), Southern African Catholic Bishops Conference (SACBC)*, Nordic Africa Institute (NAI), Institute for Commonwealth Studies (ICS). Namibia: September 2003.

Jauch, H. (2004). *Labour Markets in Southern Africa (Project on Alternatives to Neo-Liberalism in Southern Africa) October, 2004*. ANSA.

Kalusopa, T. (2011). *Developing an e-Records Readiness Framework for Labour Organisations in Botswana*. PhD Thesis, University of South Africa, Pretoria.

Kalusopa, T., & Otoo, K. N. (2013). *Developing Trade Union Strategies for Decent Work in the Context of Labour Flexibility in Africa: Foundation Chapter*. Accra: ALRN Secretariat.

Kanyenze, G., Kondo, K., & Martens, J. (2006). *The Search for Sustainable Human Development in Southern Africa*. Harare: ANSA.

Moodley, K. (2015). Political Mobilisation, Alliance Building and the Trade Union Movement. Paper presented at *ITUC-AFRICA AND TWN-AFRICA Consultative Meeting on Employment, Structural Transformation and Equitable Economic Development in Africa – Towards an African Trade Union Response to Three Decades of Neo-liberalism in Africa*, Accra, Ghana.

NALEDI. (2009). *The State of Trade Unions in Southern Africa*. ITUC-Africa, South Africa.

OATUU. (2014). Communiqué of the Tripartite Meeting of OATUU, WFTU and ICATU Held at the OATUU Headquarters, Accra, Ghana, 15 January 2014.

Rainsberger, P. K. (1998). Collective Bargaining Historical Models of Collective Bargaining in the U.S. *Steward Notes* 1(2).

SATUCC. (2017). *Study on the Current Status of Trade Unions and Their Role in the SADC Regional Integration and Development Process: An Internal Audit of SATUCC Affiliates*. Gaborone: SATUCC Secretariat.

Southall, R. (1994). *The Labour Market and Trade Unions at the South African Periphery: Lesotho and Transkei, African Affairs (1994)* (Vol. 93, pp. 565–586).

The September Commission Report 1997. Johannesburg: COSATU.

Wood, G. (2001). *South Africa Trade Unions in a Time of Adjustment*. http://www.historycooperative.org/journals. Accessed 10 Feb 2018.

CHAPTER 8

From 'Labour Dividend' to 'Robot Dividend': Technological Change and Workers' Power in South China

Yu Huang and Naubahar Sharif

China became the world's largest market for industrial robots in 2013. The robotic revolution gained pace and occurred after the 2008 financial crisis as many export-oriented firms coped with dwindling orders, rising labour costs and growing concerns over occupational safety. Unlike workers in the Global North who experienced automation in the 1960s and

Originally published in *Agrarian South: Journal of Political Economy, Vol. 6 No. 1*

Y. Huang (✉)
School of Ethnology and Sociology, The Minzu University of China, Beijing, China

N. Sharif
Division of Social Science and Division of Public Policy, The Hong Kong University of Science and Technology, Hong Kong SAR, China

P. Jha et al. (eds.), *Labour Questions in the Global South*,
https://doi.org/10.1007/978-981-33-4635-2_8

1970s against a backdrop of strong union activism, whether semi-proletarian peasant-workers in China ultimately enjoy the 'beneficial' effects of industrial upgrading is questionable. However, very little social science research has investigated how automation, in light of the negative consequences of unemployment and deskilling, can continue to be advanced. Drawing on Beverley Silver's concept of workers' power, this article explores how workers' *marketplace* and *workplace* bargaining power interfaces with technological change. The Chinese case may offer important lessons to those in the under-technologized South seeking to conceptualize strategies for social change in the context of industrial upgrading.

Introduction

In summer 2011, Foxconn Technology Groups, one of China's largest employers, declared that it would use one million robots to replace human labour over the next three years. The company, which has excelled by deploying a military-style management and has rapidly become the world's largest contract manufacturer of electronics, cranking out gadgets for Western firms such as Apple, decided to alter its mix of capital and labour (Pun et al. 2016; The Economist 2011). Although the adoption of robots proceeded at a slower pace than expected, when news came in May 2016 that the Foxconn factory in Kunshan, Jiangsu Province had retrenched 60,000 workers, over half of the total workforce, it triggered ambivalent feelings among analysts and observers there (of the shift towards use of industrial robots) (Zuo 2016). The city of Kunshan had grabbed headlines in 2014 following an explosion in a sand-blasting workshop in an auto parts factory, killing 75 people in one of the most serious recent industrial accidents. Since then, the Kunshan municipal government has been trying to shift its growth strategy by replacing humans with robots.

The trajectory of Foxconn's industrial policy change warrants academic attention because it reflects the transformations in the dynamics between the state, capital and labour as China witnesses gradual change in development strategy gradually shifting from leveraging its 'demographic dividend' to developing a 'robot dividend' (Dongguan People's Government 2014). Until the 2008 global financial crisis, China's economic growth was rooted firmly in its massive workforce, a dividend associated with a relative increase in the age and participation rate of the labour force. However, China's traditional low-end, labour-intensive and export-oriented mode of production encountered a bottleneck following the financial crisis. In 2014, China's economy recorded GDP growth of 7.4 per cent, its slowest rate of expansion since 1990 (Bird 2015). The government and media began to champion the 'robot dividend' that emphasized accelerating efforts to use automated machinery and robots in place of human labour.[1] Premier Li Keqiang, when presenting the 'Made in China 2025' policy, vowed that the government would upgrade China's manufacturing industry within a decade through 'intelligent manufacturing'[2] backed by automated factories and 'big data' to develop an innovation-driven and value-added sector (Xinhua Net 2015). Local governments in the major manufacturing bases of the Yangtze River Delta (YRD) and the Pearl River Delta (PRD) also actively echoed the central government's initiative. For example, in the city of Dongguan, where this study was conducted, the municipal government launched a policy called 'Replacing Humans with Robots' (*jiqi huanren*) and pledged to offer 10–15 per cent subsidies to qualified firms to upgrade their equipment (Dongguan People's Government 2014).[3]

In fact, Foxconn is not the only Chinese manufacturer betting on automation, as China's robotic revolution is well under way, albeit without great fanfare. China became the world's largest market for industrial robots in 2013, with demand skyrocketing to 57,096 units in 2014, a 25 per cent share of the total global supply (IFR 2015). Demand is expected to continue to rise in the foreseeable future as robot density in China, which is only 30 units/10,000 workers, remains very low, less than half of the world's average and far behind countries with higher levels of automation such as Korea and Germany (Ministry of Industry and Information Technology [MIIT], 2016).

China's robotic revolution might paint a rosy picture for the state and capital, but its impact on labour remains very controversial. As shown in the Foxconn case, automation might improve workers' well-being by taking over operations that are repetitive, monotonous and hazardous. On the other hand, in light of the lethal power of robots to cull the workforce in the world's most populous country, one might hesitate to embrace the robotic revolution without reservation. Therefore, it is surprising that the 'Made in China 2025' plan, drafted by the Ministry of Industry and Information Technology (MIIT) with the input of more than 20 other ministries, did not invite any suggestions from either the trade unions or the Ministry of Labour and Social Security and the Labour Bureaus at the provincial and local levels (Butollo and Lüthje 2017). Even though the plan saw 'labour' as factor 'cost' to be reduced, there were no assessments of the mid- and long-term impacts on the labour market or skill development (Ernst 2017). Paralleling the 'labour blind' tendency of the government agencies, labour scholars on China tend to be 'technology blind' as they focus largely on workers' misery in labour-intensive and dehumanizing environments while being slow to respond to the impact of industrial upgrading on workers (Chan 2013; Friedman and Lee 2010).

Drawing from Beverly Silver's (2003) theory of 'workers' power', this article explores contradictions between technological upgrading and labour activism in China's burgeoning robotic revolution. Countries in the Global North such as the USA, Japan and Germany achieved automated production in the 1960s and 1970s, when labour unions still wielded strong bargaining power. This process also predated the emergence of the global value chains that assign value-added tasks of R&D and marketing to the Global North and low-value jobs of Original Equipment Manufacturer (OEM) production and parts supply to the Global South (Chan et al. 2013; Lüthje 2002).[4] In contrast, China's automation took place during an economic downturn in the aftermath of the 2008 financial crisis. Chinese migrant workers, as a semi-proletarian labour force with weak trade unions and low labour protection standards, might find it very difficult to enjoy the beneficial effect of an industrial upgrading (Butollo and Lüthje 2017). However, very few social science studies have investigated the impact of automation, in light of the negative consequences of unemployment and deskilling. In this conceptual context, this article seeks to answer the following questions: (1) How did automation takes place in a country in the Global South and how did the semi-proletarian status of migrant workers make China amenable to industrial upgrading? (2) Despite the lack of protection for craft or industrial unions, how might workers' identity as 'peasant-workers' give them bargaining power that will affect the trajectory of technology-driven accumulation? The case of China, a late industrializing nation, is likely to offer important lessons for those in the under-technologized South who seek to conceptualize strategies for social change in light of weak union protection.

Technological Change and Workers' Power

Mainstream economists insist that industrial upgrading and innovation are necessary steps for establishing and maintaining competitive edge in the globalized economy (Dai and Zhang 2016; Freeman and Soete 1997). They often adopt a Schumpeterian perspective to consider innovation to be relevant only to a firm's entry into and exit from the market (Howell 2015; Li 2011), but they have largely dismissed the role of workers in the labour process as a whole. In this model, 'labour' is seen as a 'static factor of production, something that pre-exists in a raw homogenous form awaiting mobile capital to touch down and set it to work' (Taylor 2009, p. 439). Labour is not, however, a homogenous factor, as industrial upgrading might weaken some kinds of workers' power and strengthen others. Moreover, labour's reaction will also influence the path of technological change.

In the 1970s and 1980s, labour scholars explored changes in union power after automation in the Global North. Harry Braverman (1998 [1974], p. 8) lamented that the unionized working class 'lost the will and ambition to wrest control of production from capitalist hands' when automatic numerical control (NC) machines were introduced in the postwar era. Unlike Braverman, Tessa Morris-Suzuki (1988) adopts a less deterministic and more contextualized understanding of the response of the union. In her account of the automobile industry's automation process in the 1970s in Japan, the Nissan union initially played a central role in the company's policymaking and disavowed the dismissal of workers. However, entering the 1980s, an economic crisis and union split severely weakened the union's bargaining power as its members had to compromise with the employer's demand for substantial layoffs. To obtain a dialectical understanding of workers' power, Silver (2003) draws on Erik Olin Wright's concept of 'structural power' to show that industrial development does not necessarily disempower workers, although it may have divergent effects on workers' *marketplace* and *workplace* power.

Despite Silver's call to follow labour movement dynamics in the Global South, few studies have investigated the effects of technological change on labour activism in countries that have industrialized recently. Scholars studying Chinese labour issues tend to be, as noted above, 'technology blind' as they continue to prioritize research on sweatshop-like, alienating, welfare-deficient and labour-intensive working conditions (Chan 2013; Friedman and Lee 2010). Zhang's (2015) ethnographic study of the dilemmas facing the Chinese automobile industry is an exception. She shows that, while just-in-time (JIT) production methods may jeopardize workers' *marketplace* bargaining power by widening the gap between full-time and temporary workers, the automation system itself is extremely vulnerable to disruption and thus augments workers' *workplace* power. Zhang's research has helped us conceptualize the complex relationships between technological change and labour politics. However, she focuses mainly on skilled and well-paid workers in the automobile industry, but has not studied workers employed in more volatile OEM industries.

This research is based on a larger project that investigates the barriers to and incentives for adopting automation in the city of Dongguan in South China. Three months of ethnographic fieldwork was conducted between September 2015 and January 2016. The study was based on participant observations and interviews with managers in 12 firms, comprising four robot suppliers and eight robot users. Eight of these factories adopted automation in the metal processing, electronics, automobile parts, furniture and bicycle and motorcycle helmet manufacturing industries. Among them, four factories were recipients of Dongguan government subsidies under the 'Replacing Humans with Robots' programme. In addition, 51 interviews were conducted with workers, labour NGO staff and volunteers, factory owners and managers and academics and government officials. Further, 31 of these informants were directly involved in the automation process.

The Semi-Proletarian 'Peasant-Workers'

> A gust of wind blew upon us
> Lifting us up beyond the soil
> Descending upon machines and assembly lines in a distant land
> Immersed in noise, engine oil, red and black adhesives, lead powder, and rust
> We were lashed together, screwed down, and nailed tight
> We were spun around so fast
> Draining our rustic accent, howls, and hot tears
> Until our last drop of sweat was shed
> And we were ossified into a rock
> Only to be discarded along the roadside
> Crops will not grow even if we were to return to the fields
> The rocks keep piling up along the roadside
> One by one, cheek to cheek, in the cold (A Rock along the Roadside,[5] Ji 2013)

The poem vividly portrays how migrant workers, troped as soil, have their life sucked up by machines and then dispersed back to the countryside when they are no longer required in the workplace. Now, drained of all nutrients, the once-fertile soil has turned into a barren rock, unfit to grow crops. During the Chinese New Year Holiday in 2017, Dongguan captured news headlines as the top ghost town in the country. Nearly 70 per cent of its population migrated during the *Chunyun* (Lunar New Year Travel Rush) (Ye 2017). Covering an area of 2460 km^2, the city hosts over 80,000 manufacturers and has a population of 8.3 million. Of these only 1.9 million are permanent residents with urban *hukou* (household registration) and 6.4 million are migrants mostly employed in factories (Dongguan Statistical Yearbook 2015).

Not only were the migrant workers drained of their sweat and blood in the rural exodus, the 'land' in Dongguan experienced a similar process of nutrient depletion. Despite its fame as the 'world's factory' in the past, it was better known as a 'land of fish and rice' (*yumi zhixiang*), as the fertile alluvial soils of the PRD turned the area into a grain basket for Guangdong Province (Liu 2010). At the beginning of the reform era, the Dongguan government was lured into the drive for rapid industrialization and pursued an export-oriented policy called 'both ends abroad' (*liangtou zaiwai*). This implied that the production process would begin and end in international markets, a prototype of OEM production that Dongguan firms continued to adopt in the later years of the reform (Dongguan Municipal Government Office 1998). The migrant labour population increased from only 156,222 in 1986 to 1.42 million in 1995, almost equal to the population of permanent residents (Dongguan Municipal Government Office 1998). After the privatization of Township and Village Enterprises (TVEs) in 2003, the population of migrant workers in Dongguan grew to 4.33 million, almost three times that of hukou-holding residents (Dongguan Statistical Yearbook 2003).

The massive rural exodus that started in 1985 in China can be understood as a process of 'the emaciation of the rural', after the post-Mao regime abandoned the pro-rural policy and reoriented economic development to an urban-centred approach (Yan 2008, p. 25). In 1978, the Household Responsibility System (HRS) instituted two-tiered land rights: Landownership was vested at the village level while land-use rights were distributed equally and leased for family contract farming.[6] With the decline of state investment in agriculture following decollectivization, family based production experienced a range of new problems, including the deterioration of irrigation systems, the fragmentation of farm land and a need for major investments in inputs and machinery (Huang 2015). After the state lowered grain procurement prices in 1985, the urban–rural income gap began to widen and remained wider, exacerbated by the exorbitant taxes and charges that village and township governments imposed to compensate for their revenue shortfalls (Tao et al. 2011). The decline of grain production between 1999 and 2003 prompted the central government to launch incentive policies such as the grain subsidy programme (2004) and the abolishment of agricultural taxes (2006), partly contributing to the first round of a putative labour shortage (Chan and Nadvi 2014; Zhan 2009). However, sustained low prices for farm produce and the rising costs of agricultural inputs failed to deter farmers from opting for urban migration. Here, the countryside definitely serves as a reservoir for surplus labour, although during favourable seasons rural workers might enhance their *marketplace* bargaining power by choosing not to migrate.

At first glance, the rural exodus in China echoes migratory patterns that are similar to other late-industrializing countries of the Global South. However, the Chinese case stands out because of the institutionalized process of semi-proletarianization in what is known as the *hukou* system. Migrant workers, better known as *nongmingong*, are caught between being *nongmin* (peasants) and *gongren* (workers). As stated in the poem, migrants are called to work in the city but not to stay in the city. As rural hukou holders, they are supposed to return to the countryside for education, healthcare services, retirement and other socially reproductive activities. The roots of this 'spatial separation of production in urban areas and reproduction in the countryside' can be traced to the socialist era of the 1950s when it was instituted both as a population control mechanism and as a welfare package (Pun and Lu 2010, p. 497). In the reform era, the hukou system was re-deployed as a means by which authorities could maintain social stability by avoiding ghettoization. It was also seen as an excuse to legitimize low wages for migrant workers who are deprived of benefits being enjoyed by urban residents. By 2015, the average salary of a migrant worker was only 60 per cent that of an urban resident (Bai 2016).

In face of exploitative working conditions, China's migrant workers could rarely obtain the protection from the All-China Federation of Trade Unions (ACFTU), the only legal representative of workers in China (Chen 2016; Clark 2005). Set up at the founding of the People's Republic of China, the ACFTU represented urban workers employed in the *danwei* (work unit) system to guarantee workers' economic interests under socialism as well as the elimination of the capital-labour division (Chen 2009). In the mid-1990s, when the *danwei*, more commonly called state-owned enterprises (SOEs) in the reform era, had to undergo neoliberal restructuring, the ACFTU, as an organization subservient to the state, failed to prevent the lay-off of over 30 million workers. In the aftermath of the drastic reduction of union membership, coeval with the quick expansion of private sector accompanied by growing labour conflicts, the ACFTU had reached out to private- and foreign-owned enterprises which employed largely *nongmingong*. However, workplace trade unions often lacked genuine linkage to rank-and-file workers. In many of the private firms, the management tended to oppose the establishment of a trade union. Even after trade unions were forced to set up, union leaders were usually concurrent members of senior management. Hence, labour strikes in China are often launched by unorganized workers, who felt excluded from power and decision-making processes in trade unions, while trade unions that have lost their role of representing workers end up pre-empting workers' collective actions and thwarting workers' demand for the right to organize (Chen 2009).

However, it is wrong to say that the ACFTU (backed by the Chinese government) are inherently 'anti-labour'. What the Chinese state enforces is actually a 'bifurcated strategy' that restricts workers' collective rights on one hand but confers on their individual rights on the other (Chan and Nadvi 2014; Chen 2016, p. 27). However, as the migrant workers hardly constitute a unified force, even individual labour rights are hard to come by. Before enactment of the Labour Contract Law in 2008, migrant workers had to endure low wages, abusive work conditions and lack of employment security (Gallagher and Dong 2011). Even by 2015, that is, eight years after its implementation, 63.8 per cent of migrant workers had not signed labour contracts (National Bureau of Statistics 2016). Though the Labour Contract Law was drafted to stabilize industrial relations, the power imbalance between labour and capital in the legislative process influenced the final draft of the law to enlarge the permissible reasons for layoffs to include technological upgrading and management reshuffling in favour of capital (Gallagher and Dong 2011). Further, despite the significant contributions of migrant workers to urban GDP figures, local city governments lack incentives to support their labour and social rights. This is evident by their passive enforcement of labour laws, especially during economic downturns.

Nongmingong, as a quasi-identity, has trapped migrant workers in the process of 'unfinished proletarianization' as they shifted between the city and the countryside while finding no permanent home (Pun and Lu 2010, p. 498). While the *hukou* system played a major role in legitimizing the minimal costs of labour reproduction, the conditions it produced were similar to that in other countries of the Global South where workers have low incomes and weak social protection, often denied of decent wage and access to consumer goods. This may be seen as a specific characteristic of accumulation in peripheral capitalism (Jha et al. 2017).

In all, the semi-proletarian status of migrant workers' significantly affects the trajectory of technological change in the urban manufacturing sector. First, rural development and livelihoods are intimately linked to *nongmingong*'s decision of migration and indexing of labour market changes that influence industrial upgrading decisions. Second, the high turnover rate among migrant workers can affect how employers weigh the comparative costs between human labour and automated equipment. Third, without collective rights, senior workers are likely to experience the process of deskilling brought about by automation and thus will fail to prevent their replacement by machines. Some of these factors are considered in the next section.

Automation and Labour Politics

Workers' Marketplace Bargaining Power

The Myth of 'Labour Shortage'

In August 2014, the Dongguan Municipal Government passed a resolution called 'Promotion of Dongguan Enterprises for "Replacing Humans with Robots" (2014–2016).' This outlined the government's determination to transform the city from being the workshop of the world to serving as a base of intelligent manufacturing. As the policy stated, in three years' time, the government would allocate an annual fund of 200 million yuan to sponsor firms that adopt 1000–1500 automation programmes, helping to boost the per capita productivity rate from 80,000 yuan to over 110,000 yuan. Purchasing the capital equipment to automate does not alone qualify a manufacturer for the subsidy; such a firm needs to demonstrate how its industrial upgrading has fulfilled four criteria: workforce reduction, productivity increase, quality upgrade and improvement of work safety protections (Dongguan People's Government 2014).

Considering the dramatic increases in labour costs for the past few years, it is not surprising that 'work force reduction' topped the list of criteria for eligibility. According to official statistics, the city's annual average salary increased by 1.56 times in five years, from only 16,108 yuan in 2010 to 41,285 yuan in 2015 (Tang 2016). The recent round of labour shortage began in earnest as early as the summer of 2009, even though its early origins lay in the spring of 2004 (Xinhua Net 2010). Soon after the Chinese New Year Holiday in 2010, Dongguan witnessed a workforce deficit exceeding one million which was explained as a labour shortage of a stunning 30 per cent. Labour-intensive industries were hit extremely hard, including electronics, furniture, garments, toys and others (Wuhan Evening News 2010). This shortage has been explained by prevalent scholarly interpretations in the theory of the 'Lewisian turning point', which adopts an analysis of demographic change to posit new mechanisms of rural-to-urban migration. Cai Fang and his colleagues were among the first to propose such a thesis as they showed how the one-child policy took a steep toll in ending the seemingly unlimited supply of migrant labour (Cai 2007; Hung 2009). To justify the 'Replacing Humans with Robots' policy, both the media and the Dongguan government offered statistics indicating demographic change: China's working age population dropped from the peak level of 941 million in 2011 to 916 million in 2014, a decline of 25 million in three years (Li and Yang 2015; National Bureau of Statistics 2015).

The problems with the 'Lewisian turning point' hypothesis are twofold. First, it is predicated on a rigid divide between urban industrial and rural agricultural sectors and hence assumes that the subsistence-based economy of the countryside will continue to send out 'surplus' labour to the city (Zhan and Huang 2013). Here labour migration is understood in terms of the law of supply and demand of the labour markets. But this approach fails to consider migrant workers' voluntary choices or even involuntary struggles. Recently, scholars have increasingly begun to unveil the dynamics of the relationship between the urban and rural sectors in a critique of this rigid hypothesis (Arrighi 2008; Weil 2006; Zhan and Huang 2013). For example, rural 'surplus' labour is far from being exhausted. In fact, the total number of migrant workers has continued to rise, from 253 million in 2011 to 274 million in 2014, an increase of 21 million (National Bureau of Statistics 2015). In 2009, just less than one third (31 per cent) of the total rural labour force of 469 million chose to migrate. Zhan and Huang (2013) reveal how rural development, especially the rise in TVEs in the 1990s and the government's 'Developing the West' and 'Constructing the Socialist Countryside' programmes of the 2000s, contributed the major portion of income growth in the countryside. Moreover, it has been found that rural labourers prefer local nonfarm employment to labour migration if the two offer commensurable economic rewards. Zhan and Huang (2013) cogently unveil how rural development helped increase the *marketplace* bargaining power of migrant workers in the urban manufacturing sector. This is evident in the 153.8 per cent increase in wages between 2003 and 2009.

The second critique of the 'Lewisian turning point' is from the perspective of the importance of workers' struggles in elevating social and economic status (Chan 2013; Pun et al. 2016). A most inspiring case was the workers' strike at the Honda Auto Parts Manufacturing plant in Foshan in May 2010 that involved 1800 workers and lasted for 17 days, forcing management to accede to the workers' demand for a significant 32.4 to 70 per cent wage increase and democratic election of new trade union leaders (Chan 2013). In addition to the struggle for higher wages, migrant workers have been fighting for worker's rights and recognition, forcing the government to pass a series of laws such as the Social Security Law (Gallagher and Dong 2011).

Therefore, the so-called labour shortage discourse reflected workers' growing *marketplace* bargaining power rather than a real shortage in the labour supply. However, rising labour costs can also turn against workers if employers refuse to offer higher salaries, instead replacing workers with robots. Currently, the average monthly salary in the manufacturing sector in Dongguan was 4062 yuan,[7] and with social security expenditures labour costs easily exceeded 50,000 yuan per year. In comparison, industrial robots averaged less than 100,000 yuan/unit (General Administration of Customs 2015). Therefore, typically it takes only two years for employers to get their investment back from upgrading their equipment, a tempting solution to the pressing 'labour shortage' issue.

According to Dongguan government statistics, from September 2014 to December 2015, among the 1262 subsidized programmes, work force reduction totalled 71,253. Our research identified an alarming rate of job replacement. As seen in Table 8.1, a dramatic reduction in the labour force ranging between 67 and 85 per cent took place after technological upgrading in the four factories studied in this project.[8,9] Factory P cut its operational workers by 80 per cent after the introduction of robotic arms that took finished products out of the injection moulding machines, enabling one worker to manage five machines in contrast to only one worker per machine before automation. Still, the facility increased productivity by 10 per cent. The production line for bicycle helmets, cut the workforce even more dramatically, from 40 to 10.

Surprisingly, most of the workers we interviewed welcomed the encroachment of industrial upgrading, which perhaps they saw as

Table 8.1 Workforce Change Before and After Automation

Factory	*Product*	*Equipment*	*Previous workforce*	*Present workforce*	*Workforce reduction*
P	Printer transmission wheels (plastic)	Industrial robots for plastic injection moulding machine	1 worker 1 machine	1 worker for 5 machines	80%
C	Auto parts (plastic)	Industrial robots for plastic injection moulding machine	1 worker 1 machine	1 worker for 3 machines	67%
H	Bicycle helmets	Industrial robots for helmet venting hole cutting	40 workers	10 workers	75%
L	Mobile Phone LED die-cut modules	Automation system	20 workers/ line	3 workers/ line	85%

Source: Fieldwork data

inevitable 'progress'. In a focus group discussion, Meng,[10] a fourth-generation carpenter, suggested that the new automatic sculpturing machines helped reduce work intensity, lowered workers' exposure to dust and yet turned out higher quality doors. Later in a personal interview, however, he did mention a case in which veteran workers resisted reductions in salary. Another worker, Gang, who worked in an electronics factory but suffered from Myelodysplastic Syndromes (MDS), a kind of blood disorder associated with exposure to toxic chemicals, highlighted the advantages of automation:

> The automation process in Dongguan epitomizes social progress[…]. Some people are concerned about the consequences of worker displacement. I don't think that this is a problem to be worried about. I feel that the government should guarantee resource sharing. I used to be a farmer. Initially farming was manual work. The crops 100 farmers grew were not enough to feed 100 people. Now (with machines), two farmers can feed 100 people. With automation, fewer workers will be needed as per capita productivity increases.

However, after hearing about the government's subsidy to employers, the focus group participants began asking why the government did not subsidize laid-off workers. Responding to these issues raised by workers.

Mr Tan from the Dongguan government implied that it was the workers' responsibility to keep up with the 'wave':

> There is a saying that in the Yangtze River the waves from behind push forward those in the front. [...] At this time, it is difficult for the government to consider offering them humanistic care [...] such as assigning them psychiatrists. It is not feasible. Workers can only depend on themselves to learn new technology. [...] Everyone needs to cultivate themselves so as to develop a competitive edge. [...] This is a trend. [...] A society's progress comes with costs.[...] Everyone here endures the pressure of survival.

We can see here that local governments benefited from migrant workers' economic contributions but neglected their social wellbeing as they were reluctant to take responsibility for the migrants who were considered as 'non-residents'. However, Mr Tan later admitted that the government's indifference to the adverse outcomes of automation was due partly to the workers' muted reaction. 'Now for people who petition the State Bureau for Letters and Visits (*shangfang*), they do it because of wage arrears and runaway bosses. I haven't heard any case of a petition due to replacement by machines'. Mr Tan's position is revealing for two reasons: On one hand, it uncovers how little opposition there is to the machines, and on the other, it shows that worker's response and the development of their consciousness is inadequate.

High Labour Turnover

Laying off workers does not present a major problem to employers. The manager of Factory H reported that they had 240 employees in their plastic injection moulding department prior to automation in 2010 and now have only 120 workers, but they never had to ask the workers to quit.

> The high turnover rate is a very special phenomenon in China. Therefore, I adhere to the law of natural selection, separating the wheat from the chaff (*quwu cunjing*). For a corporation, you can't lose your human rights as a result of evolution. That is a fundamental social right. The turnover rate is high in China, which matches my hiring freeze initiative. This works like an ecological cycle in nature. We utilize this natural cycle to add to or reduce our workforce.

Here the manager uses the trope of 'natural selection' to deflect employers' responsibility for compensating laid-off workers. Before 2014, the turnover rate in his factory was 150 per cent, having just recently dropped to 100 per cent in 2015. Although Chinese labour law requires employers to offer severance pay calculated at one-month's salary for each year of service, in reality there are various ways by which an employer can circumvent this regulation. Currently, the minimal salary in Dongguan is only 1510 yuan. Considering the average monthly salary of 4062 yuan in manufacturing, the bulk of workers' salaries comes from overtime work. Therefore, if an employer does not offer overtime tasks to its workers, the workers might quit their jobs 'of their own free will', obviating employers' mandate to offer severance pay.

Some labour scholars on China have not paid enough attention to the relationship between labour market factors and industrial upgrading. They tend to view high labour turnover as a phenomenon that threatens workers' skill development, employers' human capital accumulation and even social stability (Huang 2012; Li et al. 2012). The 'Migrant Workers' Employment Trends Report', released by Tsinghua University, indicates that the trend in temporary employment intensified in recent years, with the average duration of continuous employment for migrant workers lasting 3.8 years in the early 2000s while dropping to 1.4 years for the cohort entering employment in 2008. What is worse, frequent job shifting has not led to upward mobility, as has commonly happened in other countries, instead apparently representing nothing more than 'horizontal' career development or 'marking time' (Tsinghua Sociology Department Project Group 2013). Over one-third of their informants reported no improvement whatsoever in this respect.

Like the 'labour shortage' factor, the high turnover rate can be utilized by employers to enforce automation that further marginalizes workers' *marketplace* bargaining power.

Workers' *Workplace* Bargaining Power

Under labour shortage conditions as well as high turnover, some manufacturers consider automation as a viable solution to reducing their reliance on skilled labour. In our visit to Factory H, the manager explained to us that previously it took six months to train a novice operator to become proficient in cutting venting holes in a bicycle helmet. Now, the same worker who is assigned to operate the robotic arm can finish the tasks very effectively in only three days. The reduction in the training period from six months to three days meant that, for employers, the ratio of the cost of training an operator to produce identical parts by conventional methods compared with the cost of using industrial robots is approximately 60 to 1. Braverman already observed this issue in his study of the automatic numerical control (NC) machinery in the post-WWII USA, when he reported the difference between training an artisanal machinist and a NC machine operator to be four years versus four months (Braverman 1998 [1974], p. 139). At that time, trade unions in the USA were still proactive and powerful so that employers had to '(in public at least) [...] conceal the downgrading' of the trained machinist 'in the interest of a smoother transition and for public relations reasons' (Braverman 1998 [1974], p. 139). If veteran machinists in the USA silently accepted their labour degradation fate, how did non-unionized workers in China react to the encroachment of automation? Our Primary data show that with the increased productivity brought by advanced machinery, workers' pay immediately changed from a piece rate to a time rate. Employers used various strategies to persuade veteran employees to accept the reality of higher productivity for the same or even lower pay-scales.

The example of Rong who worked in a factory that produced metal car seat frames is illustrative of the impact of automation on categories of workers. In 2013, the owner purchased one automatic lathe for metal punching-stamping and one for welding. The punching-stamping lathe includes a series of tools that revolve to the next tool as the previous one completes its cycle, and is capable of finishing tasks that previously required 10 small lathes to accomplish. Rong estimates that the automatic lathe produces at least 30 items per minute, compared with only five items per minute produced by the 10 small lathes combined. The automatic welding lathe can weld at three points simultaneously and even remove welding slag and polish surfaces afterwards, replacing the labour of four to five workers. However, Rong's boss did not intend to replace all the old lathes immediately because the automatic lathes are economical only for large orders. The factory still relies on the skilled senior (40+) workers to operate the small outdated lathe. When the factory owner purchased the three automatic lathes, productivity increased almost tenfold. This time, rather than asking veteran skilled workers to operate the automatic machines, he hired three younger workers to operate them. This has a bearing on the wages of workers. Now, the younger operators are paid 5000 yuan per month, almost the same as the veteran workers with more advanced skills and experience but lower productivity, leading to disquiet among veteran workers. Younger workers are preferred to veteran workers apparently because the younger workers are better able to adjust to small errors to which the machines are prone.

Factory H maintains dual payment systems for manual and robotic cutting of helmet venting holes. Manual cutting is paid at a piece rate, while robotic cutting operators are paid by time rate. At the time of the study, the latter group could produce 40 pieces per hour and were paid on average 4000 yuan per month. In contrast, manual workers produce 15 pieces per hour and are paid 5000 yuan per month in recognition of their skills. In the future, skilled workers will be replaced increasingly by robots. Currently, the factory uses the internal labour market to convert manual workers to robot operators rather than hiring younger unskilled workers from outside. The barrier is that the factory environment is noisy and dusty, making the job unattractive to younger workers.

The dilemmas of transition from labour intensive to robotic operations is reflected in the story of some veteran workers' experience with a failed strike. Jun is a third-generation carpenter and works with his father in Factory D, which specializes in manufacturing doors. The factory was set up in 2002 with fewer than 20 workers, but expanded to over 300 workers in 2009. Today it has only a little more than 100 workers. However, replacing workers was not a smooth process because the veteran skilled workers organized a strike to protest the drop in pay that automation brought.

Before the introduction of automatic lines, the factory had already launched a Taylorized approach to manufacturing that divided the production process into small steps. Jun's father had joined the factory soon after its establishment. At that time, his co-workers were all rural craftsmen who acquired woodworking skills from generations of practice. As the factory expanded, the owner found it hard to recruit a sufficient number of experienced carpenters and started to organize a division of labour, forming five door manufacturing units: feeding raw materials, cutting parts, pressing boards, assembling doors and painting. In the past, the factory manufactured conventional doors, catering to the booming real estate industry. However, after the 2008 global financial crisis, the factory owner incurred losses in the business that he chose to compensate for by attempting to extract higher profits on the product manufactured in the factory. This was the trigger for automation that leads to a drive to increase in the factory's competitiveness and shift its market from conventional doors selling at 1000 yuan per piece to high-end, fire-resistant doors with average prices of 5000–6000 yuan per piece. In order to make the fire-proof door, the factory launched automatic and semi-automatic lines for laminating, cutting and painting.

The urgency to continue automating also came with the need to reduce pollution in the workshop. Manufacturing fire-proof doors required the insertion of asbestos and gypsum plaster. Long-term exposure to asbestos increases the risks of lung cancer, while immediate exposure will cause skin irritation. In 2011, the factory owner introduced a semi-automatic veneer pressing machine that accomplished a series of tasks from glue application to pressing the asbestos and gypsum plaster together. Before automation, veteran workers in the veneer pressing unit were paid at a piece rate of about 6000 yuan per month. The first month after automation, increased productivity helped push the average salary to 8000 yuan per month.

The owner quickly began recruiting younger workers. The head of the pressing unit became angry because his unit was composed mostly of workers who had worked at the plant for more than four years and even a few who had joined the factory at its inception in 2002 while union did not exist in the firm. After a quick discussion with his fellow workers, the pressing-unit head decided to call on a strike early one morning. He successfully used his authority to gain the support of not only veteran workers but also newly recruited younger ones. They halted production for about two hours before the owner came to yell at them: 'Do you still want to work here or not? If you choose to quit today, I will settle your wages'. The veteran workers suddenly realized that they were no longer the backbone of the factory and their skills no longer automatically granted them *workplace* bargaining power. In their 40s, most feared that they would have great difficulty finding other jobs if they were fired, and quickly returned to their positions. Each striking worker was fined 100 yuan as punishment. After the strike, the owner accelerated the automation process to cover operations in painting and cutting. Later, in their bi-monthly assembly, the owner would scold the workers: 'You are just a speck. The factory won't stop without you'.

Jun attributed the failure of the strike to the lack of solidarity among the workers. In the factory, the head of each unit liked to recruit fellow workers from their hometowns, a trend that became more pronounced after the factory introduced Taylorized form of production. For example, the veneer pressing unit is composed of workers from Hunan, while the painting unit has workers mostly from Henan. As the employer introduced automation to various production units, workers from automated units installed later lacked incentives to support workers from units that had been automated earlier. Jun thought that if all the workers had participated in the strike together, the employer would have had to yield to the workers' requests. Jun did notice that, with the introduction of automation machines, veteran workers like him were no longer desirable. After the strike, the skilled workers all experienced pay cuts, while younger workers, although still earning lower salaries than the veteran workers, were paid slightly above the market rate. In a sense, automation stirred up tensions between skilled and younger workers through the process of de-skilling.

Finally, we can see from the above examples that workers do not resist deskilling but rather the unfair treatment they experience in the transition to deskilling. As semi-proletarians lacking union representation, workers were omitted from industrial policy decision making, giving free reign to employers to determine the process of industrial upgrading and to reduce salaries as they desired. Worker's semi-proletarian status in this regard has weakened their *workplace* bargaining power.

Conclusion

China, as the country with the world's largest population, is shifting from an economy based on exploiting its 'demographic dividend' to one based on possibly leveraging the upcoming 'robotic dividend'. This article shows the significant impact that this process of industrial upgrading is having on the labour force. Drawing on Beverly Silver's theory of the 'structural' power of workers, this article seeks to disentangle the complex relationship between technological change and workers' power. While a 'labour shortage' and high turnover rate might epitomize workers' increasing *marketplace* power, the rising labour costs that result might jeopardize workers' interests, as employers are incentivized to use robots to replace human labour. Moreover, employers can capitalize on the high turnover rate to avoid offering severance pay. In terms of workers' *workplace* bargaining power, in the absence of broad labour movements, the potential for initiating large-scale, well-organized resistance against deskilling might be weak.

Hence a dialectical analysis of the relation between technological change and workers' power is necessary. A dialectical approach on one hand refutes mainstream economists' notion of technological determinism that views labour as a static and passive force awaiting capital's manipulation. On the other hand, it also cautions against an opposite tendency that champions workers' power as inherently insurmountable to machines. Automation machineries have the dual effects of increasing efficiency and improving work safety on one hand and causing worker displacement and deskilling on the other. Will technological change help provoke class consciousness? How might worker activism be organized in the era of robotic revolution?

While Silver offers insightful theories to examine how workers' bargaining power interfaces with technological change, she has not systematically discussed how workers in the Global South might be affected by automation different from their predecessors in the Global North. We try to fill in this gap by introducing the concept 'semi-proletarianization' into the analysis of workers' power.

First, in the 1960s–1970s, under strong union activism and welfare state labour protectionism, industrial upgrading in the USA and Japan did bring forward the 'beneficial' effect of increased wage although the negative consequences of worker de-skilling and union weakening should not be overlooked. In contract, when the robotic revolution took off after the 2008 financial crisis in China, workers might find it hard to get a fair share of the 'robot dividends' under the backdrop of 'periphery capitalism' (Amin 1974; Jha et al. 2017) when workers' semi-proletarian status blocked their entitlement to decent wages and access to consumer goods. By far, despite the high work displacement rate we recorded in our study, robotization might still seem a lesser evil than factory shutdown or relocation to Southeast Asia. Second, for the Chinese migrant workers who are used to high turnover, the fact that the workers impacted are themselves easily able to relocate to different cities, and different factories in possibly differing industries, makes them unlikely candidates to lead a concerted effort to raise class consciousness. Third, the process of automation is not being questioned symmetrically from all angles. Mainstream discourse touts robotization as an unstoppable trend that will lead to workers' upskilling and creation of new jobs, although they have not offered any credible evidence on what kind and what percentage of workers will get job retraining and work replacement (Wu 2017; Xinhua Net 2015). In contrast, there is little symmetrical attention given to the plight of workers who are directly or indirectly impacted by such technological changes. Even the official 'Made in China 2025' plan did not include any long-term or mid-term assessment of the possible impacts of automation on labour.

Therefore, workers might easily internalize a discourse of 'progress' and view their sacrifice as an inevitable outcome rather than standing up to fight against it.

Therefore, although it is evident that automation might deteriorate Chinese workers' conditions, the rise of class consciousness faces a number of important, if not presently insurmountable, hurdles. However, we do believe in the importance of education and organization as a way to empower workers. As previously mentioned, when workers were informed of Dongguan government's policy of subsidizing firms for industrial upgrading, they immediately questioned why there was not a corresponding policy in place to subsidize displaced or de-skilled workers. In the future, we think it important to carry on our research-cum-activism work to focus on the following two areas. At the aggregate level, we would like to conduct labour market research to understand the industry, sector, regional and gender pattern of job displacement. With the help of labour activists, workers will learn how their semi-proletarian status might be taken advantage of by employers for industrial upgrading, but at the same time, they can develop informal labour organizing to request both central government and local government to not only cushion the adverse impact of automation, but more importantly, to get more income with less hours—a just share of the 'robot dividend'. At the more detailed level, we would conduct shop-floor labour process analysis to understand how advance machinery might de-skill workers on one hand, but become vulnerable to 'localized stoppage or disruption by a small group of workers' (Zhang 2015, p. 90). The large-scale adoption of automation equipment will likely create a homogenized workforce and revolutionize shop floor control, it is time for workers in the Global South to unite and fight strategically.

Acknowledgements We would like to thank Mathew Hale, Boy Lüthje, Vitor Schincariol, Kenneth Tsz Fung NG, the Agrarian South editorial team and participants at the Sam Moyo African Institute for Agrarian Studies Summer School 2017 for their valuable comments and suggestions. Earlier versions of this paper were also presented to 'The 9th Asian Regional Congress of the International Labour and Employment Relations Association (ILERA)', Beijing, 1–3 November, 2016 and the 'Workshop on Labour Geography: From Spaces of Work to Communities of Struggle', City University of Hong Kong, Department of Asian and International Relations, and Goettingen University, Germany, Department of Sociology, Hong Kong, 25–26 March, 2017.

Funding The authors gratefully acknowledge the funding support from the Institute for Emerging Market Studies (IEMS) at the Hong Kong University of Science and Technology (HKUST).

Notes

1. Authorities classify robots as either industrial robots used in manufacturing or service robots performing tasks other than industrial automation. In our research, we studied only industrial robots, which are defined by the International Organization for Standardization ISO 8373 as 'automatically controlled, reprogrammable, multipurpose manipulator[s] programmable in three or more axes, which may be either fixed in place or mobile for use in industrial automation applications' (IFR 2015). An industrial robot is a typical component of programmable automated systems. The term 'automation' denotes technology designed to replace human labour in the manufacturing process, combining industrial technologies for physical operations and computer technology for information management (Siciliano et al. 2009, p. 16). Here we use these terms interchangeably because in introducing robots, manufacturers are, at the same time, automating their production lines.
2. For a full definition of 'intelligent manufacturing' please refer to 'Guidance on National Intelligent Manufacturing Standard System Construction (2015)', jointly published by the MIIT and the Standardization Administration of China.
3. The literal translation of this policy should be 'replacing humans with machines' (jiqi huanren). However, we decided to adopt the translation 'replacing humans with robots' because the application of machines in itself does not make a firm eligible for the subsidy, although some degree of automation is required. The 2014 plan awarded subsidies to 438 firms, but only 5 per cent adopted industrial robots, while 95 per cent used non-robotic automated equipment.
4. An OEM is a company that produces parts and equipment that may be marketed by another manufacturer. For example, when Foxconn manufactures mobile phones for Apple, Foxconn is the OEM.
5. Translation by Yu Huang and Edwin Schmitt.
6. In 1982, the term of the contract was designated to be 15 years. To stabilize agriculture production and overcome the problem of further fragmentation of farmland, the principle of 'more people but no more land, fewer people but no less land' (zengren bu zengdi, jianren bu jiandi) was adopted. In 1997, the contract term was extended to 30 years (Wen 1999).
7. The average annual salary for the manufacturing sector was 48,750 yuan in 2015. See Yu (2016).

8. We were able to collect data on four out of the eight factories that adopted robots and automation systems. For the four factories from which we were not able to gather data, Factory M already had automation equipment (CNC) at the time of establishment. Therefore, there was no information on the labour force before automation. We obtained information on Factory D mostly from workers who had grievances with the owner and did not feel it would be appropriate to interview the owner. Factory J was still testing its automation line, which was not yet in production. The owner of Factory K did not want us to take notes of our conversion and did not want his factory to be reported on, even anonymously.
9. The table reflects only workforce changes in the same production line, not in the whole factory. For example, Factory L reduced labour in the production unit but increased personnel in the still labour-intense QC unit. However, it is foreseeable that with automation technology implemented in QC, the overall workforce for the whole factory will decline significantly.
10. All informants' names have been anonymized.

References

Amin, S. (1974). *Accumulation on a World Scale: A Critique of the Theory of Underdevelopment* (2 Vols). New York: Monthly Review Press.

Arrighi, G. (2008). *Adam Smith in Beijing: Lineages of the 21st Century*. London: Verso.

Bai, T. (2016, April 20). Are Migrant Workers' Wages Rising Too Fast? *People's Daily*, p. 13.

Bird, M. (2015, June 18). China's Economy Is Hitting a Wall—And It's Going to Affect Everyone. *Business Insider*. Retrieved from http://uk.businessinsider.com/data-and-statistics-on-the-china-economy-and-the-chinese-stockbubble-2015-6

Braverman, H. (1998 [1974]). *Labour and Monopoly Capital: The Degradation of Work in the Twentieth Century*. New York: Monthly Review Press.

Butollo, F., & Lüthje, B. (2017). 'Made in China 2025': Intelligent Manufacturing and Work. In K. Briken, C. Shiona, M. Krzywdzinski, & A. Marks (Eds.), *The New Digital Workplace: How New Technologies Revolutionise Work* (pp. 42–61). Houndsmills: Palgrave.

Cai, F. (Ed.). (2007). *The Upcoming Lewisian Turning Point and Its Policy Implications*. Beijing: Social Sciences Academic Press.

Chan, C. K. C. (2013). Contesting Class Organization: Migrant Workers' Strikes in China's Pearl River Delta, 1978–2010. *International Labour and Working Class History, 83*(Spring), 112–136.

Chan, C. K. C., & Nadvi, K. (2014). Changing Labour Regulations and Labour Standards in China: Retrospect and Challenges. *International Labour Review, 153*(4), 513–534.

Chan, J., Pun, N., & Selden, M. (2013). The Politics of Global Production: Apple, Foxconn And China's New Working Class. *New Technology, Work and Employment, 28*(2), 100–115.

Chen, F. (2009). Union Power in China: Source, Operation, and Constraints. *Modern China, 35*(6), 662–689.

Chen, F. (2016). China's Road to the Construction of Labor Rights. *Journal of Sociology, 52*(1), 24–38.

Clark, S. (2005). Post-Socialist Trade Unions: China and Russia. *Industrial Relations Journal, 36*(1), 2–18.

Dai, L., & Zhang, W. (2016). The Mechanism of Reindustrialization Based on the Perspective of Schumpeter Innovation. *Science and Technology Management Research, 2*, 47–53.

Dongguan Municipal Government Office. (1998). *Dongguan in Twenty Years: 1978–1998*. Dongguan: Dongguan Statistics Bureau.

Dongguan People's Government. (2014). *Announcement on Circulating Dongguan's 'Replacing Humans with Robots' Special Fund Management Policy*. Retrieved from http://www.dg.gov.cn/cndg/s1272/201408/787179.html

Dongguan Statistical Yearbook. (2003). *Dongguan: Dongguan Statistical Bureau*. Retrieved from http://tjj.dg.gov.cn/website/web2/art_list.jsp?Column Id=10000

Dongguan Statistical Yearbook. (2015). *Dongguan: Dongguan Statistical Bureau*. Retrieved from http://tjj.dg.gov.cn/website/web2/art_list.jsp?columnId=10000

Ernst, D. (2017). Advanced Manufacturing and China's Future for Jobs. In E. Paus (Ed.), *The New Technological Revolution: What Future for Jobs and Livelihoods?* Ithaca: Cornell University Press.

Freeman, C., & Soete, L. (1997). *The Economics of Industrial Innovation*. Cambridge, MA: MIT Press.

Friedman, E., & Lee, C. K. (2010). Remaking the World of Chinese Labour: A 30-Year Retrospective. *British Journal of Industrial Relations, 48*(3), 507–533.

Gallagher, M. E., & Dong, B. (2011). Legislating Harmony: Labour Law Reform in Contemporary China. In S. Kuruvilla, C. K. Lee, & M. Gallagher (Eds.), *From Iron Rice Bowl to Informalization: Markets, Workers, and the State in a Changing China* (pp. 36–60). Ithaca: Cornell University Press.

General Administration of Customs. (2015). *The Import of Industrial Robots Witnesses Volume Drop and Price Increase*. Retrieved from http://www.customs.gov.cn/publish/portal0/tab7841/info768491.html

Howell, A. (2015). 'Indigenous' Innovation with Heterogeneous Risk and New Firm Survival in a Transitioning Chinese Economy. *Research Policy, 44*(10), 1866–1876.

Huang, C. (2012). Personality and Ideal: Analysis of Temporary Employment of New Generation Migrant Workers Behavior. *China Youth Study, 11*(80–83), 108.

Huang, Y. (2015). Can Capitalist Farms Defeat Family Farms? The Dynamics of Capitalist Accumulation in Shrimp Aquaculture in South China. *Journal of Agrarian Change, 15*(3), 392–412.

Hung, H.-F. (2009). America's Head Servant? The PRC's Dilemma in the Global Crisis. *New Left Review, 60*(November–Dececember), 5–25.

IFR. (2015). World Robotics 2015 Industrial Robots. *International Federation of Robotics.* Retrieved from http://www.ifr.org/industrial-robots/statistics/

Jha, P., Moyo, S., & Yeros, P. (2017). Capitalism *and 'Labour Reserves': A Note.* Paper presented at the Sam Moyo African Institute for Agrarian Studies Summer School. Harare, Zimbabwe.

Ji, Z. (2013). The Rock at the Roadside. In Q. Xiaoyu (Ed.), *My Poems* (pp. 332–334). Beijing: China Writers Publishing House.

Li, X. (2011). Sources of External Technology, Absorptive Capacity, and Innovation Capacity in Chinese State-Owned High-Tech Enterprises. *World Development, 39*(7), 1240–1248.

Li, H., & Yang, J. (2015, July 3). Labour Force Continued to Decline in Three Consecutive Years, Labour Shortage Increasingly Intensified. *Renmin Daily Net.* Retrieved from http://politics.people.com.cn/n/2015/0703/c1001-27247829.html

Li, Y., Wu, L., & Shen, S. (2012). The Impact of Corporate Social Security Welfare on Migrant Workers' Mobility: Evidence from the Pearl River Delta of Guangdong. *Chinese Rural Economy, 9*, 61–73.

Liu, W. (2010). The Development and Historical Functions of Commune and Village Enterprises in Dongguan. *Dongguan Party History* 1. Retrieved from http://dgds.sun0769.com/dgds/shownews.asp?id=201&Url=list.asp%3FitemID%3D18&rootTitle=2010%C4%EA%B5%DA1%C6%DA

Lüthje, B. (2002). Electronics Contract Manufacturing: Global Production and the International Division of Labour in the Age of the Internet. *Industry and Innovation, 9*(3), 227–247.

Ministry of Industry and Information Technology (MIIT). (2016, May 12). *Interpreting 'Made in China 2025': Pushing Forward the Development of Robots.* Retrieved from http://www.miit.gov.cn/n11293472/n11293877/n16553775/n16553822/16633940.html

Morris-Suzuki, T. (1988). *Beyond Computopia: Information, Automation and Democracy in Japan.* New York: Routledge.

National Bureau of Statistics. (2015). *The National Economy Ran Smoothly Under the New Normal in 2014.* Retrieved from http://www.stats.gov.cn/tjsj/zxfb/201502/t20150211_682459.html

National Bureau of Statistics. (2016). *Migrant Workers Monitoring Survey Report 2015.* Retrieved from http://www.stats.gov.cn/tjsj/zxfb/201604/t20160428_1349713.html

Pun, N., & Lu, H. (2010). Unfinished Proletarianization: Self, Anger, and Class Action Among the Second Generation of Peasant-Workers in Present-Day China. *Modern China, 36*(5), 493–519.

Pun, N., Shen, Y., Guo, Y., Lu, H., Chan, J., & Selden, M. (2016). Apple, Foxconn, and Chinese Workers' Struggles from a Global Labor Perspectives. *Inter-Asia Cultural Studies, 17*(2), 166–185.

Siciliano, B., Sciavicco, L., Villani, L., & Oriolo, G. (2009). *Robotics: Modelling, Planning and Control.* London: Springer.

Silver, B. (2003). *Forces of Labour: Workers' Movements and Globalization Since 1870.* New York: Cambridge University Press.

Tang, H. (2016, February 17). Average Salary Soaring 25,000 Yuan in Six Years. *Guangzhou Daily.*

Tao, R., Liu, M., Su, F., & Lu, X. (2011). Grain Procurement, Tax Instrument and Peasant Burdens During China's Rural Transition. *Journal of Contemporary China, 20*(71), 659–677.

Taylor, M. (2009). Who Works for Globalisation? The Challenges and Possibilities for International Labour Studies. *Third World Quarterly, 30*(3), 435–452.

The Economist. (2011, August 6). Foxconn: Robots Don't Complain. Retrieved from http://www.economist.com/node/21525432

Tsinghua Sociology Department Project Group. (2013). Migrant Workers' Employment Trends Report. In S. Yuan (Ed.), *Tsinghua Sociology Review (Vol 6): Social Transformation and New Generation Migrant Workers* (pp. 1–45). Beijing: Social Science Academic Press.

Weil, R. (2006). Conditions of the Working Classes in China. *Monthly Review, 58*(1), 25–48.

Wen, T. (1999). Rural Institutional Change in the Past Half Century. *Strategy and Management, 6*, 76–82.

Wu, H. (2017, May 5). Artificial Intelligence Might Take Away Your Job, But It Will Not Take Away Human Beings' Jobs. *163 News.* Retrieved from http://news.163.com/17/0505/00/CJKPOQD200018M4D.html

Wuhan Evening News. (2010, February 21). Widespread Labour Shortage in Coastal Regions, Labour Deficit Exceeding 2 Million in the Pearl River Delta. *Wuhan Evening News.*

Xinhua Net. (2010, February 22). *Multiple Perspectives on Labour Shortage After the Spring Festival.* Retrieved from http://news.xinhuanet.com/politics/2010-02/22/content_13024222.html

Xinhua Net. (2015, July 31). *The Joy and Concerns Regarding the 'Replacing Humans with Robots: Investigation on the First 'Workerless Factory' in Dongguan, Guangdong*. Retrieved from http://news.xinhuanet.com/fortune/2015-07/13/c_1115909116.html

Yan, H. (2008). *New Masters, New Servants: Migration, Development, and Women Workers in China*. Durham: Duke University Press.

Ye, D. (2017, January 31). Big Data Showing Dongguan as the Nation's Top 'Ghost Town' in the Chinese New Year. *Nanfang Net*. Retrieved from http://kb.southcn.com/content/2017-01/31/content_164528734.html

Yu, B. (2016, July 14). The Average Salary for Last Year Debut in Dongguan. *Yangcheng Evening News Web*. Retrieved from http://news.ycwb.com/2016-07/14/content_22514028.htm

Zhan, J. (2009). Assessment on the Implementation of China's Grain Subsidy Policy. *Journal of Hunan Agricultural University (Social Sciences), 10*(4), 17–21.

Zhan, S., & Huang, L. (2013). Rural Roots of Current Migrant Labour Shortage in China: Development and Labour Empowerment in a Situation of Incomplete Proletarianization. *Studies in Comparative International Development, 48*(1), 81–111.

Zhang, L. (2015). *Inside China's Automobile Factories: The Politics of Labour and Worker Resistance*. New York: Cambridge University Press.

Zuo, M. (2016, May 21). Rise of the Robots: 60,000 Workers Culled from Just One Factory as China's Struggling Electronics Hub Turns to Artificial Intelligence. *South China Morning Post*. Retrieved from http://www.scmp.com/news/china/economy/article/1949918/rise-robots-60000-workers-culled-just-onefactory-chinas

CHAPTER 9

Labour Trends in Latin America and the Caribbean in the Current Crisis (2008–2016)

Vitor Eduardo Schincariol, Muryatan S. Barbosa, and Paris Yeros

Introduction

The world economic crisis that erupted in 2008 had a strong and negative impact on the rates of economic growth in Latin America and the Caribbean (hereafter, LAC).[1] Most countries in the region were showing a tendency towards positive and, in some cases, even accelerating growth rates in the first half of the 2000s. There was a small recovery in GDP from

Originally published in *Agrarian South: Journal of Political Economy, Vol. 6 No. 1*

V. E. Schincariol (✉) • M. S. Barbosa • P. Yeros
Federal University of ABC (UFABC), São Paulo, Brazil
e-mail: vitor.schincariol@ufabc.edu.br

P. Jha et al. (eds.), *Labour Questions in the Global South*,
https://doi.org/10.1007/978-981-33-4635-2_9

2011 to 2014, but the growth rates remained fragile: On one hand, the preceding boom had provided some space for counter-cyclical policies, but on the other, the region remained vulnerable to the collapse of commodity prices (Ocampo 2009, p. 703; Fig. 9.1).

The reasons why these specific patterns of economic growth occurred are complex, contingent on the interdependence of domestic and external factors. However, from the point of view of the sectorial composition of the region as whole, two main features stand out during the 2000s, namely deindustrialization and 'primarization', that is, the predominance of primary goods exports in response to the higher export prices led by Chinese demand (Rapoport 2013, p. 176). With the exception of Mexico and some Central American and Caribbean countries where industrialization advanced through the 'maquilas', there has been an overall decline in the manufacturing sector as a share of GDP, as well as in the share of industrial employees, and an increase of the primary goods sector as a share of the total exports (Table 9.1).

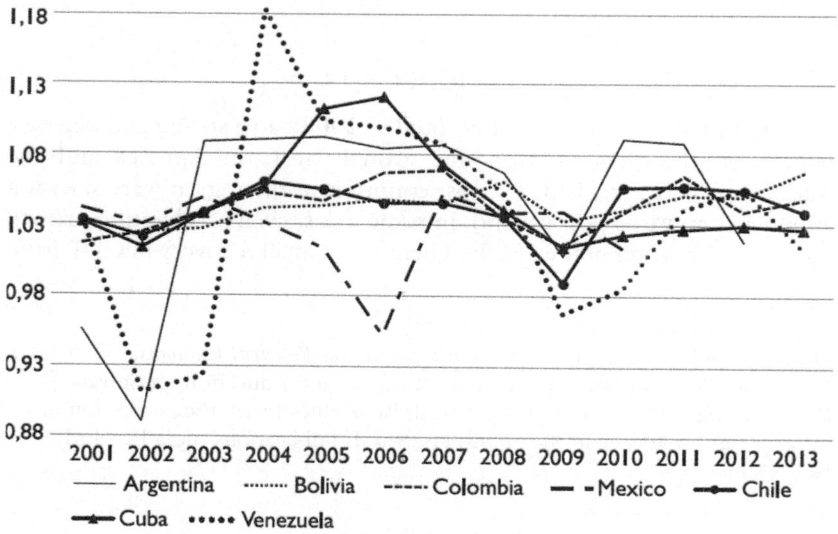

Fig. 9.1 Latin America and the Caribbean, Selected Countries, Rates of Growth of Annual Domestic Product, 2001–2013. (*Source*: ECLAC Statistics, 'Annual Gross Domestic Product (AGD) by Activity at constant prices in National Currency')

Table 9.1 Latin America and the Caribbean, Manufacturing as a Share of Annual Gross Domestic Product, Selected Countries, 2005–2014

	2005	*2006*	*2007*	*2008*	*2009*	*2010*	*2011*	*2012*	*2013*	*2014*
Argentina	0.18	0.18	0.17	0.16	0.16	0.16	0.16	0.15	0.15	0.15
Brazil	0.14	0.14	0.13	0.13	0.13	0.12	0.11	0.1	0.09	0.09
Bolivia	0.12	0.11	0.11	0.11	0.12	0.11	0.10	0.10	0.10	0.10
Chile	0.16	0.15	0.14	0.13	0.12	0.12	0.11	n.a	n.a.	n.a.
Colombia	0.14	0.14	0.14	0.14	0.13	0.13	0.12	0.12	0.12	0.11
Cuba	0.14	0.13	0.15	0.15	0.15	0.16	0.15	0.16	0.16	0.15
Mexico	0.17	0.17	0.17	0.17	0.16	0.17	0.16	0.17	0.17	0.17
Paraguay	0.12	0.12	0.11	0.11	0.12	0.11	0.11	0.11	0.11	0.11
Peru	0.17	0.16	0.17	0.16	0.15	0.16	0.15	0.15	0.15	0.14
Uruguay	0.15	0.15	0.14	0.15	0.15	0.14	0.13	0.12	0.11	0.12

Source: For Brazil, IBGE, Contas Trimestrais, Gross Domestic Product by Activity and Manufacturing, at current prices (Produto Interno Bruto e Indústria de Transformação), http://www.ibge.gov.br (accessed 15 June 2016); for others, ECLAC Statistics, 'Annual Gross Domestic Product (AGD) by Activity at current prices in National Currency'

In the countries where manufacturing advanced, a special kind of industrialization has emerged based on free trade agreements, low wages and production for the US market, hence devoid of a dynamic role in the economy (Curia 2011, p. 67). This holds also for countries in South America, such as Peru, Colombia and Chile, where the maquilas are also present, but less intensively; in these countries, the tendencies point similarly towards deindustrialization and the 'primarization' of exports. Yet, even the countries that did not sign broad free trade agreements, such as Argentina, Brazil, Uruguay and Venezuela, have come under the substantial influence of China's foreign trade, in terms of the export of raw materials and import of manufacturing goods. As a recent Economic Commission for Latin America and the Caribbean (ECLAC) survey (2016a, p. 36) observed, countries with direct and indirect exposure to China's economy face risks associated with the performance of China's economy.

The majority of the LAC countries saw upward trends in the share of primary goods exports (Table 9.2). This was the case of Argentina, Brazil, Bolivia, Chile, Colombia, Costa Rica, Ecuador, Jamaica, Paraguay, Dominican Republic, Uruguay and Venezuela. A second group, including Peru and Guatemala, showed stability, with an average of 85 and 37 per cent of primary goods as their main types of exports, respectively. A third

Table 9.2 Latin America and the Caribbean, Primary Goods as a Share of the Total Exports, Selected Countries, 2007–2014

	2007	*2008*	*2009*	*2010*	*2011*	*2012*	*2013*	*2014*	*2015*
Argentina	68.7	68.8	67.4	66.8	67.4	67.9	67.6	67.8	70.6
Barbados	52.6	52.0	29.2	28.3	65.3	55.1	58.8	55.4	38.3
Belize	91.7	98.6	98.6	98.6	91.3	97.9	91.5	82.9	77.6
Bolivia	93.0	94.2	94.2	93.6	95.9	94.7	96.0	96.4	93.1
Brazil	52.2	55.2	60.5	62.9	65.9	65.0	63.6	65.2	61.9
Chile	87.6	84.0	86.6	87.4	86.2	85.8	86.3	85.9	85.6
Colombia	59.7	67.6	70.8	76.1	80.6	82.5	82.4	82.4	75.8
Costa Rica	37.3	36.7	54.0	39.1	39.6	38.8	38.1	n.a.	46.4
Ecuador	91.4	91.3	90.8	90.2	92.1	91.0	93.3	93.9	92.3
El Salvador	24.7	25.6	27.7	27.2	31.2	28.9	26.6	24.2	23.7
Guatemala	50.3	53.0	56.8	57.3	60.7	59.4	58.7	60.8	57.3
Guyana	74.7	87.3	88.9	90.0	84.2	90.3	91.9	90.7	65.9
Honduras	70.8	n.a.	72.6	74.7	79.0	68.5	n.a.	60.3	n.a.
Jamaica	41.9	37.7	48.2	55.4	54.1	52.8	52.4	54.1	48.7
Mexico	27.9	26.4	24.0	24.0	27.6	25.7	23.7	21.2	17.1
Nicaragua	89.6	64.7	90.3	92.9	94.1	56.1	51.4	53.7	53.2
Panama	12.1	8.4	6.2	5.9	6.5	84.1	85.6	85.4	85.9
Paraguay	87.0	90.7	89.3	92.6	92.4	91.2	91.9	90.5	89.9
Peru	85.9	83.9	83.6	86.3	86.4	85.5	85.5	85.3	85.1
Dominican R.	22.2	28.6	27.6	32.3	33.1	35.0	33.9	37.9	31.8
Uruguay	68.4	71.0	74.4	74.0	72.0	75.9	75.6	76.3	74.8
Venezuela	n.a.	95.6	97.1	95.7	98.0	98.3	98.2	n.a.	n.a.

Source: ECLAC Statistics, 'Annual Gross Domestic Product (AGD) by Activity at current prices in National Currency'

group, consisting of Barbados, Belize, Guyana, Honduras, Mexico and Nicaragua, actually experienced a decline in the share of primary goods exports. Curiously, many Central American countries currently have more complex export lists than the larger economies of Argentina and Brazil. In Mexico and the Dominican Republic, primary goods tended to decrease as a share of the total exports, as a result of the high net capital inflows in the manufacturing sector, mainly coming from North American corporations. As we shall see, however, this did not translate into improved social conditions.

In political terms, between 2000 and 2015 there has been a differentiation in the region among governments that followed: (a) a nationalistic approach to economics and foreign relations; (b) a neoliberal path; (c) a mixed path; and (d) other cases. Venezuela, Bolivia, Nicaragua, Ecuador,

Uruguay and Argentina seem to be in the first group, while Costa Rica, Mexico, El Salvador, Peru, Colombia, Honduras, Belize, Panama and most of the Caribbean have been in the second, accompanied by Brazil, Chile and Guatemala in the third and Cuba in the fourth. Evidently, these classifications are subject to intense theoretical disputes, and depend on one's political assumptions (Burdick et al. 2009; Chodor 2015; Dos Santos 2016; Leiva 2008; Petras 2011; Ros 2015; Spronk and Webber 2015). However, it is clear that the emergence of centre-left parties in several countries in the 2000s was far from the general case.

In this article, we review the recent growth period in LAC countries up to the current crisis to provide an assessment of trends observed in the world of labour. Our assessment includes demographic trends, the employment structure, trends in unemployment and wages and the trajectory of social, racial and gender inequalities. We argue that the LAC region has undergone significant structural changes due to shifting positions in the international division of labour. The rural exodus has persisted, but also the industrialization patterns of the past have given way to renewed emphasis on primary goods exports, as well as new specialization patterns which favour low-paying jobs in services or industries of the 'maquila' type. The informal, or low productivity, sector has also expanded. The economic boom of the 2000s had some positive distributional effects, but made only limited inroads into the established racial and gender hierarchies, which found expression in persisting super-exploitation and extreme levels of violence and mass incarceration.

Demographic Trends

According to the United Nations Population Division, the LAC rural population peaked in 1990 and then started slowly to decline.[2] From 1950 to 1975, the rural population increased by up to 1.3 times, reaching 141 million people. This trend began to change in the 1980s, due to the decline of birth rates but also the process of urbanization. It is expected that the rural population will decline to 112 million in 2030, and to approximately 107 million in 2050. Yet, in relative terms, the share of rural population was only 19 per cent in 2015. Meanwhile, the urban population has more than doubled, from 197 to 502 million people in 1975–2015. Thus, overall, Latin American countries have become more and more urbanized in recent decades (see Fig. 9.2). These changes have not been equally distributed, and the different rates of urbanization are

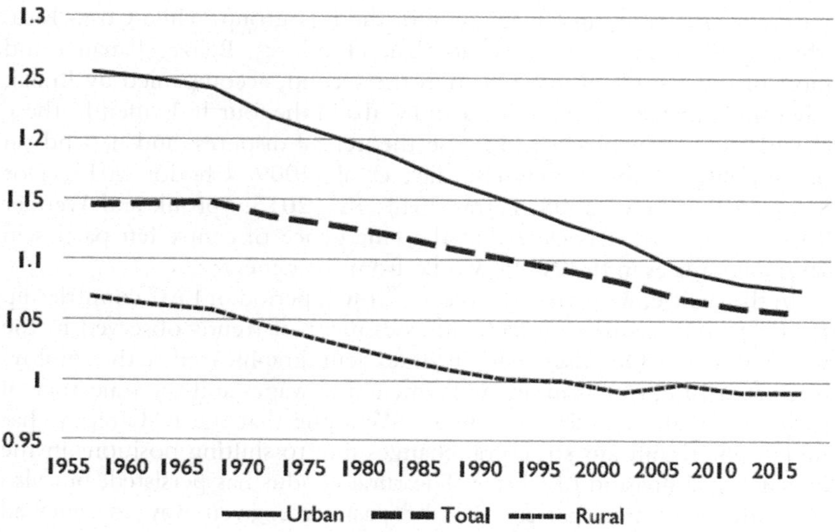

Fig. 9.2 Latin America and the Caribbean, Rates of Growth of Population, 1955–2015. (*Source*: ECLAC Statistics, 'Demographic and Social, Total Population by sex')

able to explain, at least partly, the different social conditions faced by the Latin American workers today. For example, in 1980–2015, the urban population increased by 2.14 times in Brazil, 2.29 times in Colombia, 2.91 in Ecuador, 3.39 in Paraguay, 4.44 in Guatemala.

Given current birth rates, the total LAC population will be growing for at least another 35 years, reaching approximately 781 million people in 2050. Although the rate of total demographic growth began to decline after 1970, it will reach zero only in 2050. Thereafter, the total population will begin to fall. This means that total population will be growing for many years, together within an increasingly ageing population. This situation poses the obvious challenge of coping with the high levels of poverty, high urban population rates and currently low economic growth, under conditions of a still growing and ageing population. As Milton Santos (2013 [1978], p. 57) observed, the growth model adopted added to the demographic explosion to result in an urban explosion and a concentration of both wealth and poverty in the cities (Santos 2013 [1978], p. 57).

Indeed, trends point to an increase in the population living in cities with above 100,000 people. In 2000 (the year of the last available data), this was the case for more than 62 per cent of the population in Argentina, 63 per cent in Chile, 50 per cent in Mexico, 53 per cent in Peru and 49 per cent in Brazil.[3] On the other hand, Cuba combined a lower rate of population growth (1.04 in 1955–2015) with a lower rate of urban population growth (1.37, in the same period). Cuba also had only 39 per cent of its population in 2000 living in cities with more than 100,000 people.

This condition explains, in part, the better social conditions in the island compared to LAC countries—which have had an average increase of 2.32 and 3.24 times in population growth and urban population growth, respectively, in the same period (1955–2015; see Table 9.3). Theoretically, the poor should have benefited from the fact that in 2005–2015, the rate of GDP growth was higher than the rate of population growth. However, distributional issues have qualified this, to which we will return.

Table 9.3 Latin America and the Caribbean, Rate of Population Growth and Rate of Gross Domestic Product Growth, Selected Nations, 2015/2005

2015/2005	*Population Growth*	*GDP*
Bolivia	1.16	1.63
Chile	1.09	2.06
Colombia (2014)	1.14	1.51
Cuba	0.99	1.49
Ecuador	1.17	1.46
Guatemala	1.27	1.44
Haiti	1.13	1.22
Mexico (2014)	1.12	1.23
Nicaragua	1.14	1.45
Paraguay	1.18	1.61
Uruguay	1.03	1.58

Source: Estimated by the authors from ECLAC Statistics, 'Population, by urban and rural areas, by sex' and 'Annual Gross Domestic Product (AGD) by Expenditure at constant prices in National Currency'

Employment Trends

The LAC region witnessed a process of intense urbanization, due to what Joan Robinson (1979, p. 134) once called 'the Latin America type of agri-business which monopolizes great areas of land to supply profitable markets in the West', associated with intense mechanization and land dispossession. In Mexico, Argentina and Brazil, this urbanization was once combined with a rapid process of accumulation of industrial capital in the metropolitan areas, which partly absorbed migrants from poor areas. But even so, it could not trigger a satisfactory process of economic and social development—not to mention the cases in which there was no significant accumulation at all.

The transfer of the rural population to urban areas has occurred without sufficient capital accumulation in the urban areas to compensate for the rural exodus.[4] This has created a historic impasse, whereby the labour force released from the countryside is not absorbed in adequate employment (Santos 2007, p. 42). The case of Brazil is the most radical example, as this country, with the largest territory among the LAC region, has never implemented any significant policy of land reform—in contrast to Bolivia, Mexico, Cuba or to a lesser degree Chile, Venezuela, Costa Rica and Peru.[5] As mechanization advanced in the countryside, the result has been one of rural exodus and urban poverty.

Beyond industry, 'modern services' (some of them necessary, but unproductive in material terms) historically have absorbed part of the migrant rural workers in the LAC region. Another part is taken up by so-called 'services' which are constituted by the economic activities of millions of poor working people, including domestic workers, waiters and waitresses, garage mechanics, sellers, drivers and diverse forms of self-employment—this constituting the majority of the modern urban proletariat in the LAC region (not to mention 'illegal' activities, which are more difficult to gauge).

We may begin by observing that the share of women in the total employment has been growing. In the period between 1999 and 2013, the share of women in employment increased from 53 to 60 per cent in Bolivia, from 43 to 50 in Brazil, from 31 to 44 per cent in Chile and from 38 to 55 in Paraguay. In the same period, women reached 51 per cent of total employees in Colombia, 42 per cent in Mexico and 45 per cent in Venezuela. For Latin America as a whole, the average share of women

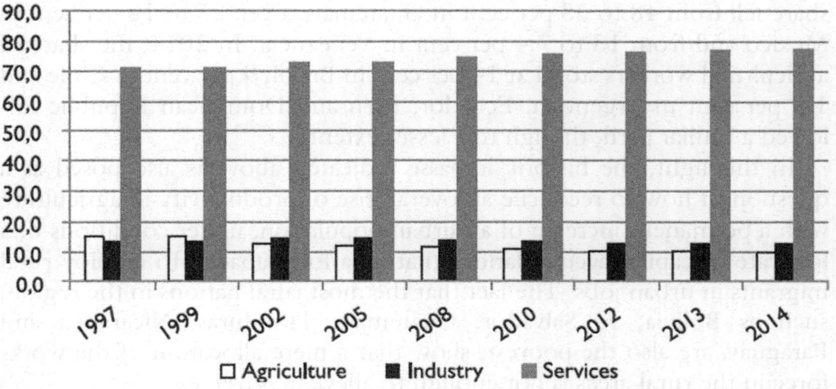

Fig. 9.3 Latin America and the Caribbean, Structure of the Total Occupied Population, 1997–2015, Weighted Average (%). (*Source*: ECLAC Statistics, 'Employment, structure of total occupied population, by main sector of economic activity and by sex and geographical area')

employed was 49 per cent in this period.[6] Latin American employees are now more or less equally divided between men and women.

Available statistics show that in Latin America as a whole the majority of the total occupied population in the recent years is being employed in the service sectors, above both agricultural and industrial sectors (see Fig. 9.3). The overall scenario of employment in Latin America in recent years is characterized by falling numbers of workers in agriculture, stagnation in industry/manufacturing and the advance of services. Among the latter, tourism became especially important to Cuba, Bahamas, Belize and other Caribbean nations, while financial services also spread generally, sometimes even as a conduit for money laundering (Bahamas, for example). Between 1997 and 2015, the share of workers employed in the services sector increased from 70 to 77 per cent, while the share of industrial and agricultural workers fell from 13.6 to 12.5 per cent and from 3.5 to 2.6 per cent, respectively (all data in weighted average).

Indeed, there has been a dramatic drop in the share of agricultural workers in almost all of LAC countries since the 1990s—a drop which was not interrupted by the 2008 crisis, including among the countries with the highest shares. In Bolivia, the share of agricultural workers declined from 40 per cent in 1997 to 29 per cent in 2014. Similarly, in 1989–2014, the share fell from 48 to 33 per cent in Guatemala, from 25 to 14 per cent in Mexico and from 13 to 7.4 per cent in Venezuela. In 2014, the share of agricultural workers stood at 14 per cent in Brazil, 9 per cent in Chile and 1.5 per cent in Argentina. Ecuador, Peru and Dominican Republic followed a similar path, though to a lesser extent.

In this light, the historic impasse indicated above is also posed as a question of how to reconcile an overall rise of productivity in agriculture with a permanent increase of an urban population, under conditions of a low rate of capital accumulation, that is, a low capacity to employ rural migrants in urban jobs. The fact that the most rural nations in the region, such as Bolivia, El Salvador, Guatemala, Honduras, Nicaragua and Paraguay, are also the poorest, show that a mere allocation of the workforce in the rural areas is not enough to alleviate poverty.

If we take into account the urban share of total employment, it is possible to see that, since 2005, there was a remarkable stability among its sub-groups, with falling rates of unemployment. Amidst the new 'populist wave',[7] some governments implemented progressive social and economic policies, but the economic structure in many of them did not suffer qualitative changes, in terms of industrialization or a return to the countryside. In fact, according to the official data, as mentioned earlier, many LAC countries increased their degree of 'underdevelopment', with the expansion of services not reflecting positive changes in production or the establishment of conditions for overcoming existing super-exploitative labour regimes.

Between 2005 and 2014, half of urban workers were employed in what ECLAC calls 'low productivity' jobs, also called 'informal', or what Santos (2013 [1978]) defined as the 'inferior circuit'. This sector presumably excludes industry and agriculture and includes mechanics, craftsmen and artisans. Over the last 10 years, the share of 'low productivity' workers declined slightly from 46 to 43.3 per cent (in weighted averages). The 'unskilled in commerce and services' have constituted the second major group of urban workers; its share fell by 1 per cent from 2005 to 2015. The third major group is constituted by the so-called 'microenterprise wage earners', whose share in the total is very stable (see Fig. 9.4).

Domestic employment fell from 6 to 5 per cent of total urban workers. 'Employers' constitute only an average of 3.5 per cent, this also being a very stable category. Indeed, since 1989, 'employers' have not been more than 3.5 per cent of the total urban population, showing that only a small fraction of the society tends to own the means of production. Figure 9.4

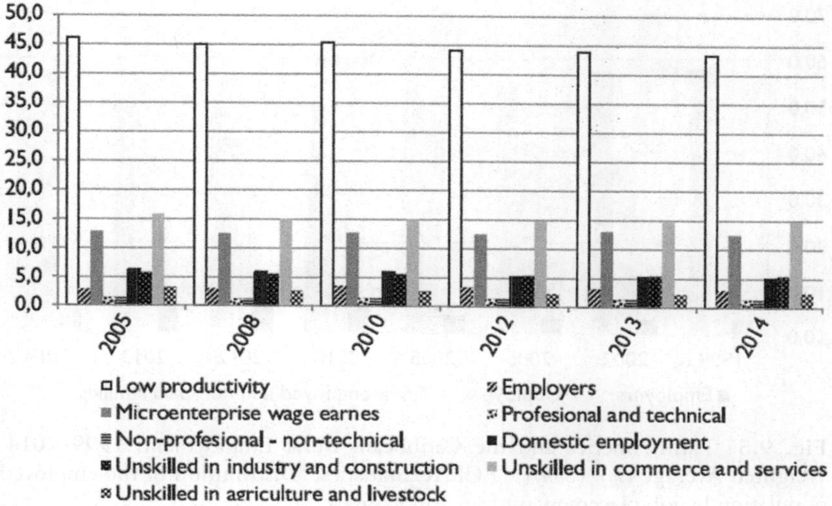

Fig. 9.4 Latin America and the Caribbean, Urban Employment, 2005–2014, Weighted average (%). (*Source*: ECLAC Statistics, 'Employment, structure of total occupied population, by main sector of economic activity and by sex and geographical area')

shows the trends relating to the types of urban work in Latin America, since 2005. There has been only a slight improvement in the 'quality' of urban jobs in Latin America (i.e., less 'low productivity') and a stable path concerning the rest.

In relation to the rural share of Latin American workers,[8] the poverty rates are, in general, higher than in urban areas (sometimes two times or more)—excluding only Uruguay and Chile, where poverty rates in rural areas are lower (there is no data regarding Argentina). Guatemala, Honduras and Nicaragua appear as borderline cases, with more than 70 per cent of the rural population living in poverty. The general differences between rural and urban areas, though diminishing in many cases, explains on the surface why the rural exodus continues.[9]

A general process of 'proletarianization' of rural working families is occurring, alongside the declining share of workers employed in agriculture. While the employers are no more than a small and stable fraction of the total, with an average share of 5.4 per cent in 2015, 'employees'

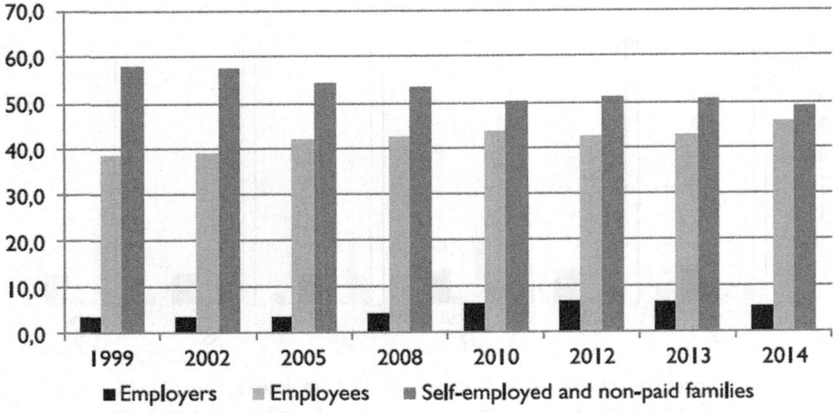

Fig. 9.5 Latin America and the Caribbean, Rural Employment, 1999–2014, Weighted Average (%). (*Source*: ECLAC Statistics, 'Distribution of the employed population by job placement and sex, rural area')

increased from 38 to 45 in 1998–2015. 'Self-employed and unpaid family workers' fell from 58 to 49 per cent in the same period. Workers specifically in agriculture, as an average share of the total rural workers, fell from 43 to 35 per cent. The share of workers in agriculture fell in Bolivia, Brazil, Chile, Costa Rica, Ecuador, Honduras, Panama, Paraguay and Uruguay; particularly in Mexico, the share of workers in agriculture dropped from 34 to 25 per cent in 1989–2000 and from 18 to 14 per cent in 2008–2015 (see Fig. 9.5).[10]

This general trend hides some differences, as some nations implemented different types of land reforms, leading to the formation of a group of 'petty bourgeois' producers with better social conditions when compared to the dispossessed. Mexico, which underwent an agrarian revolution (1910–1920), as Bolivia, which passed through a revolutionary process in 1952, and Uruguay, which had some distribution of land during the popular administration of José Battle y Ordóñez (1903–1907 and 1911–1915), all have the higher relative shares of rural employers, with an average of 11 per cent of the rural working population, in 2012. They are followed by a second group above the average, with Costa Rica and Venezuela, which also have implemented some (limited) policies of land redistribution. Brazil, Guatemala, Honduras, Panama and Dominican Republic have a share of 'employers' below the Latin American average, at 5.4 per cent in 2014. In Brazil, only 1.6 per cent of the total rural working population was considered as such, followed by Colombia and Paraguay, which stood at 3.9 and 5.1 per cent, respectively.

The average share of 'employees' in the rural areas also has shown important differences among the countries of the region. Despite the falling birth rates and continuing rural exodus (both reducing relative surplus population and the very quantity of labour), 'proletarianization' increased after 2008–2009 in Brazil, Chile, Costa Rica, Ecuador, Mexico, Panama, Paraguay and Peru, by a combination of ongoing mechanization, land dispossession and unsolved land conflicts. This process of 'proletarianization', however, did not occur in the Dominican Republic (where the rate is more or less stable since 2009), El Salvador and Bolivia (where the rate is, in fact, dropping since 2007). Bolivia has one of the lower rates of urbanization in the region, around 60 per cent, and the lowest rate of 'employees' in rural areas in 2014—only 12 per cent of the rural population, as opposed to 'self-employed' workers. The employees' rate reached 16 per cent in 2004. Apparently, some land distributions and nationalizations undertaken by the Evo Morales government had some effects in preventing the above-mentioned process of proletarianization', despite its contradictions (Dos Santos 2016, p. 198; see Fig. 9.6).

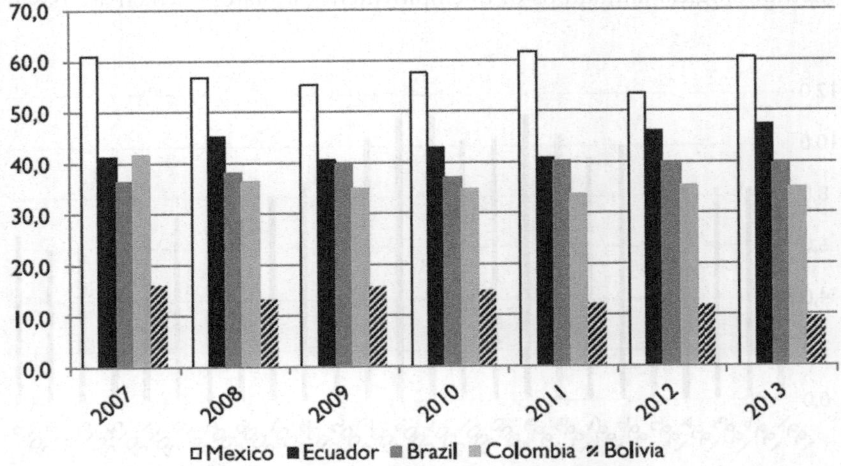

Fig. 9.6 Latin America and the Caribbean, Employees as a Share of the Total Rural Employment, Select Countries, 2007–2014, Weighted Average (%). (*Source*: ECLAC Statistics, 'Distribution of the employed population by job placement and sex, rural area, employees: total')

The general decline of workers in agriculture, in turn, was accompanied by a general increase of agricultural productivity in several LAC countries.[11] However, in Barbados, Cuba, Jamaica, Panama, Trinidad and Tobago and countries in the Caribbean, productivity remained stable or dropped. With respect to those countries which saw an increase in agricultural productivity, the increase was higher than the rate of the population growth. Within a decade, the indices of agriculture and food production increased by 43 per cent in Peru, 30 per cent in Argentina and Venezuela and 15 per cent in Mexico. Nonetheless, such higher production was not sufficient to eliminate dependence on food imports, such as in Venezuela and Bolivia, in part because it consisted of commodity exports such as soybeans.

Unemployment and Wages

The official overall rates of unemployment in LAC countries fell between 2003 and 2008 (Fig. 9.7). It was, in fact, a remarkable performance in light of the dramatic situation posed by the neoliberal tide since the 1980s. The average rates of unemployment reached 12 per cent in 2003 and fell continuously to approximately 7 per cent in 2008. We do not ignore the methodological limitations of unemployment estimates—which are based

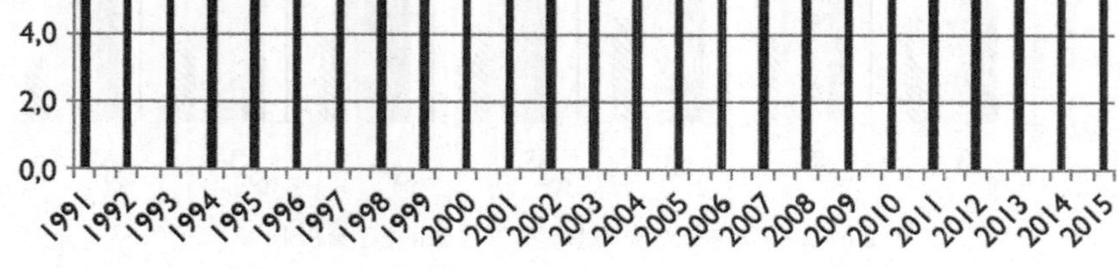

Fig. 9.7 Latin America and the Caribbean, Average Unemployment Rates, 1991–2015 (%). (*Source*: ECLAC Statistics, 'Unemployment rate by sex')

on unemployed workers who are in search of employment in the formal sector and exclude unemployed workers in the informal and rural sectors (Agenor and Montiel 2000, p. 78). A structural type of 'disguised unemployment' persisted in LAC economies during 2003–2009, perhaps at a level much higher than 8 or 10 per cent. However, the case for the official unemployment rates is still valid as a 'proxy' variable, in terms of a general analysis of the aggregate performance of these economies. Unemployment rates clearly dropped since 2003, after almost 14 years of a dramatic deterioration in labour market conditions (1990–2003). Yet, urban unemployment rates in the 15–24 age group remained the highest among all age groups, reaching an average rate of 17 per cent in 2005 and 15.1 per cent in 2014.[12]

The average rate of unemployment fell continuously between 2003 and 2015, with the exception of 2009, due to the uncertainties of the world economic crisis, the credit crunch and trade shocks. There was a slight recovery in 2010, but the crisis endured in the form of lower unemployment, even if not uniformly. Two major groups, in fact, appeared, one for which the rate of unemployment in 2015 was higher than in 2007, and another for which it was lower. But in most of the countries, official unemployment rates were lower in 2015 when compared to the pre-crisis levels, including Argentina, Cuba, Uruguay, Chile, Colombia, Paraguay, Peru and Venezuela. It is worth adding that, according to the International Labour Organization, trade union membership over these years was stable or declined, with the exceptions of Chile and Uruguay.[13]

In Cuba, where the official rate of unemployment is the lowest in the region, it more than doubled in 2009–2012, from 1.7 to 3.5 per cent, and then it dropped again, reaching 2.4 per cent in 2015 (Table 9.4). In Mexico, which had suffered a severe contraction in 2009, the unemployment rates fell continuously in 2011–2015, from 5.6 to 4.7 per cent, in 2015. On the other hand, in Costa Rica, El Salvador, Honduras, Jamaica and Brazil, the unemployment rates in 2015 were higher than in 2007, with Brazil pushing upwards the LAC average rate. This also partly explains Brazil's political instability and acute political conflicts at present.

Thus, the unemployment rates reacted distinctly after the 2008 crisis, revealing the differences in the region in terms of economic structure, foreign trade relations and domestic policies, as well as their different rates of population growth. Whether the labour market among LAC countries will converge in the following years will depend on various factors, external and domestic, including government capacity or will to manage

Table 9.4 Latin America and the Caribbean, Unemployment Rates, Selected Countries, 2006–2015 (%)

	2006	*2007*	*2008*	*2009*	*2010*	*2011*	*2012*	*2013*	*2014*	*2015*
Argentina	10.2	8.5	7.9	8.7	7.7	7.2	7.2	7.1	7.3	6.5
Bahamas	7.6	7.9	8.7	14.2	n.a.	15.9	14.4	15.8	14.8	12.0
Barbados	8.7	7.4	8.1	10.0	10.8	11.2	11.6	11.6	12.3	11.3
Belize	9.4	8.5	8.2	13.1	12.5	n.a.	15.3	13.2	11.6	10.1
Bolivia	8.0	7.7	4.4	4.9	n.a.	3.8	3.2	4.0	3.5	n.a.
Brazil	10.0	9.3	7.9	8.1	6.7	6.0	8.2	8.0	7.8	9.3
Chile	7.8	7.1	7.8	9.7	8.2	7.1	6.4	5.9	6.4	6.2
Colombia	12.2	10.7	11.0	12.3	11.8	10.9	10.6	10.1	9.5	9.2
Costa Rica	6.0	4.8	4.8	8.5	7.1	7.7	9.8	9.1	9.5	9.7
Cuba	1.9	1.8	1.6	1.7	2.5	3.2	3.5	3.3	2.7	2.4
Ecuador	8.1	7.4	6.9	8.5	7.6	6.0	4.9	4.7	5.1	5.4
El Salvador	5.7	5.8	5.5	7.1	6.8	6.6	6.2	5.6	6.7	n.a.
Guatemala	n.a.	n.a.	n.a.	n.a.	4.8	3.1	4.0	3.8	4.0	2.8
Honduras	4.6	4.0	4.1	4.9	6.4	6.8	5.6	6.0	7.5	8.8
Jamaica	5.8	6.0	6.9	7.5	8.0	8.4	9.3	10.3	9.4	9.5
Mexico	4.0	4.0	4.3	5.9	5.9	5.6	5.4	5.4	5.3	4.7
Nicaragua	7.0	5.9	6.1	7.9	7.8	5.9	5.9	5.6	6.6	n.a.
Panama	8.4	5.8	5.0	6.3	5.8	3.6	3.6	3.7	4.1	4.5
Paraguay	8.9	7.2	7.4	8.2	7.2	7.1	8.1	8.1	8.0	6.8
Peru	8.5	8.4	8.4	8.4	7.9	7.7	6.8	5.9	5.9	6.5
Dominican Republic	6.2	5.4	5.3	5.8	5.7	6.7	7.2	7.9	7.2	6.9
Trinidad and Tobago	6.2	5.6	4.6	5.3	5.9	5.1	5.0	3.7	3.3	3.5
Uruguay	11.3	9.8	8.3	8.2	7.5	6.6	6.7	6.7	6.9	7.8
Venezuela	10.0	8.4	7.3	7.9	8.7	8.3	8.1	7.8	7.2	7.0

Source: ECLAC Statistics, 'Unemployment rate by sex'

economic forces, not entirely dependent on foreign trade. In effect, the declining rates of GDP growth have impacted adversely on job creation, which decelerated from 3.1 to 0.8 per cent in 2012–2014, and which is likely to continue to decelerate for the region as whole (Economic Commission for Latin America and the Caribbean [ECLAC] and International Labour Organization [ILO] 2016, p. 11).

The performance of wages over time is a relatively good proxy of the performance of real wages in any country, and, in a broader sense, of the prevailing social conditions and the state of class relations. Real wages can be assessed according to different methodologies; here we will analyse the performance of minimum and average wages. In general, minimum wages are institutionally determined, by some criteria; while total average real wages are a sum of all wages paid, divided by the number of workers and deflated by any realistic inflation index. Of course, if minimum wages tend upwards, real average wages will also tend to rise. Both of them are subject to class conflicts; but the minimum wage, when it exists, is a legal basis for wages in general. All workers benefit from an increase in minimum wages, but among different kinds of work, wages differ. Be that as it may, both minimum wages and real wages cannot rise unless there is (a) a fall in unemployment rates and an increase in economic surplus to be divided among the classes, or (b) intensification of class struggles.

The ECLAC does not furnish data concerning average wages for all LAC countries.[14] A more detailed assessment would require data more comprehensive than those at our disposal, as well as a qualitative analysis to capture tendencies towards the erosion of working conditions, including situations of personal dependence analogous to slavery. The general performance of real wages also conceals important differences among countries. On one hand, as Ocampo observed (2009, p. 718), exchange rate appreciation was a common feature among LAC countries, which contributed to a rise in real wages, despite the deterioration in current accounts which it also caused. On the other hand, experiences have varied. In Argentina, Paraguay, Uruguay and Nicaragua, the average real wages recovered from the earlier 2001–2002 crisis, to rise until 2015. The same occurred in Brazil, but real wages dropped significantly in 2015. In Bolivia, wages dropped after 2006, and then recovered, but without reaching pre-2005 levels. The same occurred in Costa Rica, but wages recovered and were higher in 2015 than in 2009. In Chile and Colombia, the performance of real average rates showed ongoing growth. In Mexico, average rates increased from 1999 to 2007 and then stagnated. In Venezuela, real wages have been dropping since 2003, except for the short period between 2006 and 2008.

There is not a unique institutional methodology to determinate minimum wages in the LAC region.[15] Some countries have different minimum wages for different types of work (agricultural and urban employment, in Guatemala, for example), or different domestic regions (such as Mexico and Brazil). The pattern of the historical minimum wages is also not the same among the LAC countries; they are explained mainly by domestic variables, or more precisely, by the way in which every LAC country developed (or underdeveloped) and also suffered (or managed) the consequences of the changes in the international division of labour over time. It is not always possible to conceive an inverse relation between 'neoliberalism' and 'real wages', because the later also depends on broader considerations based on foreign trade and the domestic economic structure. But in the case of Brazil, Argentina, Uruguay, Bolivia, Ecuador and Mexico this inverse relation can be postulated.

In the case of Argentina, minimum wages were artificially increased during the dollarization period of the 1990s; the devaluation in 1991 was then followed by an extreme drop in real and minimum wages. Along the 2000s, during the Néstor and Cristina Kirchner governments, minimum wages recovered. In the case of Brazil, the increase in the minimum wages since 1990 was not sufficient to change drastically one of the worst concentrations of wealth in the world. During the governments of Lula da Silva (2003–2010) and Dilma Roussef (2011–2016), minimum wages were increased according to GDP growth and inflation rates. This situation, coupled with soaring exports and a decreasing rate of population growth, led to an overall increase in the real wages, as well as a decline in the Gini index.

In Mexico, from 1980 to 1993, minimum wages lost more than half of their real value, and lost further after the signing of the North American Free Trade Agreement in 1994. From 1995 to 2014, they continued to fall, under a succession of 'neoliberal' administrations, of Vicente Fox, Felipe Calderón and Enrique Peña Nieto (2000–2016). In all, by 2014, minimum wages were reduced to one-third of their value in 1980. Uruguay is in the middle ground, as it saw its real minimum wages drop drastically from 1985 to 1997, during the external debt crisis.

The emigration rates from the former so-called 'Latin American Switzerland' to other nations accelerated. Then, with the election of Tabaré Vásquez (from the left-wing Frente Amplio coalition, with former guerrilla leader Raúl Sendic as vice-president), minimum wages recovered by the successive enactment of laws (since then, the Frente Amplio has won all presidential elections).

In Venezuela, the neoliberal policies adopted during the 1990s have also had negative consequences for minimum wage policies, with wages falling from 1992 to 1999. During the first government of Hugo Chávez (1999–2001), the situation slightly improved, but not enough to prevent a new deterioration. The rise in the price of crude oil allowed the government to raise the minimum wage anew, but, as the Venezuelan economy remained largely dependent on this commodity, it was not possible to obtain a sustained rise in minimum wages, which have been declining since 2007. The recent decision by the OPEC to cut crude oil prices had a particularly dramatic impact on Venezuela, which helps to explain not only the performance of wages but also its political instability, which has intensified in the chavista government of Nicolás Maduro (since 2013).

In other 'neoliberal' experiences, such as those of Chile, Colombia and Peru, which signed free trade agreements with the USA over recent years and whose foreign trade depends heavily on commodities, the minimum wages increased during the 2000s—unlike neoliberal Mexico. From 2000 to 2014, minimum wages in Chile, Peru and Colombia increased by 49, 26 and 18 per cent, respectively, helped by soaring exports and cheaper imports, including appreciated exchange rates. It is worth noting, however, that in the 'non-neoliberal' Bolivia of the Movimiento al Socialismo (MAS), and in Ecuador, where the nationalist President Rafael Correa was elected in 2007, this pattern was also verified. On the other hand, Jamaica, Cuba and Paraguay saw their minimum wages drop after 2005 (see Table 9.5). Finally, although in real terms, most LAC countries tended to make gains in minimum wages, their rates of increase all declined after 2012.

Table 9.5 Latin America and the Caribbean, Selected Countries, Minimum Wages, 2007–2015 (2000 = 100)

	2007	*2008*	*2009*	*2010*	*2011*	*2012*	*2013*	*2014*	*2015*
Argentina	219.6	253.3	292.1	321.3	364.4	n.a.	n.a.	n.a.	n.a.
Bolivia	109.7	108.0	117.0	119.9	130.9	144.0	174.4	197.8	218.6
Brasil	154.8	160.8	172.7	182.1	182.1	197.5	202.7	203.6	203.3
Chile	118.5	118.3	124.7	127.7	129.8	133.5	139.9	145.3	149.1
Colombia	108.69	106.9	110.3	111.6	111.8	114.2	116.7	118.6	118.2
Costa Rica	100.8	99.5	103.3	105.8	107.2	109.1	110.3	112.8	116.8
Cuba	183.6	180.6	181.6	180.7	175.8	169.7	168.4	166.1	n.a.
Ecuador	135.1	146.7	152.0	161.7	170.2	179.1	190.0	196.1	196.4
El Salvador	92.7	92.9	101.9	100.9	100.8	101.9	103.1	108.1	113.3
Guatemala	117.7	111.9	117.7	122.0	130.7	134.4	135.3	137.4	140.9
Haití	64.8	56.4	72.2	114.1	105.3	107.1	124.8	129.2	128.7
Honduras	130.9	131.1	223.5	213.4	212.9	213.7	214.6	212.3	216.7
Jamaica	128.8	122.0	122.4	108.6	109.8	108.2	106.2	109.7	105.9
México	98.3	96.2	94.8	95.6	95.9	95.4	95.8	95.7	104.5
Nicaragua	131.6	141.6	165.5	174.7	182.9	190.2	200.3	210.1	224.3
Panamá	106.3	109.2	106.5	113.3	107.0	116.4	111.9	123.9	140.6
Paraguay	103.9	101.3	102.0	102.5	105.2	103.9	101.2	104.3	102.7
Perú	111.7	114.5	111.2	110.1	120.7	133.6	135.6	131.4	126.9
República Dominicana	93.8	87.7	93.9	93.5	94.6	97.3	100.3	102.7	110.1
Uruguay	159.6	176.9	194.4	196.8	227.7	252.8	256.1	166.1	273.3
Venezuela	114.4	107.1	99.4	93.8	92.9	97.0	93.4	94.1	n.a.

Source: ECLAC Statistics, 'Real minimum wage'

Social, Racial and Gender Inequalities

LAC societies continue to be highly unequal, with class relations being strongly conditioned by race and gender hierarchies, in line with the neocolonial paradigm. Born of genocide and slavery, most LAC societies are devoid of national cohesion, despite commonalities of language and religion in many countries. The national ideologies that emerged post-slavery reinstated the genocidal project, seeking to eliminate completely or reduce and suppress permanently black and indigenous peoples. Myths of nationhood evolved in the twentieth century to weave a mixed race, populist ideal under the control of the European settler element, which served the double purpose of projecting a benevolent view of the colonial past and denying black and indigenous people of their non- European origins (save for folklore). The genocidal project persisted in a sui generis neocolonial form, officially disregarding racial cleavages while organizing class relations precisely by race and propping up gender hierarchies in the interest of the same neocolonial order. The official recognition of institutionalized racism in several LAC countries in the more recent decades, on account of the emergent indigenous and black movements, has thrown the neocolonial paradigm into crisis, but has not overcome the problem.

Thus, the world of labour in the LAC region continues to be a world of severe inequalities, segregation and extreme violence. Inequalities exist between ethno-racial groups, between different sexes, between social classes and occupations, and between rural and urban populations. Black and indigenous women are generally employed in the lowest paying jobs; rural workers earn less than their urban counterparts; industrial workers earn more than service and agricultural workers; and whites are far wealthier and politically established than blacks and indigenous people. LAC societies are typically divided by a white and rich minority group—the ruling classes—and a black and indigenous majority which constitutes the bulk of the working people.

The economic boom of the 2000s followed a wave of democratic transitions in the 1980s and 1990s, which brought about a measure of relief. For example, the Gini coefficient in LAC countries generally improved during the 2000s, on account of the improved levels of employment which redistributed part of the economic surplus in the form of higher wages. Economic growth, when it occurs under minimally democratic conditions, is capable of redistributing wealth, and if this is coupled with lower population growth, the redistribution tends to be stronger. Low unemployment rates also tend to facilitate trade union organization and the strengthening of labour. This has been the recent experience of LAC countries, generally, whereby the concentration of wealth declined in 2000–2014, as unemployment rates dropped. Wealth concentration as measured by the Gini coefficient was lower in 2014 than in 2002 or 2003, in all selected nations (Table 9.6).

On the other hand, the Gini coefficients of the LAC region are still higher than the average of the 'Very High' and 'High' Human Development Nations, according to the methodology of the United Nations (2015, p. 216), whose averages stand at 0.327 and 0.397, respectively. Even the data regarding Venezuela, Mexico and Brazil, formally 'High Development Nations', remained above their poorer counterparts with regard to the Gini coefficient. Thus, excluding Uruguay, the increases in GDP and the higher wages, in most of the LAC countries in the 2000s, were not sufficient to lead to a pattern of wealth distribution similar to those existing in the majority of the 'developed' nations.

Another indication of measured improvement concerns the urban populations. Between 2000 and 2014, the rate of urban populations living in slums generally decreased, by as much as half in some cases, as in Argentina (from 30 to 15 per cent) and Costa Rica (from 10 to 5 per cent). Other countries showed slower rates of reduction, such as Brazil (from 29 to 22 per cent), Colombia (from 17 to 13 per cent) and Guatemala (from 42 to 34 per cent), while countries such as Ecuador, Panama and Suriname did not experience improvements in this regard. In Haiti, the rate actually increased from 70 to 74 per cent in 2005–2015, under the impact of the 2010 earthquake. Thus, the overall improvements did not include all nations.[16]

Racial and gender inequalities improved during the 2000s, but within the established hierarchies. According to ECLAC (2016b, p. 30), in 2014, 22 per cent of the Afro-descendants in Brazil were poor, compared to 10 per cent of Whites; in Ecuador, 42 per cent of Afro-descendants were poor, compared to 27 per cent of Whites. In Guatemala, 72 per cent of Indigenous were poor, compared to 59 of non-Indigenous; in Paraguay, 61 per cent of Indigenous were poor, compared to 30 per cent of non-Indigenous. In Bolivia, 42 per cent of Indigenous were poor, compared to 34 per cent of non-Indigenous. In all LAC countries, Indigenous were only 9 per cent of the richest quintile. Unpaid labour time performed by women was still at least twice that of men, in 2014–2015; in Mexico, women's unpaid working hours were almost three times higher than men's

Table 9.6 Latin America and the Caribbean, Selected Countries, Gini Index, 2000–2014

	Argentina	*Bolivia*	*Brazil*	*Chile*	*Colombia*	*Ecuador*	*El Salvador*	*Mexico*	*Paraguay*	*Peru*	*Venezuela*	*Uruguay*
2000	0.544	0.643		0.564	–	0.559	0.531	0.542	0.558	–	0.468	0.447
2001	0.560	0.609	0.639	–	0.567	0.539	0.525	–	–	0.525	0.486	0.452
2002	0.578	0.614	0.634	–	0.548	–	–	0.514	0.563	–	0.500	0.455
2003	–	–	0.621	0.552	0.553	–	–	–	0.536	0.530	–	–
2004	0.578	0.561	0.612	–	0.551	0.513	0.493	0.516	0.528	–	0.470	0.464
2005	0.558	–	0.613	–	–	0.531	–	0.528	–	–	0.490	0.451
2006	0.549	–	0.605	0.522	–	0.527	–	0.506	0.548	–	0.447	–
2007	–	0.565	0.590	–	0.562	0.540	–	–	0.529	0.500	0.427	0.457
2008	–	–	0.594	–	0.553	0.504	–	0.515	0.512	0.476	0.412	0.446
2009	0.510	0.508	0.576	0.524	0.557	0.500	0.478	–	0.533	0.469	0.416	0.433
2010	0.509	–	–	–	0.545	0.495	0.454	0.481	0.546	0.458	0.394	0.422
2011	0.492	0.472	0.559	0.516	0.536	0.460	–	–	0.502	0.452	0.397	0.402
2012	0.475	–	0.567	–	0.536	–	0.437	0.492	0.522	0.449	0.405	0.380
2013	0.472	0.491	0.553	0.509	0.535	0.477	0.453	–	0.536	0.444	0.407	0.383
2014	0.470		0.548	–		0.452	0.436	0.491		0.439	–	0.379

Source: ECLAC Statistics, 'Gini Index'. For Argentina and Uruguay, the data refer to urban areas

in 2014.[17] On the other hand, it is worth noting that the average working hours of employed women aged 15 and over declined in all LAC countries during the 2000s (the available data suggest that working hours have declined for all workers).[18]

Differences in education levels and incomes also remain stark, despite some improvements. In Brazil, Ecuador, Peru and Uruguay, Afrodescendent men obtained an average of 6.7 years of schooling in 2014, compared to 9.1 years among White men (ECLAC 2016b, p. 38). Afro-descendant women obtained, on average, one additional year of schooling in relation to Afro-descendant men. Yet, Afro-descendant women earned little more than half the income of Afro-descendant men (ECLAC 2016b, p. 38), while the latter received less than non-Afro-descendants in all levels of education. Even among the most educated, Afro-descendent men with a college degree earned, on average, only 75 per cent of the income of non-Afro-descendants; the earnings were still lower for Afro-descendent women with college degrees.

One of the most overlooked aspects of the recent period in the LAC region is the high level of violence that persists. On one hand, homicide rates (per 100,000 habitants) declined in the majority of the countries of the region in the 2000s. Indeed, if we consider homicide rates as being positively related to poverty, we could expect a reduction in poverty to be followed by a reduction in homicide rates. On the other hand, important cases, such as Venezuela and Mexico (since 2007), have experienced increased violence.[19] While a more careful analysis of race relations—in all cases, including the exceptions—is capable of revealing a more complex result. In Brazil, for example, while homicide rates eventually slowed, they have remained at civil war levels. In 2009, for example, at a rate of 30.5 homicides per 100,000 inhabitants, as officially reported by the ECLAC, the number of total homicides was approximately 60,000 people. Moreover, the relative share in the total homicides related to Afrodescendents, particularly young men, increased. The data show that 46 per cent more blacks died than whites in 2002, and this proportion increased to 67 per cent in 2005 and 103 per cent in 2008 (Instituto and Waiselfisz 2011, p. 154). Thus, despite the improvements in wages and inequalities measured by the Gini coefficient, black men died violent deaths at more than double the rate of whites. This suggests that the socioeconomic advances that have occurred within the established hierarchies have not necessarily improved race relations but, instead, have aggravated them. It is also interesting to note that suicide rates were higher in 2008 as compared to 2000 or 1990, in almost all LAC countries.[20]

The contradictory tendencies above in the world of labour gain even more complex dimensions if incarceration rates are considered, which increased in the majority of the LAC countries during the 2000s (Table 9.7).

Indeed, the upward tendency in the incarceration rate was widespread, excluding only Ecuador and Honduras. In Brazil, El Salvador and Uruguay, the rate of incarceration was 2.29, 2.93 and 2.49 times higher, respectively, than the rate of population growth. The fact of rising incarceration rates at a time of falling unemployment leads us to a more realistic evaluation of the type of economic growth that LAC countries have experienced. In Brazil, for example, if we add, for 2009, the approximately 60,000 people murdered to the approximately 529,000 individuals incarcerated (approximately 264 per 100,000 inhabitants), and deduct the total murdered and incarcerated from total economically active population of 99,193,885 people, the official rate of unemployment for 2009 would have to be at least adjusted from 9 to 9.5 per cent.

It lies beyond our scope here to analyse fully the dynamics of such genocidal levels of violence and incarceration, which afflict

Table 9.7 Latin America and the Caribbean, Selected Countries, Rate of Population Growth and Rate of Imprisonments, 1995–2010

Countries	*(a) Population*	*(b) Imprisonment*	*(b)-(a)*
Argentina	1.15	1.95	0.80
Bolivia	1.32	2	0.68
Brasil	1.2	2.75	1.55
Chile	1.18	2.04	0.86
Colombia	1.26	2.01	0.75
Ecuador	1.32	1.01	-0.31
El Salvador	1.08	3.17	2.08
Honduras	1.36	1	-0.36
México	1.22	1.95	0.73
Panama	1.33	1.42	0.09
Peru	1.22	1.77	0.55
Uruguay	1.04	2.59	1.55
Venezuela	1.31	1.67	0.36

Source: ECLAC Statistics, 'Prison population rate' and 'Demographic and Social, Total Population by sex'. For Bolivia and Venezuela, imprisonments in 1996–2011

disproportionally non-white youth. Much of the incarceration and violence, for example, relates to petty crimes and also the fact that the drug trade is criminalized and gun possession highly diffused. There is also a technical and institutional apparatus that feeds on repression and violence, including the diffusion of security cameras, the privatization of prisons and the setting of 'minimum goals' to justify state security budgets. To aggravate the 'public security' situation further, there has been an evolving region-wide 'war on drugs' propagated by US imperialism since the 1980s, whose effect has been to militarize the contradictions of a development model that has consistently produced a large and expanding reserve army of labour.

Conclusion

The LAC region experienced improvements in social conditions in the 2000s. However, the gradual unravelling and restructuring of industrial sectors since the 1980s, and the ongoing denationalization of economies, all contributed to an intensification of the effects of the world economic crisis that struck in 2008. The improvements in social conditions became unsustainable, both economically and politically, as implicit and fragile class/race/gender pacts came undone, especially after 2014–2015, and the ruling classes of the region—perennially fascist in their basic reflexes—reclaimed the initiative in the interest of 'public security' (Barbosa 2009).

The rural exodus persists, but the rate of population growth is decreasing. The region still relies heavily on primary commodity exports. Excluding Mexico and some smaller countries, the contribution of industry to GDP declined, while the majority of the workforce is still allocated in 'low productivity' jobs. The transition to a peripheral 'post-industrial' or 'postfordist' regime of low accumulation, based on primary production and persisting super-exploitation in new activities, has also led to an overall change in the way working people pursue their livelihoods and organize themselves.

Overall, the falling rates of population growth in the region pose a new challenge to the ruling classes: within two or three decades, an important part of the reserve army of labour will retire—and there are no grand immigration solutions here. The ruling classes in the region are likely to opt for increasingly authoritarian means to solve the question of a declining reserve army of labour—given the low capacity of producing an economic surplus for the maintenance of class and racial hierarchies—just as they have sought historically to solve the question of a bourgeoning reserve army of labour.

It has been beyond our scope here to pursue at length the sociopolitical consequences of the above structural changes. Nonetheless, by way of conclusion, it is worth noting that the consequences have been, indeed, substantial. The spread of drug production and trafficking has continued to penetrate society and politics, especially in countries such as Colombia, Mexico and Brazil, as well as the Caribbean. Meanwhile, trade unionism in many countries has subsided, together with deindustrialization, while churches have advanced rapidly among working people, especially Evangelical churches. Yet, another feature of LAC society is the often strong presence of rural movements and landless peoples' movements, both urban and rural, which serve as organizing centres of the reserve army of labour, in competition or co-existence with the expanding influence of churches. Black, indigenous and women's movements have also been on the rise, becoming among the most combative in a number of cases.

Acknowledgement We would like to thank Jorge Américo de Toledo, Sammer Siman and Yu Huang for reading and commenting on the ideas presented in this text.

Notes

1. We adopt this term for reasons of simplicity and convenience; 'Nuestra América' or 'Afro-Latin America' may be more adequate.
2. See ECLAC Statistics, 'Population'.
3. See ECLAC Statistics, 'Population in localities with 20,000 or more, and 100,000 or more inhabitants'.
4. In the case of Cuba after 1959, because of the emigrations (referring to those who left Cuba after the revolution), the already existing small population and the further reorganization led by the socialist revolution, the authorities did not face 'excessive unemployment' and were thus able to allow internal migrations (Feder 1975).
5. It has been observed in relation to Brazil that the presence of a reserve army of labour has constituted a pillar of economic expansion by means of the super-exploitation of labour (Kowarick 1981, p. 46). With regard to the land reforms and associated difficulties in Chile, Venezuela, Peru and Argentina, see French-Davis (1994, p. 194), Feder (1975) and Peralta Ramos (2007, p. 97).

6. See ECLAC Statistics, 'Relación Empleo-Populación por sexo'.
7. We use the expression 'populist' as Ernesto Laclau (2008), without pejorative connotations.
8. See ECLAC Statistics, 'Distribution of the employed population by job placement and sex, rural area'.
9. See ECLAC Statistics, 'Population living below the extreme poverty and poverty lines, by geographical area'.
10. See ECLAC Statistics, 'Distribution of the employed population by job placement and sex—rural area'.
11. See ECLAC Statistics, 'Agriculture production indices'.
12. Argentina and Uruguay had the highest urban unemployment in the 15–24 age group, at 18 and 20 per cent, respectively; see ECLAC Statistics, 'Urban open unemployment rate, by sex and age group'.
13. In Chile, particularly, the number of trade union members more than doubled between 2000 and 2013, which helps explain the growth of wages in this country, while in other countries this did not occur; see ILO Statistics, 'Trade union membership of persons employed and employees by sex'.
14. See ECLAC Statistics, 'Annual real average wages'.
15. See ECLAC Statistics, 'Real minimum wage'.
16. See ECLAC Statistics, 'Urban Population living is slums'.
17. See ECLAC Statistics, 'Unpaid Working Time by Sex'.
18. See ECLAC Statistics, 'Working hours of employed women aged 15 and over as the number of children 0 to 5 years of age in the household, urban and rural areas', and also ILO Statistics, 'Mean weekly hours actually worked per employed person by sex and economic activity'. The latter does not cover all Latin America and the Caribbean.
19. See ECLAC Statistics, 'Tasa de homicididos, por sexo'.
20. See ECLAC Statistics, 'Tasa de mortalidad por suicidios y lesiones autoinfligidas, por sexo'.

References

Agenor, P.-R., & Montiel, P. J. (2000). *La macroeconomía del desarrollo.* Mexico City: Fondo de Cultura Económica.

Barbosa, W. N. (2009). *A discriminação do negro como fator estruturador do poder. Sankofa: Revista de História da África e de Estudos da Diáspora Negra* (p. 87). São Paulo: Universidade de São Paulo.

Burdick, J., Oxhorn, P., & Roberts, K. (Eds.). (2009). *Beyond Neoliberalism in Latin America? Societies and Politics at the Cross Roads.* London: Palgrave Macmillan.

Chodor, T. (2015). *Neoliberal Hegemony and the Pink Tide in Latin America Breaking Up with TINA?* London: Palgrave Macmillan.

Curia, E. (2011). *El modelo de desarrollo en Argentina. Los riesgos de una dinámica pendular*. Buenos Aires: Fondo de Cultura Económica.

Dos Santos, F. L. B. (2016). *Além do PT. A crise da esquerda brasileira em perspectiva latino-americana*. São Paulo: Elefante Editora.

Economic Commission for Latin America and the Caribbean (ECLAC). (2016a). *Economic Survey of Latin America and the Caribbean 2016*. Santiago: United Nations.

Economic Commission for Latin America and the Caribbean (ECLAC). (2016b). *La matriz de la desigualdad social en America Latina*. Santiago: United Nations.

Economic Commission for Latin America and the Caribbean (ECLAC) and International Labour Organization (ILO). (2016). *Coyuntura Laboral en América Latina y el Caribe. Mejoras recientes y brechas persistentes en el empleo rural* (N. 14). Santiago.

Feder, E. (Ed.). (1975). *La lucha de clases en el campo. Análisis estructural de la economía latinoamericana*. Mexico City: Fondo de Cultura Económica.

French-Davis, R. (1994). The Latin American Economies, 1950–1990. In L. Bethell (Ed.), *The Cambridge History of Latin America Volume VI, Part 1, Latin America Since 1930*. Cambridge: Cambridge University Press.

Instituto, S., & Waiselfisz, J. J. (2011). *Mapa da Violência 2012. A cor dos homicídios no Brasil*. São Paulo: CEBELA, Centro Brasileiro de Estudos Latino-Americanos.

Kowarick, L. (1981). El precio del progreso: crecimiento económico, expoliación urbana y la cuestión del medio ambiente. In O. Sunkel & N. Gligo (Eds.), *Estilos de Desarrollo y Medio Ambiente en America Latina*. Mexico City: Fondo de Cultura Económica/El Trimestre Económico.

Laclau, E. (2008). *La razón populista*. Buenos Aires: Fondo de Cultura Económica.

Leiva, F. I. (2008). *Latin America Neostructuralism: The Contradictions of Postneoliberal Development*. Minneapolis: University of Minnesota Press.

Ocampo, J. A. (2009). Latin America and the Global Financial Crisis. *Cambridge Journal of Economics, 33*(4), 703–724.

Petras, J. (2011). *Social Movements in Latin America: Neoliberalism and Popular Resistance*. New York: Palgrave Macmillan.

Ramos, P. (2007). *Mónica. La economía política argentina: poder y clases sociales (1930–2006)*. Buenos Aires: Fondo de Cultura Económica.

Rapoport, M. (2013). *En el ojo de la tormenta. La economía política argentina y mundial frente a la crisis*. Buenos Aires: Fondo de Cultura Económica.

Robinson, J. (1979). *Aspects of development and underdevelopment*. Cambridge: Cambridge University Press.

Ros, J. (2015). *Development macroeconomics in Latin America and Mexico*. London: Palgrave Macmillan.

Santos, M. (2007). *Ensaios sobre a Urbanização Latino-Americana*. São Paulo: Edusp.

Santos, M. (2013 [1978]). *Pobreza Urbana*. São Paulo: Edusp.

Spronk, S. J., & Webber, J. R. (2015). *Crisis and Contradiction: Marxist Perspectives on Latin America in the Global Political Economy*. Boston: Leiden.

United Nations. (2015). *Human Development Report 2015*. New York: United Nations Development Program.

CHAPTER 10

Primitive Accumulation and Exploitative Labour Relations in Zimbabwe's Artisanal and Small-Scale Gold Mining (ASGM) Sector: The Case of Mhondoro Ngezi

Grasian Mkodzongi

Introduction

One of the major outcomes of Zimbabwe's Fast Track Land Reform Program (FTLRP) implemented in 2000 was the way it allowed landless peasants access to land and natural resources which had been enclosed and enjoyed by a few whites (Moyo 2011; Mkodzongi 2016; Mkodzongi and Spiegel 2018). After land reform, there is now improved mobility across former large-scale commercial farms which were earlier enclosed and inaccessible. Moreover, access to land and natural resources has led to an increase in natural resource extraction activities. This is especially the case with the artisanal and small-scale gold mining (ASGM), which has become

G. Mkodzongi (✉)
Tropical Africa-Land and Natural Resources Research Institute,
Harare, Zimbabwe

P. Jha et al. (eds.), *Labour Questions in the Global South*,
https://doi.org/10.1007/978-981-33-4635-2_10

a key economic activity undertaken by a socially differentiated group of people such as the peasants, unemployed youths, politicians and Chinese individuals and companies. The engagement of peasants and other unemployed people in ASGM across the world has been extensively explored by research scholars (Bryceson and Jønsson 2009; Maconachie and Hilson 2011; Hilson and Garforth 2012; Spiegel 2014; Mkodzongi and Spiegel 2018), and its contribution to the livelihoods of the rural poor is the focus of on-going debate (Bryceson et al. 2000; Mabhena 2012; Mkodzongi and Spiegel 2018). Moreover, a more recent literature has explored the forces behind the new scramble for Africa's natural resources (Moyo et al. 2019) and the expanding gold commodity frontier (Verbrugge and Geenen 2018). Others have highlighted the adverse incorporation of local communities into capitalism through the widening of commodity frontiers (Moore 2000). Debates about the 'frontier' has also escalated, with some scholars highlighting how the frontier operates, its logic and modus operandi and links to global capitalism (Moore 2000). The frontier has also been highlighted as place where a form of local democracy can eventually emerge, allowing some people to exit when better livelihood opportunities emerge (Bryceson 2018). This essay does not aim to engage with these wider debates, but it seeks to build upon some of the more recent literature which focuses on the dynamics of the global expansion of ASGM and the way in which it 'touches down' at various locales across countries and regions (Verbrugge and Geenen 2018). In particular it explores how the global expansion of gold mining and in particular ASGM has intensified exploitative labour relations, which results in the adverse incorporation of local communities into global capitalism. Under this process, the poor and vulnerable who tend to do most of the laborious work of digging and processing of ores are exploited through poor remuneration and harsh working conditions. Those who get a lion's share out of the proceeds of mining are located higher up in the ASGM value chain.

While considering the dynamics of ASGM it is important to bear in mind that miners often operate in hazardous environments such as dilapidated mine shafts which are prone to curving in and flooding. They also face periodic violence sponsored by criminal gangs who sometimes operate in collaboration with different arms of the state like the police and the military. Apart from its exploitative nature, ASGM contributes significantly to ecological destruction which has a negative impact on rural livelihoods in the long term. The essay attempts to map the interrelationship and dynamics of labour relations and environmental degradation in

Zimbabwe's ASGM sector during a new phase of primitive accumulation. It largely relies on ethnographic data gathered over a ten-year period with peasants and unemployed youths engaged in ASGM in central Zimbabwe.

Primitive Accumulation Under a New Scramble in the Extractive Sector: Conceptual Debates

According to Verbrugge and Geenen (2018), research on 'resource extraction is abound with the frontier concept. The frontier concept has been used as a 'metaphor to describe wild and unruly places' and the 'global expansion of capitalism' (Moore quoted in Verbrugge and Geenen 2018). The widening of the gold mining frontier under a new 'scramble' (Moyo et al. 2019) has not only intensified exploitative labour relations in the global resources sector, but also facilitated the 'adverse' incorporation of local communities into global capitalism as low-paid wage labourers (Hickey and Du Toit 2007). According to Moore (2000), 'capitalism should be understood as a socio-ecological system that constantly reproduces itself through the appropriation of ecological surplus (quoted in Verbrugge and Geenen 2018:2). Similarly, Moyo et al. (2019:5) have argued that the 'current scramble for Africa is shaped by important historical specificities associated with the continent's pre-colonial integration into the world economy as a slave reserve and its relatively recent history of colonial subjugation..'. They further argue that 'primitive accumulation under capitalism is not a one-off event to establish the historical conditions for expanded reproduction … imperialism has systematically deployed extra-economic and violent force to commodify both labour and land and to offload the costs of social reproduction onto the working peoples themselves'. Exploitative labour relations which dominate within the ASGM sector thus signify a process of super-exploitation characterised by the 'exploitation of labour through the appropriation of labour power far beyond the labour necessary for the social reproduction of the workforce' (Ibid:6). Similarly, in his classic study of imperialism, Bukharin (1972:96) noted that when capital is sent to foreign countries (in this case the periphery), 'it is not done because there is no employment to be had for it at home' but is done because it can be employed at a higher rate of profit in a foreign country'.

Under the unfolding gold commodity frontier, the periphery (there most artisanal mining is taking place) is a perfect zone for exporting capital at higher profit returns due to the casualisation of labour and low wages. The global expansion of the gold mining (characterised by the expansion of ASGM) due to increasing scarcity of gold (Verbrugge and Geenen 2018) has thus intensified the super-exploitation of local communities through casualisation of labour. ASGM is thus increasingly becoming the major source of gold at a time when the profitability of corporate mines has been undermined by difficult geological conditions. Under a 'widening' gold commodity frontier, wages are exploited through low wages and the levying of various rents which are intended to 'subsidise' capital in order to maintain a high rate of profit (Bukharin 1972).

The widening of the gold mining frontier through the ASGM has also left local communities vulnerable to the shocks of fluctuating commodity markets which are characterised by 'boom and bust' cycles. These cycles can take a 'few months to years, with underlying long term super cycles that can span several decades' (Niederberger et al. 2016:412). Although specific metals and minerals have their own market dynamics depending on their use and characteristics, these correlate with super cycle developments'[1] (Ibid:412). Boom and bust cycles can undermine 'profits' and thus require capital to look for areas where profits can be maximised. In the case countries of periphery provides a perfect opportunity for super profits. After the global financial crisis of 2008, gold became a safe haven for investments, as capitalists ran away from risky investments in the stock market. Investments in gold have in turn led to a steady boom in gold prices surpassing the prices of other precious metals such as PGMs which are experiencing low demand. According to Seccatore et al. (2014:662), there has been an 'increase in gold price of over 400 per cent between 2002 and 2012, due to a shift towards safe investments in a period of crisis in the global economy. This has created a rapid increase in gold production' Geenen (2015:138). The ASGM has been one the major contributors to increased production. Similarly, it has been observed that between 2003 and 2012 the price of gold on the global market increased by 18 per cent, with a decrease of 17 per cent in the first half of 2013.

The above show how gold has attracted capital investments at a time of global financial market volatility. Increasing investments have led to the unfolding global gold commodity chain which is characterised by new gold mining constellations. The new gold production network (of which a significant part is artisanal) has relied on technological innovation and cheap labour to expand and increase production and profits during a time of scarcity. Hence the expansion of the sector is characterised by synergies between corporate mines and artisanal operators. These synergies can involve tribute payment arrangements and technological transfer in order to boost production. For example some struggling corporate mines have deliberately allowed artisanal miners to access mine shafts at some of their claim areas in exchange of tribute. Others have entered into a more formal arrangement where artisanal miners are allowed access to corporate claim areas on condition that they sell their gold to the claim owners. In some places, gold mining constellations have produced mixed scenarios which require further investigation. Competition over 'scarce' gold due to ecological limitations have in some places led to conflicts between corporate mines and ASGM operators who may be encroaching on private mining claims without an agreement with the owners. In some places, illegal mining by artisanal miners has been used as a negotiating tactic in order to enter into a more formal tribute payment arrangement with claim owners. A major question to be asked is: how is the widening of the gold commodity frontier intensifying the super exploitation of local populations? In order to answer this question, one must first examine how labour is mobilised and organised in the ASGM sector. Our work in central Zimbabwe (Mkodzongi and Spiegel 2018) shows that wage labourers in mines generally work under a syndicate comprising of a few people to a large group depending on the size of the workings. On top of the syndicate is a so-called 'sponsor', a de facto employer who provides equipment and food to those who do the actual work of digging. Syndicate members are thus de facto wage labourers working under an employer who provides capital to procure tools, food and other mining equipment. Most of the mining involves hard labour, breaking rocks, removing the overburden and bringing out the ore outside pits in semi-mechanised conditions of many artisanal operators. In some places, the ore must be transported to a nearby milling station where it is beneficiated. Since most artisanal miners lack capital and equipment to mine and process gold, they rely on sponsors for them to make a living from gold mining. This desperate situation leaves them vulnerable to exploitative labour arrangements and hazardous working environments imposed by sponsors. Payment in the ASGM sector is normally based on 'gold' and not cash. The sponsor makes money by deducting an agreed percentage (as a form of agreed rent) for his equipment hired out to the miners, for milling the ore (sponsors can also be mill owners) and money advanced to miners. In many places miners can be left with a tiny percentage of the gold milled after all deductions are made. Apart from losing gold through unfair labour arrangements, miners can also lose money to sponsors through unfair pricing mechanisms. Since the sponsor can also act as a gold buyer; he takes advantage of the fact that miners are generally afraid of travelling to places that offer better prices as they can be arrested if found in possession of gold as they do not have the legal paper work to sell gold. In addition, miners may make distress sales of gold amalgam to any available buyer instead of looking for a better market because they are in need of money for their daily needs. It is generally the sponsor who gets the lion's share of proceeds of gold under artisanal production. In some places miners can end up as indentured labourers or in bondage due to their inability to pay back money advanced to them by sponsors. This can force them to work under dangerous conditions in order to pay off debts. While in some places miners are able to organise themselves without a sponsor and run a successful gold mining operation, this is very rare.

Under the unfolding gold mining frontier, sponsors have played a pivotal role in the integration of artisanal miners into global commodity circuits under conditions unfavourable to them. This process has intensified especially under the current Zimbabwean government (which has reversed local empowerment regulations) which has promoted the penetration of global mining capital into the Zimbabwean countryside under a new 'scramble' for extractives. This scramble is characterised by the increasing number of so-called 'foreign investors' of different nationalities including the Chinese. The later have become dominant players in the ASGM value chain, supplying milling equipment and sponsoring syndicates to mine on their behalf. As a result, the upsurge in Chinese investments have led to the ramping up of gold production which has boosted gold output. The Chinese have also brought in significant amount of capital which has further boosted production and deepened the exploitation of peasants and other unemployed people who have been forced to engage in ASGM as wage labourers. While ASGM has contributed livelihoods at a time of a deep economic crisis rooted in the confrontation between Zimbabwe and foreign capitalists during the implementation of radical land reforms, the ramping up of gold production in the ASGM sector under an expanding gold mining frontier signifies a new wave of primitive accumulation of capital which is yet to be fully explored in literature (ASGM produced gold has surpassed that of big corporate mines mines). Primitive accumulation has also intensified environmental degradation and pollution of underground and surface water sources. It has also led to the widespread damage to habitats, ecosystems which poses hazards to fauna and flora. These negative impacts of the widening of the gold mining frontier under a 'new scramble' (Moyo et al. 2019) cannot be fully explored here and thus require further research.

Fast Track Land Reforms and the New Gold Mining Frontier

The upsurge in ASGM activities in Zimbabwe has been largely linked to the change in agrarian structure which allowed landless peasants access to land and other natural resources which were formerly enclosed to them under a bi-modal agrarian structure inherited from colonialism. In the aftermath of the land reforms implemented in 2000, smallholder agriculture and artisanal gold mining are now intertwined (Mkodzongi and Spiegel 2018). Moreover, the implementation of the Zimbabwe's indigenisation and local empowerment regulations in 2010, in a highly charged political environment and a diplomatic stand-off with western countries, gave impetus to grassroots discourses of local ownership of natural resources natural popularised by the ruling Zimbabwe African National Union Patriotic Front (ZANU PF) (Mkodzongi 2016). Such discourses influenced the way unemployed people and peasants illegally occupied gold mines on private concessions that were deemed to be foreign owned. In some places, claim owners were either expelled or a deal was struck to allow miners access on a tribute payment arrangement. The implementation of indigenisation and local empowerment regulations thus influenced the widening of gold mining frontier by allowing peasants and unemployed youths access to gold ores that were previously in accessible to them under the colonial era agrarian structure dominated by a few white farmers. The implementation of Zimbabwe's fast track land reforms coincided with the global crisis facing the gold mining sector. The crisis is rooted in in the scarcity as major gold producing countries such as South Africa, Australia and the United States of America are facing a decline in production of gold thereby leading to the closure of major mine shafts (Verbrugge and Geenen 2018). Moreover, the increasing scarcity of gold has led to the deepening of mine shafts to reach inaccessible ores and the widening of the gold commodity frontier to remote locations in search of gold. These macro-trends have been a factor in the upsurge of the ASGM sector especially in Africa and other countries in the south. I have noted elsewhere (Mkodzongi forthcoming) how the gold commodity frontier 'touches down' (Verbrugge and Geenen 2018) in Zimbabwe. As discussed later in this essay, the advancement of the 'frontier' results in gold mining constellations which have influenced diverse socio-economic and political dynamics. For example in some places it has led to synergies between large corporate mines and artisanal gold miners and in others it has resulted in fatal conflicts over access to gold ores. These conflicts are also influenced by class dynamics and local politics which tend to favour politically connected individuals at the disadvantage of the poor.

Another fallout of the expanding 'frontier' is shown by recent work in the ASGM sector, we have explored how 'migrant workers make frontier culture' (Mkodzongi and Spiegel forthcoming; Peluso 2018), and how they resist super-exploitation by moving from one location to the other in search of better remunerative livelihoods (Bryceson 2018). The widening of the gold mining frontier during a changing agrarian situation thus signify what Moyo et al. (2019:11) have called a 'third wave of primitive accumulation which is combined with a wider scramble for mineral energy and biogenetic resources, amounting to a comprehensive scramble under neo-colonial conditions'. Across the globe, the unfolding gold commodity frontier has been largely influenced by increasing scarcity of gold and other localised socio-economic and political dynamics which are sometimes difficult to generalise. For example within Zimbabwe, radical land reforms which were followed by the implementation of local empowerment regulations shaped the way the 'scramble' has unfolded and the trajectory of the gold commodity frontier. Under these circumstances, the Zimbabwean state vacillated between on one hand, facilitating the scramble by awarding mining concessions to big mining companies especially in the platinum group metals sector (Mkodzongi 2016), and on the other hand the state also challenged the 'scramble'. It did this by demanding that foreign miners comply with local empowerment regulations (Ibid 2016) or face closure after the withdrawal and re-allocation of their mine leases. It is important to note that during the implementation of local empowerment regulations, state antagonism towards large corporate mines influenced the growth of the artisanal mining sector (gold, diamonds, chrome and other base metals) mainly dominated by 'indigenous capitalists' and the Chinese. This has led to the dramatic growth of the ASGM sector whose annual gold deliveries to the state owned company (Fidelity Printers and Refineries) surpassed that of the corporate mines in 2018. This created intra-elite conflicts over access to rents from 'extractives' and many claimed that the state is antagonistic to 'corporate' mines in favour of ASGM because high profile ZANU PF politicians had linkages with ASGM. While there is no evidence to support such claims, the government has been blamed for failing to support struggling corporate gold mines even as the ASGM sector have been allocated funds to mechanise their operations. Until recently, the ASGM sector enjoyed favourable market conditions and were able to retain a large percentage of their income from gold sales in foreign currency. In contrast, the private corporate enterprises in the sector have been forced to accept a large percentage of their income in the local bond notes[2]. Under the highly charged political environment of 'indigenisation', corporate mines found themselves facing tenure insecurity, with the state threatening to withdraw some of their claim area due to conflicts over compliance with local empowerment regulations (Mkodzongi 2016). This demonstrates how a radicalised state contested the 'scramble;' in the wider resources sector in favour of local capitalists. However, in the context of the recent political developments in the country, the indigenisation drive has been reversed in favour global mining capital which now has a free reign to extract mineral resources without the need to comply with local empowerment regulations. The Zimbabwean context demonstrates the political dynamics underpinning the scramble and the unfolding gold mining frontier.

State Landlordism and Violence in the ASGM Sector

The widespread violence experienced by miners across the gold mining areas demonstrate the way local people have been adversely integrated into the global gold production network. Our interviews with informants in Mhondoro Ngezi show how the absence of 'government' (interview with Chenga 23 November 2017) in artisanal mining areas has left miners vulnerable to violence and exploitation without recourse to justice. The state has thus played a key role in the exploitation of miners by 'sponsors' through its inability to formalise and regularise ASGM operations. The 'absence' of the state (interview with Mazora at Just Right 22 November 2018) in artisanal mining areas has led to incidences of widespread violence and exploitation of miners across the countryside with criminal gangs wielding machetes (the now dreaded Mashurugwi) roaming the countryside and terrorising artisanal miners. These criminal syndicates have taken advantage of the illegality of ASGM to rob miners of their gold and to force some to work for them under dangerous working conditions. Since some high profile politicians are also involved in artisanal mining, illegality favours them as in some places they operate with criminal syndicates to dispossess artisanal miners of their hard earned gold or unprocessed ore (interview with Meki at Etina 20 November 2018).

A report by the NewZWire news site (14 February 2019) implicates the government in the exploitation of miners as it contends that the government is more interested in gold deliveries than the safety of miners. According to the report, 'The Zimbabwe government likes to tell us that rising gold output from informal mining is a good thing, but the dozens of bodies floating inside a mine shaft near Kadoma today suggest that it isn't'. The report went on to say that it seems as if the government is 'eager to boast of rising gold output, and in the scramble among the elite to personally profit, the government is not asking how this gold is being produced, or how many are dying producing it'. Below is a table chronicling regular accidents in the ASGM with the government doing very little to address the situation.

26 September: Eight miners died after a mine shaft collapsed at Chatyoka Mine in Concession
October 2016: Four people were buried alive when a tunnel at Indarama Mine near Kwekwe collapses
May 2017: Eight die the roof of a tunnel caves in at Big Mine in Masasa area of Mazowe, two of those that died were sucked in while working on the surface
April 2018: Six die after a tunnel at the disused Old Motapa Mine caves in
April 2018: Two die when a mine shaft collapses at Jongwe farm in Goromonzi
August 2018: 14 die at Eldorado Mine near Chinhoyi after a rock fall
December 2018: Nine people are suspected of having died when Wanderers Mine near Shurugwi curves in, taking with it part of an adjacent road
February 2019: Over 50 miners die after the Cricket and Silver moon mines at Battlefields in Kadoma are flooded while miners are working underground

Source complied by author from NewZWire site and other sources

The fact that miners continue to die in mine related accidents with the government doing very little to formalise and monitor ASGM operations demonstrates how the government is implicated in the deaths of miners under the unfolding gold mining frontier. It seems the government has kept ASGM deliberately informal in order to facilitate the exploitative nature of the activity. Lack of monitoring of ASGM activities by the government has left miners vulnerable to dangerous working conditions and violent conflict which often goes unreported. Moreover many fatal accidents go unreported as some miners operate in remote locations with limited involvement of the state. Again illegality of their work further makes it difficult to report abuses to the police. The fact that sponsors can be powerful politicians or their surrogates can make it difficult to challenge them. This is why cases of widespread violence which are reported in the media have not led to a shift in government policy in terms of formalising and monitoring ASGM activities. Interviews with informants[3] show how criminal gangs that terrorise artisanal miners and rob them of their hard earned gold are protected by the police and high profile politicians who are also engaged in ASGM. A case in point is that of the current Minster of State Security (he was recently placed under sanctions by the USA government for alleged human rights violations) who, before his appointment was suspected of being involved in ASGM related violence, as noted below:

> President Emmerson Mnangagwa named one of his closest allies as National Security Minister on Wednesday. If Mnangagwa's Cabinet announced on September 7 offered a glimmer of hope for Zimbabwe's democratisation project, commentators said Owen Mudha Ncube's appointment showed a leader hankering for Zanu PF's violent past. Ncube – widely known as Mnangagwa's enforcer – has been named in violent gold wars in the Midlands city of Kwekwe, and was the leader of a notorious Zanu PF terror group known as Al Shabaab, which takes its name from its infamous Somalian cousin. (Zimlife.com 19 September 2018)

While these media reports cannot be verified, the involvement of politicians and their surrogates in ASGM sector is well documented (Mawowa 2013; Mkodzongi and Spiegel 2018). Our own work in Mhondoro Ngezi shows that high profile politicians are engaged in ASGM and often operate hand in hand with criminal syndicates[4]. Interviews also indicate that miners lose their mine shafts to politicians forcibly and routinely because of the nexus between politicians and criminal. This is done by developing and using contacts at a given mining camp to gather information about syndicates operating in the area. Once they observe that a particular mine syndicate has hit a rich gold vein, they can organise criminal gangs (locally known as *mbimbos)* or use the police to evict miners. For example interviews with artisanal miners in the Kadoma area show that once a miner hits a gold rich pit or a good sample as it is locally called, it will not take long before he/she receives 'visitors' claiming ownership of the pit. Such visitors will either demand that the miner vacate the pit or pay tribute. In some places the 'visitors' can simply be violent thugs that will dispossess you of your ore or force you off the gold rich mine. Miners are thus vulnerable to various forms of abuses by criminal syndicates that are sometimes linked to politicians or individuals with political connections.

The involvement of ZANU PF politicians in ASGM has led to claims that the government is now deliberately supporting artisanal mining at the expense of formal corporate mines as many politicians are benefiting from the growing ASGM sector. According to NeZWire (14 February 2019),

> … government has pampered the small-scale miners more than it has the larger producers. Formal gold producers spend significant amounts of money on safety and environmental compliance, but get less for their gold than informal miners do. Small scale miners get paid 70% of their gold sales to Fidelity in US dollars, paid out in cash. For larger producers, they only get to keep 55% of their earnings, if at all it is paid.

While it is difficult to verify such claims, interviews with miners in Kadoma[5] shows that high profile politicians are involved in ASGM as sponsors who often employ their surrogates to run their operations. An important point to highlight here is that in some places artisanal miners enjoy government support due to their support for the ruling ZANU PF political party. Many of them rely on their political allegiance to the party for their tenure. However, in the past artisanal miners have faced state sponsored violence under the pretext that they were criminals (Spiegel 2014)

The longstanding conflict between Dexter Nduna (see Herald Newspaper 29 December 2015) a ZANU PF politician and ACR/Breckridge, a London Stock Exchange listed company, over the ownership of Pickstone and giant Gadzema mines in the town of Chegutu demonstrates the way some ZANU PF politicians are entangled in ASGM in Zimbabwe. The politician who happens to be the Member of Parliament for the Chegutu West Constituency is known to work with artisanal mining syndicates in the Chegutu area. He supported their illegal operations at the privately owned Pickstone mine which led to a longstanding conflict with the mine owners after a mine shaft collapsed and killed some miners. At the height of the conflict, Nduna claimed that ACR/Breckridge was keeping the mine for speculative purposes since there was no mining taking place at Pickstone. He further argued that artisanal miners were contributing to national gold output and local economic empowerment by producing 100 kgs a month. In a letter written by Dexter Nduna to the Herald Newspaper, he argued that:

> ACR & Breckridge Resources are listed on the London Stock Exchange and the value of their shares hedges on the gold resources at Pickstone and Gadzema Giant Mines which claims they have continued to hold onto for the last 20 years without production for speculative purposes. This is where Black Zimbabwean Artisanal Miners came in and filled the void and delivered Gold to Fidelity counters at a rate of 100kg per month.
>
> This is well documented and unlike what the Mines Secretary deliberately ignores and chooses to be ignorant about royalties as gold tax is accruing to Government at a rate of 5 percent and 3 percent for large mines and artisanal Miners respectively. The artisanal miners have delivered more gold and value to the Government of Zimbabwe than ACR & Breckridge … Zanu-PF Party, of which I am Treasurer in the Mashonaland West Province received $3 500 into the Zanu-PF Party's Provincial Bank Account from the Artisanal Miners. This is the apex the Empowerment drive sought and brought about by the Zanu-PF Government where our very own Black young Zimbabweans are beginning to support their Party … By the way the $3 500 from the Artisanal Miners is part of the sacrifices by Zanu-PF Membership that was channelled towards the successful hosting of the 15th Annual National People's Conference. (Herald Newspaper 29 December 2015)

Dexter Nduna's letter demonstrates the political dynamics and underpinning Zimbabwe's unfolding gold mining frontier. The illegal occupation of 'dormant' privately owned mines is sometimes promoted and justified on the basis of 'black empowerment' and the financial contribution of artisanal miners to the ZANU PF political party (AllAfrica News site 9 march 2018)[6]. However, while the land reform allowed ordinary people access to mineral resources which were formerly enclosed under colonialism, access to such 'liberated' mineral resources is contested among various classes which in many places has led to conflicts.

The state itself has played a contradictory role in managing conflicts in the mining sector. On one hand, it has sided with big mines to protect their tenure rights by violently evicting artisanal miners (Spiegel 2014), while on the other it has undermined their tenure security by either confiscating some of their claim area or allowing artisanal miners to seize and operate private mines (Mkodzongi 2016). While indigenisation and local empowerment regulations have allowed the poor and unemployed people access to mineral rich ores, access to minerals has been underpinned by class struggles over 'resource rents', thus leading to violent evictions and in some places fatal conflicts. Local politicians have played the role of a comprador bourgeois representing global mining capital under a 'widening' gold mining frontier which is now dominated by artisanal mining. The widening of gold mining frontier poses new conceptual challenges, historically, the global gold mining industry relied on big monopolistic producers (Verbrugge and Geenen 2018), such producers are now facing viability challenges due to the scarcity of gold and its location in deep underground geological conditions that are difficult and expensive to extract. As a result, the current trajectory towards 'artisanally' produced gold has addressed this challenge. Rather than deepening mines in order to access ores, gold is increasingly produced by ASGM operators using rudimentary technologies and casualised labour. Such gold is cheaply produced and the risk of production has been transferred from large producers to small operators.

This process has promoted exploitation of local communities and their exclusion from accessing mineral resource rents. It has been argued that commodity frontiers can promote what has called been called 'frontier democracy'. In her study of gold rushes in America and Australia Bryceson (2018:32) has argued that a gold rush 'may encourage the evolution of frontier democracy as long as 'hierarchically organised labour circumstances do not pose a constraint'. The ideal environment for the attainment of 'frontier democracy is when 'untied, independent artisanal labourers engaged in high stakes and hazardous work, are inclined to cooperate with one another for mutual benefit'. Within the Zimbabwean context many localised socio-economic and political dynamics have influenced the way frontier democracy have unfolded and its limitations. Evidence from work in central Zimbabwe shows that gold rush sites are by their nature hierarchical, there is always a 'leader' or ad hoc committee that oversees the operations of miners. The committee has an interest in rent seeking and will end up engaging in exploitative tendencies by levying a fee to allow miners to enter a mine site. The tendency towards exploitative labour relations is thus common across gold rush sites and can undermine the mutual bonds that initially bind artisanal miners together. This can happen when new class dynamics start to emerge among the group. Several reasons can be cited for the above. First, some miners might 'strike gold' and climb high up the social ladder and hence become employers of their poor counter-parts. Second, others might remain stagnant in their status as wage labourers exploited by a richer capitalist class. Elsewhere (Mkodzongi and Spiegel 2018) we show that in central Zimbabwe shows that artisanal miners are socially differentiated, their relationships are dynamic and thus open to shifting loyalties and conflict rather than collaboration although in some places, kinship ties can be paramount in providing the bonds that keeps syndicate members together (Mkodzongi and Spiegel 2018). Third, the intervention of the state and other politically powerful actors (with a strong lobby over state policy) can also help to undermine frontier democracy as violence and extreme hardships due to loss of tenure and autonomy can undermine the egalitarian entry and exit of miners from the frontier. Within the Zimbabwean context, the ZANU PF political party encouraged unemployed youths to engage in mining in its bid to gather votes especially during elections. This promoted a temporary form of 'frontier democracy' epitomised by what some youths in central Zimbabwe called 'freedom' mining. Under freedom mining, youths could join and exit mine sites without any major problem. Moreover, the process encouraged a more democratic access to mineral resources without the need for a bureaucratic process of acquiring legal paperwork before commencing mining operations. However, interviews with artisanal miners in central Zimbabwe demonstrate that many of those engaged in 'freedom' mining end up being exploited by the more rich capitalist class involving politicians and the Chinese. Under the widening gold commodity frontier, artisanal miners are thus integrated into global commodity markets under unfavourable terms.

However, artisanal miners have not been passive victims of the new scramble under a widening gold commodity frontier. Following on Tsing (2005) and Verbrugge and Geenen (2018:2), it has been observed that 'frontiers are not ... simply destructive but creates space for something new ... the frontier becomes a zone of friction where ... new forms of governance, social norms and cultural practices emerge from the articulation of global and local dynamics'. Our work in central Zimbabwe and other locations (Mkodzongi and Spiegel 2018; forthcoming) explores the dynamics of mobility across the widening gold mining frontier. Miners fight exploitation through exiting the gold mining frontier in search of better remunerative livelihoods or better working conditions (Bryceson 2018). Fieldwork also shows that miners 'exited' the frontier in pursuit of farm based livelihoods (interview with Chipata at Just Right mine 23 November 2018), others had crossed borders to seek work in neighbouring countries and came back after a few years away[7]. While others were alternating between farming and mining as a way of spreading risks (interview with Bozo at Etina 29 November 2018). Others had become successful 'frontier' entrepreneurs having accumulated enough capital to set up milling facilities and gold buying syndicates' [8].Thus the picture that emerges is complex and requires a careful analysis. The frontier presents 'livelihood' opportunities for some, while for others it is simply exploitative and thus to be avoided. In general, artisanal miners have sought to pressure the state from below by deploying indigenisation discourses to get a fair share of resource rents at a time of great economic challenges facing the country. The state itself has gone through moments of radicalisation (Moyo and Yeros 2007) and thus promoted 'resource nationalism' through the promulgation of local empowerment and indigenisation policies in favour of local populations. This was progressive as it challenged monopoly syndicates in the mining sector to share profits with locals. However, under the neo-liberal state that has emerged after the removal of Zimbabwe's former president Robert Mugabe from power, the state has been de-radicalised under the 'Zimbabwe is open for business' mantra which has seen the reversal of indigenisation policies in order to make peace with global capital. This has thus undermined the equitable redistribution of resource rents in favour of exploitative labour relations under a widening resource frontier, mostly pronounced in the artisanal gold mining sector.

Conclusions

Zimbabwe's artisanal gold mining sector has rapidly expanded during a changing agrarian situation occasioned by the radical land reforms implemented in 2000. A major dynamic underpinning this new gold mining frontier is the upsurge in artisanal gold mining activities. These activities have been instrumental in the diversification of livelihoods among peasant households and other unemployed people. However, the upsurge in ASGM signifies a new scramble for natural resources under an unfolding gold mining frontier. The widening of such a frontier has been underpinned by exploitative labour relations, violence and environmental destruction with long-term negative consequences for local populations. While ASGM has played a major role as a source of employment and livelihoods for peasants and unemployed urban dwellers, it has also been central in the insertion of local people in the global commodity markets under unfavourable terms. This essay has demonstrated that the land reform opened up the countryside and improved mobility and access to natural resources which were previously enclosed under colonialism. However, the engagement of peasants and other unemployed poor people must not be celebrated without taking into account the negative impact of this widening gold mining frontier. There is thus a need for the government to get more involved in the 'frontier' in order to manage the violence and the exploitative labour regime underpinning the unfolding gold mining frontier.

Notes

1. Apart from deepening the exploitation of local communities, boom and bust cycles can be a major source of economic distress especially in communities where mining becomes the main livelihood activity.
2. This goes against what is observed elsewhere (Verbrugge and Geenen forthcoming), where corporate mines have 'entered into an unholy alliance with landlord states in an attempt to monopolise access to mineral-bearing land'.
3. Interview with Manaka on 24 November 2017.
4. Interview with Chikoti 25 November 2017.
5. Interview with Chenge at Lincoln Mine 25 November 2018.
6. I have explored elsewhere (Mkodzongi forthcoming) how discourses of black empowerment popularised during the former President Mugabe's tenure were instrumentalised by both ordinary people and ZANU PF politicians to engage in artisanal mining and to legitimise their illegal occupation of privately owned mine claims.
7. Interview with Chibaro at Etina 22 November 2018.
8. Interview with Tich in Harare 16 June 2016.

References

Bryceson, D. F. (2018). Artisanal Gold Rush Mining and Frontier Democracy: Juxtaposing Experiences in America, Australia, Africa and Asia. *THE PICK*, p. 31.

Bryceson, D. F., & Jønson, J. B. (2009). Gold Digging Careers in Rural East Africa: Small-Scale Miners' Livelihood Choices. *World Development, 38*(3), 379–392.

Bukharin, N. (1972). *Imperialism and World Economy.* London: Merlin.

Geenen, S. (2015). *African Artisanal Mining from Inside Out. Access, Norms and Power in Congo's Gold Sector.* Abingdon: Routledge.

Hickey, S., & du Toit, A. (2007). *Adverse Incorporation, Social Exclusion and Chronic Poverty* (CPRC Working Paper 81). University of Manchester.

Hilson, G., & Garforth, C. (2012). 'Agricultural Poverty' and the Expansion of Artisanal Mining in Sub-Saharan Africa: Experiences from Southwest Mali and Southeast Ghana. *Population Research and Policy Review, 31*(3), 435–464.

Mabhena, C. (2012). Mining with a 'Vuvuzela': Reconfiguring Artisanal Mining in Southern Zimbabwe and Its Implications to Rural Livelihoods. *Journal of Contemporary African Studies, 30*(2), 219–233.

Maconachie, R., & Hilson, G. (2011). Artisanal Gold Mining: A New Frontier in Post-Conflict Sierra Leone? *Journal of Development Studies, 47*(4), 595–616.

Mawowa, S. (2013). The Political Economy of Artisanal and Small-Scale Gold Mining in Central Zimbabwe. *Journal of Southern African Studies, 39*, 921–936.

Mkodzongi, G. (2016). 'I Am a Paramount Chief, This Land Belongs to My Ancestors': The Reconfiguration of Rural Authority After Zimbabwe's Land Reforms. *Review of African Political Economy, 43*(supl), 99–114.

Mkodzongi, G., & Spiegel, S. (2018). Artisanal Gold Mining and Farming: Livelihood Linkages and Labour Dynamics After Land Reforms in Zimbabwe. *Journal of Development Studies, 55*, 1–17.

Moore, J. W. (2000). Sugar and the Expansion of the Early Modern World-Economy: Commodity Frontiers, Ecological Transformation, and Industrialization. *Review (Fernand Braudel Center), 23*(3), 409–433.

Moyo, S. (2011). Changing Agrarian Relations After Redistributive Land Reform in Zimbabwe. *Journal of Peasant Studies, 38*(5), 939–966.

Moyo, S., & Yeros, P. (2007). The Radicalised State: Zimbabwe's Interrupted Revolution. *Review of African Political Economy, 34*(111), 103–121.

Moyo, S., Jha, P., & Yeros, P. (2019). *Reclaiming Africa, Scramble and Resistance in the 21st Century*. Singapore: Springer.

Niederberger, T., Haller, T., Gambon, H., Kobi, M., & Wenk, I. (2016). *The Open Cut: Mining, Transnational Corporations and Local Populations* (Vol. 2). Zürich: Lit Verlag.

Peluso, N. (2018). Entangled Territories in Small-Scale Gold Mining Frontiers: Labor Practices, Property, and Secrets in Indonesian Gold Country. *World Development, 101*, 400–416.

Seccatore, J., Veiga, M., Origliasso, C., Marin, T., & De Tomi, G. (2014). An Estimation of the Artisanal Small-Scale Production of Gold in the World. *The Science of the Total Environment, 496*, 3–8.

Spiegel, S. J. (2014). Legacies of a nationwide crackdown in Zimbabwe: Operation Chikorokoza Chapera in gold mining communities. *Journal of Modern African Studies, 52*, 541–570.

Tsing, A. (2005). *Friction. An Ethnography of Global Connection*. Princeton: Princeton University Press.

Verbrugge, B., & Geenen, S. (2018). *The Gold Commodity Frontier: A Fresh Perspective on Change and Diversity in the Global Gold Mining Economy*. The Extractive Industries and Society.

Princeton List of Interviews

Bozo interviewed at Etina 29/11/18.
Chenge interviewed at Lincoln Mine 25/11/2018.
Chibaro interviewed at Etina 22/11/18
Chikoti interviewed on 25/11/2017.
Manaka interviewed on 24/11/2017.
Mazora interviewed at Just Right 22/11/2018.
Meki interviewed at Etina 20/11/2018.
Tich interviewed in Harare 16/06/2016.

Web Sources

Hoax, What Hoax? Accessed at: https://www.herald.co.zw/hoax-what-hoax/. Date accessed 12 June 2019.

Mine Collapse the Body Count Is Rising in the Mines but Govt Is Only Counting the Money. Accessed at: https://newzwire.live/mine-collapse-the-body-count-is-rising-in-the-mines-but-govt-is-only-counting-the-money/. Accessed 5 June 2019.

Mnangagwa Names Violent Enforcer Owen mudha Ncube as Security Minster. Accessed at: https://www.zimlive.com/2018/09/19/mnangagwa-names-violent-enforcer-owen-mudha-ncube-as-security-minister/. Accessed 6 June 2019.

Zimbabwe: Zanu-PF Grabs Gold Mine in Mnangagwa's Kwekwe Backyard. Accessed at: https://allafrica.com/stories/201803090038.html. Date accessed 15 June 2019.

CHAPTER 11

Informal Economy in India: Persistence and Meagreness

Arup Mitra

Introduction

Considering the important role that the informal sector plays in providing sources of livelihood, particularly to the rural migrants and those residing in the urban slums, this article (a) examines the relative size and composition of the informal sector; (b) conceptualizes the supply-push segment within the informal sector; (c) estimates the well-being index of the households engaged in the informal sector across cities, and identifies important correlates and (d) delineates the recent changes relating to contractualization and ancillarization and their impact on work practices and performance. The database of the study is drawn from various sources.

Originally published in *Agrarian South: Journal of Political Economy, Vol. 4 No. 2*

A. Mitra (✉)
Institute of Economic Growth, Delhi University Enclave, New Delhi, India
e-mail: arup@iegindia.org

P. Jha et al. (eds.), *Labour Questions in the Global South*,
https://doi.org/10.1007/978-981-33-4635-2_11

The secondary data sources include the employment and unemployment survey of the National Sample Survey Organisation (NSSO) for 2004–2005 and 2009–2010 (NSSO 2012a) and the NSSO's special surveys on unorganized manufacturing enterprises for 2004–2005 and 2010–2011 (NSSO 2012b). The micro-surveys include the project sponsored by United Nations Development Programme and the Government of India (UNDP-GoI) for 2006–2007, carried out by this author and others at the Institute of Economic Growth, Delhi, in the slums of four Indian cities and also a qualitative survey conducted by the author in 2010 in a specific location of Delhi.

Several studies on the informal sector in India have been carried out in the last 20 years; a brief review of these may be found in Das (2011) and Mitra (2013). The rural labourer who is pushed out of the agricultural sector due to the lack of a productive source of livelihood and at the same time cannot be absorbed in the rural non-farm sector, or the high productivity manufacturing sector in the urban areas, is likely to be residually absorbed in the low productivity urban informal sector (Mitra 1990). Most of the earlier studies focused primarily on the relative size of the informal sector, indicating the presence of a large percentage of the workforce in low productivity activities and considerable overlaps between informal sector employment and poverty. This article goes a few steps further to understand the residual absorption of labour in the informal sector vis-à-vis the demand-induced component by adopting a stochastic frontier function framework. Moreover, based on the micro-surveys, it also focuses on the vulnerability of the workers by estimating a well-being index at the household level. All this is pursued in the backdrop of the concept 'space', that is, the overall economic structure of the city in which they reside and the variations in the nature of the informal sector across cities, identifying some of the important correlates of well-being. Also, the article addresses subcontracting practices and tries to address the paradox of rising work consignments accompanied by meagre earnings.

The Relative Size of the Informal Sector

The informal sector accounts for a sizeable percentage of the total workforce in the country. Not only the agricultural activity which primarily falls into the domain of the informal sector but also other non-agricultural activities are characterized by a large informal segment. The informal sector is usually defined in terms of low productivity activities, small size of operation, poor level of technology conceptualized in terms of a low capital–labour ratio, and unprotected factor and product markets, although an operational definition of the informal sector may not include all the attributes. Factors which impinge on a firm's decision to operate in the formal or informal sector lie in the skill and educational level it possesses. Individuals with poor human and physical capital endowment are residually absorbed in own account enterprises and other small units. Some of them remain perpetually within the informal sector, as they are not able to experience any upward income mobility. With improvement in the quality of education, there is an increase in the accessibility to market information, credit facilities, technological know-how and other information pertaining to the overall macroeconomic and policy changes, and, hence, the scale of operation expands. This, in turn, helps the unit graduate from the informal or unorganized sector to the formal or organized sector.

However, the graduation process also needs to be seen in terms of the cost associated with it. For example, if the registration procedure and the labour laws are stringent in the formal sector, then the unit may prefer to operate from the informal sector—deliberately choosing to remain small in size (Maiti and Mitra 2010). Similarly, the firm may decide to remain small so that it can take the advantage of the labour market flexibility that the informal sector offers. In such situations, the informal sector units are not necessarily unproductive in nature; rather they may be technically efficient and highly competitive.

The NSSO's estimate of the incidence of informal sector employment, defined as the proportion of informal sector employment to total employment, is high in both the rural and urban areas. In the agriculture sector, its dominance does not come as a surprise, but in the non-agriculture sector, too, an overwhelmingly large proportion of workers are engaged in informal activities. In fact, the rural–urban differences in the figures are not spectacular. The other surprising pattern relates to the gender differences: the proportion of women workers engaged in the informal sector to total women workers is lower than its male counterpart, though one would have expected it to be otherwise.

The NSSO's estimate possibly does not reflect the reality because in the definition used by the National Sample Survey (NSS) (2009–2010), the informal sector employment mainly comprises employment in the informal sector enterprises (proprietary and partnership enterprises), excluding the employees in the households, which actually should have been a part of informal sector employment. Since employment in the households is

Table 11.1 Relative Size of the Informal Sector in Percentages: All-India (2009–2010)

	Non-agriculture		
Sector	*Male*	*Female*	*Person*
Rural	73.0	64.1	71.3
Urban	68.3	60.1	66.9

Source: Based on NSS employment–unemployment data, 2009–2010 (NSSO 2012c)

quite substantial, its exclusion tends to grossly underestimate the relative size of the informal sector employment reported in Table 11.1. Furthermore, the households in order to take the advantages associated with flexibility, tend to engage women to a large extent (Mitra 2005) and, therefore, their exclusion naturally suppresses the incidence of informal sector employment among the women workers.

We may further note that the size of informal employment which includes casual or short-term contractual or irregular workers in the formal sector, in addition to the employment in the informal sector enterprises and in the households, is indeed phenomenally large. Notwithstanding these limitations, the estimates of informal sector employment provided in Table 11.1 are exceptionally high in the Indian context, particularly in non-agricultural activities.

The Supply-Push Component Within the Informal Sector

Issues concerning the residual absorption of labour in the low productivity informal sector have already received a great deal of attention in the past (see Mitra 1994). In the present context of globalization, while most countries are aiming at maximizing growth, the issue of well-being has become increasingly important. One of the crucial dimensions of well-being is access to productive employment opportunities. Thus, the concept of pro-poor growth and various other questions relating to informalization have acquired prominence in the development studies literature.

Growth that is currently taking place is accompanied by informalization such as subcontracting in the production process and various other mechanisms that tend to leave labour with less bargaining power. On the whole, the informalization process is feared to involve substantial welfare losses and deterioration in terms of governance. There is also concern on limited industrialization issues and, accordingly, it has led policy makers and researchers to debate and design policies for providing a safeguard against global imbalances. Keeping some of these concerns in mind, we make an attempt in this section to estimate the supply-push component of informal sector employment across the Indian states (see also Maiti and Mitra 2010).

Theoretically, the informal sector can grow due to supply-side factors, or demand-side factors or both. In the present specification, we have taken informal sector employment to be a function of certain demand-side factors approximated by formal sector employment in various activities. Next, we pose the question as to whether the actual (observed) level of informal sector employment is much above the level that can be explained in terms of formal sector employment. We have analysed this in the stochastic frontier function framework. The distance of actual informal sector employment from the level of informal sector employment, which can be explained in terms of formal sector employment, would represent the pressure of excess supplies. The higher the distance, the greater is the pressure of excess supplies of labour, leading to a residual absorption of labour in the low productivity activities in the informal sector.

By applying the statistical stochastic frontier function framework, we can identify, based on the cross-sectional data, the extent to which different states are above the level that can be explained in terms of formal sector employment.

As regards the estimation procedure, log transformation of informal sector employment is regressed on the log transformation of various components of the formal sector employment. Cross-sectional data used for frontier function estimation require an a priori assumption regarding the one-sided distribution of the error term taken to measure the effect of the supply-push phenomenon. In this case, we have assumed a half-normal distribution. The frontier equation is estimated by the maximum likelihood estimation technique. Data from both the survey years (1999–2000 and 2004–2005) have been used. Based on the magnitude of the error U_i, the maximum value (indexed as 100) is chosen to represent the case with a maximum supply-push effect. Mizoram (1999–2000) corresponds to the maximum effect of excess supplies of labour. After assigning a value of 100 to Mizoram (1999–2000), other states have been indexed accordingly. It is important to note that many states which had a low index in the year 1999–2000 seem to have recorded a much higher value in 2004–2005 (Maiti and Mitra 2010). On the whole, the supply-push component, or the component which remains unexplained in terms of the growth of the formal sector, is on the rise. And this is, indeed, a matter of concern, since such components within the informal sector may not be in a position to engage workers productively.

Patterns Emerging from Micro-Survey

On aspects of living standards and well-being of workers in the informal sector, not much information is available at the city level from the secondary sources. Under the project on urban poverty sponsored by UNDP-GoI, a primary survey was undertaken in four cities of different population size and economic activities (namely, Jaipur, Ludhiana, Mathura and Ujjain).[1] These cities were picked from the list of 64 cities prepared specifically for the urban renewal mission (Jawaharlal Nehru National Urban Renewal Mission (JNNURM)). The primary survey enables us to comment on certain aspects of the well-being of slum dwellers in these four cities. While Jaipur and Ludhiana are two million plus cities, Mathura and Ujjain are relatively small in size.

From the point of view of measurement, various dimensions of poverty, rather than only income or consumption poverty, need to be considered to assess well-being. However, we could consider only those dimensions which are quantifiable (Mitra 2007). The following variables have been combined to construct the household-specific well-being index: household size; child–woman ratio; per capita consumption expenditure; proportion of persons in the household who reported illness; percentage of household members who acquired at least primary-level education; percentage of members in the age group 15–59, which is a proxy for adult potential earners; percentage of working individuals; age of the household head or principal earner taken as a proxy for experience in the job market; health expenditure per capita and per capita household income. Variables, such as, household size, child–woman ratio and the percentage of ill members in the household, are likely to reduce the well-being of the household. Health expenditure per capita on an a priori basis may raise the well-being of the household if it tends to enhance productivity. On the other hand, it may reduce well-being if it is incurred at the expense of consumption of essential items. The other variables considered here are expected to enhance well-being. Since these variables are heterogeneous, it is difficult to combine them to indicate an overall living standard of the households. Hence, factor analysis was conducted, and using factor loadings as weights, variables were combined to generate a composite index of well-being.

The well-being index constructed on the basis of the factor loadings indicates that in Jaipur and Ludhiana, 26 and 32 per cent of the slum households, respectively, are located in the bottom two size classes. However, in Mathura and Ujjain, which are much smaller than the other two cities and also lack dynamism of growth, the corresponding figures are 57 and 61 per cent, respectively. It is interesting to note that these figures are substantially lower than the incidence of consumption poverty, which is 66.8 per cent in Jaipur, 43.6 per cent in Ludhiana, 75 per cent in Mathura and 88.2 per cent in Ujjain. This would tend to suggest that even when consumption poverty is high, many other facilities which are available in the cities tend to improve the well-being of the population. Second, the well-being index even among the low-income households seems to have a positive association with the city size and the nature of the city.

We may infer that the informal sector activities are relatively more productive in the industrialized or otherwise dynamic cities. On the whole, the nature of the informal sector tends to change as the city size and its economic activities change. Within the informal sector, elements of dynamism can be traced in a city which has growth potential relative to the one which is stagnant and small in size. With the similar level of skill endowment and other demographic characteristics, an individual may have the possibility of being better off in terms of real earnings in a city that has the growth momentum. So the informal sector is not uniformly stagnant; its spatial variations lay emphasis on its potential to provide better sources of livelihood in the broad context of economic growth.

However, these patterns are aggregative in nature. We may therefore like to pursue further experiments. One important line of enquiry could be relating to the factors which explain the overall well-being. Since well-being is measured in terms of a number of variables, we need to be careful in selecting the determinants so that they do not include some of the constituents of the well-being index. The right-hand side variables include: nature of employment, caste categories, duration of migration categories (the long duration migrants of more than 20 years and the natives constitute the comparison category), nature of construction of the huts and the number of rooms per household, ownership pattern, access to sanitation and water and ability to remit. As there are mainly three types of employment—daily wage, regular wage and self-employment—two dummies representing the first two categories have been included. In relation to the social groups, scheduled tribes and 'others' have been taken as the comparison category.

The analysis is carried out in a binomial logit framework: households which registered a well-being index of less than 400 are assigned 0 and those lying above the threshold limit are designated as 1. The estimation is carried out for the samples drawn from the four cities separately and also for the pooled sample.

Results suggest that households in which heads are engaged in regular wage employment correspond to higher levels of well-being, while those in daily wage employment are statistically not different from those in self-employment (see Kumar et al. 2009). In individual cities, the gender dummy does not appear to be significant, although in the pooled sample it is significant at a 10 per cent level with a negative sign. This implies that women-headed households have a lower well-being index, although in terms of marginal effect the probability of having higher levels of well-being drops marginally (-0.08) as one moves from male-headed to female-headed households.

In relation to the caste categories, we may again refer to the marginal effects. Relative to the scheduled tribes and 'others', most of the categories seem to have a lower probability of experiencing a higher well-being index. However, the extent of fall in the case of other backward castes (OBCs) Hindus, OBC Muslims and scheduled castes (SCs) measured in terms of marginal effect is higher than that for General Hindus or Muslims. However, these results hold only when we pool the data from all the four cities. Otherwise, based on individual cities, this pattern is not uniformly evident. For example, only OBC Muslims in Ludhiana and Mathura have a different impact on well-being, while the rest of the categories are statistically insignificant. However, in Ludhiana they tend to have a higher well-being, while in Mathura the marginal effect corresponding to OBC Muslims is -0.30. In Ujjain, none of the caste dummies is significant, implying that the variations in well-being across categories are not substantive. In Jaipur, both General and OBC Muslims tend to have a lower well-being index than the rest. On the whole, based on the individual city data, it is not possible to conclude that lower castes such as OBCs.

The duration of migration does not play a significant role in enhancing the level of well-being of the households as seen from the pooled data.

However, households which are able to remit and are residing in greater space (measured in terms of the number of rooms) are able to acquire higher levels of well-being. The only surprising result is in relation to access to piped water and concrete roof, which have negative coefficients. Access to piped water does not mean individual access; it could be the accessibility of the cluster as a whole. Similarly, the households with concrete roof do not seem to be better off in terms of the well-being index. On the whole, while some of the physical characteristics of the shelter and the well-being levels of the households move in the positive direction, some other do not show any such pattern. This would imply that, even in better dwelling structures, one may locate households with lower well-being index in terms of income, consumption, education, health and certain social and demographic variables. Land tenure can improve the quality of shelter but that does ensure improvement in well-being. Similarly, accessibility to piped water can be a function of the residents' association with political parties, and such political contacts are of mutual help only when well-being levels are poor (Edelman and Mitra 2006).[2]

The survival of low-income households in an anonymous urban set-up with an inadequate rural–urban continuum is a complex phenomenon. One class of literature that has grown in this respect emphasizes the role of social capital in enabling the poor to cope with uncertainties and risks. However, while social capital can enhance accessibility to jobs and earnings at the individual level, issues relating to the needs of a group of households need to be addressed in terms of a wider framework. For example, squatting on public land with no provision of drinking water and sanitation is a difficult situation involving insurmountable risks and struggles. In India, political contacts often play the role of reducing risks and uncertainties relating to land encroachment, and also help with access to basic amenities. The operation of social networks that occurs simultaneously with the struggle to access political support is a complex phenomenon.

As Edelman and Mitra (2006) noted that although political contacts yield in terms of providing access to basic amenities or ownership of land, they do hamper the long-term interests of the slum households. Since the political objectives of using these households at election time are more impelling than any social or humanitarian interest, such favours tend to tie the beneficiaries to the benefactors forever, with no genuine concern on the part of the latter for the slum inhabitants to experience upward mobility. Political contact confers short-term benefits upon slum dwellers in terms of access to basic amenities, without genuine concern for their upward mobility.

Relating to social capital, Mitra (2013) noted its significance in providing job market information. In accessing the minimum sources of livelihood, social contacts are indeed helpful to the bulk of the workers engaged in the lower rungs of the informal sector. Differences in types of network are found across activities, although most of them are informal in nature. However, in the context of the upward mobility, there is no strong evidence to confirm possibilities of improving earnings through networks. On the contrary, traditional networks tend to reduce the possibility of upward mobility by creating information asymmetry and excess supplies.

New Trends

Growth in employment and output are undoubtedly two important indicators of performance. Growth in employment has been negative at the aggregate level and in a number of industries in unorganized or informal manufacturing (Table 11.2). Nevertheless, industries, such as, textiles and leather, non-metallic mineral products and basic metal and metal products registered a positive growth rate. In this context, certain results may be highlighted from the qualitative survey conducted in 2009–2010 in Delhi. In particular, considering that the textiles group performed better, the workers' gains in this sector may be assessed. The field survey in the Sunder Nagari area in Delhi identifies workers in three types of activities: tailoring and embroidery, jewellery and packaging. Most of them receive work consignments through the contractors who supply the products to large as well as small shops. While some of the products carry the name of certain specific companies, the others are sold without any such liaison. The contractors supply the raw materials and collect the final products at regular intervals, and as per the workers, there is no dearth of work consignments. However, the wage which is offered on a piece rate basis is extremely low in comparison to the effort put in. In fact, there is evidence to suggest that the real wage rate has declined over time. Thanks to the supply of work consignments, the workers' levels of living have not witnessed any deterioration, implying, however, that much more labour hours are spent to earn the same magnitude of real income. The workers do not take the initiative to sell the products directly to the shopkeepers, as none will be willing to buy from them. This helps the middlemen extract a large sum of profit. To

Table 11.2 Growth in Employment and GVA in Unorganized Manufacturing: 2005–2006 through 2010–2011

	OAME		*Establishment*		*All*	
Industry	*Workers*	*GVA in ₹ Crore (in 2004–2005 prices)*	*Workers*	*GVA in ₹ Crore (in 2004–2005 prices)*	*Workers*	*GVA in ₹ Crore (in 2004–2005 prices)*
Food products, beverages and tobacco	-6.77	2.12	-3.39	-1.29	-5.94	0.35
Textiles and leather	2.48	15.14	0.46	9.84	1.79	12.07
Paper and products	-13.35	-4.04	15.53	23.45	-0.64	17.29
Chemical and chemical products	-17.36	-4.70	-2.04	-4.59	-10.99	2.95
Non-metallic mineral products	-4.91	2.01	11.27	9.03	3.97	7.67
Basic metals	13.34	19.06	-2.30	-12.92	2.52	-9.10
Metal products	-3.69	9.65	4.77	1.47	.82	2.54
Machinery and equipment	-26.19	-14.44	-8.65	-5.70	-12.64	-6.60
Transport equipment	-5.64	15.63	-7.70	4.20	-7.52	4.70
Other manufacturing including wood	-1.32	12.79	4.43	7.77	0.89	9.47
All industries	-2.45	9.58	1.85	5.25	-0.86	6.72

Source: Computed by the author from NSS data (NSSO 2012a, b)

Note: OAME stands for own account manufacturing enterprises (household enterprises)

bypass the middlemen, marketing assistance has to be provided to these units by the governments and civil society.

For some of the products which are sold under the name of certain specific companies, quality-consciousness exists and thus the better performers tend to receive the consignments abundantly and regularly. However, this process does not lead to any rise in wage rate, as the better performers are still large in number. In fact, it is a buyers' market—the contractors set the price and no negotiation is possible to revise it in any manner. 'Take it or leave it' is the principle which is being followed widely.

The role of civil society in this context is important. Some of the organizations are able to offer a much higher piece rate than what the contractors do. But since the work consignments collected by civil society groups are highly negligible, the workers naturally are drawn to the private contractors, such that the interventions of civil society are not able to make any dent on the ongoing rate offered by contractors.

There is no formal or informal union of workers, although each one of them is aware of the ongoing rate. While further exploitation by offering a lower rate to any of the workers is not possible, raising the rate from the workers' side is almost impossible, as collective bargaining does not take place due to the lack of coordination. On the other hand, different contractors have a strong nexus which does not allow any upward revision of the rate. Since the contractors supply the raw materials, the workers do not have sufficient motivation to access credit or marketing assistance directly so as to establish an independent enterprise.

Some of the companies which have good reputations in the market and are also able to get export consignments have followed the practice of subcontracting, and much of the products are manufactured by the home-based workers. But the benefits of growth do not trickle down, partly because of the excess supplies of workers and partly because of the middlemen's role. As quality is a strong criterion for success, these companies prefer to engage the same workers on a long-term basis, instead of adopting a high labour turnover policy. To do this, economic theory would suggest that the employers have to pay higher wages to retain workers and thus assure mutual benefit. But there is hardly any evidence suggesting a pattern favourable to the informal sector workers. There is no indication of a rise in the piece rate wage, which is a prevalent mode of payment in the informal sector. The only benefit that the workers are able to experience is regularity in employment.

The so-called informal sector, which is known for irregular employment, is emerging to offer regular employment, although only in certain specific sub-sectors. This pattern of regularity is expected to result in a positive effect in the long run. The workers taking advantage of the stability in employment conditions may get an opportunity to develop market contacts and acquire proficiency in their skill to nurture their entrepreneurial ability in the long run, which in turn may contribute to productivity growth in the informal sector. However, some of these positive developments seem to be neutralized by the informalization process followed in many components of the formal sector. Incidentally, the formal sector has adopted the informalization process at various levels, although in some of the activities the process has been followed only at the lower rungs (e.g., labourers in the industries and class four employees in various organizations, including universities and government offices).

The changes observed within the manufacturing component of the informal sector are noteworthy. Many petty enterprises, especially in the garment, leather and gems- and jewellery-related industries are now connected to the large units falling into the domain of the formal sector. Since the large units provide raw materials, one may argue that the uncertainty component faced by the small informal sector units in carrying out their operations has declined. They are not required to explore possibilities for credit assistance or production outlets; rather they have the supplies of raw materials and work consignments available at their doorsteps. All this is likely to contribute to a smooth and efficient functioning of the units. And from this, one may further conjecture that the positive effects of growth experienced by the large units can get transmitted to the micro units through the process of subcontracting and ancillarization, and thus globalization is expected to be pro-poor as well. However, our field visits in the Sunder Nagari area in Delhi bring out results, as cited above, quite contrary to this general expectation.

Conclusion

A sizeable percentage of the workers are engaged in the informal sector enterprises both in the rural and urban areas. Even after excluding the household sector which should have been part of informal sector employment, the NSS estimate for the recent year 2009–2010 is alarming. Our study examines the supply-push segment within the informal sector, so as to highlight that much of the informal sector employment is of residual type. The findings of micro-surveys are also utilized to focus on the well-being of the slum households. The silver lining is that the nature of the informal sector tends to change as the city size and its economic activities change. Within the informal sector, elements of dynamism can be traced in a city which has growth potential relative to the one which is stagnant and small in size. With the similar level of skill endowment and other demographic characteristics, an individual may have the possibility of being better off in terms of real earnings and other indicators in a city that has the growth momentum. So the informal sector is not uniformly stagnant; its spatial variations lay emphasis on its potential to provide better sources of livelihood in the broad context of economic growth.

Based on individual city data, it is not possible to conclude that lower castes such as OBCs and SCs show lower well-being levels, although from the pooled data such a tendency is evident. Duration of migration does not play a significant role in enhancing the well-being level of the households, as seen from the micro-survey data pooled across four cities. In other words, although migration may be contributing to a rise in real earnings, the overall well-being does not improve at the place of destination. This brings out several costs associated with the process of rural to urban migration.

Some of the findings from our qualitative survey are brought in to delineate the recent changes that are being observed in the informal sector. For example, how the contractualization and ancillarization impacted on the work practices and performance of the informal sector is an important aspect, indicating the positive changes as well as the welfare losses. Employment growth in the informal (unorganized) manufacturing sector has been negative between 2005–2006 and 2010–2011. Possibly, the informal sector units are not able to compete, and, thus, in an attempt to reduce labour cost, the downsizing of employment has taken place widely. Since Indian manufacturing exports have not picked up, and more obviously so from the unorganized sector due to the poor quality of the products, the advantages that Chinese enterprises could draw in the context of globalization are still a dream for their Indian counterparts. Due to the lack of modernization and inaccessibility to information and communications technology (ICT), neither product diversification has taken place nor have the enterprises been able to graduate to high-value products.

The recent efforts on the part of the Indian government to revive industry as the engine of growth rather look unfeasible, as the unorganized or informal manufacturing may not be in a position to contribute to growth and employment significantly. One of the major constraints that the informal economy enterprises face relates to the lack of physical and financial capital resulting in sluggish labour productivity growth and earnings. Even for marketing of goods, they are dependent on contractors, and in the process, it reduces their profitability significantly. Though accessibility to inputs and work consignments has gone up, the benefits tend to subside due to the practice of intermediation and the earning of incomes on piece rate basis. All this builds a strong case for the introduction of an informal sector policy, which may help reduce the welfare losses to labour employed at the lower rungs.

Many of these informal sector workers are migrants from the rural areas. Using their social capital, they access job market information and sources of livelihood in the cities. However, when it comes to upward mobility, there is no strong evidence to confirm possibilities of improving earnings through networks. On the contrary, traditional networks tend to reduce the possibility of upward mobility by creating information asymmetry and excess supplies. The struggle of these rural migrants in cities to pursue political contacts through the leaders of the clusters is enormous. But, since the political objectives of using these households at election time are more impelling than any social or humanitarian interest, political contact confers only scant and short-term benefits upon slum dwellers in terms of access to basic amenities.

The policy initiatives need to address some of these issues. In areas where social capital exists, economic policy can be combined with it to make economic policy less expensive and, at the same time, neutralize its adverse effects. Similarly, through political contacts, the voices of those in the lower rungs are expected to receive greater attention, but in reality, it is seen to have led to a low equilibrium situation. Therefore, it is imperative that political representatives of the respective constituencies work more effectively towards developing strategies for creating productive employment opportunities and decent living conditions for the rural migrants struggling in the urban set-up for a livelihood. Since many of them do not have any asset base in the rural areas, and, thus, cannot explore possibilities in the rural non-farm sector, they are rather forced to migrate to the cities. And it is pertinent that the urbanization process becomes more inclusive in the Indian context and plays a complementary role for rural development and removal of rural poverty.

Notes

1. This project and survey sponsored by UNDP-GOI were undertaken by the Institute of Economic Growth, Delhi.
2. The clusters act as political vote banks and in return, they are assured of legal tenure and accessibility to basic amenities.

References

Das, K. (Ed.). (2011). *Micro and Small Enterprises in India: The Era of Reforms.* New Delhi: Routledge.

Edelman, B., & Mitra, A. (2006). Access to Basic Amenities: The Role of Political Contact, Its Determinants and Adverse Effects. *Review of Urban and Regional Development Studies, 18*(1), 25–40.

Kumar, R., Kumar, S., & Mitra, A. (2009). Social and Economic Inequalities: Contemporary Significance of Caste in India. *Economic and Political Weekly, 44*(50), 55–63.

Maiti, D., & Mitra, A. (2010). *Skills, Informality and Development* (Institute of Economic Growth Working Paper, No. 306). Delhi.

Mitra, A. (1990). Duality, Employment Structure and Poverty Incidence: Slum Perspective. *Indian Economic Review, 25*(1), 57–73.

Mitra, A. (1994). *Urbanisation, Slums, Informal Sector Employment and Poverty: An Exploratory Analysis.* New Delhi: D.K. Publishers.

Mitra, A. (2005). Women in the Urban Informal Sector: Perpetuation of Meagre Earnings. *Development and Change, 36*(2), 291–316.

Mitra, A. (2007). Industry and Poverty: Evidence from Indian States. *The Indian Journal of Labour Economics, 50*(2), 245–256.

Mitra, A. (2013). *Insights into Inclusive Growth, Employment and Wellbeing in India*. New Delhi: Springer.

National Sample Survey Organisation (NSSO). (2012a). *India: Unorganised Manufacturing Enterprises Survey: NSS 62nd Round (July 2005–June 2006).* National Statistical Organisation, Government of India, New Delhi. Retrieved 14 May 2015, from http://mail.mospi.gov.in/index.php/catalog/108

National Sample Survey Organisation (NSSO). (2012b). *Report of the Committee on Unorganised Sector Statistics (2010–11).* National Statistical Commission, Government of India, New Delhi. Retrieved 14 May 2015, from http://mospi.nic.in/mospi_new/upload/nsc_report_un_sec_14mar12.pdf

National Sample Survey Organisation (NSSO). (2012c). *Informal Sector and Conditions of Employment in India.* New Delhi: Government of India.

CHAPTER 12

Whatever Happened to Employment: India's Recent Record from a Nationally Representative Sample

Anamitra Roychowdhury

Introduction

More than eight decades ago, John Maynard Keynes, arguably the most influential economist of the last century, remarked: 'The outstanding faults of the economic society in which we live are its failure to provide for full employment and its arbitrary and inequitable distribution of wealth and incomes' (Keynes 2010: 341). Remarkably, Keynes' observation remains exceedingly relevant in the contemporary world. Thomas Piketty's, *Capital in the Twenty-First Century* dealing with global inequality, published in 2014 (English edition) quickly became an international bestseller; likewise, most developed as well as many developing countries closely monitor unemployment rates. Considering its harmful social impact, the United Nations, under goal 8 of the Sustainable Development Goals (SDGs), seeks to achieve *full and productive employment* and decent work for all by 2030. Further, evidence suggests that the rise in radical

A. Roychowdhury (✉)
Jawaharlal Nehru University, New Delhi, India

P. Jha et al. (eds.), *Labour Questions in the Global South*,
https://doi.org/10.1007/978-981-33-4635-2_12

right-wing populist forces is linked to surge in inequality and unemployment (Burgoon et al. 2018).

Indian policy-makers, understanding the sensitivity of the aforementioned issues early on, stressed upon redistributive policies and actively designed policies for employment generation. For example, Mahendra Dev (2006: 1511) notes, 'Employment generation has come to occupy centre stage in our development planning as well as implementation. Expanding productive employment is central for sustained poverty reduction as labour is the main asset for a majority of the poor.' In this article we revisit India's record on the employment front, after it embraced market-friendly economic policies in 1991—with special emphasis on the most recent period (2011–12 to 2017–18), based on a nationally representative sample.

The importance of job creation in the Indian policy discourse may be understood from the fact that even adoption of market-oriented economic policies was justified on grounds of promoting efficiency and employment growth. As Chadha and Sahu (2002: 2012) put it, 'The proponents of economic reforms would have us believe that employment was expected to pick up primarily because the output growth was likely to pick up after economic reforms took roots.' In fact, support for such policies in India, with a vast majority of people engaged in agriculture, was garnered through the promise of introducing greater dynamism in the sector leading to rapid poverty reduction; Sen (1996: 2469) identifies this argument clearly: '[There is]a central component of the structural adjustment policies, wherein it is argued that greater liberalisation of trade and industry would shift resources towards agriculture and this would not only be more in line with India's comparative advantage but would also reduce poverty much more than earlier policies.' However, as we shall see below, expectations about economic reforms boosting employment growth have been thoroughly belied. Thus commenting on the post-reform employment trends, Mahendra Dev (2006: 1511) noted, 'Over time it has also been recognised that high [output] growth does not necessarily create employment. Labour absorption depends more on the pattern of growth (i.e., labour-intensive or capital-intensive). The experience of the last one and a half decades in India showed that employment opportunities created were inadequate in spite of rapid growth … leading to a worsening in the employment situation in the post-reform period.'

Employment stagnated even more over the next period (Mehrotra et al. 2014); in what follows, we document labour market outcomes in the most recent period (2011–12 to 2017–18), along with a brief discussion (and re-interpretation) of the employment trends in earlier phases. The detailed structure of the chapter is as follows: before discussing the labour market indicators in India, the section "Labour Market in South Asia: Broad Trends" sets the stage with a brief description of the labour market scenario in South Asia, primarily because India bears a striking resemblance, in terms of labour market indicators, with her neighbours. Section "Post-reform Employment Trends in India Until 2011–12" summarizes the broad trends in employment in earlier phases, viz. early nineties to 2011–12 and specifically scrutinizes the argument of voluntary withdrawal from labour force as an explanation for employment downturn. Section "Employment Trends and Labour Market Outcome: 2011-12 to 2017–18" presents the main findings of the study, with a detailed analysis of the most recent nationally representative employment survey data, available from the Periodic Labour Force Survey (PLFS) 2017–18. The chapter ends with some concluding observations.

Labour Market in South Asia: Broad Trends

South Asia, with a quarter of the world population, is home to around one-fifth of the global labour force (ILO 2018). Therefore, generating gainful employment in sufficient magnitude in the region would certainly put a dent on global poverty—in so far as productive employment is an effective way out of poverty. However, it would be naïve to assume that simply jacking up the output growth would be enough to meet the target of providing gainful employment; as Table 12.1 shows, there is in fact no relationship between output and employment growth in the region for the one and half decades under consideration (specifically, compare the cases of India and Pakistan).

Table 12.1 Annual growth rate: 2000–2015 (%)

Country	*Output*	*Employment*	*Labour force*
Bangladesh	5.8	1.2	1.3
India	7.2	1.5	1.4
Nepal	4	1.8	1.9
Pakistan	4.1	3.3	3.2
Sri Lanka	5.5	0.5	0.3

Source: Ghose (2019)

Table 12.2 Underemployment and unemployment rate: 2015 (%)

Country	*Incidence of under employment*	*Unemployment rate*
Bangladesh	20.4	4.1
India	11.7	3.5
Nepal	6.5	3
Pakistan	15.1	5.9
Sri Lanka	2.6	4.7

Source: Ghose (2019)

Moreover, there is little to take comfort from the fact that the growth in labour force and employment closely follow each other, implying low rates of unemployment (as brought out by Table 12.2). This is because in these countries there are no unemployment insurance benefits and people have to somehow survive, doing whatever is available *irrespective of pay and time of engagement*. Thus, in these countries lack of gainful employment manifests itself in the form of work-sharing or underemployment (of which there is significant evidence, even with problems of estimation, as observed from Table 12.2).

There is a further lacuna of using unemployment rate as an indicator to capture job scarcity. This is because lack of job opportunities may not show up as high unemployment rates; faced with faint prospects of securing employment there is a distinct possibility of simply dropping out of the labour force due to discouraged worker effect (fuelled by cost of job search and/or social barriers). In fact, there is evidence of very low labour force participation rates among women in South Asia; with female labour force participation rate (FLFPR) at 27.6%, this region remains one of the lowest in the world in terms of women joining the labour force (ILO 2018: 10).

But why does output growth fail to lift employment growth in South Asia? It is important to remember that these economies are at their early stages of development as demonstrated by their structure of workforce where 'agriculture employment still represents 59 per cent of total employment, manufacturing accounting for only 12 per cent, and services for about 24 per cent.' (https://www.ilo.org/asia/media-centre/news/WCMS_615872/lang%2D%2Den/index.htm). Historically, development trajectories of today's developed nations show that rise in manufacturing sector (as proportion to GDP) happens in the early stages of development and dominance of services comes only at a later stage. But the development experience of South Asian economies defies this trend; instead of first building a strong manufacturing base, these economies leapfrogged into services (as is evident from Table 12.3).

However, note that the services' share in employment does not match by a wide margin with its share in output, in any of the countries; the reason is the high productivity of labour in services. In other words, employment intensities of service sector output have been low and dominance of this sector in fuelling output growth in South Asian countries has led to weak employment growth in the region.

Finally, we look at the challenge of massive informality characterizing South Asian labour markets (Table 12.4). Note that except Sri Lanka (44.9%), a majority of the workforce in South Asian countries are self-employed in the informal sector, operating mainly on the principle of work-sharing and product-sharing. Further, a large proportion of workers are stuck in the informal sector on wage contracts with little security of tenure, no guarantee of minimum wages, no social security benefits and

Table 12.3 Share of services in output and employment: 2015 (%)

Country	*Output share*	*Employment share*
Bangladesh	56.6	34
India	56.5	26.9
Nepal	54.6	14.4
Pakistan	59.1	34.5
Sri Lanka	65.9	43.8

Source: Ghose (2019)

Table 12.4 Structure of employment: 2015

Country	*Share of formal employment (%)*	*Share of informal employment (%)*	
		Self-empt.	*Wage empt.*
Bangladesh	12.6	61.9	25.6
India	19.1	56	24.9
Nepal	7.7	83.2	9
Pakistan	14.4	64	21.5
Sri Lanka	37.2	44.9	17.9

Source: Ghose (2019)

no restrictions on working hours, among other things. No wonder then that the ILO (2018: 21) in 2018 finds: 72% of the workforce in South Asia employed under vulnerable conditions (i.e. own account workers and unpaid family labour) and 12.4% of workers (highest in the Asia-Pacific region) are in extreme poverty (i.e. living on less than US$1.9 per day in PPP). The discussion above shows that the labour market scenarios in South Asian countries are in many ways similar: with large gap in output and employment growth (except Pakistan), high incidence of underemployment rather than *open* unemployment (except Sri Lanka), dominance of service sector in output without matching share in employment and pervasive presence of informality. Further, their shared colonial history (except Nepal) makes a compelling case for learning from each other, through a close reading of labour market policies, about strategies that worked and draw lessons from failures. Given this background, we take up the detailed case study on India next.

Post-reform Employment Trends in India Until 2011–12

As already mentioned in Section "Introduction", since high output growth need not necessarily lead to rapid employment creation – one of the major promises of economic reforms in India were never fulfilled. This is evident from Table 12.5; output growth accelerated after economic reforms but failed to boost annual increment in employment, except for the period 1999–2000 to 2004–05 (more on this later). In fact, there

Table 12.5 Annual increase in employment (principal+subsidiary) [PS+SS] status and output

Period	*Annual output growth (%)*	*Annual empt. increase (million)*
Pre-reform		
1983 to 1993–94	5.2	7.1
Post-reform		
1993–94 to 1999–00	6.5	4
1999–00 to 2004–05	5.9	11.9
2004–05 to 2011–12	8.5	2.1

Note: Periodization on the basis of nationally representative large surveys available (1987–88 and 2009–10 survey results are avoided since these were drought years)

Source: Thomas (2012) and author's estimate

seems to be an inverse relationship between output growth and employment expansion, in the close to three decades under observation.

For example, Table 12.5 shows annual output growth in pre-reform era (5.2%) to be lower than the immediate post-reform years (6.5% between 1993–94 and 1999–2000); however, pace of employment creation in the previous period (7.1 million absolute increment yearly) prominently surpassed the later phase (4 million annual rise)[1] The employment slowdown during 1993–94 and 1999–2000 is well-established in literature (more so if we compare with the period 1977–78 to 1983–84) and is primarily due to falling employment elasticity of output over the years; as Mahendra Dev (2006: 1511) notes: 'The total employment in the economy increased at an average growth rate of close to 2 per cent per annum between 1977–78 and 1983, at 1.5 per cent between 1983 and 1988, at 2.2 per cent during 1987–94 and at less than 1 per cent between 1993–94 and 1999–2000 ... [driven by the fact that] ... employment elasticity to GDP for the economy as a whole was 0.53 in the period 1977–83 and this declined to 0.41 in the period 1983–94. The elasticity declined sharply to 0.15 in the period 1993–2000'. Further, Chadha and Sahu (2002: 2013) succinctly document that the rural segments of the workforce were worst affected by the slowdown: 'For example, under the usual (principal+subsidiary) status perspective, the decline in the growth rate of the rural workforce from 1.75 per cent during 1983/1993–94 to as low as 0.66 per cent during 1993–94/1999–2000, ... clearly indicates the substantial worsening of the employment situation in rural India. In terms of the drop in percentage points, the worsening occurred no less seriously in urban areas [from 3.27 per cent between 1983/1993–94 to 2.27 per cent between 1993–94/1999–2000] ... [These figures] points towards an overall worsening of the employment situation during the post-1993 years, and the rural workforce seems to be most grievously hit.' Therefore, employment growth may not automatically respond to output expansion.

There was, however, a dramatic turnaround in employment between 1999–2000 and 2004–05. Aggregate employment increased annually by 11.9 million and over the course of five years there were 59.5 million net additions to the workforce. Nevertheless, as Rangarajan et al. (2014: 117) put it: 'Contemporary literature has termed this phenomenon as "distress employment".' This is because around one-third of this employment expansion (18.5 million of 59.5 million; see Table 12.5 in Thomas 2012: 41) took the form of agricultural employment, precisely, during the period when rural incomes stagnated.[2] Further, an overwhelming proportion of those joining the agricultural workforce (16.9 million of 18.5 million; see Table 12.6 in Thomas 2012: 42) were self-employed females.[3] In fact, there was a dramatic rise in self-employment with 83% (49.5 million out of 59.5 million, see Table 12.4 in Thomas 2012: 40) of the newly added jobs occurring in this category. Now self-employment was typically associated with low quality jobs (Chandrasekhar and Ghosh 2006) along with a fall in the educational attainment of an average worker newly joining the workforce (Thomas 2011).There is further evidence of decline in wage growth and rising wage inequalities amidst employment improvement, when compared with the earlier period (1993–94 to 1999–2000) (Sarkar and Mehta 2010). These results led observers to conclude that the observed employment dynamism was actually 'distress driven'—in response to meagre livelihoods opportunities available in the countryside—with rural women entering the agricultural labour force to supplement their low household incomes, in order to meet subsistence needs (Abraham 2009).

Employment growth severely collapsed in the next period (2004–05 to 2011–12) merely adding 15 million to the workforce—being the lowest in any period since 1993–94 (Table 12.6)—even after registering highest output growth (8.5% per annum) in three decades (Table 12.5). This was far short of the job creation target (50 million) set by the Eleventh Five-Year Plan. Now disaggregating workers by residence and sex shows, employment growth decelerated across every segment of the workforce, except urban male (UM) (Table 12.6). Another important feature brought out by Table 12.6, is the absolute contraction of rural female (RF) workers (22 million) between 2004–05 and 2011–12. It is this decline in RF workers that primarily explains the slow growth in overall employment during the period and therefore deserves attention in details.

Table 12.6 Distribution of workers by residence and sex (principal+subsidiary) (PS+SS) status (million)

Category	*1983–84*	*1993–94*	*1999–00*	*2004–05*	*2011–12*
Rural Male	154	188 (34)	199 (11)	219 (20)	234 (15)
Rural Female	91	105 (14)	106 (1)	124 (18)	102 (-22)
Urban Male	47	65 (18)	76 (11)	90 (14)	109 (19)
Urban Female	12	17 (5)	18 (1)	25 (7)	27 (2)
Total	303	374 (71)	398 (24)	458 (60)	473 (15)

Note: Figures in parenthesis represent change in employment over previous period

Source: Thomas (2012) and author's estimate

Fall in RF workers between 2004–05 and 2011–12, was lead by an even greater decline in these workers from agriculture and allied activities sector (26.7 million) (see Table 12.2 in Thomas 2014: 16).[4] Further, the self-employed (male+female) in agriculture and allied activities registered a decline (21.3 million; see Table 12.3 in Mehrotra et al. 2014: 51) in this period. Therefore, the labour market seems to have witnessed over time two exactly opposite movements in workforce (see Table 12.6): (a) sharp rise in RF workers entering the labour market (18 million) between 1999–2000 and 2004–05 and (b) even a larger magnitude of RF leaving the workforce (22 million) between 2004–05 and 2011–12.

This withdrawal of RF from the workforce was accompanied by three events: (a) improvement in agricultural incomes in the second half of 2000s (Thomas 2012); (b) substantial improvement in rural wages due to Mahatma Gandhi National Rural Employment Guarantee Scheme (MGNREGS) and construction activities (Mehrotra et al. 2014; Thomas 2012); and (c) rise in educational attainment of RF population[5] (Rangarajan et al. 2011). These outcomes prompted observers to infer: 'The fall in female agricultural employment during the second half of the 2000s is possibly due to an improvement—and not a worsening—in the economic conditions in rural India' (Thomas 2012: 42).

Thus, the slowdown in aggregate employment between 2004–05 and 2011–12—mainly due to withdrawal of RF from the workforce—was seen as a positive development since targeted level of household income could be earned by the male members of the family *alone*, on account of improvements in the rural economy. As Thomas (2012: 42) puts it: 'A possible reason for the movement of [rural] women back to the household work during the second half of the 2000s is the improvement in the availability of income-earning opportunities for male members of the family.' Associated with this, was a jump in the RF student-population ratio (SPR) spreading even to older age groups (15–19 and 20–24 years), signifying expansion of higher education in addition to primary and secondary level education.

It is this explanation of *voluntary* withdrawal from workforce by the RF (i.e. fall in labour supply for attending to domestic duties and enrolling in educational institutions), along with no noticeable spike in unemployment rate among RF (as well as in other population segments; more on this below), that the steep decline in employment growth between 2004–05 and 2011–12, did not receive any urgent policy attention.

The basic contention of the voluntary withdrawal thesis of RF (i.e. adjustments in labour supply) can be readily checked from Table 12.7. As just mentioned, slowdown in overall employment between 2004–05 and 2011–12 was mainly on account of the absolute decline in RF workers; interestingly, attention was drawn to the fact that unemployment rate for RF, barely increased during this period (Table 12.7). The reason being a sharp decline in labour force participation rate (LFPR) of RF from 333 per thousand in 2004–05 to 253 per thousand in 2011–12 (note that LFPR for other population segments, namely, Rural Male, Urban Male and Urban Female fell as well but their magnitude of decline were far less than RF). It should be noted that the labour force (LF) captures that segment of the population who are *willing* to work (either working or engaged in job search) and LFPR is the ratio of *this* segment (LF) to total population. We also found that the number of RF actually working declined sharply between 2004–05 and 2011–12. However, unemployment rate (proportion of people engaged in pure job search to those willing to work i.e. LF)

Table 12.7 Distribution of population by their activity (principal+subsidiary) [PS+SS] status and unemployment rate

	Rural Male (RM)		*Rural Female (RF)*		*Urban Male (UM)*		*Urban Female (UF)*	
	2004–05	*2011–12*	*2004–05*	*2011–12*	*2004–05*	*2011–12*	*2004–05*	*2011–12*
LFPR ('000)	555	553	333	253	570	563	178	155
NLFR =(1000 - LFPR)	445	447	667	747	430	437	822	845
(i) Student ('000)	262	299	211	249	268	291	249	259
(ii) Domestic Duty & free collection of goods ('000)	4	3	272	353	4	3	428	461
(iii) Disabled, beggars, aged, young, sick etc. ('000)	178	143	183	146	158	142	145	126
Unemployment rt.(%)	1.6	1.8	1.8	2.0	3.8	3.0	6.9	5.2

Source: Employment-Unemployment Situation (EUS) in India, National Sample Survey Report: 2004–05 and 2011–12

was marginally higher in this period; signifying, in response to employment contraction, RF were *not* searching for jobs (for then the unemployment rate would have increased significantly). What were they doing then? Table 12.7 shows, RF simply *moved out* of the labour market and this is captured by the significant spike in the proportion of population not in labour force (NLFPR from 667 per thousand in 2004–05 to 747 per thousand in 2011–12, constituting: (i) students; (ii) attending to domestic duties and free collection of goods; (iii) disabled, young, old, beggars, prostitutes etc.).

But how can we infer that this shift out of labour force was voluntary? Rise in student population ratio (SPR) for RF from 211 per thousand in 2004–05 to 249 per thousand in 2011–12 was a positive development and therefore, considered to be voluntarily chosen due to rising aspirations. However, note that rise in SPR for rural male (RM) was also of similar magnitude but this did not result in a fall in LFPR for RM, anywhere comparable to RF. Additionally, LFPR—unlike in the case of RM—fell across *all* age groups for RF (see Table 12.19 in Appendix); therefore, fall in LFPR for older (25 years and above) rural women cannot be explained by rise in SPR. Again note that share of disabled, beggar, young, old, prostitutes and so on in RF fell by an equal magnitude to that of SPR; thus attending educational institutions cannot be a sufficient explanation for the fall in LFPR of RF (although undoubtedly it contributed to the trend).

This finding squarely underscores the importance of the second adjustment factor responsible for reducing labour supply of RF, namely, their moving out of the labour force to attend *only* household/domestic activities. Indeed, there was a sharp rise in RF *exclusively* engaged in domestic activities and free collection of goods from 272 per thousand in 2004–05 to 353 per thousand in 2011–12 (Table 12.7). And since this was associated with rise in rural wages and rural incomes, thus, the conjecture held sway that—with the rural male members, by themselves, earning enough to meet the targeted level of household income, women members *voluntarily* dropped out of the labour force to attend to domestic duties *exclusively*, due to reasons related to patriarchy.

Is there any evidence to raise doubts about this conjecture? Table 12.8 investigates this. It provides information about RF—more than 15 years age—*only* attending to domestic duties for major/most part of the year.

Note that as high as one-third of RF (32%) exclusively attending to domestic duties were ***willing to join the workforce***; this clearly shows that there was a scarcity of labour demand and some of these women may have been forced to confine themselves only to household duties, ***in the absence of labour market options.*** In fact, lack of job opportunities may be confirmed from the fact that majority of RF (51%)—attending household activities but willing to work—possessed the requisite skills necessary for the kind of jobs they were aiming. Further, 95% of these women were available for work on a regular basis. In fact, voluntary withdrawal thesis may have negatively affected RFs' prospect of joining the workforce, since 97% of such women reported to be in need of some kind of assistance to integrate with the labour market (Table 12.8).

These results raise scepticism about the voluntary withdrawal hypothesis of RF and possibilities of ***forced withdrawal*** due to 'discouraged worker effect' as a result of lack of labour market opportunities open up; consequently, their employment contraction may not be seen as a positive sign, but manifestation of a looming jobs crisis, first felt in this segment of population. Further Thomas (2014: 16) notes, rising SPR without commensurate job creation only postpones the labour market crisis: 'The growth in the population of students who are 15 years and above reduces labour supply for now, but raises the numbers of educated persons who would be demanding high quality jobs in the future.' Experience of the most recent period lends support to this apprehension; with crisis in job creation persisting– unemployment rate alarmingly rose to a 45 year high (Jha, Somesh 2019). It is to the discussion of these set of issues to which we now turn.

Table 12.8 Proportion of rural female (15 years and above age) exclusively attending to domestic duties with willingness and ability to work at household premises (%)

Willing to do specific work	32
Possessing skill for specified work	51.2
Available for regular work (Full time + Part time)	94.5
Assistance required	96.5

Source: Participation of Women in Specified Activities along with Domestic Duties, NSS Report 2011–12

Employment Trends and Labour Market Outcome: 2011–12 to 2017–18

Aggravating past trends—in a first since employment figures are recorded in India—overall employment shrank by 1.2 million between 2011–12 and 2017–18 (Table 12.9).[6] Once again this was principally driven by an absolute decline in RF workers (24.7 million; Table 12.9); although other population segments showing clear mark of employment slowdown (except urban female [UF]; Table 12.10) contributed to the trend. In fact, an approximate four-fold decline in employment growth among RM, in the current period (4.6 million between 2011–12 and 2017–18) compared to the previous period (16 million between 2004–05 and 2011–12), brings out the complete collapse of job opportunities in the rural segment as a whole (Table 12.10).

However, as a result of the employment debacle—unlike in the previous period—*open* unemployment rates across every population segment rose very sharply in the current period (Table 12.11); catching much attention of the media and policymakers alike.[7] Indeed such significant rise in open unemployment rate surprised everyone, for in developing countries like ours, there are no unemployment benefits available and people simply cannot afford to remain unemployed; job scarcity rather takes the form of work-sharing or underemployment as opposed to *open* unemployment (see Section "Labour Market in South Asia: Broad trends").

But what explains such high unemployment rates? Now, unemployment rate can be seen as the proportion of: excess supply of labour over aggregate labour supply.[8] We already noted that employment creation (i.e. labour demand) slowed down (or turned negative) in the current period in every population segment (except UF; Table 12.10). On the other

Table 12.9 Aggregate change in workforce (principal+subsidiary) [PS+SS] status (million)

	RM	*RF*	*UM*	*UF*	*Total*
2017–18	239.0	77.0	123.8	31.5	471.3
2011–12	234.4	101.6	109.1	27.4	472.5
Net change	4.6	-24.7	14.7	4.1	-1.2

Note: Employment figures are obtained through multiplying work-participation rate (WPR) of each population segment with Census Population figures

Source: Periodic Labour Force Survey (PLFS) 2017–18 and EUS 2011–12

Table 12.10 Comparative change in workforce (principal+subsidiary) [PS+SS] status (million)

	RM	*RF*	*UM*	*UF*	*Total*
2017–18 over 2011–12	4.6	-24.7	14.7	4.1	-1.2
2011–12 over 2004–05	16	-21.8	18	2.1	14.7

Source: Periodic Labour Force Survey (PLFS) 2017–18 and EUS 2011–12

Table 12.11 Distribution of population by their activity (principal + subsidiary) [PS+SS] status and unemployment rate

	RM		*RF*		*UM*		*UF*	
	2011–12	*2017–18*	*2011–12*	*2017–18*	*2011–12*	*2017–18*	*2011–12*	*2017–18*
LFPR ('000)	553	549	253	182	563	570	155	159
NLFR = (1000 – LFPR)	447	451	747	818	437	430	845	841
(i)Student ('000)	299	292	249	245	291	272	259	248
(ii) Dom Duty & free collection of goods('000)	3	8	353	432	3	7	461	467
(iii) Disabled, beggars, aged, young, sick etc. ('000)	143	151	146	141	142	151	126	126
Unemployment rt. (%)	1.8	5.8	2.0	3.8	3.0	7.0	5.2	10.7

Source: Periodic Labour Force Survey (PLFS) 2017–18 and EUS 2011–12

hand, there was a stable rise in labour supply[9] (determined by the natural growth rate of population and LFPR) as a result of the demographic structure of population (on the basis of which the so called demographic dividend argument is made in literature).[10] For example, aggregate labour supply (or total labour force) increased from 485 million in 2011–12 to 501 million in 2017–18, whereas, aggregate labour demand declined from 472.5 million to 471.3 million during this period (Table 12.9). This mismatch, therefore, resulted in an excess supply of labour in the job market, leading to a sharp rise in the overall *open* unemployment rate (from 2.5% in 2011–12 to 6% in 2017–18). Note that this thesis holds for all population segments—as their LFPRs between two periods barely changed—except RF. As for RF, LFPR sharply declined from 253 per thousand in 2011–12 to 182 per thousand in 2017–18 (therefore, reducing the pace of entry into the labour market i.e. labour supply); but then labour demand also contracted significantly by 24.7 million workers (Table 12.10), on balance, leading to an almost doubling of the reported unemployment rate (Table 12.11).

Since the continuing fall in RF employment is identified as the major cause behind fall in aggregate employment in the current period, along with lowest reported unemployment rate among all population segments, due to sharp decline LFPR—can we identify traces of *voluntary withdrawal* phenomenon among RF?

Table 12.11 shows for RF, movement out of labour force neither happened due to rise in SPR nor due to rise in the dependent segment (disabled, beggars, sick, young, old etc.) of the population (in fact, *both* declined marginally in the current period); but purely due to phenomenal rise (from 353 per thousand in 2011–12 to 432 per thousand in 2017–18) in the proportion of population *only attending to domestic duties and free collection of goods.* Can this withdrawal be voluntary in nature? Available evidence does not support this hypothesis. First, recall the four-fold decline in employment creation among RM in the current period (Table 12.10). Second, growth in rural wages decelerated significantly in the current period (Table 12.12; this is true for even the urban segment). Third, income from agriculture markedly declined in the current period compared to the previous one, inter alia, due to two consecutive droughts in 2014–15 and 2015–16 (Mahendra Dev 2018). Thus, given labour market returns and agricultural incomes, it is difficult to conceive of RM, on their own, meeting the targeted level of household income; consequently, withdrawal of RF from the labour force appears *involuntary due to lack of*

Table 12.12 Annual average growth rates in real wages of casual workers engaged in other than public works (%)

Period	*RM*	*RF*	*UM*	*UF*
2004–05 to 2011–12	6.29	7.6	5.14	5.73
2011–12 to 2017–18	3.27	2.12	3.26	2.84

Note: computed at 2011–12 prices; Rural wages deflated by CPI(RL) and Urban wages deflated by CPI(IW); 2017–18 wages are simple arithmetic mean of quarterly wages

Source: Periodic Labour Force Survey (PLFS) 2017–18 and EUS 2011–12

labour market opportunities (job scarcity is also confirmed by the near doubling of open unemployment rate among RF).

Given this backdrop, we now compare sectoral changes in employment between two periods, namely, 2004–05 and 2011–12 with 2011–12 and 2017–18 (Table 12.13). Continuing past trends agricultural employment fell in the current period as well; people in large numbers deserted agriculture for over a decade due to mechanization and non-remunerative returns from farm activities. However, decline in the present period (27.1 million) was less than the contraction of agricultural employment in the previous period (34.36 million). Even more alarming is the non-agricultural employment scenario; as already noted, aggregate employment shrunk in the present period (1.2 million) while it posted positive growth in the previous period (14.58 million), on account of, non-agricultural employment slowing down significantly in the current period (almost halved at 25.9 million) compared to the previous period (registering 48.94 million jobs) (Table 12.13).

Next major concern is the contraction of manufacturing employment (0.92 million) in the current period, in spite of government running programs (like, Skill India and Make in India) to energize manufacturing employment. Most disturbingly, expansion in construction sector employment fell by more than five times in the current period. In fact, amidst overall employment slowdown in the earlier period, construction sector came as a saviour, accounting for half (23.95 million) of non-agricultural employment expansion (48.94 million); therefore, it was considered to be the employer of last resort. However, significant slowdown in construction sector employment shows, even this sector was unable to absorb labour. Only three sectors, namely, trade, hotels and restaurants; transport, storage and communications; and other services, posted higher employment growth in the current period. However, note that their margin of expansion were nowhere near the margin of employment contraction/slowdown in other sectors of the economy—explaining the total collapse of aggregate employment in the present period.

Within this broad labour market situation, characterized by a large body of reserve army of labour (RAL) captured by the soaring open unemployment rates, let us now investigate the working conditions of those reporting employed. Table 12.14 reports the proportion of workers engaged in informal enterprises with ownership patterns either, depicting proprietary (full-liability) structure or, on partnership basis (joint-liability). Therefore, these firms do not resemble an important feature that

Table 12.13 Comparison of sectoral change in employment (principal + subsidiary) [PS+SS] status between two periods (million)

Sectors	*RM*		*RF*		*UM*		*UF*		*ALL*	
	2017–18 to 2011–12	*2011–12 to 2004–05*	*2017–18 to 2011–12*	*2011–12 to 2004–05*	*2017–18 to 2011–12*	*2011–12 to 2004–05*	*2017–18 to 2011–12*	*2011–12 to 2004–05*	*2017–18 to 2011–12*	*2011–12 to 2004–05*
Agriculture	-7.78	-6.32	-19.78	-27.16	0.58	0.59	-0.12	-1.47	-27.10	-34.36
Mining &Quarrying	0.02	-0.14	-0.15	-0.07	-0.24	0.17	-0.02	0.03	-0.39	-0.01
Manufacturing	-0.58	1.70	-3.73	-0.46	3.30	3.19	0.09	0.91	-0.92	5.34
Electricity, water etc.	0.49	0.27	-0.10	0.10	0.08	0.80	-0.08	0.22	0.39	1.40
Construction	4.18	15.59	-2.63	4.85	2.82	3.36	0.20	0.16	4.57	23.95
Trade, hotels & Restaurant	3.24	0.59	0.03	-0.05	1.98	3.05	0.59	0.50	5.83	4.08
Transport, Storage & Communications	2.58	1.53	0.03	-0.04	2.96	3.09	0.30	0.39	5.88	4.97
Other Services	3.16	2.09	1.57	0.45	3.28	4.54	3.15	2.00	11.16	9.08
Total	4.61	15.29	-24.67	-22.26	14.74	18.79	4.14	2.76	-1.2	14.58
Non-agricultural	12.39	21.61	-4.83	4.90	14.42	18.20	4.25	4.23	25.90	48.94

Source: Periodic Labour Force Survey (PLFS) 2017–18 and EUS 2011–12

Table 12.14 Share of workers engaged in informal (proprietary and partnership enterprises) sector (PS+SS) (%)

	RM	*RF*	*UM*	*UF*
2004–05	79.2	86.4	73.9	65.4
2011–12	76.2	72.7	70.4	63.6
2017–18	74.5	59.3	67.3	51

Source: Periodic Labour Force Survey (PLFS) 2017–18 and EUS 2011–12

characterizes modern firms, namely, limited liability structure. This typically restrains the capacity of informal enterprises to grow—in the absence of sourcing sufficient capital—producing a low-level equilibrium trap, in turn offering poor working conditions to those employed here.

The share of workers engaged in informal enterprises registered a fall—of varying degrees—across each population segment. Among males (both in rural and urban areas), this fall is moderate compared to the females (both areas); however, it should be kept in mind that the number of females employed is only a small fraction of the male workforce. Further, fall in share of informal sector RF workers should be interpreted with caution, since RF segment suffered an absolute employment decline in this period (Table 12.10). However, for UF, although constituting merely 7% of overall workforce in 2017–18, this decline is an encouraging trend.

Next, we examine the employment status of workers (Table 12.15). It is well known that regular wage (RW) employment are most coveted jobs, as these pay higher wages on a regular basis along with certain non-pecuniary benefits.

Note that the proportion of RW jobs increased across the board, once again rising more sharply for females compared to males. However, in interpreting these trends the caveats mentioned earlier also apply here. Additionally, it should be kept in mind that the rise in share of RW workers is in midst of a contraction in aggregate employment (specifically, RF) and marked slowdown in job creation in the working men segment (both rural and urban). Nonetheless, improvement in RW employment among UF is a welcome development.

The reason why RW employment remain lucrative to workers can be gauged from Table 12.16; essentially, because RW positions fetch around double the (monthly) income offered in a typical casual wage job, irrespective of location and sex (in fact for UF it is almost triple). This

Table 12.15 Distribution of workers according to their employment status (%)

	Rural Male			*Rural Female*		
	Self-employed (SE)	*Regular wage (RW)*	*Casual labour (CL)*	*Self-employed (SE)*	*Regular wage (RW)*	*Casual labour (CL)*
2004–05	58.1	9	32.9	63.7	3.7	32.6
2011–12	54.5	10	35.5	59.3	5.6	35.1
2017–18	57.8	14	28.2	57.7	10.5	31.8
	Urban Male			**Urban Female**		
	Self-employed (SE)	**Regular wage (RW)**	**Casual labour (CL)**	**Self-employed (SE)**	**Regular wage (RW)**	**Casual labour (CL)**
2004–05	44.8	40.6	14.6	47.7	35.6	16.7
2011–12	41.7	43.4	14.9	42.8	42.8	14.3
2017–18	39.2	45.7	15.1	34.7	52.1	13.1

Source: PLFS 2017–18

Table 12.16 Average monthly earnings in 2017–18 (Rs)

	RM	*RF*	*UM*	*UF*
Regular wage	13,533	8939	17,990	14,560
Self-employed	8955	4122	16,067	6994
Casual wage (other than public works)	6955	4498	8418	4992

Note: For Regular Wage and Self-employed, monthly income is obtained by averaging over quarterly figures. Monthly income at casual wages is obtained by multiplying daily wages by 26 days

Source: PLFS 2017–18

observation broadly holds when compared with self-employment, except for UM. However, there is wide disparity among earnings within RW category; as Anand and Thampi (2019) documents: 'In 2017–18, around 45% of regular workers earned less than Rs 10,000 per month, and about 12% earned less than Rs 5,000 per month.' Further, note that regular workers, on average, earned below the minimum monthly income of Rs. 18,000 prescribed for government employees by the 7th Pay Commission.

Additionally, Table 12.17 shows, RW workers were on average working far greater hours per week than both self-employed and casual wage workers; thus, part of the higher monthly pay RW workers received were simply

Table 12.17 Average number of hours worked in a week by different employment statuses (PS+SS)

RM			*RF*		
SE	*RW*	*CL*	*SE*	*RW*	*CL*
50.5	57.6	45.4	38.6	49.9	38.3
UM			**UF**		
58.6	60.2	46.5	41.5	52.7	40.4

Source: PLFS 2017–18

Table 12.18 Share of Regular Workers without written job contract in non-agriculture sector (PS+SS) (%)

	RM	*RF*	*UM*	*UF*
2004–05	59.4	56.8	58.6	61.2
2011–12	65.4	61.9	64.4	65.9
2017–18	71.7	58.5	72.7	71.4
Share of Regular Workers without paid holiday in non-agriculture sector (PS+SS) (%)				
2004–05	47.3	48.7	44.8	48
2011–12	51.7	48.1	49.5	49.1
2017–18	58.1	47.9	53.1	51.8
Share of Regular Workers without social security in non-agriculture sector (PS+SS) (%)				
2004–05	55.5	60.8	51.9	59.6
2011–12	56.8	63.4	53.5	56.2
2017–18	51.9	55.1	47	50.1

Note: Social Security comprise of PF/pension, gratuity, health care and maternity benefit

Source: PLFS 2017–18

extra compensation for extra effort and ***not necessarily due to higher compensation rate per unit of labour.***

Nonetheless, RW employment are still the most sought after jobs since they come with certain non-pecuniary benefits (viz. written job contracts, paid holidays and social security benefits) not available in other forms of employment contracts. However, Table 12.18 shows proportions of RW non-agricultural workers, without written job contracts and without the facility of paid holiday, are increasing overtime across every segment of the workforce, except RF. As for RF, first note that the change is marginal—although improving—when compared to other segments of the workforce; moreover, RW employment merely constitutes 10.5% of all jobs in the RF segment (see Table 12.15; least among all segments of the workforce and has to be read with the fact that employment in this segment registered sharp decline). The only improvement noticeable is the fall in proportion of RW workers without social security; however, coverage under social security may not be comprehensive and entitlement to *any one* scheme (see notes to Table 12.18) is enough to bring about the observed trend. Further, without written job contracts establishing employment status for claiming social security benefits may be difficult (although it is better than absence of social security provisions altogether). Therefore, evidence suggests that faced with a slack labour market—surrounded by large RAL—even RW jobs cannot necessarily assure quality anymore, as increasingly its content gets diluted.

Thus, located within an overall employment and (casual) wage slowdown, every segment of the workforce suffered both in terms of quantity, as well as, in terms of quality of jobs, except UF. As for UF—although constituting merely 7% of aggregate workforce—employment growth picked up alongside lesser proportion of workers engaged in informal enterprises and greater chances of securing RW employment (although content of RW jobs faded away). Thus, the recent period saw deterioration in livelihood opportunities and conditions of employment for overwhelming sections of the workforce in India.

Conclusion

With a brief description of the labour market situation in South Asia, this chapter primarily focuses on the employment trends and labour market outcomes in India, in the post-reform period. South Asian economies show striking resemblance in their development experience: (a) none of them demonstrate rapid output growth automatically pulling up employment growth (in fact, no relationship between these two variables is observable in any of the countries); (b) each country, even at their early stages of development, heavily depended on services output; however employment intensity of service sector output were low, everywhere; (c) majority of the workforce, in all countries, were located in the informal sector.

Turning to the Indian case study, we divided the post-reform period into two parts: (i) 1993–94 to 2011–12: with sub-periods according to the availability of data (dealt in Section "Post-reform Employment Trends in India Until 2011–12") and (ii) 2011–12 to 2017–18: the most recent period (examined in Section "Employment trends and labour market outcome: 2011–12 to 2017–18").[11]

Discussion of the employment trend between 1993–94 and 2011–12 clearly shows that a central promise of economic reforms, namely, acceleration in employment growth with the adoption of market-friendly policies in India was never fulfilled. Except for a brief period (1999–2000 to 2004–05), employment growth in the post-reform period was less than in the pre-reform phase (1983–84 to 1993–94). Between 1999–2000 and 2004–05, rapid growth in employment was basically driven by 'rural distress' with rural women joining the workforce, as self-employed in agriculture, in large numbers to meet subsistence needs of the household. Experience of the subsequent period with the withdrawal of RF from the labour force is explained in the literature as a voluntary move. We contested this hypothesis and showed that RF might have been forced to withdraw from the labour force in the face of job scarcity.

Turning to the most recent period it was shown that aggregate employment in fact shrank between 2011–12 and 2017–18. Again, this was driven by a fall in RF workers along with marked slowdown in employment creation in other segments of the workforce, except UF. An explanation of the soaring unemployment rates observed across the board was provided in terms of shrinking labour demand, in the face of labour supply rising at a regular (not extraordinary) pace. Specifically, rise in unemployment rate for RF, even with falling LFPR, was explained in terms of dramatic reduction in labour demand (workforce). Further fall in RFs' LFPR was found to be *solely* driven by, their *exclusively* joining household work, even in the midst of slowdown in rural (casual) wages and agricultural incomes. Thus, this withdrawal seems to be *involuntary* in nature.

Sectoral analyses suggest that manufacturing employment turned negative and most disturbingly employment growth in construction decelerated more than five times in the current period. Examining the quality of employment, although it was shown that the proportion of workers in the informal sector has come down and RW employment share is on the rise; nonetheless, it was pointed out that the RW earners were working for more hours than workers in other employment categories and the content of RW jobs were increasingly getting diluted. Therefore, both opportunities of livelihood and quality of employment seem to have deteriorated in the current period.

Appendix

Table 12.19 Age-specific LFPR

Age-groups	*RM*		*RF*	
	2004–05	*2011–12*	*2004–05*	*2011–12*
5–9	3	0	3	1
14–10	70	29	75	30
15–19	529	333	331	164
20–24	891	788	435	297
25–29	982	963	530	369
30–34	988	990	593	431
35–39	991	991	642	481
40–44	985	988	627	482
45–49	982	988	616	484
50–54	963	966	562	444
55–59	931	935	509	394
60 and >	645	649	254	213

Source: EUS-NSS, 2011–12

Notes

1. This inverse relationship continues to hold in the subsequent periods.
2. Actually, an overwhelming 38 million out of 60 million, additions in workforce took place in the rural areas (see Table 12.6).
3. Most disturbingly, 1.67 million out of the 16.9 million women joining agricultural workforce were more than 60 years old (see Table 12.7 in Mehrotra et al. 2014: 53).
4. Interestingly, overall agricultural employment, for the first time since independence, shrank by 33.3 million between 2004–05 and 2011–12 (Mehrotra et al. 2014).
5. This trend in rising educational attainment was also visible across other population segments viz. Rural Male, Urban Male and Urban Female.
6. On the issue of comparability of PLFS with earlier NSS rounds, note that, P.C. Mohanan who resigned as the National Statistical Commission chairman, categorically mentioned, 'When we [National Statistical Commission] approve a report, I am not going to give a figure which is not comparable with the other ones. Second, the concept of employment and unemployment are universally accepted. International Labour Organization pre-

scribes the standards, we all follow it.' (https://scroll.in/latest/912803/unemployment-former-statistical-commission-chief-denies-centres-claim-that-report-is-a-draft; last accessed 10 September 2019). Further, Professor R. Ramakumar (2019) pointed out that the sampling design only changed at a later stage (second stage stratification) and there are inbuilt mechanisms to correct over/under-representation of any group. Therefore, PLFS remains comparable with the earlier rounds of NSS survey.

7. In fact, there was a huge controversy over allegedly intentional delay in the publication of employment data by the Union government. The controversy arose with the resignation of the chairman of National Statistical Commission (in protest to the inordinate delay in publication of the employment report finalized by the Commission) and subsequently, leaked unemployment figures—showing highest unemployment rate in 45 years—appearing in the media. There was widespread speculation that, in an election year government was suppressing unpalatable unemployment figures. Curiously, the employment report was published within a week *after* the declaration of election results and it confirmed the high unemployment rates leaked in the media earlier.
8. This can be expressed in symbols as: $UR = \frac{L^S - L^D}{L^S}$; where, UR = unemployment rate; L^S = labour supply; and L^D = labour demand.
9. Growth in labour supply is determined by the proportion of population joining the labour force (LFPR) multiplied by the underlying population growth.
10. For example, Thomas (2014: 16) cites: 'Estimates by the World Bank show that the population aged 15 to 59 years is set to increase dramatically in India from around 757 million in 2010 to 972 million in 2030. This could potentially translate into an addition of over 200 million workers over the next two decades.' Certainly, labour supply increases due to such additions in the working age group population.
11. This periodization is done with the sole objective of giving emphasis to the most recent period rather than any pedagogic compulsion.

Bibliography

Abraham, V. (2009). Employment Growth in Rural India: Distress-Driven? *Economic and Political Weekly, 44*(16), 94–104.

Anand, I., & Thampi, A. (2019). Most Regular Jobs in India Don't Pay Well: PLFS. *Live Mint*. https://www.livemint.com/politics/policy/most-regular-jobs-in-india-don-t-pay-well-plfs-1565075309032.html. Last Accessed 8 Sep 2019.

Burgoon, B., van Noort, S., Rooduijn, M., & Underhill, G. (2018). *Radical Right Populism and the Role of Positional Deprivation and Inequality*. Paper

Presented at the 67th Economic Policy Panel Meeting, 12–13 April Zurich. https://cepr.org/sites/default/files/events/papers/995_Radical%20Right%20Populism.pdf. Last Accessed 8 Sep 2019.

Chadha, G. K., & Sahu, P. P. (2002). Post-reform Setbacks in Rural Employment Issues that Need Further Scrutiny. *Economic & Political Weekly, 37*(21), 1998–2026.

Chandrasekhar, C. P., & Ghosh, J. (2006). Working More for Less. *Macroscan.* http://www.macroscan.org/fet/nov06/print/prnt281106Working_More.htm. Last Accessed 9 Sep 2019.

Ghose, A. K. (2019). Economic Growth and Employment in South Asia. In S. Chaturvedi & S. Saha (Eds.), *Manufacturing and Jobs in South Asia: Strategy for Sustainable Economic Growth.* Singapore: Springer.

Government of India. (2006). *Employment and Unemployment Situation in India 2004–05.* New Delhi: Ministry of Labour and Programme Implementation, National Sample Survey Office.

Government of India. (2014a). *Employment-Unemployment Situation in India 2011–12.* New Delhi: Ministry of Labour and Programme Implementation, National Sample Survey Office.

Government of India. (2014b). *Participation of Women in Specified Activities Along with Domestic Duties 2011–12.* New Delhi: Ministry of Labour and Programme Implementation, National Sample Survey Office.

Government of India. (2019). *Periodic Labour Force Survey (PLFS) 2017–18.* New Delhi: Ministry of Labour and Programme Implementation, National Sample Survey Office.

International Labour Organisation. (2018). *World Employment Social Outlook.* https://www.ilo.org/wcmsp5/groups/public/%2D%2D-dgreports/%2D%2D-dcomm/%2D%2D-publ/documents/publication/wcms_615594.pdf. Last Accessed 10 Sep 2019.

Jha, S. (2019). Unemployment Rate at Four-Decade High of 6.1% in 2017–18: NSSO Survey. *Business Standard.* https://www.business-standard.com/article/economy-policy/unemployment-rate-at-five-decade-high-of-6-1-in-2017-18-nsso-survey-119013100053_1.html. Last Accessed 8 Sep 2019.

Keynes, J. M. (2010). *The General Theory of Employment, Interest and Money.* New Delhi: Atlantic Publishers.

Mahendra Dev, S. (2006). Policies and Programmes for Employment. *Economic & Political Weekly, 41*(16), 1511–1516.

Mahendra, Dev. S. (2018). *Transformation of Indian Agriculture? Growth, Inclusiveness and Sustainability.* IGIDR Working Paper 026, http://www.indiaenvironmentportal.org.in/files/file/TRANSFORMATION%20OF%20INDIAN%20AGRICULTURE.pdf. Last Accessed 8 Sep 2019.

Mehrotra, S., Parida, J., Sinha, S., & Gandhi, A. (2014). Explaining Employment Trends in the Indian Economy: 1993–94 to 2011–12. *Economic and Political Weekly, 49*(32), 49–57.

Ramakumar, R. (2019). Unemployment: Why Amitabh Kant and Surjit Bhalla Are Wrong. *Newsclick.* https://www.newsclick.in/unemployment-india-NSSO-PLFS-Amitabh-Kant-Surjit-Bhalla. Last Accessed 10 Sep 2019.

Rangarajan C., Kaul, P. I., & Seema. (2011). Where is the missing labour force?. *Economic and Political Weekly, 46*(39), 68–72.

Rangarajan, C., Seema, & Vibeesh, E. M. (2014). Developments in the Workforce Between 2009–10 and 2011–12. *Economic and Political Weekly, 49*(23), 117–121.

Rawal V., & Bansal, P. (2019). Surgical Strike on Employment: The record of the first Modi government. *Macroscan*, https://macroscan.org/cur/jun19/pdf/Surgical_Strike.pdf. Last Accessed 08 September 2019.

Sarkar, S., & Mehta, B. S. (2010). Income Inequality in India: Pre- and Post-reform Periods. *Economic and Political Weekly, 45*(37), 45–55.

Sen, A. (1996). Economic Reforms, Employment and Poverty: Trends and Options. *Economic & Political Weekly, 31*(35/37), 2459–2478.

Thomas, J. J. (2011). Locked in a Low-Skill Equilibrium? Trends in Labour Supply and Demand in India. *Indian Journal of Labour Economics, 54*(2), 195–218.

Thomas, J. J. (2012). India's Labour Market During the 2000s: Surveying the Changes. *Economic and Political Weekly, 47*(51), 39–51.

Thomas, J. J. (2014). The Demographic Challenge and Employment Growth in India. *Economic and Political Weekly, 49*(6), 15–17.

PART III

Agrarian Labour and the Semi-Proletarian Condition

CHAPTER 13

Rural Labour Unionism in Brazil: The Transformations of the National Confederation of Farm Workers (CONTAG)

Eryka Galindo and Marcelo C. Rosa

This chapter aims to examine the recent transformations in the unified rural labour unions system in Brazil. The emergence of new political actors, organised movements and agrarian policies from the Workers Party (PT) for smallholders has contributed to changes in the discourse and the modus operandi of the National Confederation of Farm Workers (CONTAG) founded in the 1960s. More specifically, the chapter draws on the emergence of the family farming agenda within the government and among the movements and on the recent role of labour courts, allowing a potential dismissal of the CONTAG's representation monopoly.

E. Galindo (✉)
Freie Universität Berlin, Berlin, Germany

M. C. Rosa
CPDA/UFRRJ, Rio de Janeiro Federal Rural University,
Rio de Janeiro, Brazil

P. Jha et al. (eds.), *Labour Questions in the Global South*,
https://doi.org/10.1007/978-981-33-4635-2_13

Introduction

This chapter aims to examine the transformation in rural unions as part of a broader analysis of the question of labour in Brazil today. Although some of the literature acknowledges that traditional forms of social organisation have dwindled in Brazil, trade unions—especially those representing rural workers—remain strong. This can be seen not only in the numbers but also in the influence that these unions have, both with state institutions and in international forums (Maybury-Lewis 1994; Pereira 1997; Carvalho 2018). The persistence of the rural unionism is directly associated with the dynamics of construction, reinterpretations and subsequent transformations in the rural worker category in the context of union organisation in Brazil. As a result of these adaptations, the representation system of rural workers is holding steady five decades after it was originally introduced.

The union rural workers system in Brazil is comprised of a network of over 4000 affiliate unions that have been grouped under a single organisation, the National Confederation of Farm Workers (CONTAG). This mammoth-like but tightly concentrated union system has been sustained by two Brazilian legal principles. The first establishes that there can be only one union for each trade in a given geographical area (a concept known as *unicidade sindical*) while the second establishes "rural worker" as a general occupational category that comprises a wide range of workers and labour relations in the rural areas.

The first section of the chapter describes the foundation of CONTAG and the political and legal transformation of the rural worker category. More specifically, we aim to explore three aspects: (1) the emergence during the 1980s of new political subjects in the countryside who joined diverse social movements and demanded recognition and representation, thus revealing the limitations of the generic category of the "rural worker" and calling into question the CONTAG system's ability to represent the collective interests of workers; (2) social transformations, a series of changes in production and economics that altered rural labour relations in Brazil, especially among wage earners; (3) a combination of these factors, which contributed to new court interpretations of the rural worker occupational category, leading, in turn, to adaptations at the organisational level among rural trade unions.

The second section examines the CONTAG's recent instrumental political division between the occupational categories of the rural worker and the family farmer with the foundation of a twin confederation named CONTAR (National Confederation of Rural Wage Workers).

Rural Unionism in Brazil: CONTAG's Structure and Role

According to Campos (2016), the National Register of Trade Unions (CNES) maintained by the Labour and Employment Ministry (MTE) lists 11,240 entities (including local trade unions, state federations, national confederations and national labour federations of diverse working categories) representing workers in 2016.[1] If only the trade unions are considered, the total is 10,817, 26.2% of which represent rural workers. This number suggests that despite rising urbanisation rates in Brazil (approximately 85% of Brazilians reside in cities and 15% in the countryside, according to the 2015 National Household Sample Survey conducted by the Brazilian Institute of Geography and Statistics), the trade unions representing rural workers remain numerous and strong. According to Ricci (2009) the rural worker unionism remains relatively influential due to the fact it was organised for so many years under a single system, that is, that of the National Confederation of Farm Workers (CONTAG). Recently, the confederation changed its name to the National Confederation of Farm Workers and Family Farmers.

Two of the various factors that contributed to maintaining such a large and diverse structure under a single umbrella organisation are *unicidade sindical* and union dues (Favareto 2007). Under the principle of *unicidade*, which was reaffirmed in Brazil's 1988 Constitution, there can be no more than a single union organisation for each professional or industrial category in a given region. In other words, there can be only one trade union for rural workers at the municipal level, one worker federation at the state level and one confederation at the federal level. This single-occupation union system is financed through the collection of monthly union dues from all affiliated rural workers. In the case of all employees, affiliates or other non-trade union organisations in the formal sector, union dues are automatically deducted from their wages. The employer is responsible for collecting the dues and transferring them to the union.

Another important features of the CONTAG system is the unification of diverse types of rural labour within a single category, that of the rural worker. At the beginning, this category mainly included rural waged workers but over time it was reconfigured and expanded to include a broader base, including small farm owners who became known as "family farmers" (Grisa and Schneider 2014).

The Legal Grounds for the Representation of the Collective Interests Rural Workers and the Founding of CONTAG

In 1931, with the passage of the Unionisation Act (Decree 19,770, 19 March 1931), Brazil introduced its first legislation on organised labour. More than a decade later, this was followed by Decree-Law No. 5452 (1 May 1943), also known as the Labour Law Consolidation Act (CLT). Although this legislation provided a legal framework for the organisation of different occupational categories, it also served as a mechanism for state interference in the operations of trade unions. These laws, however, were restricted to organised labour in cities.

In 1944 and 1945, a series of government and ministerial decrees were passed to establish a legal framework for three types of rural worker organisations: trade unions, professional associations and civil associations (Costa 1996). These edicts laid out the basic conditions for the operation of rural trade unions in Brazil and soon after, the first organisations began to form. Nonetheless, the legal status of many of these trade unions would not be officially recognised until the 1960s.

In 1962, three decades after trade union legislation was first introduced in Brazil, the statutory regulations for the Brazilian rural union system were finally instated. Ricci (2009) argues that this delay can mainly be attributed to rural employers, who held sway over government officials and their decisions, pushing to block—or at least delay—the creation of these rural union organisations. According to Medeiros (1997), until the 1960s large estate owners argued fiercely that all rural producers, which included both farm owners and wage earners working on these farms, shared common interests, thus eliminating—in their view—the need for organisations representing the collective interests of the waged workers.

In 1962, with the passage of Degree 209-A (25 June 1962), the João Goulart administration officially legalised trade unionism in the countryside. According to this decree, rural workers were divided into four different classifications: (1) crop workers, including wage workers, sharecroppers or the self-employed under a family or collective work regime; (2) farming and livestock workers, and other similar agricultural tasks; (3) workers involved in extractivism; (4) administrative employees (Costa 1996).

Although this decree was fundamental to establishing the legal grounds for the rural worker union system, it was highly criticised at the municipal and national levels—especially among sectors of the Brazilian Communist

Party (PCB)—because of this division within the worker category (Costa 1996). The separation of rural workers into four groups created the potential for two equally perilous scenarios, in the opinion of the PCB: (i) it could lead to the existence of more than one union representing rural workers in a single municipality, generating conflict among the union's members; (ii) the split category could make it harder to obtain the minimum number of affiliated workers needed to found union organisations and maintain them. Though the rural elites were also against the subdivision of the worker categories, they took a different view of the situation. These large estate owners advocated for a single, broader category of rural workers, thus avoiding the distinction between "small" and "large" rural producers. Their aim in this regard was to sidestep the touchy issue of landless workers who worked other people's lands under highly unfavourable terms—so unfavourable, in fact, that they often received no payment for their work.

The PCB came out against a single category comprising both rural workers and employers; it was also opposed to the division of the rural worker into different worker segments, as party members believed this would create obstacles for a strong worker union organisation.

As part of the process of legally recognising both rural unions and a series of worker rights, a range of political actors in the 1960s started several new unions, federations and confederations—including CONTAG. On 22 December 1963, the first CONTAG assembly was held to elect a governing body with representatives from the different political groups involved in building rural unionism. The Ministry of Labour granted legal status to the new organisation on 31 January 1964, just days before a coup d'état that would bring military rule to Brazil for the next two decades.

Military rule delivered a terrible blow to worker rights, initiating a period of repression for unions, leagues and rural associations, and of prison, torture and disappearance for union workers. According to Medeiros (1989), however, the military had no intention of putting an end to unionism. The military strategy to weaken the unions, which involved appointing military inspectors, closing down unions and repealing their charters, aimed to realign these organisations with the interests of the military government. Certain sectors within the Catholic Church were very supportive of this strategy.

CONTAG was not immune to the military's efforts to weaken unions. The first actions against the confederation came in 1964, when the military government dismissed the members of its governing body and replaced them with military inspectors. Over the next few years, a new governing body would be formed of individuals aligned with the interests of the military government. It was not until 1968 that the joint efforts of union leaders resulted in the appointment of a representatives sympathetic to the plight of rural workers on the CONTAG board. Another measure by the military government to exercise greater control over the union system was the merger of federations affiliated with CONTAG, reducing the total from 29 to just 11 (CONTAG 2003).

The military also introduced new regulations on rural union organisation. In 1965, the Ministry of Labour released Decree 71 (2 February 1965) dividing rural unions into two categories, one for employers and the other for rural workers (Medeiros 1997). Under the new edict, the different rural worker occupations established in prior legislation were combined in a single category of the rural worker, or "an individual who performs professional rural labour as an employee or as a self-employed entrepreneur, either as an individual or under a family farm or cooperative and without employees" (Decree 71). Wage workers, sharecroppers, tenant farmers and small farm owners were thus encompassed in a single category.

In 1971, Decree-Law 1166 was introduced to establish and regulate criteria for the payment of union dues. This decree provided a description of the rural worker category as a person (owner or other) working under a family farm system or independently (including rural employees). Individual assistance could be provided by third parties under the decree, provided said assistance was not paid. In addition to authorising the work of other people outside of the family in farm production, the decree introduced a new element, setting a maximum on the size of the family farm in order to avoid the large scale farmers intentions to control the unionism.

The Brazilian Constitution of 1998, ratified after the military dictatorship ended, rounds off the legislation on rural unionism. The principle of *unicidade sindical* is upheld in the Constitution. In other words, for each category—teachers, bank tellers, rural workers, and so on—there can be no more than one trade union at the municipal level, one federation at the state level and one confederation at the federal level.

The unification of a category as complex and heterogeneous as the rural worker, combined with the principle of *unicidade sindical* as established by the Brazilian Constitution of 1988, laid the groundwork for an expanded presence (the principle was now applied in all Brazilian municipalities and states) and the concentration of the entire union structure within a single system. The main implication was the reinforcement of the political influence of CONTAG within the party system in most of the rural areas of the country.

Another important aspect of the Constitution of 1988 is that it reduces government control over the founding of trade unions, eliminating the need of having a certificate of recognition issued by the Ministry of Labour to establish a trade union. However, the new Constitution granted the courts the power to determine whether the established trade unions meet legal requirements, including the principle of *unicidade* and union membership rules as established by law (Picolotto 2009). The fact that the courts were given more authority in this regard is one of two factors that would prove problematic during the recent reorganisation of the union system under CONTAG.

The "Rural Worker" Category: New Political Actors and Controversies

In addition to the legislative changes and the obstacles they created for unions, the 1970s and 1980s brought new challenges in relation to CONTAG's representation of the collective rights of rural workers. According to Cappellin (1994), scholars on unionism in Brazil during this historical period concur that traditional union organisations successfully began to mobilise in these years. The clamour for democratic freedoms grew increasingly more intense, begetting new types of political mobilisation and actions on the part of social movements (Gohn 2011, 2008). The broad alliance working to bring about the end of dictatorship and the rising struggle to guarantee rights influenced the drafting of the new Constitution. According to Favareto (2006), democratic consolidation in the 1980s contributed to the expansion and strengthening of trade unions in both the city and the countryside. The great number of worker strikes and the establishment of what would become Brazil's largest trade union (Central Única dos Trabalhadores, or CUT) in 1983 are both significant during this decade.

Under the authoritarian military regime, CONTAG exercised prudence in its trade union and political advocacy, always operating within the law and seeking legal-administrative resolutions to any conflicts (Aguiar 2015; Favareto 2006). As a result, the guiding principles of CONTAG's politics were a source of controversy among proponents of the new unionism who were members of the union opposition. It is important to note that starting in the 1970s, urban trade unions began a movement known as "new unionism" that would later spread to the countryside. As the name suggests, the "new unionism" proposed to break with the corporate influence, legalism and protection of State interests associated with traditional union practices (Aguiar 2015, Antunes and Santana 2014).

In the 1980s, Brazil saw a veritable wave of political movements that brought visibility to countryside dwellers long relegated to the background. These movements include the Landless Rural Workers Movement (MST), the National Rubber Tappers Board (CNS), the Dam-Affected Peoples Movement (MAB), the Rural Women Worker's Movements and the Rural Youth Ministry (PJR). Organisations such as these begin to formulate the demands of social groups historically ignored by both the State and by trade unions as well. In addition, these movements introduced innovative organisational practices and political activism, including an insistence on horizontal relations at the institutional level and, in the specific case of the MST, the introduction of a whole new type of land struggle in Brazil (Sigaud 2000). As observed in Rosa (2015), the pressure of these movements led to the opening of the CONTAG to other political agendas and specially to the support of the occupation of bankrupted farms to force the implementation of the agrarian reform policy.

As a range of other subjects began demanding political recognition, the shortcomings of the rural worker category came into focus, given that it was far too expansive and overlooked the diversity of the many types of people living in the countryside. New subjects were now becoming visible, including the landless workers, those affected by dams, rural women workers and farmers, extractivists and in the 1990s, family farmers.

The emergence of these movements—and with them, the new political subjects of the countryside—provided insight into the lives of rural dwellers previously relegated to the shadows. This reconfiguration breaks with the existing notion of rural worker, revealing the profound complexity of this occupational category and emphasising its lack of *unicidade* beyond the originally acknowledged difference between wage workers and small farmers.

The establishment of the National Rural Workers Department of CUT in 1988 bolstered the union opposition and created better conditions for new strategies to alter the structures associated with CONTAG. As Medeiros (1989) argues, the CUT's position with regards to CONTAG during the second half of the 1980s was to resolve the union dispute by working within the existing structures. These issues had to do with the structure of the unions but also the political positions adopted by union leadership. Their agenda included expanding democracy within the unions, ensuring union autonomy with regard to the State and challenging the principle of *unicidade sindical*.

Initially, the ideas of the new unionism—ideas that were materialised by union oppositions—played out in the push for trade union board posts and political posts within the structures of the CONTAG system. Almost immediately, the opposition began to rally around the idea of more than one institution competing to represent the workers in the category. Competing organisations began to appear at the end of the 1980s and would expand in the following decade. Some of the most emblematic examples include the Federation of Rural Wage Workers in the State of São Paulo (FERAESP), founded in 1989 (Moraes Silva et al. 2014); and, at the beginning of the 2000s, the Federation of Family Farmers of the South (FETRAF SUL/CUT), an organisation that would extend its coverage nationally a few years later and adopt a new name, the National Confederation of Family Farm Workers (CONTRAF) (Picolotto 2018).

Given these recent developments, it can be said that two different challenges to the CONTAG system took shape. The first focused on changing the system from within by vying for board posts while the other attempted to change it externally, creating new movements in the countryside, some of which were not legal entities and others that operated as trade unions but faced legal challenges.

Therefore, the entities founded outside the CONTAG system can be separated into two types: (1) non-institutionalised movements; (2) trade union organisations. At the risk of generalising, we use the term non-institutionalised **movements** to refer to those organisations struggling for people's rights in the countryside and nationwide. These are characterised by more horizontal practices and methodologies focused on local actions (in communities and rural settlements). Finally, these movements have no intention to become established as legal entities to avoid being scrutinised by the State and held legally responsible for their members' individual actions. Examples of these include the Landless Rural Workers Movement (MST), the National Rubber Tappers Board (CNS) and the Dam-Affected Peoples Movement (MAB). The bodies referred to herein as trade union organisations are those formed by union oppositions and must be established as legal entities in order to justify their actions in defence of the collective interests of a specific segment of rural workers.

Although their methods differ, these movements called into question the supposed consensus around the "rural worker" category, focusing attention on the heterogeneity of these workers and questioning CONTAG's ability to represent the full gamut of rural dwellers.

Although the principle of ***unicidade sindical*** is still embedded in the legal framework of trade union activity, the multiple segments that now currently exist within the "rural worker" category have challenged CONTAG's position as the exclusive representative of rural workers. In this regard, CONTAG has directed efforts towards preserving unity within the organisation through legal challenges to competing organisations as permitted by Brazilian law, on the one hand, and building agreements and political alliances with the different emerging segments on the other. Some authors (Rodrigues and Ladosky 2015) acknowledge that CONTAG's affiliation with CUT (in 1995) can be understood, at least in part, as an attempt to avoid conflict.

Another equally important effort is CONTAG's incorporation of new union practices and methodologies, some of which have been inspired by the social struggles of Brazil's emerging social movements. The most challenging one was the organisation of illegal land occupations in some regions absorbing some of the MST potential basis. In addition, CONTAG has worked decisively on networking while advocating for the demands of the different social actors who comprise the rural worker category, for example, claims among small producers for amendments to agricultural policy (Medeiros 1995; Rosa 2015).

Family Farming and Rural Unionism

The previous section provided an overview of how the rural worker category was gradually reinterpreted as the result of sociohistorical changes. As demonstrated before, the transformations in labour relations in the countryside contributed to political and legal changes in the concept of the rural worker. Another meaningful political shift was the decision of CONTAG to provide specific representation for family farmers so as to dispute the governmental emergent agendas on the issue.

According to Medeiros (1995), the 1980s marked a new time in the Brazilian countryside, with small farmers increasingly setting the agenda. In a context in which the political role of family farmers expanded due to the successful actions of other movements such as MST and MPA (Small Farmer's Movement) to influence the agrarian policies and secure special subsidies, the role of rural wage workers within unions decreased. These changes were accompanied by the increasing automation of farming and the resulting decline in agricultural employment. Globalisation also played a role in this process as a greater number of transnational agribusiness companies created new challenges for unions, especially with regards to collective bargaining agreements.

Although small producers were a segment of the generic rural worker category—and thus were already represented by CONTAG—trade unions and other movements began echoing their demands in the 1990s and referring to them as family farmers. Picolotto (2009) views the shift from the term "small producer" to "family farmer" as a calculated attempt to bring to mind efficiency and the significant role this group plays in food production. Family farming has also become a way to politically differentiate the groups of small holders associated with leftist agendas in rural areas.

The advocacy work of CONTAG, it should be noted, traditionally supported struggles for land reform. The confederation defended a great number of workers in a precarious situation with regards to land tenure and use—including tenant farmers, sharecroppers and squatters. At the same time, it stood behind labour rights, declaring strikes and pushing for higher salaries for rural wage workers. When CONTAG began to incorporate the demands of family farmers, its advocacy work and agenda were transformed and the organisation began to prioritise state policies for agricultural production that provided benefits for small producers, a key issue for its union members in the south and southeast of Brazil (Medeiros 1997). The focus on these regions was an attempt to regain some terrain in the areas where new emergent movements were stronger (Rosa 2015).

Therefore, the banners so characteristic of the classic struggles of rural unionism in the 1990s slowly ceded space to the family farming agenda within the leftist governments of the Worker's Party (2003–2016). The labour-related issues associated with the struggle of rural wage workers have progressively faded with the emergence of policies that facilitated credit and the compulsory acquisition by the government of family farming products in order supply the public education and health services. Other issues have been reshaped to adapt to the newly configured worker CONTAG represents. Demands for agrarian reform, for example, have become strategic for the consolidation of the family economy. Along the way, the organisation of family farming and its agenda were nationalised, bringing important changes to the regional balance of power and the organisational structure under CONTAG.

Brazilian legislation has also acknowledged the importance of family farming. In 2006, a law was enacted that established the criteria[2] for defining family farming in order for these farmers to benefit from specific public policies (Law 11,326/2006), a milestone for the struggle of social movements and trade unions in Brazil.

The Brazilian Courts and Their Interpretation of the Rural Worker Category and Union Organisation

It cannot be argued that this new configuration of the category substitutes the existing concept of the rural worker. This category remains in effect, though it has been subject to sweeping revisions.

In one reinterpretation by a Brazilian court, the notion of the rural worker is recognised as an eclectic category, that is, one comprised of different segments, with specific mention of family farmers and rural wage workers. As an eclectic category, the court ruled that trade unions founded specifically to represent rural wage workers, family farmers or other specific occupational categories did not violate the principle of *unicidade sindical*. Instead, in the view of the judges, the specificity of these trade unions ensured that they were better positioned to represent the collective interests of the different segments within the rural worker category.

Besides determining that the division of the rural worker category did not represent a breach of *unicidade sindical*, the courts found that this subdivision into more than one occupation could occur at all levels of the Brazilian union system, that is, at the level of trade unions, federations and confederations. This case law precedent had major implications for existing union organisations. With the creation, certificate of recognition and registration of the specific union organisations with the authorities, the original organisation automatically loses its right to represent the specific category of workers the new union organisation intends to represent. To provide an example, once a union of rural wage workers is founded and attains legal status in a certain municipality, the existing rural workers union immediately ceases to represent this segment (that of the rural wage workers) and only retains representation of the remaining categories.

Based on current legislation, all new organisations must meet the following requirements: (1) for the founding of new unions or the dissociation of certain workers from an existing union, an assembly must be held for the specific category the new organisation intends to represent, though there is no minimum in terms of the number of workers who must attend said assembly; (2) for the creation or division of federations, the organisational structure of said federation must have at least five affiliate unions; (3) at the level of the confederation, the requirement is at least three affiliate federations. Provided said criteria are met, any of the organisations can file to be registered with the Ministry of Labour.

As a result of court rulings such as these, the Brazilian state has recognised a plethora of trade unions, federations and confederations that specifically represent certain rural occupations, thus challenging the exclusive representation of rural workers that CONTAG has retained for over 50 years. According to the reports from CONTAG's 12th Conference, in 2013, there were 117 trade unions of rural wage workers and 16 regional unions of family farmers. All of these organisations are separate from the CONTAG system and duly registered with the Ministry of Labour, with the seal of approval of the Brazilian Labour Court (CONTAG 2018). In addition to the unions representing these two specific occupations (family farmers and rural wage workers), other occupation-specific unions in different parts of the country have obtained recognition and been officially registered by the courts in recent years. These include trade unions for cowboys (in the state of Piauí), extractivists small-scale fishermen, colliers, rural truck drivers and crab pickers (state of Paraíba), and organisations like the Farm Cooperative Workers (state of São Paulo), the Union of Persons Recruited for Rubber Extraction (state of Amazonas) and the Rubber Tappers Trade Union (states of Acre and Amazonas).

This list reveals that the subdivision of the rural worker category has not been limited to smaller bodies representing only rural waged workers and family farmers. As we have seen, there are a range of established trade union organisations that are now legally representing the collective interests of various segments within the rural worker category. A category that is now acknowledged by the labour courts as "eclectic."

Transformations and Recent Impacts for CONTAG and Rural Unionism

In response to the wave of new trade union organisations across Brazil, CONTAG opted for two autonomous and accordant union organisational structures, one specifically representing family farmers and coordinated jointly with this population and another representing rural wage workers. This vision led CONTAG to provide both political and financial support for the founding, in 2015, of the National Confederation of Rural Wage Workers (CONTAR).

The dissociation reveals that CONTAG sought to minimise the risk of representing a category as broad and diverse as that of the rural worker. By making this subdivision, CONTAG safeguarded its role as the union representing the specific segment of the family farmer—a segment with strong roots in its membership. At the same time, by supporting the establishment of CONTAR, the organisation also demonstrated its desire to continuing exercising influence over the political decisions of this new organisation (comprised of former leaders from CONTAG, federations and their affiliates). This decision to break down its representation is a clear example of "divide and conquer," (Picolotto 2018b).

The move to subdivide was thus a response to both external pressures and the rulings of the Brazilian courts, as noted in the reports of CONTAG's 12th Conference:

> The judicial branch has exercised great pressure by clearly establishing the rural worker category as an eclectic one, that is, as one encompassing more than a single specific category, and by ruling that the creation of organisations representing rural wage workers or family farmers in the countryside does not violate the constitutional principle of *unicidade sindical.* As a result of this case law, a range of organisations representing specific segments appeared outside the MSTTR (Rural Workers' Social Movement), including not only trade unions, but also federations and confederations (Contag 2018. p. 58)

The process of subdividing into smaller organisations representing specific segments is still ongoing. Although CONTAG has made its name change official, adopted new bylaws and been registered as a new union, many of its affiliated federations and trade unions have not made these changes and continue to represent the single eclectic category of the rural worker. In addition, some of the organisations that comprise the CONTAG system have expressed their disagreement or, at the very least, decided not to follow the confederation's example in subdividing the category. This shows that the topic is still a source of controversy even within the CONTAG system.

Therefore, it is possible to argue that the CONTAG system will not fully represent family farmers until all of the confederation's affiliates have registered to represent these farmers exclusively. This will take time, as acknowledged by the confederation: to date, only 560 of the 4000 rural worker trade unions affiliated with CONTAG have filed to represent either family farmers or rural wage workers specifically. This reluctance with the national splitting strategy is partially explained by the fact that most of the local leaders could not merely break their political unities into two different branches. The division tended to open the path for the resurfacing old internal conflicts leading to undesirable political disputes. In addition to these organisations, another 90 new trade unions for specific representation have been established and affiliated with CONTAG (Contag 2018). However, of the 27 federations affiliated with CONTAG, 19 have initiated the dissociation process in order to represent family farmers, while an additional two new federations have been formed.

The dissociation process could have new and unexpected ramifications, as noted in CONTAG's own reports: "with immediate and long-terms impacts that are gradually altering the state of affairs in the Brazilian countryside." (CONTAG 2018: 61). There is thus clearly a need for CONTAG affiliate organisations to opt for a specific occupation and defend its collective interests, in coordination with the government bodies. Moreover, one of the most salient topics in recent union discourse has been the need to truly represent the full range of existing rural workers of both genders and increase their visibility in society. It is also possible to argue that CONTAG's rural union leadership must draw on its reputation as a legitimate political broker—a reputation it has built by working with its membership—in order to defend itself against competing organisations, keep its members unified and guarantee its political and financial sustainability (Pereira 1997).

Conclusion

Rural unionism has experienced important changes in recent years. Although these do not radically break with some of the original principles of trade unionism (***unicidade sindical*** and the unification of a gamut of rural workers in a single category), they are at least indicative of a major change: the idea of more than one union system for a single group of workers has gained legitimacy and support.

The emergence of new political actors in the countryside has contributed to changes in the discourse and the modus operandi of unions, which have had to be increasingly more connected to a range of social subjects demanding recognition and advocacy for their agenda. At the same time, these new political actors also drew attention to the diversity of occupations and types of work in the countryside, calling into question the vision of the rural worker as a homogeneous category unified by common interests.

Another factor in these transformations included legislative amendments and court decisions against a single union system for rural workers. Though this has not created an opening for trade union fragmentation, the need to assure better conditions for the representation of the collective interests of different professional and economic categories has been established. Therefore, courts have ruled that if workers feel better represented under a specific craft union (one reserved for family farmers, rural wage earners and others), these structures are in keeping with the law and do not violate the principle of *unicidade*.

These new approaches to unionism in the Brazilian courts motivated CONTAG to choose a specific segment, family farmers, to represent. The reasons for the choice included the growing struggles for recognition among small producers, the restructuring of agricultural production and the foundation of competing union organisations.

A worthwhile question to address is to what extent the decision to represent the collective interests of family farming is part of a broader trend of recognising the diversity that the rural worker category comprises. In other words, a further analysis is necessary to determine whether the concept of family farming could prove as problematic as the rural worker category, erasing difference while lumping together a broad, diverse membership with a range of demands and disparate work conditions.

In summary, the decision to choose family farming as the exclusive segment of worker representation reveals CONTAG's attempt to maintain a broad and unified membership within its union system. Therefore, dissociation was the best option for bringing workers together, revealing that not all changes in trade unionism represent a radical break: instead, they belie an attempt to maintain the original state of affairs to the extent possible.

These recent developments provide an overview of what has remained the same and what has changed in relation to the organisation of rural unionism in Brazil. At the time of writing this chapter, profound changes are underway in Brazil, where the current president represents the interests of the ultraconservative right, supports a neoliberal agenda and has stated his opposition to the labour union system. Therefore, it appears almost certain that the situation will continue to evolve, providing new opportunities for analysis.

Notes

1. It is useful to note that employer associations are permitted under Brazilian law. The terms under which these associations operate are similar to those of the trade unions. According to the CNES survey from 2015, there are 5251 employer associations across Brazil.
2. The size of the property is limited to four times the minimum technically required to develop commercial farming. The work force has to be formed predominantly from members of the family running the business. A minimum portion of the gross family income must be generated in the farm. The law also defines as family farmers forest people, indigenous groups, quilombolas (black rural communities formed during and after slavery), small-scale fishermen and extractivists.

Bibliography

Aguiar, V. V. P. (2015). *Somos todas margaridas: um estudo sobre o processo de constituição das mulheres do campo e da floresta como sujeitos políticos. Doctoral Thesis in the Social Sciences.* Unicamp: Campinas/SP. 521 p.

Antunes, R., & Santana, M. A. (2014). The Dilemmas of the New Unionism in Brazil: Breaks and Continuities. *Latin American Perspectives, 41*(5), 10–21.

Campos, A. G. (2016). *Sindicatos no Brasil: o que esperar no futuro próximo? Texto para discussão 2262. Instituto de Pesquisa Econômica Aplicada.* Brasilia: IPEA.

Cappellin, P. (1994). Viver o sindicalismo no feminino. Revista Estudos Feministas 2 (special edition). Rio de Janeiro. *CIEC/ECO/UFRJ., 1994*, 273–290.

Carter, M. (Ed.). (2015). *Challenging Social Inequality: the landless Rural Workers Movement and Agrarian Reform in Brazil.* Durham: Duke University Press.

Carvalho, P. D. (2018). *A produção do transnacional: compilações da agricultura familiar e camponesa na Contag e no MPA.* PPG Doctoral Thesis in the Social Sciences. Belo Horizonte, UFMG.

Contag. (2003). *CONTAG—40 anos ao lado do homem e da mulher do campo.* Brasilia.

Contag. (2018). *Report from the 12th National Congress of Rural Farm Workers and Family Farmers.* Brasilia, 366 p.

Costa, L. F. C. (1996). *Sindicalismo rural brasileiro em construção.* Rio de Janeiro: Forense Universitária.

de Medeiros, L. S. (1989). *História dos movimentos sociais no campo*. Rio de Janeiro: FASE.

de Medeiros, L. S.. (1995). *Lavradores, trabalhadores agrícolas, camponeses: os comunistas e a constituição de classes no campo*. PPG Doctoral Thesis in the Social Sciences. Campinas/SP: UNICAMP.

Favareto, A. (2006). Agricultores, trabalhadores: os trinta anos do novo sindicalismo rural no Brasil. *Revista Brasileira de Ciências Sociais, 21*, 27–44.

Favareto, A. (2007). *Paradigmas do desenvolvimento rural em questão*. São Paulo: Iglu: Fapesp. 220p.

Gohn, M. da G. (2008). Abordagens teóricas no estudo dos movimentos sociais na América Latina. *Caderno CRH 21*(54), 439–455. Salvador.

Gohn, M. da G. (2011). Movimentos Sociais na contemporaneidade. *Revista Brasileira de Educação 16*(47), 333–361. Caxambu/MG.

Grisa, C., & Schneider, S. (2014). Três gerações de políticas públicas para a agricultura familiar e formas de interação entre sociedade e Estado no Brasil. *Revista de Economia e Sociologia Rural, 52*, 125–146.

Maybury-Lewis, B. (1994). *The Politics of the Possible: The Brazilian Rural Workers' Trade Union Movement, 1964–1985*. Philadelphia: Temple University Press.

Medeiros, L. S. d. (1997). Trabalhadores rurais, agricultura familiar e organização sindical. *São Paulo em Perspectiva, 11*(2) São Paulo, 65–72.

Moraes Silva, M. A., Menezes, M. A., & Ribeiro, J. D. (2014). State and Regulation of Labour Relations in the Sugarcane Fields of Brazil. In T. Marsden, J. S. B. Cavalcanti, & A. Bonanno (Eds.), *Labour Relations in Globalized Food* (pp. 167–191). Bingley: Emerald Group Publishing Limited.

Pereira, A. (1997). *End of the Peasantry: The Rural Labour Movement in Northeast Brazil, 1961–1988*. Pittsburgh: University of Pittsburgh Press.

Picolotto, E. L.. (2009). A emergência dos "agricultores familiares" como sujeitos de direitos na trajetória do sindicalismo rural brasileiro. *Mundo Agrário 9*(18). Centro de Estudios Histórico Rurales. Facultad de Humanidades y Ciencias de la Educación. Universidad Nacional de La Plata.

Picolotto, E. L. (2018). Union Plurality in the Field? Family Farmers and Paid Rural Workers in a Dispute Setting. *Lua Nova: Revista de Cultura e Política, 104*, 201–238.

Picolotto, E. L. (2018b). Pluralismo, neocorporativismo e o sindicalismo dos agricultores familiares no Brasil. *Sociedade e Estado, 33*(1), 85–115.

RICCI, R. (2009). A maior estrutura sindical do Brasil: papel do sindicalismo de trabalhadores rurais no pós-64. In B. M. Fernandes, L. S. Medeiros, & M. I. Paulilo (Eds.), *Lutas camponesas contemporâneas: condições, dilemas e conquistas—a diversidade das formas das lutas no campo* (Vol. 2, pp. 321–338). São Paulo/Brasília, DF: UNESP/Núcleo de Estudos Agrários e Desenvolvimento Rural (NEAD).

Rodrigues, I. J., & Ladosky, M. H. G. (2015). Paradoxos do sindicalismo brasileiro: a CUT e os trabalhadores rurais. *Lua Nova, 95*, 87–143.

Rosa, M. C. (2015). Beyond the MST: The Impact of Brazilian Social Movements. In M. Carter (Ed.), *Challenging Social Inequality: The Landless Rural Workers Movement and Agrarian Reform in Brazil*. Durham: Duke University Press.

Santos, M. J. D. (2001). Projeto alternativo de desenvolvimento rural sustentável. *Estudos avançados, 15*(43), 225–238.

Sigaud, L. (2000). A Forma Acampamento: Notas a partir da versão Pernambucana. *Novos Estudos CEBRAP, 58*, 255–279.

CHAPTER 14

Re-peasantization, Resistance and Subordination: The Struggle for Land and Agrarian Reform in Brazil

Bernardo Mançano Fernandes

The process of re-peasantization in Brazil occurs primarily through the peasant struggle for land and agrarian reform. Adopting a geographic method and using territorialization as a central axis of study, this article analyzes the history of peasant formation, particularly focusing on the formation of the Landless Rural Workers' Movement (MST), the peasant movement that has most contributed to the process of recreating the peasantry through land occupations. The process of re-peasantization

Originally published in *Agrarian South: Journal of Political Economy, Vol. 2 No. 3*

B. M. Fernandes (✉)
São Paulo State University (UNESP), São Paulo, Brazil

UNESCO Chair in Territorial Development and Education for the Countryside, São Paulo, Brazil

P. Jha et al. (eds.), *Labour Questions in the Global South*,
https://doi.org/10.1007/978-981-33-4635-2_14

occurring over the last 30 years is supported by data showing that more than a million families have been settled through agrarian reform. However, these fractional territorial gains have not eliminated the subordination of peasants by capitalized land rent. Using data from the most recent Agricultural Census, we highlight the situation of dependence to which Brazilian peasants are submitted. The hegemony of agribusiness has provoked a reflux in the peasant struggle for land and agrarian reform, which currently finds itself stagnant. The greatest challenge for peasant movements is the creation of a development model for their territories which would enable them to recuperate the process of re-peasantization[1].

Introduction

The idea and process of re-peasantization are central to the study of the agrarian question, as capitalist development simultaneously promotes the destruction and recreation of the peasantry. It is within this contradictory process that re-peasantization in Brazil must be situated and understood: as a process of creation and recreation of peasants determined by the actions of peasants themselves, and of capital. There are two forms of re-peasantization: the first occurs by the struggle for land and agrarian reform (Fernandes 2000; Moyo 2007; Moyo and Yeros 2005a), occurring predominately through the actions of peasant movements. The second occurs by means of the capitalist market through the purchase and sale of land, which can also be promoted by public policies such as those implemented with the support of the World Bank in several countries (Ramos Filho 2008; Sauer and Pereira 2006). These processes have deeply marked the trajectory of re-peasantization.

The current article examines the process of creation and re-creation of the peasantry in Brazil from a geographical and historical perspective, focusing on the role of the peasant movement that has most contributed to re-peasantization, the Landless Rural Workers Movement (MST). The process of territorialization, a concept not commonly used in sociological and economic analyses, is central to the analysis presented here. Land, production units, and peasant and capitalist land holdings are understood as fractions of the territories of countries. These territories are in dispute due to the distinct social relations and development models respectively promoted by peasants and capitalists. As each of these types of social relations needs a territory within which to develop, the continuation of the peasantry and capitalism effectively foment an ongoing conflict over land and resources.

These disputes have led to struggles, massacres, and wars, as evidenced by several examples in the history of the formation of peasants in Brazil. In fact, there is a geopolitical use of land and territories that is becoming increasingly significant due to recent changes in the agrarian situation, marked by the expansion of agro-fuel production and recurrent food crises. The hegemony of agribusiness, effectively consolidated in the 1990s, endangers the existence of the peasantry, while keeping a significant part of it subordinate. This reality brings new political and theoretical challenges. It is not only a struggle for land but also a struggle for sustainable food systems and the production of quality food products. The industrialization of agriculture, the intensive use of pesticides, and the expansion of transgenic crops have generated environmental problems and negatively impacted public health. These elements, central to the agrarian question in the twenty-first century, build upon classic elements, such as inequality and land concentration, which have persisted since the sixteenth century. Organized into three main parts, this article first discusses the process through which the peasantry in Brazil has been formed. It then examines the struggle for land and agrarian reform as a process of re-peasantization. Finally, it presents an analysis based on data from the latest Agricultural Census, in order to illuminate the conditions of subordination to which the peasantry are subject.

The Formation of the Peasantry in Brazil

The history of the formation of the Brazilian peasantry is marked by struggles and peasant wars, in disputes over territory and models of agricultural development. The social conflicts occurring in the countryside in the current century mark a continuity of a capitalist model of development implemented for over five centuries. Land concentration, the struggle for land, and the hegemony of capitalist agriculture are key elements of this continuity. The land occupations realized by the MST and other peasant movements are actions of resistance in the face of increasing land concentration and against exploitation and oppression that mark the historic struggle for land. Through the struggle for land, peasants seek to attain the basic conditions for a dignified life and a more equitable and just society. Intrinsic to the process of the destruction and reconstruction of peasants, or re-peasantization are five centuries of persisting *latifúndios*, land struggles, and peasant organization.

Since the arrival of Portuguese colonizers in 1500, Brazil's history has been marked by the invasion and usurpation of indigenous territory, slavery and the subordination of the peasantry in the process of producing capitalist territory. The formation of the peasantry began with the struggle against slavery, against expropriation and exploitation, which resulted in the creation of territorial disputes that have continued until the present. These struggles characterize the history of peasants and indigenous peoples and the defense of their territories. In Brazil, indigenous peoples have never been considered peasants, although they have always contributed to the formation of a Brazilian people through miscegenation with African slaves and European and Asian immigrants. It is this intersection of peoples and ethnicities that initiated the formation of a unique Brazilian peasantry. The ceaseless struggles and wars of resistance of indigenous peoples, occurring one after another, or concurrently and in constant confrontation with capitalism, have shaped the memory that helps us to understand the process of re-peasantization.

During the sixteenth and seventeenth centuries close to 350,000 indigenous people were enslaved. The hunt of indigenous peoples by colonial powers in order to enslave them was met by various movements of resistance, such as the Confederation of Tamoios and the War of the Potiguara (see Fig. 14.1). A great battle in the fight against slavery took place in the region that now marks the frontier of South Brazil, shared with Argentina, Paraguay, and Uruguay. In this territory, disputed by Portugal and Spain, religious missions were organized by Jesuit priests. The Thirty Guaraní Peoples (Trinta Povos Guaranis) lived in this territory on commonly shared land, and each Guaraní village had a sizable population of between 1500 and 12,000 members. Facing constant attacks by slave hunters and the armies of Spain and Portugal, the Guaraní maintained their resistance until exhaustion and eventual defeat. The final blow came in 1756, with a bloody massacre that led to the death of Sepé Tiaraju, a Guaraní leader who has become a symbol of indigenous resistance. At that time, the indigenous population in Brazil had been almost decimated and indigenous slavery was being substituted by African slaves (Prezia and Hoornaert 1989: 91–99).

In 1570, at the beginning of the colonial period, over 50 sugar mills had been established using slave labor. In 1584, around 15,000 African slaves toiled on sugarcane plantations. By 1597, the beginnings of a

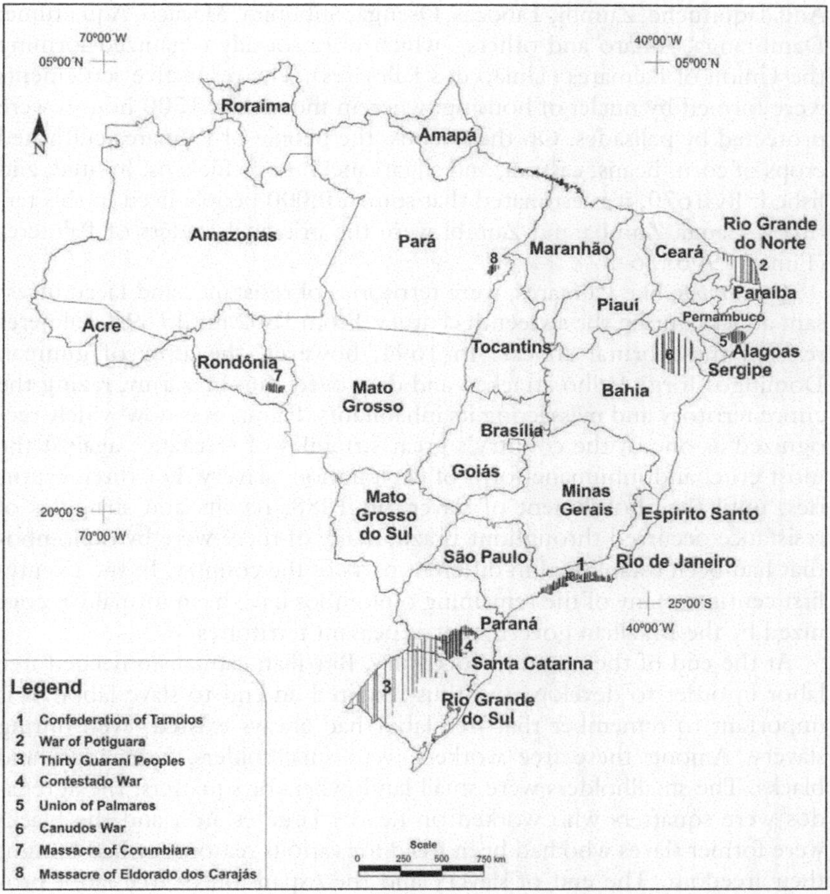

Fig. 14.1 Historic struggles for re-peasantization in Brazil. (Source: Developed by the author)

quilombo—a territory inhabited principally by escaped African slaves, but also by some indigenous people and free workers—had developed in the region of Palmares. Located approximately 70 kilometers from the coastline, in an area that today is the frontier region between the states of Alagoas and Pernambuco, Palmares was Brazil's largest quilombo (see Fig. 14.1). It comprised of several different villages—including Acotirene,

Andalaquituche, Zumbi, Tabocas, Osenga, Subupira, Macaco, Aqualtume, Dambranga, Amaro and others—which were socially organized forming the Union of Palmares (União dos Palmares). The respective settlements were formed by nuclei of housing, wherein more than 1500 houses were protected by palisades. On these lands, the people of Palmares cultivated crops of corn, beans, cassava, and sugarcane; raised chickens, hunted, and fished. By 1670, it is estimated that some 20,000 people lived in this territory. Canga Zumba and Zumbi were the principal leaders of Palmeres (Funari 1996: 26–37).

Quilombos, like Palmares, were territories of resistance and faced incessant attacks during the sixteenth century. From 1602 until 1694, Palmeres resisted these brutal attacks. In 1694, however, the army of gunman Domingos Jorge Velho attacked and destroyed Zumbi's army, razing the entire territory and massacring its inhabitants. Palmares is now widely recognized as one of the country's great struggles of resistance against the most cruel and inhumane form of exploitation: slavery. For three centuries, until the abolishment of slavery in 1888, revolts and struggles of resistance occurred throughout Brazil; many of these were by quilombos that had been established in different parts of the country. In the twenty-first century, many of the remaining quilombos have been formally recognized by the Brazilian government as peasant territories.

At the end of the nineteenth century, Brazilian capitalism needed free labor in order to develop, and thus required an end to slave labor. It is important to remember that free labor had always existed, even during slavery. Among these free workers were smallholders, agregados, and blacks. The smallholders were small landowners or squatters; the agregados were squatters who worked on nearby large estates; and the blacks were former slaves who had been freed for various reasons, or had bought their freedom. The end of slavery and the expansion of free labor promoted wage labor. Subordination began to occur through the sale of one's labor power to large landholders—the capitalists. In order to further expand the free labor force, the government incentivized the immigration of peasants from diverse countries, such as Germany, Japan, Italy, and Spain. Slaves became free because they regained control over their own labor power; the immigrants were free only because they possessed and controlled their own labor power. If, for the freed slaves, labor power was what was gained through emancipation, for the immigrants labor power was all they had left; neither had access to land (Martins 1986: 16–17). As such, the struggle for freedom and liberty now unfolded, simultaneously, alongside the struggle for land. The black Afro-Brazilian, the white European and the indigenous native converged to form the Brazilian peasantry. In constant struggle, the peasantry was being destroyed and recreated by the expansion of capitalist development, and in the process also recreating itself. Free laborers often worked as bondage workers on large farms, with their bondage ending only after a period of 38 years of service. The Land Law of 1850 instituted the principle of private property and determined that access to land was only possible through purchases in money. The latifúndio, or large landholding—a remnant of the colonial and monarchic eras—became a salient feature of the Brazilian Republic. In this context, there were two main options that remained for landless workers (that is, former slaves and immigrants): to work on large farms in order to save and buy land, or to occupy already enclosed lands which, in large part, had been illegally obtained by landowners through the falsification of land title documents. In the struggle against the private enclosure of land, there emerged diverse forms of resistance. In Bahia, peasants and former slaves, followers of Antônio Conselheiro, ended their pilgrimage and established the village of Canudos (see Fig. 14.1). Antônio Conselheiro and his followers formed a peasant movement that opposed the established order of submission imposed by the *latifundiários*, and was declared an enemy of the state (Martins 1981).

The war of Canudos was one of the first examples of the organization of peasant resistance in Brazil. Antônio Conselheiro and his followers settled on a farm in Canudos in 1893, calling the place Belo Monte. The economic organization of the settled community was realized through cooperative work, essential to the reproduction of the community. Everyone had the right to land and developed a mode of family production, ensuring a common fund reserved for use by the more vulnerable segments of the population, particularly the elderly and disabled. Approximately 10,000 people lived in Canudos—a population equivalent to the largest cities in Bahia at the time. The settlement was continuously attacked by military expeditions coming from all over Brazil. Over 5000 soldiers fought against the peasants. From October 1896, the people of Canudos were able to defend against attacks by the Brazilian Armed Forces, until the final siege and massacre of the population in 1897 (Cunha 1982).

The nineteenth century closed with a war waged against peasants by the Brazilian army, and the following century opened with yet another war. In the first decade of the twentieth century, in the border region of the southern Brazilian states of Paraná and Santa Catarina, another peasant movement emerged. In 1908, the government made a large concession to the Brazil Railway Company—a North American corporation—of a strip of land 30 kilometers wide for the construction of a railway stretching from São Paulo to Rio Grande. This was one of the first examples of foreign land grabbing in Brazil in the twentieth century. For the realization of this mega-project, the lands traversed by the railway were exploited by the company, and thousands of families where forcefully dispossessed. In 1912, in Campos Novos, Santa Catarina, a peasant movement was formed; by 1914, the movement was comprised of more than 15,000 people. The peasant families that resisted expropriation by the company were attacked by gunmen of Brazil Railway Company and troops of the Brazilian Armed Forces. The diverse localities of resistance that formed in the region become known as Contestado (Martins 1981).

Accusing the government of killing peasants and workers, and handing land over to foreign companies, peasants began to attack the large farm holdings and cities and took control of parts of the railway. The final battle took place in 1916, when 7000 armed forces, thousands of police officers, and 300 gunmen launched a series of attacks. Aircraft were used to survey lands and identify the location of peasant strongholds. Trapped by the encircling forces, the peasants were unable to access supplies, thereby marking the end of the peasant resistance (Derengoski 1987). In the same manner as Canudos, Contestado was vanquished; completely destroyed. Those massacred were peasants who believed it to be possible to overcome the iron-grip that large landholders exercised in the Brazilian countryside.

In their process of formation, peasants have always confronted or been faced down by large landowners. In the mid-twentieth century, the struggle for land and agrarian reform acquired new features, taking on new forms in the continual process of the recreation of the peasantry or re-peasantization. The formation of the Peasant Leagues (Ligas Camponesas) began around 1945 with the help of the Brazilian Communist Party (PCB), upon which they were dependent. In 1947, the government of President Dutra declared the PCB to be illegal and embarked on a campaign of violent repression of the Peasant Leagues.

Yet, they remerged in 1954 in the state of Pernambuco, this time as an autonomous organization. They expanded into 13 states, organizing a myriad of meetings and congresses, and strengthening peasant organization. The Leagues played a defining role in the struggle for radical agrarian reform as a means to end land concentration; peasants held their ground and began to realize land occupations. In 1954, the PCB created the Union of Peasants and Rural Workers (ULTAB), with the aim of coordinating the peasant associations and creating the conditions necessary to form a political alliance between workers and peasants. In Rio Grande do Sul, in the 1960s, the Landless Agriculturalists' Movement (MASTER) was formed. With the military coup in 1964, these movements were annihilated. The military dictatorship in Brazil lasted from 1964 to 1985 (Fernandes 2000).

The Struggle for Agrarian Reform: Re-peasantization

In the mid-twentieth century, the Brazilian peasantry found itself facing a new challenge: the advance of the modernization of agriculture characterized by the confluence of agricultural and industrial systems. This process represented the first phase in the formation of agribusiness in Brazil. Denominated 'conservative modernization' (Graziano da Silva 1981), this process exacerbated the situation of extreme land concentration in Brazil, and only intensified the inequality that existed between capitalist agriculture and peasant agriculture. In the following decades, market, financial and technological systems coalesced with agroindustrial systems consolidating the formation of agribusiness as the model of development of capitalist agriculture.

The military regime created a series of instruments for the expansion of capitalist agriculture, instituting various policies of land concessions to large corporations, principally for the appropriation of land in the Amazon region (Oliveira 1987, 1988). The annihilation of peasant movements occurred concomitantly with the establishment of trade unions which were defended by the Catholic Church, political parties and the federal government. Conditions were created to institutionalize peasant organizations and subordinate them to government control.

The process of creation of national rural union began en 1962, with the regulation of rural unionization, introduced with the intention of transforming peasant organizations into unions that could later form federations and be integrated into a confederation. The Brazilian Communist Party (PCB) and the Catholic Church wrestled with peasant organizations, trying to rein them in and control them through means of subordination, with the hope of having political control over the future confederation. In December 1963, in an agreement between these institutions, the National Confederation of Agricultural Workers (CONTAG) was created, and consolidated itself as an independent peasant institution (Medeiros 1989). The various attempts to eradicate peasant movements ultimately proved to be unsuccessful, since they were continually being reborn in different forms, thus proving re-peasantization to be a process with significant popular support. Not only was re-peasantization a form of resistance, it was also an inherent element of capitalist agricultural development.

Emerging in the 1960s, Christian-based Communities (CEBs) were important social spaces wherein workers encountered conditions conducive to organizing and fighting for their rights and against injustice. By the mid-1970s, they had been established all across the country, in both rural and urban areas. Through the popularization of the teachings of Liberation Theology, these communities became spaces of political socialization, liberation, and popular organization. In 1975, the Catholic Church created the Pastoral Land Commission (CPT). Working in conjunction with parishes from the outskirts of cities and in rural communities, the CPT became the principal organizer of the new peasant movements that emerged during the military regime, in what can be considered a new phase of re-peasantization.

In order to suppress the struggle for land and avoid carrying out an agrarian reform that would have redistributed lands to peasant families, consecutive military governments worked to restrict the advance of the peasant movement. It was precisely the severity and extent of political oppression that led to the emergence of a new peasant movement in Brazil: The Landless Rural Workers Movement (MST). This is a contradiction that can also be understood using the very logic inherent in capitalist development in agriculture. Capital, even though it constitutes the hegemonic social relation, does not configure only one social relation, that is, wage labor. In the process of unequal and contradictory development and expansion, capital both destroys the peasantry and promotes re-peasantization. This is one way to understand the genesis of the MST, but the principal way is through the movement's own actions.

The struggle for survival has long been the aim of peasant resistance. In 1978, 110 landless families began to organize, and on 7 September 1979, they occupied Macali farm in the municipality of Ronda Alta, in the southern state of Rio Grande do Sul (see Fig. 14.1). This land occupation inaugurated the process of the formation of the MST. The lands of the Macali farm were remnants of land struggles that had taken place in the 1960s, when MASTER had organized encampments in the region. The history of the struggle for access and control over these lands had been recorded in the memory of the peasants who were now participating in an even greater struggle: the struggle for the restoration of democracy (Medeiros 1989).

In the early 1980s, several land occupations took place in the states of Rio Grande do Sul, Santa Catarina, Paraná, São Paulo, and Mato Grosso do Sul. These occupations united workers and initiated the formation of the MST, culminating in the foundation of the movement with the realization of its first national meeting in January 1984. The MST was formed in interaction with other institutions, especially the Catholic Church, through the CPT. Learning from the history of peasant organization, the MST built its autonomy.

Through the occupation of land, the MST effectively territorialized itself across all of Brazil's geographic regions, becoming a national movement in less than a decade. Territorialization is a process of multiplication of fractions of territory that occurs by the organization of groups of families that occupy and conquer land. Agrarian reform in Brazil has historically been realized by means of land occupations. In its almost 30 years of existence, the MST is the peasant movement that has realized the greatest number of land occupations, and, in the process, has transformed the action of occupation into one of the principal forms of re-peasantization in Brazil. The process of the MST's formation is comprised of three distinct periods. The first encompasses the gestation and birth of the movement, from 1978 to 1985, during which the MST territorialized itself primarily in the regions of the south and southeast. During this period, the movement defined its principles and form of organization, and adopted land occupations as the primary means by which to access land, thereby, defining its mode of re-peasantization.

The second period, between 1985 and 1990, marked the territorialization and consolidation of the MST in all regions of the country. The creation of an organizational structure, made up of committees of coordination and direction and a secretariat, were conceived on the basis of the practices of the historic peasant organizations and, principally, the lived experiences of families that organized committees and nuclei in the encampments and resettlement areas. Challenges faced, and practices tested, in the initial period of struggle became points of reference that outlined and guided the forms of organization and activities of the movement. In this way, landless peasants created their own body of representation, becoming a socio-territorial movement—in other words, a movement which has, as its primary objective, the acquisition of a fraction of territory.

The MST's second National Congress, in 1990, marked the beginning of the third period of the movement's formation, characterized by its institutionalization. At that time, the roots of its organizational structure had already been firmly established, including representative bodies and forms of organizing activities. In establishing, consolidating, and expanding its structure, the MST intensified the resistance of the landless peasantry. In the prior period of formation (1985–1990), the MST territorialized significantly; it grew from a movement organized in just five states to a more substantial movement of national character. Since 1990, there have not been any substantive changes in the MST's organizational structure. In this period, the movement was confronted by numerous repressive state policies that created obstacles for land occupations and the development of the areas conquered. The massacres of Corumbiara in the state of Rondônia, on 9 August 1995 and Carajás on 17 April 1996 (see Fig. 14.1), are but two examples of state repression and violence against the MST (Fernandes 2000). Since 1996, the movement has faced many other challenges related to the multidimensional nature of development, as well as challenges more specifically related to recent changes in the age-old agrarian question.

The central challenge of peasant movements is to guarantee the process of re-peasantization, that is, the reproduction of their members and territories. The reproduction of peasant territories is achieved through the implementation of pro-peasant policies in the areas of agricultural production, processing, marketing, education, health, housing, roads/transport, and technology. However, the dramatic changes occurring in the agrarian question over the last two decades have greatly affected peasant movements, and resulted in a significant reflux in the struggle for land and agrarian reform. This reflux has had much to do with the fact that the governments of Fernando Henrique Cardoso, Luís Inácio Lula da Silva, and Dilma Rousseff opted for a conservative agrarian reform, while investing significantly in the expansion of an agribusiness model that has ensured the perpetuation of land concentration and low incomes for peasant families (Fernandes 2013). Even though several progressive public policies were implemented, such as the Food Acquisition Program (PAA) and the Program of Education for Agrarian Reform Settlers (PRONERA), these have not been sufficient to change the agrarian situation so as to improve the lives of the majority of the peasant population.

Also, significant changes in the global energy matrix have led to the expansion of the areas used for the production of sugarcane and soybean (Fernandes et al. 2010) and intensified the process of land grabbing by foreign multinationals (Borras and Franco 2012; Clements and Fernandes 2013). This has, in turn, impacted peasant farming in Brazil, which has been relegated to the margins of public policies in the agro-energy sector and constantly threatened by the expansion of commodities. In addition to its own territories being threatened by agribusiness, the peasantry confronts agribusiness by occupying *latifúndios*. In the last 10 years, there has been an increase in the number of conflicts between peasant movements and agribusiness (DATALUTA 2013).

The majority of conflicts between the peasantry and agribusiness occur in regions where agribusiness is expanding on the lands of the latifúndios, principally for the production of sugarcane, orange, soybean and planted forest like eucalyptus. Over the past two decades, over one million families have engaged in land occupations; of these, 60 per cent have been organized by the MST. Between 1979 and 2013, over a million families have been settled through agrarian reform. This is indicative of a strong process of re-peasantization in Brazil (see Table 14.1). Nonetheless, it is important to note that only half of the families settled were the result of land expropriation, expressing a de facto process of re-peasantization. Although in the last decade the participation of the urban population in land occupations has increased, the number of land occupations has decreased. The government has instead prioritized the regularization of land titles for existing small farms, transforming them into peasant territories. Regularization of land titles accounts for the greatest part of the total area

Table 14.1 Geography of rural settlements: Policies for the acquisition of land, 1979–2013

Policy	*Projects*	*%*	*Families*	*%*	*Area (ha)*	*%*
Expropriation	5486	61	527,560	49	19,954,180	25
Regularization	1307	15	312,974	29	52,791,308	65
Purchase	525	6	53,659	5	1,579,364	2
Recognition	1200	13	91,859	9	3,328,073	4
Donation	134	1	15,384	1	435,844	1
In acquisition	305	3	68,458	6	3,187,163	4
Total	8957	100	1,069,894	100	81,275,932	100

Source: DATALUTA (2013)

of land obtained by peasants through agrarian reform. Land can also be granted by the act of 'recognition', which is by states of the federation that adopt settlement projects. The purchase of land is a policy used, in some cases, to resolve conflicts, while donations of lands occur by means of institutions that support agrarian reform (see Table 14.1).

Although peasant families have gained access to over 80 million hectares of land through occupations carried out by peasant movements, like the MST, this has not altered the fact that land concentration in Brazil remains among the highest in the world. Gaining access to land promotes re-peasantization, but the major challenge for peasants is to remain on the land.

Resistance and Subordination

Capitalized land rent is a social relation utilized by capital to appropriate the wealth produced by the peasantry. In this section, we analyze data from the 2006 Agricultural Census in order to elucidate the condition of subordination affecting the Brazilian peasantry, which endangers the.

process of re-peasantization. According to the Brazilian Institute of Geography and Statistics (IBGE), Brazil possesses 8,514,876 sq. km of land. This is marked by extreme regional and territorial inequalities (IBGE 2009a, b). These inequalities play a role in maintaining a highly concentrated land structure, as evidenced by a Gini index of 0.854. Most of Brazil's lands are under the domain of large national and multinational corporations. These companies exert significant influence and effectively control agricultural development policies, by capturing the large majority of the resources destined for agricultural credit, monopolizing the markets on all scales, and directing the application of technology for increasing agricultural production. Primarily producing commodities, agribusiness in Brazil also constitutes a hegemonic power that determines the planning of agricultural production and subordinates peasants who are responsible for the majority of food production destined for the domestic market.

Brazil is one of the largest and most important agricultural producers in the world. In 1996–2006, of the total territory, 330 million hectares were used for agriculture and livestock production, according to the Agricultural Census. In 1975–1985, this agricultural area covered 375 million hectares, meaning that over the last 30 years, Brazil has used between 39 and 44 per cent of its territory for agricultural production, representing one of the greatest areas dedicated to agriculture in the world. The persistent inequality that marks the country's rural territory becomes more evident when one compares data on peasant farming with that of agribusiness. The Census registered a total of 5,175,489 agricultural landholdings nationwide; of these, 84.4 per cent (4,367,902) were family units and 15.6 per cent (805,587) were capitalist holdings. The total area occupied by the family units was 80,250,453 hectares, while the area occupied by capitalist holdings was 249,690,940 hectares. Although agribusiness or capitalist agriculture used 76 per cent of the total agricultural area, gross annual production amounted only to 62 per cent of the total, or R$89 billion (US$45 billion). The gross annual production from peasant agriculture, on the other hand, was 38 per cent, or R$54 billion (US$28 billion), using just 24 per cent of the total area.

While using just under a quarter of all agricultural land, peasant farming accounts for 74 per cent of the total number of persons working in agriculture (12,322,225 people). In contrast, agribusiness employs about 4,245,319 people, or 26 per cent. This disparity is even more evident when considering that, in the territory pertaining to agribusiness, only two workers on average are employed per 100 hectares cultivated, while in territory pertaining to peasants, the average ratio is 15 people per 100 hectares. This discrepancy is related to the fact that the majority of people who gain a livelihood from peasant agriculture live in the countryside, and the majority of those who are employed by agribusiness live in the city. In the same way, this difference reveals the distinct forms of use of rural territories. While for the peasantry, land is a place of production and housing, a place to call home, for agribusiness, land is merely a place of production. These distinctions are important characteristics for understanding the different models of territorial development promoted by the peasantry and agribusiness.

When we analyze data regarding the respective participation of peasant and capitalist landholdings in terms of the value of total agricultural production, the disparity between these two models is equally as pronounced. According to an analysis conducted by Alves and Paulo (2010), only 8.19 per cent of establishments (423,689 of 5,175,489), are responsible for generating 84.89 per cent of the total value of production. This means that 91.81 per cent, or 4,751,800 of the total number of establishments are responsible for just 15.11 per cent of the total production value. This data demonstrates the correlation between territorial concentration and the concentration of wealth. The situation is even worse when one considers that 11.3 million people living in 3,775,826 establishments receive a mere 4.03 per cent of the total wealth produced from agricultural production, and that the families of over 2,014,567 establishments have annual revenues equal to only half of the minimum wage, or less. The majority of the agricultural establishments receiving the lesser portion of the wealth generated corresponds to peasant agriculture.

Despite this obvious disparity, peasant agriculture is responsible for 70 per cent of beans, 87 per cent of cassava, 38 per cent of coffee, 46 per cent of corn, and 34 per cent of rice produced in Brazil. Moreover, peasant agriculture accounts for 59 per cent of pork, 46 per cent of chicken, 30 per cent of beef and 58 per cent of milk produced. The disparity between peasant and capitalist agriculture is also evident when analyzing the production of different food products. For example, 1.57 per cent of the establishments that produce corn account for 68.31 percent of the total corn production, and 19.59 per cent of the establishments producing milk account for 73.3 per cent of total milk production. This concentration of production has produced differing attitudes toward the development of agriculture in Brazil. Some think-tanks defend that the farmers who produce less should be eliminated. Others defend the expansion of policies, such as agrarian reform and agricultural credit, which would increase the participation of these marginalized peasant farmers, thus promoting greater access to land and income generating opportunities.

The Brazilian agrarian paradox is stark: 74 per cent of producers receive only 15 per cent of agricultural credit and possess just 24 per cent of agricultural land, yet produce 38 per cent of total production value. On the other hand, agribusiness receives 85 per cent of all agricultural credit, controls 76 per cent of the agricultural area, produces 62 per cent of the total production value, and employs 26 per cent of the total number of people employed by agriculture. In the first example, on much less land, a greater number of people, who receive very little agricultural credit, divide a small share of the wealth produced, that is, the share that capital allows to stay in the hands of peasant farmers. In the second example, using vast extensions of land, fewer people receive a greater share of the resources used for agriculture and of the wealth produced. This same group also maintains a significant share of the wealth produced by the peasantry, through capitalized land rent, because agribusiness commercializes the majority of food products produced by peasants. The peasant class of over 2 million families, while contributing to 38 per cent of gross production, receives a monthly income of less than US$15 dollars and is forced to depend on government assistance to survive.

Inequality is often only exacerbated by government and private policies implemented through the development projects of national and transnational corporations. Other institutions, such as labor unions and peasant organizations, also participate in the process of territorial development, but on a smaller scale and with limited power. In most cases, these institutions do not initiate development projects, but rather submit themselves to the projects presented by the state and by capital. Subordinated workers and peasants confront an assailing capitalism that manifests itself through government policies in support of agribusiness, predominantly determining the logic of territorial planning and development. The confrontation which constantly occurs between these opposing postures generates permanent class conflicts which, when examined, allow a better understanding of the particularities of each of the respective development models. We can conceptualize these differences more clearly by analyzing various elements of the agrarian question. These elements will vary from country to country, as each possesses different variables that may be more or less predominant than others. In the case of Brazil, two of the principle problems which threaten the process of re-peasantization are the reflux of land occupations and the capitalization of peasant land rent.

Conclusion

The history of the formation of the Brazilian peasantry, and its geography, demonstrates that its existence is much more dependent on the actions of peasants organized in peasant movements than those of capital, which subordinates the peasantry and seeks to permanently maintain this state of subordination. Despite the gains, successes and learning, Brazilian peasant movements have not yet been able to articulate the elaboration of a national project for peasant agriculture. They remain hostage to a model of agribusiness development promoted by governments of both the political Left and Right. The ideology created and promulgated by agribusiness has blinded even leftist intellectuals who have come to believe that the development of peasant agriculture cannot be thought of outside of the agribusiness model. Thus, the agribusiness model is viewed as a totality, and the peasantry as simply an attachment of the capitalist model.

It is this conception of agribusiness that led to the creation of a new concept which has attempted to replace the concept of peasantry. In the 1990s, in the context of neo-liberalism in Brazil, the concept of 'family farmer' or 'family farming' (agricultura familiar) emerged. With its emergence, the process of the destruction of the peasantry went from being a strictly physical process to an ideological process as well. The concept of family farming appeared as 'modern', in contrast to the concept of peasant, which seemed to connote 'backwardness', as has been analyzed in the works of Abramovay (1992) and Lamarche (1993, 1998). Family farming is one of the new expressions appropriated by agrarian capitalism in an attempt to mischaracterize the peasantry. The emergence of the concept impacted agrarian reality visibly, with the creation of public policies, such as the National Program for Strengthening Family Farming (PRONAF), and a national socio-territorial movement, the Federation of Family Farm Workers (FETRAF). The new concept sought to conceal the differences between non-capitalist family social relations and capitalist relations, masking the existence of the permanent conflicts.

The concept of family farming, now well established, has been incorporated by peasant movements, although without the modern/backward dichotomy in which the term originated. In fact, every peasant is a family farmer and every family farmer is a peasant. The reaction of peasant movements to the concept, especially the MST, was positive, steering clear of the dichotomy that is frequently employed by government institutions. This is also a part of the process of re-peasantization: the response of the peasant movement was to recover the concept of peasant by associating it to the concept of family farmer. In fact, it is not through the use (or non-use) of such concepts that the peasantry is differentiated, but rather the condition of subordination of peasants to the model of capitalist development. The greatest challenge for peasant movements is to overcome this condition of subordination, of peasants seeing themselves as appendices of a capitalist model, and to construct an alternate model of development for peasant agriculture. Only by overcoming this way of looking at agricultural development will the peasantry be truly emancipated. This is the paradigmatic debate that is being waged today by institutions, yet the predominance of the vision of agrarian capitalism has prevented changes in public policy. The reflux in the struggle for land and agrarian reform is one example of how the peasant movement has thus far failed to alter the correlation of forces and shift the dominant agricultural paradigm. This is the current reality of the agrarian question in Brazil.

Note

1. Translated by Elizabeth Alice Clements

Bibliography

Bibliography

Abramovay, R. (1992). *Paradigmas do capitalismo agrário em questão*. São Paulo/ Campinas: Editora Hucitec/ANPOCS and Editora da Unicamp.

Alves, E. R., & de Paulo, D. (2010). Ganhar tempo é possível? In J. G. Gasques, J. E. R. V. Filho, & Z. Navarro (Eds.), *A agricultura brasileira: Desempenho, desafios e perspectivas* (pp. 275–290). Brasília: IPEA.

Borras, S. M., Jr., & Franco, J. C. (2012). Global Land Grabbing and Trajectories of Agrarian Change: A Preliminary Analysis. *Journal of Agrarian Change, 12*(1), 34–59.

Clements, E. A., & Fernandes, B. M. (2013). Land Grabbing, Agribusiness and the Peasantry in Brazil and Mozambique. *Agrarian South: Journal of Political Economy, 2*(1), 41–69.

Cunha, E. (1982). *Os Sertões*. São Paulo: Abril Cultural.

da Graziano Silva, J. (1981). *Modernização dolorosa*. Rio de Janeiro, Zahar Editores.

da Ramos Filho, E. S. (2008). *Questão agrária atual: Sergipe como referênia para um estudo confrontativo das políticas de reforma agráriae reforma agrária de mercado, 2003–2006*. PhD thesis, Universidade Estadual Paulista 'Júlio de Mesquita', Presidente Prudente, São Paulo.

DATALUTA (Banco de Dados da Luta pela Terra). (2013). *Relatório Brasil*. Presidente Prudente: Núcleo de Estudos, Pesquisas e Projetos de Reforma Agrária.

de Medeiros, L. S. (1989). *História dos movimentos sociais no campo*. Rio de Janeiro: Fase.

de Oliveira, A. U. (1987). *Amazônia: Monopólio, expropriação e conflitos*. Papirus: Campinas.

de Oliveira, A. U. (1988). *Integrar para entregar: Políticas públicas e Amazônia*. Papirus: Campinas.

Derengoski, P. R. (1987). *Os rebeldes do Contestado*. Porto Alegre: Tchê Editora.

Fernandes, B. M. (2000). *A formação do MST no Brasil*. Petrópolis: Editora Vozes.

Fernandes, B. M. (2013). A reforma agrária que Lula fez e a que pode ser feita. In E. Sader (Ed.), *Dez anos de governos pós-neoliberais no Brasil* (pp. 191–206). São Paulo: Boitempo Editorial & Flacso Brasil.

Fernandes, B. M., Welch, C. A., & Gonçalves, E. C. (2010). Agrofuel policies in Brazil: Paradigmatic and territorial disputes. *Journal of Peasant Studies, 37*(4), 793–819.

de Funari, P. P. A. (1996). Arqueologia de Palmares: Sua contribuição para o conhecimento da história da cultura Afro-Americana. In J. J. Reis & F. d. S. Gomes (Eds.), *Liberdade por um fio: História dos quilombos no Brasil* (pp. 26–51). São Paulo: Companhia das Letras.

IBGE (Instituto Brasileiro de Geografia e Estatística). (2009a). *Censo agropecuário, 2006: agricultura familiar: Primeiros resultados—Brasil, grandes regiões e unidades da federação.* Rio de Janeiro: IBGE.

IBGE (Instituto Brasileiro de Geografia e Estatística). (2009b). *Censo agropecuário, 2006: Brasil, grandes regiões e unidades da federação.* Rio de Janeiro: IBGE.

Lamarche, H. (Ed.). (1993). *A agricultura familiar: Uma realidade multiforme.* Campinas: Editora da Unicamp.

Lamarche, H. (Ed.). (1998). *A agricultura familiar: Do mito a realidade.* Campinas: Editora da Unicamp.

Martins, J. d. S. (1981). *Os camponeses e a política no Brasil.* Petrópolis: Vozes.

Martins, J. d. S. (1986). *O cativeiro da terra.* São Paulo: Hucitec.

Moyo, S. (2007). A terra Africana e as questões agrárias: Os casos da luta pela terra no Zimbábue. In B. M. Fernandes, M. I. M. Marques, & J. C. Suzuki (Eds.), *Geografia Agrária Teoria e Poder* (pp. 105–149). São Paulo: Expressão Popular.

Moyo, S., & Yeros, P. (Eds.). (2005). *Reclaiming the Land: The Resurgence of Rural Movements in Africa, Asia and Latin America.* London: Zedbooks.

Prezia, B., & Hoornaert, E. (1989). *Esta terra tinha dono.* São Paulo: FTD.

Sauer, S., & Pereira, J. M. M. (2006). *Capturando a terra: Banco Mundial, políticas fundiárias neoliberais e reforma agrária de mercado.* São Paulo: Editora Expressão Popular.

CHAPTER 15

Peasants of Manipur: Agrarian Change, Land Tenure and Emerging Patterns of Re-peasantization in India

Ch. Priyoranjan Singh

and Hanjabam Isworchandra Sharma

Introduction

The economies of the north-eastern region of India that are in the periphery of developmental processes in the post-independence period are some of the most backward in the country.[1] In the absence of industrialization and the strengthening of the agrarian base, fast population growths have led to land hunger, agricultural involution, and massive occupational diversification into the tertiary sector, which has been fed by huge

Originally published in *Agrarian South: Journal of Political Economy, Vol. 2 No. 3*

C. P. Singh (✉) • H. I. Sharma
Department of Economics, Manipur University, Imphal, Manipur, India

P. Jha et al. (eds.), *Labour Questions in the Global South*,
https://doi.org/10.1007/978-981-33-4635-2_15

investments in the unproductive sectors. As the tertiary sector has not commensurately absorbed incremental population growths, increasing dependence on land and agriculture for pathways out of poverty are still persistent, as amply reflected in the marginalization of holdings and insignificant emergence of entrepreneurial and capitalist farming.

However, there seems to be a qualitative shift in the way that peasants conduct their production and reproduction in the face of limited resources and alternative employment opportunities. Adjusting to changing demand patterns through changed cropping patterns; minimizing overdependence on external resource inputs; bringing down the costs of production; innovating and fine-tuning the institutional framework of land, labour, and credit markets—these are some of the qualitative changes in the peasant's world that are re-ordering the very structure of production, distribution and appropriation.

This article attempts to highlight some critical agrarian changes that are taking place in the fertile valley region of the state of Manipur, in north-eastern India, which has a history of being the most agriculturally advanced state in the entire region. The focus is on how peasants are seeking survival autonomies through farming intensification and diversification that are crucially grounded on mutual trust and co-operation at the community level; and how age-old tenurial systems are giving way to new ones that serve community purposes, leading to value addition at the community level with very little room for undue private expropriation. 'Back to the farm' as a neo-idiom seems to be re-emerging among the peasantry, which until recently appeared to have given up farming as a primary occupation.

The study is based primarily on recent findings of village-level surveys in the most productive district of the Manipur Valley. The first part examines the land ownership and holding pattern, which, along with the structure of occupations, suggests the non-emergence of land-based polarization among the peasantry. The second part looks into the emerging nature of land tenure and how it is symbiotically linked with village- and State-level structural changes in the economy. The final part makes some tentative conclusions on some emerging dimensions of re-peasantization and the importance of culture and values in the re-shaping of institutions that are favourable to re-peasantization.

Land and Non-polarized Resource Control Structures

The peasant mode of production (van der Ploeg 2008) is defined by a constant search for value addition and employment in the context of limited resources and by social and material resources being processed and controlled by those in the labour process. Interrelations among actors are essentially governed by 'local cultural repertoire' and gender relations. Ownership and land holding structures in the village of Wabagai show how land is both private as well as communal, in the sense that ownership control over land has visibly become subservient to the use of land by the community.

The village is located in the most agriculturally advanced district of the valley. The river Sekmai runs through the village, and has been the main reason for favourable crop culture. The village had a population of 5268 persons and 1027 households when the survey was conducted in 2010. The village has a high literacy rate of 81.18 per cent and is well-connected by a state highway on its southern boundaries. A wetland and lake, the Kharung Pat, is contiguous to its northern boundaries. The lake and the wet lands with their rich aqua and vegetative resources along with some 755 acres of paddy land have historically been the basis of village sustenance and development. However, fixity of land, population growth, and land hunger has led to only 37.49 per cent of households owning paddy land and 46.25 per cent of households having operational holdings (Tables 15.1 and 15.2) in paddy land. The rapidly growing productive base of the

Table 15.1 Land ownership in Wabagai village by size class

Size-class (in acres)	*Number*	*Area*	*Avg. area*	*Gini coefficient*
0–1	116 (30.13)	70.98 (10.63)	0.61	0.367
1–1.5	120 (31.17)	148.8 (22.28)	1.24	
1.5–2	33 (8.57)	61.38 (9.19)	1.86	
2–3.5	77 (20.00)	198.77 (29.77)	2.58	
3.5–5	34 (8.83)	150.80 (22.58)	4.44	
5+	5 (1.30)	37 (5.55)	7.4	
Total	385 (100.00)	667.73 (100.00)		

Source: Census survey

Note: Figure in parentheses indicates percentage

Table 15.2 Operational holding in Wabagai village by size class

Size class (in acres)	*Number*	*Area*	*Avg. size*	*Gini coefficient*
0–1	148 (31.16)	91.70 (12.14)	0.62	0.348
1–1.5	160 (33.68)	198.40 (26.27)	1.24	
1.5–2	58 (12.21)	105.42 (13.96)	1.82	
2–3.5	73 (15.37)	188.03 (24.90)	2.56	
3.5–5	29 (6.11)	125.76 (16.66)	4.34	
5+	7 (1.47)	45.84 (6.07)	6.55	
All size class	475 (100)	755.15 (100)		

Source: Census survey

Note: Figure in parentheses indicates percentage

village consists in cash cropping on paddy land and other non-paddy land and fisheries on colonized land in the wetlands or village land.

The land ownership pattern shows that intergeneration transfers and subdivisions have resulted in extremely small landholdings without any visible sign of capitalistic land accumulation or polarization. Sale of land has been historically rare as reported by the villagers. Almost 90 per cent of landholdings are no more than one hectare. Only five families owned land above two hectares. Land ownership of an average size of 0.61 acres constitutes 30.13 per cent of landholdings, while another 31.17 per cent is composed of landholdings of 1.24 acres. Families owning about one hectare of land, the institutionally determined pre-colonial subsistence holding size, constitute 20 per cent of landowners. The Gini coefficient is 0.367.

The problem of utilization of land for productive purposes has to be seen as an historically evolved phenomenon and also as having material and non-material components. There are different modes of productive organization in different contexts that give rise to differing rights, duties, and obligations, leading to a particular pattern of property rights. The most important basis for inequality is the distribution of land with which leisure and enjoyment of status and authority are associated (Myrdal 1968). Historical dynamics and the structural evolution of the economy have led to agricultural involution and marginalization of ownership as well as operational holdings, without any visible rise of an agrarian capitalist class thriving on economies of scale or on pure feudal extraction based on landownership and interlocking markets.

The land ownership structure in the village exhibits the virtual absence, if not complete absence, of the conditions for the emergence of exploitative production relations based on the control over land and the land lease market or through the interlocking of land, labour, credit, and product markets. This will become clearer in a later section which will refer to the structure of operational holdings and the nature of tenancy.

In India, unlike trends in the developed countries, landholding households have increased while the average area operated by them has decreased steadily since the 1950s. The relative share of marginal landholdings has increased dramatically and that of large and medium declined, while the size groups located in the middle (small and semi-medium) have more or less remained constant (Thorat 1997). In Manipur, small and marginal holders dominate, and the medium and large landholders are virtually disappearing.

In Wabagai village, only 7.58 per cent of operational holdings are above one hectare, as compared to about 10 per cent in terms of land ownership in the same size class. In other words, about 92 per cent of landholdings are marginal and small in terms of average size. Marginal holders constitute 31.16 per cent of operational holders with average holding size of 0.62 acres, and small holders constitute 33.68 per cent with average size of 1.24 acres. There are only seven households (1.47 per cent) operating on an average size of 6.55 acres (2.64 hectares), classified as semi-medium holders. The Gini coefficient is 0.348. The village does not therefore even have medium and large holders, as seen in the rest of India. The village therefore shows no signs of consolidation and expansion of operational holdings, the rise of big farms and the commoditization of agriculture.

The occupational structure of the village, reflecting macroeconomic structures in the state, provides insight into the nature of the change that is taking place in village agriculture and how re-peasantization seems to be emerging in the village. Occupational profiles of heads of households (Table 15.3) show that 60.76 per cent consider agriculture as their primary occupation (excluding the old and disabled), while 40.59 per cent had secondary occupations, of which 82.22 per cent considered agriculture as a secondary occupation. In other words, among the bulk of agricultural household heads with secondary occupations, agriculture continued to provide a part of their livelihood.

Among those who considered agriculture as a primary occupation, 27.46 per cent were in paddy cultivation, 9.74 per cent in fisheries, and 7.26 per cent in cash cropping. Animal husbandry as a primary occupation

Table 15.3 Primary occupation of head of the household in Wabagai

Occupation	*Male*	*Female*	*Total*
Agriculture			
Paddy cropping	282 (27.46)	0	282 (27.46)
Cash cropping	74 (7.21)	0	74 (7.21)
Animal husbandry	10 (0.91)	0	10 (0.97)
Fish farmer	100 (9.74)	0	100 (9.74)
Agri. labourer	73 (7.11)	2 (0.19)	75 (7.30)
Subtotal (Agriculture)	539 (52.43)	2 (0.19)	541 (52.68)
Non-agriculture			
Construction and manufacturing	94 (9.15)	3 (0.29)	97 (9.44)
Govt. services	97 (9.44)	1 (0.10)	98 (9.54)
Other services	130 (12.67)	21 (2.04)	151 (14.71)
Subtotal (Non-agriculture)	321 (31.26)	25 (2.43)	346 (33.69)
Old and disabled	130 (12.66)	10 (0.97)	140 (13.63)
Total	990 (96.40)	37 (3.60)	1027 (100)

Source: Field survey
Note: Figure in parentheses indicates percentage

was insignificant, at 0.97 per cent, and agricultural wage labour accounted for a comparatively low 7.3 per cent. Crop diversification into high-value commodities is catching on fast in the village, as 34.14 per cent of household heads with agriculture as primary occupation are into cash cropping, fisheries, and animal husbandry. This is further evident from the fact that members of the households who are economically active are more into non-cereal agriculture, both for primary as well as secondary occupations. Among family members, 53.37 per cent have non-paddy agriculture as primary occupation and 69.9 per cent as secondary occupation. The younger generation are obviously entering into high-value crops more than the older generation and also finding casual jobs as agriculture labourers (21.44 per cent), which is much higher than the village average of 7.3 per cent.

Given the limited land resources of the village, vertical and horizontal occupational diversification within village families are but inevitable. Main occupations of household heads show that 33.69 per cent are into non-agricultural activities. However, in the overall portfolio of multiple occupations among the villagers, agriculture still takes priority. How this has been made possible in the limited land resources of the village can be seen from the nature and structure of tenancy in the village and the change that has taken place towards more intensive utilization of land, based on both rent and non-rent community relationship structures.

Land Tenure and Structural Changes

There is a large lease market in the village with an incidence of tenancy standing at 34.95 per cent, as against 9.9 per cent in India (Vaidyanathan 2010), reflecting high levels of land hunger in the absence of alternative employment opportunities. The tenure groups in Table 15.4 have been divided into four. Pure owners are those who cultivate on their own land and do not lease in or out. Combined owners cultivate on their own land, but lease out some land. Combined tenants cultivate both on own and leased in land. Pure tenants cultivate only on leased in land. Pure owners constitute 48.41 per cent, pure tenants 27.09 per cent, combined owners 13.15 per cent, and combined tenants 6.33 per cent. There are only 26 pure non-cultivating landlords in the village, 57.7 per cent of which are in the land ownership size class of less than 1.5 acres. The land market in the village is obviously heterogeneous, and sharply polarized categories of landlords and tenants do not exist, as is the case in many parts of India (Rao 1974).

The macro characteristics of the lease market is that over one-third (34.95 per cent) of the cultivators are leasing in land and among landowners, 23.9 per cent are leasing out land and only 8.05 per cent leased in

Table 15.4 Size class and pattern of agricultural tenancy

Size class (in acres)	*Tenure group*					*Rent receiver*
	Pure owner	*Combined owner*	*Combined tenant*	*Pure tenant*	*Total*	
0–1	78 (32.10)	23 (34.84)	1 (3.23)	46 (34.07)	148 (31.16)	9 (34.62)
1–1.5	84 (34.57)	15 (22.73)	5 (16.13)	56 (41.48)	160 (33.68)	6 (23.08)
1.5–2	20 (8.23)	9 (13.64)	10 (32.26)	19 (14.07)	58 (12.21)	0
2–3.5	42 (17.28)	12 (18.18)	9 (29.03)	10 (7.42)	73 (15.37)	7 (26.92)
3.5–5	16 (6.58)	6 (9.09)	4 (12.90)	3 (2.22)	29 (6.11)	4 (15.38)
5+	3 (1.24)	1 (1.52)	2 (6.45)	1 (0.74)	7(1.47)	0
Total	243 (100)	66 (100)	31 (100)	135 (100)	475 (100)	26 (100)

Source: Census survey

Note: Figure in parentheses indicates percentage

land. There is clearly a preference among land owners to lease out land rather than lease in. In this village of marginal and small landowners, all size classes seem to be interested in the lease market on the supply side, irrespective of the size of their land. In fact, 57.7 per cent of the pure landlords that lease out land are in the size class of 1.5 acres and below, with the upper size classes accounting for a lower 42.3 per cent. An almost equal 57.56 per cent of owner cultivators lease out land in the same size class. Also, in the relatively larger uppermost size class, 10.61 per cent of the owner cultivators lease out land, in spite of their meagre land. In this village, therefore, it is not necessarily the case of the larger land owners renting out more land, but it is more a case of land owners of all types and sizes being interested in the land lease market rather than cultivating themselves.

Preferences for leasing out land among smallholders in Asia and Africa has been attributed to inherent difficulties in the enforcement of hired labour, especially in operations covering widely scattered parcels of land. Thus, smallholders find it more profitable to lease out land because of scale diseconomies arising from the use of hired labour (Binswanger and Rosenweig 1986), so that family farms become most effective. The persistence of small family farms in Asia and Africa has also been attributed to these reasons. Some of the major reasons given by the villagers for leasing out are rising costs of cultivation, investment opportunities in agriculture and non-agricultural activities, cultural obligation to help out a near one with subsistence land, debt servicing, consumption emergencies arising out of health, and other ceremonial events.

On the demand side, the reasons are clearer, although some 30 reasons have been identified in the Indian context (Jodha 1981). First, as 62.51 per cent of the households do not own land, there is huge competition among the landless to lease in even the smallest piece of paddy land at least to provide for subsistence paddy and create the safety net for the extreme levels of uncertainties in other casual employment. A Sangam (0.64 acres) of paddy land, at the productivity level in the village, provides just the bare rice consumption needs of a family of five members,[2] the average family size in the village. A Marak (1.24 acres) of land on the other hand leaves some surplus paddy to meet extreme cash needs in health and other emergencies. This is the reason why 75.55 per cent of pure tenants are concentrated in the lowest land size classes of 0–1 and 1–1.5 acres, being essentially subsistence holders. Second, there is an upsurge in cash cropping on paddy land, as irrigation has become more efficient in the village and as community norms are fast shifting away from mono-cropping of paddy on paddy land only and cash cropping on other land. Use-right of paddy land is thus providing the opportunities to produce three to four crops annually and offering high degrees of employment and income to the younger generations which are being confronted by ever tightening job markets in the state. The forces working on the demand and supply sides of the land market and determining the structure of land tenure are visible from the contractual arrangements in the village, which has caught on in other villages though at varying degrees.

Historically, most tenure contracts in Manipur have been of the straightforward fixed-kind rent type between the lessor and the lessee, with terms being highly favourable to the lessee (Singh 2005a). Share cropping tenure had virtually disappeared on the advent of colonial rule with the introduction of private property in land. In the post-colonial period, while the bulk of the tenure arrangements had remained the fixed-kind rent type, agricultural census data began to record usufruct mortgage types of tenure arrangements. In the mortgage tenancy arrangement, the mortgagee pays no interest on cash given to the landowner during the pendency of the debt, but has the use rights over the land and does not pay rent. The mortgagee can cultivate the land or lease it out to others and receive rent from the cultivator. Once the debt is settled, the land reverts to the owner. This type of tenure is now significantly emerging in many villages. Share cropping is very rare in the State, as this arrangement is socially considered exploitative and against the cultural core of avoiding taking advantage of the weaknesses of the other (Singh 2005b).

Agricultural tenancy is one of the oldest institutional arrangements of the rural economy, evolved in order to facilitate adjustments in agricultural factor markets. In post-green revolution India, improvements in irrigation and factor markets and technological change have drastically changed the implications and the nature of tenancy. Commercial tenancy, what Lenin called 'entrepreneurial renting', is on the rise in advanced agricultural areas such as Punjab and Haryana, and subsistence tenancy is still widespread throughout the country. Commercial tenancy is viewed as promoting allocative efficiency, whereas subsistence tenancy consists in compulsive and involuntary participation in the transaction, as the returns from tenanted land are hardly commensurate with the effort that the tenant invests due to high rent (Swain 1999).

There is a large amount of literature in India on which types prevail, where, and for what reasons (Iqbal Singh 1989; Narayana and Nair 1989;

Swain 1999). Share cropping has been found to be the dominant mode of tenancy in backward regions, as a means of risk hedging under conditions of high uncertainty, especially in low irrigation density areas. On the contrary, fixed rent types of tenancy are found in developed agricultural regions where technological advancements have reduced uncertainties and new classes of entrepreneurial tenants, who are themselves a new product of technology, are capable of bearing risk and are able to pay rent in advance, as in the Punjab (Singh 1989). Subsistence tenancy and renting, as well as entrepreneurial tenancy and renting, both exist in the village, but their cultural and economic moorings are indeed certainly peculiar.

The structure of tenancy contracts in the village (Table 15.5) shows that share cropping is hardly acceptable in the scheme of things in the village, as only three peasants (1.8 per cent) sharecrop. The traditional fixed rent tenure, at 41.57 per cent, is still holding ground but usufruct mortgage tenure, at 56.63 per cent, has come to hold sway in the village, which has strong implication for agriculture and agrarian relations in Manipur valley.

Fixed rent contracts are an age-old land tenure type in the state that existed mainly between the absentee landlords settled in the capital and the peasants in the villages. As populations grew and the economy diversified, rent-receiving landowners also emerged faster in the villages during the colonial and post-colonial agrarian scene. Rent rates of 12 Pots a Paree (12 sacks a hectare) during the pre-colonial days endured right up to the late 1970s, when the green revolution had started setting foot in many parts of the valley region. The rent rate was on average roughly 20 per

Table 15.5 Nature of tenancy in Wabagai village (in numbers)

Size class (in acres)	*Cash mortgage*	*Kind*	*Share cropping*	*Total*
0–1	26 (55.53)	21 (54.47)	0	47 (100)
1–1.5	40 (65.57)	20 (32.79)	1 (1.64)	61 (100)
1.5–2	14 (48.28)	13 (44.83)	2 (6.89)	29 (100)
2–3.5	10 (52.63)	9 (47.37)	0	19 (100)
3.5–5	3 (42.85)	4 (57.15)	0	7 (100)
5+	1 (33.33)	2 (66.67)	0	3 (100)
Total	94 (56.63)	69 (41.57)	3 (1.80)	166 (100)

Source: Field survey

Note: Figure in parentheses indicates percentage

cent of produce. After the 1980s, rents have steadily risen, either in tune with yield growths, the ratio remaining more or less constant, or in the case of subsistence tenancy on inferior land, higher rent-to-produce ratios. Rents have risen to as high as 30 Pots a Paree in intra-village transactions in pockets of the valley, where better irrigation facilities have made multiple cropping possible. Land owners do not receive rent on crops other than paddy that is grown by the lessee, a social norm that favours the tiller of the soil rather than the owner of the land. In case of absentee landowners of the urban area, rent has stabilized at 20 Pots a Paree. This is one of the reasons why peasants in the State try to sell land to urbanites who care more for capital appreciation rather than kind rent. Urban lessors also rarely evict tenants, whereas rural ones can assume self-cultivation in any season. The rent rates are, however, not enforced in times of less than normal production, as cultural and village norms takeover and fair rent reductions are accepted by both parties.

Mortgaging in land by providing cash credit to the owner and its rise is a recent phenomenon underscoring the degree of land hunger and lack of institutional credit in the state. The bargaining normally starts from the owner's side for consumption credit, investments, or for pure usury. Sickness, children's education, and social ceremonies, like marriages and mortuary rites, are some of the prime reasons for mortgaging out. Seed money for cash cropping or other non-agricultural activities, including petty contract work in the state's booming infrastructure sector, or outright bribes for government jobs, are some of the areas of investment. At the ruling five per cent per mensum rate of interest in the rural informal credit market, usury has also been a great attraction to many landowners who lack the stomach for physical work and desire to taste the waters of the highly lucrative rural credit market, without losing land.

The mortgage land market works favourably in many ways for both the lessor and the lessee. The lessor gets instant credit that can be used at will and the lessor gets land to cultivate for a minimum of two years and employment and income for the family without having to buy scarce land at exorbitant prices, if at all land is on sale, which is rare.[3] A hectare of land is mortgaged for ‘80,000, and petty peasants lease in the smaller parcels of land with smaller amounts (0.64 acre at ‘20,000 for lucrative cash cropping, e.g.) which they are able to save from cash income from casual daily work, into which most families have vertically and horizontally diversified in the village or outside.[4]

All Manipuri villages and professions have the informal institution of mutual chit funds known as Marup, wherein monthly savings are pooled in by members, the total monthly collection going to members according to needs or by lot. Even the poorest of the poor subscribe to these funds and are the source of bulk funds/credit for the peasantry. The recent implementation of institutional credit to even non-land owning peasants through the Kishan Credit Cards is also feeding the mortgage lease market in the villages, where the scheme has hit the ground and where multiple cropping practices are encouraging banks to be liberal.

In the village lease market in Wabagai, 70.21 per cent of the mortgage tenants are in the size range 0–1.5 acres, having invested between ‘20,000 and ‘40,000 for use rights for a minimum of two years and up to the date of repayment of the original mortgage amount. Thus, in the largest segment of the lease market (56.63 per cent), in the 0–1.5 acres size class, it is the small parcels of land and their rapid circulation which are feeding both the demand and supply sides of the market. Comparatively bigger landowners are also mortgaging out land instead of cultivating it themselves, as perceived advantages of farm and non-farm activities differ across size class of land ownership.

The important issue here is why, in the emerging structural change in land tenure from fixed rent to mortgage types, peasants as well as landowners are exhibiting preferences for a vitiated mortgage tenure system in place of the time-tested fixed-kind rent tenure system. The motivations are varied yet rooted in risky rational choices. For the more enterprising landowners, the prime motivator is obtaining immediate cash for higher return investments in fisheries and cash cropping, without permanent land alienation. Many have colonized the wetlands as fisheries at low costs by constructing earthen ring bunds, or dug small-scale fishery ponds on homestead land, with handsome returns that pay off debts in a short time and without losing the mortgaged land. Income from fisheries range from ‘60,000 to ‘200,000 per annum on farms ranging from 0.60 acres to five acres, which is far above the income that a farmer gets from equivalent areas of paddy land (the gross paddy income from the best land of 0.60 acres was less than ‘20,000). Some 9.74 per cent of the village households have fisheries as the main occupation and another 11.94 as secondary occupation. In other words, over one-fifth of the village households have diversified into fisheries. Data on indebtedness among the households shows that 12.65 per cent of the borrowings were for fisheries and another 49.65 per cent for agriculture, including leasing in land and other inputs.

There is thus a strong indication that credit through mortgaging out land for investments in fisheries was one of the prime factors for the emergence of a mortgage lease market in the village in the face of low returns on paddy cultivation, especially in the case of the comparatively bigger landholders.

Many, especially among the younger generation, also reported mortgaging out parcels of land in order to finance cash cropping on remaining paddy and other land. As the mortgage debts are of small amounts, even if the new ventures fail, as it often does in a volatile cash crop vegetable market, most landowners are able to pay off, being more economically sound than the landless.

On the demand side, the marginal mortgage tenants are motivated mainly by food and employment security and the availability of low interest agricultural credit, formal self-help group funds, or the more widespread informal mutual funds. Community based efficient irrigation has enabled them to raise three crops per season and motivated them to mortgage in land and seek survival autonomies, rather than face the highly uncertain casual labour market in the state.

The emergence of mortgage tenancy has led to intensification in agriculture and higher value addition to village income, based on the fundamental community resource of land. In the absence of institutional credit, larger landowners have used mortgage credit to colonize the wetlands with fisheries in areas adjacent to the village, which are fast drying up due to ecological disturbances. These wetland fisheries of larger scale, of up to five acres, are the commercial farms that provide employment to villagers round the year in the gathering of grass feeds from the wetlands that are highly suitable for the variety of 'Grass Carps' that are mainly reared. Villagers on canoes provided by the farm receive half the daily wage in gathering grass from the wetlands. The farm thus depends mainly on cheap local resources rather than factory feeds, to reduce costs and compete with imports from far away fisheries in Andhra Pradesh that are flooding the local fish market. Many smaller farmers have also raised fish farms of smaller scale on homestead land. Thus, mortgage tenancy on the one hand has ensured access to land to the landless; it has at the same time enabled the landowners to branch out to more lucrative agriculture on under-utilized land resources in the village, thereby expanding the productive base of the village and increasing value addition.

The intensification of land use in the village has been helped by another type of innovative land tenure in the village, which is not based on direct payment of rent but on mutual benefits, community principles of co-operation and a primal sense of pride in having helped out a fellow villager, governed by what van der Ploeg (2008) calls the 'local cultural repertoire'. This type of production and land relation was observed on over one-fourth of cash cropped land in the village.

Traditionally, vegetables are planted on small parcels of homestead land or on non-paddy land known as Inkhols, specifically devoted to vegetables. As land is becoming scarce, irrigation is improving, and demand for high-value vegetables is on the rise, cash cropping on paddy land has been on the rise. As vegetable cropping has boomed in the village, 78.22 per cent of vegetable cash cropping is carried out on paddy land (Table 15.6). About one-third of the paddy land vegetable cropping is carried out by landless and marginal farmers who had worked as agriculture labourers on those lands during the Kharif paddy season.

These farmers do not pay rent, and their obligation is only to carry out the first preparatory tillage for paddy cultivation, just after reaping their last crop, which can be done with comparative ease, as the soil is still loose. The landowner gains in that crop rotation improves the fertility of the soil and garners social capital as a benevolent person, though there is a bit of quasi-rent involved in the transaction in terms of costs of preparatory tillage. The average size of the this type of land being only 0.62 acres or the traditional measure of a Sangam, the cost of preparatory tillage for the average farm would be about one tractor hour or five man days. At the prevailing daily wage rate of '100, and the lower range of cash crop income being '60,000 to '70,000, the quasi-rent involved is quite nominal. Obviously strong traditional and social norms underpin this tenure system, rather than pure economic considerations of rent or other forms of expropriation.

Table 15.6 Land utilization pattern of cash cropping in Wabagai

Type of Land		*Number of Households*	*Area (acres)*
Paddy	Own	53	41.85
	Others'	47	20.10
Non-paddy		30	17.25
Total		130	79.20

Source: Field survey

The social norm of not paying additional rent to the landowner on non-paddy crops has also enabled tenants (holding 34.95 per cent of land) to offer their fallow paddy landholdings, under the nose of actual landowners, to fellow peasants and landless labours, while gaining in the cost of preparatory tillage. This social norm and tradition has also worked on the landowners to offer fallow paddy land in return for preparatory tillage. As the proportion of landless agricultural labour is quite low in the village at 7.3, elements of labour tying are involved in the transaction, whereas labour tying as an institution has not historically existed in Manipur in any significant form. The form of labour tying during the pre-colonial period, in the form of the King's sharecropper, abruptly ended with monarchy in the advent of colonial rule, being exogenous to the general peasantry. Another form of labour tying is indeed emerging in Manipur, whereby the employer buys labour in advance in a debt contract which is highly risky and more favourable to the labourer. Exchange labour is the main form of labour through which rice cultivation is conducted, and the underlying principle is that one should put in one's labour in the process, thereby blurring the hierarchical distinction between the master and the serf, one of the cultural cores of the Manipuries. Thus, if a rich peasant does not himself participate in the labour process, he finds it hard to get labour and suffers greatly in production and productivity. The essential point here is that co-operative and communitarian value systems strongly dictate crucial aspects of production, distribution, and expropriation among the Manipuri peasantry.

The quasi-tenurial mechanism in cash cropping is increasingly leading to more intensive use of paddy lands which are otherwise left fallow after one crop, thereby giving access to land to the landless and marginal peasants with very little rent obligations. This type of tenure accounts for one-fourth of cash cropped land in the village. Vegetable cropping on seasonal fallow paddy land with nominal rent obligations but with high returns have enabled many towards self-employment and more dignified survival autonomies, especially among the landless. It is in this sense that we had earlier suggested that land is private as well as communal and that ownership control of land has visibly become subservient to the use of land by the community in a given context. Cultures and values indeed provide many safety valves to those at the margins and help communities to regenerate themselves in times of stress. 'Back to the farm' neo-idioms seem to be re-emerging not only because of favourable conditions as well as compulsions, but also because of community actions based on co-operative behaviour and the suppression of undue private expropriation.

Search for Survival Autonomies in a Peasant's World

Wabagai village is experiencing rapid expansion and growth in agricultural activities. These have been labour driven and achieved through farming intensification on formerly underutilized land resources and innovative expansion into wetland. In the process, new resources are being created or expanded at the individual as well as community levels. Growth and development is not based on takeovers of land and scale expansion, but on running efficient small farms under co-operative behaviour and collective action. In a context where the gains from labour process are not significantly being appropriated by any distinct social category, incentives for farming are on the rise in the village. Some of the important reasons can be identified in a preliminary way.

Assuring efficient irrigation through collective community action has been at the core of cropping intensity and crop diversification in the village. A barrage on the river Sekmai was built in 1983, and double cropping in paddy was a distinction in the village. As maintenance and the canal system deteriorated and as demand far outstripped supply, the village had stopped double cropping of paddy. But in the last decade or so, the village has found its own alternative way in water management and resource conservation and expansion. In the lean winter season, villagers dammed up the Sekmai River and ensured irrigation to the vital cash crops. The local Member of Legislative Assembly recently built a small concrete dam there. Local clubs and NGOs have also stepped in to help provide lift and pump irrigation. Besides, the community maintains complex traditional diversion canal and channel irrigation systems. Damming up the river at strategic points and maintaining the complex irrigation channels is a collective community affair, and contributions are irrespective of farm or family size or types of crops. The result has been total irrigation in all the farms of the village (Table 15.7). The village does not double crop paddy anymore and has diversified into more lucrative cash crops after the first crop of paddy.

The outcome of better irrigation has been the widespread adoption of modern inputs and time-saving machinery and the acquiring of knowledge. High-yielding seed varieties are used by 78.11 per cent of farmers, the rest using flood resistant local varieties on farms located in

Table 15.7 Irrigation by source in Wabagai (in numbers)

Size class (in acres)	*Canal*	*Lift/Pumpset*	*Traditional diversion channels*	*Total*
0–1	83 (56.08)	51 (34.96)	14 (9.46)	148 (100)
1–1.5	94 (58.75)	46 (28.75)	20 (12.50)	160 (100)
1.5–2	39 (67.24)	13 (22.42)	6 (10.34)	58 (100)
2–3.5	42 (57.54)	27 (36.98)	4 (5.48)	73 (100)
3.5–5	19 (65.52)	6 (20.69)	4 (13.79)	29 (100)
5+	4 (57.14)	2 (28.57)	1 (14.28)	7 (100)
Total	281 (59.16)	145 (30.53)	49 (10.31)	475 (100)

Source: Field survey

Note: Figure in parentheses indicates percentage

flood prone areas. Because of high maintenance costs, bullock power has been mostly substituted by farm machinery that are owned mainly for hiring out, as requirements on small own farms are far less than the capacity of the machinery. Competition among owners has ensured that the cost of hiring-in is lesser than the maintenance cost of plough cattle.

Growth, however, has been fuelled by easier formal credit flows, self-help group funds, and informal mutual funds. For all households, 69.44 per cent of borrowings were institutional. Farmers were making good use of credit, as only 31.62 per cent of credit was for consumption while 68.38 per cent was invested into crops, fisheries, and industries.

The overall result was high levels of employment, as 42.49 per cent of the entire population is economically active, with 70.35 per cent being self-employed and 17.23 per cent being casual workers. The rest had salaried jobs. The high degree of self-employment only shows how villagers are striving towards survival autonomies, mainly within agriculture and to a lesser extent in industry. The low level of agricultural labour, at 7.3 per cent, indicates such survival autonomies. Industry is limited to barely 59 households, mainly in rice milling and handloom and handicrafts, but out of these households, 82.75 per cent are engaged in farm activities for over six months. Interestingly, only 8.06 per cent of these industries were financed formally, whereas 45.16 per cent were self-financed.

The most important factor contributing to agricultural development is perhaps the institutional framework in land and labour in the village and the favourable ways in which the community adepts.

In developing countries, communities are defined by groups of people tied by mutual trust, based on intense personal relationships, and take forms like tribes and villages tied by blood and locational affinities. In these communities, especially of the Southeast Asian types, principles of mutual help, income, and work-sharing for generating subsistence to all members are strong and 'economic rationality in terms of individual profit and utility maximization does not operate in a community of this definition' (Hayami and Yoshihisa 2003: 328). In such traditional communities, the contractual forms of labour and land utilization governing resource utilization have historically obtained deep-rooted social codes of income and work sharing. Where there are strong sanctions or losses upon violating these social norms, the community guides the individual to co-operate voluntarily and to increase efficiency and reduce cost associated with the division of labour. In other words, landlord and tenant relationships are 'solidified within the total community relationship' (Hayami and Yoshihisa 2003: 328).

Land is not a means of extraction in the village, it is rather a means of community welfare. Larger landowners rent out small parcels of land rather than accumulate holdings. In spite of unequal distribution of landownership, tenure mechanisms have been evolved to create and maintain an agrarian structure that is fundamentally based on family-based farms. Traditional norms in developing countries of helping out the landless, as underscored by Hayami and Yoshihisa (2003), as well as scarcity of labour in peak labour cycles, have led to the emergence of the new tenure form of quasi-rentals to the landless for cash cropping during the fallow season on paddy land. In this seasonal contract, the landless labourer does not suffer any wage reduction on the labour obligation on the landlords' land, but has some claim on the landlords' land at nominal rent obligation. In this new form of clientalization, 'a special case of dyadic ties' (Scott 1972: 8), both gain, with labour appropriating almost the entire produce. Exploitative labour tying has not been historically a social norm among the Manipuri peasantry. As such, this quasi-rental tenure constitutes a fine-tuning of the institutional framework of land that offer access to unused land of the landowner to the landless at highly favourable terms that are non-exploitative and are based upon cultural cores and social norms of co-operative behaviour. The result has been a structural shift in production towards higher income and employment-generating cash crops and higher farming intensification on fixed village land.

The rise of mortgage tenancy is another example of adaptive institutional change in land tenure where conflicts between community principles of income and work-sharing and individual profit motives are being ironed out. Mortgaging out small parcels of land has enabled landowners to mobilize village savings outside of scarce formal credit for agricultural diversification into high-value cash crops on fallow paddy land and fisheries in the wetlands, thereby expanding the productive base of the village and value addition at the individual and community levels. Cash cropping and fisheries considered as main occupation account for 16.95 per cent of agricultural households, and 47.22 per cent as secondary occupation.

The colonization of common property land resources by private individuals, mainly by the landed on the wetlands, is not being objected to by the villagers. Direct employment on the farm, indirect employment in the gathering of fish feeds and marketing of fish are some of the reasons given for not objecting. Besides, none is restricted from colonizing on the wetlands, and growth of these larger commercial farms has helped the growth of lower-scale homestead farms within the village. Fish farming paddy landowners have further helped the colonizers by letting out small parcels of land under mortgage or quasi-rental tenures to the landless under community sharing principles. This, perhaps, has weighed politically upon landowners to be more liberal in giving marginal peasants use rights to fallow paddy land for cash cropping with nominal quasi-rent, thereby giving birth to a new tenure arrangement. In some sort of quid-pro-quo understanding and co-operation at the community level, this is leading to farming intensification and expansion in paddy land as well, as the wetlands.

The village still relies mainly on the pool of village labour, with rare intrusion by the recently emerging gang labour culture in the state. Family and exchange labour are the two main forms of labour in the village. Labour exchange takes place mainly within the cultivating households, and hired labour occurs only when exchange balances are not achieved due to differing family or farm sizes, or for other reasons. However, due to labour scarcity in peak labour cycles, a nascent type of labourer seems to be emerging in the village. These are the landless labourers who are given access to fallow paddy land for cash cropping by landowners and landholders. In a reverse case of expropriation, labour power seems to be exacting access to land at highly favourable terms and returns, in exchange for assured labour services to the land owner without any wage rate concession. In the net, farming intensification has gained and labour is better off.

The village seems to have achieved certain degrees of institutional change in land and labour relations that has enabled the peasantry to respond productively to changing demand patterns by transforming cropping patterns and farm diversification. More interestingly, this has been brought about by minimizing overdependence on external resource inputs and bringing down the costs of production. For example, the fishery feeds are based on cheap local produce and labour rather than costly factory feeds, and vital irrigation is based on communal labour and mutual co-operative behaviour rather than paid formal irrigation.

A comment is necessary regarding the traditional banking and credit institution of Marup. Historically, these were village level material funds, based on mutual trusts and co-operation, provided to member households to meet costly requirements of life cycle events, like birth, death, and marriage. For example, the Singel Marup to meet the material requirements of mortuary rites—such as firewood for cremation, bamboos to erect Pandals or covered ceremonial space, rice for ceremonial feasts and other needs—was provided to the beneficiary by the members of the Marup, irrespective of inequity in the number of deaths in member families. Eventually, the institution became monetized and adapted to various economic needs. Run mainly by women, the emergence of various forms of this institution as a savings and indigenous banking mechanism through mutual trust and co-operation has been responsible for the impetus given to agriculture in the village as well as in the State, especially in the absence of formal credit. In spite of moral hazards leading to breakdowns, the institution in various forms has endured through strong social sanctions and isolation of defaulters at the village level. The village community has thus found its own ways out of formal credit market failures by evolving various institutional forms through mutual trust and co-operation, although these institutions are far from being able to meet the rising credit needs of the village. The essential issue here is that the rise of these mutual funds and informal banking system has marginalized the role of professional money lenders; and that through these mutual funds the peasants themselves have become both lenders as well as a borrowers, thereby largely doing away with credit linked market interlinking that empowers the landed or the rich for undue appropriation.

Though the emerging dominance of mortgage tenancy in the village as well as quasi-labour rental tenancy needs more rigorous examination on the matter of efficiency and real impacts on village agriculture, one can only conclude that the emerging land system is more pro-peasant than pro-profits. There has been a massive marginalization of the workforce in the post-liberalization phase: marginal workers increased by 329 per cent during the census years 1991–2001, from 66,621 to 285,849 during the decade. Underemployment and casualization of rural labour, therefore, had grave consequences on the survival autonomies of the rural poor. Survey data from an adjacent Tezpur village show that 45 per cent of agricultural labour households had four to five occupations (Lisam 2010). Increasing access to land through quasi-rentals or mortgage tenancy has had the impact of greater stability in income and employment, and, as such, on survival autonomies. On the other hand, the landed in the villages had little options for accumulation through the tertiary and secondary sectors. New opportunities in the farm sectors are being successfully exploited by both landowners and the landless for value addition at the individual as well as at the community levels, thereby creating conditions that are favourable to re-peasantization.

While data needs to be generated more rigorously in defining the nature of agrarian change in the village, some tentative conclusions can be drawn from the village level dynamics on issues relating to re-peasantization. In situations of food and employment stress, culture and social norms are capable of innovating and fine-tuning the institutional frameworks of land, labour, and credit markets that re-order the very structure of production, distribution, and appropriation. Mutual trust and co-operation at the community level can lead to survival autonomies through intensification and diversification in farming. Resource expansion with increasing output and employment that add to value at the community and individual levels is possible in smallholder-based peasantries.

Notes

1. According to the Ministry of DONER and NEC (2008), the region has to grow at 11.8 per cent on average to come into parity with the national average by 2020.
2. As per NSS norms, a person requires 207 kg of rice per annum.
3. The price of paddy land ranges from about six to eight lakhs per hectare in the village.
4. Survey data from a neighbouring village show that 45 per cent of agricultural labour households had four to five occupations; see Lisam (2010).

References

Binswanger, H. P., & Rosenweig, M. R. (1986). Behavioural and Material Determinants of Production Relations in Agriculture. *Journal of Development Studies, 22*(3), 503–539.

Hayami, Y., & Yoshihisa, G. (2003). *Development Economics.* New Delhi: OUP.

Jodha, N. S. (1981). Agricultural Tenancy: Fresh Evidence from Dry Land Areas in India. *Economic and Political Weekly, 16*(52), A118–A128.

Lisam, S. (2010). *Problems of Agricultural Labour in Manipur in the Postliberalization Period.* PhD Thesis, Manipur University.

Ministry of DONER and NEC. (2008). *NE Vision 2020, Vol. 1.* www.indianchamber.org/northeast/Vision2020. Accessed 16 Nov 2013.

Myrdal, G. (1968). *Asian drama.* London: The Penguin Press.

Narayana, D., & Nair, K. N. (1989). *Heterogeneity, Mobility and Dynamics of Contractual Arrangements in the Agricultural Labour Market in an Irrigated District.* Working Paper No. 230, Centre for Development Studies, Trivandrum.

Rao, V. M. (1974). Village Lease Markets for Agricultural Land: Some Approaches for Analysis, Economic and Political Weekly. *Review of Agriculture, 9*(26), A55–A62.

Scott, J. C. (1972). The Erosion of Patron–Client Bonds and Social Change in Rural Southeast Asia. *The Journal of Asian Studies, 32*(1), 5–37.

Singh, I. (1989). Reverse Tenancy in Punjab Agriculture: Impact of Technological Change. *Economic and Political Weekly, 24*(25), A86–A92.

Singh, Ch. P. (2005a). Manipur's Economy: Historical Roots and Structural Evolution. *Eastern Quarterly, 3*(3), 149–159.

Singh, Ch. P. (2005b). *Agrarian Structure and Production Relation in Manipur.* PhD Thesis, Manipur University.

Swain, M. (1999). Agricultural Tenancy and Interlinked Transactions, I: Neoclassical and Marxist Approaches. *Economic and Political Weekly, 34*(37), 2657–2666.

Thorat, S. (1997). Trends in Land Ownership, Tenancy and Land Reform. In B. M. Desai (Ed.), *Agricultural Development Paradigm for the Ninth Plan Under New Economic Environment* (pp. 678–689). New Delhi: Oxford and IBH.

Vaidyanathan, A. (2010). *Agricultural Growth in India: Role of Technology, Incentives, and Institutions.* New Delhi: OUP.

van der Ploeg, J. D. (2008). *The New Peasantries: Struggles for Autonomy and Sustainability in an Era of Empire and Globalization.* London: Earthscan.

CHAPTER 16

Changing Forms of Wage Labour in Zimbabwe's New Agrarian Structure

Walter Chambati

Introduction

This chapter examines the changing nature of farm wage labour in the context of the extensive redistributive land reform since 2000. Despite being largely associated with large-scale capitalist farms (LSCFs) in sub-Saharan Africa (Barrett et al. 2005; Sender and Johnston 2004), this research argues that farm labour markets did not collapse as a result of reallocation of land compulsorily acquired from the LSCFs to mostly peasants who have been characterized as a class that does not hire wage labour. Existing alongside an expanded farm self-employment base (Chambati 2011; Chambati and Moyo 2004), the diverse forms of farm wage labour that emerged from the new agrarian structure tend to differ in their nature and character to those found in LSCFs.

The literature on agrarian labour relations since the Fast Track Land Reform Programme (FTLRP) which began in 2000 has tended to argue that agrarian labour markets in Zimbabwe, particularly their importance as

W. Chambati (✉)
Sam Moyo African Institute for Agrarian Studies (SMAIAS), Harare, Zimbabwe

P. Jha et al. (eds.), *Labour Questions in the Global South*,
https://doi.org/10.1007/978-981-33-4635-2_16

the major source of formal wage employment, have been reduced by the redistribution of land to peasants.[1] Various studies sought to quantify the numbers of formal farm jobs lost through retrenchments on the redistributed LSCFs lands (FCTZ 2002; Hellum and Derman 2004; Magaramombe 2003; NRC 2003; Rutherford 2004; Sachikonye 2003), erroneously claiming that all LSCF farm workers had been retrenched (e.g., NRC 2003). Indeed, many studies based their analyses on overstating numbers of the pre-existing LSCF farm workers, with one study suggesting that over 600,000 workers had been employed (JAG/RAU 2008), as opposed to the 350,000 farmworkers reported in various official records (CSO 1999, 2000).

The post-FTLRP literature on the emerging agrarian labour regime and relations also continued to be silent about the changing nature of wage and family labour among the peasantry, with the implicit suggestion that farm wage labour as a whole had declined (Chambati and Moyo 2004). Meanwhile, the few studies on wage labour considered the new jobs created by resettled farmers (whether as new commercial farmers or peasants) as being limited, both, in scale (in terms of numbers) and in terms of their financial value (Hartnack 2015; Magaramombe 2003; Sachikonye 2003). The presumed lack of capital and requisite skills among new black farmers, compared to the LSCFs, was considered to reflect an inherent lack of capacity to hire both new and former farm workers who were retrenched from their jobs. The slow recovery of agriculture since 2000 was generally seen as limiting the agricultural development (productivity, exports, etc.) given the pessimistic view about small-scale farming (The World Bank 2006) and by implication the prospects of formal farm wage labour and beneficial family labour were considered bleak.

Notwithstanding this narrative, a few existing studies on the post-FTLRP agrarian labour relations have broadly noted the increasing trends in 'hiring in' wage labour and 'hiring out' of family labour among the new land beneficiaries, alongside the expansion of the scale of family labour applied on their farms. The number of permanent, casual and family workers used in the agricultural production units has risen, as has the share of peasant households and small capitalist farms utilizing these forms of labour (Chambati 2009, 2011; Moyo et al. 2009; Scoones 2015; Scoones et al. 2010). However, such studies have failed to examine in detail the variations in forms and quality of agrarian labour in the newly resettled areas. Moreover, the extremely limited and exclusive definition of farm 'work' conceived as 'wage work' that is often used, obscures the scale of 'paid work' that includes both cash wages and in-kind payments (Ibid.) that obtains. Altogether, the focus on LSCF-based forms of formal wage labour has obscured the diverse labour relations which have emerged and limited the assessment of agrarian labour relations in the new labour markets, and the differing relations found between various classes of farmers (Chambati 2011, 2013; Moyo et al. 2009).

Knowledge gaps also exist on the labour management practices that contribute to the overall quality of employment, such as the nature of contracts for full- and part-time workers, segmentation of labour by gender, skills and commodities produced, and methods of supervision of farm labour. Quite crucially, such research has not assessed the changing nature of the residential labour tenancy system as it operates among both the new and former farm workers and its implications on farm labour supplies to the new many smaller-scale employers.

The underlying problem with the post-2000 literature on agrarian labour was that it overlooked the fact that a new more complex and diverse agrarian structure had emerged, reconfiguring agricultural production, market relations and labour (Moyo 2011a, 2013). Thus, the new farmers were established under the two settlement models (A1 and A2 schemes) promoted by the FTLRP were assumed to be homogenous forms of organizations in terms of their labour relations, while the A2 farmers were often characterized as 'poor employers' (Masiiwa and Chipungu 2004; Mutangi 2010; Sachikonye 2003). The suggestion that all of the new farmers had similar production capabilities related to poor wage labour relations obscured the fact that the new and diverse forms of agrarian labour were emerging.

The current tri-modal agrarian structure is characterized by three modes of the social organization of production, namely, the peasantry, middle-to-large capitalist farms and agro-industrial estates. They were found to be highly differentiated in their agricultural practices, production market integration and labour utilization patterns. This change reflected a substantially reconfigured agrarian labour market (Moyo 2004; Moyo and Yeros 2005, 2011a, b). This increased differentiation of landholdings, production patterns and access to markets was increasing the social differentiation between farms, with critical implications for a complex web of agrarian labour relations (Moyo 2011a, b, c, 2013). Different classes of farmers constituted the new and diverse labour markets. Sources of wage labour came from a wider rural and urban population as well as from the former farm workers, whereas the new peasantry and the persistent land short and/or landless people from Communal areas (Chambati 2009, 2013; Chambati and Moyo 2004).

The absence of systematic empirical work on agrarian labour at the farm level, focusing on the differentiated landholdings and land use patterns and agricultural production in the redistributed and Communal areas, and, consequently, on the evolving differentiation of labour utilization and remuneration patterns, obscures our understanding of the specific nature of Zimbabwe agrarian labour regime/relations and its implications for wider social reproduction.

This study utilizes micro-level survey data of farms allocated land under the A1 and A2 schemes, (which are also referred to here as new farm households). The data were collected in Goromonzi and Kwekwe districts by the African Institute for Agrarian Studies (AIAS) in 2006 and again 2014 to outline the changing forms of wage labour since 2000.[2] A farm labour survey conducted by the author in the same districts provided further insights into the new agrarian labour markets. These two districts provide an opportunity to examine the differentiated outcomes of redistributive land reform, which are characterized by contrasting socio-economic and agro-ecological patterns. Goromonzi district is located in a high potential agro-ecological zone, which is near to major agricultural markets in the capital city, Harare and endowed with high per capita public infrastructures, which influences the agricultural production patterns and labour relations. In contrast, Kwekwe district is located further away from Harare in a dry and low potential agro-ecological zone, with gold mining, a key feature of the district's economy.

After this introduction, the next section discusses the context of wage labour in the LSCFs prior to the FTLRP in order to provide a basis upon which to evaluate the changes and continuities in agrarian labour markets. This is followed by an examination of the differentiated sources of farm (wage) employment that have arisen in the two districts studied since 2000. The next two sections expose the character of permanent and casual labour that is utilized by the landholders and how the labour is recruited and mobilized to work in the farm units. The conclusion summarizes the main findings.

Wage Labour in Large-Scale Capitalist

Farms Before the FTLRP

The agrarian labour regime that evolved from settler colonization onwards largely remained unaltered due to limited land redistribution until 2000. It consisted of landless and/or land short permanent and casual wage-workers employed in the 4500 LSCFs that occupied 11.2 million hectares of prime land and mostly self-employed family labour on 16.4 million hectares of Communal area land held by one million peasant households (Moyo 2011a). Few peasants also hired wage labour in their farm units (Adams 1991; CSO 1998). Wage labour lived on small portions of the LSCFs in farm compounds providing permanent labour and, in some cases, with access to land for minor production for own sustenance, and accommodated casual workers from surrounding Communal and other areas. These workers, which were stabilized as permanent labourers and full-time residents on LSCFs' compounds, had insecure agricultural and residential tenure rights that were linked to employment on the farm, constituting a form of 'residential labour tenancy' (Moyo 2011a). The dependency relations generated by latter weakened the bargaining power of farm labourers and was deployed to entrench the control over them by LSCFs in both work and off-work relations (Amanor-Wilks 1995, 2000).

Initially, labour force comprised of foreign migrant labour from Nyasaland, Northern Rhodesia and Mozambique. But as land dispossession took its toll from the 1960s onwards, the composition of the labour force on the LSCF began to be tilted towards domestic migrants. (Arrighi 1970; Palmer 1977). By 2000, the share of foreign farm workers was down to 10 per cent (FCTZ 2000; General Agriculture and Plantation Workers' Union of Zimbabwe [GAPWUZ] 2002) from about 60 per cent in 1956 (Clarke 1977).

The same LSCF employed permanent or full-time labourers continuously. Different variants casual or part-time labour included seasonal and contract labourers. Seasonal labourers were employed for a fixed time period ranging between 3 and 8 months in any period of the 12 months. Most workers initially gained employment as seasonal workers prior to being 'promoted' to the stable permanent employment by guaranteeing access to labour from their families (Gibbon 2011; Rutherford 2001). Contract work was the most informal type of wage labour ranging from a few hours to a few days. This comprised of piecework, which entailed performing a certain magnitude of work (e.g., weeding 0.5 hectares of a maize field in exchange for an agreed wage) and time-rated work, which involved labour being hired for a specific number of hours, which is rewarded with a daily wage. Its extent in the LSCFs was not clear since it has neither been documented nor captured in the official statistics (Adams 1991).

Many permanent workers were semi-proletariats who combined wage labour with independent agricultural production in the Communal areas (Moyo and Yeros 2005; Moyo et al. 2000; Yeros 2002). One study estimated that 40.5 per cent of the male permanent workers had access to Communal areas, where they also farmed (Vhurumuku et al. 1998). Nonetheless, labour immobility characterized permanent work, as many of the workers and their families spent their lifetimes working on a single LSCF.

Around 2000, the total LSCF labour force numbered 313,879 workers, split between 167,459 permanent workers and 146,420 casual workers (CSO 2001). While permanent workers accounted for 76 per cent of the LSCF labour force in 1983, it had dropped to 53 per cent in 2000 (CSO 1984, 1997, 2001). There was structural change in the agrarian labour market from a previously large permanent force to the casualization of farm labour after the 1990s. This trend was driven by the new Economic Structural Adjustment Programme (ESAP), the introduction of flexible labour laws and by the growth of capital intensive horticultural production systems and extensive wildlife land uses (Moyo 2000). These processes were a result of the decline in the production of labour intensive grain crops in the LSCFs that began in the 1970s and intensified in the 1980s (Loewenson 1992). Women were mostly employed as marginal and seasonal workers, constituting 65 per cent of the casual labour force and only 10 per cent of the permanent workers in 2000 (CSO 2001). Agricultural labour was unevenly distributed with LSCFs in wetter Mashonaland provinces employing on average between 75 and 174, while the employment levels were between 17.5 and 42 workers in the Midlands and Matebeleland provinces (Commercial Farmers Union, n.d.).

The 1980s were characterized by rising real wages in the agricultural and mining sectors on account of state intervention in the labour markets (Amanor-Wilks 1995). The ESAP reversed these gains and real wages in LSCFs declined by more than 1.6 times between 1990 and 1997 (Kanyenze 2001). Government in terms of the Minimum Wages Act of 1980 set post-independence wages, but ESAP introduced collective bargaining where employers and employees negotiate wages through their respective unions (GoZ 1993). Since the farm workers trade union was weak, LSCFs dominated the determination of wages and ensured that they remained very low (Loewenson 1992). Minimum wages from the collective bargaining exercise protect permanent and seasonal workers only, and exclude pieceworkers.[3]

The wages paid to permanent and seasonal workers were based on a skill grading system defined through collective bargaining.[4] By the year 2000, most of the permanent farm workers (82 per cent) were classified as unskilled workers (CSO 2001). The skills also informed the hierarchical organization of workers on LSCFs. These consisted of clerical staff, foreman, supervisors and gang leaders that mediated work relations between the general workforce and the owners/managers. Farm labourers were also segmented according to commodities produced on a single LSCF especially in the Mashonaland Provinces, which had diversified commodity production (Gibbon 2011). The employers at the farm level determined remuneration for contract workers.

In comparison, the farm workers were the lowest paid within all formal employees and never had enough to meet subsistence requirements, even by the Poverty Datum Line (PDL) standard. In 1997, about 70 per cent of farm workers were below the PDL, while average monthly wages were about 51 per cent of the PDL (Kanyenze 2001). Female labourers received substantially lower wages than males. Wage subsidies provided by LSCFs including food rations and other non-farm income generating activities did not reverse their precarious living conditions of farm labourers (McIvor 1995). Even the free accommodation in the farm compounds was of poor quality, lacking ancillary social services and featured by overcrowding that exposed residents to respiratory diseases (Magaramombe 2001; Tandon 2001).

Although cases of labour abuse declined substantially after 1980, physical violence, racism and long working hours beyond the regulated time for the same pay were documented in the literature up to 2000 (Amanor-Wilks 1995, 2001; Tandon 2001). Remnants of the master–servant type relationships endured in some LSCFs (Loewenson 1992) and frequently reported in the media. Farm workers were however not passive victims of exploitation in LSCFs but resisted in various ways including strikes, absconding from work, thefts and voting with the feet (Rutherford 2001; Tandon 2001).

New Agrarian Labour Markets at the Local Level

The increased number of farm households and/or potential employers since 2000 transformed the farm labour markets. Access to more and better quality land also expanded the possibilities of families to utilize their own labour for independent agricultural production. The few LSCFs were redistributed to mostly new peasant households and small-to-medium scale capitalist farms whose relative distribution differs from district to district depending on the local dynamics of land reform.

In Goromonzi, the FTLRP enlarged the number of farm households from 20,253 in 2000 to 23,626 in 2014 (MLRR 2014). The majority of the new farm households were 1673 A1 land beneficiaries that added to the existing peasantry composed of 19,976 households in the Communal areas. The A2 land beneficiaries joined the ranks of the small-to-medium and large capitalist farms, 778 and 89, respectively. About 16 agro-estates are part of the new agrarian structure in the district. The new peasantry in the A1 farms, own an average of 19.39 hectares (combining grazing and arable land) compared to 3.72 hectares for the old peasantry in the Communal areas. Land sizes in the small-to-medium capitalist farms were almost three times those of the new A1 peasantry. With an average land size of 493.8 hectares, the new LSCFs are 20 per cent smaller than those in this category are in 2000. The agro-estates had the most expansive land sizes (in excess of 1400 hectares) among the farming classes. Overall, the land controlled by the LSCFs was downsized from 61.8 per cent to 29 per cent. In contrast, the peasantry increased their share of land from 31.7 per cent to 44.87 per cent during the same period. Compared to the national situation and experience in other districts (including Kwekwe; Chambati 2013; Moyo 2011a), the peasantry in Goromonzi got a smaller share of the land distributed due to high demand for the larger sized A2 plots in this peri-urban district. Agro-estates in Goromonzi, which include private agribusiness companies, state farms, mining companies and church and trust institutions control about 8 per cent of the land area.

The FTLRP in Kwekwe created 3586 and 266 new A1 and A2 farm households, respectively, on 308,495.6 hectares of land formerly belonging to mainly white LSCFs (MLRR 2014). The A1 scheme had increased the number of peasant households from 29,066 in 2000 to over 33,801 by 2014 accounting for 98.6 per cent of the farm units in the district (Ibid.). The share of the land area controlled by them increased dramatically from 52.5 per cent to 71.2 per cent between 2000 and 2014. The first phase of land redistribution in the early 1980s in Kwekwe had already increased the shares of land held by peasants by 10.1 per cent. Peasant households from Communal areas own an average of 13.7 hectares of land (combining both arable land and shared grazing land rights). Those in old resettlement and new A1 farms access more arable and grazing land averaging 63.1 hectares and 48.4 hectares, respectively.

Between 2000 and 2014, the new A2 farms joined the category of medium capitalist farms that were composed of small-scale commercial farms (SSCFs). This slightly increased the share of the medium-sized capitalist farms in the total number of farm households in the district from 0.4 per cent to 0.76 per cent. In relation to the total land area, the medium-sized capitalist farms also increased their share from 1.4 per cent to 4.11 per cent. The medium capitalist farms, which now include the old SSCFs and small-to-medium A2 farms owning on average 145.2 hectares, are defined by their reliance on hired in their agricultural production units. The large capitalist farms (now including remaining black and white LSCFs and the large A2 farms) now account for 0.6 per cent of the farm households and 16 per cent of the total land area controlled (Ibid.). The new large capitalist farms in the A2 scheme on average own relatively less land (537.2 hectares) compared to the remaining LSCFs (937.9 hectares; Ibid.). The agro-estates in Kwekwe are largely not of the agro-industrial type that are vertically integrated into the global market chains and highly capitalized. Rather they include wildlife conservancies and both public and private farms (MLRR 2014). The agro-estates now control 7.6 per cent of the land area, came down from 17.2 per cent in 2000. Agro-estates in Kwekwe, like others nationally, control large swathes of land averaging over 3000 hectares per unit but employ less wage labour than the others do (Chambati and Moyo 2004).

Agricultural Production Patterns

Most of the main 15 agricultural commodities produced in the country including food, oilseeds, export and horticultural crops, as well as livestock are found in Goromonzi (Moyo 2013; The World Bank 2012). Food crops (maize and small grains) are the common in A1 and Communal area households (AGRITEX 2015). Wheat is predominantly produced by A2 and LSCFs that have access to irrigation (Ibid.). A2 farmers dominate Soybean production, while farmers in the Communal areas mostly grew sunflower (Ibid.). Specialized crops, such as seed maize, seed soybeans and barley, are the preserve of LSCFs. All the classes of agricultural producers grow tobacco, but A1 form bulk of its grower base. Few peasants are linked to export horticulture, but they do dominate domestic horticulture (AGRITEX 2015). Livestock production activities include beef, dairy, pigs, goats and poultry production. Large beef herds are found in the A2 and LSCFs, while A1 and Communal areas keep few cattle mainly for draught power.

Although agriculture is the main employer in Kwekwe, it competes for labour with alluvial gold mining. The agricultural commodities produced in Kwekwe are less diverse than those of Goromonzi. The A1 farmers produce maize, groundnuts, sunflower, while edible beans, soya beans, wheat and potatoes are dominated by A2 farmers. Dairy farming is still undertaken by the remaining LSCFs. A2 and LSCFs dominate large beef herds in Kwekwe. Maize production is pervasive in the Communal areas, alongside cotton, groundnuts, rapoko, millet and sorghum (AGRITEX 2013).

Changing Agrarian Labour Force

Nationally, self-employed labour (84.1 per cent) has remained the largest share of agricultural workers while permanent and casual workers accounted for 7.4 and 4.5 per cent, respectively (ZIMSTAT 2013). Yet, the character of hired labour has changed since the FTLRP. On account of the larger land sizes and better agro-ecological conditions, the demand for farm labour could be expected to higher in the new peasant households in the A1 scheme than the old peasantry in the Communal areas. While the A2 scheme expanded the potential number of farm wage employers in the category of existing capitalist farms.

The allocation of the hired and family labour was different across the A1 and A2 farm units in both districts examined. Hired workers were the major source of labour in the A2 farms, which in addition to producing food crops were also more integrated into the production of cash and/or export crops than the A1 farms. Approximately, 73 per cent and 57 per cent of the labour for key tasks on the farm, including cultivating, weeding, harvesting, fertilizer application and, pest disease control was supplied by hired labour in Goromonzi and Kwekwe districts, respectively (AIAS 2014). The reverse was true for the A1 where unpaid family labour supplied the majority of the labour for the key farm tasks, 70.8 per cent and 84.6 per cent in Goromonzi and Kwekwe, respectively (Ibid.).

Differentiation was also apparent in the forms of labour employed by the A1 and A2 farm units. In Goromonzi, about 86.8 per cent of the surveyed A2 households hired permanent workers compared to 31.7 per cent of the A1 households (Ibid.). Only 8.0 per cent of the households in the Communal areas employed permanent labour. An average of 5.5 permanent workers were hired in the A2 farms as compared with to 0.9 per cent and 0.2 per cent workers in the A1 and Communal areas, respectively (Ibid.). Casual labour hiring was more pronounced in the A1 (60 per cent) and Communal area (38.2 per cent) than permanent labour hiring. Similar patterns of labour use were also deduced from the new farm households in Kwekwe district, where over 81.2 per cent of the surveyed A2 households hired permanent labour compared to 21.8 per cent in the A1 farms (AIAS 2014). The average 2.7 permanent workers per farm in the A2 farms were at least four times of those hired in the A1 and Communal area. Again, casual labour was also the most common form of hired labour employed across the different farming classes in Kwekwe district. These average employment levels in the new farm units in Kwekwe were however lower than those found in Goromonzi farm households, which is characterized by more intensive land uses.

The majority of the total number of permanent workers are employed by the surveyed farm households in the A2 capitalist farms (51 per cent), and the remaining LSCFs (11 per cent) in Goromonzi (ZIMSTAT 2015). The Communal areas and A1 farms there employed 17 per cent and 21 per cent of the permanent labourers, respectively. Most of the casual labourers (87 per cent) were employed in the A1 scheme. Whereas in Kwekwe, the A1 farms employed the majority of the total number of permanent workers (55 per cent) are employed on A1 farms, the A2 and LSCFs account for 12 per cent and 3.0 per cent, respectively. Communal areas in Kwekwe hired 25 per cent of the permanent labour force. The majority of total number of casual labourers (71.8 per cent) are employed in the A2 farms.

As in the past, women's representation in the permanent workforce (17 per cent) remains well below that of men and they constitute majority of casual labour across both districts. Females were 17 per cent of the permanent labourers in Goromonzi, but were the majority of the casual labourers (56.3 per cent). In Kwekwe, women were the majority of farm labourers (62.3 per cent) hired by all classes of farms, and yet, they were only 6.1 per cent of the permanent workforce. Discrimination of women in the farm labour markets, as elaborated later, continues to characterize the new agrarian labour markets.

Another feature of the new labour markets is that some landholders (23.1 per cent), especially those within the peasantry also hire out their labour to other farm households (AIAS 2014). This implies that access to land is not only factor that influences the participation of households in farm labour markets. Since land reform in Zimbabwe provided limited post-settlement support to the new farm households, some enter farm labour markets to mobilize finance to acquire inputs for their household production as outlined later.

By expanding the number of farm units, the FTLRP has enlarged the opportunities of wage employment especially in the A2 farms, while access to smaller land sizes by the peasantry has also added to the total number of family labourers. The majority of the new employment opportunities generated are however in the casual forms of farm labour. In Kwekwe, a total of 26,995 workers were employed in the entire farm units and 85.5 per cent of them were casual labourers (ZIMSTAT 2015). These employment levels in the A1 and A2 farm units represent an increase from the 1100 and 800 full- and part-time workers employed in Kwekwe LSCFs around 1999 (Interview, District Extension Officer, 24 March 2015). For Goromonzi district, the estimated 4665 permanent and 16,619 casual workers that are now employed in the new agrarian structure (ZIMSTAT 2015) represent an increase from the approximately 3900 and 6950 permanent and casual labourers in the old LSCFs around 2000, respectively.[5] However, due to the reduced farm sizes, the average numbers of labour employed per farm unit are relatively lower than those found in the LSCFs nationally—36 and 32 permanent and casual workers per farm before the FTLRP, respectively (CSO 2000). Overall, the differentiated patterns of land redistribution during the FTLRP at district level influenced the new local agrarian structures generated and subsequently the agrarian labour relations. In Kwekwe, the FTLRP emphasized the allocation of land to smaller-sized A1 farm units compared to the larger sized A2 farm units. At the district level, this promoted the more the growth of family labour than hired labour, which is predominantly deployed in the smaller-scale A1 farm units. A2 farm units, which are reliant on hired labour, got the larger share of land redistributed in Goromonzi than the A1 farms. The labour use patterns are influenced by the land use potential across the different agro-ecological regions that characterize the district studied. Goromonzi, which has diversified land uses than Kwekwe districts, tends to employ more hired labourers per farm unit. Whereas food production is now the dominant land use, the A2 farm units which are more integrated to the cash and export production (Moyo et al. 2009; The World Bank 2012) dominate the employment of hired and also maintain more permanent employees than the A1 farms. In what follows, the chapter uncovers the precise character of permanent and casual labour hired in the new agrarian structure.

Forms of Agrarian Wage Labour

New farm households still hire in the broad categories of labour that were found in the old LSCFs. Yet, both the permanent and casual wage labour today is qualitatively different from before 2000 in terms of the degree of formality, types of contracts offered and how are they organized to perform work in the new farm units. Segmentation of labour according to the enterprises and skills—a prominent feature of diversified LSCFs—is no longer as elaborate. Women's accommodation in the more full-time forms of works still retains the character of the past. Moreover, the composition of the labour force in terms of history of working in the LSCFs and its age dimensions has also been changed following the FTLRP.

Permanent Labour Hired In

The same employer continuously employed permanent or full-time farm workers. They included former farm workers and new farm workers. The former farm workers accounted for 23 per cent and 24.3 per cent of the labourers surveyed in Goromonzi and Kwekwe districts, respectively. Many new entrants (30.3 per cent) into the farm labour markets were unemployed prior to their current jobs. Others were transitioning from self-employment in the agriculture sector (10.3 per cent), non-agricultural sector (4.5 per cent), urban employment (12.9 per cent), mining jobs (5.8 per cent) and from school (21.3 per cent) to farming. Nonetheless, among the new farm workers, 15.0 per cent had entered farm labour markets earlier as permanent (8.4 per cent) and casual labourers (6.5 per cent) in the Communal areas.

Today, the permanent workers are relatively younger than those found in the LSCFs, with an average age of 34 years. Former permanent workers were on average 15 years older than new permanent farm workers in both districts. The older former permanent workers are the ones who started as part-time workers, before being employed permanently. New permanent workers were also more educated compared to the former farm workers.[6] In Goromonzi, 43.5 per cent of the former farm workers had completed only part of the primary education compared to only 7.8 per cent among the new permanent workers. Most of new permanent farm workers (37.7 per cent) completed secondary education. In Kwekwe, 20 per cent of the former farm workers did not attend any school and 32 per cent completed part of primary education, whereas among the new permanent workers, 38.6 per cent attended secondary school but did not complete and 28.2 per cent completed this curriculum. These findings are reflective of the poor access to educational facilities in the former LSCFs (McIvor 1995; Nyagura and Mupawaenda 1994; Waeterloos and Rutherford 2004) and also indicate the capacity of new permanent workers to assimilate agricultural skills.

Most of the permanent workers surveyed (78.9 per cent) had oral employment contracts. In Kwekwe district, the incidence of oral agreements was over 87 per cent of the workers in A1 and A2 farm units. Differentiated patterns were observed in Goromonzi, as 46.8 per cent of those employed on A2 farms had written contracts compared to 18.4 per cent in the A1 farms. It is important to note that an earlier Collective Bargaining Agreement spelt out in Statutory Instrument 323 of 1992 recognized oral contracts for permanent and seasonal workers, but the new Statutory Instrument 116 of 2014 which replaced it now explicitly requires written employment contracts. Many employers were therefore in conflict with the law and less than 45 per cent provided statutory benefits such annual leave for instance.

Women accounted for 8 per cent and 5.8 per cent of the permanent workers in Goromonzi and Kwekwe. Data provided by the FTLRP land beneficiaries also showed women were 10.3 per cent of the permanent employees (AIAS 2014). There was however differentiation in the recruitment between the districts and within the different settlement models. In the A2 farm households in Kwekwe, 7.8 per cent of the permanent workers were women. While among the small-scale A1 producers, there were 20 women out of the 31 permanent workers in the same district. The A1 farms of Goromonzi employed only two women for every 16 men in the permanent workforce. Representation of women was however relatively higher in the A2 farms where they accounted for 28.6 per cent of the 495 workers. Hence, the marginalization of women in the (farm) labour markets that is also common elsewhere (Maertens and Swinnen 2009; Sender et al. 2006; Yaro et al. 2016) was not reversed by land reform and the feminization of part-time labour persists. Patriarchal structures, which sideline women from active involvement in the full-time sections of the farm labour force it could be argued, have been resilient even in the context of land reform and women's position in the labour markets therefore remains peripheral. Furthermore, women still remain burdened with attending to their reproductive roles that might conflict with full-time farm labour employment (Naidu and Ossome 2016; Tsikata 2016).

New farm employers deployed permanent workers in variegated positions, ranging from general hands to other specialized skills such as tractor driving. The majority of them were employed as general hands. The A2 farms in Goromonzi district were an exception as they had a wider spread of permanent employees engaged in skilled work activities and leadership roles (e.g., supervisors and foremen). At least 75.5 per cent of the permanent workers in the A1 scheme in both Goromonzi and Kwekwe were employed as general hands. Again, patriarchal discrimination was apparent, as the majority of the women were located in the lower rung of permanent work as general hands, 75 per cent and 83.4 per cent in Goromonzi and Kwekwe, respectively.

The fragmentation of labour into different enterprise sections commonly found in the (former) LSCFs (Gibbon and Riisgaard 2014; Loewenson 1992; Selwyn 2015) was reported by only 29.1 per cent of the permanent workers interviewed. These labourers were clustered into field crops, horticulture, livestock, engineering and transport and irrigation sections on the farms. This practice was more noticeable in A2 farms were an equivalent 40.4 per cent of the permanent workers in both districts were attached to specific enterprises. Only 24.5 per cent and 9.4 per cent of the permanent workers on in the A1 farms in Goromonzi and Kwekwe, respectively, reported such practices. Limited enterprise diversification in new farms also conditioned the labour segmentation along commodity lines. The crop diversification index averaged on 0.36 among the A1 and A2 farm households in the two districts (AIAS 2014).[7]

Furthermore, the management structures are not as elaborate as in the past, particularly in the A1 farms. The LSCFs had different layers of management headed by an overall farm manager. Below the manager were administrative and clerical staff, section foremen for the different enterprises, supervisors and team leaders of labour groups and so on. Less than 23 per cent of the workers on A1 farms in Goromonzi had managers or supervisors at their workplaces. Even fewer percentages of permanent employees in A1 farms in Kwekwe reported existence of managers. Consequently, the employers were also the managers in the A1 farms. Daily task allocation, for instance, that was previously carried out by foremen is now largely performed by the A1 employers as indicated by 71.7 per cent and 79.2 per cent of the permanent workers in Goromonzi and Kwekwe, respectively.

Divergent patterns were however exposed in the A2 farms where 57.4 per cent and 34 per cent of the workers in Goromonzi and Kwekwe had a manager at their place of employment, respectively. Other managerial functions were also relatively more common in these farms than they were on the A1 farms. In the A2 farms, the managers had oversight over all the operations on the units, including supervising the different layers of management beneath them. Other managerial functions they performed included land use planning, preparation of farm budgets, marketing plans and development and allocation of work schedules, whereas in the A1 farms, allocation of labour tasks was the predominant managerial function; the other functions performed by some managers in A2 farms were not institutionalized. Nonetheless, the managers were not qualified as those in former LSCFs since 39.3 per cent of them in Goromonzi's A2 farms had no formal agricultural qualification, while certificates and diplomas were possessed by 37.8 per cent and 20.7 per cent, correspondingly. The few managers in the A2 farms of Kwekwe had certificates (41 per cent) and diplomas (25 per cent) and the remaining 12.5 per cent had no formal training in agriculture.

As such, the allocation of daily tasks in A2 farms in Goromonzi was not only the responsibility of the employers (34 per cent), but also involved managers (31.9 per cent), supervisors (23.4 per cent) and foreman (10.6 per cent) while in Kwekwe, employers perform this responsibility (53.3 per cent) and are assisted by managers (26.7 per cent) and foremen (15.6 per cent). The mugwazo system (31.3 per cent) or designated daily working hours (68.7 per cent) were used to assign tasks to workers. Up to 57.3 per cent of the permanent farm labourers had a working day that went beyond the maximum legislated eight hours. In both Goromonzi and Kwekwe districts, a larger share of permanent workers in the A2 farms reported more working hours, 46.8 per cent and 80.9 per cent, than those employed in the A1 farm households, 34.7 per cent and 69.8 per cent, respectively. Less than half of those characterized by eight hour plus working day received either overtime pay or additional off duty days.

Many new farm employers were thus extracting unpaid labour contributions through extended working hours.

About 16.6 per cent of the permanent farm workers also performed part-time farm wage jobs for other employers while holding a permanent job on one farm. Such a practice termed as 'moonlighting' showed differential trends in both these districts., with Goromonzi having a higher share of permanent workers involved (29.3 per cent) compared to Kwekwe (4 per cent) in moonlighting. Limited farm job opportunities curtailed this practice in Kwekwe. There was no significant difference in the share of multiple-job holding permanent workers in A1 and A2 farms. Moonlight permanent workers indicated that they performed part-time jobs for other employers during their off days (77.1 per cent), after knocking off from their regular job (11.4 per cent) and some even absconded work (11.4 per cent). Both male (50 per cent) and female (27.5 per cent) workers were involved in this practice in Goromonzi. In Kwekwe, 7.2 per cent and 16.7 per cent of the male and female workers practiced moonlighting. Since males are ascribed as the 'primary' income earners for the household by the intra-household patriarchal institutions (O'Laughlin 1998; Potts 2000, 2012; Tsikata 2009), they tend to dominate moonlighting. While female involvement points to the increasing pressure on them to also contribute to the rising demand for income after subsidies for social services, such as health and education, were withdrawn at the onset of neoliberalism (Bryceson 1980; Yaro et al. 2016).

Yet, these processes are neither new nor unique to the redistributed LSCFs (Rutherford 2001). The scale of the practice in terms of numbers of permanent farm workers involved in the practice of 'moonlighting' this prior to 2000 has not been adequately documented. But, the history of labour control in the former LSCFs, especially through the farm compound institution (Loewenson 1992; Tandon 2001) suggests that it was not pervasive. For instance, some former farm workers in Goromonzi district noted that LSCFs adopted strategies that discouraged workers from leaving the farm during their off days, including farm compound bars and stores that provided credit, as well as soccer fields. Farm labour could thus be easily summoned to attend to emergencies, such as fire outbreaks during their rest days. The length of employment with the current employer was at least 1 year for all the interviewed permanent workers. On average, each of the workers had been employed for a period of 5 years at their place of employment.[8] Over 27 per cent had spent more than 5 years in their current job. When the length of employment was compared with the year, the workers started providing wage labour in the redistributed LSCFs, the survey data reveal that the majority of the workers (56.4 per cent) had not switched their first jobs. These data suggest the stabilization of permanent workforces by the new range of producers, partly due to the continued deployment of residential labour tenancy as discussed below.

Other peripheral strategies reminiscent of the practices in the old LSCFs which tie labour to the farms include the provision of cash loans and credit purchases of agricultural produce deductible on wages (Loewenson 1992). About 10.6 per cent of the permanent workers had received loans from their employers, which were deducted from their wages over a couple of months. Close to 20 per cent regularly bought agricultural produce from their employers on credit. This was significantly associated with workers from Goromonzi (46.8 per cent) than those in Kwekwe (12.2 per cent). Credit was also available through on-farm shops operated by a few of the employers, which 4 per cent of the labourers received credit from.

Farm wages were paid either as cash or as a combination of cash and kind for both permanent and casual labourers. Rather than collective bargaining, the wages received were an outcome of the individual negotiations between the worker and the employer. The collective voice of workers was therefore fragmented and wage determination was tilted in favour of the employers. Between 2012 and 2014, monthly wages for the surveyed permanent workers increased from US$56 to US$79. Against the Statutory Instrument 116 of 2014, which stipulated the minimum wages for farm labour, a substantial number of them were being paid below the statutory minimum wages, 40.5 per cent, 38.5 per cent and 46.5 per cent in 2012, 2013 and 2014, respectively. The patterns were not significantly different across the districts. Nevertheless, the A2 farm units had relatively lower proportions of those earning below the minimum wage (30 per cent) compared to A1 farm units (53 per cent) during the same period. On a positive note, the evidence does not suggest the existence of gender discrimination in the payment of wages.

Not only were monetary wages low, permanent and casual labourers (30.5 per cent) also faced challenges in receiving them. Permanent workers in A2 farms experienced delayed wage payments (48 per cent), irregularity in the payment of wages (40 per cent) and not receiving wages in full at once (12 per cent). During the survey, 19.1 per cent of the permanent workers were actually owed part of their wages. Responses to these poor working conditions include theft of farm produce and absenteeism at work to perform maricho[9] elsewhere. Agrarian capital has thus sought to limit disruptions to accumulation processes by introducing work attendance and production bonuses, which were received by 10.1 per cent and 12.6 per cent of the permanent workers in Goromonzi and Kwekwe, respectively.

Diverse benefits akin to a 'social wage' for workers were also observed in the field. The provision of accommodation was most common and received by 91 per cent of the permanent workers. Despite the exploitative tendencies of the residential labour tenancy, farm employers are enjoined by law to provide housing to permanent and season labourers or pay an allowance of US$35 per month (GoZ 2012). Some permanent farm labourers also received monthly food rations, including maize grain and cooking oil, 56.1 per cent and 35.4 per cent in Goromonzi and Kwekwe districts. To limit delays during work breaks as workers prepared their own meals, food was also provided to 34.2 per cent of the permanent workers during working hours. Beyond these, other benefits such as land for food production and electricity covered less than 30 per cent of the workers.

Casual Labour Hired In

Casual or part-time labour indicates employment ranging from a few hours to couple of months. The former is commonly referred to as contract work, which is differentiated into piecework/maricho and time-rated work. At law, those employed for a continuous period ranging from three to eight months are officially designated as seasonal labourers (GoZ 1993).

Roughly, the distribution of female workers rose four fold in the casual labour compared to the levels observed in the permanent labour category. Their representation levels were 46.8 per cent in Goromonzi and 44.6 per cent in Kwekwe among the pieceworkers. Among the seasonal labourers, it was 45 per cent and 19.4 per cent, respectively.

Again new entrants dominated the casual labour force, accounting for least 77 per cent of workers employed as both seasonal and pieceworkers in both districts. Most of the part-time workers in Goromonzi (39.1 per cent) were unemployed prior to their farm jobs. About 14.4 per cent of them were previously employed as farm wage labour in the Communal and other rural areas. The remaining group consisted of unpaid family farm labourers, school leavers (23.2 per cent) and an equal share of 7.2 per cent of those retrenched from urban employment and transitioning from self-employment in the non-agricultural sector. Similar patterns existed in Kwekwe, except for an additional group of retrenched mineworkers (15 per cent).

New part-time workers also had attained a superior level of education compared to former farm workers. Only 16.7 per cent and 4.0 per cent had completed secondary education among former farm workers in Goromonzi and Kwekwe. In contrast, among new part-time farm workers, 34.8 per cent and 20.3 per cent had completed part of the secondary education and completed the same, respectively. The average age patterns were also comparable to those observed among permanent workers, with former workers being 12 and 15 years older in Goromonzi and Kwekwe, respectively.

Farm households mainly hired part-time labour for two tasks in the production process, namely, weeding (80 per cent) and harvesting (58.2 per cent), which according to them need to be performed timeously (AIAS 2014). The other farm tasks, including land clearing, marketing, and pest and disease control were cited by less than 22 per cent of the households. Some piecework tasks were also segmented by gender, such as the preference of women for maize threshing and winnowing, and male dominance in transporting harvest from the fields.

Verbal employment contracts were also dominant among casual labourers, involving 86 per cent of them. Seasonal labourers in Goromonzi commanded the largest share (26.3 per cent) that had written employment contracts. Also in Kwekwe, seasonal labourers were more likely to possess written contracts (12.9 per cent) compared to pieceworkers (7 per cent).

Contract work is the dominant form of part-time labour in the new farms. Seasonal labourers, which represented half the share of the LSCF labour force, are now confined to the new and old LSCFs. Contract work is further differentiated into time-rated and task-rated work/piecework. For time-rated work, workers employed for an agreed number of hours per day are paid a daily wage. This was equivalent to supplying on average eight hours of work in exchange for a daily wage of US$4. In contrast, task-rated/piecework or mugwazo entails the delivery of a certain task irrespective of the amount of time spent on the work and the wages are pegged depending on the type of task. For instance, wages for weeding are pegged per hectare of area weeded, whereas for harvesting it can be set by the number of bags harvested. Seventy percentage of the casual labourers indicated that land clearing, weeding and harvesting were undertaken on the basis of mugwazo, while the other tasks, such as maize threshing and packaging outputs for the market, were time rated.

Close to two-fifths of the pieceworkers could not accomplish their mugwazo as individuals. Workers from Kwekwe more commonly reported work overload (45.9 per cent) than those from Goromonzi did (30.8 per cent). Most of them (70.6 per cent) had to summon the help of family members in order to receive the requisite wage for the task. For the remainder, the piecework spilled into the second day. The latter is reminiscent of the ticket system in the colonial LSCFs, where most workers worked for 45 days in order to receive a monthly wage (Rubert 1997). In the former case, employers not only exploit the labour of the pieceworkers but also are able to indirectly exercise control over the labour of the family of the workers hired for the wages of one person. There is a continuum between paid and unpaid labour in the performance of piecework. What is termed piecework, therefore, sometimes includes both paid and unpaid labour contributions. Their combination enables the delivery of piecework in shortest possible time that would otherwise take a single person more time and thus limit the aggregate wages that could be earned over a given period of time. Yet, this also implies that the farm employers for the wage of an individual exploit more people and the existing piece wage rates are much lower when spread over the number of people who actually contribute to the delivery of the task.

Pieceworkers are either hired individually or as part of a group. The hiring of group labour occurs in two dimensions. First, employers rely on an individual labourer to mobilize other workers. Though working as a group, all members of the group are paid individually and accountable to the employer. Second, are self-organized groups that provide specialized labour services, such as tobacco curing and grading, involving mostly male workers (Chambati 2011; Chambati and Moyo 2004). Senior former farm workers normally led these groups and negotiated contracts with employers. A single wage is paid for the work performed and leaders share the payment among group members. Nearly, 26.6 per cent and 19.7 per cent of the pieceworkers in Goromonzi and Kwekwe sometimes participated in these groups.

Many workers surveyed (51.8 per cent), spent relatively short periods of time—between one to seven days—on a job before moving on to the next employer. By its very nature, part-time work, especially piecework and time-rated work involves working for many farm employers per season. Moreover, 75 per cent of pieceworkers changed employers on a seasonal basis. Like in the former LSCFs, seasonal labourers had relatively stable employment since over 63 per cent of them in both Goromonzi and Kwekwe worked for the same employers every season. The average distances travelled to the nearest and furthest employer for pieceworkers in

Goromonzi were 0.74 kilometres and 3.72 kilometres, respectively. Pieceworkers in Kwekwe travelled relatively longer distances to their nearest and furthest employers, 1.51 and 6.14 kilometres correspondingly.

The wage rate received by pieceworkers for most of the tasks averaged US$4 in both districts and did not vary by the settlement type. However, further investigations exposed the differentiation of the daily wage payments by the type of the tasks and the commodities. For instance, in maize production, arduous tasks such as weeding and digging holes for planting commanded a wage of US$5 compared to US$3 received for fertilizer application and planting. The wage rate for weeding in maize was US$5 per 0.25 hectares, while in tobacco it was US$5 per 0.06 hectares (Interview with extension worker, Goromonzi, 7 July 2012). It was also observed that beyond weeding, tasks in cash/export crops, such as tobacco and soybeans, attracted higher wages (US$5) for similar tasks than in food crops, such as maize (US$3). There was no significant difference in the piecework monthly income during the peak seasonal period realized by male and female part-time workers in both districts. During peak periods, there is intense competition for casual labour and offering food is deployed as an incentive to attract labour. Indeed, 72.4 per cent and 51 per cent of the pieceworkers received meals during their contract period in Goromonzi on top of the cash wages.

Given that less than 20 per cent of the farm households were endowed with functional irrigation infrastructure across both districts, rain-fed agricultural production predominates (AIAS 2014). The demand for part-time wage labour is therefore seasonal, peaking at the onset of the rainy season in October and reaching a plateau in December (Fig. 16.1). Thereafter, it declines partially, before it begins to rise again during the

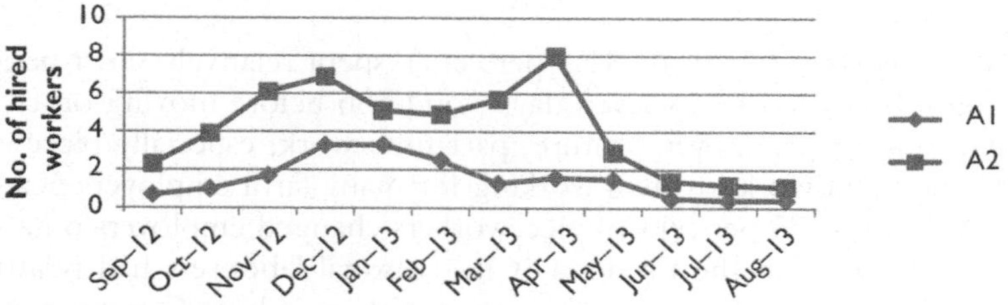

Fig. 16.1 Recruitment patterns of part-time labourers by A1 and A2 farm units. (Source: Compiled from AIAS (2014))

harvesting season around April. Most part-time farm labourers therefore experience slack time between June and September after the harvesting season. The average number of days worked by pieceworkers and time-rated workers in Kwekwe was relatively lower than by those in Goromonzi district.

The slack time provides flexibility not only for part-time labourers, but also for family labour to allocate some of their labour to non-farm rural income earning opportunities during the dry season. The proliferation of multiplex non-farm labour activities that have been argued to signify the decreasing importance of farm labour by some analysts (Bernstein 2014; Bryceson 2000; Rigg 2006), could in fact be considered to be inevitable due to the seasonality of agriculture (Moyo 2016).

At least 30 per cent of the farm workers were also involved in other non-farm income earning activity. Encompassing more pieceworkers than permanent and seasonal workers, the activities included trading in natural resources. The nationalization of land tenures on redistributed LSCFs opened access to natural resources previously enclosed in freehold properties and protected by trespass laws (Mkodzongi 2013). The activities were also structured by the resource availability in the different locales. In Goromonzi, the commonly reported activities were trading in river sand and thatching grass, both used in the construction of houses, cited by 20 per cent of the farm workers. Widespread gold deposits in Kwekwe meant that alluvial panning attracted 44.2 per cent of farm labourers.

In sum, the new permanent and casual labourers found in the A1 and A2 farm units are distinguishable from those found in the old LSCFs in terms of the degree of formality and working conditions. Yet, the differences across the new farm units have seen the A2 farms to some extent mirroring the pre-2000 forms of labour. The focus now shifts to how the labour is recruited and mobilized is the new farm units.

Recruitment and Mobilization of Agrarian Wage Labour

This section provides evidence, which shows that the recruitment of individuals and/or households into agrarian labour markets, as before 2000, continues to be influenced by access to land. However, land access alone is not the only determinant that compels people into farm labour markets as some peasants who received land during the FTLRP also sell their labour to other farm units, alongside their own household agricultural production. The sources of farm labour are now diversified than before involving migration beyond the nearby Communal areas to include other rural locations further away and urban areas.

Access to Land and Sources of Farm Labour Supply

Less than 10 per cent of the peasantry received land allocations during the FTLRP (Moyo 2011a, 2013). This means that there are some rural people who are still either land short or landless and these constitute the labour reservoir for the new capitalist farms. Land reform experiences elsewhere also show that landlessness is not totally eradicated (Borras 2005; Bush 2002; De Janvry 1981) and inequalities in land access alongside other factors continue to drive farm labour markets (Cousins 2009).

The farm labour is being mobilized from the Communal areas within and outside the districts, as well as from the local A1 farmers and the former farm workers. Most of these labourers are either separated from or have inadequate the means of production for their social reproduction. Access to land was mentioned by most farm workers as one of the main challenges they were facing in their social reproduction (63.1 per cent), outside of the low wages reported by 95.3 per cent. Many farm workers aspire to own their independent piece of land in the future for the social reproduction (42.8 per cent) rather than a better paying job (16.7 per cent). Overall, 33.4 per cent of the farm labourers interviewed did not have access to any land to grow crops across all rural areas. Landlessness was relatively higher among those in permanent employment (36.9 per cent) than among casual labourers (29.9 per cent). Both male and female farm workers faced challenges of landlessness, 34.4 per cent and 30.3 per cent, respectively.

The land sizes owned by farm workers were also small, with 21.1 per cent controlling less than 0.5 hectares of arable land. Another 23.3 per cent of the farm workers possessed less than two hectares of the land. Besides those who formally own FTLRP (9.1 per cent) and Communal areas (31.9 per cent), land and tenure insecurity characterizes land accessed through 'self-provisioning' in the FTLRP areas (1.2 per cent; Moyo 1995), leased from land beneficiaries (16.3 per cent) and small plots of land in the peripheries of the old farm compounds (20 per cent). Amidst labour shortages, A1 landholders sometimes restrict the production of cash crops such as tobacco in old compounds to prevent labour from being autonomous in their social reproduction and thus continue to supply them labour (Chambati 2013).

Informal leasing from FTLRP beneficiaries also tends to be based on dynamic short-term seasonal agreements, whose renewal is not obvious. In fact, about 9.4 per cent of the farm workers in Goromonzi who had been allocated land to grow their own crops by land beneficiaries, no longer had access to such land. However, in Kwekwe district, all of the farm workers who had access to informal land allocations for beneficiaries still maintained this access at the time of the survey. Indeed, informal land leasing by farm workers is under threat as land beneficiaries are increasingly seeking to enter the recently state sanctioned joint ventures with various resource rich agrarian capital.

Nonetheless, the proletarianization of rural labour is not only contingent upon landlessness and/or land shortages (Moyo and Yeros 2005; O'Laughlin 2002). The A1 farmers entered farm labour markets to mobilize resources for their own farms. Semi-proletarianization of rural labour therefore continues, albeit with more autonomy derived from land ownership (Chambati 2013; Moyo and Yeros 2005). Farm labourers are therefore fragmented by the ownership of means of production (especially land), with those having access to land more likely to be partially integrated into the labour markets.

Continuities and Changes in Residential Labour Tenancy System/ Labour Stabilization

The long established strategy of stabilizing labour force on LSCFs through the provision of on-farm residency in farm compounds linked to employment (Magaramombe 2001; Sachikonye and Zishiri 1999; Tandon 2001; Visser and Ferrer 2015) is being replicated in differing degrees in the new A1 and A2 farm units. Residency for farm workers, observed in the surveyed farms, included the old farm compounds on farms resettled under A1 and A2 schemes, new labour compounds constructed by the landowners, homesteads of landowners, own A1 plots and neighbouring Communal areas. Such a labour tenancy arrangement mostly affects those farm workers who do not live in their own independent accommodation.

Close to 63 per cent of the farm workers surveyed indicated that their accommodation was tied to their employment at the farms. Eighty-three per cent and 92.2 per cent of the permanent workers in Goromonzi and Kwekwe, respectively, lived in such accommodation. Seasonal labourers were the second-most affected, with 50 per cent and 58.1 per cent in the two districts living in such accommodation. Less than 33 per cent of the pieceworkers had this kind of relationship and the majority's employment was delinked from their residency.

The old farm compounds on A1 farms had the least share of farm workers (40.9 per cent) who reported residential and employment linkages, yet this encompassed over 75 per cent of those in old A2 compounds, new farm compounds and the homestead of landowners. The farm compounds in A1 farms belong to the state and landholders have limited power to control labour resident there. Moreover, in the old A1 farm compounds, the power to enforce the residential labour tenancy is also dispersed among the many beneficiaries that reside in any given farm. In contrast in the A2 farms, the farm compound falls under the control of the landowner in whose subdivision it lies. The fewer beneficiaries in A2 farm offers relatively more latitude, including using the law to evict 'truant labourers'. In general, the public land tenures offered to the new landowners do not enable them to totally enforce the residential labour tenancy (Chambati 2011; Moyo 2011a) and thus sometimes face stiff resistance from the farm labourers.

Contract workers resident in the old farm compounds sometimes face pressure from the landowners in the farms they stay to provide labour services to them, especially during peak periods. Over 31 per cent of the contract workers in Goromonzi had received eviction threats from their residency, mainly for not providing labour to the new farm units (54.1 per cent). Only 3.1 per cent of the pieceworkers faced eviction threats in Kwekwe. None of the permanent workers had received eviction threats from their residency since 2000 in the same district, while it was recorded from 7.2 per cent of the permanent labour in Goromonzi. Some A1 and A2 land owners in Goromonzi also conducted 'employment audits' in the old farm compounds to identify the residents who are not supplying them labour (Chambati 2013). Those who are found not be supplying labour are evicted as happened at Maruva farm in 2014.[10]

The new compounds on the other hand are an effort to re-establish the control of labour under a single owner, in order to provide possibilities to enforce the tenancy relationship. Due to reduced demand for wage labour per unit among smaller-scale landowners, the new compounds tend to have fewer housing units (not more than 10 in farms surveyed) compared to the massive compounds that sometimes housed over 100 families in the Mashonaland provinces. An estimated 24.3 per cent of the landowners had constructed new farm compounds for their permanent workers and families (AIAS 2014). These new compounds in Goromonzi were only found in A2 capitalist farms (38.5 per cent). While in Kwekwe, 11.5 per cent and 19.4 per cent of the A1 and A2 farms had them, respectively (AIAS 2014). Beyond the permanent workers, the new farm compounds also guarantee access to labour of their families who were also employed as pieceworkers during peak seasonal periods.

A new dynamic entails the housing of permanent employees within the homestead of the landowners, which was practiced by 43.9 per cent and 54.2 per cent of the landowners in Goromonzi and Kwekwe, respectively. This scenario was more prominent in the A1 farms where 82.4 per cent in Goromonzi and 80.8 per cent in Kwekwe reported it (AIAS 2014).

Conclusion

This chapter has shown that the nature of agrarian capitalism as reflected by the extent of the reliance of hired labour in agricultural production units has been changed by land reform. The diversified agrarian structure that is dominated by the peasantry has resulted in the increase in number of wage labour opportunities. This expanded agrarian labour market exists alongside the growing use of family labour, especially in peasant households. Yet, most of the wage labour opportunities generated across the different farm units are part-time in nature and thereby extending casualization of labour trends noticed in the LSCFs throughout the post-independence period. Rather than being mobilized in large batches per farm unit, as was the case in the LSCFs, the new downsized farms recruit relatively lower averages of workers per farm unit.

Both the permanent and casual forms are qualitatively different from those found in LSCFs especially regarding the degree of formality of the work. Indeed, the more formal types of employment are mostly found in the new small-to-medium and large capitalist farms. Furthermore, the skills base is also diffused containing a mix of new entrants into the farm labour markets and those previously employed in the LSCFs prior to the FTLRP. The dominance of the peasantry both in terms of the land controlled and the number of agricultural production units in the redistributed lands have also meant that family labour was the dominant source of employment.

Landlessness and/or land shortage continues to be a key characteristic of farm wage labourers as in the past suggesting the persistence of the labour reserve dynamic. Enlarged land access in the context of limited agrarian financing has meant that even some land beneficiaries participate in the agrarian labour markets, thereby perpetuating the process of semi-proletarianization but with greater autonomy provided by land ownership in comparison with those who are landless (Chambati 2013; Moyo 2013). Indeed, access to land provides a choice in the social reproduction strategies for those who have it and they can deploy it to bargain for better wages. Unlike the landless, they have the option of disengaging from the labour markets and survive by farming their lands. Moreover, land can be utilized to mobilize resources for their own farming by renting out their land to farm workers and others, as field data revealed (Moyo et al. 2009), as well as commodifying some of the natural resources found on their lands.

There is continuation of the super-exploitation of agrarian wage labourers that is reflected by the payment of poor wages and the institution of the residential labour tenancy in the old farm compounds and through the construction of new compounds to guarantee labour supplies. Women continue to be relegated to the irregular part-time labour, although their share has slightly improved in the full-time labour at least in the districts studied. The majority of the farm labourers in the new labour markets resist exploitation through enhanced labour mobility and the 'freedoms', which have been expanded by the new land tenure and which offers less power to the new landholders to control labour as the LSCFs could do.

Beyond the farming classes, agrarian labour markets are also differentiated across districts. As shown in this chapter, the FTLRP did not reverse the uneven development of agrarian labour markets. The areas in higher potential agro-ecological regions and thus diverse production continue to have more pronounced labour markets than those in the lower potential agro-ecological zones have. Therefore, the manifestation of agrarian capitalism is driven with various factors and chief among them is the land use patterns, which are also occasioned by the agro-ecological potential of the district. Farm units in Goromonzi, which were involved in the production of diversified labour intensive commodities, dominate the use of hired labour compared to the extensive livestock-oriented production in the drier district of Kwekwe. Whereas the differentiation within and across A1 and A2 farm sectors are propped not only by land sizes, but also by access to other agrarian resources, such as finance, which affect the land use and mix of commodities produced and in turn the use of hired and family labour, as well as the quantities applied.

Notes

1. The FTLRP redistributed land using two models; namely the A1 and A2 schemes. The A1 scheme was intended to expand the small-holder farming sector (commonly called the Communal Area sector), to cater for the landless, unemployed and disadvantaged peoples from communal, urban and other areas. On average, the A1 beneficiaries were given 5 to 6 hectares of arable land for farming and 7 to 15 hectares per household for grazing. There are 146,000 A1 household land allocations in the country (Moyo 2011a, b, c, p. 512). The A2 scheme sought to expand commercial farming to blacks. It comprises individually held farm units ranging in size from the small 50 hectares to large-scale A2 units (at around 400 to 1500 hectares). Their average size was about 330 hectares in 2003 (Utete 2003). Farm sizes vary according to natural regions, with those in drier suited for extensive livestock production getting the larger land sizes. By 2010, the A2 model was made up of small-, medium- and large-scale commercial farms and there were about 25,000 A2 farms nationwide, meaning that the former 4500 LSCFs have been subdivided into approximately 171,000 farm units (a 30 fold increase; Moyo 2011a, b, c, pp. 512). The households who got land under the FTLRP are generally referred to as new farm households in the literature and in this chapter. The A1 and A2 schemes added to the other land existing categories, which are Communal Areas—the areas gazetted for smallholder farming since the colonial period; LSCFs, SSCFs—areas gazetted to promote black commercial farms since the colonial period and the Old Resettlement Areas—lands where people were resettled during the first phase of the Land Reform and Resettlement Programme, mostly early years after independence.
2. Data were collected from 402 landholders in Goromonzi and Kwekwe districts by AIAS in 2014 while the farm labour survey interviewed 200 farm labourers in each district in 2017.
3. Noteworthy is that piecework in Zimbabwe is outlawed in most industrial sectors (e.g., engineering, iron and steel industry), except agriculture.
4. The grades of farm workers ranged from grades one to seven, from the least skilled general hands to the highest level, which comprised clerks, senior medical orderly and maintenance operatives in the LSCFs.
5. Employment for the year 2000 is based on estimates from CSO (2000).
6. In both districts, there was a statistically significant association at 95 per cent level of significance between the education level and employment history in the LSCFs. Goromonzi: Chi-square = 15.74, p = 0.03, N = 99 and Kwekwe: Chi-square = 21.54, p = 0.00, N = 105.
7. Crop diversification index measures the extent to which farm households produce a diverse range of crops. It is n calculated as CDIi = 1-S (aij/Ai)2

where CDIi = crop diversity index; aij = area planted to jth crop in the ith location; j = 1 Ai = total are planted under all crops. The index is zero for monocropping and moves towards 1 as the level of diversity increases (Shahidullah et al. 2006).

8. Standard deviation was 5 years based on 199 interviews.
9. Maricho is a derogatory term used to describe daily wage work and is normally associated with the poorest segments of the rural society.
10. Name of the farm has been changed to protect the identity of the respondents.

References

Adams, J. (1991). The Rural Labour Market in Zimbabwe. *Development and Change, 22*(2), 297–320. https://doi.org/10.1111/j.1467-7660.1991.tb00413.x.

AGRITEX. (2013). *District Annual Plan, 2014.* Harare: AGRITEX.

AGRITEX. (2015). *Goromonzi District Annual Report.* Goromonzi: AGRITEX.

AIAS. (2014). *Land Use, Agricultural Production and Food Security Survey: Trends and Tendencies, 2013/14 (Mimeo).* Harare: Sam Moyo African Institute for Agrarian Studies (SMAIAS).

Amanor-Wilks, D. (1995). *In Search of Hope for Zimbabwe's Farm Workers.* Harare: Dateline Southern Africa and Panos Institute.

Amanor-Wilks, D. (2000). *Zimbabwe's Farm Workers and the New Constitution.* Retrieved from www.africaaction.org/rtable/ded0002.htm

Amanor-Wilks, D. (2001). *Zimbabwe's Farm Workers: Policy Dimension.* Harare: Panos Institute.

Arrighi, G. (1970). Labour Supplies in a Historical Perspective: A Study of Proletarianisation of African Peasantry in Rhodesia. *Journal of Development Studies, 6*(3), 197–234.

Barrett, C. B., Besfuneh, M., Clay, D. C., & Reardon, T. (2005). Heterogeneous Constraints, Incentives and Income Diversification Strategies in Rural Africa. *Quarterly Journal of International Agriculture, 44*(1), 37–60.

Bernstein, H. (2014). Food Sovereignty Via the 'Peasant Way': A Sceptical View. *Journal of Peasant Studies, 4*(6), 1031–1063.

Borras, S. M., Jr. (2005). Can Redistributive Reform Be Achieved Via Market-Based Land Transfer Schemes? Lessons and Evidence from the Philippines. *Journal of Development Studies, 41*(1), 90–134.

Bryceson, D. F. (1980). The Proletarianization of Women in Tanzania. *Review of African Political Economy, 7*(17), 4–27.

Bryceson, D. F. (2000). Peasant Theories and Smallholder Policies. Past and Present. In D. Bryceson, C. Kay, & J. Mooij (Eds.), *Disappearing Peasantries?* (pp. 1–36). London: ITDG Publishing.

Bush, R. C. (2002). *Counter-Revolution in Egypt's Countryside: Land and Farmers in the Era of Economic Reform*. London: Zed Books.
Chambati, W. (2009). *Land Reform and Changing Agrarian Labour Processes in Zimbabwe*. MM thesis, University of Witwatersrand, Johannesburg.
Chambati, W. (2011). Restructuring of Agrarian Labour Relations After Fast Track Land Reform in Zimbabwe. *Journal of Peasant Studies, 38*(5), 1047–1068.
Chambati, W. (2013). The Political Economy of Agrarian Labour Relations in Zimbabwe after Redistributive Land Reform. *Agrarian South: Journal of Political Economy, 2*(2), 189–211. https://doi.org/10.1177/2277976013493570.
Chambati, W., & Moyo, S. (2004). *Land Reform and the Political Economy of Agricultural Labour*. Harare: African Institute for Agrarian Studies (AIAS) [Mimeo].
Clarke, D. G. (1977). *Agricultural and Plantation Workers in Rhodesia*. Gwelo: Mambo Press.
Commercial Farmers Union. (n.d.). *An Overview of the Agriculture Sector*. Harare: CFU.
Cousins, B. (2009). Capitalism Obscured: The Limits of Law and Rights-Based Approaches to Poverty Reduction and Development. *The Journal of Peasant Studies, 36*(4), 893–908.
CSO. (1984). *Indicator Monitoring Labour Force Survey*. Harare: CSO.
CSO. (1997). *Statistical Yearbook*. Harare: Central Statistical Office.
CSO. (1998). *Statistical Yearbook 1997*. Harare: CSO.
CSO. (1999). *Labour Force Survey*. Harare: CSO.
CSO. (2000). *1999 Indicator Monitoring Labour Force Survey*. Harare: CSO.
CSO. (2001). *Agricultural Production on LSCF 2000*. Harare: CSO.
De Janvry, A. (1981). *The Agrarian Question and Reformism in Latin America*. Baltimore/London: The Johns Hopkins University Press.
FCTZ. (2000). *Survey of Commercial Farm Worker Characteristics and Living Conditions*. Harare: Farm Community Trust of Zimbabwe.
FCTZ. (2002). *Report on Assessment of the Impact of Land Reform Programme on Commercial Farm Worker Livelihoods*. Harare: Farm Community Trust of Zimbabwe.
General Agriculture and Plantation Workers' Union of Zimbabwe (GAPWUZ). (2002). *Report on the Survey of Displaced Farm Workers in Zimbabwe*. Harare: General Agriculture and Plantation Workers' Union of Zimbabwe.
Gibbon, P. (2011). *Experiences of Plantation and Large-Scale Farming in 20th Century Africa*. Copenhagen: Danish Institute for International Studies.
Gibbon, P., & Riisgaard, L. (2014). A New System of Labour Management in African Large-Scale Agriculture? *Journal of Agrarian Change, 14*(1), 94–128.
GoZ. (1993). *Statutory Instrument 323*. Harare: Government Printers.
GoZ. (2012). *Collective Bargaining Agreement*. Zimbabwe: Agricultural Industry.

Hartnack, A. (2015). *Cultivations on the Frontiers of Modernity: Power, Welfare and Belonging on Commercial Farms Before and After Fast Track Land Reform in Zimbabwe*. Unpublished PhD thesis, University of Cape Town, Cape Town, SA.

Hellum, A., & Derman, B. (2004). Land Reform and Human Rights in Contemporary Zimbabwe: Balancing Individual and Social Justice Through an Integrated Human Rights Framework. *World Development, 32*(1), 1785–1805.

JAG/RAU. (2008, May). *Land, Retribution and Elections: Post-Election Violence on Zimbabwe's Remaining Farms 2008*. A report prepared by the Justice for Agriculture (JAG) Trust and the Research and Advocacy Unit.

Kanyenze, G. (2001). Zimbabwe's Labour Relations Policies and Implications for Workers. In D. Amanor-Wilks (Ed.), *Zimbabwe's Farm Workers: Policy Dimension* (pp. 86–114). Panos Southern Africa: Lusaka.

Loewenson, R. (1992). *Modern Plantation Agriculture: Corporate Wealth and Labour Squalor*. London: Zed Books.

Maertens, M., & Swinnen, J. F. M. (2009). Trade, Standards and Poverty: Evidence from Senegal. *World Development, 37*(1), 161–178.

Magaramombe, G. (2001). Housing, Sanitation and Farm Worker Settlements. In D. Amanor-Wilks (Ed.), *Zimbabwe's Farm Workers: Policy Dimensions* (pp. 115–136). Lusaka: Panos Southern Africa.

Magaramombe, G. (2003). *Resource Base and Farm Production: Farm Labour Relations Use and Needs* (Discussion Series Paper). Harare: AIAS.

Masiiwa, M., & Chipungu, L. (2004). Land Reform Programmed in Zimbabwe: Disparity between Policy Design and Implementation. In M. Masiiwa (Ed.), *Post-Independence Land Reform in Zimbabwe: Controversies and Impact on the Economy*. Harare: FrederichEbert Stiftung and University of Zimbabwe.

McIvor, C. (1995). *Zimbabwe: The Struggle for Health: A Community Approach for Farm Workers*. London: CIIR.

Mkodzongi, G. (2013). New People, New Land and New Livelihoods: A Microstudy of Zimbabwe's Fast Track Land Reform. *Agrarian South: Journal of Political Economy, 2*(3), 345–366.

MLRR. (2014). *Data Excel Sheets*. Harare: Ministry of Land Reform and Resettlement.

Moyo, S. (1995). *The Land Question in Zimbabwe*. Harare: SAPES Books.

Moyo, S. (2000). *Land Reform under Structural Adjustment in Zimbabwe: Land Use Change in the Mashonaland Provinces*. Uppsala: Nordiska Africainstitutet.

Moyo, S. (2004). *The Overall Impacts of the Fast Track Land Reform Programme*. AIAS monograph.

Moyo, S. (2011a). Three Decades of Agrarian Reform in Zimbabwe. *The Journal of Peasant Studies, 38*(3), 493–531.

Moyo, S. (2011b). Land Concentration and Accumulation by Dispossession: Redistributive Reform in Post Settler Zimbabwe. *Review of African Political Economy, 38*(128), 257–276.

Moyo, S. (2011c). Changing Agrarian Relations after Redistributive Land Reform in Zimbabwe. *Journal of Peasant Studies, 38*(5), 907–934.

Moyo, S. (2013). Land Reform and Redistribution in Zimbabwe since 1980. In S. Moyo & W. Chambati (Eds.), *Land and Agrarian Reform in Zimbabwe: Beyond White Settler Capitalism* (pp. 29–78). Dakar: CODESRIA.

Moyo, S. (2016). *Family Farming in Sub-Saharan Africa: Its Contribution to Agriculture, Food Security and Rural Development* (Working Paper No. 150). Brasília: International Policy Centre for Inclusive Growth (IPCIG). Retrieved from http://www.fao.org/3/a-i6056e.pdf

Moyo, S., & Yeros, P. (2005). The Resurgence of Rural Movements under Neoliberalism. In S. Moyo & P. Yeros (Eds.), *Reclaiming the Land: The Resurgence of Rural Movements in Africa, Asia and Latin America* (pp. 8–66). London/New York: Zed Books.

Moyo, S., & Yeros, P. (2011a). The Fall and Rise of the National Question. In S. Moyo & P. Yeros (Eds.), *Reclaiming the Nation: The Return of the National Question in Africa, Asia and Latin America*. London: Pluto Press.

Moyo, S., & Yeros, P. (2011b). After Zimbabwe: State, Nation and Region in Africa. In S. Moyo & P. Yeros (Eds.), *Reclaiming the Nation: The Return of the National Question in Africa, Asia and Latin America*. London: Pluto Press.

Moyo, S., Rutherford, B., & Amanor-Wilks, D. (2000). Land Reform and Changing Social Relations for Farm Workers in Zimbabwe. *Review of African Political Economy, 84*(18), 181–202.

Moyo, S., Chambati, W., Murisa, T., Siziba, D., Dangwa, C., Mujeyi, K., & Nyoni, N. (2009). *Fast Track Land Reform Baseline Survey in Zimbabwe: Trends and Tendencies, 2005/06*. Harare: AIAS.

Mutangi, G. (2010). *The Changing Patterns of Farm Labour after the Fast Track Land Reform Programme: The Case of Guruve District. Livelihoods After Land Reform in Zimbabwe. Livelihoods After Land Reform Project* (Working Paper No. 13). Cape Town: PLAAS.

Naidu, S., & Ossome, L. (2016). Social Reproduction and the Agrarian Question of Women's Labour in India. *Agrarian South: Journal of Political Economy, 5*(1), 1–27.

NRC. (2003). *Displaced and Forgotten*. Harare: Global Internal Displacement Project.

Nyagura, L. M., & Mupawaenda, A. C. (1994). *A Study of the Factors Affecting the Education of Women and Girls in Commercial Farming Areas of Zimbabwe*. Harare: Ministry of Education.

O'Laughlin, B. (1998). Missing Men? The Debate over Rural Poverty and Women Headed Households in Southern Africa. *Journal of Peasant Studies, 25*(2), 1–48.

O'Laughlin, B. (2002). Proletarianisation, Agency and Changing Rural Livelihoods: Forced Labour and Resistance in Colonial Mozambique. *Journal of Southern African Studies, 28*(3), 511–530.

Palmer, R. (1977). *Land and Racial Domination in Rhodesia*. London: Heinemann Educational.

Potts, D. (2000). Worker-Peasants and Farmer-Housewives in Africa: The Debate about 'Committed' Farmers, Access to Land and Agricultural Production. *Journal of Southern African Studies, 26*(4), 807–832.

Potts, D. (2012). *Whatever Happened to Africa's Rapid Urbanisation?* London: Africa Research Institute.

Rigg, J. (2006). Land, Farming, Livelihoods and Poverty: Rethinking the Links in the Rural South. *Journal of World Development, 34*(1), 180–202.

Rubert, S. (1997). Tobacco Farmers and Wage Laborers in Colonial Zimbabwe, 1940–1945. In A. Jeeves & J. Crush (Eds.), *White Farms, Black Labor: The State of Agrarian Change in Southern Africa, 1910–1950*. Portsmouth/Oxford/Pietermaritzburg: Hienemann, James Currey, University of Natal Press.

Rutherford, B.'l. (2001). *Working on the Margins: Black Workers, White Farmers in Post-Colonial Zimbabwe*. Harare/London: Weaver Press & Zed Books.

Rutherford, B.'l. (2004). Desired Publics, Domestic Government, and Entangled Fears: On the Anthropology of Civil Society, Farm Workers, and White Farmers in Zimbabwe. *Cultural Anthropology, 19*(1), 122–153.

Sachikonye, L. (2003). *The Situation of Commercial Farmers After Land Reform in Zimbabwe* (Report). Harare: Farm Community Trust of Zimbabwe. Retrieved June 1, 2017, from http://citeseerx.ist.psu.edu/viewdoc/download?doi=10.1.1.590.2155&rep=rep1&type=pdf

Sachikonye, L., & Zishiri, O. J. (1999). *Tenure Security for Farm Workers in Zimbabwe*. Harare: Friedrich Ebert Stiftung.

Scoones, I. (2015). *Sustainable Rural Livelihoods and Rural Development*. Rugby/Winnipeg: Practical Action Publishing/Fernwood Publishing.

Scoones, I., Marongwe, N., Mavedzenge, B., Murimbarimba, F., Mahenehene, J., & Sukume, C. (2010). *Zimbabwe's Land Reform: Myths and Realities*. Harare/Oxford: Weaver Press/James Currey.

Selwyn, B. (2015). Capital–Labour and State Dynamics in Export Horticulture in North-East Brazil. *Development and Change, 45*(5), 1019–1036.

Sender, J., & Johnston, D. (2004). Searching for a Weapon of Mass Production in Rural Africa: Unconvincing Arguments for Land Reform. *Journal of Agrarian Change, 4*(1–2), 142–164.

Sender, J., Carlos, O., & Cramer, C. (2006). Women Working for Wages: Putting Flesh on the Bones of a Rural Labour Market Survey in Mozambique. *Journal of Southern African Studies, 32*(2), 313–333.

Shahidullah, S. M., Talukder, M. S. A., Kabir, M. S., Khan, A. H., & Elahi, N.-E. (2006). Cropping Patterns in the South East Coastal Region of Bangladesh. *Journal of Agricultural Rural Development, 4*(1–2), 53–60.

Tandon, Y. (2001). Trade Unions and Labour in the Agricultural Sector in Zimbabwe. In B. Raftopolous & L. Sachikonye (Eds.), *Striking Back: The Labour Movement and the Post Colonial State in Zimbabwe 1980–2000* (pp. 221–249). Harare: Weaver Press.

The World Bank. (2006). *Agricultural Growth and Land Reform in Zimbabwe: Assessment and Recovery Options* (Report No. 31699-ZW). Harare: Author.

The World Bank. (2012). *Recovery and Growth of Zimbabwe Agriculture.* Retrieved from www.networkideas.org/focus/may2008/fo28_globalisation.htm

Tsikata, D. (2009). Gender, Land and Labour Relations and Livelihoods in Sub-Saharan Africa in the Era of Economic Liberalisation: Towards a Research Agenda. *Feminist Africa, 12*, 11–30. Retrieved from http://www.feministafrica.org/uploads/File/Issue_12/fa12_feature_tsikata.pdf.

Tsikata, D. (2016). Gender, Land Tenure and Agrarian Production Systems in Sub-Saharan Africa. *Agrarian South: Journal of Political Economy, 5*(1), 1–19.

Utete, C. M. B. (2003). *Report of the Presidential Land Review Committee, under the Chairmanship of Dr Charles M.B. Utete, Vol 1 and 2: Main Report to His Excellency the President of the Republic of Zimbabwe, Presidential Land Review Committee (PLRC).* Harare: Government Printers.

Vhurumuku, E., McGuire, M., & Hill, V. (1998). *Survey of Commercial Farm Worker Characteristics and Living Conditions in Zimbabwe: Verification Report.* Harare: Agricultural Labour Bureau, Farm Community Trust of Zimbabwe and USAID FEWSNET.

Visser, M., & Ferrer, S. (2015). *Farm Workers' Living and Working Conditions in South Africa: Key Trends, Emergent Issues, and Underlying and Structural Problems.* Based on a Research Project Commissioned by the Pretoria Office of the International Labour Organization, Pretoria.

Waeterloos, E., & Rutherford, B. (2004). Land Reform in Zimbabwe: Challenges and Opportunities for Poverty Reduction Among Commercial Farm Workers. *World Development, 32*(3), 537–553.

Yaro, J., Awetori, J. T., & Bawakyillenuo, S. (2016). *An Assessment of Determinants of Adaptive Capacity to Climate Change/Variability in the Rural Savannah of Ghana.* Accra: Springer International Publishing.

Yeros, P. (2002). *The Political Economy of Civilisation: Peasant-Workers in Zimbabwe and the Neo-colonial World.* PhD thesis, University of London, London.

ZIMSTAT. (2013). *National Report.* Retrieved from http://www.zimstat.co.zw/sites/default/files/img/National_Report.pdf

ZIMSTAT. (2015). *Labour Force Survey Report.* Harare: ZIMSTAT.

CHAPTER 17

Re-organizing Peasant Labour for Local Resilience in China

Tsui Sit, Erebus Wong, Kin Chi Lau, and Tiejun Wen

Double Cost-Transfer to the Global South

In the early years of the twenty-first century, emerging countries, such as Brazil, Russia, India, China and South Africa (BRICS) had once 'risen up' and then pursuant to crises erupted in core countries in recent years, have again fallen into stagnation. The core countries are essentially constructing a global system that facilitates the smooth 'double transfer' of the

This article is an outcome of the Sub-project on 'International Comparative Studies on National Security in the Process of Globalization', led by Dr. Sit Tsui, Southwest University, which is under the Major Project on 'A Study of the Structure and Mechanism of Rural Governance Basic to the Comprehensive National Security' led by Professor Wen Tiejun, Renmin University of China. Originally published in *Agrarian South: Journal of Political Economy, Vol. 6 No. 1*

T. Sit (✉)
Institute of Rural Reconstruction of China, Southwest University,
Chongqing, China

P. Jha et al. (eds.), *Labour Questions in the Global South*,
https://doi.org/10.1007/978-981-33-4635-2_17

economic and political costs to semi-peripheral and peripheral countries, in Immanuel Wallenstein's sense (Wallerstein 2011).

Global crises have continuously erupted inside core countries, referred to as 'implosion' by Amin (2013). After the sub-prime crisis erupted in the USA in 2007 and developed into the Wall Street financial crisis in 2008, core capitalist countries fell into financial or debt crises one after the other. The USA, Europe, Japan and so on have successively initiated multiple attempts of quantitative easing, creating enormous amount of excessive liquidity. On the one hand, it has pushed up the price of energy, raw materials and food commodity globally, thereby successfully exporting the cost of economic crisis to countries of physical economy. On the other hand, while continuously exporting inflation, they effectively sustain low interest rate and low inflation at home. Furthermore, during the crisis, core countries have increased their external debt on a large scale, yet most of them would certainly not implement institutional changes in accordance with requests by the creditor countries. On the contrary, they even transform the debts into asset trades, thus expanding the capital market which does not bear the obligation of debt repayment.

These two phenomena of the new century give warning to all the interest groups in developing countries that are subject to the soft power of the West and infatuated by its 'invisible hand'. Only hegemonic

E. Wong
Kwan Fong Cultural Research and Development Program, Lingnan University, Hong Kong, China

K. C. Lau
World Forum for Alternatives, Dakar, Hong Kong, China

Global University for Sustainability, Hong Kong, China

Department of Cultural Studies, Lingnan University, Hong Kong, China

T. Wen
Institute of Rural Reconstruction of China, Southwest University, Chongqing, China

Institute of Advanced Studies for Sustainability, Renmin University of China, Beijing, China

Institute of Rural Reconstruction of the Straits, Fujian Agriculture and Forestry University, Fuzhou, China

countries having the backing of international institutions and occupying the high table in financial-monetary dominance can create the unprecedented 'miracle' of wealth in the history of economy. The approach of core countries—the higher the debt the more outrageous the expansion—is completely opposite to the situation of developing countries in the latter part of the twentieth century. As debtor countries, these countries not only have to comply with the demands of creditor countries to carry out 'institutional reform' but are also encouraged to sell off their valuable assets in order to repay debts with interest, that too in terms of US dollars. This clearly indicates that the international order of so-called liberalism, proudly flaunted after the World War II, has already been thoroughly overturned by 'neoliberalism' in the stage of financial capitalism.

The core, relying on global financialization, expands credit on a large scale in order to sustain its unipolar hegemony. They manage to do this by three types of borrowing: (a) to borrow for consumption (borrow money for their limitless consumption); (b) to borrow for investment (borrow money to possess our resources and acquire our industries); and (c) to borrow for war (arms race, instigating conflicts and killing civilians).

It is true that certain emerging countries, such as Brazil and Venezuela, made improvements in their domestic well-being by hitching a ride on this short-lived opportunistic profiteering arising from rise in prices of resources. Other super-sized countries with physical economy like China could also deploy measures to deal with the onslaught of global crises to maintain a temporary footing. Yet, these emerging countries should not forget even for a moment that international institutional power is still concentrated in the hands of the core, which, in order to deal with the global crisis arising from innate contradiction of financial capitalism, have adopted many tactics similar to the 'Hand of God' trick in the soccer field. These tactics are not targeted at resolving the structural contradiction of financial capitalism, but they continuously make use of the asymmetry in international institutions to extend their advantage to extract enormous profit from the semi-periphery and periphery in the global system on the one hand, and to transfer out the political and economic costs to non-core countries on the other hand.

People are more or less aware of the transferred economic costs already. However, regarding political cost-transfer there is often too much ambiguity and vagueness. What needs to be emphasized is that globalization of today is based on nations as competing units. Therefore, political cost-transfers have mainly been embodied in the support that core countries provided, through soft power and smart power, to the various colour and floral revolutions in peripheral countries, essentially pretexts for the strategic deployment of denationalization. The outcome is often that core countries are able to protect their monetary geopolitical strategic interests at low cost, while the countries that have become peripheral under the dominance of Eurocentric ideology have mostly 'failed' in the global competition. Only a few vested interest groups in these peripheral countries can share some handouts in accordance with their contributions to the core, while the people at large have to bear the enormous cost of failed governance and even collapsed state. In some cases, the tragedy of population displacement and casualties among innocent civilians are also witnessed.

Undoubtedly, we also have to give importance to the increasingly serious class contradiction within core countries. Wealthy societies in Europe, the USA, Japan, South Korea and so on are becoming increasingly polarized in terms of wealth allocation. Western social science has, because of the strong growth of the middle class, once challenged the concept of 'class', in the Marxian sense, in classical political economy. Yet in wealthy societies, middle class is shrinking. A small population from the wealthiest class disproportionately takes up most of the increase in national wealth. This may be called the institutional asymmetry of financial capitalism. Regarding this structural asymmetry, some Western progressive academics have descriptions on the phenomenon, but seldom investigate its root deep in financial capitalism (Piketty 2014; Sassen 2014). Yet class contradiction in the core does not necessarily reveal itself in the form of class struggle. On the one hand, international asymmetry has allowed the countries of the core to extract enormous profits from the periphery. When these profits flow back to the society of core countries, regardless of how unfair the allocation is, the lower middle-class people would still be able to share a small portion. Hence, though a majority of them could enjoy proceeds from the global system, they would still prefer a state system of financial capitalism that engages in international competition. On the other hand, ideological machines (including media, cultural industries and academics) have strived to hide the structural source of class contradictions and ease the class confrontational mood. Consequently, the discontent among lower middle class has often expressed itself by way of various kinds of identity politics, such as religious or ethnic confrontations, xenophobia and others. Right-wing populism and even fascism are generally on the rise in Europe, the USA and Japan and non-constructive radical politics is showing its face in different countries. All these have roots deeply ingrained in the system of financial capitalism.

The Global South, in general, has different conditions even though they witness identity politics. But within this chaos created by global financial capitalism, their social contradictions would be more often expressed as direct antagonism towards their own government. The key reason is that these countries, unlike the core, could get as much political and economic gain globally on the one hand and transfer crisis outwards on the other. Therefore, the return they enjoy and the risk they bear in the international contest are highly asymmetrical, and this is manifested directly as domestic social contradictions.

Core countries can engage in 'transfer of political cost', the main substance of which is monetary-geopolitical-military strategic deployment in character. Such a strategy comprises of all kinds of smart power and soft power moves, to topple governments in peripheral countries which are seen as barriers to the optimization of interests of the core. Alternatively, such countries could be denationalized, hollowed out of sovereign substances. Political and economic instability of opponents is on the one hand beneficial to the capital of core countries for acquisition of valuable assets; on the other hand, it also induces international capital to flow back to core countries. An aspect of denationalizing is to reduce a country's capability in adjusting its economy to combat the destructive flow of capital. This is done by knocking out the relatively competitive state capital even as its national capital is not yet competent to compete in the international sphere. This strangles the country's international competitiveness in the long term.

In this context, the producers of knowledge and public opinions in these countries lack proper understanding of their situation because they are under the spell of the hegemonic power of the core. They simply blame it on the backwardness of their own country's economic system and see it as inferior to the advanced systems of developed countries. As a result, economic and social contradictions are then rendered into political contradiction. Furthermore, some of these movements have been launched to serve the core's geopolitical strategy.

In the South, China, relatively speaking, was better positioned to deal with the double cost-transfer from the core countries. In the following, we will elaborate how China negotiates with the global financial crisis of 2008 through a large scale investment into the rural areas.

China's Responses to the Global Financial Crisis of 2008

In New China's 60-year history of modernization and industrialization, as a rule, capital intensive urban industry has been able to achieve a 'soft landing' (Wen 2012) whenever the cost of economic crisis could be transferred to the rural sector, and the status quo has been maintained. When costs have not been transferrable to the rural sector, however, the urban sector has experienced a 'hard landing' (Wen 2012), leading to major reforms in fiscal and even economic systems. The recent example is China's response to the global financial crisis of 2008 and her continued negotiation with its repercussions.[1]

In the late 1990s, macroeconomic fluctuation has led to deterioration and crisis in rural governance (Dong and Wen 2008). Since 2003, the ruling party has reiterated the importance of the sannong problem, referring to peasants, villages and agriculture as the most important of all problems. In 2005, the policy of New Socialist Countryside has been listed as the first major strategy in China's future development.

Since then, a series of pro-rural policies has been implemented, and the rural sector has been given a chance to rehabilitate. The regulatory function of its labour pool for industrialization has partly been restored. The function of the county economy as the second capital pool besides the urban sector has been strengthened. It has played a positive role in enhancing the sustainability of development and rectifying the long-lasting structural imbalance of the national economy, in terms of industrial over-capacity, capital excess, labour surplus, disparities between coastal regions and hinterland, rural-urban polarization as well as income inequality.

Between 2003 and 2008, investment into the rural sector was over RMB 1473 billion.[2] The fiscal investment into the sannong problem during 2003 and 2009 has accumulated to RMB 3096.752 billion, that is, an average of RMB 15,000 per household. This has substantially increased the capital stock in the rural capital pool. Infrastructure investment has provided a great number of local non-agricultural employment opportunities. The once heavily debilitated regulatory function of the rural labour pool has thus been restored.

Second, pro-rural investment has stimulated rural consumption demand. During 2000 and 2003, the annual increase of retail sales volume in rural consumer goods market below county level was only about RMB 100 billion. In 2004, its number doubled to RMB 231.2 billion. It is estimated that the big push by the New Socialist Countryside would increase the rural retail sales volume of social consumer goods annually by about RMB 400 billion, that is, an annual increase of over 2 per cent in GDP (Huang 2005).

Third, as significant resources are flowing back into the rural sector and the tension between the peasants and grass-root governments is being mitigated, the contradictions and conflicts in rural communities are centred on disputes about general benefits. The rural sector at large has become more stable and would be the social base of the sannong as a vehicle to bear the cost of another crisis transfer. These have been the vital conditions affording China ample leeway to deal with the 2008 global crisis. China maintained a high GDP annual growth rate from 2003 to 2007, but the national economy became increasingly dependent on the international market in this period. In 2006, this dependence was estimated to be at 66 per cent. This fared unfavourably in comparison with other countries. Between 1980 and 2001, the dependence on trade in economies, such as the USA, Japan, India and Germany, were within 14 per cent to 20 per cent (Shen 2004). In this condition of general over-capacity, China could only 'use the future over-capacity to digest the present over-capacity' (Lang 2010). In other words, China has no more space to deal with its over-capacity in the future.

The global credit crunch of 2008 caused China's unbalanced economy and export-dependent sectors to be hit hard instantly. The contribution of export to GDP growth dropped from 2.6 per cent in 2007 to 0.8 per cent in 2008. International capital in commodities future markets increased after the sub-prime crisis pushed up primary product prices. China suffered a serious instance of imported inflation (Wang 2008). The Producer Price Index (PPI) rose from 5.4 per cent in 2007 to 8.1 per cent in 2008. The monthly Consumer Price Index (CPI) reached 8.7 per cent. Long-lasting insufficient domestic demand and over-dependency on export and investment had made China's economy highly susceptible to external crisis. The GDP growth rate declined to 9 per cent. This was still considered a respectable growth figure, but compared with previous years, it was just a step away from recession.

Just like in the financial crisis of 1997 and 1998, the Central Government's response was to stimulate domestic demand by positive fiscal investment. The planned scale was up to RMB 4 trillion by the end of 2010. Even though the government was successful in resuscitating the economy, the rescue measures of 1997–1998 were skewed in favour of urban interests, leading to the over appropriation of rural resources. The rural sector had to bear much of the institutional costs, which gave rise to an escalation of social conflicts.

In contrast, the rescue measures of 2008 and 2009 emphasized investment in the rural sector, which was a continuation of the Central Government's Sannong New Deal since 2003. Two of the three factors of production (namely, capital and labour) have flowed back into the rural sector in a significant way and partly restored the regulatory function of the rural labour pool. Moreover, a second capital pool (the first being in the urban sector) has been in the process of being constructed in the rural economy at a county level. Hence, there was a major difference between two national measures dealing with external crises. In the face of the financial crisis of 1997 and 1998, new public debt was mostly spent on infrastructure, whereas in 2008, investment allocation of RMB 120 billion was allocated as: RMB 10 billion in public housing, RMB 34 billion in rural livelihood and rural infrastructure, RMB 25 billion in railway, highway and airport, RMB 13 billion in medical care, education and culture, RMB 12 billion in energy efficiency, environmental and ecological preservation and RMB 6 billion in supporting entrepreneurship initiatives and industrial structure adjustment, and RMB 20 billion was advanced from the 2009 budget for reconstruction after disaster. It is obvious that most of the new funds were used in livelihood-related projects and over one-third in rural projects. Only RMB 25 billion was spent on infrastructure (Wen 2012). Despite continued government investments, rural society has been confronted with the problem of brain drain and weakening self-organization capability.

Attenuation of Rural Grassroots Self-organization Capability

Because the Central Government finally removed the agricultural tax in 2004–2006, rural China entered into a post-tax era characterized by an essential structural change. Since the rural population is increasingly composed of the elderly, women and the very young, the capacity of the sannong as shock absorber and social regulator is thus weakened considerably. Young and prime labour forces with higher human and natural resources stock (potential surplus value stock) have been migrating out of rural China over the last two decades. New generations of migrant workers from rural regions tend to settle in cities as the new rural population are excluded from land redistribution when the neoclassical conjecture of 'the scale economy of land' is now being legalized as a formal policy. As a consequence, the rural labour force that is left over comprises women and the aged (Wen and Yang 2012). Whether it is the elderly and women who are left behind in villages, or the first generation of workers who have endured multiple exploitations and returned from cities, the human resource stock is too low to be attractive to external capital seeking to capitalize on cheap human resources. In other words, the capitalization of the rural surplus labour force is necessarily untenable, even if the ageing rural sector is willing to be capitalized on so as to seek development opportunities. The question of how the rural inhabitants who were left behind can become agents of rural sustainable development has become a great challenge in the post-tax era. The crux seems to hinge on how the rural labour force reservoir may be resuscitated. What should be emphasized is the essential change in the social fabric has taken place as a result of the outward drain of rural human resources.

Since 1989, the contribution of agriculture to GDP and peasant's household income has been declining. After the decline of township village enterprises, peasant households seeking comprehensive returns had to adjust their labour portfolio which was increasingly oriented towards cities in order to seek short-term cash income to maintain reproduction. This resulted in a massive flow of migrant workers from the rural areas into cities. These workers mostly comprised surplus labour forces from rural households that owned a small number of assets (the usage right of a small parcel of arable land). In this way, they were different from the working class as defined in classical political economy, which arose from being expropriated of the land. Such migrant workers endured irregularly paid wages, accepted employment without social benefits and consciously suppressed consumption in order to collect a cash income higher than that obtained from rural labouring. What underpinned this practice was the particular form of land ownership that was in place. Arable land is collectively owned by a rural community and distributed within the village. Meanwhile production subcontracting has been determined according to the size of the household. This has been the real foundation of China's ability to maintain low labour costs for 20 years. The so-called comparative advantage theory has failed to explain China's ascendency because there was no shortage of developing countries with a huge population base but which could not replicate similar economic outcomes.

Nevertheless, the Government policy of New Socialist Countryside, with its stress on investment inputs to the countryside and to agriculture, reinforces the money-oriented solution to the crises. Ironically, it is this same money-orientation that destroys the social fabric of communities. The following example of the rural reconstruction effort of the Puhan community offers possibilities beyond government efforts from above. Puhan believes that the cultural regeneration of the community with a reintegration of young people in the village and agricultural community is a more resilient way.

Puhan Rural Community

Initiated in 2003 by Zheng Bing, Yongji Peasant Association is the first peasant association in China officially registered under the Ministry of Civil Affairs. A primary school teacher for over 10 years in Zaizi Village of Shanxi province in north China, Zheng organized science and technology training courses for local peasants. Recognizing that if peasants did not have common interests, it would be very easy for them to be disbanded, she decided to organize them.

As the Asian financial crisis revealed the fragility of the bubble economy, Zheng quit her teaching job and in 1998 began to devote herself to organizing cultural and economic activities based on grassroots women's collectives. With the support of the Women's Federation of Yongji City, she launched a women's club, which was named the Center for Women's Cultural Activities and Women's Association. When male peasants showed interest in the association, they were also accepted as members, and the base of the association became larger and larger. Formally established in 2003, the Yongji Peasant Association now has 3865 members from 35 villages in two counties, namely, Puzhou County and Hanyan County. It organizes six technological service centres, a handcrafts cooperative, a youth farm and an ecological agriculture zone (Sit 2011; Zhao and Yang 2007; Zhou 2012). Some of these efforts are described below.

Towards an Ecological Agriculture

Although the fertilizer-based cooperative agriculture can make profit, Puhan makes efforts in transforming agriculture from chemical to ecological agriculture. On the one hand, it runs four retail stores which sell fertilizers and provide technological advice to peasants. Thirty per cent of its profit goes to the whole community. On the other hand, Puhan has been experimenting on organic farming for several years. Once a local government official asked Zheng Bing, 'you have done so well for ten years, but why don't you build a factory and set up a business company?' Zheng Bing responded, 'every mu[3] of land is a factory, if we do it well, it will bring more profit than running a factory. And the environment can become better. Why do we have to build a factory?' 'You won't see any factory. Our offices are on the second floor of peasant houses' (Chen 2012; Han 2012).

In 2008, Puhan designed a 10-year plan for the future. One of the targets is to convert 50,000 mu of its 80,000 mu arable land into organic farming. They persuade the household one by one to improve the quality of soil. Gradually, they persuade every household to begin organic farming from one to three mu. In 2011, Puhan has successfully converted 3000 mu into organic farming. Hong Kong business company, Mecilla, wanted to purchase organic cotton but did not believe Puhan could produce organic cotton. A Swiss organization, Helvetas, was sent to investigate. It finally agreed to cooperate with Puhan after discovering lots of coccinella septempunctata linnaeus on the land. The purchasing price is 20–30 per cent more than the market price. Mecilla even requested for 30,000 mu to grow cotton, but Puhan declined the offer, as they believed that monoculture will bring harm to the land and ecology. They had paid high costs to learn the negative effects of mono-culture. In 2006 and 2007, over 60 per cent of land was invested in growing asparagus. But in 2008, a big pest disease destroyed nearly all asparagus (Ren 2013). In 2012, they successfully practiced ecological agriculture on nearly 10,000 mu. Zheng Bing remarks, 'being peasants, we must cultivate our feelings for the land. Is it possible if human beings take pills (referring to chemical fertilizers) everyday?' (Zheng 2012). A simple and alternative calculation is provided for the peasants. During the slack farming season, a peasant normally goes out to work in the city. He can earn RMB 60–70 per day. Then he spends two days' wages for a bag of chemical fertilizers. If he spends one day to make compost, such as mixture of weeds, grass and soil, after several months, he can save money because he does not need to buy any chemical fertilizers. It is even cheaper than goat manure and cow manure which cost more than RMB 100. In this way, a peasant can save money and the soil is greatly improved (Zheng 2012).

Association of Organic Agricultural Cooperatives

Forty professional cooperatives are established on a voluntary basis, of which 20 cooperatives are registered and the other 20 are non-registered. Before 2007, the association has 28 professional cooperatives. After the law of cooperative was announced, the government gives each cooperative a grant of RMB 30,000–50,000. Some cooperatives were formed just because they wanted to apply for the government grant. However, they did not do any cooperative activities after receiving the government grant. So Puhan decided not to do any more cooperative registration.

Every cooperative has between 20 and 150 households, with 100 and 150 mu of land. The cooperatives focus on cultivation of cotton, asparagus, bean, apple, persimmon, almond, peach, walnut, pear, hawthorn, cedrela sinensis, jujube, corn, pepper, sweet potato and sesame. There are also poultry cooperatives with focus on producing chicken, pig, cow, sheep, rabbit and fish. Other activities under taken are the cultivation of vegetables, watermelon production and small-scale industries, such as spinning, weaving, embroidery and others. There are 12 staff members who monitor the activities of cooperatives with one staff member taking charge of 50–150 households. They provide services and assistance to the cooperatives in order to promote the transition to organic agriculture (Ren 2013). In 2005, they organized study tours to Nanjie Village of Hehan Province and Scientific Village in Sichuan Province, which practice modern large scale agriculture and eco-tourism. After returning home, they concentrated 1850 mu of land in order to copy the above models. However, the experiments of land concentration completely failed (Ren 2013). Thereafter, they adopted a decentralized way of household management of land. One cooperative is generally composed of 20–100 households with groups of 3–5 households each. The agreement is to carry out examination of five standards: examination of fertilizers, usage of pesticides and selection of seeds, technological trainings, quality control and marketing. But individually, each cooperative has its own management of land and production. In other words, each farming household controls and manages its piece of land. Any kind of cooperation is based on voluntariness and commitment (Ren 2013).

The association provides some benefits in order to encourage peasants to adopt organic farming. The association owns three agricultural machines, which are used for ploughing, tillage and sowing. The market service charge is RMB 30 per mu, but they only charge RMB 10 per mu in the first year, and it is free of charge in the second year. They produce organic seeds at RMB 10 per mu, while the market price is RMB 40 per mu. They even provide some tools for members (Ren 2013).

It takes about 20 minutes from the community to Yongji City, and about 40 minutes to Yuncheng City by car. Organic agricultural products are fixed at only 20 per cent higher than the market price. The idea is to let the people enjoy good and healthy food, while money and profit are not the first priority.

Youth Organic Farm

In the face of rural youth exodus, the core group has mobilized their sons and daughters to return to the rural areas since 2008. For example, Han Lei, the son of Zheng Bing's classmate, was persuaded to work for the association after graduation at Yuncheng Agricultural College. Against his original dream of being a government official in the small city, he has explored another lifestyle in the countryside. Another example is Liang Xiaoli, whose mother is a core member of Hongliang Handicraft Cooperative. She found a job in the supermarket in the city after she graduated. Later she found it was unnecessarily expensive to lead a city life with boredom. She decided to go back to her native village.

In 2008, Zheng Bing recruited more than 20 young people and then a youth organic farm was set up. They contracted about 28 mu of land. Each is required to cultivate 1 mu and to take record about progress. They are also required to do collective farming. They did experimental organic farming for three years. In 2010, after having a good harvest of organic cotton on some experimental farmland, they promoted the relevant techniques and skills to other farming households. The target is to gradually improve the fertility of soil. Now the Farm has 53 young staff members who are doing experimental organic farming on 68 mu of land at a monthly salary of around RMB 800–1000 (Chen 2012; Han 2012).

Every young staff member is also requested to collect a monthly charge for garbage collection, that is, RMB 2, from each village. At the beginning, they were not willing to do it as they thought it was not a decent job. They considered themselves as educated people, and they felt embarrassed when it was related to dirty work. Then Zheng Bing and other senior staff arranged a series of meetings for the young staff to discuss with village heads, village cadres and garbage collectors. They taught the young staff how to conduct household interview through the process of garbage collection. In that way, the young staff can understand more about the reality of different peasants and also pay respect to physical labourers. Afterwards, every month the young staff arranged a lunch meeting for garbage collectors to show their appreciation. Gradually, the young staff identified with peasants and workers. They are no longer arrogant outsiders in the eyes of villagers (Zheng 2013).

Han Lei and Liang Xiaoli have changed their minds and behaviours after working with peasants for several years. Han Lei was sent by Zheng Bing to attend a youth training course organized by James Yen Rural Reconstruction Institute in 2006. He felt surprised when he found fellow classmates from prominent universities such as Peking University and Tsinghua University willing to collect urine and faeces to make organic compost. He thought he could do better than them, as his major subject was agriculture. Now he is in charge of the Youth Organic Farm and is the leader of the young team. He organizes many collective activities such as hiking and camping on the mountains for young colleagues. He even mobilizes his classmates and friends to go back to the village (Chen 2012).

Liang mentioned that she felt very upset when she returned to home village. In the dominant discourse, a successful model of a rural youth should lead a decent city life and never return to any village. Liang has gradually overcome these prejudices about shame and failures through learning together with young colleagues, senior staff and peasants. She found it interesting to learn ecological farming in the actual cotton field and apple land, even though it is hard work (Liang 2011).

Puhan intends to complete 30,000 mu of organic soil conversion by 2018. Puhan cooperates with the Rural Youth Training Program of Liang Shuming Rural Reconstruction Centre to introduce zero-waste Natural Farming Fermentation Bed technology to 600 livestock farming households. Laoshi Farm, named after a famous rural reconstruction movement leader, Liu Xiangbo, becomes not only a demonstration farm of natural farming and husbandry but also a model of rural youth engaged in organic agriculture. By raising livestock at the scale of 5 pigs, 5 goats and 20 chickens, each household can convert 10–15 mu of corn and wheat into organic farming using compost made with fermented manure. Apart from that, the participants are encouraged to document and learn traditional knowledge and skills such as making sesame oil by stone grinder, natural dyeing and weaving, paper cutting, and so on (He 2017).

Social and Cultural Activities

Puhan aims to let economic activities and public services go hand in hand. They redistribute the profit through providing public services and organizing social and cultural activities for women, children and the elderly.

In 2011, the net profit was about RMB 2 million. Sixty per cent of the profit came from the organic agricultural cooperative association, 20 per cent from the fertilizer cooperative, 10 per cent from the handicraft cooperative and 10 per cent from other sources. In 2012, collective consumption and marketing generated an income of RMB 5 million. They divided the net profit from the cooperatives into three parts: 60 per cent to members, not through cash, but through other methods. They did not grow rice, so they made collective purchase of rice. A profit of 30 per cent went to the whole community, and particularly to those sectors which did not have much income. Ten per cent of cash bonus went to all members (Zheng 2013).

Hongliang Handicrafts Cooperative not only re-activates traditional knowledge, such as spinning, weaving, dyeing and embroidery, but also organizes social activities for the elderly. The members are mainly middle-aged women who frequently visit the elderly to learn from them. Now there are around 200 members, with RMB 1000 for each share, but the maximum is five shares (Zheng 2013).

There are more than 2000 people who are aged above 65. It is impossible to build a big elderly care centre. The elderly people are invited to be teachers of the handicrafts cooperatives and of summer camps. The elderly people are also encouraged to learn to use computers to communicate with young people such as their grandchildren. For the elderly who cannot take care of themselves, matching services are provided with some middle-aged women providing in-door services for the elderly who are differently abled (Liang 2017).

Children summer camps are also organized. Children are taught the local knowledge, such as how to recognize different seeds and plants, and how to grow cotton and weave. Children have more opportunity for social interaction with the elderly. One of the slogans is that 'you, I, he or she do not exist on one's own, we exist as a family. Fame and fortune are not our goals, but only truth, kindness and beauty' (Liang 2017).

Conclusion

Other than the usual approach of providing more urban jobs, an alternative more socially and culturally beneficial to society in the long term is to enhance local resilience against globalization and reactivate rural communities to promote jobs as well as reincorporate young people. Though the Chinese government's central policy of 'New Socialist Countryside' attempts to absorb the crises of overproduction and unemployment through large scale domestic investment in basic infrastructure and social welfare in rural areas, it does not necessarily strengthen local resilience. Local resilience evolves through initiatives from below for social transformation through self-organization, popular participation, reciprocity and ecological practices. The efforts from the above should be integrated with the efforts from below.

Based on Puhan's experiences, the major functioning vehicle at the grassroots level should be comprehensive rural community cooperatives. Besides ensuring effective investment, rural regions can also be better organized to benefit the majority of peasants, including women, the elderly and the handicapped.

Puhan works hard to keep 'the identity and reality of peasantry' alive: living on land as a way of life and means of livelihood, supported by small-scale manufacturing industries. It adopts collective management of the commons such as land resources and labour power. Puhan has established several cooperatives against the trend of individualization and privatization. The goals are neither to be an agri-business nor to be subject to them. The basic social structure is family units working hand in hand with community management. The practices of organic farming embody the values of ecology and ethics, becoming more and more important. Rural-urban interaction and cooperation are carried out through fair trade of farm products.

Apart from economic business, there are various cultural and social activities. Marginalized groups such as women, the elderly, the youth and even the handicapped are encouraged to be involved in activities of community building. Particularly, the youth education and leadership training becomes the priority task for the future of rural society.

Through cultivating on the land and working with peasants and workers, the youth have gradually taken a different perspective on nature and social relations. They no longer consider the countryside as a failure and a shame. They no longer dislike physical labour such as farming and garbage collection. They have learned not only ecological agriculture and skills of handicrafts but also the importance of self-organization and cooperation. Hence, they are no longer so self-centred and market-oriented.

All these are carried out with an understanding of the importance of the cultivation of social relations that form the basis of interdependence, mutual support and recognition, reaffirming the genuine wealth of the people, rather than monetary value determined by capitalistic relations. Hence the social organization of labour and peasants forms an important part of the strategy to build an alternative to a merely finance driven approach.

Acknowledgements The Major Project is funded by the National Social Science Foundation of China (No. 14ZDA064). The authors thank Alice Chan for translation of some parts of this article.

Notes

1. Wen Tiejun analyses the ten cyclical economic crises that China experienced since 1949 till now. Retrieved from http://our-global-u.org/oguorg/en/series-no-5-chinas-real-experiences-professor-wen-tiejun-on-ten-cyclicaleconomic-crises-in-china-1949-2016/
2. Data sources: China Statistical Year books. Due to limited data in several years, the actual total fund investment is estimated to be more than RMB 1790.
3. The unit of land in China is mu. 15 mu is 1 hectare.

References

Amin, S. (2013). Implosion of the European System. In *Implosion of Contemporary Capitalism* (pp. 89–104). New York: Monthly Review Press.

Chen, T. (2012). Rush Towards Puhan Rural Community. *Nanfengchuang, 1*(18), 34–36. Retrieved 24 September 2012, from http://www.nfcmag.com/article/3586.html.

Dong, X., & Wen, T. (2008). Macro-Economic Fluctuations and Crisis of Rural Governance. *Management World, 1*(9), 67–75.

Han, Y. (2012). *Primary Village School Teacher Quitted to Organize Cooperative and Become Head of Peasant's Association After 14 Years.* Retrieved 31 March 2012, from http://www.chinanews.com/gn/2012/03-31/3790253.shtml

He, Z. (2017). Puhan Rural Community: An Experiment of Integrated Peasant's Association. In Z. He & T. Wen (Eds.), *Rural Reconstruction Movement in Contemporary China* (pp. 87–102). Beijing: Dongfang Publisher.

Huang, H. (2005). Building a New Socialist Countryside—The Countryside is a Neglected Dynamic Element of Domestic Consumption. *Outlook Weekly*. Retrieved 23 November 2005, from http://www.agri.gov.cn/jjps/t20051123_500588.htm

Lang, X. (2010). US Is Making China the Second Japan. *China's Logistics and Purchasing, 12*, 38–39.

Liang, X. (2011). *Speech on the National Forum on Peasant Cooperatives*. Liang Shuming Rural Reconstruction Centre.

Liang, S. (2017). Service Economy for Noah's Ark—The Case of Yongji. In L. Chengping & D. Jie (Eds.), *Ten villages ten leaders* (pp. 31–56). Beijing: Dongfang Publisher.

Piketty, T. (2014). *Capitalism in the 21st Century Capital in the Twenty-First Century*. Cambridge, MA: Belknap Press.

Ren, M. (2013). *Yongji Peasants of Shanxi Province Build Up a Model of Peasant Cooperative*. Retrieved 7 March 2013, from http://finance.china.com.cn/stock/20130307/1315556.shtml

Sassen, S. (2014). *Expulsions: Brutality and Complexity in the Global Economy*. Cambridge, MA: Harvard University Press.

Shen, J. (2004). China's Foreign Trade Exceeded 60%: Five Suggestions for Its Rationalization. *Xinhua News*. Retrieved 21 September 2004, from http://news.xinhuanet.com/fortune/2004-09/21/content_2001979.htm

Sit, T. (2011). Double Task. *Signs: Journal of Women in Culture and Society, 36*, 577–588.

Wallerstein, I. (2011). *The Modern World-System I: Capitalist Agriculture and the Origins of the European World-Economy in the Sixteenth Century*. Berkeley/Los Angeles/London: University of California Press.

Wang, J. (2008). Concern about the Turning Point of Situation of Growth and Inflation. *Macroeconomic Management, 1*(8), 11–13.

Wen, T. (2012). *Eight Crises: Lessons from China (1949–2009)*. Beijing: Dongfang Publisher.

Wen, T., & Yang, S. (2012). Local Governance and Rural Development Under the Background of the Structural Change of Rural Society in China. *Theoretical Investigation, 6*, 76–80.

Zhao, L., & Yang, L. (2007). Women Don't Waste Their Life. In C. S. Hing, L. K. Chi, D. Jinhua, & C. H. Mei (Eds.), *Colors of Peace—108 Stories of Women* (pp. 626–635). Beijing: Central Compilation and Translation Press.

Zheng, B. (2012). *A Speech Delivered at the Conference on the Local Integrated Peasant's Association*. Beijing: Beijing Peasant's Consultation Centre.

Zheng, B. (2013). An Interview with the Authors Conducted in Fujian Province in October 2013.

Zhou, C. (2012). Introduction to Puhan Rural Community of Yongji City of Shanxi Province. *Integrated Peasant's Association Newsletter, 2*, 16–19.

CHAPTER 18

Insurgent Working Class Self-Organization Outside the Wage Labour Relation: Land and Livestock in the City

Ricardo Jacobs

Introduction

The monumental Marikana mineworker strike (and ensuing massacre) and the unprecedented unprotected farm worker strike in the commercial farming districts of the western cape of 2012 marked a turning point in working class self-organization in post-apartheid South Africa. Almost 45% of the total strikes in 2012 were wildcat or unprotected strikes (Annual Industrial Action Report 2012). These strikes were part of a broader global wave or "cycle of struggles" beginning around 2010 and including a wide repertoire of actions from street demonstrations and strikes to food riots and other forms of protest (Nowak 2019, 25; Silver 2003, 59). In South Africa, the Marikana and Farmworkers' strikes unfolded through self-organized worker committees operating outside of trade unions at the point of production and at the community level (streets) encompassing the entire sphere of social reproduction. These two

R. Jacobs (✉)
University of California, Santa Barbara, CA, USA

P. Jha et al. (eds.), *Labour Questions in the Global South*,
https://doi.org/10.1007/978-981-33-4635-2_18

strikes collapsed the analytical distinction between work and home, connecting the workplace to households and the sphere of social reproduction of workers, and highlighting the consequential role of women (Benya 2015, 557). While insurgent worker self-organizations have been seen as a central moment in the struggles of labour vis-à-vis capital, worker self-organization outside of the capital wage labour relationship has been largely ignored.

This chapter examines working-class self-organization outside the sphere of capitalist production, focusing on a land occupation site for livestock raising in the city of Cape Town that developed a radically democratic and egalitarian organizational form. Drawing on fieldwork conducted between 2009 and 2017, I argue that the land occupation is an instance of *land reform from below* with immanent progressive potential for anti-capitalist change. Moreover, the land occupiers' combined experience of historical land dispossession resistance and contemporary anti-neoliberal struggles has produced what I call an "urban agrarian politics" in the twenty-first century. Reliance on the past and present resistance shapes their collective agency in challenging the prevailing unequal property relations. The chapter argues that what looks like an ad hoc, locally focused and unsustainable land occupation is part of the broader demand of labouring classes for agrarian transformation in urban areas of South Africa. Collective action to resist eviction from the land by the state and private capital, the formation of an autonomous organization by the land occupiers, the rules and procedures they developed, provides us a window into the independent self-organization of the urban semi-proletariat. These land occupations puncture the dominant narrative in the literature on South Africa and beyond that urbanization without industrialization dislodged new urban classes from historical agency á la Mike Davis (2004).

The land occupation examined in this chapter began in a low-profile and unstructured form in the 1980s, and organically developed into a radically democratic and egalitarian organizational form. This is visible from the way in which they make decisions around the allocation of land (including setting equal plot sizes), their fledgling system of solidarity and cooperation, and how they interact with the local informal market and aspire to supply food to the working class.

The actors who spearhead these land occupations are urbanized and proletarianized but they chose to pursue quintessentially "peasant" forms of livelihoods. Put differently, the emergent forms of class struggle are spearheaded by workers with a dual (peasant/proletarian) character, what

I previously characterized as an "urban proletarian with peasant characteristics" (Jacobs 2018) and what Sam Moyo referred to as the generalized semi-proletarian condition in cities (Moyo et al. 2019). Thus, the urban land occupations are indicative of the semi-proletarian condition operative in cities, that became more widespread under neoliberalism (Moyo and Yeros 2005), with the expulsion of "billions of people from the formal economy into the informal grey zones" (Fraser 2014, 59; Tsikata 2009).

With the semi-proletarian condition no doubt widened and deepened with neoliberalism, it is an ongoing characteristic of working-class formation in South Africa and most of the global South. This argument is in line with one of the central contentions within the world-systems perspective—that is, that profitability in the capitalist world-economy has always depended on the externalization of part of the costs of reproduction of labour onto the households of workers themselves and therefore has always tended to operate on the basis of "semi-proletarianized households". The possibility of a labouring class primarily dependent on the sale of their labour power is impossible for a large section of the population in cities. Seen from this perspective, land occupations in the City of Cape Town are indicative of the semi-proletarian condition that has been a permanent feature in South Africa, where urbanization and proletarianization have been largely decoupled.

Independent worker and peasant self-organization has a long history in South Africa with interaction between the two spheres of production (urban and rural) that have been mutually reinforcing. The peasant revolts of the 1960s and the subsequent wildcat strikes by migrant peasant labour in the 1970s are examples of peasant and worker independent self-organization (Kepe and Ntsebeza 2012; Mamdani 1996). In the twenty-first century, both the Marikana and farm worker strikes united workplace and community struggles through independent self-organization and politics (Cottle 2017; Wilderman 2015). Moreover, these struggles drew together the working poor, migrant workers, seasonal labour and the reserve army of the unemployed. Spatial relations (location and place) became a critical factor within these strikes, particularly social relations that striking workers maintained outside of the workplace (Nowak 2019, 26). The sphere of social reproduction is an important site of struggle and contestation, linking the active and reserve army of labour that is often contained within the same household or urban space.

The politics of the urban semi-proletarian is placing land for urban farming as a central part of the twenty-first century agrarian struggles in

South Africa. These land struggles are often hidden or simply submerged by the monumental struggles for housing and "service delivery" in the city. Despite the neglect by scholars and activists alike, this form of politics in the city is becoming an important alternative for both the active and reserve army of labour.

The chapter is organized around the self-organization and accompanying class struggle of an urban semi-proletariat. Section "Research Method: Actuality and Potentiality" will briefly outline the research method. The next section will discuss the dynamics of space, location and the emergent forms of class struggle and independent self-organization in the city and rural towns, specifically focused on the mineworker and farm worker strike of 2012. Section "Urban Land Occupations, Independent Self-Organization and Remapping the City" and "Urban Agrarian Politics" are the empirical core of the chapter and will discuss how an analogous form of independent self-organization outside the capital wage relation is remapping the city. These sections explore the unfolding urban agrarian politics that form an integral part of what has been termed the "rebellion of the poor" (Alexander 2010). The last section offers a brief conclusion on the self-activity of labouring classes and anti-capitalist alternatives.

Research Method: Actuality and Potentiality

My fieldwork was conducted between 2009 and 2017 at three land occupation sites, in densely populated areas of the city of Cape Town. The urban land occupiers engaged (or actively sought to engage) in agrarian activities despite being culturally, socially and economically assimilated into the city. Long-term urban residents, they can be divided into those that maintain direct links to the countryside continuing to invest in rural homesteads and agrarian activities and those with mixed or weak ties to the countryside. They fall into five categories:

1. those involved in livestock raising in both urban areas and on their communal land in the countryside;
2. those who take their livestock, particularly cattle, to the countryside for lack of grazing space in the city as a reprieve;
3. those who transport some of their livestock back to the communal land in the Eastern Cape either for sale, as a stock of wealth and for lineage reproduction;

4. those who are permanently embedded in the city but remit to the rural areas on a regular basis; and
5. those who are permanent urban residents with no ties to the countryside.

The chapter will be based on one of the land occupations that best illustrates worker self-organization outside the sphere of capitalist production—the Zabalaza land occupation site (Table 18.1).

The land occupation sites should be seen in the context of both actuality and potential, a method of inquiry for investigating how social processes unfold. As Bertell Ollman (2008, 13) explains "Investigating potential is taking the longer view, not only forward to what something can develop into but also backward to how it has developed up to now". This provides us with a method of investigation to study a process as it unfolds, with all its messiness, contradictions and limitations, disrupting the scholarly impulse to search for "pristine" cases. Gillian Hart adds another important layer to our method of investigation drawing attention to the "political stakes", that is new insights of "possibilities for social change" produced by focusing on the self-activity of subaltern classes (Hart 2018, 375). To put it differently, what are the political stakes of our research and theorization. Alternative theorizations emerge out of real existing class struggles, often neglected in the social science scholarship.

Table 18.1 Land occupation site in the city of Cape Town

Zabalaza small scale farmers	
Year of occupation	1985
No. of individuals/ households	180
Size of land	71 ha
Plot sizes	30 × 50 metres
Ownership	**Private**: 1985–2000: NuWay Housing Development (PTY) LTD **State**: 2000–present Department of Human Settlement
Main land use	Livestock
Affiliation	Rural: Food Sovereignty Campaign (FSC) African Farmers Association of South Africa (AFASA)

Dynamics of Space, Location and New Forms of Class Struggle

The Marikana strike is trumpeted as a defining moment in the capital/wage labour conflict in post-apartheid South Africa (Alexander et al. 2012, 9/195; Neocosmos 2016, 136). What is often less remarked upon about the Marikana strike is the predominantly rural character of the Marikana workers, as well as the important role that the unemployed and the community (shantytowns), particularly women, close to the mines played during the strike (Naicker 2016; Bruchhausen 2015; Ntswana 2015). New geographies of labour and spatial configurations are important in structuring independent worker politics and self-organization outside the point of production and also outside of existing trade unions and social movements. Shinning the spotlight on the sphere of social reproduction allows us to disentangle labouring classes household composition where the employed and unemployed coexist within the same households and informal settlements. The divide between workers and non-workers are blurred, because they live in spaces that are intertwined. Women were central actors during the strike and after the massacre by organizing marches against police brutality demanding justice and the withdrawal of the military and police from the Marikana informal settlement (Benya 2015; Ntswana 2015). In her pathbreaking ethnography, Asanda Benya shows the Marikana, and arguably, the farm worker strike collapsed the dividing line between home and work. The strike was about both the workplace and household (particularly the role of women) "where they produce mine labour at no cost to capital", externalizing the cost of social reproduction onto already impoverished families and their communities in both urban and rural areas (Benya 2015, 557). The mineworker strike was also made possible by community solidarity and a form of internal community politics.

An important feature of capital is the production of space and the shaping of spatial relations. The connection between the social structure of capitalism and the spatial structure of the town/city was vividly demonstrated during the mineworker and farmworker strikes (Katznelson 1993, 146; Smith 2008, 7). Moreover, the two major strikes represent a significant shift in worker agency, and a new cycle of struggle starkly unveiled the depth of the South African crisis. Some of the broad features of the crisis include the ever growing spatial relocation of surplus populations from rural to urban areas, precariousness of work, externalization of the cost of social reproduction, poverty, inequality and a crisis of accumulation (Hart 2013; Ashman et al. 2011; Bond 2019). Jobless economic growth, rising unemployment and precariousness of work have led many scholars to conclude that the point of production is becoming a less important terrain of struggle and that we have to shift our attention to the sphere of social reproduction. Binary framings like these obscure the real existing relations and interconnections between the employed, underemployed and unemployed in two ways. First, the employed, underemployed and unemployed are linked through precariousness in the wage relation and crisis of social reproduction. Second, the employed, underemployed and unemployed are linked and involved in class struggles at the workplace and community level as deftly demonstrated by Benya (2015) in the case of the mineworker strike.

In De Doorns where the farm worker strike started in the Western Cape, the strike was preceded by intense and violent service delivery protests directed at the local government. The spatial shift, expelling farm workers from their houses on the farm to informal settlements, allowed agricultural capital to shift the cost and risks of global competition onto workers. A Report by the Bureau for Food and Agricultural Policy (BFAP) strikingly illustrates that while South Africa's agricultural labour force is highly productive, most farmworker households are food insecure. One of the key demands of farm workers was an increase in wages from R69 a day to R150 a day. Notwithstanding, economists showed a farm worker family of two adults receiving each a wage of R150 per day would be unable to afford "an energy adequate and nutritional balanced daily food intake" (BFAP 2012, 49).

The geographical shift of agricultural labour to poor informal settlements and low-cost housing areas in the outskirts of town created the condition for worker agency and self-organization. Instead of being isolated on different farms, agricultural workers were now concentrated in a single space—informal settlements—creating the conditions for organizing outside of the gaze of the farm management and owners. The mining industry, on the other hand, had historically relied on migrant labour that was housed in single sex compounds that served as "the foundation of the infrastructure of control over black labour" (Bezuidenhout and Buhlungu 2010). These single sex compounds at the point of production was a space intended by capital to control labour, but at the same time it was a space recreated through workers agency, inverting the logic of capital, and ultimately culminating in the formation of the militant National Union of

Mineworkers in the 1980s. In post-apartheid South Africa workers increasingly shifted away from the compound system as the dominant form of worker housing to squatter settlements. The workplace became embedded in the relations of the squatter settlements and low cost housing areas. The landscape became spaces and places filled with agency (Nowak 2019, 8).

The Marikana workers continue to combine wage labour and strong ties to the countryside by investing in rural housing and livestock, retaining their "rural based solidarities and cultural identities" (Beinart 2014; Reddy 2015; Bruchhausen 2015; Neocosmos 2016; Capps 2015). Migrant labour continues as a source of cheap labour and profitability for the mines in South Africa and international capital as well as at the forefront of a new wave of labour militancy. In spite of agrarian activities being undermined by capitalist agriculture and ongoing waves of accumulation by dispossession, migrant workers retain a rural outlook and perspective (Delius 2014; James and Razak 2014).

The urban land occupiers and migrant labourers represent different configurations of the semi-proletarian condition; nevertheless, they are linked through relational processes (Hart 2006). Beverly Silver analytically distinguishes between direct and indirect relational processes. Direct relational processes exist when actors at different locations are aware of and actively promote links among each other whereas indirect relational processes refer to when actors in different locations are "linked behind their backs by systemic processes" [of the capitalist world economy] (Silver 2003, 26–27). Relational processes are an important component in the new wave of insurgent working class self-organization. It is spatial relations that link the workplace and community in a dynamic way forcing us to examine strikes beyond the workplace and the "social dynamics of worker self-organization" at the sphere of social reproduction or community level.

Instead of a permanent stable urban worker in the city reliant on the sale of their labour power (cf. Arrighi 1970) what we are observing are semi-proletarians in the city reconfiguring the urban built environment and urban spaces of social reproduction. Migrant labour has been consequential in shaping the trajectory of urbanization and proletarianization by connecting the urban and the rural (Hendricks et al. 2013; Mamdani 1996). As such, urbanization and proletarianization has to be understood in the context of the structure and processes of capitalism and the agency of workers' struggles over physical space and livelihoods in the city (Platzsky and Walker 1985). In sum, while migrant workers in the platinum mining industry represent the continuity (and evolution) of the earlier configuration of the dual character of labour, urban land occupiers raising livestock on the edge of the city represent the latest reincarnation of the long-term tendency to reproduce a labouring class with dual characteristics or generalized semi-proletarianization.

Urban Land Occupations, Independent Self-Organization and Remapping the City

This section will examine the organizational characteristics of the Zabalaza occupation and will put forward the argument that the occupation is an instance of "land redistribution from below" with immanent progressive potential for anti-capitalist agrarian change. First, I will explore how being neither fully peasant nor proletarian nor capitalist in logic, the Zabalaza land occupation has a progressive potential visible from the way in which they organize themselves, make decisions (particularly around the allocation of land), and from their fledgling system of solidarity and cooperation. Second, the progressive potential is visible in how they interact with the local informal market and aspire to supply food to the working class in ways that contribute to the livelihood and welfare of the community in a more fundamental way than commercial farming. Third, it is visible in the way in which the internal organizational dynamics of the Zabalaza farmers has limited the extent of internal class differentiation.

Decision-Making and Plot Allocation

The Zabalaza occupation started with one individual settling on the land for his livestock to graze. Initially the occupiers were not visible to the general public or the state because their activities were hidden behind the bushes and trees. Gradually more households joined the occupation and in 1996, they formed a voluntary farmers association. The National African Farmers Union (NAFU) was instrumental in them forming the farmers' association. The latter association unfortunately collapsed and in the early 2000s, they formed the Zabalaza Farmers Association (ZFA). Today the association consists of a membership of 180 household and a list of 150 individuals waiting to be allocated a plot.

A key feature of the associations is their autonomous organizational form. Notwithstanding the fact that NAFU assisted in the formation of the earlier farmer association and that individual Zabalaza farmers are members of various political parties, both the associations remained autonomous from political parties and NGOs. The impetus to form these organizations was the need to address various problems that the farmers were experiencing, including how to allocate new plots. As discussed in more detail below, the ZFA developed procedures for the democratic allocation of land and a system of solidarity and cooperation.

The Zabalaza Farmers Association's organizational structure consists of a six member executive committee and four subcommittees (plots, security, disciplinary and worker) on which non-executive members are co-opted to serve. The primary task of the plot committee is to allocate plots and ensure that farmers adhere to the policies of the organization. The security committee's primary task is to patrol at night to prevent livestock theft. The disciplinary committee's task is to resolve boundary disputes or conflicts over ownership of animals or theft of livestock by members of Zabalaza. Finally, a worker committee is tasked to represent the interests of workers who are employed by the Zabalaza farmers. However, the fact that workers are not directly represented on the executive committee or the four sub-committees limits their democratic participation and the organization's accountability.

Accountability and democratic participation happens through monthly general meetings (assembly form) on an open plot where the executive committee reports to and receives its mandate from the members. More than 100 people normally attend these meetings, which usually take place on late Sunday afternoons. This form of autonomous organization was significantly disrupted by the state from 2010 onwards, a point elaborated on below.

The Zabalaza occupiers seek to maintain the farm as a place exclusively for agricultural activities and exclude the use of land for informal housing. The first occupiers have considerably bigger agricultural plots. An increase in membership prompted the organization to reduce the plot sizes and give access to more farmers. A person or household regardless of gender, disability, age or ethnicity who wants to farm has to apply to the committee with a certified copy of his/her identity document, contact details and clearly state what type of farming she or he wants to practise. As the members of the executive committee explain:

> Once the executive accepts your application a farmer is allocated a plot. Plot sizes that are allocated to each farmer are approximately 30 metres x 60

> metres in size. At that time the committee thought that was an appropriate size to make a living and also to ensure that everyone can have a piece of land. (Interview, Zabalaza executive committee, 2012)

After the formal allocation of the plot, a farmer has to sign a commitment form; and he or she is given one month to fence the site and three months to start with livestock farming or crop production. The plot sizes are clearly very small, particularly for livestock farming. A typical plot is divided into a structure for housing, kraals for cattle, sheep or goats and pens for pigs. Land for grazing is very limited at Zabalaza and most farmers have to take their herds for grazing in the open fields in the different residential locations adjacent to Zabalaza or have to plant crops for grazing at their own plots. The former often resulted in their animals being impounded by the City of Cape Town or livestock theft.

Some Zabalaza farmers employ workers who are often precariously employed, with poor living and work conditions. Nevertheless, workers are not precluded from becoming farmers. Disputes between workers and plot "owners" are sometimes resolved in favour of the workers. For example, Abraham and Melvyn both made the transition from worker to farmer after declaring a dispute to the executive committee, or in the case of Melvyn declaring himself the owner of the farm after the former plot owner who brought him to Zabalaza to work, decided to sell all of his pigs and leave Zabalaza. After a three-year absence, the farmer returned and wanted to reclaim his plot. The matter was referred to the executive committee who ruled in favour of Melvyn, who now farms with pigs, chickens and vegetables at Zabalaza (Focus group Interview with workers, 2012).

Solidarity and Collective Support

Since the state does not supply Zabalaza farmers with agricultural resources or extension support, solidarity plays a critical role for the success of the ZFA. In the mid-1990s, the organization implemented a fledgling system of solidarity and collective support to assist farmers with limited resources. As the chairperson of Zabalaza explains:

> We had a system for example in cases where people who did not have livestock [but who wanted to farm] were lent a pig (sow) and a boar to breed. Once the sow is pregnant and has piglets the sow and boar would be returned to the owner. The piglets would remain the new farmer's property.

> We assisted each other to build our farming activities. (Interview, Chairperson of Zabalaza, 2012)

As an organizational ethos, this system of solidarity and cooperation lasted from the mid-1990s to 2009 when it was discontinued as an organizational practice, as there were cases of new farmers who were reluctant to return the pigs that were borrowed. This in part could be attributed to the fact that the principles of the system were not adequately explained to new entrants or developed as a conscious political principle of the association. The end date of the practice also coincides with when the state initiated efforts to evict the Zabalaza occupiers. In a focus group held in 2012 with farmers who employ workers, it was argued that "cooperation and working together are being constrained by the uncertain situation, so farmers do not know if they are staying or moving to another place" (Farmers with workers, focus group, 2012). In the same focus group, it was argued that another barrier to cooperation was the fact that many farmers did not know each other. Today, cooperation and solidarity—including purchasing feed together, exchanging equipment and pooling transport—is more likely to develop amongst clusters of two or more farmers, rather than being driven by the general ethos of the organization.

In 2012, in a renewed effort to overcome these barriers, the executive committee started a system of organizing groups of 10–15 farmers every second week so that they can get to know each other and facilitate joint efforts (Fieldnotes, July 18, 2012). Moreover, the association negotiates agreements with some companies like Parmalat for farmers to access their waste material or organize training for farmers. Finally, solidarity was fostered in less direct ways. For example, Petula and her household for the past four years organized a party for the children of Zabalaza with her own money and resources; between 100 and 200 children attend the event. In 2014, the executive committee decided to support the initiative of Petula.[1]

Links to the Local Informal Market

The Zabalaza occupiers' links to the informal market in the working-class areas of Cape Town provide them a degree of insulation from the vagaries of the formal capitalist market. Prabhat Patnaik, in discussing what constitutes commodity production, contends that there must be "a coercive force" or a "degree of economic coercion" upon the commodity producer. Seen from this perspective, the Zabalaza occupiers are not engaged in commodity production proper because they are not subjected to the coercive force that commodity producers are subjected to and personal relations remain intact (Patnaik 2015, 120–122). Moreover, Zabalaza farmers' production is oriented to meeting the everyday needs of the local working class. Thus, the Zabalaza land occupation is fundamentally different from most state sanctioned land reform projects in South Africa. The latter are firmly locked into large-scale formal distant national and global agricultural commodity markets, which in part explains their limited success (see Greenberg 2015; Jacobs 2009). In contrast, the Zabalaza farmers are intimately linked with the informal economy in the City of Cape Town and some of the rural areas in the Western Cape. Tata Bongani, for example, was already firmly entrenched in the local informal economy—selling milk and goats to residents of Khayelitsha—prior to coming to Zabalaza. The informal street food market seller makes up the biggest group that buys livestock from the Zabalaza farmers. Some farmers also double as informal street food market sellers. As Pumla explains, it is more profitable for her to cook and sell prepared meat in the informal street food market:

> So for example my meat value might be R6000 ($600)–R7000 ($700) but I would have to sell it for R1500 ($150) if I decide to sell a whole pig to other street vendors. If we are selling a whole pig, we can only sell to the black [people] market and street vendors, and we get a very low price. (Pumla, interview 2012)

The Zabalaza occupiers see the formal market as unjust, discriminatory and undemocratic in contrast to the informal market. This experience is vividly captured by Tata Bongani who also sells his cattle at the auction in Cape Town, arguing that it is structured in a way that does not favour small scale or black farmers.

> For example when they look at you and your address, they would give you a lower price. They would give a price of R2000 or R6000 which is less than the actual value of the cattle. (Tata Bongani, interview, 2014)

The majority of the farmers sell their livestock to what they call "the black market"—by which they mean the growing black population living in both informal and formal housing in Cape Town and nearby rural towns. A number of farmers also purchase pigs for breeding from other black small-scale farmers in rural towns like Hopefield, situated some 120 kilometres from Cape Town. Another important component of the local market for Zabalaza farmers is meeting the demand for livestock and poultry among recent migrants from rural areas of the Eastern Cape who require livestock for African traditional practices and ceremonies. Although people are migrating to the cities, they do not abandon their traditional practices from the rural areas and make them a part of their lives in the cities. In terms of supplying the cultural or traditional market, goats and other livestock units are slaughtered for different cultural ceremonies and practices. Some traditional healers have specifications of what type and colour chickens they require for their ceremonies. As Sakumzi explains, for example, goats are slaughtered during male initiation or traditional healer ceremonies and various other cultural practices:

> Like for a firstborn child you have to slaughter a goat. If it's a boy you slaughter a male goat, if it's a girl you slaughter a female goat. My market is Langa, Gugulethu, Nyanga and Khayelitsha. (Sakumzi, interview, 2014)

Agricultural production is geared to meet their own food needs and to supply working class demand. Livestock is sold to street vendors selling meat, butchers and petty traders within the townships. Every farmer determines his/her own price that can be negotiated with potential buyers. A study about livestock farmers situated in Green Point in Khayelitsha has found similar links with the informal market (Lugogo, no date). This allows the farmers to delink from the dictates of the formal agro food market. Gonjeman one of the Zabalaza farmers captures it as follows:

> We want to achieve something in life and also to satisfy human or family needs. Both go hand in hand. Our primary objective is to provide for our family and supply the informal market with food. The informal market is a huge market. The farmers cannot keep up with the supply. Our prices are lower than the formal market [the retail commercial chains] like Shoprite, Brutos and Meatrite...Informal market participants come to Zabalaza because they cannot afford to purchase from the formal market, it's too expensive if you do not buy in bulk or on a larger scale. (Gonjeman, interview 2012)

What Gonjeman demonstrates is that land at Zabalaza is both a "production and consumption unit" and that "capitalist profit maximizing" is not their primary objective. It is the social reproduction or consumption needs of the household that determines production. As Vergara-Camus, using Armando Bartha's socio-economic peasant unit, contends:

> The peasant produces use values that he or she transforms into commodities in order to acquire money with which to acquire other use values. Within this context, money is not capital, it is simply a means of exchange…even the monetary surplus sometimes generated by peasant units should not be considered as capital accumulation. (Vergara-Camus 2014, 168)

This formulation aptly encapsulates the meaning of land and agricultural production at Zabalaza. The extra income generated is normally used for extended consumption like Gonjeman, who used the sale of pigs to organize a 21st (coming of age) party, and Doman, who used his farming income to pay for his daughter's college education.

Land Redistribution from Below in the City: A New Alternative?

Much ink has been spilled on land reform in South Africa despite its dismal record. Notwithstanding the limitations outlined above, the Zabalaza case provides us with a potential model for progressive land redistribution from below that is a much-needed alternative to the stalled government run land reform programme. This should not be conceived in the ideal typical triumphalist sense but the immanent progressive tendency from which we can develop alternatives rooted in the everyday struggles of social forces like the Zabalaza land occupiers.

In South Africa, land redistribution for agricultural purposes has been limited (Hendricks et al. 2013; Cousins 2013; Jacobs and Hart 2014). While only 10% of agricultural land has been redistributed, a number of state-driven land-reform projects collapsed, as agricultural production either declined or was discontinued. In part, this failure is attributed to the neoliberal restructuring of agriculture, the agro-food system and the "untransformed agrarian class structure" that severely limits the efficacy of land reform in South Africa (Jacobs 2012; Greenberg 2015; Cousins 2013). Scholars and agrarian social movement activists are increasingly calling the prospects for successful land reform within a neoliberal capitalist framework into question. What these scholars and activists propose is an anti-capitalist agrarian change framework that at a minimum should be based on "human needs, social equity and participatory democracy"

(Jacobs 2012, 178). This requires the building of an independent agrarian social movement and a clearer understanding of the social forces that would lead this struggle in urban and rural areas.

Agrarian struggles continue apace despite the non-existence of a national movement proper, since the collapse of the national Landless People's Movement. Many of these agrarian struggles are happening through the independent self-organization of subordinate classes in both rural and urban areas. Moreover, the struggle for urban land is also a contestation about how urbanization should proceed and the geography of cities should be shaped. Redistribution of land from below is one way in which occupiers such as those at Zabalaza are reconfiguring the geography of the city.

Reclaiming part of the city for agricultural livelihoods, the land occupiers are breaking down the dividing line between rural and urban and the sphere of production and social reproduction. Moreover, it shifts the policy terrain of land reform in South Africa that up to now has been framed in a narrowly statist way. The real existing struggles of the land occupiers open up new fields of possibilities and point us to an alternative trajectory of agrarian transformation beyond capitalism. By occupying land, the fundamental basis of the existing property relations are questioned and the socialization of land from below based on use rights to land through labour is brought to the forefront (cf. Tomba 2019). Instead of the state being conceived as the only mediator of land reform, and as some proposals suggest, vesting ownership of land in the state that manages it on behalf of society, the socialization of land from below transfers use rights to independent democratic self-governing bodies. To put it differently the division of land by democratically elected bodies at a local level—which the Zabalaza land occupation embodies—is not part of the imagination of scholars, policymakers and activists alike. It also poses the fundamental question, "what type of state is necessary for anti-capitalist agrarian reform"? These alternative forms of land reform from below have not received much attention by movements and policy-oriented scholars, but they are nonetheless essential signposts indicating the way towards alternative trajectories beyond capitalism.

Urban Agrarian Politics

In the previous sections, I argued that the Zabalaza occupiers are urban semi-proletarians; that the land occupation is an instance of "land reform from below" with immanent progressive potential. Moreover, I argued they are the early twenty-first century reconfiguration of the semi-proletarian condition engendered by capitalist development in South Africa, which recurrently creates a labour force with a dual peasant/proletarian nature. In this section, we will focus on the agrarian politics of the urban semi-proletarian in the twenty-first century as seen through the experience of the Zabalaza occupiers. A central argument in this section is that the alliance forged with agrarian social movements played a decisive role in the radicalization of the politics of Zabalaza. Secondly that their politics is shaped by a combination of worker experience of urban politics and landless peasants/workers in the countryside, which in turn led to a confrontational politics with mining capital and the state. The combined experiences of the history of resisting past dispossessions and contemporary struggles produce what I will describe as an urban agrarian politics in the twenty-first century.

A specificity of the urban semi-proletarian, as seen from the Zabalaza case, is that they tend to gravitate towards alliances with agrarian movements. In the late 1990s, they sought out an alliance with NAFU, a farmers' union. In 2009, they became part of the Agrarian Reform for Food Sovereignty Campaign, popularly known as the Food Sovereignty Campaign (FSC), an agrarian social movement whose members include forestry communities, small scale farmers, farm workers, landless peasants and rural dwellers operating in the Western and Northern Cape province of South Africa. In their search for assistance against an impending threat of eviction by the state, the Surplus People Project introduced the FSC to the Zabalaza farmers. As a consequence, the Zabalaza farmers participated in the local protest by small-scale farmers in the rural areas of the Northern Cape that was a defining moment setting the stage for an enduring alliance between rural and urban farmers and landless workers. An organizational unity between rural and urban was forged, revolving around access to land for agricultural livelihoods and agricultural worker (land and labour) rights through direct action.

The question arises whether this unity is constitutive of the alliance between urban workers and peasants as envisaged within the classical Marxian discourse. Since the Zabalaza occupiers are urban workers, one can argue that it fits within the Marxian conceptualization. However, one key difference is that the organizational unity is between a resident urban semi-proletarian, which also makes it an alliance between an urban landless peasantry and rural landless peasantry. The Zabalaza occupiers are moving us away from conceptualizing the unity between town and country in the strict old rural/urban dichotomies. As E.P. Thompson (1978, 149) argues, it is "in the process of struggling [that classes] discover themselves as classes". The Zabalaza occupiers eventually joined and at one stage became leaders of the FSC. This transformed their politics and practice from petitioning the state to militant collective action.

"We fight for land" invoked by the Zabalaza occupiers defines the agrarian politics of an urban semi-proletariat, premised on the return of land dispossessed during colonial and apartheid capitalism. This type of invocation was markedly different in early 2009 at Zabalaza when there was more of an appeal to the state to allow them to farm (Participant observation, 2009).[2] Collective action by the Zabalaza occupiers as they mobilized against the threatened eviction by the state and capital led to a further validation and entrenchment of their peasant characteristics.

> Apartheid is far from over. If apartheid was over, we would have been equal and things would have been distributed on an equal basis. That's why we are still landless. In South Africa we have a situation where a white farmer is farming on 20 – 30 000 ha of land, behind him that he does not even see… Why can't the government at least give some of this land to the poor farmers. (Zabalaza farmers employing workers, focused group, 2012)

The Zabalaza occupiers' first militant action occurred when they successfully stopped MacSands, a company mining sand, from mining sand on the farm. This radical action was a turning point in the politics of the Zabalaza farmers visibly radicalized in this instance by the rural members of the food sovereignty campaign. MacSands, a black economic empowerment (BEE) company was issued a permit in September 2009 to mine sand on the farm. For the Zabalaza farmers sand mining posed a threat to their livelihoods and they communicated this to the FSC. On World Food Day—October 16, 2009—a major confrontation unfolded between MacSands and the Zabalaza occupiers. The FSC 16-member task team, the majority of whom were rural farmers and activists, in solidarity went to the Zabalaza farm demanding that the mining company cease all mining activities until the Zabalaza occupiers have a clear understanding of what the mining permit entails and the impact it will have on their livelihoods (Participant observation, 2009).

The mining company of course refused to concede to the demands and the FSC members quickly mobilized the female members and workers employed at Zabalaza, burning tyres in the road. The flames of resistance were sparked, as tyres were set alight in the tradition of many struggles in urban South Africa. The trucks responsible for transporting the sand, subcontracted by the mining company, decided to leave immediately, fearing that their vehicles would be set alight. The rest of the Zabalaza occupiers were standing on the hill, holding back from participating, but watching as this struggle was unfolding in front of their eyes. The police and firefighters were swiftly on the scene, uncharacteristically suggesting that the farmers and sand mining company enter into a dialogue. An agreement was brokered between the farmers and MacSands on terms favourable to the occupiers. This was the first victory registered by the farmers and also the first time they faced eviction not by the state, but by a private company. This was the beginning of joint protest action in the city between urban occupiers and rural landless peasant, farm workers and forestry communities in support of the Zabalaza occupation.

This type of militancy is analogous to what Mahmood Mamdani refers to as "the rural in the urban", when discussing the way in which rural peasant migrant workers were at the forefront of radical industrial action, particularly in the historic Durban strike action of 1973.

> Just as migrants carried forms of urban militancy from the towns to reserves in the 1950's, so they did the flame of revolt from the rural to the urban in the coming period: the so-called decade of peace that followed Sharpeville came to an end with the predominantly migrant strikes of 1972–74, at first in Durban, and then on the Reef and the Cape. (Mamdani 1996, 220–221)

In the case under consideration here, the rural radicals were not migrants, but rather farmers residing in rural areas who facilitated the radicalization of the Zabalaza farmers, helping them to overcome the barriers to collective agency through direct action and struggle. This small but significant victory transformed the basis on which the Zabalaza occupiers engaged with the state. The political and organizational boundaries between rural and urban also shifted substantially in favour of solidarity giving shape to a new type of agrarian social movement politics. Similarly, the Zabalaza occupiers reinvigorated the FSC, particularly when they officially adopted land occupation as a legitimate form of land reform.[3] The transformation from alliance towards active member was solidified when Joseph, a precariously employed Zabalaza occupier, became the national convener of the FSC in 2012. This episode points to key differences and similarities between the migrant peasant worker and the urban semi-proletarian.

A key similarity between the urban semi-proletarian and migrant peasant worker is that both rely on land (agricultural production) and wage labour for social reproduction. Migrant peasant workers of the twentieth century played a central role in labour and urban community struggles and in land struggles in the countryside. Essentially, they operated as "conveyor belts between urban activism and rural discontent" (Mamdani 1996, 220). The Zabalaza occupiers, as emphasized earlier, are decidedly urban residents, that don't want to be dislocated from the city. Therefore, they rejected any offer by the state that would relocate them to rural areas far away from the city. The political activism of the resident urban semi-proletarian involves the entire household within a single geographical (urban) space. This was particularly evident with the Zabalaza occupiers' resistance against the state's attempt to evict them, when the entire household of occupiers participated in the different protest actions (Participant observation, 2010). Whereas migrant peasant workers' struggles were directed at both capital and the state, in the case of the Zabalaza occupiers, notwithstanding the conflict with MacSands, their struggles are primarily against the state.

Conclusion

Insurgent worker self-organization at the point of production and urban spaces of reproduction is indicative of the co-presence of different temporalities that give rise to a counter politics in cities in South Africa and the global south more broadly. The Zabalaza case illustrates the point that class is both about socio-economic location and a political category connected through political agency.

Neoliberal capitalism gives rise to new geographies of labour and spatial relations that creates the basis for new forms of insurgent worker self-organization. The concentration of semi-proletarian labour in squatter settlements is the basis for the emergence of a new wave of independent politics and insurgent worker self-organization among the Marikana mineworkers and seasonal farmworkers in the Western Cape. Massive rural-urban migration and semi-proletarianization sets the basis for a new form of insurgent worker self-organization through urban land occupations for livestock raising. Like the Marikana and Farmworker struggles, the experience of the Zabalaza land occupiers provides a starting point from which to unearth the basis for anti-capitalist change.

The land occupation in the city through independent semi-proletarian self-organization has also shifted the spatial parameters of the agrarian question. This is indicative, as an editorial of the *Agrarian South* journal has concluded:

> The semi-proletariat never abandoned the agrarian question, or the land question. The demand for land has expanded in rural areas, where land continues to be seen as fundamental to social reproduction of the household, while the same demand has also expanded to urban areas for the purpose of housing as well as urban agriculture. (Agrarian South 2012, 8)

Insurgent semi-proletarian self-organization is a critical component of both the labour and agrarian question, particularly in the global south, in the twenty-first century.

Notes

1. In a study of women in urban agriculture in the Cape Metro, Peter Jacobs and Tembi Xabi, similarly shows how "production for solidarity forms a core part" of urban women farmers, "building collective or social solidarity institutions", "instead of a exclusive commercial orientation" (Jacobs and Xaba 2008, 196). This further points to the importance of cooperation and solidarity emerging through the self-activity of producers in the city.
2. A common refrain was that the "government encourages us to do something for ourselves, now that we are doing something they want to evict us". This is markedly different from "when I was growing up, my family had land, and the government took it… They did not ask for it, they take it. So I take back this land" (Zabalaza Occupier, quoted in Mersha 2012). The latter militant approach only emerged during the course of collective action.
3. As one of the Zabalaza occupiers who was part of a delegation of the FSC at the United Nations climate change Conference of the Parties (COP) 17 in Durban articulated "Land occupations are the new way of doing land reform… We must force the government to *give back our land*" (Zabalaza farmer, quoted in Mersha 2012)

References

Agrarian South: Journal of Political Economy, Editorial. (2012). The Agrarian Question: Past, Present and Future, *1*(1), 1–10.

Alexander, P. (2010). Rebellion of the Poor: South Africa's Service Delivery Protests—A Preliminary Analysis. *Review of African Political Economy, 37*(123), 25–40.

Alexander, P., Lekgowa, T., Sinwell, L., & Xezwi, B. (2012). *Marikana: A View from the Mountain and a Case to Answer*. Johannesburg: Jacana.

Arrighi, G. (1970). Labour Supplies in Historical Perspective: A Study of the Proletarianization of the African Peasantry in Rhodesia. *Journal of Development Studies., 6*(3), 197–234.

Ashman, S., Fine, B., & Newman, S. (2011). *The Crisis in South Africa: Neoliberalism, Financialization and Uneven and Combined Development.* Socialist Register.

Beinart, W. (2014). A Century of Migrancy from Mpondoland. *African Studies, 73*, 387–409.

Benya, A. (2015). The Invisible Hands: Women in Marikana. *Review of African Political Economy, 42*(146), 545–560.

Bezuidenhout, A., & Buhlungu, S. (2010). From Compounded to Fragmented Labour: Mineworkers and the Demise of Compounds in South Africa. *Antipode, 34*(2), 237–263.

BFAP. (2012). *Farm Sectoral Determination: An Analysis of Agricultural Wages in South Africa*. A Report by Bureau for Food and Agricultural Policy. December. https://www.hopcal.co.za/wp-content/uploads/2018/04/article_files_61_bfap-farm-sector-determination-report-draft-17-dec.pdf

Bond, P. (2019). South Africa Suffers Capitalist Crisis Déjà Vu. *Monthly Review, an Independent Socialist Magazine, 70*, 8. https://monthlyreview.org/2019/01/01/south-africa-suffers-capitalist-crisis-deja-vu/.

Bruchhausen, S. (2015). Understanding Marikana Through The Mpondo Revolts. *Journal of Asian and African Studies, 50*(4), 412–426.

Capps, G. (2015). Labour in the time of platinum. *Review of African Political Economy*, 42:146, 497–507.

Cottle, E. (2017). Long Waves of Strikes in South Africa: 1900–2015. In O. Balashova, I. D. Karatepe, & A. Namukasa (Eds.), *Where Have all the Classes Gone? A Critical Perspective on Struggles and Collective Action*. Munich: Rainer Hampp Verlag.

Cousins, B. (2013). Smallholder Irrigation Schemes, Agrarian Reform and 'Accumulation from Above and from Below' in South Africa. *Journal of Agrarian Change, 13*(1), 116–139.

Davis, D. (2004). Planet of Slums: Urban Involution and the Informal Proletariat., *New Left Review, 26*, 5–34.

Delius, P. (2014). The Making and Changing of Migrant Workers' World (1800–2014). *African Studies, 73*, 313–322.

Department of Labour. (2012). *Annual Industrial Action Report 2012*. Republic of South Africa. https://www.gov.za/sites/default/files/gcis_document/201409/industrialreport2012a.pdf

Fraser, N. (2014). Behind Marx's Hidden Abode: For an Expanded Conception of Capitalism. *New Left Review, 86*, 55–72.

Greenberg, S. (2015). Agrarian Reform and South Africa's Agro-Food System. *The Journal of Peasant Studies, 42*(5), 957–979.

Hart, G. (2006). Denaturalizing Dispossession: Critical Ethnography in the Age of Resurgent Imperialism. Antipode. Volume 38, Issue 5, pages 977–1004, November.

Hart, G. (2013). *Rethinking the South African Crisis: Nationalism, Populism, Hegemony*. University of KwaZulu-Natal Press, South Africa.

Hart, G. (2018). Relational Comparison Revisited: Marxist Postcolonial Geographies in Practice. *Progress in Human Geography., 42*(3), 371–394.

Hendricks, F., Ntsebeza, L., & Helliker, K. (2013). Land Questions in South Africa. In F. Hendricks, L. Ntsebeza, & L. Helliker (Eds.), *The Promise of Land: Undoing a Century of Dispossession in South Africa* (pp. 1–23). Johannesburg: Jacana Media.

Jacobs, P T. (2009). Questioning Pro-poor Responses to the Global Economic Slump, *Review of African Political Economy, 36*(122), 611–619, https://doi.org/10.1080/03056240903346210

Jacobs, P. (2012). Whither Agrarian Reform in South Africa? *Review of African Political Economy, 39*(131), 171–180.

Jacobs, R. (2018). An Urban Proletariat with Peasant Characteristics: Land Occupations and Livestock Raising in South Africa. *The Journal of Peasant Studies, 45*(5–6), 884–903.

Jacobs, P., & Hart, T. (2014). Pro-Poor Rural Development in South Africa. In T. Meyiwa, M. Nkondo, M. Chitiga-Mabugu, M. Sithole, & F. Nyanjoh (Eds.), *State of the Nation 2014: South Africa 1994–2014: A Twenty-Year Review* (pp. 158–170). HSRC Press.

Jacobs, P., & Xaba, T. (2008). Women in Urban and Peri-Agriculture: Sustaining Livelihoods in the Cape Metropolitan Area. *Agenda: Empowering Women for Gender Equity, 22*(78), 186–197.

James, D., & Rajak, D. (2014). Credit apartheid, migrants, mines and money. *African Studies*, 73: 3. 455–476.

Katznelson, I. (1993). *Marxism and the City*. Oxford: Clarendon Press.

Kepe, T., & Ntsebeza, L. (2012). *Rural Resistance in South Africa: The Mpondo Revolts after Fifty Years*. Cape Town: UCT Press.

Mamdani, M. (1996). *Citizen and Subject: Contemporary Africa and the Legacy of Late Colonialism*. Princeton University Press: Princeton.

Mersha, S. (2012). "Land Occupation as a Strategy for Agrarian Reform and Climate Justice". *Grassroots International*. https://grassrootsonline.org/in-thenews/newsarticlesland-occupation-strategy-agrarian-reform-and-climate-justice/

Moyo, S., & Yeros, P. (Eds.). (2005). *Reclaiming the Land – The Resurgence of Rural Social Movements in Africa, Asia and Latin America*. London: David Philip, Southern Africa, Zed Book Ltd.

Moyo, S., Jha, P., & Yeros, P. (2019). Introduction: The Scramble for Land and Natural Resources in Africa. In M. Sam, P. Jha, & P. Yeros (Eds.), *Reclaiming Africa: Scramble and Resistance in the 21st Century*. Singapore: Springer.

Naicker, C. (2016). Worker Struggles as Community Struggles: The Politics of Protest in Nkaneng, Marikana. *Journal of Asian and African Studies, 51*(2), 157–170.

Neocosmos, M. (2016). Editorial Introduction: The Marikana Moment, Worker Political Subjectivity and State Violence in Post-Apartheid South Africa. *Journal of Asian and African Studies, 51*(2), 135–142.

Nowak, J. (2019). *Mass Strikes and Social Movements in Brazil and India: Popular Mobilisation in the Long Depression, Studies in the Political Economy of Public Policy Series*. Cham: Palgrave Macmillan.

Ntswana, N. (2015). Striking together: Women workers in the 2012 platinum dispute. *Review of African Political Economy, 42*(146), 625–632.

Ollman, B (2008). Why Dialectics? Why Now?. In Ollman, B and Smith T (eds). 2008. *Dialectics for the New Century*. Palgrave Macmillan. New York.

Patnaik, P. (2015). Defining the Concept of Commodity Production. *Studies in People's History, 2*(1), 117–125.

Platzsky, L., & C. Walker. (1985). *The Surplus People: Forced Removals in South Africa*. Ravan Press. Johannesburg.

Reddy, N. (2015). Understanding the Labour Crisis in South Africa: Real Wage Trends and the Mineral-Energy Complex Crisis. In V. Satgar (Ed.), *Capitalism in Crisis: Class Struggles in South Africa* (pp. 211–244). Johannesburg: Wits University Press.

Silver, B J. (2003). *Forces of Labor: Workers' Movements and Globalization since 1870*. Cambridge Studies in Comparative Politics. Cambridge University Press.

Smith, N. (2008). *Uneven Development: Nature, Capital and the Production of Space* (3rd ed.). London: The University of Georgia Press.

Thompson, E. P. (1978). Eighteen-Century English Society: Class Struggle without Class? *Social History, 3*(2), 133–165.

Tomba, M. (2019). *Insurgent Universality: An Alternative Legacy of Modernity*. New York: Oxford University Press.

Tsikata, D. (2009). Gender, Land and Labour Relations and Livelihoods in Sub-Saharan Africa in the Era of Economic Liberalisation: Towards a Research Agenda. *Feminist Africa, 12*, 11–30.

Vergara-Camus, L. (2014). *Land and Freedom: The MST, the Zapatistas and Peasant Alternatives to Neoliberalism*. London: Zed Books.

Wilderman, J. (2015). *From Flexible Work to Mass Uprising: The Western Cape Farm Workers' Struggle*. SWOP. Society, Work & Development Institute, Working Paper 4, April. https://www.global-labouruniversity.org/fileadmin/books/SWOP__FarmWorkers_-_Jesse_Wilderman.pdf

CHAPTER 19

Changing Labour Relations in Commercial Agrarian Landscapes in Ghana

Joseph Kofi Teye, Gertrude Dzifa Torvikey, and Joseph Awetori Yaro

Introduction

In recognition of the importance of employment creation in transforming agrarian landscapes and improving the livelihoods of smallholder farmers (Hall 2011; De Shutter 2011), employment generation is one of the key goals of recent agricultural commercialization programmes being adopted by governments in the Global South (Cotula et al. 2009; Li 2011; Sitko and Jayne 2014). Consequently, within the past 20 years, when large-scale land acquisitions have become prominent in many developing countries, many researchers continue to ask questions on the connection between land acquisitions, employment and labour relations (Hall et al. 2017; Chambati et al. 2018; Gyapong 2019). Various models of commercial agriculture, including plantations and medium-scale commercial farms, have been critiqued in the literature for their specific features that have bearings on employment and labour practices (Smalley 2013; Tsikata and Yaro 2014; Yaro et al. 2017).

J. Kofi Teye (✉) • G. D. Torvikey • J. Awetori Yaro
Centre for Migration Studies, University of Ghana, Accra, Ghana

P. Jha et al. (eds.), *Labour Questions in the Global South*,
https://doi.org/10.1007/978-981-33-4635-2_19

In Ghana, although smallholder commercial agriculture remained the dominant form, with cocoa being a good example of a commercial crop produced by smallholders (Teye and Torvikey 2018), plantation and medium-scale models of agricultural production, which have gained currency in recent discussions of agrarian change, exist. Historically, the Ghanaian state has supported the establishment of plantations with the state itself having had several of such farms (Graham 1993; Teye and Torvikey 2018). Oil palm is one of such crops that has continued to be produced under the plantation model and these plantations are mostly linked to outgrower schemes. In some cases, outgrower/contract farming schemes were instituted to assuage the negative effects of land dispossession (Akyeampong and Hippolyte 2012).

Medium-scale commercial farms have also existed in Ghana alongside plantation models. In recent years, the horticultural sector, in particular, has seen the emergence of several medium- to large-scale farms. This is partly a result of immense intervention by the state, donors, and NGOs who seek to promote fruit export so as to diversify the economy and improve livelihoods in rural areas (Torvikey 2018; Teye and Torvikey 2018).

Historically, many of the commercial farmers have relied on both family labour and non-family labour arrangements, such as sharecropping, labour tenancy, caretaking arrangements, and by-day labour use. Ghanaian commercial farmers have, since the colonial era, relied on family labour where husbands, wives, children and other relations are involved in producing on the household farm. However, family labour became scarce due to the increasing land commodification and commercialisation in commodity producing areas (Amanor 2010). In the cocoa sector, the reliance on household labour, often unpaid, was also weakened by contestations over inheritance practices that do not favour wives and sons who might have contributed significantly to the establishment of cocoa farms (Hill 1963). In some cases, sons out-migrated to seek lands to produce cocoa on their own account (Amoah 1995). The challenges associated with the use of family labour resulted in increased reliance on other labour arrangements, such as hired labour, sharecropping and caretaking arrangements to sustain production. These labour practices remained popular in cocoa and oil palm producing areas. The structure of production and agrarian change favoured migrants' access to land, especially through sharecropping and caretaking arrangements.

In recent times, global and local labour practices have shaped the production of old industrial crops, such as oil palm, and new ones such as mango, pineapple, coconut, citrus, banana, papaya and others (Krumbiegel et al. 2017). Due to the export and industrial features of these crops, it is expected that marked changes would occur in the agrarian areas that produce them. However, there is little understanding of how employment opportunities and labour relations have changed in different agricultural landscapes in Ghana. Relying on primary data collected as part of the Land and Agricultural Commercialisation in Africa (LACA) project, we examine the nature of employment and labour relations in two case studies, carefully selected to represent large-scale plantations and medium-scale commercial agricultural models in Ghana. Our findings suggest that there are both continuations and departures from old labour relations and practices. While earlier researchers have attempted to generalize employment relations for different agricultural models, we argue that employment and labour relations in different agricultural landscapes are shaped not only by features of the different agricultural models but also by intergenerational and gender norms.

The Case Studies

The two cases examined were NORPALM Company limited which represents a plantation model and Somanya mango farms which represent a medium-scale commercial farming model. NORPALM acquired the National Oil Palm Limited (NORL) which was established in 1965 as a wholly state owned enterprise. The divestiture was effectively completed in 2000. Currently, Norpalm AS and PZ Cussons Ghana Ltd hold 68.6% and 31.4% shares respectively. It had 4500 hectares of nucleus farm and a milling capacity of 30 tons per hour and about 80,000 metric tons of Fresh Fruit Bunches (FFB) per year. It employed 284 people. Although it did not operate direct outgrower schemes, it has contractors who sourced palm fruits from a number of farmers.

The medium commercial agriculture model site is located at Somanya in the Yilo Krobo District in the Eastern Region of Ghana. The area is known for its commercial production of mangoes for the local market and for export. Mango production was on smaller scale until it got a boost in 1997 when the Adventist Development and Relief Agency (ADRA) and the United States Agency for International Development (USAID) provided interventions in the sector with the objective of reducing poverty and increasing agricultural incomes (Yidu and Dzorgbo 2016). The mango farm sizes in the area ranged from a hectare to several hundred hectares.

Data Sources

The data for this work were culled from the Land and Agricultural Commercialisation in Africa (LACA) research project. To compensate for the weaknesses of dichotomous research approaches (see Tashakkori and Teddlie 2010; Teye 2012), a sequential mixed-methods research design was adopted to collect data from households and key informants in three farming communities where outgrower, plantation and medium-scale commercial farming models were dominant. During the first year of the research, we undertook non-participant observations, qualitative interviews and focus group discussions in selected farming communities.

Non-participant observations were employed to understand the agro-ecology, infrastructure of the farming areas, nature of farms, and the living and working conditions of employees of these agricultural entities. The non-participant observation ran concurrently with informal discussions. During the farm visits, for instance, informal discussions were held with labourers that were found working on these farms. Key informant interviews were conducted with selected farm managers/owners. The issues discussed with these informants include: ownership structure, history of their farms, level of production, processing and value chains, marketing of produce and employment. Other key informants were chiefs and officials of district assemblies, who were interviewed on various issues, including land tenure, displacement and compensation. At least ten in-depth interviews were conducted with the various key informants (i.e. farm managers, chiefs and officials of district assemblies) in each study community.

The Focus Group Discussions (FGD), conducted in year one, were held with local people in the farming enclaves. For each of the farming areas, one focus group discussion was held with men and one with women in a group of 6–10 participants drawn from households in the area. The aim of the focus group discussions was to provide a natural setting for various people to discuss the impacts of agricultural activities on livelihoods in the area. Themes discussed in the FGD include effects of land acquisitions and investments on: employment; settlement and migration; access to the commons; infrastructure and livelihoods.

Year two of the research project was devoted to the quantitative data collection and analysis. Based on insights gained from the qualitative results in the first year, a structured questionnaire was designed and used to collect data from a sample of 423 households of which 141 were selected from the plantation area, 140 from commercial farming area and the rest from outgrower area.

In year three, qualitative and participatory methods were used to collect data to fill gaps in the data collected during the previous years. During this third year, further in-depth interviews were conducted with different categories of farmers and non-farmers to provide data for analysing the local impacts of each agricultural model. Seven households were purposively selected in each of the farming areas for these comprehensive interviews which focused on life histories of farmers, their spouses and their adult children. In each selected household, the farmer or household head was interviewed. These interviews, provided information on the intra-household (i.e. gendered and intergenerational) dynamics of farming. Although data was collected from three farming communities, this chapter is based on the data collected from only plantation and commercial farming areas.

Nature of Employment and Labour Arrangements

Both the plantation and medium scale commercial farming models have generated some form of employment for farm workers who live on-farm or commute from their homes. In each of these farming areas, different categories of workers were employed for different activities. NORPALM, which operates a plantation model, provides enormous employment opportunities to the nearby communities and beyond on the plantation and the processing plant. At least one member of almost all the households surveyed had working stints with NORPALM. As the fourth largest oil palm producer in Ghana, this firm has the capacity to employ different categories of workers, including managers, drivers, security personnel, and slashers. There are different types of workers, notably permanent, casual, contract, and field contractors and their workers. The company has oversight responsibility over the permanent, casual, and contract workers who are paid directly by the company. The field contract employees work for field contractors who pay them after receiving bulk payment from NORPALM. The terms of payment for field contract workers is fixed by NORPALM to prevent workers from being cheated, but the company does not check other benefits, such as social security payments and input for work. Outsourcing of labour tasks by companies therefore come with loses of labour rights to employees of subcontractors showing ever growing insecurity to labour in emerging capitalist tactics of reducing cost of production. It is only those who work at the mill and factory site who consider themselves permanent junior workers but there are no permanent workers in the nursery department. Some workers in the nursery department are engaged throughout the year but they are still considered casual workers. Consistent with findings of Obeng, Wrigley-Asante & Teye (Obeng et al. 2015) in the export processing zones of Ghana, 'permanent casual work' is a common feature of the agricultural production schemes in Ghana. A third category of workers is the seasonal workers employed when workloads are high.

Wages at NORPALM are uniform among the same categories of workers irrespective of gender, age, length of work and type of work. This is because of casualization and the contract system, which prevents social mobility within each category except between categories. For instance, all slashers take the same wage irrespective of gender and length of work because casualization means all workers are considered new workers all the time. However, wage differences exist between different categories such as slashers and supervisors or nursery work and processing work. Unlike the situation in the past where there were many permanent workers, the company currently employs more casual workers for a period of three months and then lays them off and rehires some of them for further three month contracts. Permanent jobs in NORPALM are usually taken by men mainly from urban areas and who are better educated than the people in the local community. Interviews showed that women are more likely to be hired on casual basis because their services are mainly required during harvesting period. Although wage discrimination does not exist in this formalized plantation model, the ability to secure employment into more remunerating categories of employment stratifies different people according to gender, education and skills. Less educated women and men therefore end up with casual harvest and slashing jobs, while the well-educated and skilful persons secure more permanent and higher paid tasks.

Apart from NOPALM, individual oil palm farmers who mostly sell their produce to NOPALM also employ both permanent and casual workers. In many cases, each farmer employs a farm manager and a few workers on permanent basis while several casual labourers are employed for specific tasks, such as weeding, harvesting palm nuts, and carrying load. For instance, 65-year-old MRA, a wealthy oil palm farmer with 225 acres of oil palm and 103 acres of rubber, has eight permanent employees and some casual workers.

Unlike wealthy oil palm farmers who employ some permanent workers, poor oil palm farmers hire labourers on daily basis (by- day) though most of the poor farmers complained about rising labour cost, which is affecting their ability to hire labour. For instance, JJ, an 80-year-old farmer talked about this in the following words:

> We hire labourers but the cost is rising now. In the past, labour was cheap but now it is quite expensive. In the past, we fed the labourers and deducted the cost from their wages and that was the practice. But now, they will want to be paid fully. It is costly because in this era, if one decides to give a labourer GH 10.00 to weed, they would not agree because it is not enough for their daily upkeep (JJ, 80 years old, poor oil palm farmer)

Similarly, MNH, a small-scale oil palm farmer, stated that he only employed a few labourers on his farms due to financial constraints.

> Apart from the children who help on the farm, we use hired labourers on some few occasions. We pay labourers according to the workload. We pay them GHS40 for between 100 and 120 palm fruit bunches harvested. I normally employ 3 labourers due to financial constraints (Life history interview, Pretsea, June 20th, 2015).

The medium-scale commercial farming model at Somanya also provides employment opportunities to people in the area and from other parts of Africa, as mango farming is generally labour intensive. The leaders of the Mango Growers Association reported that they have advised that each farmer should employ at least two permanent labourers to help manage the mango farms. However, only wealthy mango farmers with farm sizes larger than five acres tend to employ permanent farm workers. Farmers with smaller farms prefer giving out contracts to labourers on temporary basis, as this helps them to manage the cost of production. Thus, temporary employment, albeit with different variations is the commonest form of recruitment for mango production. The first type of labour arrangement is the situation whereby a farmer contracts farm hands to perform specific tasks. Contract work is used by farmers as a response to the rising cost of by-day labour which was more inefficient. With the contract type of labour, the workers determine the rate of work and since the work is charged per the task, they tend to do it faster so as to move on to another contract. The second type of labour used on the mango farms is 'by-day' where labourers are paid to work for the day and take fixed amount of money per day. By-day labour is mainly used for harvesting, which requires many workers. After the harvesting period, the workers cease to work and may only return the next harvesting season. Many by-day workers are women since it is women who are mainly engaged in harvesting the mangoes. Women are deemed to possess skills that are suitable for mango handling. The segmentation and segregation of work is associated with the gendered division of labour at the household and community. The perpetuation of this makes women more unstable in their working relationships with the farm owners. A farmer describes the categories of casual labourers used on his farms:

> I hire labour sometimes and they are mostly men. Sometimes, I work with the person on the farm for two weeks and they are paid 15 cedis a day. The women who come to work on the farm are not hired. They just come to help and I give them maize for free (CHR, 50-year-old mango farmer).

CHR's statement above captures a variant of 'by-day' work, where women who are not hired to work visit the mango farms during harvesting period to work for 'free'. However, the farmers compensate the women by giving them some of the harvested mangoes. These women would sell the mangoes after the day's work in order to get cash. The fact that the women would have to sell the mangoes makes this informal exchange arrangement uncertain since the women require time to be able to sell the mangoes to make money. This arrangement can also deepen further exploitation of female labourers since they may have to sell the mangoes at very cheap prices to prevent spoilage. This arrangement also mean that the farm owners cut labour costs by recruiting less number of seasonal labourers for harvesting while making allowance for the so called 'uninvited' female labourers. Women's lack of resources to engage in autonomous production is one of the reasons why they are the exploited in these types of labour relations.

An important feature of the casual or 'by-day' work is the fact that some of the casual farm labourers are farmers themselves but they sometimes take on casual farm jobs so as to earn some money to support their activities. The wage work gives these farmers some money to invest on their farms and also their households in times of need. Another form of labour arrangement is the situation where commercial mango farmers give out portions of their land to poorer and landless farmers for food crop production so that the beneficiary farmers will help maintain the mango trees by weeding. This arrangement is, however, fading out as the beneficiary farmers, according to interviewed farm owners, do not properly maintain the mango trees.

A few farmers also employ a few permanent workers, such as Farm Managers, who carry out all activities on the farm, including supervision of other workers. All the few permanent workers seen on the mango farms were men. A farmer explained that since permanent labourers are required to reside on the mango farms, most farmers would not want to employ women permanently because their spouses will accuse them of having sexual relationships with the women. Some farmers also believe that it will be odd to employ women who are not their wives permanently. The statement below by some mango farmers highlight why women are less likely to be employed as permanent workers on the mango farms:

> I only hire male workers. I don't take females on permanent basis because you can't make friends with them if they are not yours but men can easily make friends with each other in the line of work. Currently, I have four permanent labourers who are all males. I have worked with one for about nine months now, two of them have been with me for two years while the other one is four years now (WA, 64-year-old mango farmer, Somanya).

Some farmers also explained that they do not take women as permanent workers because many of the daily tasks such as spraying and weeding are very difficult, and cannot be performed by women. These findings indicate that consistent with findings in other parts of the world (Sen and Batliwala 2000), both the gendered segregation and segmentation of work and conditions of work on the farms are functions of the sexual division of labour that classify women and men as having the ability to perform certain tasks better. In terms of the dichotomy between permanent and casual work, in the cases that have been discussed, the former is more framed in the residential pattern and a reason why women cannot do it (Nyantakyi-Frimpong and Kerr 2017). Similar labour practices have been reported in the cocoa producing zones of Ghana (Okali 1983; Amanor 2010).

Heavy reliance on migrant labour is one of the features of agricultural production in the commercial farming area. On the mango farms, the majority of the farm labourers come from the same Krobo area. However, many other migrants are from the Volta, Northern, Upper East, and Upper West Regions of Ghana. A few labourers come also from West African countries, notably Burkina Faso, Niger and Togo. Those from Burkina Faso were particularly numerous on two of the farms visited. This trend of migrant labour sources shows a continuation and perpetuation of the labour migrant stream that started during the peak of the cocoa production era in the colonial times. Migrant labour has always been preferred because of the willingness of migrants to work under poorer conditions, their flexibility especially with regard to living on farms with limited freedoms, and their acceptance of comparatively lower wages compared to indigenes (see Hill 1963; Hunter 1963). Social networks are crucial in enabling this flow of migrant labour into commodity production regions in Ghana. Box 19.1 elaborates on the role of social networks in labour migrants flow into the mango producing region:

Box 19.1 Role of Social Networks in Recruitment of Migrant Farm Labourers

Three labourers from Burkina Faso were found working on one of the farms visited. These labourers, aged, 21, 23 and 32 are AL, MSU and TNK. They have all attended some basic school in Burkina Faso and so can speak English. TNK was the first to arrive in Ghana in 2010. He first stayed in Accra where he has worked with some building contractors as a labourer. While in Accra, life was very difficult for him because he did not get any work to do on many of the days. One day, he visited a friend in Ashaiman and he told him that he was going to Somanya to work as a labourer on a mango farm. TNK followed this friend to Somanya and the friend introduced him to the farm manager. Having worked there for one year, TNK went to Burkina Faso and brought his two cousins AL and MSU to come and do the same work.

Similar to the cases of TNK and his brothers in the case above, most of the migrant labourers reported that they have been recruited through social networks, which are very important in explaining the movements and survival of vulnerable people. The reliance on migrant labourers for farming, especially in the forest belt has been an age old phenomenon

(Addo-Fening 1997; Hill 1961, 1963). The structure of the economic development that privilege Southern Ghana over Northern Ghana made the latter a labour reserve for the commodity producing belt (Scully and Britwum 2019; Plange 1979; Grischow 1998; Abdul-Korah 2008).

Differences in the Level of Employment Generation by Different Agricultural Models

While both the plantation and commercial farming models generate employment, there are differences in the level of employment opportunities created by these farming models. Table 19.1 presents the distribution of persons aged 10 years and above in the sampled households according to direct employment and type of agricultural models. The findings indicate that the percentage of the workforce employed (casually or permanently) in the plantation and commercial farming models were respectively 19.42% and 20%. While the commercial model has more employees working on permanent basis than those who work on casual basis, the plantation model has more employees in the casual category than in the permanent category. For instance, while 16.6% of people in the commercial area work permanently on the mango farms as against 3.4% working on temporary basis, the plantation model has more people working on casual basis than permanent basis (11.99% versus 7.4%).

The findings are consistent with secondary data obtained from NORPALM, which operates a plantation model. As shown in Table 19.2, a majority of employees of NORPALM are contract workers employed on

Table 19.1 Distribution of household members aged 10 years and above by employment status and agriculture model

Agriculture model	*Employment in the agricultural models only*			
	N	*Percentage of permanent workforce in the agricultural models*	*Percentage of casual/ temporary workforce in the agricultural models*	*Total*
Plantation focal area	448	7.43	11.99	19.42
Commercial focal area	461	16.63	3.37	20.0
TOTAL	1385	11.28	7.33	18.61

Table 19.2 Employment Statistics for NORPALM

Category of employees	*Total*
General Manager	1
Assistant Mangers	9
Senior Staff	31
Unionized Staff	134
Casual Workers	91
Factory Contractors	4
Factory Contract Workers	54
Field Contractors	40
Field Contract Workers (Casual)	1500

Source: Human Resource Department of NORPALM, 2013

casual basis, though in practice many of them work more or less permanently without the associated rights. Our in-depth interviews show that the company, in its early days of operations, made workers permanent after three months of working with the company but this has changed to casualization over the past ten years following the introduction of and proliferation of labour agencies into the Ghanaian landscape. Workers now renew their contracts every three-six months when the contracts expire.

In the literature, the reasons why farms shift more of their workforce into casual category include labour shortages, a fall in producer prices, seasonal demands of the crop in question, demands for farm flexibility from globalised buyers or an attempt by farmers to escape their duties as employers towards permanent staff (Poulton et al. 2008). The oil palm sector is highly seasonal requiring specific tasks at particular times, which means labour needs vary requiring higher recruitments for slashing and harvesting on-farm, and also higher number of factory hands during harvesting period for the processing plant. This calls for fewer permanent workers using a division of labour that taps the special skills of different labour categories. In the past when the state guaranteed permanent employment in these corporations, workers were multipurpose swinging between slashing, harvesting and factory tasks without a clear division of labour. In a neoliberal dispensation, these old arrangements have given way to optimal systems using casualization and labour agencies which have the added advantage of absolving the company of other liabilities such as workers welfare benefits which constitute significant costs of production. However, these new forms of casualization are clearly associated with exploitation of workers and abuse of their rights (Obeng et al. 2015).

Conditions of Work and Average Wage for Permanent and Temporary Employees in the Agricultural Models by Gender

Given the different categories of employees and the variations in the number of hours that different workers work, there are variations in the conditions of service. Across the two models, different labourers receive different rates of remuneration. In the plantation farming area, for instance, permanent workers have better conditions of work (e.g. accommodation, medical care, higher salaries etc.) than casual and contract labourers. Some of the permanent workers earn quite high salaries. For instance, a farm manager earns between GHS1500 and 2000. On the other hand, the casual workers receive very low wages. As of 2013, workers in the nursery department of NORPALM work from Monday to Friday and earn wages between GHS160 cedis and GHS120 cedis at a daily wage of GHS8.40p. The wages of casual and contract workers are paid based on the number of days of work within the month. Social security contributions are deducted and paid to Social Security and National Insurance Trust (SSNIT). Wages are uniform among the categories of workers irrespective of gender, age, length of work and type of work. This is because of casualization and the contract system, which prevents social mobility within each category except between categories. Some contract workers expressed the view that they are not satisfied with the amount paid them but since they have no option and avenue for redress they accept it. Given the low wages, most casual workers complement their wages with own farm food production and non-farm activities, such as construction work and trading. Some women also grow vegetables within the company plantation-. Some workers are also provided with accommodation and this helps them to save money for things that they have to buy. While women at managerial and supervisory levels of the permanent category are granted leave with pay when pregnant, those belonging to the casual and contract group have leave without pay. Hence, pregnant casual workers normally stay and work until they are due before proceeding on leave. They are however engaged when they return from maternity leave. Salary levels of labourers working on individual farms are also lower than what is paid by NOPALM. However, people working for such farmers also sometimes get free accommodation and other benefit such as soft term loan.

Conditions of service at the commercial farming area also vary according to type of employment. The wage of labourers varies considerably from one farm to another, and it also varies within the same farm. The permanent labourers tend to receive salaries ranging from as low as GHS50 per month to a little above GHS200 per month. Majority of casual labourers receive about GHS10 per day. However, the labourers who are fortunate to get contracts usually charge according to the kind of work and the size of the farm. One farmer reported that she pays about GHS25 to a labourer in order to get her two-acre farm sprayed. The possibility of gaining more income as a contract labourer gives a better understanding of the reasons why some labourers do not want to be hired on permanent basis. The permanent labourers are disadvantaged, with the meagre salaries they take monthly, but they have the advantage of having a regular source of income. Some of the farm workers complained about low salaries. OSA, a farm manager, echoes his sentiments about this in the following words:

> As a Farm Manager, I receive GHS200 a month and this is not adequate at all. I have wife and children. I complained bitterly and my employer says he will do something about it. I also get a little support for food purchase. Whenever our boss is around and we tell him we need food, he provides for us. He usually provides maize and rice (OSA, Farm Manager, Somanya).

Another farm manager made similar statement as follows:

> I have been working for more than 13 years, but I collect just about GHS200. If you go around, hardly will you find someone earning more than GHS200. That is how these mango farmers cheat us. The only reason why we still work here is that because we know the work, we get contracts to work on different farms. So for that matter, if it is not the time for harvest, we work here from Monday to Thursday and use the rest of the week to handle the contracts we get elsewhere.There was a time when we wanted to stop working on this farm because we were suffering so he [the farm owner] had to agree that we come to work up to Thursday, except during the harvest time (TRA, Farm Manager, Somanya).

Other farmers complained about low salaries but also indicated that they get other benefits such as free food, water and accommodation. Some labourers also mentioned that during the harvest period, they are sometimes given mangoes that are considered not good for export or for sale to the processing companies, which they sell for additional income. Another challenge faced by labourers in the commercial mango production area is the fact that some farm owners do not have money to pay them until during the harvesting time. In some cases, farmers do not pay the total amount that would have accrued to contract workers:

> Payment is a problem for us because sometimes we work without salaries until the crops are harvested although we occasionally receive money for sustenance. Just like we have returned from the farm today, if we are fortunate and there is some money, we are given a little to manage; like GHS20 or GHS50 to use for our daily affairs so that when we harvest, the promised salaries for the work done will be paid. Because of that, daily records are kept on the number of days, hours and the type of work. We the labourers will be happy if a law is passed to regulate our payment. The farmers get the money from the mangoes but are reluctant to let go. When they get the money, paying the salary becomes an issue (KBA, Farm Labourer, Somanya).

One reason for the very low salaries is the fact that there are no labour associations, and this means that individual labourers will have to negotiate with their employers for better conditions. Yet, unemployment in the area affects the negotiating capacity of these labourers. Despite complaints about exploitations, some of the labourers believe that their livelihoods have improved.

Across models, permanent employees of the commercial model received USD 112 while their counterparts in the plantation model received USD 107 as monthly wage. However, managers who work on formal plantation firms, such as NOPALM, receive better salaries than managers on the individual farmers' farms, such as in the commercial farming areas. At the time of the study, some of the managers at NOPALM received as high as GHS2000 monthly while those working as managers in the commercial farming area received about GHS350 monthly wage. Thus, most of the benefits in the plantation model go to top managers while farm labourers are poorly paid. Such low wages offered to farm workers have been reported elsewhere. Ironically, while farm labourers complained of low wages, farmers in both study sites, complained about labour scarcity as a result of youth outmigration and rising cost of casual labour. The demand and supply factors of labour have also caused changes in labour terms and conditions. For instance, in the past, by-day labourers went to work as early as 6 am and closed around 6 pm. However, they now insist on working from 8 am to 12 noon. In addition, all workers now demand that the farmer should feed them (Gyapong 2019).

Use of Family Labour and Intra-Household Dynamics of Labour Arrangement

The use of family labour by individual mango farmers and oil palm farmers varied with the wealth of the farmer and the farm size. Poorer smallholder farmers depend more on family labour while richer and more established farmers tend to hire labour. Wives, children and other members of the household provide constant labour on farms. While the labour of wives is usually deemed as a conjugal duty, and that of children is mainly deemed as a way of effecting intergenerational knowledge transfer in the agricultural household as the children undergo training in agricultural production. Almost all the farmers in the study communities in both farming areas acquired their farming skills through participation in the household's farms in the past. For instance, MAM, a wealthy farmer in the mango commercial farming area worked on his parents cocoa farms in the Ashanti region. When he lost his formal job through retrenchment in the 1980s, he came back to the village to work on his uncle's fruits farm for several years. He acquired skills in fruit farming that became useful for him when he started his own mango farm. He reported that uncle also gave him resources, including money to set up his farm. He now expanded his farm from one hectare to about 250 hectares.

In other cases, smallholder farmers rely on family labour because they do not have adequate resources to hire workers. Some smallholder farmers also parsimoniously use hired labour but only for tasks they deemed difficult and time-consuming. NNH, who has a hectare of a mango farm, uses family labour for tasks such as watering, pruning and spraying. He however hires labour for weeding, planting and harvesting. His son, who was in the university during the time of the study described the tasks they perform as follows:

> When the mangoes were planted, we used to go to the farm to water the plants, to prune and spray. Sometimes, I carried the knapsack sprayer and followed my father while he sprayed. We sometimes helped in harvesting too (Life history interview, SSM, 25 years old, Somanya, 14 May 2015)

Other smallholder farmers use family labour on some farms and a combination of family and hired labour for other crops. Atipu cultivates two acres of mango works on that farm with his wife. However, on his maize and cassava farms, he employs on average five labourers for tasks such as weeding and planting. The literature on agrarian labour in smallholder agriculture has mainly focused on its unpaid nature, especially of wives and children (von Bülow and Sørensen 1993). In our study areas, we found that the unpaid family labour is waning and giving way to a form of remuneration for children in particular in agricultural households. In these smallholder commercial agriculture production households, children reported receiving wages for the tasks they carried out on household farms. For instance, an 18-year-old Senior High School student works as a labourer on farms in his community for payment. In addition, when he worked on the household's farm, he was paid for some specific tasks. He explained this when he said:

> We [children] work on the household's farm as labourers. We are paid when we carry the debris after weeding. I have been receiving payment for some works I do on our farms for the past three years (Life history, Pretsea, 5 May 2015).

The labour of wives has also undergone some changes. Generally, wives received no pay for their labour on the family's farms. However, they are partly, and sometimes totally in charge of processing and marketing the farm produce. Husbands sometimes compensate wives with farms they create purposefully for them which wives controlled. Some smallholder farmers segmented the tasks on farms and using family or hired labour when it is necessary. An oil palm farmer recounted the labour practices:

> You know, no one can work on that land alone so my sister, nephews and nieces help me on the farm. When it gets to certain stages we go in for hired labour to help us, especially for harvesting. After harvesting, my sister and nephews transport the fruits to the buyers at Norpalm. Whatever we get from the day's sale, we deduct our expenses from it and each family member who worked on the farm receives some payment (Life history, JBA, 47 years, Pretsea, 17 May 2015).

The shift from unpaid household labour to paid household labour for specific tasks on smaller farms shows a fast changing agrarian landscape. Farmers who paid their adult children may do this to motivate them to work on the farm. Labour scarcity and rising costs in agrarian areas make the payment for adult children labour a pragmatic strategy since in the past, especially in the forest belt, children often protested the demands their family made on them by out-migrating to work autonomously (Amoah 1995; Amanor 2010). In another vein, the resistance to the exploitation of family labour also shows in family members deserting family farms and either working on other farms for wages or taking new jobs outside the family's economic activities. The changing labour relations in both the plantation and commercial farming areas indicate that even farmers with small landholdings are obliged to pay for family labour which is often not discussed in agrarian labour studies. The commercialization of family labour is a response to the changing social relations of agricultural production in the rural communities.

Although family labour is still used by wealthy large-scale farmers, it is not as prominent as the earlier literature on agrarian labour suggest. With regard to children working on large-scale farms, many wealthy large-scale farmers have been able to sponsor the education of their children and as such, those children are not interested in farming in the countryside. In a few cases, however, the sons of some wealthy farmers have returned to the countryside to work on their parents' farms as farm managers. Some of these sons reported that they did not get jobs after school or lost their jobs in urban areas and had returned to take farm management positions in their parents' farms. For instance, MTE, the son of a mango farmer in Somanya, returned to work on his father's farm after he lost his job in Accra.

> I started working for my father for the past two years. I used to come and assist him on the farm occasionally in the past when I was in Accra. I lost the work I was doing and so I returned. I work with my father on contract basis so I don't have a regular pay (MTE, 37 years, University Graduate, Son of farmer, Somanya).

It is clear that the son of this wealthy farmer took the work for convenience sake and expected a type of income that is not usually present in agricultural production of the kind his father operated. Other educated sons who worked on the farms of their large-scale commercial farms had already worked on the farms since childhood and often combined with schooling. These are mainly seen as successors and therefore, even though they received no payments, they considered the final handing over of the entire farm to them as the natural course to compensate them for their investment in the farm.

With reference to the role of wives on large-scale farms, our findings indicated that many of the women who worked alongside their husbands at the initial stages of the farming enterprise are likely to be 'pushed out' of the farm by their husbands when the farms expand and their husbands become wealthier. Our interviews show that at the initial stages of the farming enterprise, many wives of smallholder farmers cook for labourers, and render other unpaid services on the farms. The wives also sometimes combine farming with trading and often the serve as the main aggregators of crops from the household farm. The income from their trading activities are sometimes invested in the family farming, mainly for hiring labour and buying input. However, as the farms expand and the husbands become richer, they tend to change the labour practices that required the services of their wives. For instance, those wealthy farmers who provide food for labourers would contract local food vendors to provide the food in lieu of asking their wives to do so. As noted already, the wealthier farmers with increasing incomes are able to hire labour to replace unpaid family labour, especially that of wives. In a few cases, the wives, having been pushed out of their roles related to farming, are reassigned roles such as local marketing of the crop and also trading. However, this is not particularly a positive outcome for wives as they complained that they were not only pushed out from the farms but also their husband no longer discussed the operations of the farms with them. Indeed, many of the wives of the wealthy farmers did not know the locations of the new lands their husbands acquired, the amount spent on the acquisition, the terms and conditions of such acquisitions and other general farm management issues. Additionally, the women did not know the terms and conditions pertaining to the supplies that their husbands sent to the buyers. Consequently, women's power in the household weakened with increasing wealth of their husbands and the opportunities that the farms brought. The farming history of 60-year-old MAT and his 50-year-old wife (AA) illustrates this scenario. When MAT started his farm in the late 1980s, he cultivated fruits on one hectare of land as he didn't have money. The wife was working with him on the farm. She reported that she used to fetch water into barrels that were used to irrigate the crops. She was also taking care of their children and going to market to sell some of the fruits from the household farm. She went to the market four times a week, often waking up as early as 12 midnight. During the time of our research, MAT was a wealthy farmer with a farm size of 250 ha on which he had several crops including mango, papaya, citrus, cocoa, plantain, cassava, oil palm, coconut and others. The wife reported that as the husband became very rich and employed 10 permanent and over 60 casual workers, she was no longer given any chance to work on the farm: *"I used to go to the farm a lot but it got to a stage he said he needs his privacy and therefore stopped me"*. AA is now a trader but knows very little about her husband's farms. MAT confirmed his wife's exclusion from the farming enterprise. He also reported that he took major asset acquisition decisions without recourse to his wife and gave the following explanation:

> I have a plot in Kumasi, Adoagyir and Doboro. I am building on those plots. If my wife asks me, I would tell her but it is not necessary for her to know what I am doing with my plots. All that matters is that what she wants, I do it for her. There is no need for us to go into an agreement about anything.

AA reported also that although it was proper for her husband to take decisions with her, she would not pursue the matter for the sake of conjugal peace since asking for accountability would be deemed 'impolite' and a case of 'meddling' in his affairs. She also noted that the expansion of the farm has further pushed her husband away from taking domestic responsibilities that he used to do:

> When I married my husband and at the early stages when the farm was small, he used to help me pound fufu but now, if I make a mistake of telling him to help, he may say something that would be too painful to bear. You know when men become rich, their wives can no longer ask them to help with any house chores. The wives cannot even get access to them to chat. So there is nothing I can do.

Similar to the findings in the commercial farming area, the wives of some of the wealthy oil palm farmers reported cases in which their husbands 'locked them out' of the family's farming enterprise. For instance, MM's wife has her own 15-acre oil palm farm but mainly engages in trading while her husband deals with production and marketing issues on the 400-acre farm. She reported that they used to work together on the large plantation but the husband pushed her away when he became wealthier.

During in-depth interviews, the wealthy farmers who pushed their wives out from gaining from the farms usually justified their actions on the grounds that "women are greedy and if they know what we earn, their demands would be high". Wealthy male farmers said women are too inquisitive and therefore they did not want them to be near the farm to 'worry' them and other workers. Some other farmers, discouraged the women from coming to the farm since they claimed that women are too 'fragile' and therefore unable to stand the stress of farming. Yet other farmers reported that they pushed their wives from the farms in order to diversify household's economic activities. The findings resonates with the concept of 'housewifization' which was used by Mies (1986) to explain how the labour of wives shifts during the course of the development of the farms.

While some researchers tend to present family farming in terms of unitary model whereby all actors are working for the common benefit of the family wealthy farmers generally end up cheating their wives in the sharing of the family cake from farming. Consistent with cases reported elsewhere, the exclusion of women from direct farm management reduces their control over how household income is spent (Waswa et al. 2012). Recent scholarship has shown that in many cases, women who have been marginalized in the sharing of proceeds of farming may resist marginalization by withdrawing their labour-power from the household and either cultivating their own cash crops elsewhere or working for wages on neighbouring farms (Watts 1994; Prowse 2012; Smalley 2013). In many of the cases presented, the women who have been marginalized rather go into trading as many of them reported that they have no lands to farms on. The findings also show that the increasing commercialization of agriculture increased the marginalization of women in agrarian households. This scenario shows how agriculture commercialization and its attendant resource enclosures can deepen social differentiation in households and push women further back into reproductive roles (Levien 2017).

Conclusion

Social relations of production are in constant shifts in agrarian Ghana and often in tandem with the transformations in the rural areas. In this chapter, we argued that there is an emergence of new labour practices and the continuation of old ones. These changes are occurring as result of the changing social relations of production, socioeconomic conditions and global labour standards. These changes affect the structure of household production, family labour relations, the labour relations between labourers and farm owners. The changing labour relations reflect pre-existing gender and class relations. Although agricultural commercialization presents both men and women with the employment opportunities which is important for economic empowerment (see Sen 1999), the ability of poor families to benefit from these are constrained by their levels of skills, education, and wealth status. Also, the need to combine formal work with domestic and reproductive roles affects women's participation in production circuits with higher wage potentials. The increasing casualization of labour in formal large farms is a source of worry in getting people out of poverty in the context of increasing scarcity of land and land values. Casual labour in more equitable land distribution scenarios where small and medium-scale farms dominate can be more beneficial as wages from seasonal labour is used as investments and coping mechanisms for smaller farmers. Our evidence shows that the failure of income to rise in accordance with rising inflation and cost of living in an economy characterized by increasing proletarianization deepens poverty and reduces livelihood opportunities of the poor categories of society. Low incomes and poor employment benefits due to poor labour regulations or the lack of enforcement of such regulations in a neoliberal landscape compounds the woes of the poorer segments of the labour market. While workers benefit more when they are protected by the state, state enforcement of welfare measures such as minimum wage, are not strictly enforced at the informal sector. As noted elsewhere, farm worker trade unions have been constrained by dispersed nature of the agricultural workforce (see Cramer et al. 2008).

The findings also suggest that whilst both husbands and wives work equally on the family farms of poor households, wealthy male farmers are likely to lock out their wives from the households' agricultural enterprise due to unequal gendered power relations. The findings are consistent with previous findings on intra-household decision-making which suggests that women tend to be given control over family decision-making only in poor households where resources are difficult to manage. Additionally, while children from poor families may receive limited or no payment for their labour on the farm, some sons of wealthy farmers are returning to farming villages to work as highly paid managers of their fathers' farms. This is because commercialization of agriculture introduces a new dynamic into how farms are conceptualized as business entities quite differently from the peasant production mode which serves mainly household consumption prerequisites.

While it is widely known that different agricultural models require different labour needs and arrangements, we tracked the changes in labour practices and relations in two sites that are synonymous with each of the models. We have also mapped out the labour practices that have remained the same and why they have not changed. Additionally, we discussed the new directions in the labour relations pertaining to gender and class and how these affected the social relations of production. The findings in this study demonstrate that labour is as important as land in agricultural production and therefore its changing dynamics must be studied to put into sharper perspectives the trajectory of agricultural development. The conclusions could serve as a guide to policy makers to critically examine the evidence of the impacts of agricultural commercialization and the changing fortunes of farmers on gender and class relations while linking these to land and labour.

References

Abdul Korah, G. B. (2008). Ka Bie Ba Yor: Labor Migration Among the Dagaaba of the Upper West Region of Ghana, 1936–1957. *Nordic Journal of African Studies, 17*(1), 1–19.

Addo-Fening, R. (1997). *Akyem Abuakwa 1700–1943: From Ofori Panin to Sir Ofori Atta. No. 19* (Trondheim Studies in History, African Series No.1). Department of History, Norwegian University of Science and Technology.

Akyeampong, E., & Hippolyte, F. (2012, April). The Contribution of African Women to Economic Growth and Development: Historical Perspectives and Policy Implications Part I: The Pre-Colonial and Colonial Periods. *Policy Research Working Papers.* https://doi.org/10.1596/1813-9450-6051.

Amanor, S. K. (2010). Family Values, Land Sales and Agricultural Commodification in South- Eastern Ghana. *Africa, 80*(1), 104–125.

Amoah, J. E. K. (1995) Development of Consumption, Commercial Production and Marketing, Cocoa Outline Series 1, Accra: Jemre Enterprises Limited.

Chambati, W., Mazwi, F., & Mberi, S. (2018). Agrarian Accumulation and Peasant Resistance in Africa. In *Inclusive Development in Africa: Transformation of Global Relations.* Dakar/Pretoria: African Institute for South Africa & CODESRIA.

Cotula, L., Vermeulen, S., Leonard, R., & Keeley, J. (2009). *Land Grab or Development Opportunity? Agricultural Investment and International Land Deals in Africa.* London/Rome: IIED/FAO/IFAD.

Cramer, C., Oya, C., & Sender, J. (2008, November). *Rural Labour Markets in Sub-Saharan Africa* (Policy Brief, 1). SOAS, Centre for Development Policy and Research.

De Shutter, O. (2011). How Not to Think of Land-Grabbing: Three Critiques of Large-Scale Investments in Farmland. *The Journal of Peasant Studies, 38*(2), 249–279.

Graham, Y. (1993). *Law, State and the Internationalisation of Agricultural Capital in Ghana: A Comparison of Colonial Export Production and Post-Colonial Production for the Home Market*. PhD Thesis, University of Warwick.

Grischow, J. D. (1998). *A History of Development in the Northern Territories of the Gold Coast, 1899–1957*. A Doctor of Philosophy thesis submitted to the Department of History, Queen's University, Ontario, Canada.

Gyapong, A. Y. (2019). Land Deals, Wage Labour, and Everyday Politics. *Land, 8*(94), 1–21.

Hall, R. (2011). Land Grabbing in Southern Africa: The Many Faces of the Investor Rush. *Review of African Political Economy, 38*(128), 193–214.

Hall, R., Scoones, I., & Tsikata, D. (2017). Plantations, Outgrowers and Commercial Farming in Africa: Agricultural Commercialisation and Implications for Agrarian Change. *The Journal of Peasant Studies, 44*(3), 515–537.

Hill, P. (1961). The Migrant Cocoa Farmers of Southern Ghana. *Journal of the International African Institute, 31*(3), 209–230.

Hill, P. (1963). *The Migrant Cocoa- Farmers of Southern Ghana: A Study in Rural Capitalism*. Cambridge: Cambridge University Press.

Hunter, J. M. (1963). Cocoa Migration and Patterns of Land Ownership in the Densu Valley Near Suhum, Ghana. *Transactions and Papers (Institute of British Geographers), 33*, 61–87. Wiley.

Krumbiegel, K., Maertens, M. and Wollni, M. (2017). *The Role of Fairtrade Certification for Wages and Job Satisfaction of Plantation Workers* (RTG 1666 Global Food Discussion Paper No. 100). Revised Draft: Göttingen: Germany.

Levien, M. (2017). Gender and Land Dispossession: A Comparative Analysis. *The Journal of Peasant Studies, 44*(6), 1111–1134.

Li, T. M. (2011). Centering Labor in the Land Grab Debate. *Journal of Peasant Studies, 38*(2), 281–298.

Mies, M. (1986). *Patriarchy and Accumulation on a World Scale: Women in the International Division of Labour*. London: Zed Books Ltd..

Nyantakyi-Frimpong, H., & Kerr, R. B. (2017). Land Grabbing, Social Differentiation, Intensified Migration and Food Security in Northern Ghana. *The Journal of Peasant Studies, 44*(2), 421–444.

Obeng, F. A., Wrigley-Asante, C., & Teye, J. K. (2015). Working Conditions in Ghana's Export Processing Zone and women's Empowerment. *Work Organisation, Labour & Globalization, 9*(2), 64–78.

Okali, C. (1983). *Cocoa and Kinship in Ghana: The Matrilineal Akan of Ghana*. London: Kegan Paul for the International African Institute.

Plange, N. K. (1979). Under Development in Northern Ghana: Natural Causes or Colonial Capitalism? *Review of African Political Economy, 15/16*(May–December), 4–14.

Poulton, C., Tyler, G., Hazell, P., Dorward, A., Kydd, J., & Stockbridge, M. (2008). Commercial Agriculture in Africa: lessons from success and failure.

Background paper for the 'Competitive Agriculture in Sub-Saharan Africa' study. World Bank: Washington D.C.

Prowse, M. (2012). *Contract Farming in Developing Countries: A Review. À Savoir, 12, February 2012*. Agence Française de Development. Available at: http://www.afd.fr/webdav/site/afd/shared/PUBLICATIONS/RECHERCHE/Scientifiques/ A-savoir/12-VA-A-Savoir.pdf

Scully, B., & Britwum, A. O. (2019). Labour Reserves and Surplus Populations: Northern Ghana and the Eastern Cape of South Africa. *Journal of Agrarian Change, 19*, 407–426.

Sen, A. (1999). *Development as freedom*. Oxford: Oxford University Press.

Sen, G., & Batliwala, P. H. (2000). "Empowering Women for Reproductive Rights", in H.B. Presser and G. Sen (eds.) *Women's Empowerment and Demographic Processes: Moving beyond Cairo*. Oxford University Press, Oxford, pp. 15–36.

Sitko, N. J., & Jayne, T. S. (2014). Exploitative Briefcase Businessmen, Parasites, and Other Myths and Legends: Assembly Traders and the Performance of Maize Markets in Eastern and Southern Africa. *World Development, 54*, 56–67.

Smalley, R. (2013). *Plantations, Contract Farming and Commercial Farming Areas in Africa: A Comparative Review* (Land and Agricultural Commercialisation in Africa (LACA) Working Paper 055). Sussex: Future Agricultures.

Tashakkori, A., & Teddlie, C. (2010). Putting the Human Back in "Human Research Methodology": The Researcher in Mixed Methods Research. *Journal of Mixed Method, 4*(4), 271–227.

Teye, J. K. (2012). Benefits, Challenges, and Dynamism of Positionalities Associated with Mixed Methods Research in Developing Countries: Evidence from Ghana. *Journal of Mixed Methods Research, 6*(4), 379–391.

Teye, K. J., & Torvikey, G. D. (2018). The political economy of agricultural commercialisation in Ghana: A Review. *Agriculture Policy Research in Africa Working Paper: WP/015/June 2018*. University of Sussex: Brighton.

Torvikey, G. D. (2018). Labour Casualisation and Youth Employment in Ghana's Formal Private Sector. *IDS Bulletin, 49*(5), 31–44.

Tsikata, D., & Yaro, J. A. (2014). When a Good Business Model Is Not Enough: Land Transactions and Gendered Livelihood Prospects in Rural Ghana. *Feminist Economics, 20*(1), 202–226.

von Bülow, D., & Sørensen, A. (1993, March). Gender and Contract Farming: Tea Outgrower Schemes in Kenya. *Review of African Political Economy, 56*, 38–52.

Waswa, F., Gweyi-Onyango, J. P., & Mcharo, M. (2012). Contract Sugarcane Farming and Farmers' Incomes in the Lake Victoria Basin, Kenya. *Journal of Applied Biosciences, 52*, 3685–3695.

Watts, M. J. (1994). Life Under Contract. In P. D. Little & M. J. Watts (Eds.), *Living Under Contract: Contract Farming and Agrarian Transformation in Sub-Saharan Africa* (pp. 21–77). Madison: University of Wisconsin Press.

Yaro, J. A., Teye, J. K., & Torvikey, G. D. (2017). Agricultural Commercialisation Models, Agrarian Dynamics and Local Development in Ghana. *The Journal of Peasant Studies, 44*(2012), 538–554.

Yidu, P. K. D., & Dzorgbo, D. S. (2016). The State and Mango Export Crop Production in Ghana. *Ghana Social Science Journal, 13*(2), 185–208.

CHAPTER 20

Adivasi Women, Agrarian Change and Forms of Labour in Neo-liberal India

Archana Prasad

This chapter elaborates the different dimensions of the gendered nature of semi-proletarianization and proletarianization of the adivasi social groups after the period of neo-liberal reforms. It shows that the integration of the adivasis in general, and adivasi women in particular, has been a result of agrarian distress and macro-economic trends that have structured the patterns of dispossession, displacement and urbanization in the last two decades. In doing so, the chapter contradicts the view which holds that communitarian structures have been playing an important part in the division of labour within adivasi communities. This chapter also contests the view that there is an autonomous sphere of existence of the subsistence economy of the adivasis and that the role of the adivasi women is largely

Originally published in *Agrarian South: Journal of Political Economy, Vol. 5 No. 1*

A. Prasad (✉)
Jawaharlal Nehru University, New Delhi, India

P. Jha et al. (eds.), *Labour Questions in the Global South*,
https://doi.org/10.1007/978-981-33-4635-2_20

confined to unpaid labour within the sphere of subsistence. As the analysis here shows, the blurred boundaries between subsistence and commercial activities have ensured that there is hardly autonomous space for the adivasi households to carry out their activities, which has several implications for the life of adivasi women. Lastly, the chapter counters the oft-repeated proposition that communities and communitarian structures can stand in opposition to the labour market and protect the interests of the adivasi women if they are democratized. It is shown here that both matrilineal and patrilineal communities have similar degrees of semi-proletarianization and proletarianization of adivasi women, although such a process is influenced by regional trends and landholding patterns. Thus, the thesis that communitarian production and distribution systems guide the class formation process does not, in fact, hold in the case of most adivasi regions. Rather, the labour market is guided by macro-economic processes that often neutralize the influence of these structures.

Introduction

This chapter addresses the changing forms of labour amongst adivasi women in the context of agrarian transformations in neo-liberal India. 'Adivasi' is a politically charged term and a form of self-expression used by 'tribes', which have been protesting against being exploited and marginalized for the last two centuries. In constitutional terms, many of the groups describing themselves as 'adivasis' are also known as Scheduled Tribes.[1] Their trajectory of development has been ridden with processes that have led to their historical semi-proletarianization since the time of colonial capitalism. This has been a long process entailing the dispossession of adivasis from their lands and their integration into the labour market under different stages of capitalism. While reviewing the debates and the processes of contemporary proletarianization and semi-proletarianization[2] of adivasi people, this chapter shows that. there has been a qualitative change and intensification of these phenomena in the last three decades. One of the most significant differences between earlier times and the present has been the gendered nature of the processes of proletarianization and semi-proletarianization.

The impact of state-led processes of dispossession and urbanization of adivasi households has been fundamentally characterized by changes in the labouring patterns of adivasi women. Scholarship on the character of this impact has largely ignored the gender dimension because it has taken a rather romantic view of the status of adivasi women in their communities. In such an analysis, community has been given greater prominence than class in the determination of the division of labour. Thus, prominent scholars have suggested that adivasi societies do not fit into a prototype classification of peasantry and proletariat—their division of labour is determined through communitarian principles and customary laws (Agarwal 2010).[3] The position of women is located by anthropologists within such customary laws, and it is suggested that adivasi women have enjoyed equal status with their male counterparts in both patrilineal and matrilineal societies. This has implications for understanding the division of labour within adivasi societies. From this perspective, community structures are democratic and egalitarian and have a fundamental role in structuring the division of labour and the functions performed by women (Kelkar et al. 2005). Community structures are also seen as deterrents to the adverse integration of adivasi people into the labour markets. This argument forms the core of the anthropological and historical work on adivasis today. However, the analysis in this chapter shows that this conclusion may not be valid: Communitarian structures have little bearing on the division of labour in contemporary times. Rather, the penetration of the labour market in adivasi societies has been structured by macro-economic processes of dispossession and the two-decade-long agrarian crisis. The position of women is fundamentally affected by these factors (Prasad 2010).

The second strand of scholarship, whose arguments are reviewed and contested by this chapter, states that there is something in the form of a 'household subsistence' as an autonomous mode of production that has escaped both feudalism and capitalism. The ability of this household subsistence economy to reproduce itself has structured the agrarian transition of intermediate classes which, according to this view, retained their control over both capital and labour. Thus, autonomous spaces have been created and the social structures within such systems have not been altered much by the penetration of capital. Hence, these authors conclude that capitalism does not exist within adivasi societies and that they are only integrated into the larger system through 'circuits of capital' (Shah 2013). Such an argument has similarities with the previous perspective that privileges community structures as the foundation of the division of labour. Since adivasi household subsistence economies enjoy an autonomous space, they also retain the authority to structure the division of labour according to community norms. This creates an advantageous position for women, since communitarian structures are inherently more egalitarian than the labour market.

However, as will be shown here, such an understanding is fraught with historical inaccuracies and misreads the way in which capital moulds the labour process in local economies. It ignores the larger dialectic between agrarian societies and political processes which lead to dispossession and accumulation. These processes are fundamental to structuring the integration of adivasi people into the labour markets. In this sense, 'social structures of accumulation' (Harris-White 2013) are not independent of class relations and play a limited role in influencing the division of labour in the current times. Hence, while patriarchy, religion and caste may be mediators in the capital–labour relationship, they are not necessarily independent of the class-based structures of accumulation. Rather, they form different layers of overlapping structures of accumulation and generate their own politics vis-à-vis the state. This chapter shows that the position of adivasi women is integrally related to this process of mediation and commercialization of subsistence which determines and influences their integration into circuits of capital through the labour market.

This chapter is divided into four parts. The first section explores the agrarian distress and increased patterns of dispossession that have occurred due to the neo-liberal reforms. In this context, the role of communitarian institutions in structuring the division of labour is explored in the second section. Using examples from both patrilineal and matrilineal communities, the chapter contests the view of egalitarian communitarian structures and shows that the traditional division of labour within these social groups lays the foundations for their adverse integration into the labour market in the pre-neo-liberal period. Following this, the third section analyses the question of property rights and structural inequalities, with particular focus on women. This section particularly problematizes the relationship between women and control over land. In this sense, the different patterns of proletarianization and semi-proletarianization of adivasi women are influenced by both broad macro-economic processes and these structural inequalities which have been largely ignored in the literature so far (Kothari and Srivastava 2012; Padel and Das 2010). The state-level decadal census of 2001 and 2011 is used to analyse the changing occupational structure in adivasi societies and locates the gendered pattern of adivasi proletarianization and semi-proletarianization within this context. In particular, it focuses on the structure of the labour market and the participation of adivasis, particularly adivasi women.

Within this broad framework of gendered labour participation, the last section of this chapter follows the changes in the labouring patterns of different patrilineal and matrilineal communities using census data for individual 'Scheduled Tribes'. The analysis is used to interrogate the argument that social and communitarian structures still play an important role in structuring the division of labour in adivasi societies.

Neo-liberalism, Agrarian Distress and the Patterns of Dispossession

The advent of neo-liberal reforms from the early 1990s was based on four policy initiatives that influenced a three-decade-long agrarian crisis and the patterns of labour in adivasi regions. First, the removal of subsidies for agricultural inputs by a neo-liberal state and of quantitative trade restrictions in all agricultural products changed the very nature of agricultural production. The cost of agricultural production increased substantially, and this resulted in indebtedness leading to more than two million farmers' suicides since the mid-1990s. Furthermore, the deceleration of agricultural growth has also led to a lack of decent jobs in the agricultural sector, thus severely impacting on the prospects of adivasi workers, particularly women, who largely depended on neighbourhood work for paid employment. This displacement of livelihoods is one of the essential elements which propelled an increasing number of women into casual wage labour (Padhi 2012; Prasad 2010).

The second important factor has been the paradigm shift in natural resource and land management. One of the main features for these environmental regulations was the change they effected in the land use pattern by allowing big projects inside adivasi regions, which were predominantly forested areas. The diversion of forestlands for non-forest purposes altered the pattern of land use and influenced the trend of growing landlessness. The area of forestland diverted for large industrial projects increased from about 21,000 hectares per annum in 1990–1999 to about 71,000 hectares per annum in 2006–2008. This increasing pace of diversion created its own patterns of dispossession and landlessness. The number of adivasi households which had no access to cultivated land increased from 32.1 per cent in 1999–2000 to 38.4 per cent in 2011–2012. At the same time, the number of landholdings below one hectare decreased from 42.2 to 38.7 per cent and the landholdings between one and two hectares also decreased from 16.2 to 14 per cent between 1999–2000 and 2011–2012. This shows the growing inequity within the adivasi societies. The regional variations in the pattern of differentiation are shown in Table 20.1.

Table 20.1 Patterns of access to cultivated land, 1999–2012

Percentage change of access to cultivated lands by Scheduled Tribes, 1999–2000 to 2011–2012							
State	*Population*	*Landless*	*0.01–0.40 ha*	*0.1–1.0 ha*	*1.01–2.0 ha*	*2.01–4.0 ha*	*More than 4.01 ha*
Chhattisgarh	30.6	−0.2	4.5	3.9	6.1	−11.7	−2.7
Gujarat	14.8	4.8	−16	11.5	−1.9	−2.7	−1.1
Jharkhand	26.2	14.5	7.6	−25.9	−5.8	−1.2	0.1
Madhya Pradesh	21.1	11.9	−5.9	−2.3	1.3	−3.1	−1.8
Maharashtra	9.4	−0.5	5.6	−2.8	−6.5	1.7	2.5
Odisha	22.8	6.4	−5.7	−0.6	−1.3	0.8	0.5
Rajasthan	13.5	5.8	3.4	−8.8	−1.9	0.2	1.4
Arunachal Pradesh	68.8	8.7	−12.1	−9	7.2	8	4.2
Assam	12.4	18	−4.1	−13.4	−2.2	1.8	−0.1
Manipur	35.1	14.3	−13.8	−3	1.3	0.2	1
Meghalaya	86.1	14.2	7.7	−8.4	−11.8	−1.5	−0.3
Mizoram	94.5	10.6	2.3	6.6	−16.1	−3.4	0
Nagaland	86.5	0	9	1.8	−17.9	4.1	2.9
Tripura	33.1	−1.6	−1.8	3.4	0.7	−0.7	0
All India	8.2	6.5	−1.5	−3	−2.2	0.6	−0.3

Source: Calculated from different rounds of NSSO, *Employment and Unemployment Survey amongst Social Groups*

The diverse patterns of dispossession influence the trends of semi-proletarianization and influence women's labour in the post-reforms period. The data in Table 20.1 show that there is a clear divide between the patterns in the northeast, central and eastern India. The mineral states of Jharkhand and Madhya Pradesh have also seen a spurt in landlessness. The most significant differentiation is seen in the state of Arunachal Pradesh where the increase in landlessness is accompanied by an increase in the number of landholders with more than two hectares of land. Within this broad trend, there is a third tendency in states such as Gujarat and Chhattisgarh which have seen a spurt in marginal landholdings. This largely indicates changing agrarian relations, especially with the adoption of commercial and corporate farming in these regions by the state governments (Mehta 2005; Prasad 2014).

The third important feature of agrarian change has been the rapid process of urbanization. The census data for 2011 clearly show that the decadal rate of growth of urban population amongst the Scheduled Tribes has been higher than the overall growth of Scheduled Tribe population between 2001 and 2011.

Table 20.2 shows that the decadal rate of growth of the adivasi population in the urban areas is almost twice that of the adivasi population in the rural areas. It is also significantly higher than the decadal growth rates of the population at the state level. This clearly indicates a rapid pace of urbanization which has influenced and structured the changes within rural India.

The fourth trend which exemplifies the agrarian distress and its impacts on forms of adivasi labour is household migration. As the latest migration data show, the number of Scheduled Tribe migrant households in urban areas increased from 2.9 to 6 per cent between 2001 and 2011.

This rise in household migration has usually been interpreted as associational migration (or migration for marriage) by women (NSSO 2010, p. 17). However, a recent survey shows that almost all women migrating to the city are also forced to look for work even if the main reason for their migration may be associational. The survey found that about a third of all female long-term migrants were looking for work in the areas in which they migrated. The survey also shows that at least 59 per cent of the circular short-term migrants were women workers (Agnihotri et al. 2013, p. 5). These data indicate that the level of migration of adivasi women is a substantial proportion of all women migrants. Also, the increase in household

Table 20.2 Decadal growth in urban adivasi population, 2001–2011

		Decadal growth of population		
State	*Percentage of adivasi population*	*Total*	*Rural*	*Urban*
Chhattisgarh	30.6	18.2	15.4	68.2
Gujarat	14.8	19.2	16.8	45.7
Jharkhand	26.2	22	21	32.3
Madhya Pradesh	21.1	25.2	24.7	32.1
Maharashtra	9.4	22.5	20.3	37.9
Odisha	22.8	17.7	16.8	33.4
Rajasthan	13.5	30.2	29.4	43.6
Arunachal Pradesh	68.8	35	30.3	63.8
Assam	12.4	17.4	16.2	42.2
Manipur	35.1	21.8	12.1	216.8
Meghalaya	86.1	28.3	27	35.1
Mizoram	94.5	23.4	17.8	29.4
Nagaland	86.5	-3.6	-15.4	75.7
Tripura	33.1	17.5	15.5	93.7
All India	**8.2**	**23.7**	**21.3**	**49.7**

Source: Census of India (2011), highlights of census data, Scheduled Tribes

migration shows that agrarian distress has led to a drying up of agricultural employment and labour mobility, the patterns of which are yet to be fully explained.

Communitarian Institutions and the Labour Processes

The developments within the agrarian economy outlined above contextualize the contemporary debates on the status of women and the nature of the division of labour within adivasi communities. Anthropological and sociological approaches have focused on the relatively egalitarian division of labour within adivasi societies since historical times.[4] This division of labour is largely structured by the contingencies of household subsistence. Since adivasi women take up a pivotal role in fulfilment of these needs, they are seen as having greater freedom especially with respect to their sexual relations and their choice of partners.

However, a closer assessment of the customary laws governing community institutions reveals a different picture and shows that adivasi societies, in most cases, follow the same traditional division of labour that structures the position of women. There are both patrilineal and matrilineal adivasi social groups in India whose relations of production differ slightly because of their property structure. Though there is diversity within cultural systems, certain common principles exist within patrilineal adivasi societies across regions, such as the Gonds of central India (Hajra 1993) and the Mizos of Northeast India (Gangte 2008).

In almost all cases, women are considered the 'property of men' and have virtually no inheritance rights. This factor structures the access of women to both land and natural resources. Surveys of women in central and northeast India have revealed that patrilineal societies have been subject to a traditional division of labour, where women have assumed most of the burden of unpaid family labour, on and off the field. Although the work patterns of women have been diverse in different local and communitarian settings, some commonalities exist with respect to the forms of their labour (Nongbri 1998; Prasad 2005). The first characteristic is that most of the unpaid subsistence work is carried out by women. However, in most cases the unpaid labour has itself been integrated into the labour market, because of the commercialization of subsistence itself. Since most of the adivasis own marginal landholdings, it has been largely the women who have worked in agriculture, while men usually have gone out for higher paid labour, travelling to cities and also to other states as both agricultural labourers and non-agrarian labourers. This has structured the division of labour.

However, women have also not been confined to family or household labour. They work in the farms of the neighbourhood and undertake short-term daily migration to farms of richer farmers. Thus, we see thatthe Baiga women of Madhya Pradesh, central India, work on the fields of adivasi Gond peasants, who own large holdings on the fringes of the forests. Similarly, the women of Dumka in Jharkhand cross the river to Bengal to work on higher productivity farms. The local mobility of labour has thus been gendered and is often embedded in hegemonic communitarian structures. Hence, it is not surprising that in the case of many forest-dwelling adivasi communities practising swidden cultivation, women are not allowed to touch either the plough or the axe. By the same measure, the men consider employment in local agriculture, especially as farm servants on the fields of large and middle peasants in the same vicinity, as a lowly job only to be performed by women. Their long-distance migration has been largely in green revolution states and has fetched a much higher wage than local agricultural labour.

In terms of forest produce, while women and children undertake the collection of almost all produce, the use of this produce is mainly confined to household and family needs. In contrast, it is the men who largely control the sale of commercially valuable produce and negotiated its price with local traders in the weekly market. In this sense, custom and customary institutions create a divide between the subsistence and commercial economies, even though such a divide may not have existed in actuality because of the integration of the adivasi household into the labour and commodity markets (Prasad 1998, 2011, Chapter 4). Adivasi women also have an interface with markets, as they sell fuelwood and forest produce in order to buy household essentials. Hence, the household subsistence has also been integrated into the local market system and commercialized in a way that has made the boundaries between subsistence and commercial economies blurred. In this sense, adivasi women have been almost always integrated into the seasonal agricultural labour and forest produce commodity markets, albeit at a lower scale than men. However, their degree of proletarianization has remained partial, as they are also dependent on cultivation for their livelihood needs.

While it is expected that the patrilineal system will be discriminatory towards women, the matrilineal society has been considered to be a more egalitarian one. Here, the lineage is traced through the female line, and traditionally the inheritance is also to be determined through this lineage. The best cases of matrilineal tribes are the Garo, Khasi and Jaintia of Meghalaya, who live in the different district autonomous councils under the Sixth Schedule (Marak 2000; Phei 1974). The village courts formed under these acts are almost always dominated by village councils and chiefs who are the male elders of the community and decide the local cases with respect to inheritance, marriages, divorce and other matters concerning the daily life of these tribes. However, the pattern of matrilineal ownership gives far more autonomy and decision-making power to the male agnates and husbands of the family, much more than any woman enjoys. Although the mother is considered the head of the family, and the youngest daughter is the inheritor of the family property, this property is only held under certain conditions. For example, if a Garo heiress (or the nokna, the female head of the family) deserts her husband she loses the right to her property. In the event, the property will be temporarily held by the husband, and if the husband takes a second wife, then this property will become a part of her ancestral property. Furthermore, the nokna must marry from her paternal lineage in order to be declared an heiress. If she chooses to have a separate house, she loses her right. Thus, the burden of maintaining the purity of the 'clan' lies with the woman, thus affecting her social mobility and personal choice. The same burden does not lie with a man in the patrilineal system.

It should also be noted that the male head (or the husband of the matriarch) in the matrilineal system has an important influencing role and is in a stronger position than the female head (wife of the patriarch) within the patriarchal community. In other words, the position of men in a matrilineal system is far stronger than the position of women in a patrilineal system. The father and husband are considered the guardians of the children and managers of the property of the wife or the heiress. When a daughter refuses to support her widower father, he receives a share of the property. Furthermore, the maternal uncle, husbands and sons play a key role in the management of the property and often have de facto control. This, in turn, structures the division of labour within matrilineal societies as well. While the mobility of male members is common, it is the women who stay at home even under matriliny. In this situation, the burden of subsistence falls on the women in matriliny as well (Nongbri 2000). The discussion above shows that communitarian structures are part of a larger structure of patriarchal oppression. Their rules and authority mediate the relationship between adivasi women and the market. However, the intensification of processes of dispossession since the 1990s weakened these structures and significantly reduced their influence on structuring the division of labour.

Structural Inequalities, Women and Property Rights Since the 1990s

The impacts of neo-liberal policies and communitarian customs on the status of adivasi women are reflected in women's control over and access to land. Information on gender-disaggregated statistics on access to land is both problematic and difficult to obtain. The only source appears to be the Agricultural Census of India, which is conducted by the Department of Agriculture and Cooperation. These data provide no information on landless households, but provide information on operational holdings (or people actually cultivating the land). These data may indicate how much control women exercise over lands in cultivating households. This limited information can be used to make a gendered analysis of the structural inequalities within the agrarian economy.

The latest Agricultural Census (2011–2012) with respect to the operational holding of adivasi women is shown in Table 20.3. It is clear that close to 89 per cent of the women have no control over their lands, even though their households may have some access to the land.

Furthermore, this has been the trend over the last decade, as shown in Table 20.4. Taken together with the data above, this shows that even though there has been a marginal decadal increase in women's land control in all categories, the net result is that an average of only 11 per cent of the women control any land.

If these data are correct, they raise crucial questions about the gendered character of landlessness and its impact on the proletarianization and semi-proletarianization of women. If landlessness is defined as the lack of access to land or property rights, then most adivasi women are landless by the virtue of their gender. Given this fact, the role of adivasi women in agriculture can be that of an unpaid agricultural worker, if the nature of family labour is disaggregated. In this context, it is possible to surmise that the increased adverse integration of adivasis into the labour market also

Table 20.3 Percentage of operational holdings operated by adivasi women

States/ UTs	*0.1–1 ha*	*1–2 ha*	*2–4-ha*	*4–10 ha*	*Above 10 ha*	*All size groups*
Arunachal Pradesh	21.05	10.53	8.82	7.14	16.67	10.28
Assam	3.08	4.08	4.76	Neg	Neg	3.65
Chhattisgarh	14.47	11.82	10.09	8.65	6.25	12.40
Gujarat	14.85	15.83	15.60	16.00	20.00	15.28
Jharkhand	10.03	8.72	5.51	4.48	Neg	3.16
Madhya Pradesh	11.35	8.98	8.57	8.44	11.76	9.88
Maharashtra	18.04	16.44	8.94	12.86	14.29	16.20
Manipur	3.45	4.55	8.33	Neg	0.00	4.69
Meghalaya	35.29	32.76	37.50	37.50	Neg	34.45
Mizoram	12.00	10.00	10.00	Neg	Neg	10.87
Nagaland	16.67	15.00	10.42	8.97	12.00	10.11
Odisha	4.95	4.17	4.24	4.76	Neg	4.63
Rajasthan	6.91	5.68	4.71	3.80	Neg	5.98
Tripura	9.92	7.41	7.14	0.00	0.00	9.20
All India	**11.93**	**11.30**	**10.41**	**8.82**	7.21	**11.32**

Source: Agricultural Census of India (2011–2012)

Table 20.4 Percentage decadal change in operational holdings operated by adivasi women, 2000–2012

	0.1–1 ha	*1–2 ha*	*2–4 ha*	*4–10 ha*	*Above 10 ha*	*All Sizes*
Arunachal	-0.38	-4.47	0.49	0.48	Neg	-0.30
Assam	0.12	2.21	3.29	Neg	Neg	1.12
Chhattisgarh	2.91	2.41	2.02	1.87	1.25	2.66
Gujarat	3.00	4.32	4.96	5.36	-5.00	3.83
Jharkhand	10.03	8.72	5.51	4.48	Neg	3.16
Madhya Pradesh	2.88	1.96	2.02	1.96	4.07	2.49
Maharashtra	1.43	1.37	-4.95	0.13	-2.38	0.99
Manipur	3.45	0.00	8.33	Neg	Neg	3.13
Meghalaya	7.86	11.71	20.36	23.21	Neg	11.23
Mizoram	0.24	2.86	2.31	Neg	Neg	1.66
Nagaland	-3.33	-7.22	-0.30	3.09	6.12	2.42
Odisha	-0.06	0.11	0.14	0.51	Neg	0.16
Rajasthan	4.68	3.43	2.94	1.60	Neg	3.76
Tripura	0.45	0.79	-1.27	Neg	Neg	-0.17
All India	**2.16**	**2.81**	**2.59**	**1.96**	**1.65**	**2.51**

Source: Calculated from different years of Agricultural Census in India (2011–2012)

signifies the conversion of unpaid work into wage labour. However, this may not be a welcome step because it shows that women are disempowered both as unpaid family labour and also as wage labour in the labour market.

Adivasi Women and Labour Markets Under Neo-liberalism

The patterns of integration of adivasi women into the labour market have to be considered in the above context. The data presented below show that the macro-level tendencies in the transformation of adivasi work patterns are gendered in character and are conditioned by the rising differentiation within the adivasi societies. Although adivasi women have always shouldered, equally or disproportionally, the burden of meeting household subsistence and other needs, the pattern of their work seems to have changed in the period of the neo-liberal reforms. The graphs below illustrate the relationship between work participation rate[5] and labour force participation[6] of adivasi men and women in comparative perspective. The work participation rate refers to those who perform at least 30 days of work in the 365 days before the reference period for which the survey has been done. The long-term trends in the work participation rate of adivasi men and women are shown in Figs. 20.1, 20.2, 20.3 and 20.4.

The data shows that there has been a steady decline in the male and female work participation rates in almost all years except 2004–2005, which were considered years of distress. It is obvious that poor working families looked for low-paid work, and women who ordinarily did unpaid work in homes and family farms were forced into the labour market. It also shows that the number of adivasis getting work for at least 30 days a year had declined. However, this does not mean that adivasis were not in the labour market. It is interesting to note that the labour force participation rate (LFPR) (or the number of people in the labour market, both employed and unemployed) remained stagnant in the case of both men and women, even though the work participation declined, especially after the neo-liberal reforms. As shown, there is a sharp decline in rural and urban female LFPRs after 2004–2005. But in urban areas, the LFPR of men remains almost stagnant. Further investigation is needed to show whether men are willing to work at lower wages and, thereby, pushing adivasi women out of the labour market. But available evidence shows that

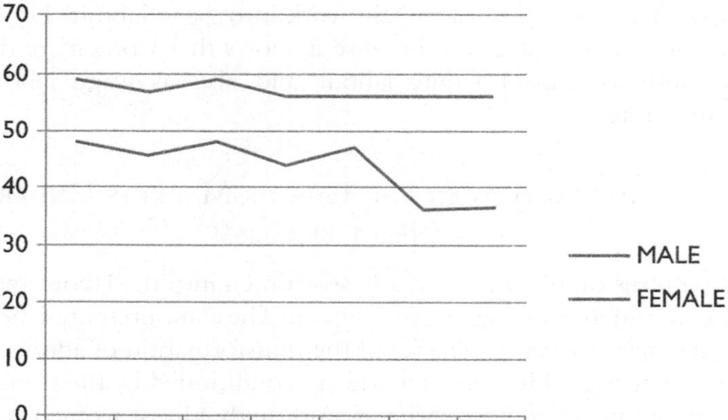

	1983	1987–88	1993–94	1999–2000	2004–05	2009–10	2011–12
MALE	58.8	56.7	59.1	55.8	56.2	55.9	55.7
FEMALE	47.8	45.4	48.2	43.8	46.4	35.9	36.4

Fig. 20.1 Rural work participation rate by gender. (Source: Calculated from different rounds of NSS data)

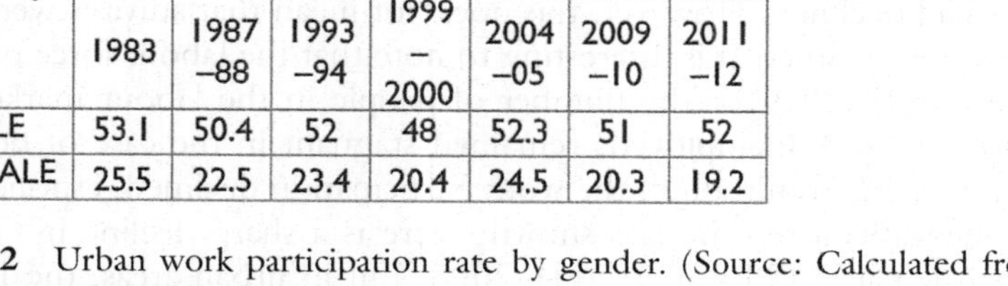

	1983	1987–88	1993–94	1999–2000	2004–05	2009–10	2011–12
MALE	53.1	50.4	52	48	52.3	51	52
FEMALE	25.5	22.5	23.4	20.4	24.5	20.3	19.2

Fig. 20.2 Urban work participation rate by gender. (Source: Calculated from different rounds of NSS data)

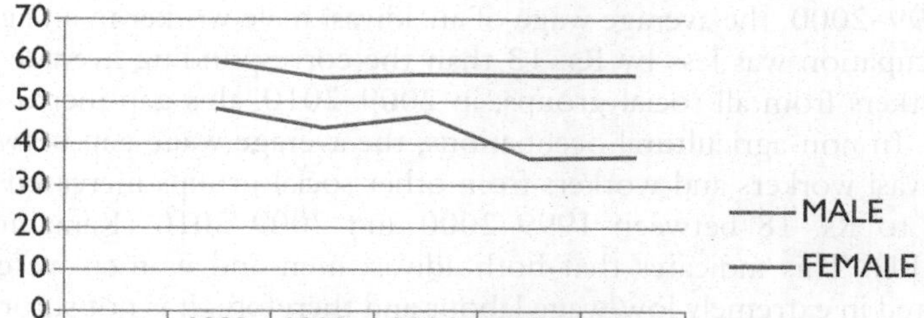

	1993–94	1999–2000	2004–05	2009–10	2011–12
MALE	59.5	56.4	56.8	56.9	56.5
FEMALE	48.3	43.9	46.6	36.2	36.9

Fig. 20.3 Rural labour force participation rate by gender. (Source: Calculated from different rounds of NSS data)

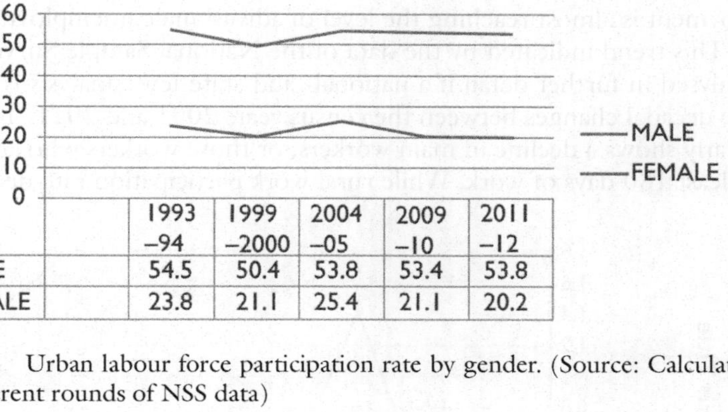

	1993–94	1999–2000	2004–05	2009–10	2011–12
MALE	54.5	50.4	53.8	53.4	53.8
FEMALE	23.8	21.1	25.4	21.1	20.2

Fig. 20.4 Urban labour force participation rate by gender. (Source: Calculated from different rounds of NSS data)

wages for both adivasi men and women are low when compared to non-adivasi populations. Hence, it is possible to surmise that adivasi men are willing to work at a lower rate than their counterparts in the rural areas.

There is virtually no data on the gender wage gap within adivasis. But discrimination between adivasis and others in agricultural wages is shown by a recent study. The study states that in 1999–2000, the daily wage earned by an adivasi male worker in an agricultural occupation was just Rs. 33 and that in 2009–2010, it increased to Rs. 73. Compared with all social groups at constant (2009–2010) prices, the authors surmise that in

1999–2000, the average wage of an adivasi male worker in an agricultural occupation was less by Rs. 13 than the corresponding average wage for workers from all social groups; in 2009–2010, this gap increased to Rs. 14. In non-agricultural occupations, the average wage gap between male adivasi workers and workers from other social groups increased from Rs. 11 to Rs. 18 between 1999–2000 and 2009–2010 (Karat and Rawal 2014). This indicates that both adivasi men and women were concentrated in extremely low-wage labour and therefore, it is not surprising that men may have been replacing women in circumstances of declining non-agricultural wage labour options.

But it is important to note that this does not necessarily mean that women are no longer entering the labour market. Figure 20.5 shows that an increasing number of women who entered the labour market were unable to find work. It is also evident, when comparing Figs. 20.5 and 20.6, that the unemployment rate of adivasi women may have surpassed that of adivasi men in the urban areas. In rural areas, too, women's unemployment is almost reaching the level of adivasi male unemployment.

This trend indicated by the data of the National Sample Survey can be analysed in further detail if a national- and state-level analysis is done for the decadal changes between the census years 2001 and 2011. Table 20.5 clearly shows a decline in main workers, or those workers who are getting at least 180 days of work. While rural work participation rate declined for

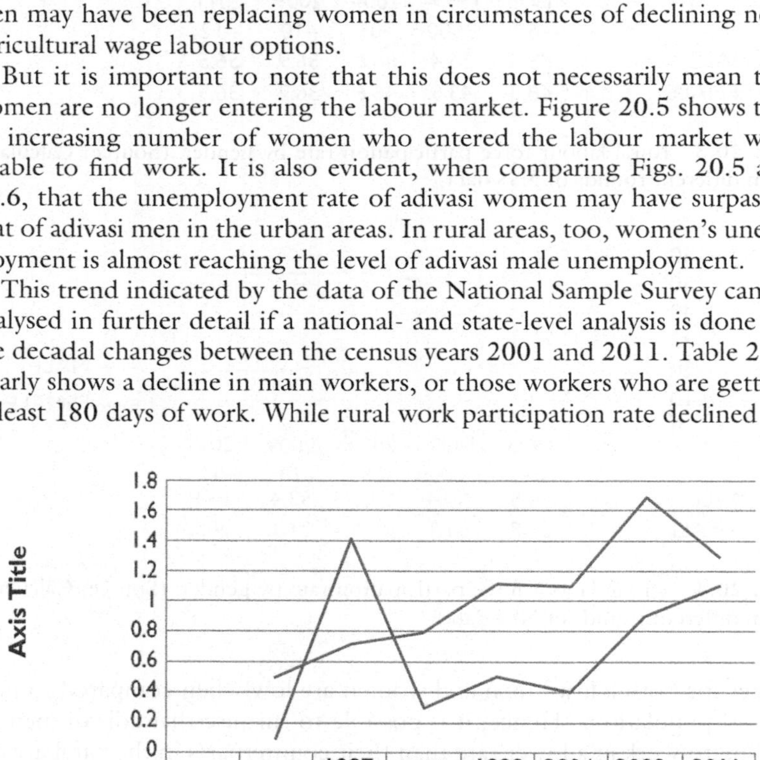

	1983	1987–88	1993–94	1999–2000	2004–05	2009–10	2011–12
MALE	0.5	0.7	0.8	1.1	1.1	1.7	1.3
FEMALE	0.1	1.4	0.3	0.5	0.4	0.9	1.1

Fig. 20.5 Rural unemployment rates by gender. (Source: Calculated from different rounds of NSS data)

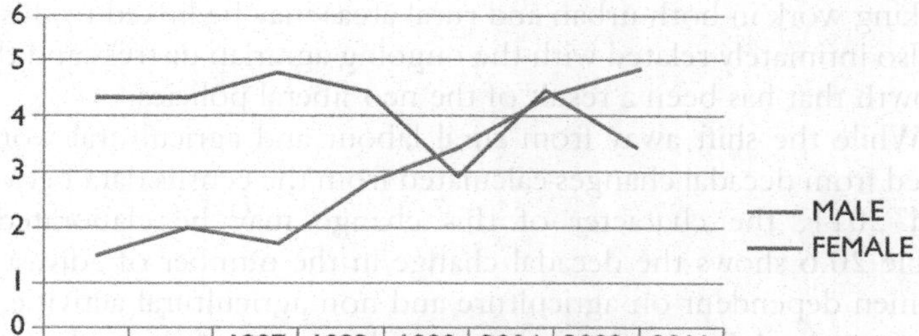

	1983	1987 –88	1993 –94	1999 –2000	2004 –05	2009 –10	2011 –12
MALE	4.3	4.3	4.7	4.4	2.9	4.4	3.4
FEMALE	1.5	2	1.7	2.8	3.4	4.3	4.8

Fig. 20.6 Urban unemployment rates by gender. (Source: Calculated from different rounds of NSS data)

Table 20.5 Decadal changes in work participation rates and main workers, 2001–2011

	Work participation rate			*Main workers*		
	Total	*Male*	*Female*	*Total*	*Male*	*Female*
Total	-0.39	0.68	-1.31	-4.16	-7.33	-0.69
Rural	-0.40	0.53	-1.28	-4.72	-8.02	-1.17
Urban	2.58	3.04	2.66	-1.04	-1.97	1.83

Sources: Calculated from Census of India (2001, 2011), Schedule Tribe Tables.

women, it has gone up marginally for men. At the same time, the work for adivasi men has declined in both urban and rural areas, but for adivasi women there appears to be a slight increase in urban work participation rates. This indicates that agrarian distress has broken the shackles of the community and that more and more adivasi women are seeking wage work in the labour market. It is interesting to note that the number of marginal women workers seeking work in the labour market has increased by about 8.18 per cent in the rural areas in the last decade. Significantly, this figure has come down by about 5.16 per cent for adivasi men.[7] Seen together with the slight increase in rural work participation rates of adivasi men, it may be concluded that adivasi men were finding more jobs in the agricultural sector than women. At the same time, the sharp rise in women seeking work in both urban and rural areas may be linked to this factor. It is also intimately related with the ongoing agrarian distress and the jobless growth that has been a result of the neo-liberal policies.

While the shift away from rural labour and agricultural work is indicated from decadal changes calculated from the census data between 2001 and 2011, the character of this change may be elaborated further. Table 20.6 shows the decadal change in the number of adivasi men and women dependent on agriculture and non-agricultural activities for their subsistence. Adivasi men and women have started depending more and more on non-agrarian work for their labour. It is also significant that the rise in urban non-agrarian work is driven by the sharp rise in female non-agricultural main and marginal workers. In the rural areas, too, non-agricultural employment amongst workers registered an increase in the last decade. This shows that agrarian distress has impacted the work patterns of women and that the changing relationship between agrarian and non-agrarian work forms the structural context of adivasi women's integration into the labour market. It also explains the sharp rise in adivasi women seeking work in the labour market and reflects the fact that the proletarianization of the adivasis is driven by the proletarianization of women at a greater degree than that of men. This is largely because the women were greatly responsible for farming activities, while adivasi men traditionally migrated for labour. The changing relationship between agrarian and non-agrarian labour is also exemplified in the recent farmer's survey of the National Sample Survey. The survey clearly shows that the LFPR of women in agriculture underwent a seasonal decline by 2.83 per cent (reflected in figures on marginal agricultural work), even between the months of July–December 2012 and January–June 2013, in its principal status (i.e., those getting more than 180 days of work in agriculture). It is also significant that if all work, principal and secondary status, is taken together, the seasonal decline in dependence on farming was 4.15 per cent for adivasi women and only approximately 1.61 per cent for adivasi men.[8] This again begs the question of whether women were being pushed out of labour market because men were being employed in low-wage agricultural jobs in an economy with jobless growth.

At a regional level, however, there are patterns that indicate multiple trajectories and diverse trends between 2001 and 2011.[9] The first trend that comes to the fore is the shift from 'main' to 'marginal' work amongst adivasi women workers and growing proletarianization of women within the rural economy. For example, in states like Rajasthan, the decadal

Table 20.6 Decadal change in classification of workers by industry, 2001–2011

	Main agricultural			*Main Non-agricultural*			*Marginal-agricultural*			*Marginal Non-agricultural*		
	Total	*Male*	*Female*	*Total*	*Male*	*Female*	*Total*	*Male*	*Female*	*Total*	*Male*	*Female*
Total	-2.51	-2.46	-2.84	2.51	2.46	2.84	-3.90	-3.74	-3.26	3.90	3.74	3.26
Rural	-0.83	-0.72	-1.19	3.64	0.72	1.19	-3.48	-3.70	-2.83	3.48	3.70	2.83
Urban	0.73	1.20	-1.30	-0.73	-1.20	1.30	-4.17	-1.65	-5.88	4.17	1.65	5.88

Sources: Calculated from Census of India (2001, 2011), Schedule Tribe Table.

decline amongst main adivasi women workers has been by 5.31 per cent. But it is important to note that the rise in marginal work has largely been in the rural sector, with 12.19 per cent rise in agricultural labour, which is about 1 per cent higher than the overall national increase of 11.37 per cent. Yet, despite this significant trend, it is also important to note that most adivasi women still depend on low-wage agricultural labour for their livelihoods. In Rajasthan alone, employment has declined by 2.66 per cent, but this is lower than the average of 2.84 per cent for adivasi women. In fact, there is an increase in the main rural adivasi women workforce in a state like Madhya Pradesh by 1.29 per cent, but this is accompanied by an increasing rate of landlessness amongst adivasi families (11.9 per cent, as per Table 20.1), thus indicating a growing proletarianization of adivasi women within the rural economy itself. The second state-level trend shows that the overall trend in non-agrarian work of women workers in rural and urban areas is increasing in both the main and marginal categories. This is evident in some eastern and central Indian states, such as Jharkhand, Odisha and Chhattisgarh. In these three states, the decline in employment for adivasi main workers is at a much higher rate than for adivasi women, in both rural and urban areas between 2001 and 2011. In Jharkhand, main rural work for adivasi men declined by almost 20 per cent, while for women it only declined by 6.63 per cent, whereas in both Odisha and Chhattisgarh it declined by approximately 11–12 per cent for men and by only about 4.5 per cent for women. This was accompanied by only marginal changes in the main adivasi women workforce in the urban areas.

However, what stands out is the increasing marginality of work in both urban and rural areas in these three states, specifically an increase in marginal work from 4.5 to 6 per cent for adivasi women and from 10 to 20 per cent for adivasi men. This difference is a result of the greater dispossession of lands through growing landlessness and marginalization of landholdings. This is reflected in the rate of increase in the number of women agricultural workers in these states (from 7 to 14 per cent), which is double the rate of increase of adivasi men agricultural workers (from 4 to 9 per cent). But the average in all these states, except for Chhattisgarh, is lower than the all-India average of 11.37 per cent for adivasi women agricultural labourers and 7.31 per cent for adivasi men agricultural labourers. This can be contrasted with the rates of increase in non-agricultural work, ranging from 4.6 to 9 per cent, which are much higher than the all-India average of 3.4 per cent. What is even more telling is the increase in non-agrarian work, which is largely in rural areas and much higher than the all-India average of 2.74 per cent for rural adivasi men. But since most of this work is seasonal in character, it is possible to surmise that men are getting much less regular work than women in these three states. Is it possible then to conclude that the burden on adivasi women to ensure survival of households is increasing? Although the data indicate this, further investigation is needed to confirm the same.

A third trend is seen in most of the Northeast Indian states, where there is a rise in non-agricultural urban work by more than 15 per cent in each state. This rise is indicative of the higher than average growth rates of urban adivasi populations in these states. But one of the main features of this increase is that though adivasi women seem to be taking to non-agrarian work, the rate of increase of such work is much higher for men than for women, sometimes even exceeding 25 per cent. In contrast, the rate of decadal increase of women's non-agrarian work remains within single digits. At the same time, the number of adivasi women workers depending on agricultural labour has increased in all states, except Tripura and Manipur. The pattern of landlessness in Tripura and Manipur shows contrasting trends. While there is a considerable increase in landlessness in Manipur (approximately 14.2 per cent, as per Table 20.1), in Tripura there is a decrease in landlessness by 1.6 per cent. Hence, in Manipur, the increase in women farmers may actually highlight contract farming, another mode of semi-proletarianization. However, even in these states, there is a considerable increase in non-agrarian work amongst women. These emerging trends in the northeastern states are in stark contrast with the central and eastern states, as the burden of proletarianization and semi-proletarianization seems to be borne by both adivasi men and women. The differences in these patterns largely emerge from the land-holding patterns and the nature of control that women enjoy over cultivable land (as shown in Tables 20.3 and 20.4).

The discussion above shows the multiple ways in which the labour markets have penetrated adivasi societies and highlights the multiple regional patterns influencing the fundamental transformation of the work of adivasi women that is taking place. The changing forms of labour being undertaken by these women show a broad secular trend of proletarianization and semi-proletarianization of adivasi women. At the same time, the growing patterns of resistance to the increasing dispossession in adivasi-dominated regions also strengthened patriarchal communitarian identities, which often disregarded the gendered nature of dispossession (Prasad 2016).

Community Structures and Labour Markets

It is pertinent to ask whether communitarian structures have been able to withstand and resist the process of proletarianization and semi-proletarianization. This question is particularly significant because reformation of community structures has been considered a panacea for bringing about gender equality in adivasi societies (Agarwal 2010; Kelkar and Nathan 2003; Krishna 2009). This argument assumes that the community will counter the negative impact of the market, if democratized, and form the basis for an egalitarian social order. However, an analysis of the labour market participation of individual matrilineal and patrilineal adivasi communities shows that customary laws and communitarian authority may not have much influence on the current forms of labour practices by adivasi women. This analysis takes into account some of the major patrilineal adivasi communities, such as Bhil, Gond, Santhal and Khondand, and also two of the main matrilineal communities, namely, Garo and Khasis (which also include Jaintia) from Meghalaya.[10] A comparison of the decadal changes between 2001 and 2011 is shown in Table 20.7.

The percentage of main workers has declined in all cases except the matrilineal adivasi communities, such as the Khasis and Garos. Table 20.7 shows a substantial increase in main work for Garo women in the urban areas, and for Khasi women in both rural and urban areas. Thus, while there is a secular decline amongst the patrilineal communities, it is the matrilineal communities in which the decline in main work is the slowest. Although this maybe largely because of regional differences, one interesting fact is that the decline of main work amongst all women workers is evident in Meghalaya (the main home of Khasi and Garo), but the trend is not replicated at a micro level for the Khasis.

Is it then possible to argue that matrilineal communitarian structures help to preserve employment opportunities? A closer look at the data does not give us a clear answer to this question, as the trend amongst the Garos is different. Here, the main work for urban Garo women has substantially increased, whereas for rural Garo women it has decreased. The process of intrusion of the market into Garo society has been documented (Fernandes et al. 2008), and this has also impacted the character of operational landholdings. While inheritance is decided through the matrilineal line, the control and management of the land is actually done by men. This traditional system has undergone a change with the intrusion of private property. Garo families have begun to give individual ownership of lands to their sons. In this sense, although the inheritance line remains female, the system is more or less patriarchal in character (Marak 2000).

Within this broad context, it is also clear that fairly major occupational changes have taken place between both patriarchal and matrilineal adivasi groups. The first trend to be noticed concerns most patriarchal adivasi social groups, for which the degree of proletarianization amongst women is much greater, as is seen in the enormous increases in the percentage of adivasi women agricultural labourers. In the period 2001–2011, agricultural labour amongst the Bhil and Gond women of Chhattisgarh has increased by about 22 and 12.86 per cent, respectively. It should be noted that these decadal changes are much higher than the overall average of the state and, therefore, reflect greater rural proletarianization of adivasi women in these communities. A similar trend is seen for the Santhal of Jharkhand and the Khond of Odisha, amongst whom agriculture labour has increased between 7 and 8 per cent in 2001–2011. Furthermore, in the same period there has also been an increase of some non-agricultural labour amongst adivasi women in patriarchal communities. For the Bhils of Chhattisgarh and the Khonds of Odisha, this increase varies from 11 to 11.67 per cent, whereas for the Gonds of Chhattisgarh and the Santhals of Jharkhand it hovers between 4 and 5 per cent. Nonetheless, all these trends indicate a proletarianization of adivasi women in the central and east Indian belt. They also show that the patriarchal community has not been able to resist the neo-liberal labour market.

A similar conclusion may also be reached for the matrilineal communities of the Northeast. There has been a loss of work in farming and agricultural labour for Garo and Khasi adivasi women. Agriculture labour amongst the women of these two communities declined in the range of 0.23–0.53 per cent between 2001 and 2011, but rose in the case of non-agricultural work between 6 and 8.5 per cent in the same period. These trends show that the character of proletarianization may have regional differences, but community-based differences only exist in terms of the degree and the geographical location of a particular adivasi community. Hence, it is safe to argue that the impact of social structures is neutralized by the larger integration of adivasi regions into the labour market.

Conclusion

This chapter elaborates the different dimensions of the gendered nature of semi-proletarianization and proletarianization of the adivasi social groups after the period of neo-liberal reforms. It has shown that the integration of the adivasis in general, and adivasi women in particular, has been a result of agrarian distress and macro-economic trends that have structured the patterns of dispossession, displacement and urbanization in the last two decades. In doing so, the chapter has contested the proposition that communitarian structures play an important part in the division of labour within adivasi communities. A closer micro-level analysis of particular social groups also confirms the gendered character of the consolidation of working class formation in adivasi societies due to the penetration of the labour markets. However, the processes of proletarianization and semi-proletarianization of women have multiple trajectories that are structured by the character of landlessness and dispossession.

The second proposition contested by this chapter is that there is an autonomous sphere of existence of the subsistence economy of the adivasis. Within this perspective, it is also assumed that the role of the adivasi women is largely confined to unpaid labour within the sphere of subsistence. However, as the analysis in this chapter has shown, the blurred boundaries between subsistence and commercial activities have ensured that there is hardly autonomous space for the adivasi households to carry out their activities. This has implications for the life of adivasi women in several ways. The semi-agrarian character of their labour ensures that, although they are liberated from communitarian structures, they face adverse inclusion into labour markets, as shown by both the macro- and micro-level analyses in this chapter. In this sense, the proletarianization of adivasi women and the forms of their labour are firmly shaped and affected by the circuits of capital.

Lastly, this chapter counters the oft-repeated proposition that communities and communitarian structures can stand in opposition to the labour market and protect the interests of the adivasi women if they are democratized. The analysis of this chapter has shown that both matrilineal and patrilineal communities have experienced similar degrees of semi-proletarianization and proletarianization among adivasi women. However, the nature of such a process is influenced by regional trends and landholding patterns. Thus, the thesis that communitarian production and distribution systems guide the class formation process does not, in fact, hold in the case of most adivasi regions. Rather, the labour market is guided by macro-economic processes that often neutralize the influence of these structures. Hence, a more rigorous class analysis of adivasi societies is needed if the intensity and the gendered character of adverse inclusion of adivasi households into labour markets are to be considered under contemporary neo-liberalism. Given this conclusion, further studies need to explain why the growth of a neo-traditional patriarchal communitarian identity coexists with the phenomenon of proletarianization of adivasi women and how it has affected patriarchal authority.

Notes

1. The Constitution of India defines 'Scheduled Tribes' under Article 342 as people with 'indications of primitive traits; a distinctive culture; shyness in contact with community at large; geographically isolated and backward'. This definition has been critiqued by activists and scholars and the term 'adivasi' is instead used as a form of self-expression and a positive political identity.
2. Both these terms are much debated in the literature, but this debate is beyond the scope of this chapter. The term 'proletarianization' here refers to processes of dispossession and accumulation which force people to forgo their control over all means of production and enter the labour market as wage labourers in either urban or rural areas. The term semi-proletarianization refers to processes of accumulation and displacement of livelihoods that force small-scale producers to depend on wage labour or disguised wage labour for a large part of their livelihoods, even though they may control some means of production, such as land.
3. This trend and argument has been mainly present in the work of anthropologists and the advocates of the perspective that communitarian management is the best alternative to neo-liberalism. Agarwal (2010), for example, argues that a mere reformation in communitarian rules and structures can bring about substantial changes in gender equations and women's empowerment.
4. Colonial and post-colonial anthropological perspectives and monographs provide enough evidence of this. For example, see Elwin (1939) and Singh (1988). For a survey of literature and debates on gender issues in adivasi societies, see Xaxa (2004). For a critique of anthropological perspectives, see Prasad (2011).
5. 'Work participation rate' is defined as the percentage of total workers in the total population. 'Workers' are defined as persons who are engaged in any economic activity or who, despite their attachment to economic activity,

abstained themselves from work for reasons of illness, injury or other physical disability, bad weather, festivals, social or religious functions or other contingencies necessitating temporary absence from work. Unpaid helpers who assist in the operation of an economic activity in the household farm or non-farm activities are also considered as workers.

6. 'Labour force participation' refers to the population which supplies or offers to supply labour for pursuing economic activities for the production of goods and services and, therefore, includes both 'employed' and 'unemployed' persons/person-days. 'Labour force participation rate' (LFPR) is defined as the proportion of persons/person-days in the labour force to the total persons/person-days. These ratios are given in per 1000 of persons/person-days.
7. Calculated from Census of India (2001, 2011, Table B-1).
8. Calculated by Thiagu Rangarajan from unit-level data from NSSO (2015).
9. All state-level trends are calculated from Census of India, Primary Census Abstracts, Schedule Tribes (2001, 2011).
10. All data analysis in this section uses the individual tribe data of Census of India (2001, 2011).

Bibliography

Agarwal, B. (2010). *Gender and Green Governance: The Political Economy of Women's Presence Within and Beyond Community Forestry*. Oxford: Oxford University Press.

Agnihotri, I., Mazumdar, I., & Neetha, N. (2013). Summary of Findings: Gender and Migration Negotiating Rights—A women's Movement Perspective. *Economic and Political Weekly, 48*(10), 54–64.

Agricultural Census in India. (2014). *Agricultural Census in India, 2010–2011*. New Delhi: Department of Agricultural Cooperation, Ministry of Agriculture, Government of India.

Census of India. (2001, 2011). *Registrar of Census, Census of India 2001 and 2011, Scheduled Tribe Tables*. Retrieved from www.censusindia.gov.in.

Elwin, V. (1939). *The Baiga*. London: John Murray.

Fernandes, W., Pereira, M., & Khatso, V. (2008). *Tribal Customary Laws in Northeast India: Gender and Class Implications*. Guwahati: North East Research Centre.

Gangte, P. (2008). *Customary Laws of Meiti and Mizo Societies*. New Delhi: Akanksaha Publishing House.

Hajra, D. (1993). Authority Structure and Mode of Social Control Among the Gonds. In K. S. Singh (Ed.), *Tribal Ethnography, Customary Law and Change* (pp. 185–194). New Delhi: Concept Publishing House.

Harris-White, B. (2013). *Dalits and Adivasis in India's Business Economy: Three Essays and an Atlas.* New Delhi: Three Essays Collective.

Karat, B., & Rawal, V. (2014). Scheduled Tribe Households: A Note on Issue of Livelihoods. *Review of Agrarian Studies, 4*(1), 159–167.

Kelkar, G., & Nathan, D. (Eds.). (2003). *Gender Relations in Forest Societies: Patriarchy at Odds.* New Delhi: Sage Publications.

Kelkar, G., Nathan, D., & Walter, P. (Eds.). (2005). *Gender Relations in Forest Societies in Asia.* New Delhi: Sage Publications.

Kothari, A., & Srivastava, A. (2012). *Churning the Earth: The Making of Global India.* New Delhi: Penguin India.

Krishna, S. (2009). *Genderscapes: Revisiting Natural Resource Management.* New Delhi: Zubaan.

Marak, J. (2000). *Garo Customary Law and Practices.* New Delhi: Akansha Publishers.

Mehta, J. (2005). Agribusiness in India. In *Alternative Economic Survey* (pp. 67–78). New Delhi: Daanish Books.

National Sample Survey Organisation. (NSSO). (2010). *Migration in India, 2007–2008, Report No. 533.* New Delhi: Ministry of Statistics and Programme Implementation, Government of India.

National Sample Survey Organisation. (NSSO). (2015). *Situation Assessment of Agricultural Households, January– December 2013.* New Delhi: 70th Round Survey NSSO.

Nongbri, T. (1998). *Problems in Tribal Society: Some Aspects* (RGICS Paper No. 47). New Delhi: Inter-India Publications.

Nongbri, T. (2000). Khasi Women and Matriliny: Transformations in Gender Relations. *Gender, Technology and Development, 4*(3), 359–395.

Padel, F., & Das, S. (2010). *Out of This Earth: East India Adivasis and the Aluminium Cartel.* New Delhi: Orient BlackSwan.

Padhi, R. (2012). *Those Who Did Not Die: The Impact of Agrarian Crisis on Women in Punjab.* Los Angeles/London/New Delh/Singapore/ Washington, DC: SAGE.

Phei, K. (1974). *Principles of Khasi Law.* Shillong: Don Bosco.

Prasad, A. (1998). The Baiga: Myth and Reality. *Studies in History, 14*(2), 325–348.

Prasad, A. (2005). More Marginal than the Marginalised. In K. Shakti & B. Pati (Eds.), *Exploring Gender Equations: Colonial and Post-colonial India* (pp. 405–418). New Delhi: Nehru Memorial Museum and Library.

Prasad, A. (2010). Neoliberalism, Tribal Survival and Agrarian Distress: The Experience of Two Decades of Reform. In Alternate Survey Group (Ed.), *Two Decades of Neoliberalism: Alternative Economic Survey* (pp. 111–138). New Delhi: Daanish Books.

Prasad, A. (2011). *Against Ecological Romanticism: Verrier Elwin and the Making of an Anti-modern Tribal Identity* (2nd Rev ed.). New Delhi: Three Essays Collective.
Prasad, A. (2014). The Gujarat Model of Adivasi Development. In S. Teesta (Ed.), *The Gujarat Mirage: A Collection of Informed Arguments* (pp. 69–82). New Delhi: Prism Books.
Prasad, A. (2016). Adivasis and the Trajectories of Political Mobilisation in Contemporary Central India (mimeo). In R. Meena (Ed.), *First Citizens* (pp. 307–336). Oxford: Oxford University Press.
Shah, A. (2013). The Agrarian Question in a Maoist Guerrilla Zone: Land, Labour and Capital in the Forests and Hills of Jharkhand, India. *Journal of Agrarian Change, 13*(3), 424–450.
Singh, K. S. (1988). Tribal Women: An Anthropological Perspective. In J. P. Singh, N. Vyas, & R. S. Mann (Eds.), *Tribal Women and Development* (pp. 3–10). Jaipur: Rawat Publications.
Xaxa, V. (2004). Women and Gender in the Study of Tribes in India. *Indian Journal of Gender Studies, 11*(3), 345–367.

Index[1]

[1] Note: Page numbers followed by 'n' refer to notes.

P. Jha et al. (eds.), *Labour Questions in the Global South*,
https://doi.org/10.1007/978-981-33-4635-2

T

The manufacturer's authorised representative in the EU is Springer Nature Customer Service Centre GmbH, Europaplatz 3, 69115 Heidelberg, Germany. If you have any concerns regarding our products, please contact ProductSafety@springernature.com

Printed and bound by CPI Group (UK) Ltd, Croydon, CR0 4YY
30/09/2026
02225457-0020